709.47Mas   BM
Massie, Suzanne,
Land of the firebird: the beauty   1980

W9-BNG-868

DISCARD

The Beauty
of
Old Russia

ALSO BY SUZANNE MASSIE
The Living Mirror: Five Young Poets from Leningrad
Journey (with Robert Massie)

LAND OF THE FIREBIRD

SUZANNE MASSIE

SIMON AND SCHUSTER · NEW YORK

COPYRIGHT © 1980 BY SUZANNE MASSIE
ALL RIGHTS RESERVED
INCLUDING THE RIGHT OF REPRODUCTION
IN WHOLE OR IN PART IN ANY FORM
PUBLISHED BY SIMON AND SCHUSTER
A DIVISION OF GULF & WESTERN CORPORATION
SIMON & SCHUSTER BUILDING
ROCKEFELLER CENTER
1230 AVENUE OF THE AMERICAS
NEW YORK, NEW YORK 10020
SIMON AND SCHUSTER AND COLOPHON ARE TRADEMARKS OF SIMON & SCHUSTER

DESIGNED BY EVE METZ
COMPOSITION BY DIX TYPESETTING CO. INC., SYRACUSE, N.Y.
MANUFACTURED IN THE UNITED STATES OF AMERICA
BY FAIRFIELD GRAPHICS
COLOR INSERT PRINTED BY LEHIGH PRESS, PENNSAUKEN, N.J.

1 2 3 4 5 6 7 8 9 10

LIBRARY OF CONGRESS CATALOGING IN PUBLICATION DATA

MASSIE, SUZANNE.
    LAND OF THE FIREBIRD.

    BIBLIOGRAPHY: P.
    INCLUDES INDEX.
    1. ART, RUSSIAN—HISTORY.   I. TITLE.
N6981.M42   709'.47   80-12860

ISBN 0-671-23051-4

Grateful acknowledgment is made for permission to reprint the quotations on these pages of this work:
    Pages 67–68. Excerpt from hymn "O Wondrous Miracle" in *Ivan the Terrible* by Robert Payne and Nikita Romanoff (T. Y. Crowell) Copyright © 1975 by Robert Payne and Nikita Romanoff. Reprinted by permission of Harper & Row, Publishers, Inc.

(continued page 491)

BELLEVILLE PUBLIC LIBRARY

For the Russians I have loved
and
my mother, whose tales first
inspired me to seek the land of the Firebird

CONTENTS

CONTENTS

ACKNOWLEDGMENTS

SO MANY PEOPLE have helped in the preparation of this book in various ways that to list them all would be impossible. I want them to know that I thank them all, and have been most grateful for every suggestion and contribution.

Over the years, there have been many Russian friends, both here and in the Soviet Union, who have generously contributed their knowledge of their country, their books and suggestions, their encouragement and their love. This book, in a very real way, is theirs as well as mine.

I especially wish to express my gratitude to Zoya Trifunovich, Russian Department, Barnard College who, from the outset, encouraged me in my work, provided me with many details and suggestions for research and carefully read the manuscript, and to John Malmstad, Slavic Languages Department, Columbia University, who also read the manuscript and provided me with many valuable suggestions and thoughts, his special enthusiasm and knowledge of the Futuristic Movement and great help in the thorny problems of transliteration. I also thank Elizabeth Valkenier, Senior Fellow of the Russian Institute for generously sharing her knowledge of "The Wanderers" and Russian Realist art of the 19th century. It is from her exactingly researched book *Russian Realist Art* that the section on "The Wanderers" was largely drawn. Also I thank Alan Fletcher, of the Juilliard School of Music for his valuable help in the research for the music section, Marilyn Swezey for her many stimulating thoughts as well as her knowledge of the art of Fabergé, Linda Gerstein, Professor of History, Haverford College, Patricia and Clive Barnes, Nikita Romanoff, Natalya Sharymova, Valery and Irina Kuharets of the Russica Book Shop, George Riabov, Catherine Wolkonsky, Antoinette Roubichou, Musa Navrosov, William Mills

9

Todd III of Stanford University and Philip Evola of the Institute of Fine Arts, New York. I remember also the help and encouragement given to me over the years by my two dear friends, the late Evgenia Ouroussow Lehovich and the late Max Hayward of St. Antony's College, Oxford.

I am also most grateful to my husband, Robert Massie, who took the time to patiently read and edit my pages while working on his own book, my children, Robert and Susanna for their faith and support, and especially Elizabeth, for her cheerful understanding of the conflicting demands of the author-mother. Thank you also to my friend Janet Kellock, who typed the entire manuscript and always sustained me in moments of discouragement.

Finally, my thanks go to Diana Vreeland, and to Suzanne Gauthier of the Metropolitan Museum, who first invited me to prepare the lectures which were the genesis of this book, and, at Simon and Schuster, Nan Talese, whose enthusiasm first brought it into being, Dan Green, and my editor, Susan Bolotin, whose encouragement and constructive suggestions were of enormous help.

NOTE ON STYLE

THERE IS no universally accepted method of transliteration. I have in general followed the Library of Congress method, with certain exceptions: for instance, *y* for final *ii*, and *yu* and *ya* for Russian я and ю. Soft and hard signs are omitted. I have also made several other exceptions in order to make the text as clear as possible to a lay reader. These exceptions are especially evident when the names of persons are now so well known and accepted in one spelling that to change them would only serve to confuse. These include Diaghilev (not Dyagilev), Tchaikovsky (not Chaikovsky), Mussorgsky (not Musorgsky), Chaliapin (not Shalyapin), Potemkin (not Potyomkin), and Rublev (not Rublyov) and the names of many members of the World of Art group whose names are generally rendered in their French form. This is also the case for the Bolshoi (Bolshoy) Theater.

All tsars have been rendered in English form; otherwise, all first names are rendered in the Russian fashion with the exception of Peter and Alexander.

The old Russian name Feodor, by the 19th century generally spelled Fyodor, was retained in the case of the patronymics of the tsarinas, i.e., Maria Feodorovna. Standard Webster spelling has been used for a few Russian words that have passed into the English language, such as borzoi, borsch, blini.

Place names are anglicized: Dnieper and not Dnepr.

In quotations I have occasionally left misspellings and incorrect transliterations because they add to the color and authenticity of travelers' accounts.

I have omitted notes, but have attributed all quotations, and all works from which these quotations are taken are listed in the bibliography. In describing customs, street scenes, markets, and so on, my rule has been never to rely on a single description as fact. Only after finding several similar accounts in different sources did I then quote the most colorful eyewitness version.

INTRODUCTION

ALL MY LIFE, in different ways, I have enjoyed and loved Russian culture. It began, I think, in those songs and fairy tales I first heard from my mother, who had spent six eventful years, from 1914 to 1920, living in Russia.

It was she who first introduced me to Petrushka, the puppet cursed with a human heart, who, sad and alone, locked in a dark room, silently cried out his despairing love for an unfeeling ballerina who spurned him and caused his destruction. In the books Mother gave me, I met princes wearing turned-up boots, who rode through Russian forests, talked to animals and braved the strongholds of the cunning witch Baba Yaga and the evil sorcerer Kaschei the Immortal. In the darkness of those deep forests, the Hunchback Horse was ready to carry the pure-hearted to their life's desire, the gray wolf became a friend, and the Firebird's feathers gleamed. As a child, I devoured these stories, which seemed more alive to me than my own life.

Over the years I found joy and inspiration in Russian poetry, prose, art, architecture, music, dance and even the sound of the language. I studied the history, I visited the land many times, I learned the language. Led by the feathers of the Firebird, beyond the stories of cruelty, beyond the gray monotony of the land of today, I always found beauty.

This book grew from lectures I gave at the Metropolitan Museum of Art in 1976, where, for the first time, I tried, in pictures and words, to weave together

13

the many threads of the civilization that had so interested me. It was then that I found that despite the multitude of books on the subject, there was no single volume that gave a sense of the whole, now-vanished culture of old Russia. It is for this reason that I have tried to introduce in this book so many different facets. It is my hope that my readers may be stimulated to explore these facets further, and to compare their impressions with mine.

Through the years, I have met many people who shared my admiration for the artistic traditions and culture of this great land, fragmented by the blows of history. And yet, the artistic achievements of Russia are often viewed as isolated phenomena, and not as vital offshoots of a society that had achieved much and, had it not been destroyed, could have achieved much more. For reasons, some understandable, and others difficult to understand, it is the darker side of Russia's history which has most often been emphasized, not only in the Soviet Union, but also in the West. As a result of this lopsided concentration, the picture of old Russia that has emerged is too often a stereotype, lacking in depth and accuracy.

Nations, like individuals, have the right to be judged not only on their faults and failings, but also on their achievements and glories. There was injustice in old Russia, as there was and is in every nation. But it was a many-textured society, characterized also by a full measure of grace and beauty. Today, more than ever, the injustice remains, but the beauty is gone. Therefore, in this book I have concentrated on describing that beauty which the Russians once knew how to create, what they loved and admired and how they once lived and rejoiced.

Russian culture has much to offer us. The Russians know the darker side of humanity, but they also understand the extraordinary capacity of the human soul for sacrifice and love, and they have the ability to accept both sides of man with greater equanimity than we in the West. They know how to take a long view, something we have all but forgotten in our anxious desire for immediate gratification. (It is a glimpse into the profound differences between our cultures to know that in Russian, the words "frustration" and "sophistication" do not exist.) The Russians have valued humility rather than pride. They have approached God in a spirit of meekness; they have loved nature. They have revered poets and poetry with a passion equaled by few other peoples, and have produced a poetic literature of extraordinary richness and variety. Their knowledge of suffering and their understanding of human weakness have made their 19th-century novels probably the greatest in world literature. They gave depth and feeling to formal movements and *divertissements* intended only for the aristocracy of Europe and turned ballet into an uplifting and popular art, one that is particularly modern. Their music has stirred hearts all over the world. These manifestations of beauty which old Russia produced so brilliantly, permeated by the spiritual qualities of the Russian people, are perhaps what we most need to rediscover now, to offset the coldness and impersonality of an increasingly heartless, technological and materialistic modern world.

O

NCE UPON A TIME *very long ago there was an orphan girl named Marushka. She was a quiet, modest and gentle maiden. None could embroider as beautifully as she. She worked with colored silks and glass beads, making for one, a shirt, for another a towel, or a pretty sash. And she was always content with the money she received, however small.*

The fame of her skill reached the ears of merchants beyond the seas. From near and far they came to see her marvelous work. They gazed and were amazed, for they never thought to find anything so beautiful. One after another, they tried to persuade Marushka to come away with them, promising her riches and glory. But she would only lower her eyes and reply modestly: "Riches I do not need and I shall never leave the village where I was born. But of course I will sell my work to all who find it beautiful." And with that, although they were disappointed, the merchants had to be content. They left, spreading the story of her skill to the ends of the earth, until one day it reached the ear of the wicked sorcerer Kaschei the Immortal, who raged to learn that there was such beauty in the world which he had never seen.

So he took the form of a handsome youth and flew over the deep oceans, the tall mountains and the impassable forests until he came to Marushka's cottage.

He knocked at the door and bowed low to her, as was the custom. Then he asked to see the needlework she had completed. Marushka set out shirts, towels, handkerchiefs and veils, each more beautiful than the other. "Kind sir," said she, "whatever pleases you, you may take. If you have no money now, you may pay me later, when you have money to spare. And if my work should not find favor in your eyes, please counsel me and tell me what to do, and I shall try my best."

Her kind words and the sight of all that beauty made Kaschei even angrier. How could it be that a simple country girl could fashion things finer than he, the great Kaschei the Immortal, himself possessed. And he took his most cunning tones and he said:

Come with me, Marushka, and I will make you Queen. You will live in a palace built of precious jewels. You will eat off gold and sleep on eiderdown. You will walk in an orchard where birds of paradise sing sweet songs, and golden apples grow.

"Do not speak so," answered Marushka. "I need neither your riches nor your strange marvels. There is nothing sweeter than the fields and woods where one was born. Never shall I leave this village where my parents lie buried and where live those to whom my needlework brings joy. I shall never embroider for you alone."

Kaschei was furious at this answer. His face grew dark and he cried, "Because you are so loath to leave your kindred, A bird you shall be, and no more a maiden fair."

And in an instant a Firebird flapped its wings where Marushka had stood. Kaschei became a great black Falcon and soared into the skies to swoop down on the Firebird. Grasping her tight in his cruel talons, he carried her high above the clouds.

As soon as Marushka felt the power in those steel claws and realized she was being taken away, she resolved to leave a last memory of herself.

She shed her brilliant plumage and feather after feather floated down on meadow and forest. The mischievous wind covered the feathers with grass and leaves, but nothing could rob them of their glowing rainbow colors.

18

As the feathers fell, Marushka's strength ebbed. And although the Firebird died in the black Falcon's talons, her feathers continued to live, down on the ground. They were not ordinary feathers, but magic ones that only those who loved beauty and who sought to make beauty for others could see and admire.

RUSSIAN LEGEND

709.47
Mar
258825

Belleville Public Library

19

1. TO SERVE GOD AND UPLIFT HUMANITY

> Countries no doubt have gender—and that of Russia is
> essentially feminine. . . . It is this strong femininity of
> hers which accounts for Russia's peculiar fertility. Give
> her the start, the seed . . . and she mothers it in her
> own peculiar way to quite astonishing results.
>
> Henry Charles Bainbridge

IT WAS PRINCE VLADIMIR of Kiev who made the decision which was to have the most profound effect on the course of Russian history and culture. The ancient *Primary Chronicle* relates that in 987 Vladimir received various emissaries who wished to persuade the pagan prince of the benefits and glories of the religion practiced in their lands. First came the neighboring Bulgars who urged, "Though you are a wise and prudent prince, you have no religion. Adopt our faith and revere Mahomet." When Vladimir inquired what was the nature of their religion, they answered that they believed in God and that Mahomet promised that, if they were faithful, they were assured of complete fulfillment of their carnal desires after death. According to the Chronicle, this appealed to the lusty Vladimir, who had married four times and had several hundred concubines. But when the Bulgars went on to explain that Moslems were not permitted to drink, Vladimir rejected them, exclaiming, "Drink is the joy of the Russes. We cannot exist without that pleasure." Then came the Germans, as emissaries of the Pope, saying, "Your country is like our country. . . . Our faith is light. We worship God, who

21

has made heaven and earth, the stars, the moon and every creature while your gods are only wood." The Jewish Khazars arrived explaining that they believed in one God, the God of Abraham, Isaac and Jacob. But upon learning that they were condemned to wander the world, Vladimir rejected them, asking, "Do you expect us to accept this fate also?" The Greeks sent a philosopher who expounded learnedly and recounted to Vladimir the history of the whole world. The Greek deeply impressed Vladimir with his erudition and his especially vivid description of the torments of hell for the unbeliever.

Still perplexed, Vladimir sought counsel among his nobles and elders, who advised him to send ten "good and wise" men to go see for themselves how each faith was practiced. When his men returned from their travels, Vladimir listened to them carefully. In Germany, they reported, although they had seen many ceremonies performed in German temples, they had seen "no glory there." But in Constantinople, when they were taken to the huge Cathedral of Hagia Sophia, with its interior completely decorated with mosaics of pure gold shimmering in the light of ten thousand candles, they were spellbound. "We knew not whether we were in heaven or earth and we are at a loss to describe it. We only know that God dwells there among men, and their service is fairer than the ceremonies of other nations. For we cannot forget that beauty." Shortly after, in 988, Vladimir was baptized and decreed that henceforth the Kievan land would adopt Christianity in its Eastern, or Greek, form rather than its Western, or Roman, form.

Constantinople, which the Russians called Tsargrad, was then the most important political and cultural center of Europe. Heir to the Roman Empire, it commanded vast lands comprising parts of Italy, the Balkan Peninsula, the Aegean archipelago and all of Asia Minor. The literary and state language of the Byzantine empire was Greek. Constantinople served as the preserver of Christian thought as well as the ancient arts of Greece and Rome for a still backward Western Europe. Nowhere else were ideas more diverse and dynamic than in Constantinople, whose civilization blended the ancient and modern, the most immense luxury with the most extreme asceticism.

The Eastern liturgy is one of the most beautiful and original creations of the Byzantine culture. The impression of supreme beauty that so profoundly touched Vladimir's emissaries still moves observers to this day. Profound and poetic, it is a dramatic palace style with great mystical depth which, with overwhelming magnificence, attempts to bring about the union of heavenly and earthly existence. Rich with ornaments and vestments, resplendent with gold and precious stones, perfumed with incense, it appeals profoundly to the senses and the imagination, embracing and enveloping the beholder with awe and warmth.

The Russians embraced this Eastern Christianity joyfully, with all the exuberance of their nature. So many churches were built in Kiev that less than fifty years after the conversion a visitor to the city recorded that their number was nearly four hundred. The Russian word for Orthodox is *Pravoslavie*, which means "true worship" or "right glory." They called their churches "the palaces of God." But the Russians did not simply imitate the Byzantine rite. Instead they quickly humanized Byzantine formality, incorporating artistic traditions of Russian folk art and music and bringing to their new church ancient Slavic traditions of community and brotherly love. So peaceful were the pagan Slavs that they had no god of war. The Christian Russians approached God humbly, in a spirit of tenderness, seeking in their worship those spiritual ideals which they admired in life—compassion, nonresistance, gentleness and humility.

Russian folklore and early written documents exalt personages endowed with meekness and humility. From the beginning the Russians placed great importance on the role of suffering in Christian life. Two of the most revered figures of the early Christian Russians and the first two saints canonized by the church were Boris and Gleb, two sons of Vladimir. When Vladimir died in 1015, their elder brother, Svyatopolk, decided to seize their principalities and assassinate his brothers. Boris was not willing to resist evil with evil and offered no resistance. He dismissed his retinue, then he prayed, saying, "I do not resist. I do not refuse." Calmly, he lay down on his couch and waited for the assassins who came and, says the Chronicle, fell upon him "like wild beasts," running a sword through his heart. His seventeen-year-old younger brother, Gleb, upon hearing the news, wept and prayed for his father and brother. Following his brother's example, in his turn he was murdered without resistance.

For centuries, Boris and Gleb were the patron saints of Russia and the greatest popular heroes. They were called the "Passion Bearers," symbolizing voluntary acceptance of suffering and death and peaceful nonresistance to injustice. This meekness and acceptance of fate in imitation of the deeds of Christ is an essential Russian ideal that runs like a golden thread through Russian life and art up to our own century. The Russians were the first to stress the humble aspect of Christ's nature, which was emphasized neither in Byzantium nor in the West until the time of Saint Francis, some two hundred years after the martyrdom of Boris and Gleb.

The father of Boris and Gleb, Prince Vladimir, was revered and canonized, not only because he was the man who first adopted Christianity for Russia, but because from the first he placed great emphasis on the compassionate social implications of Christianity. Banquets and feasting always held a great place in Russian life. Vladimir, called "The Bright Sun" in Russian folklore, was a genial host and after his conversion made his banquets an expression of Christian brotherhood and love. Whenever he held great feasts with his court, he sent wagons loaded with bread, meat, fish, vegetables and mead through the city to be distributed to the poor and the sick. Nowhere else in Europe were there such highly organized social services as in 10th-century Kiev. Deeply conscious of the Christian law of mercy, when he introduced the Byzantine legal code in Kiev, Vladimir mitigated its savage and brutal features; in ancient Kiev, there was no death penalty, no mutilation, no torture. Vladimir for a time even refused to execute robbers until the church convinced him that it was fitting for him to punish criminals after due process of law.

For the Slavs, the destinies of man, animals and plants were all blended into one; they blossomed and died together. For them, beauty lay primarily in an all-embracing, all-encompassing nature. To their church, the Russians brought this close feeling for nature. The Earth was the ideal of Eternal Womanhood, and so in Russia, there never was the extreme Latin veneration and cult of the Virgin as the Virgin of Purity but more importantly as the Virgin of Motherhood, fertility and compassion; the Virgin was rarely portrayed without a child. Permeated by this sense of unity with nature and the earth, the Russians interpreted Christian rebirth quite literally as the beautifying and transfiguration of human life. The church building itself had a twofold meaning. It embodied the significance of the Resurrection and was also part of the natural world, blending harmoniously into the landscape. The terminology of church architecture reflected this double significance; a dome was called "the head" or "forehead"; the drum, "the neck"; the rounded gable, "the shoulder"; the sectional vaulting below the drum, "the bosom." There were also such homely terms as "melon," "belt" and *kokoshnik* to describe architectural details.

Cathedrals and churches quickly became the landmarks of all Russian principalities, towns and villages. In the vast, flat spaces of the land, they raised their cupolas like beacons of fire, calling attention to heaven. The most important public events took place either in them or in front of them, for the people felt at home both inside and outside the church. Often they assembled for services in the open air in large numbers, watching the "holy action" through open doors.

In Byzantium there never was the love for a multitude of domes that developed in Russia. For the Russians, the number of domes had symbolic significance. One dome symbolized God as the head of the church; three, the Trinity; five, Christ and the four Evangelists; nine, the nine choirs of angels. Twelve smaller domes surrounding the main one signified Christ and His Apostles. All domes carried a cross, usually the Orthodox cross with a slanting beam across the bottom arm and often another near the top to indicate the places where the sign was hung above Christ's head and the place of His feet. In later centuries, a crescent moon at the foot of the cross signified a victory over the Moslem Tatars.

In the earliest Russian churches, the domes were rounded, like those of Byzantine churches, but very quickly they took on their distinctive onion-bulb shape. A practical explanation is that this shape was more suited to heavy snowfalls, but there are more poetic explanations. One is that the cupolas assumed their characteristic shape to catch the prayers of the faithful and send them to heaven. Another is that they took the form of the helmets of Kievan soldiers because Russia was the last line of defense of the West against the East, and her churches stood like soldiers, protecting the West from annihilation.

Russian churches are square in plan, with a wide central space covered by a dome, representing the dome of heaven. There are no pews or chairs, for Orthodox worshipers consider it a lack of respect to sit in the presence of God; they stand, however long the service. This gives to Orthodox worship an informality that does not exist in Western churches. Seated in neat rows, Western worshipers are not only obligated to stay through the entire service but can barely move without causing a disruption. In the Orthodox Church, worship is timeless and unhurried. People move about, come and go as freely as they wish. They do not view themselves as Christian soldiers, but as children in their Father's house.

From their earliest history, the Slavs always have had a strong clan mentality. Among all the European peoples only they, Iceland, and a few Balkan clans have preserved personal patronymics until our own day. Every Russian, besides his Christian name, bears as a second name a derivative of his father's* and simple people called themselves only by this name. Family names came into general use in Russia only in the 18th century.

---

* These patronymics, a distinctive feature of Russian life and a sometimes confusing problem for readers of Russian novels, are formed by adding the suffix *vich* for a man and *ovna* for a woman, to the father's name. Thus Ivan Petrovich means Ivan, son of Peter.

The whole Russian people once thought of themselves idealistically as a single, immense family, with the tsar as a father. Russian peasants, down through the centuries, addressed everyone, even strangers, in terms of kinship—father, mother, brother, sister. The individual life was only a fleeting moment in the life of this great clan. In their church, Russians found a full sense of this *sobornost,* or feeling of community. Orthodox worship was a family affair; lord and peasant stood side by side. God, in the person of his priests, appeared in church and moved freely among his people.

Russians believed that God was not only a God of truth but of beauty, who revealed Himself to His people through the beauty of art, and throughout the centuries, nowhere was the lavishness of the Russian personality, the love of ornamentation and decoration more opulent and beautiful than in their churches. Statues, considered "graven images," are not permitted within an Orthodox church, so Russians filled their churches with icons, tempera pictures of religious scenes and figures painted on wood. They are everywhere: on the great screen protecting the altar, on the walls in special shrines; there is hardly a corner where the congregation does not feel the benign eye of a saint upon them. They remind the congregation of the invisible and comforting presence of whole companies of heaven at the liturgy.

The symbolic spatial frontier between earthly and heavenly existence is a screen, completely decorated with icons, called the iconostasis, which conceals the sanctuary and both connects and separates the priests and the congregation. The iconostasis has three doors. The central door is called the "Royal Door" and it is opened and closed during the service to signify many things—the creation of the world, Christ's enthronement, His birth and the Resurrection. During Easter week the door remains open all the time; closed, it signifies the expulsion from Paradise. Only priests—and the tsar during his coronation—were permitted into the sanctuary. No woman, not even the tsarina, has ever been allowed behind the Royal Door.

In the Russian church, the iconostasis assumed a great importance. It grew taller and taller until it nearly reached the ceiling, encasing three tiers and, in the larger churches, five tiers of icons, so that a person entering the church was immediately confronted with a solid wall of brilliant pictures. In later centuries, the iconostasis itself was so ornately decorated with gilded frames and elaborate carving that it commanded almost as much attention as the icons themselves.

On the iconostasis, icons are arranged in a special order. First are the icons of Christ, the Archangel and the Apostles, then Christ between the Virgin and John the Baptist, then saints of the months and feast days. The panels may be moved and changed, thus revealing the mystical events which are symbolically taking place unseen behind the screen in the Kingdom of Heaven. In the interior of the church various iconographical scenes are also arranged according to a precise plan, so that the whole church forms one great icon or image of the Kingdom of God and the very walls seem to open out into eternity.

Icon painting as it was developed in Byzantium was a strongly stylized art, done according to precise rules. The colors and lines were not meant to indicate nature but rather, as John of Damascus wrote, "Icons are open books to remind us of God . . . if a pagan asks you to show him your faith, take him into a church and show him your icons. . . . The icon is a song of triumph and a revelation . . . an enduring monument to the victory of saints and the disgrace of demons." Artists aimed to show that men, animals and plants could be rescued from their state of earthly degradation and restored to their heavenly image. The shape of a face was altered—the mouth made smaller, the nose thinner—to emphasize the spiritual nature of the subject, whose eyes testified to the perfect peace of the next life.

The Orthodox believe that it is possible to recognize the presence of the Holy Spirit in a man and to convey it to others by artistic means. Therefore, the function of the icon painter had much in common with that of a priest, and although it was important for an icon painter to be a good artist, it was essential for him to be a good Christian. Those who painted icons had to prepare themselves spiritually: fast, pray, read religious texts, for it was a true test, not only a pictorial work in the usual sense.

As the Russians humanized everything in the Byzantine church, they humanized the icon form as well, working more independently, suffusing their icons with nature and bright colors, painting saints with compassionate and tender eyes, filling their icons with life, love and on occasion even humor. From the 10th to the 17th centuries, Russian painting was almost entirely icon painting, and through the centuries several independent schools of icon painting grew up, each with its own distinctive style and colors. Novgorod developed in the 13th and 14th centuries a school of painting which was one of the three great schools of painting in all Europe. The artists of Novgorod had a particular talent for colors. Their icons were distinguished by lively scenes and brilliant unmixed hues— blue, yellow and green, with a vibrant vermilion predominating.

27

For an Orthodox worshiper, icons were far more than paintings; they were the palpable evidence of things hidden and a testimony to the possibility of man's participation in the transfigured world which he sought to contemplate. The role of icons was not static but alive, a dynamic means by which man could actively enter into the spiritual world, a song of faith to man's spiritual power to redeem himself by beauty and art. So magnificent were the Russian churches with their decorated interiors, so mighty the music of Orthodox choirs unaccompanied by any instruments, that many foreign ambassadors were awestruck upon setting foot in these palaces of God and, like those earlier Russians in Constantinople's Hagia Sophia, said that they felt they were in heaven.

This power of perceiving the beauty of the spiritual world and of expressing this beauty in worship has been a particular gift of Russia. Man, the Russians believed, found his most profound fulfillment and was most himself when he glorified God. In the act of worshiping God, a divine energy was released which permitted him to surpass himself and to participate in the divine life, even on earth.

The Orthodox liturgy continually inspired poetry, music and art, for, unlike the Catholic liturgy in the West, it was from the beginning the possession of the whole Christian people, who worshiped together not in Latin or Greek but in their own Slavic tongue. Russian thought and ideals entered into the tradition borrowed from Orthodox Byzantium and became the basic source of Russian culture. Throughout the centuries, the Russians, even in their secular art, were to preserve their view that art is above all a divine gift whose essential purpose is to serve God and to uplift humanity.

2. RADIANT AND MANY-COLORED KIEV

O Russian land, you must mourn
remembering your early age, your early princes.
The Lay of Igor, 12th century

THE KIEVAN KINGDOM which so creatively took on the Christianity of Byzantium was ruled from the city of Kiev. Called in Russian sagas "the Mother of Russian cities," Kiev stood at the crossroads of the great river routes linking Constantinople and Byzantium with the West; it was chief among a group of principalities which then covered most of the south and center of Russia. The Kievans were prosperous traders, taking honey, amber, wax and furs down their meandering rivers to Constantinople, from which they returned with silks and objects of art. Great Kiev, "the radiant and many-colored," stood high on the banks of the river Dnieper. The city in the 10th and 11th centuries was one of the wealthiest and most animated cities of Europe—larger than Paris, which at the time had eighty thousand inhabitants, and twice as large as the small city of London.

In its greatest days, the Kievan kingdom was governed by a number of chivalrous princes whose heroic deeds, along with those of their brave knights, or *bogatyry* still live on in the sagas and songs of the Russian people. Vladimir, "The Bright Sun" and Christianizer of Russia, had around him such fabled *bogatyry* as Ilya Muromets, Alyosha Popovich and Dobrynia Nikitich, who formed a sort of Russian counterpart to King Arthur's Knights of the Round Table. These men, who were often of very humble origin, caught the imagination of their countrymen. Their exploits of valor and strength passed into legend and the *byliny*, or epic songs, of early Russia.

The greatest of the Kievan princes was Yaroslav the Wise, the sixth of the prolific Vladimir's twelve sons. Yaroslav reigned as Grand Prince of Kiev from 1019 to 1054. Under him, the kingdom lived in peace and reached its highest state of splendor. In Kiev there were schools, hospitals and numerous public baths. Yaroslav was deeply religious, says the *Primary Chronicle*, "devoted to priests and especially monks," and he founded many churches. Outside the city was formed the Monastery of the Caves which, supported by Yaroslav's sons, grew to be the first great spiritual center of the Orthodox Church and a center for learning.

Wanting to rival Constantinople, Yaroslav had constructed Golden Gates at the principal entrance of the city. With their gilded copper mountings, which shone blindingly in the sun, they were more impressive than those of the Byzantine capital itself.

In 1037 he determined to build for Kiev its own Cathedral of Hagia Sophia.* Yaroslav laid the foundation stone for the great church which was of red granite set in pinkish cement. Pillars of marble were brought from the Crimea. Cruciform, with five apses and naves and thirteen cupolas, it was constructed at the point where lines drawn from each of the city's four gates intersected. To help in the building and decorating of his cathedral, he brought to Kiev skilled craftsmen from Greece and Constantinople, thus establishing what was to become a tradition. Hagia Sophia was the first in a long line of artistic and architectural collaborations between Russian and foreign artists. With these first foreign artists who came to Kiev to work on Hagia Sophia, as with many others who were to follow them in the centuries to come, a strange phenomenon occurred. Although they arrived as fully formed artists with ideas of their own, such was the strangely magnetic and inspiring effect of their contact with the Russian land and taste that the work they created in Russia was completely different from anything they had created in their native lands.

* Cathedral of the Holy Wisdom.

Nowhere in Western Europe at that time did there exist such a splendidly vivid cathedral. Russian and Greek artists decorated the interior of the church with mosaics of gold and many colors; more than 117 shades were used to achieve various artistic effects. In the conch of the altar, under a dome dominated by a huge figure of Christ and the Archangels, was a sixteen-foot-high image of the Virgin, set against a shimmering background of golden mosaics. When the light of the flickering oil lamps caught the golden and colored cubes of glass, these great mosaic figures seemed almost to move and come alive.

Wall paintings became a feature of Russian churches. At Kiev's Hagia Sophia were not only Biblical scenes, but on a panel running alongside the outer face of the gallery a painting showing Yaroslav followed by his seven sons in order of seniority, his wife and three daughters, all in single file, presenting a model of the cathedral to the Savior.

Like the Emperor of Constantinople, Yaroslav had the passageway connecting the church to his palace decorated with paintings. Exuberant and decidedly unreligious, they showed 130 merrymaking figures. There were scenes of hunting, which Yaroslav loved, of jugglers, comedians disguised as fantastic animals, charioteers preparing for a race, folk dancers and musicians.

Yaroslav was a noted scholar who, says the Chronicle, "read continually day and night." He collected hundreds of books and made of his collection a permanent library. He assembled scribes and translated books from Greek to Slavic and even wrote many himself. Fluent in five languages, he recommended to his children the usefulness of learning foreign tongues.

Under Yaroslav, Kiev became a cosmopolitan artistic center. Artists and craftsmen from southern, eastern and western cultures came there to work, mingle and exchange ideas. These skilled Russian craftsmen were famous throughout the world for their fine cloisonné enamels of brilliant hues, their *niello* (engraved and decorated metalwork) and delicate gold and silver filagrees. The potters, woodcarvers, painters and bridge builders were known for their excellence; fine linens and wools woven in Kiev were sold as far as India.

Russia was then an integral part of Europe. Children of Kievan princes married sovereigns or princesses of the ruling houses of England, Germany, France, Sweden, Hungary and Byzantium. Yaroslav's wife was the daughter of King Olaf of Sweden and his three daughters all married kings. Elizabeth became the Queen of Norway, Anastasia the Queen of Hungary, and Anna the Queen of France when she married Henry I in 1051. Queen Elizabeth II of England traces her ancestry to Yaroslav through this marriage.

Anna spoke three languages; and at the time of her marriage was able to write her own name on the marriage contract, while her husband, though King of France, could only make an X. (Upon her arrival in Paris for her wedding, Anna remarked that the banquet offered to her seemed tasty enough, but rather sparse compared to the higher standards of Kiev—she was offered only one soup; at home she was accustomed to being given a choice of five.) She continued to sign state documents, and when Henry died in 1060 and she became the ruling queen, she signed her name "Anna Regina" in Slavic characters.

Kiev's code of laws, the *Russkaya Pravda,* was unusually humane by medieval standards. Corporal or capital punishment was seldom used. There were no hereditary castes or classes. Peasants were free and could move about as they wished. Farmland was given or bequeathed with little restriction. Lord and peasant worshiped together. In those far-off days a spirit of optimism and freedom reigned in the land.

Although the greatest, Kiev was not the only important city of early Russia. The city of Vladimir, on the banks of the Volga River in the principality of Vladimir-Suzdal, boasted in the 11th century a series of magnificent churches and palaces, all now vanished, which were accounted wonders of the age. The elegance of its art and architecture mingled Russian elements with those of the Caucasus, to which Vladimir was linked by its water trade routes to the Caspian Sea and the marriage of its rulers with Caucasian princesses.

In the north stood the crustily independent city-state of Novgorod with its "little brother," the city of Pskov. Novgorod was the heart of a huge trading empire which at its height stretched from the Baltic to the Urals. The prosperous Novgorod merchants traded in both Europe and Asia. So frequent were the trading contacts of these merchants with the Swedes that they maintained their own Orthodox church on the Swedish island of Visby. Sadko, the traveling hero of Russian fairy tales, who, they said, even visited the Kingdom of Neptune, was a merchant of Novgorod.

The prosperous citizens of Novgorod developed a distinctive architectural style, suited to their independent spirit and their snowy environment, a style which impressed itself all over Russia. It is they who are often credited with designing the first onion-shaped dome. Their churches were sturdy and simple with white walls almost devoid of windows, decorated inside with a burst of colorful frescoes. The comfortable mansions of their rich merchants had thick whitewashed walls and wide courtyards. Although Paris did not attempt to pave its streets until 1184, both Kiev and Novgorod, possessed almost a century before, roadways made of oak laid across oak foundations. Intricate systems were devised for running off melted snow, with underground wooden pipes sewn tightly together with birch bark. Citizens of Novgorod, the majority of whom could read and write, jotted down their thoughts on thin, delicate birch-bark scrolls.

By the 11th century Novgorod had principles of self-government, including a *veche*, or town assembly, which any free man could attend, convened simply by the ringing of a special large bell, the proud symbol of the city's independence.

In early Kievan days, Novgorod was ruled by a son of the Kievan Grand Prince and the *veche*, but in 1136 the Novgorodians simply rejected princely rule altogether and calling themselves "Lord Novgorod the Great" decided to govern themselves.

From then on, if the Novgorod *veche* decided that it needed military assistance, it simply hired a prince by contract and placed tight restrictions on him. Princes elected by the *veche* were not permitted to own any estates in the domains of Novgorod and could not dismiss any town officials without the consent of the *veche* and a court ruling. The *veche* also reserved for itself the right to dismiss the prince whenever it wished.

So independent were the men of Novgorod that when a certain prince of Kiev wanted to put his son on the throne, the *veche* sent back his emissaries with this message: "We were sent to you, O Prince, with the following instructions, that our city does not want either you or your son. If your son has two heads, let him come." Novgorod defied all enemies with the ringing challenge, "Who can stand against God and Great Novgorod?"

The last of the great princes of Kiev was Vladimir Monomakh, the grandson of Yaroslav the Wise. Vladimir's mother was a Greek princess; his wife, Gytha, an Englishwoman, the daughter of the last Anglo-Saxon prince of England. Prince Harold II, who had been forced to abandon England after the Battle of Hastings, had come with his family to live in Kiev as an emigré.

Vladimir, who ruled from 1112 to 1125, was the last prince to rule a unified Kievan realm and he occupies a position in Russian history comparable to that occupied in English history by good King Alfred. His golden sable-bordered cap of state was carried in the coronation of every Russian tsar down through the last, as a symbol of the continuity of the ideals of ancient Kiev. Brave and chivalrous, Vladimir left his children a touching will describing his life and values, which gives a striking picture of the vigorous life of this Russian prince. He speaks of long journeys, of many battles and perils: "At Chernigov I bound wild horses with my bare hands or captured ten or twenty live horses with the lasso and besides that, while riding along the Ros, I caught these same wild horses bare-handed." While hunting, "two bisons tossed me and my horse on their horns, a stag once gored me, one elk stamped upon me . . . a boar once tore the sword from my thigh, a bear on one occasion bit my knee cap, another wild beast jumped on my flank and threw my horse with me. But God preserved me unharmed."

He advised his children: "Fail not one single night to kneel to the ground three times, in the case you cannot do so more often . . . pray unceasingly even while riding, better," he says, "than thinking idle thoughts." He counsels them never to shed blood except in battle, to judge the poor in person and give alms generously, and bids them, "Give to the orphan, protect the widow, and permit the mighty to destroy no man." Finally, he wrote, "Without fear of death or war or of wild beasts, do a man's work, my sons, as God sets it before you. If I suffered no ill from war, from wild beasts, from flood, or from falling from my horse, then surely none can harm you and destroy you unless that too, be destined of God . . . the protection of God is fairer than the protection of man."

Because Russia is a flat country without sharp mountain ranges to slow an invader, Kiev was constantly exposed to attack from successive waves of fierce nomads who wandered the broad steppe of the south. Vladimir Monomakh speaks of his many campaigns fighting against the Polovtsy or Kuman tribes that made a raid into Russian territory every year, killing, burning, and taking away women and children into captivity. Both princes and *bogatyry* were continually fighting against these warlike tribes; from these unceasing battles great patriotism and love of country were born in the Russian people. It was during the chivalrous days of Kiev that the beloved and poetic concept of "the Russian land" was born, of not merely territory but a motherland. Like a litany, over and over it appears in all the songs, legends and sagas of old Russia. The glory of Kiev with its generous spirit of nobility and freedom remained the golden dream of the Slavs, a poignant memory of what once was and might have been.

3. "THIS HAPPENED FOR OUR SINS"

The black earth under the hooves
was strewn with bones
was covered with blood.
Grief overwhelmed the Russian land.

The Lay of Igor

THE GREATNESS AND PROMISE OF KIEV lasted two hundred years and then came to a sudden and violent end. After the death of Vladimir Monomakh, despite the warnings of the church, the Kievan princes feuded for many years among themselves. Disunited, they were unprepared to face the cataclysm that engulfed them.

Near the Gobi Desert lived a strong and prolific Asiatic people, the Mongols. In the middle of the 12th century, one of the world's most terrifying warriors rose to become their leader. His name was Temuchin, but he is better known in history as Genghis Khan, which means "limitless strength." In 1211, with 100,000 fearless and pitiless horsemen, Genghis broke through the Great Wall of China and conquered a million people. Forcibly conscripting thousands of Chinese engineers and technicians, he swept through Central Asia into Persia, through the mountains of the Caucasus and into the Russian steppe. Fleeing before them, the fierce nomadic Polovtsy tribes sought the aid of their old enemies in Kiev, warning, "Today they have taken our land; tomorrow they will take yours." An alliance was formed and seven Russian princes and their armies faced the Mongols on the banks of the river Kalka near the Sea of Azov in 1223. The Mongols seemed to be in retreat when suddenly the Polovtsy fled in terror, leaving the Russians to be destroyed. Most of the princes and many of the brave *bogatyry* perished. The Mongols killed them in a gruesomely imaginative way. They built a platform over them, then held a feast on the platform, crushing their victims to death.

The Mongols disappeared as swiftly as they had come. For fourteen years Russia heard nothing of them; say the chronicles, "Only God knew whence they came and where they went." The respite was deceiving and brief. In 1227, Genghis had died, but his son, Ugedey, the new Great Khan, granted to one of Genghis' grandsons, Batu, the whole territory from the Urals to the Dnieper. In 1236 with an enormous army of some 200,000 men, each traveling with eighteen spare horses, Batu and the Mongols returned like a plague to Russia. These horsemen were terrifying in appearance. A chronicler wrote of them that they had "broad and flat visages and cruel looks, thin hair upon the upper lip and pit of the chin. Light and nimble bodies with short legs, as if they were naturally made for horsemen, whereto they practice themselves from childhood, seldom going afoot about any business. Their speech is very sudden and loud, speaking as it were, out of a deep and hollowed throat."

The Mongols lived for war. They were capable of staying on horseback for days on end without tiring. If they found themselves without food, they drew blood from their horses' veins and drank it. With their bows they could shoot as skillfully facing backward as forward and unquestioningly obeyed the terrible discipline of their leaders. Genghis Khan had organized his warriors into groups of ten and ordered that if any of the ten were taken captive in battle, those who returned would be executed. They gave no quarter. "Regret," said Genghis, "is the fruit of pity." Despising all other races, believing that it was their destiny to conquer the world, the Mongols advanced inexorably, burning and killing everything in their path. Swiftly they came up the Volga and prepared to attack Novgorod. Only a miracle of nature spared the city. The spring had melted the ice of the surrounding marshes and made them impassable for horsemen, so the Mongols wheeled and went south, ravaging all before them, and in 1240 rode down on Kiev. They used the domes of the Cathedral of the Assumption built by the first Vladimir as a target for their catapults. Then their battering rams broke through the walls and the terrifying warriors flowed into the city. The neighing of horses and the screams of the dying filled the air. Churches where the people had taken refuge were stormed and all in them destroyed.

Having crushed Kiev, the Mongols crossed the Carpathians and defeated the Hungarians. Poland was laid waste. Although they were momentarily routed by the Czechs and Austrians, they reached the Adriatic and prepared to attack Western Europe, which lay trembling before them. Then fate took a strange turn, and Europe was spared. In Mongolia, the Great Khan was poisoned—by a jealous woman, according to legend. As it was the Mongol custom to elect the new Khan from among his kinsmen, Batu turned back his troops and withdrew to the East, finally establishing his capital in Saray on the lower Volga. This Mongol stronghold came to be known as the Golden Horde, from the Mongol word for camp and because yellow was the imperial color of the Khan and his clan.

The Russian land was conquered and covered with blood. Every Russian town had been burned and sacked. A chronicler of the time, lamenting the destruction of the city of Ryazan, wrote, "And they burned this holy city with all its beauty and wealth . . . the churches of God were destroyed, blood spilled on the altars. . . . And not one man remained alive in the city. All were dead. All had drunk the same bitter dregs. And there was not even anyone to mourn the dead. Neither father nor mother . . . nor children . . . nor brother . . . nor relatives. And this happened for our sins."*

Of great Kiev nothing survived. Gone were the books and libraries and most of the churches of Yaroslav. The craftsmen and artisans were taken into slavery; some were later seen as far away as China. The Mongols of the Golden Horde used them to make rich ornaments and decorative objects for the courts of their rulers. A Russian craftsman made for the Great Khan an ivory throne inlaid with precious stones, metalwork and carving. Russians were conscripted by the thousands into Mongol armies; in the 14th century a Russian guards division was formed in Peking. Only in folk tales remained allusions to the wooden and stone palaces in which the princes of Kiev had once held court, to the shining glass windows, the great banqueting halls and the decorations in mosaic and paint that adorned their walls. A Minorite friar, Giovanni de Piano Carpini, who passed through Russia traveling to China in 1246, wrote that Kiev had only two hundred houses left and that in the Russian territory he saw only ruins and a countryside littered with piles of human skulls and bones.

* A Russian legend tells that rather than submit to the Mongols the city of Kitezh sank into the lake with all its inhabitants. On Midsummer Eve, the story continues, one can see the lights of the city blinking in the depths. In 1905 Rimsky-Korsakov used this legend as the theme for his opera *The Invisible City of Kitezh and the Maiden Fevronia*.

A few brave princes struggled on. One was Daniel of Galicia, who desperately appealed to the Pope and Frederick II, the Holy Roman Emperor, for help. There was no response from Europe. Courageous princes who tried to resist their conquerors were summoned to Batu's headquarters and poisoned.

One light in the darkness was Alexander of Novgorod. During the time that the Mongols were ravaging Russia, certain European powers decided that the time was opportune for invading Novgorod and seizing it for Catholicism. In 1236 the Swedes, incited by a new Pope, attacked, but Alexander conquered them and was from thenceforth known as Alexander of the Neva or Nevsky. In 1241–42 the Teutonic Knights invaded and once again Alexander Nevsky was victorious, defeating them in the famous battle on the ice of Lake Peipus.

Because of his courage and his victories, the Mongols respected him above all others. In 1247 when the Mongols sent envoys to Novgorod to collect tribute, the independent men of Novgorod refused, but Alexander persuaded them that the odds were hopeless. By traveling frequently to the Golden Horde, he was able to hold off the Mongols by tribute and persuasion so that Novgorod was never destroyed by the Mongols. In 1263 a number of towns refused to pay tribute and drove the Mongols away. Enraged, the Mongols assembled a large army which was already on its way when Alexander set off and once again succeeded in begging them off. He died on the return journey. His death was announced in the cathedral of Vladimir by the Metropolitan with these moving words, "My dear children, know that the sun of Russia has set." Yet thanks to Alexander's wisdom and restraint, Novgorod remained the only great free city in Russia, and the Novgorodians were able to maintain constant contacts with the West. Lord Novgorod became a member of the German Hanseatic League, and the city remained a center for independent art and architecture until the 16th century, when it was finally subjugated by a Muscovite tsar, Ivan the Terrible.

With the exception of Great Novgorod, for two hundred years Russian principalities and city republics survived only by total, humiliating subservience to their Asiatic rulers. And even after, as the Mongol domination was gradually broken, their successors, known as the Tatars,* continued to ravage Russia throughout the 15th and 16th centuries. Each year they would ride forth from

---

* Tatar or Tartar, as it is often spelled, was the name given by the Russians to the southern part of the Golden Horde in which the Turks predominated. Eventually, the Mongols themselves came to be called "Tatars" in the Russian chronicles.

their strongholds in the Crimea through the narrow Isthmus of Perekop in roving bands which had no purpose other than to take captives. In the summer, when the river beds were dry, they would ride in silently, surround villages and descend on them. The horsemen carried leather thongs to drag away men prisoners. On the sides of their horses were slung great baskets made like bakers' panniers to carry away children, for their prized booty were young boys and girls whom they sold to the Turks or other neighbors. Galloping through the towns, they swept up children in their baskets; a sick child was dashed to the ground or against a tree.

As late as 1571, the Crimean Tatars reached Moscow. Accounts of the day say they killed 200,000 people and that the rivers were swollen with bodies; 130,000 people were carried off into slavery. A Jewish merchant who sat at the entrance of the Isthmus of Perekop saw so many captives pass through that he asked if there were any people left in Russia. Russians were sold in the markets of Kaffa to all parts of Asia Minor, Africa and even some parts of Europe. At the court of the Medicis there were Russian slaves, and many Egyptian babies were sung to sleep with Russian lullabies.

For two centuries a great silence fell over the Russian land. All contacts with the West were severed. Russia virtually disappeared from the map of Europe. Earlier, as the Slavs had expanded and absorbed the land, they had fallen into two natural divisions: the Great Russians in the north and the Little Russians in the south. After the Mongol invasion, the Little Russians were cut off from the Great Russians. While the Great Russians became vassals of the Mongols, the Little Russians, who later were known as Ukrainians, were taken over by the Poles and the Lithuanians. The Russians retained an abiding fear of the East and a resentment of the West that had deserted them in their hour of dire need. Kiev was never to recover, and the Russia that emerged from the Mongol invasions was greatly changed. When, after two hundred years, the Tatar yoke was finally shaken off, the Russians had taken on some of the characteristics of their conquerors. From the Great Khans they had learned the art of despotic rule. Even their appearance had altered. Among the blue-eyed Slavs appeared the slanted black eyes of their conquerors, and it was through these eyes that Russia began once again to look out at the world.

4. HOLY MOSCOW: THE THIRD ROME

So RUTHLESSLY had the Mongols dismembered Russia that the nation had almost lost its sense of identity. Two-thirds of the population had perished. Survivors of the terrible holocaust had fled into the forests. Only one force still kept the flame of national consciousness alive—the Orthodox Church. Despite everything, the Christianity of Kiev survived and remained a living memory in the hearts of the people.

During the years that followed the invasions, monks and holy men roamed the land like shepherds to comfort and help frightened survivors or withdrew into the forests to meditate. Holy men sometimes wandered for twenty or even fifty years before founding a monastery; Saint Paul Obnorsky lived for three years in the trunk of a tree. Gradually others followed them to their retreats and over the years hundreds of new churches and monasteries grew up. Miraculously, the Mongols, so bloodthirsty in war, were tolerant toward all religions. They often spared holy men of any faith. Until they themselves became Moslems and all tolerance vanished, their khans indiscriminately attended both Christian and Moslem services.

The church, which had withstood the invasions, re-emerged stronger than before. The two centuries following the invasions, as Russia strove to reassert its national identity, became the Golden Age of Russian spirituality, the greatest age of icon painting and the church arts. During those years the church was Russia, and Russia was the church. Even after the Mongols were gone, the teaching and spirit of the Orthodox Church, which had come to stand for the Russian nation itself, remained the dominant influence in art and architecture until the end of the 17th century.

• • •

As the church grew in power, so did the city of Moscow. In Kievan times, Moscow was only a small trading post in the wilderness, hardly mentioned in the chronicles until 1147. In 1272 Alexander Nevsky gave it to his youngest son, Daniel. After the invasions, Moscow began to grow in importance; however, the princes of Moscow looked no longer to the West as had the princes of Kiev, but to the East. The Mongols governed by granting warrants to Russian princes, and acting under this power, the princes collected tribute. The Mongols kept a permanent mission at the court of the Muscovite princes. When the Great Khan made one of his visits to Moscow, he demanded that the prince approach him on foot, with his cap in hand filled with oats, from which the Mongol's horse would feed. As subservient vassals, the Moscow princes made regular trips to the Golden Horde, bringing their tribute and prostrating themselves in the prescribed manner, beating their heads to the ground five times before the Great Khan.

In return for this subservience, the Mongols permitted the Muscovite princes to rule their domains as they wished. Over a hundred years a series of cunning, persevering and ruthless princes fought with their brothers and relentlessly annexed or acquired neighboring principalities. Steadily, their riches and power grew.

Recognizing the growing power of Moscow, in 1326, the Metropolitan of the Russian Orthodox Church decided to move his seat from the city of Vladimir to Moscow. With him he brought the prestige and power of the church which radiated all over Russia. The church began to draw the loyalty of various parts of the country toward Moscow. Moscow became "the holy city" and its princes assumed the role of the defenders of the faith.

Around Moscow grew up a ring of fortified monasteries, all unified under the faith. There are no orders in the Orthodox faith; all the monks and nuns of the land are simply members of one great brotherhood, and these monasteries were far from being simply refuges for mystics and ascetics. Many were walled cities capable of defending themselves, with many hundreds of monks and nuns. Monasteries came to possess vast lands; satellite villages and towns grew up under their protection.

Humble monks, who in the words of the ancient chronicles, "bore upon themselves the humiliation of Christ, not having a city here, but seeking a future one," always were revered by the Russian people. Now, more than ever, they seized a position in the popular imagination which they never lost. Through the years their ideals were taken up by many Russian writers, including in the 19th century both Tolstoy and Dostoevsky. Such a monk was Saint Sergius of Radonezh (1314–92), who became the patron saint of Moscow. Following the Mongol invasions, Sergius withdrew into the forests. After several years, as his small dwelling became known, people gathered around him because of his holiness. He became known as a *starets*, or elder, a special figure in Russian Orthodoxy, one that Dostoevsky immortalized in *The Brothers Karamazov*. The *starets* is a man of profound spiritual wisdom, guided by direct inspiration of the spirit. His special gift of "charisma" enables him to see in a practical way the will of God in relation to each person who consults him.

Around Sergius was formed the Troitsky or Holy Trinity Monastery, forty-five miles northwest of Moscow. In the 14th century, the Troitsky (or Troitse-Sergeieva) Monastery became what the Monastery of the Caves had been for the Kievan kingdom—a dynamic center of spiritual teaching and the greatest religious house in the land. Within the walls of this monastic city were schools, craftsmen's shops and artistic studios. In this golden age of Russian religious art, painters carried the iconographic form to its perfection. Andrei Rublev, Russia's greatest religious painter and one of the world's great artists, entered the Troitsky Monastery and lived there as a monk. Rublev died in 1430. His deep faith radiates from his paintings. They are full of innocence and tenderness, distinguished by their great delicacy of line and harmonious colors, soft yellows, rich browns and celestial blues. One of the masterpieces of the Orthodox icons, the Holy Trinity, was painted by Rublev in honor of Saint Sergius, whose contemporary he was.

Sergius inspired a great colonizing advance of monks into the dark northeast forests of Russia. He was a revered figure whom princes came humbly to consult. And yet, even when he was abbot of this huge monastery complex, in the great tradition of Russian humility he lived always as a peasant in the poorest of clothing. When princes came to seek his advice, they found him in old felt boots and in worn clothes heavily patched and saturated with sweat. At the height of his fame he still worked in the kitchen garden. Often visitors could not believe that the simple man before them was actually Sergius.

Monks were in close contact with the people. They were sometimes merchants and they traveled along the great rivers of Russia. Monasteries were hospitable, distributing food to the poor and giving bread, meat and fish to all who came to them. Intensely patriotic, these rugged monks did not shrink from opposing princes, and it was they who among people and rulers urged defiance of the Mongols. Sergius is called the "Builder of Moscow" because he urged upon its princes resistance against the invader. Encouraged by the saintly Sergius, it was a Muscovite prince, Dmitry, who won the first victory over the Mongols at Kulikovo on the Don in 1380 and became known as the hero Dmitry Donskoy. Before the battle, Dmitry went first to consult with Sergius at the Troitsky Monastery. Sergius himself carried the most holy icon of Russia in the church procession before the troops set off.

Bolstered by the prestige of the church, the city of Moscow grew rapidly. By the 15th century the frontier settlement had grown to a city of 100,000 people. It grew in circles, like a tree adding rings to its trunk. It was a walled city within a walled city, with many fine churches and wooden mansions. Almost in the exact center of the city and dominating it high above the river was its heart—another walled city, which came in 1331 to be called the Kremlin, from the Mongol word *kreml*, which meant "fortified." The word today is associated only with Moscow, but originally every regional capital had its own fortified central kremlin. In Moscow, the Kremlin was the citadel both of the church and of its new defenders, the Moscow princes, and there they established their power.

When in 1453 Constantinople fell to the Moslem Turks, Moscow proudly declared itself to be the "Third Rome," the last bastion of the true church in all Christendom. The first Rome, it was argued, had fallen to the barbarians because of heresy; the second, Constantinople, had been captured and pillaged by infidels. "The Third Rome will stand," said the new doctrine, "and a fourth there shall not be." Shortly after, the Metropolitan was raised to the rank of Patriarch. The ruler of Moscow was declared to be not only the defender of the last true faith, but the successor of the Byzantine emperors and Caesars of Rome and, by authority of his rank, "similar to God in Heaven."

After the death of his first wife, the reigning Grand Prince of Moscow, Ivan III, in 1472 sought to consolidate his new rank by marrying Zoe Palaeologina, niece of the last emperor of Byzantium.

Women have often played an important role in Russian history. Zoe, who took the name Sophia, was both intelligent and ambitious and in her twenty-one years as Ivan's wife she exercised a great influence on the arts at the court. She had been raised in Rome as a ward of the Pope, and her stay there had exposed her to the most sophisticated culture of the time. When she arrived in Moscow she spoke not only her native Greek, but had mastered Latin and Italian as well. With her she brought from Rome and Constantinople a large retinue of priests, scholars, artists and architects. She carried to Russia her Greek and Latin books, priceless manuscripts, icons and art. For Ivan she brought a magnificent ivory throne made in Persia as well as the emblem of the Byzantine emperors for a thousand years—the Double Eagle—which Ivan adopted as the symbol of Russia. Sophia gained for herself the right to receive ambassadors and entertain visitors and she introduced into the court the elaborate court etiquette, full of the pomp and glitter of Byzantium. Far removed from the simple and direct relations of the Kievan princes, access to the Muscovite sovereign now took on great ceremony, which included bowing of the head to the ground, walking backward while still bowing, and kissing of hands and robes.

To emphasize Moscow's new position as the center of the true faith, Sophia enthusiastically urged her husband to embark on a vast building program of new and magnificent churches in the Kremlin. In the 15th century the Italians were the most famous builders of the day, called on for construction projects all over Europe. Spurred by Sophia, Ivan sent a mission to Italy to recruit the best architectural talent to be found. From Bologna his first emissaries brought back Ridolfo Fioravanti, a man famous far beyond the borders of Italy. Cities and reigning dukes were clamoring for his services, and it was a compliment to Moscow that he decided that he could best exercise his talents there. Fioravanti was a true Renaissance man—not only was he an architect, but also an engineer, a hydraulics expert and a master of military fortifications, pyrotechnics and metal casting. In addition to all this, he was also a talented magician who dazzled Ivan's ambassador with tricks, apparently turning water into wine before his eyes. The citizens of Moscow regarded him as a wizard possessed of fabled powers.

In 1488 other emissaries brought back Pietro Antonio Solario and Marco Ruffo of Milan, and in 1493 another Milanese, Alevisio Novy, along with a whole company of other engineers and architects. Working beside the Russians, these men were put in charge of the Kremlin reconstruction. Fioravanti taught the Russians how to make good mortar and organized a plant for brick manufacturing. Most probably it was he who acted as consultant for the building of the Kremlin walls; the work was supervised by architects and engineers from Milan. The walls are of brick, twelve to sixteen feet thick, interspersed with passages and storage rooms, nineteen towers and five rose-colored doors. These great walls, coupled with its elevated location, made the Kremlin almost impregnable.

Everywhere else in Europe Italian architects masterfully imposed their own Renaissance style, but not in Russia. From the beginning, the Italians followed Russian models and built according to Russian standards and taste. As had happened in Kiev with the craftsmen from Byzantium, the land exerted its own magnetism over the Italians. As they worked with Russian architects and artisans, the new Kremlin cathedrals became a microcosm of the styles that existed throughout the land.

Ivan III asked Fioravanti to study carefully the Uspensky Cathedral in Vladimir, built in 1158, and to use it as his model for the Uspensky Sobor, or Church of the Assumption (or more correctly, Dormition), in the Kremlin, which was to be the new coronation church for the rulers of Muscovy. Fioravanti went not only to Vladimir but also to the cities of Rostov and Yaroslavl, thoroughly absorbing the principles of their architecture. The church was completed in 1479, so successfully that it served as a model for other important Russian churches in later times. Russian artists covered every inch of the interior of the church with magnificent frescoes on gold backgrounds in the Byzantine style. The pillars were painted in zones, as in Egyptian temples. On the columns were gigantic figures of martyrs, archangels in armor and figures of the New Testament. The entire west wall was occupied by a huge painting of the Last Judgment.

In the cathedral was placed the premier icon of the land, the Virgin of Vladimir, or the Virgin of Tenderness, the miracle-working icon which Saint Sergius carried in the procession before Dmitry Donskoy's victory over the Mongols. The Russians believed Saint Luke to be the first icon painter. Although this masterpiece, commissioned in Byzantium by a son of Vladimir Monomakh in 1132 for a church he was building, is assumed to be the work of one of the greatest Greek masters, the artist is unknown and the Russians continued to attribute it to Luke. The spirit of this magnificent Virgin with her sad and tender eyes is so profoundly Russian that it quickly became the most beloved icon in the land, on which the Russians called in times of danger. It also set the standard for representations of the Virgin and Child that later native artists attempted to attain.

Over the years, the Uspensky Cathedral became a treasure house of church art. The iconostasis was a glowing wall, a fabulous display of the finest icons of Russian and Byzantine medieval masters brought to Moscow by the Grand Princes from Great Novgorod, Pskov, Kiev and Constantinople. The images were encased in gold, they wore breastplates of gold and silver, golden collars and pendants of diamonds. In the haloes of the saints, thousands of precious stones, gleaming like small stars, flashed with sparks of fire. In the crown of the miraculous Virgin of Vladimir, whom all approached with many genuflections, were emeralds as large as walnuts; on her shoulder, an enormous priceless diamond.

The Metropolitans and Patriarchs of the church were buried in the Uspensky Cathedral. The silver casket in which, after his coronation, a tsar placed his last will and testament was kept there, as was the canopied wooden throne used as the coronation chair for all Russian rulers. Legend claims that this throne was made for Vladimir Monomakh, but more probably it was ordered by Ivan the Terrible for his coronation. Originally gilded, its entire surface of twelve walnut panels is intricately carved with scenes from the life of Monomakh. The throne is supported by strangely lifelike carved figures of mythical savage beasts and it is justly considered one of the finest examples of medieval wood carving.

Only a few yards away from the Uspensky Cathedral, on the site of an existing church, architects from Pskov built a new Church of the Annunciation with white walls and five gold cupolas which was to be the baptismal and marriage church of the tsars. Small and intimate, it became the favorite chapel of the wives and sisters of the Muscovite rulers. The floor is paved in mosaics of jasper and agate, the walls covered by frescoes and the iconostasis decorated with the work of the master icon painters Theophanes the Greek and Andrei Rublev. The icons and iconostasis in this church were so dazzling that in the 17th century a visiting churchman, Paul of Aleppo, deacon of the Syrian Metropolitan Macarius, was moved to write: "No goldsmith could evaluate the great stones, diamonds, emeralds, rubies, set upon the icons and haloes of Our Savior and Our Lady. The jewels glow in the darkness like coals. The gilding of the icons was pure gold. Many-hued enamels executed with the finest art arouse the admiration of the discerning observer. The value of the icons in the church would fill several treasuries."

In a simultaneous burst of architectural activity, palaces and churches went up side by side. Marco Ruffo began the Palace of Facets, which Antonio Solario completed in 1491; the Terem Palace was completed in 1508. The Granovitaya, or Palace of Facets, took its name from the diamond-shaped pattern of its facade, reminiscent of the Pitti Palace in Florence and the Castella in Milan. The most striking feature of this palace was an enormous reception hall, 77 feet long and 70 feet wide, dominated by a single massive central gilded pillar that occupied the entire second story of the palace. The base of the pillar was surrounded by shelves forming a great buffet on which the rich treasures of ancient gold and silver plate and vessels from the royal household were displayed at great banquets and receptions. Here ambassadors were received, Patriarchs invested, great victories celebrated.

In 1505 Alevisio replaced the old Church of the Archangel Michael with a new one, which was to serve as a burial place for the rulers of Muscovy. There all the rulers of Russia until the 18th century were interred, each in a brass-covered coffin surmounted with a figure painted in a long white robe and the halo of Imperial investiture.

Along with these three great churches, the Kremlin included seven other churches, a monastery, a convent, the Palace of the Patriarchs, a treasury and council chambers. Important boyars also built their private chapels and great wooden mansions within its confines.

The walled city of the Kremlin with its complex of forts, armories, palaces, cathedrals and cloisters was at the height of its grandeur during the 16th and 17th centuries, and the splendor of this miniature city within a city was extraordinary. Windows and pillars differed in design and color. A multitude of cupolas in gold and bright colors crowded each other like bubbles. Gold, silver and later, in the 17th century, colored tiles that gleamed like brilliant fish scales decorated the walls. When the sun shone upon its gilded roofs, its domes and tents of many colors, it was difficult to discern from afar whether these were indeed buildings or whether perhaps a flock of brilliant-plumed firebirds had landed and spread their fiery feathers under the sun.

5. INSIDE AND OUTSIDE THE WALLS OF THE KREMLIN

Inside this citadel, behind the great walls, the tsar reigned supreme, "like the tree of paradise planted by God," a combination of khan and pontiff. All peasants and merchants who did not remove their hats with respect when passing before the Terem Palace, where the all-powerful ruler lived, were whipped. Noblemen were required to stop their carriages and sleighs a certain distance from the Imperial apartments and to surrender their arms before entering.

The three palaces of the tsar were connected with gardens, terraces and covered passageways. They were a maze of low corridors, sinuous little rooms and vaulted chambers. Brightly painted designs covered every inch of the walls. Rich frescoes, glorifying the deeds of the princes of Russia, mythical beasts and an infinite variety of garlands, vines and flowers bloomed on the walls and ceilings in a riot of color, red, green, blue and gold. Huge tiled stoves lavishly decorated with animals and flowers reached to the ceiling and warmed the chambers. The windows were of mica, often colored. In the semidarkness, the rooms glowed as if in a kingdom under the sea.

Throne rooms and reception rooms were approached by narrow, well-guarded outside staircases, on which only two or three people could pass abreast at one time. A deep silence reigned inside the palace, as if it were uninhabited. A visitor passed sentinels and guards immobile as statues. Ushered into the tsar's presence, he found all standing in total silence. The tsar received sitting on any one of his collection of sumptuous thrones. The Shah of Persia sent Ivan the Terrible a golden throne set with 2,000 jewels. Tsar Alexis' throne was set with 876 diamonds and 1,223 rubies. Above the throne hung an icon of the Virgin, and to the right, one of the Savior; Biblical scenes were painted on the surrounding walls, all framing the tsar like a god in a temple. On either side of him stood tall bearded warriors, in high white fur caps and white kaftans of velvet or satin and carrying shining axes. Surrounded by these guards, his sumptuously dressed gentlemen in gold and jewels, his clergy in their dark habits, the tsar in state inspired a kind of religious terror, like a fierce divinity. Bowing to pass through the low doorways, the boyars prostrated themselves before him, saying, "Do not order me to be punished, order me to say a word before you."

In the Gold Room, or tsar's study, where he received his council of nobles each day, a small window called the "Petitioner's Window" opened onto the courtyard of the palace. Each day, a small box was lowered from this window, into which the people could deposit their supplications and petitions.

This tsar worship reached its apotheosis in the 17th century. Like a divinity, the tsar showed himself to his subjects only on important occasions. In crown and golden robes, he would appear at the top of the Red Staircase which led into the courtyard so that his awestruck subjects might see "the light of his eyes." A contemporary print shows one of these royal processions with the onlookers, including the soldiers in ranks, all prostrated on the ground.

In the 16th and 17th centuries when the tsar married, couriers were sent all over the kingdom and all eligible girls of marriageable age were presented to them. The couriers made the first choice; the most beautiful among all the maidens of the kingdom were sent to Moscow. Vasily Ivanovich, the father of Ivan the Terrible, made his choice from among fifteen hundred girls, and Ivan the Terrible from among two thousand. A stern circular warned the boyars not to hide their daughters. Ivan sent the following circular in 1536, when he was sixteen years old: "From Ivan Vasilievich, Grand Prince of all the Russias, to the city of Lord Novgorod the Great, our patrimony, to the princes and boyar children living within 50 and to 200 versts from Novgorod, I have sent envoys and asked them to examine your daughters who might be suitable brides for us. As soon as this letter will reach you, those who have unmarried daughters must leave immediately for Great Novgorod. Those among you who should hide your daughters and shall not bring them to our boyars shall bring a great disgrace and punishment upon themselves. Be certain to circulate this letter among yourselves, immediately, without so much as keeping it an hour in your hands."

The maidens were brought to Moscow where they slept in special houses, in dormitories twelve to a room. In each room there was a throne upon which the tsar seated himself. Each girl knelt before him, and when he had gazed upon her as long as he wished, he dismissed her by throwing a handkerchief embroidered with pearls and gems on her bosom. Ivan narrowed his choice first to three hundred, then to two hundred and one hundred, until finally only twelve remained. They were minutely examined by midwives and doctors.

Because of this selection, which seems out of a fairy tale, it sometimes happened that quite humble girls became tsarinas. The imperial fiancée, once chosen, was given gifts, she was rebaptized, her name was changed, and a crown was placed on her head. She was then turned over to the sisters and close female relatives of the tsar and to the noble ladies, the boyarinas. But the memoirs of the day testify to the anguish of some of these young women whose beauty elevated them to a throne. They were prey to the fierce jealousies and silent hatreds of those who were former intimates of the tsar and who feared being dispossessed by the new family of the tsarina. Poison, which played an active role in the power struggles at the court, took the life of several maidens chosen by the tsar. Barren tsarinas were dispatched to convents; a Russian folk song laments their plight:

You palace of stone, palace of white stone,
Palace of purple,
Will I nevermore walk here?
Will I no longer sit at cypress tables,
No longer taste sweetmeats,
No longer eat the white swan,
No longer hear the tender words of my Tsar?

No wonder that a saying in the land held that it was not good to bring one's daughter to the beauty contest of the tsar; far better to throw her in the river than allow her to enter the upper apartments of the *terem*.

The word *terem* comes from a word for a Russian house, but it also came to mean the Russian custom from the mid-16th century to the early 18th century of keeping women, especially highborn women, in seclusion. This was not a Slavic tradition—on the contrary, women enjoyed a great degree of independence in the Slavic culture; rather it was one of the trappings of Byzantium and the East, which the rulers of Muscovy took along with their court ritual.

The women of the Kremlin palaces were never admitted to the company of men except for their close male relatives, the clergy and especially privileged courtiers. They passed their lives secluded in special quarters. The house of every nobleman of the time had its *terem*, or female quarters. In the palace of the tsar, the upper apartments of the female court were completely separate from those of the tsar. In the time of Alexis, in the mid-17th century, this female court numbered over three hundred women.

There they lived like birds in a gilded cage. Their special apartments were furnished with oriental luxury—Persian rugs, tapestries from Bokhara, Byzantine enamels. Along the walls great chests painted red and blue with locks of silver served as seats, beds and wardrobes. In these chests the tsarinas and boyarinas stored their precious furs of sable and blue fox, their red *sarafans* sparkling with pearls, their dresses of gold cloth, their long gauzy veils which were attached to their long plaits and fell in large folds over their shoulders. There they placed their hats of sable embroidered with precious stones and their ceremonial *kokoshniki*.

The *kokoshnik*, a high-peaked or rounded headdress which gracefully outlined the face and was characteristic of old Russia and the elegance of Russian women, perhaps had its origin in the diadems of ancient Greece. In Russia, married women always wore a headdress because, according to ancient Slavic custom, they were obliged to hide their hair from strangers. Maidens wore open diadems and their hair plaited in a single braid down their backs. In each region the shape of the headdress differed. *Kokoshniki* were variously embroidered with gold and silver thread, precious stones and pearls. Pearls completely covered the *kokoshniki* of the north regions, where river pearls abounded.

On the shelves of the rooms were placed beautifully bound religious books and enameled and jeweled caskets to hold necklaces, bracelets and clasps of diamonds. There was a quantity of toilet objects, mirrors, wooden and ivory combs, brushes, pots of white and red cosmetics. The ladies spent hours painting and making up. A visiting clergyman of the 16th century wrote, "They are extremely beautiful, tall, with great dark eyes, exquisite hands and fine fingers. Unfortunately, they paint themselves with all sorts of colors—not only their faces, but their eyes, necks and hands. They put on themselves red, white, blue, black or other somber colors. They apply cosmetics so thickly and strangely that everyone notices it at once. To make themselves more beautiful, they blacken their teeth with preparations of mercury, and have even discovered the secret of blackening the white of their eyes."

As for scent, musk and ambergris were not much esteemed at the Russian court; cinnamon brought from the East was the preferred Imperial aroma. Ladies rested and slept and ate fatty things so as to achieve the rounded shape that was the ideal of beauty. The word for "thin," *khudaya*, comes from the superlative of the Russian word for "bad." Ivan the Terrible once contemptuously refused a woman, saying she was too thin and that he hated leanness in women. According to Samuel Collins, an ebullient Englishman who was the doctor of Tsar Alexis in the 17th century, "The beauty of their women they place in their fatness. . . . A lean woman they count unwholesome, therefore those who are inclined to leanness give themselves over to all manner of epicurism on purpose to fatten themselves, and lie abed all day long drinking Russian brandy (which will fatten extremely), and they sleep and afterwards drink again. . . ."

The tsarina and her boyarinas were forbidden to show themselves in public. When they fell ill, male doctors attended them in a darkened room and diagnosed them by feeling the pulse of a wrist covered with a gauzy cloth.

A network of secret passageways connected the churches, convents and palaces of the Kremlin. The tsarina went out into the interior of the palace only at dusk. Screens or large pieces of cloth were held up on either side of her passage to shield her from the eyes of strangers. If she chanced to go out in a carriage, she was accompanied by a whole escort of serving men. Her carriage had bladder skins for windows, which permitted her to look out without being seen.

The long days were spent attending endless religious services or stitching fine embroidery. A suite of chambers was reserved for embroidery and became a school of art of its own. Icons on cloth and church linens of all sorts were embroidered with such skill and delicacy that, masterpieces of thread and needle, they still stir the wonder of the observer.

To relieve the tedium of life in the *terem*, in the household of the tsarina, among the boyarinas of noble birth who were ladies in waiting to the sovereign, there were also merry young country girls whom the tsarina called "my cousins" or "my sisters." There were lady jesters, male and female dwarfs, clowns, Ethiopians, young Kalmucks with slant eyes and turned-up noses, and old blind men who sang epics and legends of Russia or told stories of princes in love, of sorcerers and enchanters. In their enclosed gardens, the ladies played on swings and see-saws. They were permitted to watch the banquets of the tsar unseen through special grilled windows that overlooked the hall. At carnival time, they peeked from behind the screened windows of the Terem Palace at the games and sports on the Moskva River and watched as men fought bears with a spear in single combat. Sometimes a white bear was let loose on the ice and attacked by dogs.

The seclusion of the *terem* was broken only occasionally at great banquets when especially distinguished guests were honored by having the tsarina—or in the case of a nobleman, the boyarina—appear. Dressed in her most gorgeous attire, she gracefully descended the staircase of the *terem* quarters bearing a golden cup in her hand. She touched the cup with her lips and then offered it to every guest. Then, while she stood at the place of honor, each guest was permitted to greet her with a respectful kiss.

• • •

Life behind the walls of the Kremlin, with all its intrigues and drama, was a world apart. Few saw the inside of those hushed and secluded palaces.

It was the great square under the walls of the Kremlin that was the bustling center of the life of the people. Russians had a great fondness for the color red, which was thought to bring good fortune. So much so, that in old Russian, the word for "red" and "beautiful" was the same. The corner in each house where, with a small lamp burning before them, the icons were hung was called the "red" corner. Women painted their cheeks bright red and plaited their long braids with red ribbons. Red or Beautiful Square was the heart of Moscow street life. In Muscovite times, and indeed right up until the Revolution of 1917, it was not the glum, empty, forbidding place of today, but a huge, lively, open marketplace where one could buy anything from a cabbage to rare icons and silks, and savor the colorful and boisterous life of the people.

People from every corner of the land brought their goods to the great marketplace in Moscow. An English visitor in the mid-16th century wrote of the number of villages between Moscow and Yaroslavl, "so well filled with people that it is a wonder to see them," and that "the ground is well stored with corne which they carry to the city of Moscow in such abundance that it is a wonder to see it. You shall meet in a morning seven or eight hundred sleds coming or going . . . that carry corne and fish. . . . Some that fetch corne that at least dwell a thousand miles off and their carriage is on sleds. They bring thither fishes, furs, and beasts' skins . . . furs, sables, martens, beaver, foxes white and black and red, minks, ermines, miniver. From Novgorod come flax and hemp and much wax and honey."

The abundance was staggering. The variety of fruits and vegetables found in the Moscow marketplace amazed Adam Olearius, a member of the Duke of Holstein's embassy to Moscow in the 17th century. He writes that vegetables were arranged in large baskets under the open sky. There were apples of many varieties, pears, cherries, plums, red currants, asparagus thick as a thumb, cucumbers, onions and garlic—but, Olearius said, the Russians were not interested in lettuce or salad and laughed at the Germans, saying that they ate grass. Russians grew sweet and perfumed melons in enormous quantities. The secret of their excellence, it was explained, was that the seeds were planted in horse manure and straw after being softened in rainwater or milk, and at night the mounds were covered with mica against the frost.

Grouse, wild ducks and geese were numerous and inexpensive, and the quantities of cranes, swans and small birds, like thrushes and larks, were such that these birds were considered almost without value. Sheep and cattle were plentiful and cheap. In the large fish market, foreigners marveled at the great barrels of live fish, some brought from great distances.

The Mongols had imposed their civilization in many ways, but most particularly in commerce. The Russian words for money, customs, treasury, trunk, tavern and posting house are all words of Asiatic origin, as are the names for many articles of clothing (*kaftan, bachmak, armyak, teflya*). They introduced new food habits to the Slavs, bringing in cabbages and yoghurt. Merchants brought Eastern influences and habits along with their goods, and Russian merchants preserved their Eastern look and customs well into the 19th century. In drawings of the early 17th century they look a little like Persian gentlemen with their sumptuous kaftans, tall-peaked hats and high-heeled boots with pointed toes.

Until the 18th century, Russian trade was primarily with the Middle East, especially Persia, and from the East the Russians took a love for fairs and bazaars, and adopted the Eastern custom of grouping market stalls to make it easier to find special goods. In the 16th and 17th centuries, bazaars were rows, or *ryady*, of icon sellers, rows of gleaming gold and silver fabrics from the East, of Arabian silver, Frankish swords, copper and Damascus steel. The metalwork of Russian craftsmen was famous. Objects were embossed and chiseled with great skill and distinguished by their fine workmanship and mechanical perfection.

In the great marketplace of Red Square, itinerant peddlers and merchants mingled their cries with the chants of blind beggars singing for alms. Bear handlers wandered through the streets with their trained animals that were taught not only to do every kind of trick but also to act as chief characters in impromptu plays. Traveling in bands of thirty to sixty, colorfully dressed jesters, minstrels and musicians called *skomorokhi* performed. No one knows where these wandering performers originated; some say perhaps in Byzantium, which was famous for its mimes and actors. They had first appeared in Russia at the courts of Kiev as singers and storytellers, and later the tsar and great boyars often kept them as clowns and jesters. In the market squares, groups of *skomorokhi* put on their performances, singing songs and composing commentaries on people and events. They danced and encouraged people to join with them. To give puppet shows, the *skomorokh* would simply fasten a large piece of cloth on the lower part of his body, and then, folding it in a special way, he would raise it above his head to make a portable puppet theater. Their principal characters—Petrushka, his bride, the Gypsy and the Robber—were so popular that they passed into Russian folklore, but so ribald and boisterous were their antics that in the mid-17th century they shocked the Patriarch. The *skomorokhi* were banned and the people forbidden to dance, play games, wear costumes and masks, and even to play musical instruments. This ban was so contrary to the fun-loving nature of the Russians that it could neither be enforced nor endured, and happily, it disappeared in less than twenty years.

On Red Square was the tribune called the Lobnoe Mesto, or Place of the Brow, called by the chroniclers "the umbilicus of the world," where the tsar delivered speeches and Patriarchs blessed the people. On the square was also a multitude of small chapels and churches (some accounts say as many as fifteen), the tsar's zoo and public baths. Hardly a foreigner failed to note the national propensity for drink, for also on Red Square were numerous *kabaki*, or public taverns. *Kvas*, a mildly fermented beer made of black bread and various flavorings, was the national popular drink. Vodka brought from Poland appeared for the first time in the 16th century. Many wines were imported from France, Hungary, Rumania and the Rhine, as well as from Astrakhan and the Crimea. Anthony Jenkinson, an English merchant captain of the 16th century, marveled at the great variety of Russian beverages: "the juice of a berry called in Russian *Malieno*, which is of a marvellous sweet taste and of a carmosant color, which berry I have seen in Paris. [This was the raspberry, which, as his description

55

shows, Jenkinson had not seen in England.] The second is called *Visnoua* [cherries] because it is made of a berry so called and it is like a black gooseberry; but it is like in couler and taste to the red wine of France. The third meade is called *Amarodina* or *Smorodina* [currants] of a small berry much like a small rezon and groweth in great plenty in Russia. The fourth is called *Chereunikyna*, made of the wilde blacke cherry. The fifth meade is made of hony and water with other mixtures. There is also a delicate drinke drawne from the root of the Byrch tree, called in the Russe toong *Berozevites* which drink the noblemen and others use in Aprill, May and Iune which are the three moneths of springtime; for after those months the sappe of the tree dryeth and they cannot haue it."

The city was divided into quarters. The nobility lived in one quarter, the merchants in another; the armorers, the falconers, the musketeers and the bell ringers each had their own quarters, as did the foreigners and the Tatars. In the Great Field south of the city, the Nogay Tatars brought herds of horses to sell, sometimes ten thousand at a time. Workers in different trades all worked and lived in their own areas—tilemakers, bell founders, gold and copper workers, and because of this there were many special markets throughout the city. All the crafts divided themselves into specialties; those who made clothing, for instance, into sheepskin coat makers, tailors, hatters and *sarafan* makers. In all, in the 16th and 17th centuries, about 250 crafts were to be found in Moscow, including a small army of culinary specialists who made pancakes, pastry, jelly and jam, candy and gingerbread. Some districts in Moscow today preserve these old names: *Bronnaya* (Armor), *Khlebny* (Bread) and *Kalachny* (Fancy Bread).

Both rich and poor, and even the tsar, lived by preference in wooden houses. Russians thought quite correctly that wood was better suited to their climate than stone as the condensation from the steam of the tiled stoves used for heating made stone rooms damp and cold.

By the 16th century and perhaps even earlier, the Russians had devised an efficient system of prefabricated houses far in advance of anything of the kind in Europe. It was almost an essential service, for Russian cities were constantly threatened by fire. Moscow suffered serious conflagrations no less than twenty-seven times in the 16th and 17th centuries and houses had to be rebuilt quickly.

All the carpenters and cabinetmakers of the city lived in a region called the Pokrovskie Gates, and in this quarter was located a celebrated wood market where timbers for houses were sold. Foreigners found this practice of prefabrication amazing; Olearius wrote: "Those who have their houses burnt have this comfort withal—that they may buy houses ready built at a market for that purpose and in a short time set up where the former stood." More than a hundred years later, another Englishman wrote: "Among the curiosities of Moscow, I must not omit the market for the sale of houses. It is held in a large open space, in one of the suburbs and exhibits *ready-made houses.*" Logs of various lengths and widths were all clearly marked and numbered for easy assembly and a buyer simply specified the number of rooms needed and ordered the parts. "And," he continued, "it may seem incredible, that a dwelling may thus be bought, removed, raised and inhabited within the space of a week."

As the streets were muddy or covered with snow, people went about in a great variety of gaily decorated and carved carriages and sleighs, some in the shape of deer, birds and swans. The daughters of boyars and wealthy merchants rode about in summer in closed carriages lined with red satin. The trappings of the horses of the wealthy were very grand. Colorful saddles were covered with Moroccan leather or velvet embroidered with gold; the frontlets were silver-mounted. Horses were decorated with wolf, fox or marten tails, and wore necklets and bells that made them jingle down to their very hooves; an important gentleman could be heard coming a long way off.

Olearius wrote that Russian women were "well proportioned," but painted their faces strangely, and that the men were mostly corpulent and greatly esteemed "great beards and great bellies." These hefty noblemen dressed, a bit like onions, in many layers. First they popped a cap of silk and gold thread set with pearls on their heads and covered this with a wide cap of black fox. They wore collars set with pearls and precious stones and then a long silk shirt which reached down to the knees and was girdled at the waist by a belt through which they thrust the fork and spoon which every Russian always carried with him. Over this, they wore a long kaftan of golden cloth, then another long garment edged with fur and over it all they threw a long cape brooched and sewn with pearls. Their boots were of soft leather embroidered with pearls. Well-to-do ladies also wore overgarments edged with fur, and high decorated *kokoshniki* or fur hats. All ladies of all classes obligatorily wore earrings and, since all children looked alike with their hair cut in the same way, little girls could be distinguished only by their brass or silver earrings.

In Muscovite Russia, up to the time of Peter the Great, pearls were worn on the clothes of nearly all well-to-do Russians. Boots and gloves were heavily sewn with pearls; women's headdresses were covered with them; pearls were used profusely in the church for decorating vestments, crosses and icons. The pearl mussel was found abundantly in many streams, in the north in Archangel and in most of the rivers that flowed into the White Sea, as well as in Lake Ladoga, Lake Onega and the Volga watershed. Bluish in color, northern Russian pearls had a maximum size of twelve grains and, although they did not equal oriental pearls, they were highly esteemed, not only by the peasants, but by the nobility and even the royal family.

Golden, honey-colored amber, the petrified resin of trees, whether clear as a ray of sunlight or dark and flecked, was always beloved of the Slavs. From their earliest days of trading along their rivers, they brought, along with their honey and furs, quantities of amber to trade in Constantinople. Necklaces, bracelets and beautifully wrought objects were made of this light, warm material. Russians revered it, believing that amber was formed from the tears of the people shed over the tombs of fallen heroes, and they wore it close to their bodies, as they believed that it preserved good health.

In those Muscovite times, the church was so important that nearly every phase of daily life was colored by it. In the 16th and 17th centuries, church laws were considered as binding on every devout citizen as the laws of the state.

Every trade and occupation had its patron saint. The years were counted by the church calendar, which dated from the creation of the world and thus began in September. (The church fathers argued persuasively that the world had to have been created in September, or else how could there have been apples to tempt Eve?) Days were divided not according to hours but by the time of services. In the early 16th century, Sylvester, a stern monk and as thoroughly pleasure-hating as any Puritan, compiled a detailed manual called the *Domostroy* (Foundation of the Home), which dictated in minute detail how domestic life should be lived according to the directives of the church. This book prescribed prayer all day and even all night. Dancing, singing and unedifying chess were prohibited. Laughter itself was frowned upon. Woman was an instrument of the devil, and the entire family owed obedience to its master. Not limiting himself to moral dictums, Sylvester also included directives on sewing, cooking, embroidering and preserving food. Devout families, especially boyar families, were expected to obey these rules precisely. Given the exuberant Russian nature, it is difficult to see how these stern dictums could be carried out.

In 1662 there were more than two thousand churches, monasteries and private chapels in Moscow. Every fifth house, wrote Olearius, was a chapel, as every magnate "builds a private chapel and maintains a priest at his own expense." A common sight in Red Square were the unemployed priests who stood beside the Spassky Gate offering their services to those who owned these private chapels. Icons were in great demand; mountains of them were sold in the marketplace. The nobility and wealthy merchants wanted icons for their chapels and the entire population wanted them for their homes, as many icons as possible and especially those of the Virgin or particularly revered saints who were believed to possess supernatural powers. The icon was the inseparable companion of every Orthodox Russian from birth to death. No important event was complete without the blessing of an icon. Especially revered family icons were passed down through generations.

Foreign visitors were not only baffled by this custom but often shocked, thinking it idolatry. An English visitor in the 16th century wrote in horror, "he who comes to his neighbor's house doth first salute his saints . . . to their painted images they use much idolatry that the like was never heard of in England."

The length and magnificence of Russian church services overwhelmed foreigners, even Orthodox Greeks, as did the austerity of the long fasts which were strictly observed by everyone from the tsar down to the simplest peasant. Many of the visiting Greeks complained bitterly in their writings, saying that living among such hardy people was almost equivalent to suicide. Who but the Russians, they asked, could manage to stand for such long hours in church and deprive themselves of almost all food during the seven weeks of Lent? Englishmen found the custom of moving freely about in and out of church very disturbing; people, said one, "gaggle and cackle like geese."

In the city, elaborate religious processions were very frequent. Anthony Jenkinson, among many others, described the colorful procession which took place in Moscow on Palm Sunday:

The procession began with the arrival of a large tree fastened to sleds and hung with apples, figs, raisins and many other fruits "abundantly." Perched in the tree were five boys in white vestments who sang sweet hymns. The tree and its occupants were followed by young men who carried thick wax tapers and a great lantern to insure that the candles would never go out. They were followed by others carrying two long banners and "six copper plates, thin and full of holes," and then by six men carrying large icons on their shoulders. More than a hundred priests in gorgeous white vestments embroidered with sapphires, precious gems and "fair and oriental pearls great as peas" filed by, followed by "one half of the Emperor's men."

The climax was the arrival of the Metropolitan, seated sidesaddle on a horse covered with white linen to the ground, with the horse's ears extended with cloth to look like a donkey's ears. On his lap, the Metropolitan carried a magnificent holy book decorated with a gold crucifix. In his right hand he carried a large golden cross with which he "unceasingly" blessed the people.

Thirty men all dressed in red spread garments before him and, as soon as the horse had passed, quickly ran ahead and spread them down again. Jenkinson says that these men were priests' sons and that they were rewarded by the emperor with new garments for their labors. One of the tsar's men held the horse by the head while the tsar himself, on foot, wearing his crown and robes of state, led the horse by its bridle rein, while in his hand he carried a large palm branch. Then followed all the emperor's noblemen dressed in their golden garments. The procession wound through Red Square to St. Basil's and into the Kremlin, going from church to church within the citadel, before filing into the palace as the church bells pealed.

Russians loved bells. Although bells were never used inside the church, but only outside in belfries, Russians took great delight in ringing them not only before, but at various moments during, the service. Each day at dawn, and sometimes before, the bells pealed, summoning people to worship.

Paul of Aleppo wrote during his visit to Moscow in 1655, "nothing affected me so much as the united clang of all the bells on the eves of Sundays and great festivals and at midnight before the festivals. The earth shook with their vibrations and like thunder, the drone of their voices went up to the skies. At celebrations all the bells sounded together, beginning with the bells of Great Bono belfry in the Kremlin and then taken up by the bells of the Tower of Ivan the Great and followed by all the bells of the forty times forty churches of Moscow, booming and rolling in unison over the city."

The city lived by this constant chiming of the bells, while over the bright cupolas of the city flew thousands of white pigeons, which the Russians loved and considered the living emblem of the Holy Spirit.

6. A REBEL IN HIS OWN LAND

ALL THIS BUSTLING LIFE of the capital was, until the middle of the 16th century, virtually unknown to Europeans, who since the Mongol invasions had almost completely lost Russia from view. To be sure, a few hardy visitors trickled through. One of these was Baron Sigismund von Heberstein, who was sent to Moscow in 1517 as Ambassador of the Holy Roman Emperor. How the Russians felt about Westerners was emphatically demonstrated when Grand Prince Vasily received von Heberstein. In an episode which quite ruffled the dignity of the Ambassador, von Heberstein was required to sit through a long period of silence, during which he noticed a large silver basin placed on a table by the ruler's elbow. The basin was filled with water, and after greeting the Ambassador the Grand Prince ceremoniously washed his hands of contact with an unclean Western Catholic.

Heberstein made two visits and when he returned to Europe he wrote in tones of shock and horror of the bizarre customs of the "barbarian" Russians, about the terrible cold, of how the women loved to be beaten by their husbands (as proof their husbands loved them), how Russians loved to be slaves and had no talent for freedom. From von Heberstein's book, published in 1549, Europeans took all their stock impressions of Russia, impressions so titillating and tenacious that they persisted for hundreds of years as the absolute truth. Some still persist.

The English, in the mid-16th century, knew nothing of Russia. To them, Muscovy was so mysterious and remote that Englishmen of Shakespeare's time believed that Russians worshiped the idol of a golden woman and practiced cannibalism. The country, it was confidently declared, was full of strange creatures, like the "baronets," or vegetable lamb, a creature with the exact shape and appearance of a lamb but growing like a plant on a stalk attached to its stomach. The land was populated with "Scyths," who received strangers warmly and afterward killed them and drank their blood mingled with milk.

But in 1553, in the time of Edward VI, the English, looking with envy at the wealth which the Spaniards and Portuguese had found in the New World, determined to go and seek new riches for themselves. The intrepid explorer Sebastian Cabot, governor of the Company of Merchant Adventurers, was convinced that a new route to the fabled wealth of Cathay and the Indies could be found by a northeast passage around the North Cape of Norway. Encouraged by Cabot, a group of English merchants outfitted at great expense three ships, the *Bona Esperanza,* the *Confidenza* and the *Edward Bonaventure.*

These three ships were to sail beyond the last outpost of civilization in the northeast, beyond which no English ship had ever sailed except for a mythical voyage in the days of King Alfred. Their holds were filled with English woolens, "all manner of artillery," and provisions of tea, hard biscuits, salt pork and cheese to last many months. The captain of the *Bona Esperanza* and the admiral of the little fleet was Sir Hugh Willoughby, "a most valiant gentleman and well-born," who had fought the Scots under Henry VIII. Richard Chancellor, a widower with two little sons, was the captain of the *Bonaventure.*

Although Cabot had strictly warned his captains to stay always within sight of each other, in terrible winds and fogs off the coast of Norway near the Lofoten Islands Willoughby's ship and the *Confidenza* were lost to view. Chancellor never saw them again. After searching for them in vain, he and his men, a small company of forty-eight which included a minister, two merchants, a surgeon, a carpenter and "seven gentlemen adventurers," all agreed that they must continue, "to make proof and trials of all adventures."

So the *Bonaventure* sailed on alone through the unknown icy waters where, silent and forbidding, desolate islands of barren stone rose up from the sea. At last, three months later, on August 24, Chancellor came to a place "where he found no night at all, but a continual light and brightness of the sun, shining clearly upon a huge and mighty sea." Guided by the light, he sailed into a great bay. Fishermen in their boats, seeing the strange ship approach, fled in terror, and when he landed, people fell before him and offered to kiss his feet.

But where was he? When Chancellor inquired of the governor of the place, he was informed that he had landed at Colmagro on the river Dvina; that the country he had accidentally happened on was called Muscovy, ruled far and wide by their mighty Tsar. Chancellor asked to be taken to this ruler, and after a delay of many weeks, during which the governor secretly sent couriers to inquire whether permission might be granted, Chancellor and his men received an invitation. By this time deep snow covered the ground and they were taken off in sleighs, driven by bearded drivers wrapped in sheepskin coats who spoke a totally strange language, across the mysterious land.

Over snow and ice, through tundra and dark forests, they sped to an unknown destination. Along the way during this "strange and troublesome journey," Chancellor noted many rivers, the large and spacious woods, "a great store of fir trees, a wood very necessary and fit for the building of houses," and "wild beasts bred in those woods, as buffes, bears and black wolves, and another beast unknown to us, but called by them russomaka." It was apparent that the mysterious ruler of the vast land was very powerful. At the posting stations, people fought to give them horses as soon as they knew that the Tsar had commanded their presence.

At last, after a journey of more than fifteen hundred miles, the Englishmen arrived at their destination and gazed with astonishment at a strange wooden city —"Mosco" with a great "castle" high above it. In amazement, Chancellor wrote that "it was as greate as the Citie of London" and inhabited by 200,000 people. It seemed "rude and without order" with strange but "not unhandsome" churches. Searching for China, Richard Chancellor and his little band had unexpectedly stumbled onto a new world that both amazed and shocked them.

In the strange city they were again made to wait, guarded and kept away from the populace. Finally, after twelve days they were brought into the fortress for an audience with the great Tsar himself. Chancellor's men were awestruck by the unexpected splendor that suddenly confronted them, for "being entered within the gates of the court, there sat a very honorable company of courtiers, to the number of one hundred, all apparelled in cloth of gold down to their ankles; and there hence being conducted into the chamber of presence our men began to wonder at the majesty of the Emperor. His seat was aloft, in a very royal throne, having on his head a diadem or Crown of gold, apparelled with a robe all of goldsmith's work and in his hands he held a scepter garnished and beset with precious stones, and besides all other notes and appearances of honor there was

63

a majesty in his countenance proportionable with the excellence of his estate. On one side of him stood his Chief Secretaries, and on the other side the great Commander of Silence, both of them also arrayed in cloth of gold; and there sat the Council of one hundred and fifty in number, all in like sort."

The travelers were so astonished by the glittering sight that they were nearly "dashed out of countenance." But such was Chancellor's steady character that he retained his composure and "nothing dismayed" courteously greeted the Tsar "after the manner of England" and delivered the letters he carried from young Edward VI to the twenty-four-year-old Tsar Ivan Vasilievich, who was to be remembered in history as Ivan the Terrible.

• • •

The ruler who so impressed Chancellor's men is the one who, of all the Muscovite rulers, also most powerfully impressed the imagination of his countrymen and the world.

In Russian, Ivan is not called "the Terrible," but something very different —*Grozny*, from the word *groza*, or thunder. This word has a mighty and even awe-inspiring patriotic ring. It means variously "worthy of respect" or "awesome." Ivan was an extraordinary tsar, and his reign of fifty-one years was the longest in Russian history. He inspired respect, fear and pity. He was complex, tortured and, in his later years, very probably insane.

The stories of his life sound like legends. His father was Grand Prince Vasily, whose first wife had been childless. Because of her barrenness, he divorced her when she was forty-seven and sent her to a nunnery. He took as his second wife a beautiful young Lithuanian princess, Elena Glinskaya, then living as a refugee at the Russian court. When, on August 23, 1530, she was delivered of a son and heir, there was immense rejoicing in the Russian land. More ominously, there were also reports of strange lightning and crashes of thunder.

The new little prince was baptized with great ceremony at the Troitsky Monastery. He was christened on the tomb of Saint Sergius, named for John the Baptist* and put under the special protection of the Trinity. But when he was four, his doting father died. When he was eight, his mother, who was then in her late twenties, died suddenly and mysteriously, perhaps of poison. Her death terrified Ivan. Russia was then ruled by two rival boyar families vying for power,

---

* In Russian John becomes Ivan.

THE VIRGIN OF VLADIMIR.
Icon,
early 12th century.
Page 45

THE CHURCH OF THE VIRGIN OF THE INTERCESSION ON THE NERL,
Bogolyubovo. 1165.   *Page 32*

ANASTASIS. DESCENT INTO HELL, detail. The Saints
Paraskeva, Gregory the Theologian, John Chrysostom,
Basil the Great. Pskov, Early 15th century. *Page 27*

VIEW OF THE KREMLIN CHURCHES.   *Page 44*

ICONOSTASIS. Church of the Archangel Michael,
Kremlin.   *Page 45*

WEST PORTAL. Church of the Annunciation,
Kremlin.   *Page 46*

INTERIOR. Terem Palace, Kremlin. *Page 46*

CATHEDRAL OF SAINT BASIL'S, Red Square, Moscow. 1555–60. *Page 69*

CROWN OF TSAR MICHAEL ROMANOV. 1627–28. *Page 79*

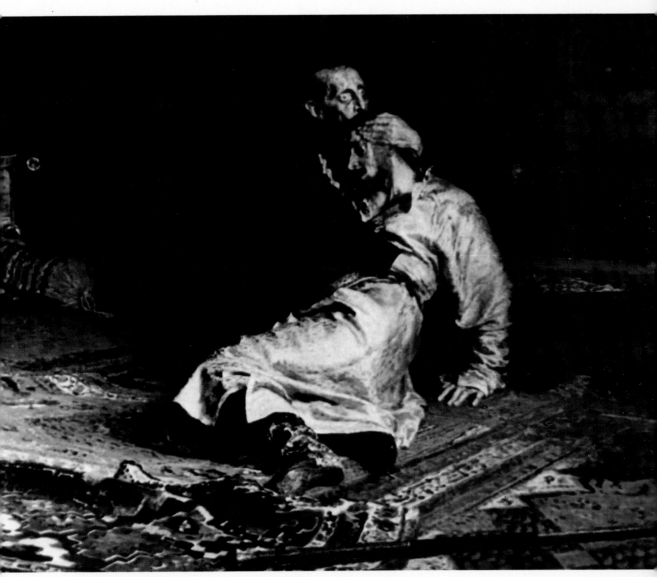

IVAN THE TERRIBLE AT THE DEATH OF HIS SON. Ilya Repin. 1885.   *Page 74*

RUSSIAN WOMEN OF THE SEVENTEENTH CENTURY IN CHURCH, detail. Mikhail Ryabushkin. 1889.
Page 51

RIZA (priest's garment), detail. Velvet, linen, gold thread, pearls, rubies, emeralds, diamonds. Middle 17th century. *Page 83*

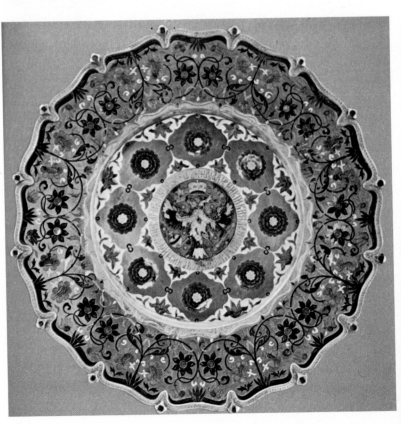

PLATTER. Enamel and gold, translucent enamel, rubies. 1667. *Page 83*

PETER I AT THE BUILDING OF ST. PETERSBURG. *Valentin Serov. 1907. Page 98*

SUMMER PALACE OF PETER THE GREAT, St. Petersburg. Architect: Domenico Trezzini. 1712–39. *Page 101*

CHURCH OF
THE HOLY
TRINITY IN
NIKITNIKI,
Moscow.
1643.   *Page 87*

THE CATHEDRAL OF SAINTS PETER AND PAUL, St. Petersburg.
Architect: Domenico Trezzini. 1712–39.   *Page 101*

SUN DIAL FOUNTAIN, Peterhof Park.
VIEW OF THE PETERHOF PALACE.
Architect: Jean-Baptiste Alexandre
LeBlond. 1715.   *Page 105*

who behaved, in the words of the chronicles, "like wild beasts." Although Ivan was Grand Prince, these regent boyars humiliated and tormented him, treating him and his deaf-mute only brother, Yury—in Ivan's words—like "menials." While the boyars sacked the tsar's treasury, Ivan remembered, "I was suffering privations, lacking everything even to food and clothing." One of these boyars in Ivan's presence insolently stretched his booted feet on his father's bed. Ivan's earliest friend was threatened with death and sent to distant exile in a monastery. One night, a terrified Ivan was awakened by soldiers filling his room. The soldiers were not there, as he feared, to kill him, but to murder the Metropolitan, who was trying to escape the wrath of the current boyar regent.

These boyars set Ivan an example of unprincipled barbarity for which they and the nation were to pay dearly later. During his childhood, Ivan saw nothing but cruelty, intrigue and treachery. But he watched and waited, always understanding his true power. At thirteen, he suddenly asserted himself. One day when the current regent came to call on him without retainers, Ivan had him seized and turned over to the kennel keepers, who clubbed the regent to death.

As a boy, Ivan read everything he could find—church history, Roman history, Russian and Byzantine chronicles. His heroes were the Biblical kings David and Solomon and the emperors of Rome and Byzantium—Augustus, Constantine and Theodosius. He directed the Metropolitan Macarius of Moscow to study the accounts of the history and rituals of the rulers of Byzantium in preparation for his coronation, and even plunged into these researches himself. At sixteen he announced to his council of boyars that he intended to be crowned, not only as Grand Prince, but for the first time in Russian history as Tsar and Autocrat.*

His coronation took place on January 16, 1547. Crowds of boyars, dressed in robes of cloth of gold, sprinkled him three times during the ceremony with a shower of gold and silver coins as a sign of the prosperity that was to mark his reign. There was great rejoicing, bells pealed all over Russia. Less than three weeks later, he married a girl whom he had chosen from among the hundreds brought to Moscow for his inspection. Legend suggests that he had already fallen in love and simply arranged to have all the eligible maidens of the kingdom summoned in order to deflect criticism. His choice fell on Anastasia Zakharina-

* From tsar came the derivatives tsarina or tsaritsa for the wife of the tsar, tsarevna for his daughter and tsarevich for his son.

Romanova, the fatherless daughter of a popular but not very important boyar family. Tradition has it that the Romanovs had descended from a certain Slavic Prince Kobyla, who had entered Russia from a region now known as East Prussia in the 13th century.* At the wedding, Ivan and Anastasia stood on a red damask cloth bordered with sables. As tradition demanded, Ivan drank from a beaker of wine, then threw the glass to the floor and crushed it with his heel. Two weeks after the wedding, the young couple, accompanied by an entourage, set out on their honeymoon, a pilgrimage on foot to the Troitsky Monastery. There they spent the first week of Lent attending services and praying devoutly on the tomb of Saint Sergius.

Anastasia was beautiful, gentle and clever. Ivan adored her. He trusted her so completely that when he went off to battle, he publicly kissed her on the steps of the cathedral and entrusted her with the keys to the jails. As a youth, he was headstrong and willful, but Anastasia, according to the description of the English Ambassador, Jerome Horsey, "became wise, and of such holiness, virtue and government as she was honored, beloved and feared of all her subjects. He being young and riotous, she ruled him with admirable affability and wisdom."

Together they had six children: three daughters and three sons. Two daughters died in infancy and their eldest son, Dmitry, was the victim of the kind of nightmare tragedy that seemed to surround Ivan's life. When he was a year old, his nurse slipped while she was carrying him on a landing by the river, and the baby fell into the water and was drowned. Anastasia was delivered of two more sons and another daughter, who eased the royal couple's sorrow. But, far worse, in 1560, thirteen years after they were married, Anastasia herself died, mysteriously stricken with an unexplained illness that wasted her in six months.

Ivan's heart was broken. At her funeral he wept so bitterly and noisily that those who accompanied him had to hold him up. After her death, he changed greatly and sank into a life of dissipation and drinking. He became increasingly suspicious. Since the use of poison was frequent among the restive and jealous boyars, Ivan became convinced in his grief that such nobles had robbed him of

---

* The name first appears in historical records in 1347 when Andrei Kobyla was a trusted servitor attached to the court of the Grand Prince Simeon of Moscow. The line underwent several changes of name. Kobyla's fifth son was known as Feodor Koshka, and his sons known as Koshkin. The branch of the family descended from Zakharin Koshkin was called later simply Zakharin. In the 16th century, Roman Zakharin had a son named Nikita Romanovich, and after him the family were called Romanov.

his beloved wife. His grief turned to rage and paranoia, increasing over the years to a mad obsession that made him see traitors everywhere. Implacably, he hunted them down, innocent or guilty. Many years later in one of his famous letters to Prince Kurbsky, who accused him of terrible crimes, Ivan was to cry out, "If you had not robbed me of my white heifer, none of this would have happened!"

In speaking of Ivan's reign, historians often refer to his "good" and "bad" periods. His "good" period coincided with the thirteen years when he was happiest. He married again seven times, officially three times and unofficially four times, but Anastasia was his only real love and perhaps the only friend he ever had.

Ivan had many gifts, among them an unusual memory and considerable literary ability. His thundering correspondence with Prince Kurbsky from 1564 to 1579 shows his talent for the telling phrase. He was one of the most educated men in Russia. He could quote easily by memory from many Biblical and historical texts. He knew Russian history well and was always interested in events in Europe. He possessed a large library, which included books of Yaroslav the Wise and Greek, Latin and Hebrew manuscripts gathered from all over Europe and the Near East. He engaged foreign scholars to translate rare manuscripts to show the world what literary riches there were in Russia and dispel the notion that it was an ignorant and uncultured land. It was Ivan, too, who in 1554 had the first printing press brought to Russia.

Throughout his life Ivan had an unceasing love for music. He enjoyed part-singing, was a competent choirmaster and even wrote hymns. Two hymns are definitely attributed to him, both written when he was a young man. Both are grand and filled with deep religious feeling. One is addressed to Saint Peter the Metropolitan, who became one of the saints of Moscow, and the other to the miraculous Virgin of Vladimir for whom Ivan had a special veneration and before whom he often prayed. For the Virgin, he composed a hymn to be sung on June 23, the feast day celebrating the bringing of the icon to Moscow. In this hymn of six long strophes, each gaining in power and more triumphant in tone, he addresses the Virgin regally as one sovereign to another, sure that the Virgin heard his prayers. Called "O Wondrous Miracle," it includes these lines:

Wondrous is thy mercy, O Sovereign Lady:
For when the Christians implore Thee on their knees to deliver them from awful ruin,
Then invisibly dost Thou pray to thy Son and by this holy image saved the people.

O ye Christians, rejoice and sing forth.
Rejoice, O joyous one, the Lord is with Thee, grant us thy great mercy.
The bishops and priests, the Tsars and princes,
The monks and clergy and all the people, women and children, glorify thy intercession,
The lords and the Russian warriors kneel before thy holy icon.
They glorify Thee and sing forth unto Thee.
Rejoice, O joyous one, the Lord is with Thee, grant us thy great mercy.

From Great Novgorod, Ivan collected the most famous singers of the time, and in 1551 he appeared at the Council of the Realm with recommendations for the teaching of music in schools all over the country. His whole reign was a golden age for the development of Russian music, in which he played a crucial role.

Ivan was a collector with a keen interest in the arts of the jeweler, the enameler and the goldsmith. He had a gift for discovering craftsmen of talent and inspiring them to create their best. He bought great stocks of gold and silver vessels in Germany and summoned to Moscow from Novgorod artists and artisans skilled in embellishing icons.

Thanks to Ivan's interest in the arts, the Armory Palace or, as it is called in Russian, the *Oruzheinaya Palata*, in the Kremlin, which had been created as an arsenal in the late 15th century, greatly expanded its activities. It became a network of workshops of icon painters and of gold- and silversmiths.

The 16th century in Russia was a century of artistic experimentation. Architecture, icons and all the decorative arts flowered in a highly imaginative and distinctive manner. The artistic achievements of this century became the nucleus of Russian national art, remaining a vital source of inspiration from which artists of later centuries drew.

Under Ivan, the wise and learned Metropolitan Macarius of Moscow undertook an immense literary project—the encyclopedic compilation of various types of Russian writings. This enormous work, which was begun in 1543 and finished in 1564, included a monumental encyclopedia of all known world history in twelve volumes (six volumes were devoted to Russia). There was extensive rewriting and copying of the chronicles with special attention to biographies of Russian rulers, folklore, and many stories. Executed in Ivan's palace workshops, this encyclopedia included 10,000 miniatures, many of them in color, and drawings and engravings of architecture, costumes, utensils, arms and armors both of princes and common people; in all, 27,000 folio pages.

To celebrate his victory over the Tatars of Kazan in 1552, Ivan ordered the building of a great church. Of all the works of art which he encouraged, this cathedral was the most splendid. It was to be called the Cathedral of the Virgin of the Intercession, after the feast day falling on October 1, 1552, when Ivan's troops took Kazan, one of the last Mongol strongholds. Ivan was young, victorious and happy in love. His first son had also been born on that day, and the church was intended to be a hymn of joy, an affirmation of gratitude and of faith in the Virgin.

The two architects from Pskov whom he chose, Barma and Postnik, were instructed to build something new and astonishing in Red Square, on the site of an existing small church built in the 12th century. Ivan deliberately wanted it to be placed in the large marketplace where all the people gathered and to be the crowning glory of all the chapels and little churches that already existed on the square. The Tsar ordered that it be built in the shape of the eight-pointed star of the Virgin as a cluster of domed chapels of different heights and colors connected by galleries. Each chapel was to be dedicated to the saint whose feast day coincided with one of the days of the eight decisive victories over the Mongols. The chapels were to include eight altars (the architects finally included nine).

The church was begun in 1555 and consecrated in 1560. In a strikingly original way, the architects incorporated all the features of Russian wooden churches and translated them into masonry. The result was startling and beautiful. An exotic legend says that Ivan had the architects blinded so that they would never create anything so beautiful again, but this colorful story has no basis in historical fact.

The cathedral came to be popularly known as St. Basil's because a Holy Fool, Basil, had been buried in the cemetery of the existing church. Holy Fools, viewed by the people as prophets and miracle workers, were very common in those times. With flowing hair and beards, often naked and wearing self-imposed chains, they wandered across the land fearlessly denouncing, even to princes, injustice wherever they saw it. Ivan honored Basil, and with Anastasia visited him on his deathbed in 1552. After the funeral, Ivan accompanied the bier to the small cemetery of the existing Church of the Trinity. The new church was to be built over the cemetery, but Ivan ordered that Basil's bones and his tomb with the chains lying on top be left untouched. After Ivan's death, Basil was canonized and a chapel erected to him adjoining the church. In time, the whole cathedral came to be called popularly by his name.

The cathedral was embellished later in the exuberant style of the late 16th and early 17th centuries. Although the basic structure stayed the same, in Ivan's day it was more sober. Onion domes, each with distinctive facets and patterns, were added, as were arcading and roofing over the galleries and tent roofs over the staircases. It was painted in rich colors that gave it the effect of folk embroidery, and in the 17th century, colored tiles were added for decoration. With its eight cupolas and eleven steeples, its domes like pineapple tops, bell towers like artichokes, and spirals colored like the pulp of many fruits, it is a structure which bewilders and enchants the eye, a creation so unique that it has become for the Western world a symbol of Russia itself.

• • •

Under Ivan, Moscow became a thriving metropolis, the largest city in Russia. Unusually, for a Russian of his time, Ivan understood and appreciated the value of foreign cultures, both those of the East and those of the West. It was the young Ivan, in the full flush of his victory over Kazan, who received Richard Chancellor and his mariners when they "discovered" Russia. Chancellor made a second trip and, thanks to his steady nerves and diplomatic skill, returned to England with a Russian Ambassador who brought with him rich gifts of gold and many rare sables, including two live sables with golden collars, for the English sovereign. The Ambassador was such a strange and exotic sight that he was constantly followed about London by gaping crowds.

In the following years, lured by the possibilities of trade, this first band of sturdy Englishmen was followed by others. Three English doctors and an apothecary were sent to Russia at Ivan's request, and he accorded the English special trading privileges. Elizabethan ships were largely rigged with ropes from Russia, considered the best in the world.

These early visitors noted approvingly that the Russian soldier was extremely hardy and could get along with little in the field, and that Russians were excellent chess players. Otherwise, ignorant of the language and history, condescending toward customs which seemed to them unworthy of respect, they were appalled by much of what they saw in Muscovy and found little good to say about it. Russian music seemed strange—completely exotic, with "no beauty in it"; the Orthodox religion nothing but idolatry and superstition. As with many other Western visitors who followed them, they were so totally confident of the superiority of their own culture that they dismissed Russia as a "rude and barbarous kingdom," wreathed in darkness and ignorance, neither civilized nor part of the Western family of nations.

Ivan's reaction, however, was different. He became such an Anglophile that he was sometimes scornfully called "the English Tsar" by his countrymen. In his later years, he carried on a lively correspondence with Queen Elizabeth and, as his paranoia grew, even offered her the startling suggestion that they accord each other the privilege of mutual refuge. He talked of going to England and even proposed marriage to her; she refused. In his last years he tried to persuade her to send one of her relatives, Mary Hastings, to become his eighth wife.

During their stay in Russia, Chancellor and his men were entertained by Ivan at prodigious banquets. Feasting and banquets played an important part in the life of every class in Muscovy. Social life revolved around great banquets held on feast days when friends and relations made merry together, sometimes getting very drunk. During these festivities, jugglers and musicians entertained; beggars were fed in the antechamber. Even daily meals were so copious and lengthy that it was an inviolate national custom for everyone to take a long nap in the afternoon.

These banquets reflected a Russian love of lavishness and magnificence and were given not only to impress but because of their intrinsic dramatic splendor. Their appeal was sensual and exuberant and this same love of lavishness shows also in the decorative arts of the time.

At Christmas in 1557 Chancellor attended a banquet for seventeen hundred people, all of whom were served in vessels of gold. Next to Ivan sat the twelve-year-old Prince of Kazan, the Tatar kingdom that had been conquered by Ivan five years before. Among the guests were the Metropolitan, the Tsar's male relatives, various ambassadors and strangers, "both Christian and heathen," while in adjoining halls dined two thousand Tatars who had come to offer themselves for the Tsar's wars.

Ivan regularly gave such banquets for hundreds and even thousands of people. He was a showman who loved scenic effects, and his banquets were spectacles. In huge halls among ornamented and painted pillars, long tables were set up in rows, with ten tables to each row and twenty places at each table. At the end of the hall, special tables were set up on a dais for the Tsar and his favorites. Sometimes Ivan ate at a table made of massive gold.

For the guests, long benches were covered with brocade and velvet, and on occasion Ivan even provided golden robes and mantles edged in ermine for his guests to wear. The Tsar sat on a high carved throne decorated with tassels of pearls and diamonds. The wall behind him was hung with icons. His throne rested on legs carved like lions and the back was a huge double eagle, painted and gilded with outstretched wings.

Placed i the middle of the great hall were huge oak tables with heavy carved legs. Piled in profusion on these tables, or if the banquet was held in the great chamber of the Granovitaya Palace, on the immense buffet at the central pillar, was a mountainous display of gold and silver dishes from the Royal Treasury. Some of the bronze, silver and copper basins were so large and heavy that they needed twelve and even twenty men to carry them. Many of the vessels were of strange design, in the shape of unicorns, lions, roosters, peacocks, storks, ostriches and even a large rhinoceros. They were made of gold and silver, encrusted with precious gems. Some goblets were made of carnelian, others of ostrich eggs, coconuts and reindeer horn trimmed with gold.

When the Tsar appeared, everyone bowed. Ivan was tall, high-shouldered and broad-chested. His full beard was auburn, and his blue eyes, everyone agreed, were so piercing that their glance could make strong men tremble and women faint. He wore long brocaded robes, richly embroidered and sewn with pearls and precious stones, and red kid boots banded with silver. Over his shoulders rested a great gold filagree collar ornamented with miniature enameled icons of the Savior, the Virgin, the Apostles and the Prophets. A large ornamented golden cross hung on a chain about his neck. He proceeded slowly through the company to his place and there inclined himself to each side, then recited a long prayer aloud, crossed himself and blessed the food. Before the banquet began, he broke bread and sent a piece to each of his noblemen, calling each name aloud and saying, "Ivan Vasilievich, Emperor of Russia and Grand Duke of Muscovy, doth reward thee with bread." Upon receiving the bread, each man stood and thus, Chancellor says, the Tsar was able to ascertain the presence of his household.

There was a multitude of servants. Alongside the great buffets laden with golden dishes stood two gentlemen with napkins on their shoulders who each held in his hands a cup of gold set with pearls and precious stones. When the Tsar was disposed, after the cup had been tasted, he drank it at a draught. All the gentlemen who waited on him were dressed in gold. At the great banquets of Ivan, servants changed their garments several times during the dinner. Chancellor noted at a banquet that he attended that Ivan himself changed his crown before dinner and during dinner wore two different crowns so that Chancellor saw him wear three crowns in one day. At first, servants were in purple kaftans with golden embroidery. They retired in double rows to the kitchen and returned carrying several hundred roast swans on golden trays. The Equerry Carver and his helpers carved them; the Tsar crossed himself, offered morsels to distinguished guests and oversaw the distribution to the other guests. Upon arriving at each place, the bearers announced, "The Tsar gives you this," and the person rose. Similar custom was followed as the beverages were poured. The swans were followed by several hundred roasted peacocks whose tails were spread fan-shaped on the trays. Then came various *kulebyaki* (meat and fish pies), cheese and dumplings.

The servants passed large gold and enameled *kovshi* (drinking vessels) full of mead, juniper and cherry spirits to clear the palate. Then came various foreign wines—French burgundy, and French white wines, Muscat and Hungarian wines, Canary, Alicant and Malmsey. Drinking every cup of wine offered was considered obligatory courtesy for every guest, a feat which sorely tried many a foreign ambassador. During the dinner, musicians played the *gusli*, a zitherlike instrument, and jesters entertained. For later courses, the servants changed into bright brocaded dolman jackets, arriving with trays laden with storks with sweetmeats, black cock in saffron, spiced crane, goose with millet, cocks dressed with ginger, hazel grouse with plums and boned chickens. Then came several soups, both fish and poultry broths. There was another rest while guests consumed honey, black currant and sugar liqueurs. Next came roast meats and giant fish, taken from the White Sea and brought alive across the country in enormous barrels, a trip which took several weeks. Large whole sturgeons were arranged on golden trays so that they looked like winged dragons with wide-open jaws. And there was still more—hares with noodles, quails and larks in onion and saffron. For dessert, the servants retired again and came back in coats of white velvet embroidered in silver and trimmed with sable. Some carried gilded and decorated trees from which hung cakes and sweetmeats, while others carried pancakes, fritters, jellies and creams, and creations made of sugar in the form of lions, eagles and birds and even miniature Kremlins. Among the birds and cities of sugar were piles of apples, berries and preserved nuts.

For the guests these banquets were tests of endurance as they customarily lasted five or six hours; to celebrate after Kazan, Ivan held a banquet which lasted three days. At last, at the end of the feasting, the Tsar dismissed each man once again by name, as he had summoned them at the beginning, a feat of memory Chancellor found astonishing.

• • •

Because in the Orthodox Church divorce on the grounds of barrenness alone was not permitted, the Patriarch of Jerusalem had opposed the marriage of Ivan's father to his mother and laid down then a terrible curse: "If you should do this wicked thing, you will have a wicked son; your states will become prey to terrors and tears; rivers of blood will flow; the heads of the mighty will fall; your cities will be devoured by flames." In the last sixteen years of Ivan's reign, all these dire predictions came true. His anxiety and uncontrollable fears continued to mount. He was consumed with the idea that his mission was to rid the world of evil, and he saw traitors and evil everywhere.

To subdue the independent citizens of Novgorod, he waged bloody purges in the city, killing sixty thousand citizens. He pillaged and murdered all over the land and formed a group of six thousand handpicked men called the *Oprichniki*, who, loyal to him alone, wandered the land stealing and murdering while ostensibly rooting out "traitors." In a century distinguished by bloodshed and atrocious cruelty everywhere in Europe, Ivan's atrocities have passed into legend, magnified by the exotic distance of Russia and the haunted personality of the Tsar who visited his nightmare terrors upon his people.

As he grew older, his large eyes perpetually darted about nervously; his beard grew grizzled. His uncontrollable rages grew more frequent; when he was angry, he foamed at the mouth like a stallion and appeared mad.

One day, in the fortified settlement of Alexandra Sloboda, the Tsar fell into an argument with his beloved eldest son and heir, Ivan, who was then twenty-eight. Some accounts say that the father accused the son of being a traitor, others that the Tsar had insulted his son's pregnant wife. Their words grew heated. In a rage, Ivan raised the heavy iron staff he always carried and prepared to strike him. Boris Godunov, one of Ivan's most faithful courtiers, rushed forward and seized Ivan by the arm. Ivan jabbed at Boris, wounding him. Then, enraged, he brought down the heavy end of his staff on his son's skull, striking him on the temple. Young Ivan fell, bleeding profusely. Stunned, shocked, Ivan threw himself on his son, embracing and kissing him and trying to stop the bleeding. He screamed for a doctor. When the doctor arrived, he found Ivan, deadly white, crying, "I have killed my son!"

The Tsar and his entourage, dressed in black, set out with the body from the settlement. Ivan walked the entire distance of seventy-five miles back to Moscow beside the coffin.

At the funeral in the Church of the Archangel Michael, streams of jewels were poured into the coffin before it was closed. Ivan threw himself upon it uttering terrible screams. Giles Fletcher, another English Ambassador writing in the 16th century, said "that he meant him no mortal harm when he gave him the blow may appear by his mourning and passion after his son's death, which never left him until it brought him to his grave."

Ivan could no longer sleep. At night he tossed so violently that he sometimes fell to the floor and slept there. Or he would wander, howling, on the church steps and banging on the doors that were closed to him. For many months he would not show himself to the people. During the last two years of his life, his expression was somber and melancholy. In the middle of conversations he would fall into fits of weeping or into bursts of hysterical laughter.

Even at the end there were omens. In 1584 a strange comet in the shape of a fiery cross appeared in the sky and hung motionless over the Kremlin. Upon seeing it, Ivan said, "This sign foretells my death." A large black bird appeared, cawing over Moscow. Ivan summoned sixty witches from Lapland, but all their spells and auguries were in vain and they gloomily predicted that the day of his death would be March 18.

In his last days, sick and failing, Ivan had himself carried daily into his Treasure Chamber where great heaps of gold, pearls, emeralds and rubies lay among vessels of gold plate and gold cups enriched with gems. Russians loved jewels, regarding them with awe, almost as if they were alive, and valued them not only for their intrinsic decorative beauty but for the mystic reservoirs of strength they were believed to possess.

Sir Jerome Horsey, the English Ambassador to Ivan's court, tells the dramatic story that on the day that Ivan was to die he summoned Horsey and his noblemen to the Treasure Chamber. He called for precious stones and jewels and spoke to those assembled about their fabled properties. He showed them lodestones, which possessed "the great and hidden virtue" of helping mariners guide their ships and kept the tomb of the Prophet Mohammed suspended in the air in the Mosque of Derbent. He asked for needles to be touched to them so that they would cling together in the air like a chain. He then said, "Take this fair coral and turquoise you see; take them in your hand. Of their nature, they are oriental colors. Put them on my hand and arm. I am poisoned with disease; you see they show their virtue by their change of pure color into pall; they declare my death." For many hundreds of years, people believed that the unicorn's horn could take away poisons and restore health, so Ivan called for "his staff royal, a unicorn's horn garnished with fair diamonds, rubies, sapphires, emeralds and other precious stones rich in value," to be brought. He asked his physician to scrape a circle with this staff on the table and to put several spiders within the circle. One after another the spiders all died and others outside the circle scurried away. "It is too late," said Ivan, "it will not preserve me."

Then, Horsey continues, Ivan said, "Behold these precious stones. The diamond is the Orient's richest and most precious. I never affected it; it restrains fury and luxury and abstinence and chastity; the least parcel of it in power will poison a horse, much more a man.' Points at the ruby. 'O! this is most comfortable to the heart, brain, vigor of man, clarifies congealed and corrupt blood.' Then at the emerald. 'The nature of the rainbow; this precious stone is an enemy of uncleanness. . . . The sapphire I greatly delight in; it preserves and increaseth courage, joys the heart, pleasing to all the vital sense, precious and very sovereign for the eyes, clears the sight, takes away bloodshot and strengthens the muscles and strings thereof.' Then takes the onyx in hand. 'All these are God's wonderful gifts, secrets in nature and yet reveals them to man's use and contemplation as friends to grace and virtue and enemies to vice. I faint, carry me away until another time.' "

It was the last time that Ivan would contemplate his jewels. After this visit to the Treasury, Ivan felt a brief new surge of strength. In the evening, he called for his chessboard and his favorites, Boris Godunov among them, to play. During the game he was suddenly seized and fell backward in a faint. There was a great outcry. One courtier sent for vodka, another for marigold and rosewater; another called the priest and the doctors. It was all too late. On March 17, 1584, almost precisely as the witches had foretold, Ivan the Terrible, says Horsey, was "strangled and stark dead."

A contemporary, summing up the tragic end of his bloody and tormented reign, wrote, "and later, as if it were a terrible storm come from afar broke the repose of his good heart and he became a rebel in his own land." Historians still argue about his reign, but one thing is certain: More than any other tsar, he passed into the folklore of his country. Songs were sung about him and legends grew in which he was revered, and even mourned. In the popular imagination, he is seen as a heroic and tragic figure standing in the moonlight, wrapped in shadows.

7. THE FIRST ROMANOVS

IVAN WAS SUCCEEDED BY FEODOR, the last of his sons by Anastasia. Feodor had been weak from birth, and at thirty, he was a gentle but feebleminded man whose greatest joy was ringing bells. After a reign of fourteen years, he died; his death, wrote the chroniclers sadly, was "the withering away of the last flower of the Russian land." Feodor was the last of a line of rulers that stretched back to the days of ancient Kiev. Russia was now without a dynasty.

The Council of the Realm met and considered many candidates. One of the least likely was Boris Godunov. Although he had been the close adviser and friend of Ivan the Terrible and his sister had been married to Tsar Feodor, Boris was a commoner and half-Tatar. But, perhaps stage-managed by Boris himself, the army and a loud city mob noisily demanded that he be elected Tsar. Finally the Patriarch, accompanied by the high clergy and boyars, went to find Boris, who was modestly in seclusion in the Monastery of Novodevichy just outside Moscow, and begged him to accept the crown. Dramatically, Boris refused. He had to be asked many times before "with deep humility" he agreed to become the new Tsar. He was crowned with great pomp in 1598.

To commemorate his election as Tsar and his hopes of founding a new dynasty, Boris ordered the construction of the Bell Tower of Ivan the Great at almost the exact center of the Kremlin. It became the highest of all the multicolored domes, cupolas and towers, rising five stories to a golden dome 33 feet in diameter. Including its golden cross, the Tower reaches 320 feet into the sky; its deep foundation is said to extend to the level of the Moskva River. Among its thirty-three bells, Boris had placed the famous bell of Lord Novgorod the Great that in days of old had summoned its citizens to town meetings; Ivan the Terrible had taken it away as a symbol of his total subjugation of the city.

Boris was actually a capable and even progressive tsar. He was interested in foreign ideas, brought foreigners into Russian service and continued the active relations with England begun by Ivan the Terrible. But his reign was beset with bad fortune. Very soon boyars began to plot against him and circulate rumors of corruption. Twelve years after the event, they came to accuse him of having murdered young Prince Dmitry, the last son of Ivan by his seventh wife. Although the young Prince almost certainly died accidentally, Boris could not seem to counter these rumors, and he reacted by imprisoning rival boyars. During three successive years Russia suffered severe famines. Boris energetically tried to dispense food and behaved so compassionately that he was called "Boris the Bright-Souled," but the peasants continued to flee the countryside in droves. Boris was forced to institute the first laws tying them to the land, thus beginning the institution of serfdom which was gradually enacted into permanent law by 1649.

Boris shares the fate that befell Richard III of England. In both cases, historical fact has been overwhelmed by the power of art. Both rulers were very enlightened for their day; both were accused of committing horrible crimes of which they were almost surely innocent; both were immortalized by the greatest literary figures of their respective nations. Shakespeare, writing in the time of the Tudors, transformed the tall and noble Richard of York into a foul, hunchbacked monster. Pushkin made Boris into a haunted, guilt-ridden murderer, an image indelibly reinforced by Mussorgsky's powerful opera based on Pushkin's tragedy. Boris' reign, which had begun in triumph, was to last but seven years.

In 1603 a young man claiming to be the murdered Tsarevich Dmitry appeared, and with the help of dissident boyars invaded Russia at the head of a Polish army. Boris at first repulsed these attacks, but he died unexpectedly in 1605. An eight-year period of Russian history known in English as the Time of Troubles and in Russian as *Smutnoe Vremya*, or "Confused Time," had begun.

When Dmitry reached Moscow, Boris' sixteen-year-old son, Feodor, a handsome and intelligent boy of great promise, was clubbed to death and his beautiful daughter Xenia banished to end her years in a convent. Dmitry was declared Tsar, but his reign lasted less than a year. His introduction of Western customs at court and his pronounced un-Russian behavior quickly discredited him. It is said that his refusal to cross himself constantly, to take naps and to visit the baths convinced everyone that he could not possibly be a true Russian. He was killed, and his ashes were loaded into a cannon and shot back toward Poland.

There were more invasions. In five years, four tsars sat in the Kremlin, all swiftly overthrown. The Swedes invaded and seized Novgorod, a second false Dmitry appeared, robbers roamed the land and the Poles occupied Moscow and captured the Kremlin. With the land in chaos, two popular heroes arose. One was Prince Dmitry Pozharsky and the other a wholesale meat dealer from Nizhny Novgorod named Kuzma Minin. Together the two men managed to raise a national militia, repulse the invaders and recapture the Kremlin. A statue dedicated to them stands in Moscow to this day.

The most representative Council of the Realm ever assembled, composed of boyars, clergy, merchants, Cossacks and free peasants, was called together to choose a new tsar. Their choice finally fell on the grandnephew of Ivan the Terrible, a descendant of Ivan's beloved Anastasia, Michael Romanov. Michael was then sixteen years old, living in semi-exile with his mother in a monastery two hundred miles from Moscow.

A great procession of people came to this young man, begging him to be their ruler. He refused many times "with tears and great wrath." His mother insisted that he was too young, but the crowd finally prevailed and Michael promised to come to Moscow.*

The constant wars had devastated the country. The roofs of the Kremlin palaces were burned and windows smashed. Much treasure had been stolen and it was Russia's richest merchant family, the Stroganovs, dealers in silk, caviar and Siberian furs, that provided the wherewithal to equip Michael's retinue. It was the custom for each tsar to have a new crown made for his coronation. Despite the sad state of the treasury, a splendid crown was fashioned for Michael, made of solid gold and studded with large clear rubies, emeralds, diamonds and sapphires. With the placing of this crown on the head of young Michael, there began a new dynasty which was to rule Russia for more than three hundred years.

---

* A Russian legend relates that while Michael was living in the monastery, Polish forces roaming about central Russia had the idea of seizing him. A heroic peasant, Ivan Susanin, guided the Poles to their doom in the trackless forest. Glinka in 1836 used this legend for his first opera, for which another Tsar, Nicholas I, suggested the title: *A Life for the Tsar.*

Michael ruled for thirty-two years. Although he was bored with public affairs, he chose capable advisers and peace gradually returned to the land. During his reign, the tall, Gothic-looking towers on the Kremlin walls were erected. The most famous of these, the tower above the Spassky Gate with its great clock, was designed in 1625 by Christopher Galloway, an Englishman, and adapted to the national taste by a Russian architect, Ogurstev. Michael also began a complete renovation of the royal palaces of the Kremlin, which had been almost totally destroyed during the upheavals.

Michael was serious. In public, he rarely permitted himself a smile or a laugh. However, in private he was a good deal merrier, keeping many jesters and dwarfs at his court, all dressed in bright blue and red. He loved to sing folk songs and his particular pride was an organ which he had ordered from Holland. Delicate in health, he made few public appearances. When he did, he was so weighted down with the golden robes of state that he had to be supported. When unexpectedly his two oldest sons died in 1645, Michael was so overcome with grief that he wept constantly and only a few months later, on July 15, 1645, Michael himself died of a stroke. The cause of his death, the doctors said, was all the tears he had shed over his beloved sons.

•   •   •

The 17th century in Russia was an exciting and inquisitive time. New ideas were introduced into the isolated land of Muscovy, ideas whose full effects were to explode dramatically only in the 18th century.

The second Romanov Tsar, Alexis, presided over this changing world. A contemporary of Charles II of England, he ruled for thirty years. A product of the old, he flirted with the new, exhibiting in himself the tendencies of both. Like his father, Michael, he came to the throne at sixteen, and was raised in the traditions of old Muscovy. He grew to be an athletic young man, six feet tall. He spent much time in the country and developed a passion for hunting and falconry, a knightly sport at which he became so expert that he wrote a manual of instruction for falconers. At seventeen, he chose an old-fashioned and very religious girl, Maria Miloslavskaya, as his wife and was himself so devout that he came to be called "the Pious." So sincerely did he follow the precepts of the church that at the age of twenty, persuaded by the stern Patriarch of the time, it was he who officially banned the *skomorokhi* and all amusements. (It was an action that Puritans of Europe would have approved; this austere period in Russia occurred during the same years that Cromwell was banning Maypoles and the theater in England.)

Alexis' devotion to the church was so extreme that his English doctor, Samuel Collins, wrote of him: "He never misses divine service. If he be well, he goes to it, if sick, it comes to him in his chamber. On fast days he frequents midnight prayers, standing four, five, six hours together, prostrating himself to the ground, sometimes a thousand times and on great festivals 1500. In great fast, he eats but three meals a week; for the rest a piece of brown bread and salt, a pickled mushroom or a cucumber, and drinks a cup of small beer. He eats fish but twice in the great Lent and observes it seven weeks altogether. In fine, no man is more observant of canonical hours than he is of fasts. We may reckon he fasts eight months in twelve."

Yet Alexis was full of contradictions. His character was in general so amiable and kind that he earned himself many devoted friends, but he also had a temper so fierce that when it exploded he rained down abuse on the heads of his courtiers and on one occasion physically booted his uncle out of the boyar council. And the man who fasted so strenuously and spent hours at religious services also loved pomp, spectacle and luxury.

Under Alexis, court ceremonial became ever more complicated and the flowery rhetoric of address absurdly long and elaborate. Such importance was put on the correct use of the Tsar's lengthy titles that the accidental omission of even a single word could be severely punished. On one occasion, the shortening of the Tsar's titles on a state paper became the cause of a war with the Poles. Like a "sparkling sun" Alexis sat on a throne of silver gilt, his scepter and crown covered with jewels, surrounded by his lords clothed in ermine. Ceremonial robes grew so heavy that it was almost impossible to move in them.

Tsar Michael had begun the rebuilding of the demolished Kremlin palaces, and under Alexis they reached their highest degree of luxury. The windows, portals and parapets of the newly rebuilt Terem Palace were of white stone, covered with carved foliage and figures of beasts and birds painted in bright colors. Polish and other foreign architects were summoned; the walls of the palace were covered with gilded leather and the ceilings were ornamented with precious metals. In Alexis' bedroom the benches were upholstered in Venetian velvet and the curtains of his large carved four-poster bed were of brocade and silk. The coverlet was embroidered by his daughters, and in this great bed, wrote Collins, "the Tsar lies in no sheets, but in his shirt and drawers under a rich sable cover."

Alexis loved to hear stories of travel in remote parts of Russia and kept storytellers permanently at his court. It was he who began the postal system in Russia and in the mid-17th century sent the first trade expeditions to China. As a result Chinese tea caravans began to come regularly to Russia and tea quickly grew so popular that it became the national beverage. Even during the time of his ban on amusements, he refused to give up his storytellers or his contacts with foreigners who brought him the Western mechanical marvels that he enjoyed. At his favorite summer residence at Izmailovo outside Moscow, there were cages for animals and very un-Russian windmills and pavilions. It seems oddly symbolic that at a time when new ideas were springing up in the land, the Tsar's greatest passion, along with his falcons, was gardening. He sent for seeds and rare plants from many countries, and at Izmailovo proudly produced such rareties as Hungarian pears, Bokhara melons, figs, cotton and pepper. He was especially delighted with a rare species of highly scented rose that had been brought to him from Belgium.

All over Europe in the 17th century, styles of decoration grew ever more ornate. The altars of Spanish churches were massively ornamented with gilt, and English silver with elegant flourishes. The French of Louis XIII's time wore clothes covered with ruffles and collars heavy with lace. In Russia, the decorative arts reached a peak of splendor. The church, which used an enormous quantity of beautiful objects for its services, inspired the creation of dazzling gold and silver work, enameling, book illustration, embroidering and carving.

It was a Russian custom to encase icons in special frames called *oklady*, made of gold and silver, which covered the entire icon until only the hands and face of the saints would show. The Moscow goldsmiths made of these *oklady* a unique art form. Coverings for icons were chiseled or engraved on sheets of gold and silver and embellished with colored enamels. Icons were hung with collars of precious metals, crowned with haloes of pearls and jewels and decked with earrings. Chains of pearls and jewels were hung on wires of gold across their foreheads.

Jewelers, calligraphers, printers and miniaturists all worked to make gospels and prayer books as beautiful as possible. Holy books were richly bound in tooled leather or covered with plaques of ivory or filigree work. The artists mingled artistic ideas of East and West into a new and original national style. Slavic motifs of ivy-shaped leaves with curled red, blue, green or gold backgrounds were combined with a whole variety of oriental motifs, Persian, Arabic and Indian. Fantastic mythical animals and dragons, birds and snakes mingled with brightly colored foliage and flowers.

Church vestments were covered with pearls and jewels and sewn with shimmering sequins of fish scales. In the embroidery studios which were under the supervision of the tsarina, embroideresses stitched altar cloths, icon covers and shrouds of Christ; they embellished them with pearls, jewels, and gold and silver threads so beautifully that they rivaled the paintings of the iconostases and the walls.

During the reign of Alexis, the artistic activities of the Armory Palace reached their height. Under an outstanding administrator, Bogdan Khitrovo, the Armory Palace became the headquarters of nearly everything that concerned the fine arts and crafts. Khitrovo was a soldier, diplomat, judge and builder, who although not creative himself had a gift for understanding the problems of artists and craftsmen. He knew how to manage and encourage, and he was open to new ideas. In the twenty-six years that he was supervisor, the Armory Palace expanded into a vast network of studios and workshops specializing in various arts, a remarkable artistic institution whose influence spread across the land.

Western ideas were being brought to Russia from Poland and the Ukraine, as well as by other foreigners from many lands who were arriving in Russia in increasing numbers. Khitrovo encouraged the artists of the Armory to study not only the arts of the East, but also those of the West, encouraging them to create their own distinctive style. There were armorers who specialized in the embellishment of the Tsar's weapons and trappings and the household vessels of the Imperial household. The artists of the icon chamber not only painted icons but designed emblems and standards, furniture and furnishings. They designed textiles, made maps, painted frescoes and illuminated manuscripts. Promising young artists were brought from various parts of Russia and apprenticed to artists at the Armory, thus establishing the Tsar's Icon Painting School. The most gifted artist of the time was Semyon Ushakov, whose talent was such that he was appointed court painter at the age of twenty-one. Ushakov was extremely interested in Western religious painting, which he studied closely while developing his own original style. Sometimes called the Slavic Raphael, he enjoyed a privileged position at court much as Cellini did in Italy, designing gold and silver vessels for the Imperial family as well as painting frescoes and icons.

Alexis' personal taste had a great influence on developing the style of decoration peculiar to his reign. He loved greens and blues. Because of his preference, the enamels of his day were executed in a delicate harmony of greens, blues, whites and yellows, occasionally accented with reds. He was interested in the Orthodox East and the styles of Constantinople, so Turkish designs of tulips, leaves and pink flowers bloomed on enameled objects. Niello and filigree also achieved a new rich look and were used for many purposes. The Tsar's passion for magnificence and opulence extended to all religious articles. Caskets which enclosed saintly relics were made of enameled gold or ivory; chalices, basins, and ewers were all of chiseled or enameled gold, as were crucifixes, candelabra and censers. Large and dazzling jewels were used to achieve the maximum richness of effect. As the iconostasis with its tiers of icons rose higher and higher, the tiers were decorated with frames of gold and silver or carved and gilded wood. Altars were covered with panels of ornamental gold and silver; the Royal Doors were covered with sheets of stamped gold.

Ironically, the church arts reached a peak of lavishness and beauty never again matched just at the time when the church was losing its total domination over the artistic culture of the land. In 1652 the newly appointed Patriarch Nikon, an energetic man whose ambition it was to have the Russian church recognized as the one true Orthodox faith among the Eastern rites, precipitated a crisis. Nikon sought to reform the Russian service, removing the deviations from the ancient Byzantine Greek service which had crept in over the centuries. He undertook to make corrections in the prayer books and in matters of ritual. Some of these changes were very minute, but every word in the prayer book had come to have its traditional meaning. Nikon also prohibited the building of churches with Russian-style tent roofs or more than five cupolas.

Many people saw these changes as an attack on the true church and on Russian life itself. Calling themselves the "Old Believers," they broke with the established church, never to return, causing a schism that was never healed. The struggle continued for years. Groups of Old Believers barricaded themselves in their churches. Many were ready to suffer exile and even death for the sake of crossing themselves with two fingers in the old way, instead of with three fingers as prescribed by the new. The schism had enduring and sad effects. The official church was cut off from many of its most sincere and intelligent followers. It lost the unity and independence that had been its greatest strength, and was finally so weakened that it was forced to turn to the state for support. In the next reign, when the old Patriarch died, a new one was not appointed and the church came to be ruled by a synod under the close supervision of the tsar.

For the first time since before the Mongol invasions, a Western wind was again blowing steadily across Russia. Throughout the 17th century, more and more foreigners were arriving, bringing with them their habits and ideas. When Ivan the Terrible annexed Novgorod in 1571, he transferred much of its population to Moscow, including a group of Hanseatic merchants. For them and the German metalworkers captured in his Livonian wars, he established a settlement in Moscow which came to be known as the Nemetskaya Sloboda or German Suburb. This was not necessarily because all of the inhabitants were German. Many of Ivan's Scottish, French and Swedish mercenaries also came to settle there when they retired from service. Rather, it was because the Russian word for German, *Nemtsi*, comes from their word *nemoy*, which means "dumb," or unable to speak, or, "not mine," i.e., foreign. Among the Russians at first, all these strange foreigners came to be lumped together as *Nemtsi*.

When Richard Chancellor arrived in 1553, he had counted three hundred foreigners at court. The Englishmen who came to trade were subsequently followed by the Dutch. In 1571 when the Tatars descended on Moscow, burning and killing, a group of seven hardy English doctors and apothecaries escaped the slaughter by hiding in the cellars of their houses in the German Suburb. By the beginning of the 17th century, Olearius counted a thousand foreigners living in the German Suburb; a few years later others simply wrote that there was "a multitude." By 1652 the streets were filled with a varied collection of people— Tatars, Bulgarians, Armenians, Serbians, alms collectors from Palestine, Italians from Genoa and Venice, Swedes and Scots. A large Greek colony maintained its own Greek monastery near the Kremlin and eventually came to have its own quarter. Foreigners, overflowing the Suburb, were living all over the city.

The Orthodox church fathers grew so alarmed at this growth of heretical influences that in 1652 they prevailed upon Alexis to found a new and larger foreign quarter on the Yauza River on the eastern outskirts of Moscow. Foreigners were each given a plot of land according to their profession and trade. In 1650, after Cromwell had overthrown King Charles I, Tsar Alexis welcomed many Royalists. Bearing great Scottish names, Drummond, Ogilvey, Crawford and Leslie, they entered the Russian service; among them was the daring soldier of fortune Patrick Gordon. The Tsar's personal physician for nine years was Dr. Samuel Collins, son of the Vicar of Braintree, who had studied at Cambridge and taken his medical degrees in Padua and Oxford. Foreign embassies multiplied. In 1664 the English Restoration poet Andrew Marvell arrived in the train of the Earl of

Carlisle, an English Ambassador, bringing beautifully composed Latin epistles which he delivered to the Russian court.

The Polish invasions of the Time of Troubles and the continuing wars with Poland during Alexis' reign, which finally culminated in the return of the city of Kiev and the Ukraine to Russia, brought a multitude of Ukrainian scholars, noblemen, merchants and mercenaries to Moscow. Along with their taste for Western painting, the Poles brought many innovations—in fashion, the use of feathers for decorating hats. In the 1650's Tsar Alexis appointed Semeon Polotsky, a Ukrainian monk and poet and one of the most learned men of his time, to the influential post of tutor for his children, both boys and girls.

The purpose of the church fathers in putting all the foreigners in one place was to keep ideas from spreading; in fact the opposite happened. The German Suburb became a miniature European city where Russians could study European customs and habits. By the late 17th century, the German Suburb comprised one-fifth of the city of Moscow. It had straight, broad avenues lined with prim rows of trees, squares and fountains. Two- and three-story houses were built in the European manner, decorated with cornices, pilasters, columns and large glass windows. Flowers bloomed in European gardens dotted with pools and pavilions. There was a theater where Tsar Alexis went to see a performance of *Orpheus* and which later inspired him to build a theater of his own. The Ukrainians and Poles founded an academy in the Western model in 1685 that taught Greek and Latin. A few daring avant-garde Russian nobles even began to shave their beards, wear Western clothes and smoke tobacco.

Despite these foreign innovations, Tsar Alexis, as most Russians, still preferred to live in a wooden house. In the late 1660's, at a time when new ideas of architecture were beginning to reach Russia, he had constructed at Kolomenskoe the most Russian of all palaces. Built entirely of wood, and set on a bluff on a bend in the river, the palace was a series of 270 interconnected dwellings and rooms of various shapes and sizes. Like the palace dwelling of a tsar in a Russian fairy tale, it was a marvel of wood architecture, which incorporated all the varied Russian forms. It had a hundred onion domes, towers, tents and spires; heart-shaped gables, arches, balconies and staircases, all gilded or painted in bright colors of blue, green and red, with multitudes of decorative birds and medallions carved on its pillars and eaves. Three thousand mica windows gleamed in the sun and Semyon Ushakov covered the interior walls with paintings.

Although outside it was totally Russian, inside the palace there were some daring foreign departures—mirrors, furniture in the Western style and many of the mechanical devices that Alexis loved, including a throne flanked by a pair of ferociously performing lions. Kolomenskoe was the crowning glory of Russian wooden architecture and it was never duplicated. In its day it was called the eighth wonder of the world.

By the end of the 17th century, new churches and buildings constructed in Moscow were losing their totally Russian look. Multistoried buildings of stone and masonry, painted in bright colors set off by white columns, reflected the new influences brought in from Poland and the Ukraine. This new architecture, known as Moscow Baroque, had only a brief vogue; it was both an end and a beginning, a harbinger of even more dramatic changes that were to revolutionize the old Muscovite way of life.

The older Tsar Alexis grew, the more even this model of Orthodox piety began changing his habits. In 1669 his devout wife of the old school died. Alexis, who was then only forty, looked for a new wife. He liked to visit the home of one of his closest advisers, Artemon Matveev, a cultured and enlightened boyar who read Latin and Greek and had Homer, Aristotle and Virgil in his library. Matveev had married the daughter of a Scottish family, Mary Hamilton, and in their house there were frequent musical entertainments which broke with Muscovite custom. The ladies present wore Western clothes and mingled freely with the guests. At one of these evening gatherings, Alexis spied Matveev's ward, Natalya Naryshkina, the daughter of a modest landed proprietor of Tatar origin who lived in a remote part of Russia. Natalya had come to Moscow for her education and was living in the Matveev household. She was tall, dark-eyed and raven-haired. Alexis was charmed. "Tell the little pigeon," he said to Matveev, "that I will charge myself with finding a husband for her." The next day, the royal ring was sent, and Natalya was summoned to the Bride Show. At their wedding on February 1, 1671, in a great break with tradition, instrumental music was played.

Thereafter, even at court, the seclusion of the *terem* began to crumble. Alexis doted on his young wife and never liked to be without her. She shared his amusements, accompanied him to church and even rode about occasionally in an open carriage.

The court became a strange mixture of Russian and Western customs. For the first time, Alexis appointed a court portrait painter, and in 1671 had his likeness painted and later those of Natalya and his leading courtiers. He, who had always loved the dramatic spectacle of church and court ceremonial, now began openly to patronize the theater. With the permission of his confessor, he built a theater at his palace at Preobrazhenskoe. A troupe of German actors gave performances of the stories of Judith and Esther which lasted many hours, after which music and feasting continued on through the night. To please Natalya, Alexis encouraged playwriting and even built in the Kremlin itself an Amusement Palace whose exterior walls were decorated with murals in his favorite shades of green. He subsidized the first Russian troupe of actors, thus beginning a long tradition of Imperial support for the theater.

Alexis had had thirteen children by his first wife, but all his sons, with the exception of two, had died in infancy. Of the two who remained, Feodor was sickly, and Ivan had a speech defect and was nearly blind. So it was the crowning joy for the Tsar when on May 30, 1672, the bells of the Kremlin announced to the land the birth of a new prince, a healthy boy who was named Peter.

For Russia, it was the decisive event of the 17th century. The stage was set for change. Now the principal player had arrived.

8 · THE GREAT PETER

T SAR ALEXIS was so overjoyed and proud at the birth of his healthy son by his young Natalya that he took the unprecedented step of sending embassies to the courts of Europe to announce the happy event. A two-hundred-pound ceremonial gingerbread, stamped with the Double Eagle, was baked, the largest such gingerbread ever recorded in Russia. Cannons were fired and bells rung all over the land. So perhaps it was natural that all his life Peter loved noise, fireworks and explosions. He was a curious and inventive boy, brimming with physical energy—and will.

Suddenly, after this joyous beginning, in 1676 at the age of forty-seven Alexis died after a short illness, leaving his young wife and four-year-old son unprotected. Although he had earlier designated his eldest son by his first wife as his heir, Feodor was so frail that everyone had supposed that the sturdy father would outlive the son. Almost as soon as Alexis had been laid in his tomb in the Cathedral of the Archangel Michael, bitter feuds and struggles for power erupted between the rival families of his first and second wives. Six years later Feodor died, and in an uneasy truce between the warring clans Peter and his retarded half brother, Ivan, were named as joint tsars. Despite the truce, the struggles for power continued and the mark of these incessant and often bloody intrigues remained with Peter his whole life. He grew to hate the Kremlin with its palaces of dusky rooms and labyrinthine corridors which for him held nothing but memories of terror and danger. When he was ten years old, the palace guards revolted and brutally murdered the supporters of his mother. The good Artemon Matveev was seized and before Peter's eyes thrown onto the spears of the palace guards in the courtyard. His mother's brother was dragged from his hiding place and massacred. Peter, his two small sisters and his mother withdrew to the country house of Tsar Alexis in the village of Preobrazhenskoe outside Moscow.

Infrequently, for ceremonial occasions, Peter was brought back to the Kremlin. There, young Peter sat on an especially built double throne side by side with the feeble Ivan, flanked by twelve giant guards with battle-axes. Warily he listened as his clever and relentlessly ambitious older half sister Sophia, acting as regent, whispered instructions to him through the curtain.

In the country, Peter was left to roam the grounds and the streets of the village entirely on his own. His friends were the village boys, and he quickly became their leader. He loved to play soldier, and before he was twelve, he was permitted to construct a wooden fortress on the grounds of the house where his family lived, complete with towers, bastions and earthworks. He learned masonry and worked along with the laborers. He learned how to shoot a cannon and, enlisting his father's falconers and huntsmen, the grooms and some clerks' sons for his war games, he drilled them and engaged them in battles. The boyars' sons, hearing of all these interesting activities, soon came from Moscow along with their servants to join these games. They, too, were all quickly enlisted. One of Peter's friends brought out a clever fellow named Alexander Menshikov, whom, legend says, he had met selling meat pies in Red Square. Menshikov became Peter's best friend and closest lieutenant. By the time Peter was in his teens, he had two companies of about three hundred soldiers, all dressed in bottle-green uniforms, which he had designed. These men, whom he called his "merry company," became the nucleus of the Preobrazhensky and Semyonovsky Guards, the elite units of the Russian Army until the time of the last tsar.

While he still was very young, Peter adopted the principle that was to rule his actions all his life: advancement should be based on merit and not on rank. (Until he felt he was sufficiently skilled, he served as a private in his own regiment.) This startling innovation in a society in which every morning the nobility were used to being received by the tsar according to a meticulous gradation of rank and precedence was a totally revolutionary concept.

One day when he was fifteen and rummaging about the Romanov storehouses, Peter came across a sailboat of unusual design. It was English, even possibly a gift from Elizabeth I to Ivan the Terrible. Peter put it on a river and searched out an old Dutch boat maker to teach him how to sail it. It was a revelation, a boat that sailed against the wind, something that Russians had not known before. For Peter, it was the beginning of a consuming passion for boats and the sea which lasted all his life. Because of this passion, the history of Russia was to be dramatically changed.

Peter grew to be a giant—over six feet seven inches tall, with a giant's physical appetites, strength and endurance. With his strong hands he could roll up silver plates like parchment, fell trees, shoe a horse. His mechanical talent and insatiable curiosity were extraordinary. All his life, whenever he saw pieces of mechanical equipment, clockwork or navigational instruments, he could usually guess their purpose at a glance and take them apart and reassemble them. All practical things fascinated him. After he learned masonry, he studied carpentry. Eventually during his lifetime he became skilled in fourteen specialties. He could pull a tooth, cast a cannon and cobble boots. As he grew up, more and more he frequented the German Suburb, observing Western customs. In the quarter, he became friendly with a Genevan soldier-adventurer, François Lefort, and the canny Scottish mercenary General Patrick Gordon, who had come to seek his fortune in Russia in the reign of Alexis. With these and other earthy companions, male and female, he also learned to drink prodigiously, make love, smoke and revel in coarse practical jokes.

Peter had an extraordinary capacity for drink, and like his father, when his ferocious temper exploded he terrified everybody. But he was also able to sober quickly, forget his anger and turn coolly to serious matters.

When his half brother, Ivan, died in 1696, Peter became at twenty-four sole ruler of Russia. From the beginning he had a strong sense of his mission as Tsar. That was, in his own words, "to break the bonds of inflexible customs of Muscovy and to lead his country toward a new day which shall be better than this." He dreamed of retrieving in one bold stroke what he saw as two centuries lost to the Mongol domination. Because of his observations and admiration of life in the German Suburb, he concluded that the best way for Russia to close this gap of centuries was a sweeping adoption of Western culture and technology. The very next year after his brother's death, he made the startling decision to go and see Europe for himself. No tsar had set foot outside his dominions for over six hundred years; no tsar had ever been seen in the West.

In March 1697, led by Peter's Genevan General Lefort, the friend and adviser of his youth, a Grand Embassy of some two hundred and seventy persons set out for Europe. There were ambassadors with their suites of young nobles wearing long furred coats and hats covered with pearls and jewels, accompanied by trumpeters, drummers, interpreters, merchants and jesters. There were Cossacks, halberdiers and guardsmen with gleaming weapons, and even a Caucasian prince armed with a jeweled scimitar. Lefort was dressed as a Tatar khan and attended by ten gentlemen in flowing robes, fifteen servants, an orchestra and four dwarfs. As for Peter, dressed as a sailor, he went incognito as the "volunteer and seaman Peter Mikhailov." The Embassy traveled by sleigh; Peter proceeded by sea to Königsberg. While he was waiting for the grand company to arrive, not wasting a minute, he took a course in gunnery from a Prussian engineer and got his master's certificate.

It is easy to imagine the amazement of Europe at the sight of this exotic company from the East, but it is hard to believe that anyone was fooled for long by Peter's transparent incognito. His size, his piercing eyes, his authority, marked him as a very unusual seaman. Also he behaved strangely. He demanded to see and examine everything, everywhere. He would stop people on the streets and abruptly ask, "What is it?" "Show it to me," as he unceremoniously examined a lady's watch or removed a man's wig. In Hanover, where Peter was a guest of Sophia the Electress, he danced with the court ladies and mistook the ribs of their corsets for bones. "The bones of these German women are devilishly hard!" exclaimed the Tsar.

Then, leaving the cumbersome Grand Embassy to follow behind him later, Peter took ten companions and sailed down the Rhine and by river and canal to Holland and proceeded to settle himself in the little shipbuilding town of Zaandam, not far from Amsterdam. In Zaandam, living on the edge of the dikes in a tiny house rented from an old carpenter, Peter slept doubled up in a small Dutch-style bed built into the wall and kept the potatoes for his supper in a drawer under his bed. Dressed as a Dutch sailor, he went to work in the local shipyards. The Dutch were simply astonished at his size and exclaimed that they had never seen "such running, jumping and clambering over the shipping." No one believed his incognito, and after only eight days, people were flocking down to the little dock to see him at work. Peter always hated to be stared at and, when traveling, tried to avoid being seen. In this case, he escaped by moving himself inside the high walls of the East India Company shipyard in Amsterdam and there, left in peace for three months, he learned how to build a frigate and received a shipbuilding certificate from the head of the dockyards.

After a few months some of the Embassy proceeded to England, where they were followed around the streets of London by gaping Londoners. When Peter visited Parliament he insisted on climbing to the uppermost galleries so that he could observe the proceedings unobserved; again, this was not a very successful evasion. In Deptford on the Thames, Peter continued his shipbuilding training. After meeting him, a somewhat stunned Bishop Burnet of Salisbury wrote, "After I had seen him often and conversed much with him, I adored the depth and providence of God that had raised such a furious man to so absolute an authority over such a great part of the world."

While traveling in the West, Peter filled many notebooks with his observations. Everything interested him; everything had to be recorded. He worked in a paper factory where he learned to make excellent paper; he learned the art of engraving. He learned how to cut up whale blubber in Texel, and human anatomy and surgery in Leyden. As the months passed, he traveled to Cleves, Leipzig, and to Dresden where he carefully studied the art galleries, and then on to Vienna. He meant to continue to Venice, but the Grand Embassy was cut short by a revolt of the palace guard in Moscow and Peter hurried home to deal with the uprising with ferocity.

He never lost his love for European travel, and in later years he went back to Amsterdam, Hamburg, Copenhagen and Lübeck. He visited Württemberg to see where Martin Luther had thrown an inkpot at the devil and wrote succinctly in the visitors' book: "The story is false. The ink stains are new." In 1717 he visited Paris. He jumped into cabs and roamed all over the city to look at everything. He went to observe the workers in the Arsenal, only a street away from where he lived in the former mansion of the Duke of Lesdiguières in the Marais section. He visited the Gobelins tapestry factory and the Jardin des Plantes, watched carriage makers and the metal founders at work. He picked up the seven-year-old Louis XV in his arms. To her great astonishment he burst into Madame de Maintenon's bedroom to take a look and have a conversation with the last and most famous mistress of the Sun King, Louis XIV. He did not think much of Versailles, which he said looked like a "pigeon with the wings of an eagle." About Madame de Maintenon he made no such ungallant comments.

On all his tours, wherever he passed, he collected people and engaged them into his service—workmen of every sort, engineers, surgeons, artists. In England he recruited British seamen, gunners, goldsmiths, astronomers and mathematicians. On his first Grand Embassy alone, over eight hundred people skilled in various specialties were hired and sent back to Russia.

Already as a radical young man frequenting the German Suburb, Peter had scandalized the conservative clergy and the boyars by smoking tobacco and shaving off his beard. A beard in Russia was serious business, the mark of a real man and a true believer. Russians had a religious respect and veneration for their beards, all the more so because beards distinguished them from strangers. Boyars kept theirs long and silky, combing them carefully and spreading them out on their wide chests. They thought that clean shavedness made men look like apes. (In fact, Peter's mustache and clean chin gave him the look of a cat, and he was often so caricatured in the art of the people.)

When Peter got back from his Grand Embassy and started to change his people's ways, he began with that symbol of old Muscovy, the beard. At Preobrazhenskoe he sat with shears and personally cut off the beards of all the boyars present. From then on, anyone who appeared at court with a beard was shaved by the court fools. Barbers were posted at the gates of Moscow and all entering males, excepting priests and peasants, were compulsorily shaved.

In conservative Moscow the Tsar's actions were regarded with sheer horror and as a sin. Men hid their shaven beards under their pillows. John Perry, an English engineer engaged by the Tsar, tells that he met one of his newly shaven Russian carpenters and asked him jokingly what he had done with his beard, whereupon the man put his hand on his bosom and pulled it out from under his shirt, telling him that when he returned home he planned to keep it to have it laid in his coffin and buried along with him so that he might give a proper account of himself to Saint Nicholas. Later Peter relented a little and allowed men to pay a tax for the privilege of keeping their beards—a hundred rubles a year for noblemen and one kopeck from common people. But, despite Peter's efforts, to this day the beard has remained a symbol for Russians of the old ways—and the true faith.

Peter also cut off the long sleeves of men's kaftans and ordered that Western-style jackets, cocked hats and buckled shoes were to be worn from then on. Patterns of men's clothes in the English fashion were hung at all the gates of the city of Moscow and all persons who brought goods and provisions into the city had to have clothes made according to those patterns. Those who were found passing the gates in long habits either had to pay a fine or kneel down and have their coats cut off even to the ground. Perry reports that "it occasioned mirth among the people, being done with good humor, and soon broke the custom of wearing long coats, especially in Moscow and other towns wherever the Tsar came." Once again, clergy and peasants were exempt from the rule.

Peter made war on the seclusion of women. Women were henceforth to cast off their veils and head coverings, and dress in the English and French fashion with tight waists and décolletage. But far more significant, he also made fathers and guardians swear that they would not marry young people against their wills and that a bridal pair might see each other freely for six weeks before marriage. In the event that they did not please each other, they were to be allowed to break the engagement. Abolished were the *terem* and the carriages and sledges with tightly drawn curtains. He even established a special order for women, the Dames of St. Catherine.*

No more were men to carouse exclusively at stag dinners. After his visit to Paris, Peter decreed that *Assemblées* were to be held. (And so that it would be precisely clear to his subjects what he meant, in his decree he gave a careful explanation: "It is a French term which cannot easily be rendered in Russian by a single word. It implies a number of persons who have got together either for pleasure or to discuss business. Friends can see each other . . . and pass the time agreeably.") Men and women were to meet in Western dress to drink tea, lemonade and brandy, to eat preserves and chocolate and to dance Polish and German dances. There was no option about attending these new gatherings; if any lady demurred because of an excess of modesty, soldiers were sent to fetch her. As in everything, Peter set the example himself, even carrying mugs of beer to the orchestra.

All this was nothing less than the complete overturning of the traditions and habits of centuries. But clothes, beards and dancing were only the surface of Peter's revolution. Peter's mind teemed with ideas and innovations. The hundreds of changes that Peter made in the lives of his subjects were great and small; no detail of his subjects' lives seemed too trivial for his interest.

As Russia had no modern army, he determined to create one. Russia had no navy, so Peter built one. He founded schools of navigation and mathematics, geography, politics and medicine, philosophy and astronomy. He introduced the potato and encouraged the breeding of native Russian horses. He began the first

---

* The Order of St. Andrew, Russia's highest decoration and comparable to the Order of the Garter in England, was a direct result of Peter's first visit to the West. Saint Andrew was chosen because in ancient Russian legends Andrew had come to pre-Christian Kiev to preach to the Slavs. Peter realized that, instead of rewarding victorious generals with vast estates, it was much cheaper to present them with a ribbon and a diamond order. The first recipients were his closest lieutenants, Menshikov and Sheremetev. He did not award one to himself until eight others had received it and until he felt he had merited it.

Russian newspaper and ordered the printing of six hundred books—including a guide to the writing of compliments, proposals of marriage and invitations. He brought foreign actors and musicians to Russia and had a theater built on Red Square. Soon after he introduced the manufacture of writing paper, a simple Russian invented a lacquer for paper far superior to anything in Europe except Venice. He introduced lace-making and tapestry-making industries.

When Scythian art was first found in Siberia and brought to him, Peter ordered it to be collected and saved for the state. He opened mines for semiprecious stones in the Urals and sent Bering off to explore Siberia. He changed the calendar* to conform with that of Europe and reformed the Russian alphabet, which remained, with few exceptions, as he changed it until 1918. The Muscovite court ritual was eliminated—no more bowing to the ground and kissing of robes and feet. He sent hundreds of promising Russians to Europe to learn first navigation and engineering and then art. He called them his "fledglings" and selected them from every walk of life. From his group of "fledgling" painters emerged three artists of distinction, all of humble birth—Ivan Nikitin, Alexei Antropov and Andrei Matveev. (Matveev, who studied for twelve years in Leyden and Antwerp, painted a very human portrait of the Tsar.)

Peter tried to open grammar schools to all classes, but in this, as in many of his most forward-looking innovations, he was opposed by the very people he had most hoped would support him. For the conservative boyars and clergy, it was quite simple: these reforms were heresy. The Anti-Christ was on the throne with smoke billowing out of his mouth.

During all this time of overturning the traditions of centuries, Peter was also fighting a continual war with the Swedes, which finally culminated in what is considered one of the twenty great battles of the world. In 1709, at Poltava in the Ukraine, Peter decisively defeated the Swedes, previously considered invincible, and thus established Russia as a great European power. When peace came, Peter was given the title "the Great" and proclaimed Russia's first Emperor.

The remarkable Tsar even found time for a great love. She was a simple Livonian orphan girl named Martha Skavronskaya, brought up as a servant in the

---

* While the various countries of Western Europe had all changed to the Gregorian calendar during the 18th century, Russia remained on the Julian calendar, which Peter had adopted, until 1918. This calendar put Russia eleven days behind the rest of Europe in the time of Peter, twelve days in the 19th century and thirteen days in the 20th century.

house of a Lutheran minister who married her off at sixteen to a Swedish dragoon in Marienberg. The dragoon disappeared somewhere during the wars and Martha was taken as a booty of war by a Russian soldier. Legend says that she was brought to the commander, Count Sheremetev, dressed only in a shift, and that he threw a soldier's cloak around her and then bought her with a few coins. She was first attached to his household as a servant, but later Peter's closest friend and lieutenant, Menshikov, spied her and brought her into his household, perhaps even as his mistress. It was in Menshikov's house that Peter first saw her in 1702.

Peter had been married at seventeen at his mother's insistence to a Muscovite boyar's daughter, Evdokia Lopukhina. Evdokia was a quiet, conservative girl, brought up strictly in the old traditions. There was nothing wrong with her except that they never got along and Peter did not love her. In 1698, when Peter was twenty-six, she was retired to a convent, the equivalent of divorce. Peter had had several mistresses by the time he met Martha. He was thirty and she was twenty, a merry and warm girl with a great sense of humor. She was also understanding, maternal and very stable. Most important, she was not afraid of him or of his fearful rages which terrified even his bravest men. In 1704 Martha gave birth to their first son. Mother and child were baptized in the Orthodox Church at the same time; Martha took the new name of Catherine. Peter lived with her on and off for seven years before, as he put it, he "had time to marry her." When they did officially marry in 1711, he gave her as a wedding present an ivory chandelier which he had turned himself.

Together they had twelve children, including six sons, three named Peter and three named Paul. All their children died in childhood except for two daughters, Anna and Elizabeth. For any ordinary human being, the loss of ten children would be a major event, one that would overshadow a life. But Peter was so titanic a figure that this personal tragedy is passed over in histories, if it is noted at all, as a small detail, hardly worth mentioning.

A beautifully inlaid wooden cradle made in the shape of a boat still stands in the nursery of Peter's simple Summer Palace in St. Petersburg. It is sadly eloquent, as are the paintings of a whole series of vanished bright-eyed children with round squirrel cheeks. One little Peter managed to survive until he was four years old. When this child died, Peter locked himself in his room and would not come out for several days. Everyone was terrified. Finally he permitted only Catherine to enter and after some time he emerged with his arm around her, saying, "We have grieved too long. Let us be on with the affairs of state."

Catherine traveled with him often and shared many of his military campaigns. Peter was subject to epileptic-like convulsions, perhaps caused by the terrible shocks of his childhood. Only Catherine was not afraid during the convulsions that racked his great body. She would take his head in her lap and caress him tenderly until the tensions and the pain fell away and he fell asleep. She could not write, but when he was away, she dictated streams of affectionate letters and sent him his favorite foods. (Peter hated foreign foods, "foreign poisons" he called them, and loved hearty Russian dishes like cucumbers and pork soaked in sour cream.) Although they were separated for long periods of time, their love endured. Even after Peter crowned her Empress Catherine I, she remained simple, unassuming, always liking to make her own pickles and jam, wanting nothing more than to love him.

All his life Peter was in constant motion, traveling, warring, inspecting, building. In his swift sleigh in the winter, he could cover a hundred miles in a day. During his entire reign, he never stayed longer than three months in one place. A painting by the late-19th-century artist Valentin Serov captures the relentless vigor of this giant. He is striding purposefully ahead, with an architect struggling to keep up with him. One can feel the wind behind him and sense the urgency in the step of the great man who was always in a hurry, as he oversees his most ambitious project, the building of St. Petersburg.

Louis XIV, then the most powerful monarch in Europe, decided to celebrate his power by building a single grandiose palace. It was typical of Peter and perhaps his grandest vision that he decided to build a whole city, a new capital which would face the West and symbolize his aspirations for his country. He decided to found his city in a remote unprepossessing place at a far northwestern corner of his vast realm, choosing the site solely because of its proximity to the sea—and to Europe.

From Lake Ladoga, the largest lake in Europe, the Neva River flows into the sea. At the mouth of the Gulf of Finland, it divides into four arms to form an extensive marshy delta. Under a pale northern sky, an archipelago of islands lies between these waterways and their tributaries, a desolate region of dark forests and silver-gray marshes stretching out toward the sea.

Long before, these lands had been part of the great domain of Lord Novgorod the Great, but the Swedes had taken them and held them through most of the 17th century. Peter, always dreaming of the sea, resolved to have them back and so he did, seizing them from the Swedes in 1702. On May 16, 1703, on an island in the river that the Finns called the Isle of Hares, Peter cut two pieces of sod with a bayonet borrowed from a soldier and laid them crosswise on the marshy ground declaring, "Here shall be a town." Afterward, he laid the first stone of what was to be the Peter and Paul Fortress, had a trench dug and buried a casket containing relics of Saint Andrew and some golden coins. On the first yards of earthworks he placed a stone that had been blessed and sprinkled with holy water. Legend says that during this ceremony an eagle soared over the head of the Tsar and landed on two birch trees that had been tied together to form an arch to mark the position of the future gateway to the fort. The eagle was captured, Peter bound its wings and it perched on his hand during the ceremony. Afterward the eagle became a pet and Peter named it "The Commander."

His new city was to be called a Dutch name, Sankt Piterburkh, after his patron saint. But from the first, and up to this day, its inhabitants called it simply "Piter."

If Peter considered the difficulties of construction at all, it was only to dismiss them. And the difficulties were extraordinary. The Swedish enemy was close, but nature was a far more formidable adversary. Placing the city on the same latitude on the North American continent would mean creating a new capital on the upper shores of Hudson Bay. The climate is terrible. The river is frozen six months of the year. The islands of the delta are marshy. The city had to be built on wooden piles sunk into this shifting swampy ground. Thousands of peasants, prisoners and soldiers were pressed into building—Finns, Estonians, Karelians, Swedes, Tatars, Cossacks and Kalmucks; even exiled robbers and thieves were brought out of banishment for the task. Every year 40,000 men were commandeered, 150,000 in all. In the beginning they had few tools; they dug with their hands and carried the dirt away in the tails of their shirts. They slept in the open air in the marshes and drank foul water. So many died that it was said the city was built on bones. Nothing mattered; Peter wanted his city immediately. It took thousands of French workers with all the skill and technology available to France, then the leading country of Europe, forty-seven years to build Versailles. St. Petersburg was built almost at a stroke. Only seven years after Peter laid his cross on the ground, he had a city. In 1712 it became the new capital of Russia and in 1714, according to a census ordered by the Tsar, had 34,550 buildings. (One has to assume that they counted every structure, however rough.)

Ten days after he laid the first stone, Peter, with the help of a few army carpenters, built himself a cabin of pine logs in just three days. It had three rooms and a small entrance; the outside was painted to look like brick. There he lived with Catherine for five years while construction was going on, even after many of his nobles lived in far grander houses. When he had to entertain officially, he did so in a local tavern opened by an enterprising German, or later in his friend Menshikov's palace.

When the King of Sweden, Charles XII, heard that his enemy Peter was building a new city, he said arrogantly, "Let the Tsar tire himself out with founding new towns. We will keep for ourselves the honor of taking them later." After Peter utterly defeated the Swedes at Poltava in 1709, he was able to exult, "Now indeed we can lay the foundation of Sankt Piterburkh." Thousands of Swedish prisoners were sent off to continue the construction of the city. In 1710 Peter decreed that thereafter no more stone or brick was to be used for building anywhere else in the empire and that all nobles and landowners would henceforth be obligated to build houses for themselves in St. Petersburg at their own expense.

All through its construction and growth, the new city continued to be plagued by nature. Disastrous floods periodically almost overwhelmed the city. In 1705 the whole city was several feet deep in water. In 1721, because of a great flood, all the streets were navigable and, a story goes, Peter risked drowning in the Nevsky Prospect. As in Moscow, ravaging fires swept through the wooden buildings. In winter, wolves roamed the streets at night, and in 1715 a lady was devoured in broad daylight not far from Prince Menshikov's palace.

Peter dreamed of a clean Dutch city, like Amsterdam, intersected with navigable canals and tree-lined streets, open to the water and the fresh wind. He carefully specified the size, style and location of the houses for the nobility, merchants and traders, artists and artisans. Humble people were to have one-story houses with four windows and a dormer, more prosperous merchants and traders larger houses with two rows of windows, dormers and a balcony.

He wanted it to be a city of ideas. There he created the first learned academies of Russia, the first libraries. He staffed his educational institutions with teachers from the West and intended St. Petersburg's contacts with all that was good in the West to be fruitful.

From the very first Peter imported hundreds of foreign engineers, architects, artists and workmen who worked closely together to help in the construction and beautification of his city. The original fortifications of the Peter and Paul Fortress were built after plans by Gaspard Lambert, who had been a pupil of the great French military architect Vauban. Domenico Trezzini, an Italian from Lugano who had been in the service of the Danish court, was recruited to come to work with the Russian architect Ustinov. Trezzini was followed by his son, Pietro Antonio, and his nephew, Giuseppe, and among them they were to devote fifty years of their lives working on St. Petersburg.

Trezzini and Ustinov working together designed the Peter and Paul Fortress and church with its 400-foot tower surmounted by a gilded spire made entirely of wood that stretches more than 197 feet into the sky.* It was a startling architectural landmark in a country dominated by the cupola, a striking statement of Peter's determination to break with national traditions. Seen from across the Neva, under the pale northern sun, with its golden spire reflected in the icy water, it is an unforgettable sight, a distinctive St. Petersburg landmark.

Along the banks of the Neva, Trezzini in 1710 made plans for a Summer Palace for Peter and in 1711 for a Winter Palace. Trezzini built two Winter Palaces for Peter, the first of wood and the second of stone.

Peter, said one of his contemporaries, "loved more to employ his money on ships and regiments than sumptuous buildings and was always content with his lodgings when he could see his fleet from his window." Certainly he was the only monarch in Europe who insisted that his private residence be built next to a shipyard, ordering that the Winter Palace be constructed next to the Admiralty. There Peter often dined, always insisting on naval rations of smoked beef and beer, which he ate to the sound of a fife and drum playing in the central tower.

Although Peter's simple Winter Palace was replaced in later reigns by a much grander structure, Peter's Summer Palace remains today. It is a sensible, solid two-storied house built in the style decreed by Peter for his nobles, more like the house of a solid burgher than that of a tsar. In every way, it bears the strong stamp of its owner. Built where the Neva River and the Fontanka Canal meet, at the far corner of the Summer Gardens, surrounded by water on two sides and with a little dock for Peter's boat, it seems almost to be growing out of the water. The windows of all fourteen rooms are wide and latticed, letting in the wind, the sun and views of the water. Inside, the light, bright rooms are clean as salt air, another world from the vaulted ceilings and mica windows of old Muscovite dwellings which Peter had learned to hate in his childhood.

* The original spire as conceived by Trezzini was more baroque and Danish in appearance. It burned when struck by lightning in 1756 and was replaced by the slimmer spire that is seen today.

Touchingly, Peter always loved to surround Catherine with luxury, even though she did not demand it. For her apartments on the upper floor of the Summer Palace, he ordered Chinese silk wallpaper woven with gold and silver and parquet floors inlaid with ivory and mother-of-pearl. Flemish and German tapestries were bought for her, Venetian and English mirrors reflected her beautiful new dresses. In her reception room, a gilded throne is surmounted with the double eagle and a crown; above it the painted ceiling represents "The Triumph of Catherine."

On the lower floor, which Peter occupied, it is a different story. The apartments are spacious but starkly simple and modest, with shining wood floors devoid of rugs. The ceilings are not unusually high. Strangely, despite his great height, Peter did not like high ceilings. When he happened to be lodged in some lofty apartment, he ordered a low canvas ceiling to be put in. The walls are paneled with dark wood, much of which Peter laid himself, and neat blue and white painted Dutch tiles. Peter's favorite room was the Turnery; on the great stove of painted tiles, Russian ships sail boldly, among them the first Russian sixty-gun sailing ship, which had been built according to Peter's design. In this workshop-room are compasses and, Peter's pride and joy, an instrument made for him by the famous Dinglinger in Dresden, showing the time and the direction, speed and force of the wind and worked by lines connected to the weather vane on the roof. There is no hint of crests or majestic seals in his reception room, only a few chairs, a sturdy Russian oak table, a massive carved Dutch cabinet of dark wood and the great Admiralty chair on which Peter sat. Covered in gold velvet, it is austere and yet awesome—its arms end in carved human hands and the feet are shaped like eagles' talons. All the rooms Peter occupied reflect their owner; they are decisive, planned for efficiency and in a striking way, even today, very modern.

Among the French summoned to St. Petersburg was the gifted architect and landscape artist Jean-Baptiste Alexandre LeBlond, a pupil of the great Le Notre, who designed the gardens of Versailles. Peter's General Lefort had engaged him on one of his talent searches in Paris. Peter met LeBlond in Germany and was delighted with him. He wrote enthusiastically to Menshikov, "Welcome LeBlond in a friendly manner and respect his contract: for he is better than the best, and a real wonder, as I could see in no time." LeBlond was to become the new Architect General of St. Petersburg, the only stipulation being that, in exchange for a free hand in his work, he should openly and without holding anything back impart his knowledge and experience to his pupils. He arrived in St.

Petersburg in 1716 with his wife and six-year-old son and a veritable Grand Embassy of French talent. There were painters and sculptors, as well as French engineers and assistants of his own, plus a covey of French craftsmen—scabbard makers, coach smiths, a saddler, a typefounder, silk and wool dyers, stonemasons, and a party of nine tapestry workers from the Gobelins, who were to start the industry in Russia.

Among all his other interests, Peter somehow found time to be interested in gardens. First, always mindful of practical things, he ordered gardens to be planted with medicinal herbs on one of the islands, which for this reason was later named Apothecary's Island. But as early as 1704, he decreed that ornamental Summer Gardens, "better than the King of France's," should be planted and be "open to all people."

Naturally he plunged enthusiastically into planning of these gardens himself. He sent off for books from Holland, including the *Book on Flower Gardens* (with figures), *Five Books of Gardening* and *The Book of Roman Gardens*. Orders flew to Moscow for "the seeds and roots for a kitchen market garden to be sent along with thirteen lads trained as gardeners." Even in the middle of battle he did not forget his gardens. Before the battle of Narva, he ordered that "flowers of all sorts to be sent from Izmailov and more of those which are scented." Before the battle of Poltava, he ordered craftsmen in fountains to be found, and sent off himself for "roots of white lilies." From Hamburg chestnuts were brought and trees from all over Russia. Lilac bushes came from Lübeck and tulip bulbs and flower seeds from Amsterdam. Envoys were sent to find statues in Italy, Germany and Holland. By 1710 there were already beautiful gardens with many trees, some planted by Peter himself. In these gardens Peter and Catherine held receptions, receiving their guests by candlelight.

The Russian architect Zemstov had first laid out these gardens, but as soon as LeBlond arrived he too was set to work to further embellish the Summer Gardens. LeBlond sent for more trees from all over Russia: "Limes, oaks and fruit trees, elms from Moscow and Kiev, cypresses and firs from the south." He collected roses from distant parts of the realm as well as sweet peas, spirea and lilies. He built a conservatory for orange, lemon, bay and clove trees and aviaries shaped like pagodas in which rare birds of all kinds twittered. To the royal menageries were added a blue monkey, a porcupine and various sables.

It was LeBlond's precept that "fountains and water are the soul of a garden, and make the principal ornament of it; these animate and invigorate . . . and give new life and spirit." So he conceived grottos of rockwork, cascades and pyramids of water. Benign stone monsters adorned pools and basins where strange fish swam. He used his great engineering skill to plan pipes and aqueducts. To feed the fountains, a water tower was constructed on the banks of a creek which was widened and deepened and became known as the Fontanka Canal. The Swan Canal was dug to drain the gardens and a little river nicknamed the Moika (from the Russian word *myt*—to wash), where the townspeople came to do their laundry, was also widened and deepened and connected to the Fontanka. Thus the thirty-seven-acre gardens were enclosed in a sparkling frame of waterways.

LeBlond was responsible for the grandest feature of the street planning of the city. He cut the two great prospects which radiated from the Admiralty: the Nevsky, nearly three miles long, and the Voznesensky. The Nevsky was built entirely of stone by gangs of Swedish prisoners, who also had to clean it every Saturday. LeBlond had many more ambitious plans, but the man whom Peter called "his Paradise" died an untimely death of smallpox when he was barely forty, after only three years in Russia.

Many others came to help build St. Petersburg. They came from Germany, from Prussia, from Holland and Italy, from England and Flanders and Scotland. The eager welcoming of foreigners that began in the time of Peter the Great was to remain a happy tradition until 1918. Many of the foreigners who first came, and who continued to come, to give Russia their talents were, in turn, inspired by her. Many grew to love their adopted land, married, began families, made great careers and stayed in Petersburg all their lives. They, in fact, became Russians. One of the charms of Petersburg to this day is that many people living there still have Russified Western names of those distant German, French, Danish and Scottish ancestors. All these gifted and energetic foreigners gave the city a "European" look. But, as in the Kiev of Yaroslav and the Moscow of Ivan III, from the first day of their arrival, they worked with Russians and had to adjust themselves to Russian standards and taste. The result of this happy marriage of combined talents and imagination has a unique splendor and beauty, a spirit all its own that has never been duplicated. In this, St. Petersburg bears certain similarities to another city only a few years older—New York. Kiev was the golden dream of the Slavs, forever killed by the Mongols. Moscow, the middle child of the 14th century, was spawned in the years of Tatar domination and Russian isolation. St. Petersburg was Russia's graceful international offspring of the 18th century.

As old Moscow had been ringed with monasteries, so like a necklace of jewels palaces grew up around St. Petersburg. Prince Menshikov employed a German architect, Schädel, to build him a palace retreat at Oranienbaum, some twenty-five miles from Petersburg. Peter's first country retreat was typically a little log cabin that he built himself at Strelna, just a few miles outside the city limits. There he had a little tree house in a large linden tree where he loved to sit, smoking his pipe and looking at the sea. But as he also liked to go to Kronstadt, on the island of Kotlin in the Gulf of Finland, to inspect his growing navy, and wanted to have Catherine with him, he asked LeBlond to design for him two palaces, one at Strelna and one at Peterhof.

At Peterhof, for his "Versailles on the sea," LeBlond decided upon a site commanding a magnificent view of the bay, the island of Kotlin and the Finnish coast far away. The park and buildings were mainly constructed in a single year. In his impatience it is said that Peter felled many of the trees himself, swinging his axe with a force that none of his men could equal. For Peterhof, LeBlond designed splendid water gardens. Just below the palace, he constructed an extraordinary fountain. From an upper terrace forty feet above the sea, drawing water through wooden pipes from thirteen miles away, he divided a high cascade from which water rushes down over six wide steps around a grotto in two arms into a lower basin. There, representing Peter's victory at Poltava, he placed a huge statue of Samson wrenching open the jaws of a lion, from whose mouth a stream of water leaps forth to a height of eighty feet. The entire marvelous fountain complex, called the "Wicker Basket," is the design of a French *fontenier* who came to Russia with LeBlond. It is in the form of a perfectly geometrical pyramid, composed of hundreds of jets of water of varying height from many sources which merge together in one great volume and flow like a mountain torrent to the sea.

Dispersed throughout the gardens were many other marvelous fountains. One was called the "Mountain of Gold" because water flowed over a flight of gilded steps which, when illuminated, gave the appearance of a cataract of gold. For the "Chess Board" water cascaded over a gigantic black-and-white marble checkered surface. Because Peter loved practical jokes, throughout the formal gardens "surprise" fountains were placed—large mushrooms that suddenly sprinkled the unwary when they stepped on a secret stone, artificial trees that sent forth a silvery stream of water from each leaf, and a spectacular Sun Dial fountain that gradually expanded its jets of water and turned in a circle.

At one point, Peter felt that the upper gardens were too formal and lacking in educational value, so, accordingly, statues of the characters of Aesop's fables were disposed about the gardens. Peter ordered that metal plates bearing an explanation and the moral of the story be placed under each for the edification of his subjects.

For the park LeBlond also designed three delightful pavilions, a Marly, a little Hermitage and Mon Plaisir, a one-story red-and-white pavilion with windows and a broad terrace overlooking the blue sea.

Just as in the Summer Palace, in Petersburg, the kitchen at Mon Plaisir is small and modern with a central stove with counters surrounding it, designed so that only one cook could manage everything. Food was passed through a window into the dining room, prompting a visitor to remark that Peter was probably the only monarch in Europe to get his food really hot. Peter loved Mon Plaisir and preferred to live there even when the larger palace was built.

It was at Mon Plaisir that one of the last scenes of the great tragedy of Peter's life was played. Peter had one surviving son, Alexis, by his first wife, Evdokia. Father and son never got along. The son feared the father, and the father grew to despise the son. As Alexis grew older, he became the center of many plots by the conservative clergy and boyars to overthrow Peter and overturn his reforms. A famous painting by the 19th-century artist Nikolai Ge shows the confrontation of father and son at Mon Plaisir. Disappointment and resentment mark the face of the Tsar sitting impatient and angry, his legs crossed in their tall boots. Evasiveness and weakness are written on the face of the pale thin son who stands, averting his face and looking at the floor. Peter issued Alexis an ultimatum: either follow him loyally and support his reforms or retire from the world and become a monk. Alexis vacillated and continued to be used by others. In the end, everyone involved was arrested. Everyone was ruthlessly questioned. The trail always led back to Alexis. Finally, reluctantly, Peter arrested and imprisoned Alexis in 1718. In prison, he was "questioned" with the knout and during the questioning he died. One story says that on the day after Alexis' death Peter went to christen a ship showing no sign of emotion. Another story says that his eyes were full of tears.

As he grew older, Peter was often ill. Against medical advice, he embarked on an inspection of the Ladoga Canal and then went on to visit ironworks in the far north, where, as usual, the Tsar set an example by digging out a huge chunk of ore. Then leaving Petersburg on another tour, he saw a boatload of soldiers in the shallows of the Gulf. Unthinkingly, characteristically, he plunged into the icy water to save them. Upon his return, he fell gravely ill and never recovered. Peter died at fifty-two, exhausted. In January 1725 he was buried in the church of the

Peter and Paul Fortress in a simple white marble coffin under the great chandelier turned by his own hand. From that time on, tsars were no longer buried in the Church of the Archangel Michael in the Kremlin but laid to rest in identical white marble coffins alongside the great Peter.

In twenty-nine short years, Peter the Great had revolutionized his land and turned it forcibly toward the West. Bewildered and stunned by the tornado that had descended upon them, many of his people did not understand him and considered him a devil. Yet his love for his country and his people was total. In his energy, endurance and imagination, he was supremely Russian; without any doubt, the greatest tsar that Russia ever had. Gavrila Derzhavin, the 18th-century Russian poet, asked, "Was it not God, who in person, came down to earth?"

Certainly after him nothing was ever the same again. To this day, controversy over his reforms is still fresh and sharp. In his headlong rush to sever the links with the past, he threw out much that was good along with the bad. The church had been above the monarch; he subordinated it to the state and the church lost forever its independence and something of its close and unique relationship with the people. By exempting the clergy and the peasants from his Westernizing reforms, he began a cultural schism between classes which had never existed, a schism never fully healed. For more than a century after him, for the upper classes what was Western became fashionable; what was Russian became lowly, unworthy and plebian. Even for a time among the aristocracy the great Russian language that Jerome Horsey, Elizabeth of England's Ambassador in the 16th century, had called the "richest and most copious language in the world" was no longer good enough. In the century that followed Peter, this cultural division was to intensify and artificially divide the people who had always thought of themselves, whether rich or poor, as one family under God.

As for Peter's beloved city, willed into being where none should have existed, over the years it continued to grow and spread over the islands. As it grew, it combined wide avenues and green parks with stately buildings and sparkling fountains. Successive rulers made Peter's dream eternal in stone, and St. Petersburg one of the most beautiful capitals of Europe. Just as Peter would have wished, his city became a center of ideas and the inspiration for many of Russia's greatest artists. Wrote Madame de Staël, the distinguished 19th-century French lady of letters: "The founding of St. Petersburg is the greatest proof of that ardor of the Russian will which does not know that anything is impossible."

9. ELIZABETH: BRIGHT COLORS AND GILT

Lᴛ ɪs ᴀɴ ɪʀᴏɴʏ ᴏꜰ ʜɪsᴛᴏʀʏ that Peter, the most masculine of rulers with the spartan tastes of a soldier, was to be succeeded by a series of women. During the rest of the 18th century, Russia was ruled by four empresses. Two of them were exceptional: Peter's daughter, Elizabeth, and a little princess from Germany who came to be called Catherine the Great. In the fifty-five years of their combined reigns, these two women, totally opposite in taste and temperament, were both in their different ways to lay the foundations for the flowering of Russian culture that was to come in the 19th century.

It was Elizabeth, Peter's daughter, who brought Russian exuberance and lavishness back into style. It did not happen right away. Russia had to wait sixteen years after Peter's death for its opulent Elizabethan age to begin.

Peter had given Tsar Alexis' marvelous wooden palace of Kolomenskoe to his Catherine, and there Elizabeth was born on December 10, 1709, the day after Peter returned to Moscow to celebrate his great victory over the Swedes at Poltava. The Tsar was so delighted that he postponed the victory parade in Moscow to come to see her. Elizabeth made her first public appearance at the age of two at her parents' wedding as a tiny, rosy bridesmaid. She was a child of love, and loving she was all her life. Her parents doted on her and she grew up in a warm, cozy atmosphere. Along with her Russian and Karelian nurses, she was also provided with a French governess, so she grew up speaking French and knowing the manners of the West. But she remained a passionate Russian; all her life she loved Russian folk traditions and customs more than any others and was sincerely and piously devoted to the church.

Elizabeth was gay and pretty with bright blue eyes, "merry as a bird's," and luxuriant auburn hair. By twelve she already had a lovely figure. Despite her beauty, she was unspoiled and irrepressibly lively, and delighted in putting on shows at Peter's masquerades. At receptions, she was a delicious sight wearing jewels in her hair and little wings made of colored gauze and whalebone, the mark of a princess not yet come of age. She was Peter's joy and pride; he wanted nothing less for her than that she be Queen of France.

The French, casting their practiced and discerning eyes over potential brides for their boy king, Louis XV, did agree that by age fifteen Elizabeth was indeed one of the prettiest princesses in Europe; on a scale of eighteen, they rated her number two. But they would have none of her, haughtily implying that the daughter of a peasant woman, born out of wedlock, was not good enough for a descendant of the Sun King. This was lucky for Elizabeth; she surely would have been miserably unhappy in the rarefied and sterile formality of the French court. She was too Russian.

By the time Elizabeth was sixteen, her doting father was dead. At seventeen, she was betrothed to the Prince of Holstein Gottorp, only to have him die of smallpox shortly before their wedding. One year later, her beloved mother and only sister were also dead. At eighteen, suddenly she was alone.

Her twelve-year-old half nephew, son of Peter's disappointing son, Alexis, was named Tsar Peter II. The grandmother of the new Tsar, Evdokia, Peter's cast-off first wife, returned in triumph to Moscow. Elizabeth was considered a possible threat to the succession, so, as her father had been, she was sent from the court to live in the countryside outside Moscow. There, like Peter, she was left to her own devices, and everyone soon realized that there was nothing to worry about. Elizabeth had no thought of power and wanted only gaiety and pleasure. She spent her time playing, dancing and singing with peasant girls and became an excellent horsewoman. Young Peter II hated St. Petersburg. "What am I to do," he cried, "in a place where there is nothing but salt water?" The court was moved temporarily back to Moscow. Together, the beautiful, high-spirited Princess and the handsome teen-aged Tsar went happily galloping off to the pleasant fields and forests of the countryside, hunting and hawking. But at age fifteen, Peter died of smallpox on the day he was to marry. Again, Elizabeth was passed over in favor of Peter the Great's niece, Anna, a morose and cruel lady who surrounded herself with foreigners.

Anna was jealous, but Elizabeth was always affectionate, good-tempered and careful to be unthreatening. She was a sparkling asset to court life, dazzling all eyes. The Spanish Ambassador wrote of her admiringly, "the eyes are flamey, the neck most white, and the figure extraordinary!" Elizabeth loved dancing, drove a troika, rode at breakneck speed. She was always visiting the barracks of the Preobrazhensky Guards, acting as godmother to their children and showering them with presents. As she grew up, in the people's eyes Elizabeth became a kind of Cinderella figure. They loved her for her generosity, her vivid beauty, but most of all because she was so Russian.

People gossiped about her romances. With all her vitality and sex appeal, men adored her. She adored them back. She found just as much joy in the company of a groom as that of a nobleman. One day in 1731 when she was twenty-two and attending services at the court chapel, she suddenly heard a splendid new voice in the choir. She asked to be introduced to the talented new singer. He was tall, with a bronzed complexion, black hair and the expressive black eyes of a poet; a Ukrainian named Alexei Razumovsky. Alexei was from a small village north of Kiev, the son of a rustic Cossack shepherd. Alexei was a dreamer and his father was continually enraged at him because he was always trying to read. One day when, as often happened, his father was drunk, Alexei was caught once again with a book. In a rage his father threw an axe at him, narrowly missing his head. After that, the boy went to live with the village priest, and his beautiful voice soon made him the finest singer in the choir. One day a court envoy passing through the town heard him sing and brought him back to sing in the court chapel. There, when he was twenty-three, Alexei met Elizabeth. Very soon after, she attached him to her own household as a bandura player. During her lifetime, the ebullient Elizabeth's interest was sometimes briefly captivated by other men, but her heart, once given, was true. Alexei and Elizabeth were devoted all their lives, a story of peasant and princess, of Catherine and Peter in reverse.

In 1741 the morose Empress Anna died after a reign without distinction or drama. Once again, Elizabeth was passed over, this time in favor of three-month-old Ivan VI, nephew of Anna, who was barely Russian at all. But this time Elizabeth was urged by the Guards to take power as the true daughter of Peter. At dawn one morning, accompanied by her friends and supporters, the Guards, she walked down the Nevsky Prospect to the palace where she woke Ivan's mother, saying, "Come, my sister, it is time to arise." Elizabeth was proclaimed Empress. Tiny Ivan and his family were banished. Elizabeth refused to kill her opponents; she stayed the anger of the Guards against the foreigners who had been in power, but little Ivan was to suffer a tragic fate. Later, in a Russian version of the man in the iron mask, he was forced to spend many years in solitary confinement; not even his guards were allowed to speak to him, and he ended his life in madness.

Anna had surrounded herself with foreigners; her lover and closest adviser was a much detested Baltic German. After sixteen years of this Germanic influence, Elizabeth gave Russia back to the Russians. To the delight of her countrymen, she dismissed the foreign chiefs of the government ministries and replaced them with Russians.

By nature Elizabeth was spontaneously warmhearted and generous. Early in her reign she drafted a decree abolishing capital punishment which her advisers would not permit her to make into law, so she simply commuted every death sentence during her reign. She is credited with providing her soldiers with such warm uniforms that it helped to cut down the casualties of war. She even offered to help earthquake victims in Portugal when Russia had no diplomatic relations with that country. An inveterate romantic, she stood as godmother to numbers of children, for whom she also gave gay parties. She often persuaded unwilling parents to give their consent to love matches and then also provided dowries.

Elizabeth detested reading, thinking it bad for the eyes, and hardly ever read anything herself except religious books printed in especially large type. Her ministers found it very hard to get her to work over state papers, especially since she would often stay up all night chattering and gossiping with her ladies while they tickled her feet to keep her awake, and generally went to bed at seven in the morning. She often left letters unanswered, even two written by the hand of Louis XV himself. But then, perhaps, woman that she was, she remembered that once she had not been considered worthy enough for him. Although she was incurably pleasure-loving and frivolous, she was also an astute judge of people. She spoke French fluently and managed in German and Italian; diplomatically she always made it a point to address foreign ambassadors in their own tongue. She chose good advisers, balancing them between the Russian and European factions at court, and with her charm and warmth was able to make them work successfully together. Secure in the hearts of many men, Elizabeth pursued the lavish pleasures she loved so much with the boundless vitality of a daughter of Peter the Great.

A very Russian magnificence and opulence ruled in the court led by the beautiful, extravagant Empress. Huge balls for as many as four hundred couples were given once, and sometimes twice, a week. There were masquerades of all kinds. Elizabeth had beautiful legs of which she was extremely proud, so she decreed masquerades called Metamorphoses, to which men had to come dressed as women and women as men. She often dressed as a Dutch sailor in memory of her father. In summer there were hunting parties and picnics. Yachts and gondolas decked with flags would sail among the islands of St. Petersburg, headed by boatloads of musicians. All would disembark for refreshments at some island where there might be swings and merry-go-rounds. In the winter there were sleigh rides and wild tobogganing down the ice slides which Russians loved so much. One time at the palace, so a story goes, she had all the windows opened on a cold winter's night and water poured over the floors. When it was frozen, everyone ice-skated in the long galleries.

Because of her beloved Razumovsky, Ukrainian dishes and music suddenly came into favor at court. In Ukrainian costume, her hair dressed with flowers and bright-colored flowing ribbons, she danced wild Ukrainian and Russian dances with him. No less an authority than Catherine the Great later wrote of Alexei that "he was one of the handsomest men I ever saw." Although no unequivocal proof exists, many believed that Alexei and Elizabeth were married on November 14, 1742, the year she was crowned Empress. There are rumors that they had as many as six children together, all of whom died.

Alexei Razumovsky was surely one of the finest favorites in history. He was noble and generous and wisely never meddled in politics or intrigue. The only negative thing that anyone could find to say about him was that he had a rather national tendency on occasion to drink too much. Alexei was profoundly religious, gave immense sums to the church, encouraged the building of churches, and sent missionaries to Siberia and the Caucasus. He is credited with sending to the north of Russia the missionaries who succeeded in converting 360,000 people. Because of his love and talent for music, he became the first important patron of literature and the arts. He provided munificently for his family. His brother, Kyril, nineteen years younger, was given a splendid education in Russia and Europe and became Hetman of the Ukraine. Kyril became immensely wealthy and was a great gourmet. He would go off to his dwellings in the Ukraine with six chefs, one of them the great Barridian from France.

Both brothers were so generous that they kept a permanent open house for rich and poor alike. Catherine the Great wrote in her memoirs, "I know of no other persons, who amidst such boundless favors at court were so universally beloved as these two brothers. Riches and honors never turned their heads and boundless luxury with all their adjuncts never spoiled their hearts. They remained cool-headed and soberminded in the very midst of the whirlpool of intrigue."

Alexei Razumovsky's interest and support of music was continued by his nephew, Andrei Razumovsky, who was Ambassador to Vienna during the reign of Alexander I. Andrei, a charming and learned man, built himself a grand palace in Vienna with a gallery full of Canova sculptures and an orangerie and rare plant collection famous throughout Europe. He was a talented musician who kept the best string quartet in Europe in his permanent employ, assuring them a lifetime income. He took lessons from Haydn and on occasion played second violin in the quartet. Razumovsky became the friend of Ludwig van Beethoven and not only supported him financially but put his string quartet at the composer's complete disposal night or day. In gratitude, in 1808, Beethoven dedicated the Razumovsky Quartets (Opus 59) to his patron, who had also suggested the Rondo on a Russian Theme in the first movement of the first quartet. Beethoven also dedicated his Fifth and Sixth symphonies to Razumovsky, among others.

Elizabeth's life mixed lavishness with coziness and informality in a style that is one of the greatest charms of the Russians. She had the ability to enjoy life exuberantly and completely, with no sense of moderation or caution. Like her father and her grandfather, the Empress had a fierce temper and when she exploded she would rain earthy curses down upon the heads of the hapless. After the storm was over, she could unself-consciously and simply admit her mistakes. She loved to eat and worried not a whit about her figure. She would have pâtés of Périgord and truffles sent to her by her ambassadors from France, but then she bewildered her Alsatian chef because most of all she loved plain and hearty Russian dishes—cabbage soup, blini, and pickled pork and onions washed down with Kvas. She delighted in preparing these dishes for herself and Razumovsky in the little kitchen at Mon Plaisir. Sometimes she would invite foreign ambassadors and do all the cooking herself.

Elizabeth had a very Russian love of nature and taste for movement. Today, we see impressive Elizabethan stone palaces, but Elizabeth never really lived in them; they were completed only at the end of her reign. She preferred the countryside, especially around Moscow, and spent most of her time outside of St. Petersburg, living like a nomad in an extravagant folk tale. Like her father, she was always on the move, traveling from one place to another at reckless speed.

Once every three years the entire court migrated to Moscow, 24,000 people with 19,000 spare horses, plus all their belongings. Elizabeth made many pilgrimages to monasteries and holy places. She liked to do this on foot, in the holy Russian tradition, but as she managed only a mile or two each day, the distance to the Troitsky Monastery, only forty-five miles away from Moscow, might take all summer. The court simply camped, living under tents.

For her incessant traveling, she had dozens of sleighs and carriages. One was a golden carriage with panels of cherubs and flowers by Boucher, ordered in 1757 in Paris by Razumovsky. For the winter, one of her sleighs was scarlet, decked with silver and lined with marten fur, with silk cushions and covers of the same soft silver-gray fur.

Her large sleighs were traveling rooms, fitted with doors, windows, stoves and beds, and were drawn by twelve horses. When she covered the four hundred miles between Moscow and Petersburg, the road was leveled and smoothed in advance. Sturdy Russian horses for four weeks in advance were fed only oats, and the teams were changed in a flash by specially designed harnesses. Foreigners always complained that Russian coachmen drove at breakneck speed; Elizabeth loved it and spurred them on. It normally took about a week for normal travelers to accomplish the distance between the two cities; it is said that Elizabeth managed it in twenty-four hours.

To accommodate her and satisfy her love for change, wooden palaces appeared and disappeared with bewildering speed. Some of the stories are breathtaking, even for the Russians, who were accustomed to working quickly with wood. Once Elizabeth decided that the available rooms in the Kremlin were too dark and Gothic; she wanted something brighter. Many hundreds of carpenters were dispatched to Moscow from the Petersburg shipyards. When they arrived, the architect was ready with a plan. They set to work at dawn and then worked all through the night by torchlight. The lodgings were ready for Elizabeth in twenty-four hours. Some of these places were built only to be destroyed a few weeks later by fire. Sometimes they were built so rapidly that disasters occurred. Catherine the Great wrote in her memoirs of her days in Elizabeth's court that she was in one such wooden palace when suddenly, in the middle of the night, it sank down many feet because it had been built on frozen ground. She was spirited out just before the walls collapsed entirely. Catherine also tells that once Elizabeth was camping with the court outside Oranienbaum when a storm blew up. She remained there, unperturbed, even when the wind blew out the torches and the driving rain soaked everything. It did not bother Elizabeth, but it bothered the German-born Catherine, who turned up her nose and said that the food was swimming in rainwater and everybody's clothes were soaked. These contrasts that Russians found normal and even joyous, continually shocked fastidious foreigners. Some years later, Madame de Staël, upon observing this characteristic of the Russians, wrote perceptively, "It is magnificence Russians want, not day-to-day ease. When they cannot have luxury, they will go without essentials. There is no comfort in the English sense in Russia. . . . When the poetry of riches is lacking, they drink mead, lie on a board, travel night and day in an open cart without regretting the luxury to which they are accustomed."

The age of Elizabeth was a time of bright colors and gilt, of gaiety and extravagance. Yet Elizabeth's constant demands for parties and entertainments were allied to a real love for music, painting and the theater. From her magnificent caprices, her generosity and enthusiasm for the performing arts, Russian opera, ballet and theater were born.

Elizabeth and Razumovsky shared a great love for music, and Elizabeth's reign is often called the "Age of Song." At her accession, which took the form of a Roman proclamation, it was said that Elizabeth burst out singing. During her lifetime, she collected folk songs and even wrote a tune called "In the Village of Pokrovskoe," which was included in the first songbook compiled in Russia. For her coronation, she had a five-thousand-seat opera house constructed on the banks of the Yauza River in Moscow.

To please Razumovsky, she brought Italian and German singers to Russia and summoned Ukrainian choirs to accompany them. The Imperial Chapel was crowded with Ukrainians. Choirboys were trained both in Russia and in Italy, sent to Bologna and Venice. When they returned from abroad, many rose to high musical positions at court. In Elizabeth's reign, two Ukrainians became directors of the Court Chapel. Dmitry Bortniansky, born in Elizabeth's time, became under succeeding rulers the most famous musical personage of 18th-century Russia and the music he composed the perfect embodiment of the Italo-Russian style that was born in Elizabeth's reign.

During the reign of Empress Anna, a Russian Ambassador had heard the works of the Neapolitan composer Francesco Araja and had invited him to come to Petersburg to be the director of a newly formed Italian opera company with seventy singers. In Elizabeth's time, Italians arrived in even greater force, bringing with them tenors and male sopranos. As they were reluctant to go to the expense of bringing masses of choir singers, these Italian directors used Russian voices. Operas became very popular. At court, they were given once a week and for every important occasion. To insure a full audience, Elizabeth firmly extracted a fifty-ruble fine from those who were invited and did not appear, which sounds very like something her father would have done.

In 1756 the first independent impresario, Giovanni Locatelli, arrived from Italy and took a lease on an opera house in the Summer Garden. It was called the Italian Free Theater to differentiate it from the court theater which only members of the court could attend. Seats were open to all; the aristocracy could rent boxes for three hundred rubles a year and were responsible for decorating boxes according to their taste with lace and pictures. Elizabeth helped Locatelli by giving him a subsidy and often visited the public opera house performances incognito.

Numerous Italian operas were translated and performed in Russian, but in December 1751 the first opera composed to an original Russian text had its premiere. This libretto was written by Fyodor Volkov, the son of a rich leather merchant in Yaroslavl. As a young man, Volkov had come to Petersburg for a visit and there heard opera for the first time. Inspired by the experience he hurried back to Yaroslavl, built a theater for a thousand people and formed his own company, acting as author, actor, stage manager, decorator and carpenter all rolled into one. Naturally, Elizabeth heard about this enterprising fellow and his company and she sent for Volkov and his brother. His whole company was provided with fine cloaks and asked to present a comedy with musical interludes at court. Eventually, the company moved to Petersburg entirely. Two of Volkov's company became famous actors. Dmitrievsky, the son of a priest, was subsequently sent abroad to study in Paris and London with the greatest actors, including the famous Garrick in London. Another, a Yaroslavl barber by trade who proved excellent in comic roles, was placed in the Corps of Cadets. Alexander Sumarokov translated French plays and wrote original plays which were performed by the Corps of Cadets, and also served as Russia's first theater critic.

At court every week the Imperial Corps of Cadets with their officers gave theatrical performances. Elizabeth followed every detail. She provided rich costumes and sometimes went backstage to help with the costuming and makeup herself. On occasion, she even went so far as to lend her own jewels to the cadets who performed female roles.

In 1756 a public theater was opened. "All decently clad persons" were admitted without charge, and seats were distributed according to rank. By 1760 fifty original Russian plays were in repertoire, and in the capital there were also companies of French, German and Italian actors.

All her life Elizabeth loved dance, of all the arts the one that best expressed her exuberant nature. A contemporary wrote that she was "the best dancer of her time" and that she "gave an example to the court of correct and graceful dancing."

Dancing in the Russian court had its beginnings in Peter's time. Typically the practical Tsar pressed captured Swedish officers into service as the first dancing masters. At their *Assemblées*, the gigantic Peter and his Catherine often danced together and astonished everyone with their spirited grace and skill.

For her larger and more elaborate festivities, in 1734 Empress Anna brought a French dancing master, Jean-Baptiste Landé, to St. Petersburg to teach the imperial cadets to dance at court receptions and in 1736 Landé put on his first ballet with a hundred cadets. The talent of the Russians was immediately apparent; Landé declared that nowhere in Europe had he seen the minuet danced with such grace. He also noted the love of ordinary Russian people for dance, and he asked if he could form a permanent company. Choosing twelve boys and girls, all children of palace servants, he organized a school with a three-year program to train soloists. The school was held in the upper rooms of the Winter Palace where Landé and his wife also lived.

Under Elizabeth, Landé expanded his activities greatly. He was appointed court *maître de ballet* and under his direction the ballet became a fixed institution and his court school the foundation of the Imperial Academy of Dancing, which was to become world famous. For Elizabeth's coronation, Landé and his students performed a long ballet in the new theater she had constructed in Moscow. The ballet was choreographed by Antonio Fusano, the best Italian dancer of his day, who had arrived in St. Petersburg in the reign of Empress Anna and had instructed Elizabeth in dancing.

By the time Landé died in 1745, his students had attained a high degree of competence in their new art. Elizabeth wrote to Empress Maria Theresa of Austria to request that Franz Hilferding van Weven, who had the reputation of being an innovative choreographer, come to Russia "to perfect ballet and add new elements." Hilferding accepted quickly and went on to have a great influence on the development of Russian ballet, introducing to St. Petersburg the *entrechat quatre* and the pirouette.

Times had changed since Peter's day. No more did Russians have to go and beg for artistic talent in Europe. European artists of all kinds were flocking to St.

Petersburg, attracted by the sparkling court and munificent Imperial patroness who so much appreciated their talents.

At Elizabeth's court with its incessant masques and balls, everybody wanted to outshine everyone else. It was a time of rustling dresses embroidered with silver and gold, of furs and feathers—and most of all, jewels. In Elizabeth's day the jeweler's art reached incredible heights; parade swords, powder flasks, bracelets, earrings and agrafes, orders, snuffboxes, scent bottles, all were lavishly strewn and studded with gems and iridescent brilliants.

Razumovsky launched the fashion for diamond shoe buckles and belts for men, as well as for blazing diamond epaulets which held the jeweled decorations which rested on broad masculine shoulders. At Catherine II's wedding to Peter III, a nobleman appeared in a suit whose back was decorated with a tree of diamonds, complete with spreading branches and leaves. Court ladies were covered with jewels and never went out without wearing precious stones. Hairpins, aigrettes and magnificent earrings were worn in particular abundance; the neck was usually left bare. Cleverly hinged ribbons of diamonds were made to tack onto dresses. Jewelry was often made in whole sets; a bandeau for the hair, bracelets and earrings all matching. Snuffboxes were the rage and became an art form of their own. The snuffboxes of 18th-century Russia have winding fanciful flourishes like the carved doorways of the palaces. One nobleman had a different box made for each day of the year. Elizabeth gave Razumovsky a golden snuffbox: on its lid, a large, dazzling yellow diamond representing the sun sends out its rays of brilliants over the sensually bare-breasted likeness of Elizabeth.

Beginning in Elizabeth's reign, many foreign jewelers came to Russia— some first as apprentices; many stayed their whole lives, working to supply the huge demands of their Russian patrons. Nowhere else in Europe was their art so well understood or so enthusiastically appreciated. In these creations of unsurpassed beauty, a Russian warmth and ebullience combine with the blazing beauty of the stones to make these creations unique.

It was the heyday of the colored gemstone in the bright Russian hues that Elizabeth loved—red rubies, green emeralds, deep-blue sapphires combined with diamonds. The Russian love of nature and flowers that had brightened the walls of the Kremlin palaces and churches now blossomed into sparkling gems to adorn white shoulders and glistening curls. Instead of real flowers, bouquets of many precious stones, each different in color, shape and character, were worn on the bodices of gleaming silk dresses. Tiny jeweled flies or bees or jeweled flowers nestled among delicate green enamel leaves so artfully made that the flowers moved and the leaves rustled. There were brooches, wreaths and earrings of tulips, roses and narcissus, aigrettes of diamonds in the form of sparkling fountains. Suspended gems swung at the slightest movement, catching the light at each coquettish turn of the head. Jewelers searched for new devices to make the light beams refract the transparent deepness of the crystals, and gave diamonds new luster by putting colored foil under them to give nuances of rose or yellow. (Many people could not afford real stones; it hardly mattered, since jewelers were so clever that they found ways to make imitations so perfect that it was almost impossible to tell the false from the real.)

In Elizabeth's time, most of these precious gems were old; many still came from the East but Peter had started a search for native mineral deposits. Jasper, malachite, lapis lazuli, rock crystal, carnelians, agates and chalcedony were found during his reign; by the end of the 18th century the superb amethysts of the Urals with their distinctive deep rich color were discovered and quickly became known throughout Europe. By the end of the 19th century, the continuing Russian passion for minerals and jewels was such that regular mining expeditions were sent to the Urals. In the period from 1820 to 1850 marvelous wealth was found. Rich deposits of emeralds, topazes, rubies, chrysolites and alexandrite were discovered and Russia became the richest country in the world for its resources of precious stones.

. . .

One of Peter's unrealized ambitions was to found a porcelain factory in Petersburg. With her love for parties and dinners, it was natural that Elizabeth determined to pursue this dream of her father's. In 1744 she hired Kristen Hunger, a professional German porcelain painter who was then working in Stockholm, and brought him to Petersburg. At great expense, she dispatched a caravan to China with instructions that they find some way to discover the precious secret of porcelain making from the Chinese. The Russian officer in charge, along with an Armenian silversmith who accompanied him, managed to bribe a Chinese potter with a thousand rubles to show them his recipe book and demonstrate his skill. Something was obviously lost in translation, because when they came back to Petersburg neither could make porcelain. The German was a disaster. In six years of working in Russia, he was able to produce only a half dozen cups, all failures. The whole enterprise looked hopeless.

Hunger was very secretive. He probably had good reason to be, since he

119

did not know very much. Against his will he had been obliged to reveal the elements of his craft to a young Russian assistant, Dmitry Vinogradov. Vinogradov, the son of a priest, had been educated in Moscow and abroad, and worked as a surveyor of mines. Vinogradov set about to remedy the situation. He had to learn everything and do everything himself. In the factory he composed colors, repaired the ovens, made experiments with temperatures and finally found the chemical formula for porcelain paste. In 1751, on the day he was to produce something for Empress Elizabeth's Name Day, probably from nervousness Vinogradov got quite drunk and was kept at work only with great difficulty. But, after this shaky start, by 1752 he and his craftsmen had become so expert that they were making fine porcelain figurines and dishes. Elizabethan porcelain is fresh and colorful. The graceful forms of flowers, garlands of roses and berries decorate cups and basins. In 1753 Vinogradov began making beautiful enameled snuffboxes, which Elizabeth sent off as presents abroad.

Jean Gottfried Müller, a master craftsman from Meissen, was engaged in 1758. With his help, Russian porcelain quickly became the rival of Meissen itself. By 1762 there were twelve porcelain factories in Russia; in the 19th century there were fifty, and Russian factories were producing some of the finest porcelain in Europe.

A friend of Vinogradov, Mikhail Lomonosov, was the greatest intellectual figure of Elizabeth's age. Lomonosov, a remarkable scientist and thinker, was decades ahead of his time in his investigations into thermodynamics and physical chemistry. In 1736, the Academy of Sciences had asked that a group of well-trained students from all over the land be transferred to St. Petersburg from theological academies. Lomonosov, the son of peasants and schooled by the church, arrived in Petersburg at twenty-five. He was subsequently sent to Germany for further study. There he acquired the finest scientific training of the time. He returned to Russia and pursued both science and literature. He studied the stars from a little observatory in what had been Peter's *Kunstkammer** and he pioneered experiments in physical chemistry. He and a colleague duplicated the

---

* *Kunstkammer:* a cabinet of curiosities embracing both natural and man-made objects. This was the name given to the private museums, open to the public, established by German princes after 1500. The Elector of Saxony founded a famous *Kunstkammer* in Dresden in 1560, which Peter first visited in 1698. When he returned to Russia, Peter founded a similar museum in St. Petersburg and encouraged his subjects to visit it by offering free wine.

experiments with electricity of their contemporary Benjamin Franklin. They produced thunder machines that brought electrical charges into bottles during thunderstorms, dazzling St. Petersburg society.

Not only a brilliant scientist, Lomonosov was also a poet, essayist, dramatist and historian. He wrote a history of Russia and gathered material to send to Voltaire for his biography of Peter the Great. Deeply interested in institutions of higher learning, he and Count Ivan Shuvalov founded the University of Moscow in 1755. Lomonosov also proposed the idea of an international academy to develop more scientific methods of navigation.

Lomonosov deeply loved Russia and the Russian language, in which he saw "the splendor of Spanish, the vivacity of French, the strength of German, the tenderness of Italian and the power of expression of Latin and Greek." He wrote a Russian grammar which served as a basic text until the 1830's. He also composed numerous patriotic odes. Because of his work, he is considered the founder of the classical literary Russian language and paved the way for the great national forms of expression in the century that followed.

Sadly, Elizabeth's pleasure-loving court had little appreciation of the talents of this great man. His scientific genius was never understood in his own time and his works remained unpublished. In his own day he was primarily known for a mosaics factory, the first of its kind, which he founded in Menshikov's old palace at Oranienbaum. In his later years, in disappointment he turned to drink and died a ruin in 1765, shortly after Catherine II had become Empress, leaving a body of work much of which remained undiscovered until the early 20th century.

• • •

The architectural mastermind of Elizabeth's reign, Francesco Bartolomeo Rastrelli, enjoyed a far happier fate. In an unusually felicitous marriage between patron and artist, Elizabeth not only understood him, but gave him total freedom to exercise his genius. For twenty years, from her coronation in 1742 until her death, he was her court architect; he and his disciples designed every major building both inside and outside the capital.

Born in Paris, Rastrelli arrived in Russia at the age of sixteen with his father, Carlo Bartolomeo Rastrelli, an Italian artist and sculptor who had been recruited by Peter's energetic General Lefort. The elder Rastrelli made a series of portrait busts of the great men of Peter's day and a life-sized wax figure of the great Tsar himself. To his son he gave his love for sculpture; the younger Rastrelli later used full-length figures in a dramatic manner to adorn the facades and roof-tops of his buildings. From the time Rastrelli arrived, with the exception of two trips abroad in the reign of Empress Anna to complete his artistic education, Russia was his life. As a young man Rastrelli carefully studied the churches of Moscow and the fortified monasteries surrounding it. He traveled all over Russia and spent long periods in Novgorod, Pskov and Vladimir, absorbing the lessons of their architecture; he was able to design a five-domed church effortlessly.

Because of her Russian tastes, Elizabeth suggested to Rastrelli that he re-turn to the architectural period which preceded Peter, and that he study the Moscow Baroque churches and buildings built in her grandfather's, Tsar Alexis', reign. She also issued an order that the Uspensky Cathedral in the Kremlin was to be the prototype for all future churches. Rastrelli incorporated this form in the design of his most elegant baroque churches. Assimilating Elizabeth's ideas with his own genius, he succeeded in creating something new for the Russian 18th century which can be called Elizabethan Rococo, a style which vividly proclaimed the spirit of the fairy-tale court of which Elizabeth was queen.

There are echoes of Paris and Vienna in his buildings, but they are not, as so many people mistakenly call them, "European." Their zest and exuberance are entirely Russian; nothing like them exists anywhere else in the world. Rastrelli's buildings are noted for their imposing size, something very important to Rus-sians, perhaps because, seen or unseen, for them there is always the knowledge deep in their souls of the immense land stretching to infinity. Only a large build-ing seems to make a human statement in defiance of such overwhelming space. From the Russians he also learned how to obtain striking effects by disposing many windows of uniform size and shape in rectangular lines.

Rastrelli's buildings stress the horizontal rather than the perpendicular, perhaps because he sensed, as a Russian poet wrote,

It seems the very land in Russia
Takes height as an impertinence.

The low massive lines of Rastrelli's buildings do not contradict, but rather har-monize with, the broad expanse of sky and land which is uniquely Russia.

His materials were dictated to him by the land. In Petersburg there was very little stone available but great quantities of lumber, fine brick and plaster.

Rastrelli used these humbler materials brilliantly. He whitewashed the walls of his buildings and painted them in glowing hues. His colors are those that Elizabeth also loved—orange, pink, pistachio, emerald and turquoise, set off by white columns, silver cornices and golden domes. Like the bright painted wooden houses of the north, they are meant to be seen in winter. Under the snow, they are magical sights.

Rastrelli trained many gifted pupils; notably Prince Dmitry Ukhtomsky, who went on to found in Moscow an architect's school and influenced a whole group of architects, and Savva Chevakinsky, who worked with Rastrelli in Petersburg, designing the blue-and-white Nikolsky "Sailors' Church." Among the magnificent buildings Rastrelli designed in Petersburg were the Stroganov Palace, which was originally orange and white; the turquoise Anichkov Palace, which he redid for Razumovsky; and the blue-and-white Smolny Cathedral with its five domes visible all over the city. Considered by many to be his masterpiece, Smolny was meant to be an entire complex of buildings including a convent, where Elizabeth planned to retire during her last days. Rastrelli's model for the cathedral shows how carefully he had intended the silhouette to resemble the great monasteries of medieval Russia. The multitude of domes and lanterns painted blue and white with details of silver which he planned would have re-created the impression of churches rising behind the fortified walls of an older monastery. The complex was never finished; only the Smolny Cathedral and his plans and sketches endure.

Rastrelli enlarged the palace at Peterhof which LeBlond had designed, showing great restraint so that his more fanciful creations would blend with the sober plan of LeBlond's. To the main palace he added two wings, with golden cupolaed chapels at either end. The fountains were embellished, and the whole palace was repainted a dark pink, Elizabeth's favorite color. Inside, Rastrelli redid the interiors with carved statuary and delicate tracery of scrollwork of wood and iron. He conceived a Cabinet of Modes and Graces where portraits were placed of the 328 loveliest women of Elizabeth's court, painted by the Italian painter Rotari, who came to Russia in 1756.

For Elizabeth, Rastrelli designed two gigantic new palaces: the Catherine Palace, named in honor of her mother, at Tsarskoe Selo, and the huge Winter Palace in St. Petersburg.

A story of its origins is that Peter's wife Catherine planned its construction as a surprise for her husband. Although Peter always preferred to be near the water, she chose a peaceful wooded place overlooking the silver marshes, in the countryside some fifteen miles southeast of Petersburg. During the two years he was away, she had a country house built and planted a garden. Then she enticed Peter out for a ride in the country and to his surprise a house came to view in a place he had never seen. The story says that the Tsar was delighted and threw his arms around her saying, "Never has my Catherine deceived me or given me wrong opinion. I perceive that she was anxious to show me that there are spots around St. Petersburg which are delightful without being aquatic and well worth embellishing!"

No one knows whether this actually happened, but it is known that from 1708 the place belonged to Catherine. On the site there was a two-storied wooden building 100 feet long with sixteen rooms on each floor, all designed and decorated in the Dutch style. After Peter's death, the name was changed from Saarskoe Selo (from the Finnish word meaning "high place") to Tsarskoe Selo, or the Tsar's Village. Catherine left it to her daughter, Elizabeth, who, even when she was a young woman with modest financial resources, engaged the architect Zemstov to make repairs and embellish the gardens.

In 1749 Rastrelli began a grand total reconstruction. As Elizabeth insisted that he keep as much of the original construction as possible, Rastrelli enlarged the original palace by extending the wings. Facing the garden, he designed an enormous three-storied building with a facade that stretched 978 feet in length. Five golden cupolas crowned the northeast corner of the building, which he painted in bright blue and pistachio and accented with white. All along the facade, enormous carytids support on their shoulders the pilasters of the upper floors. Gilded statues stood on gilded balustrades. It all looked so opulent that the villagers believed that the roof and all the ornamentation were actually made of gold.

Under the direction of Rastrelli and Chevakinsky, all the leading decorators of the day, both Russian and foreign, worked on a series of magnificent rooms which stretched in a sumptuous line to form one uninterrupted suite of apartments, framed by beautifully carved wooden doorways of warm linden wood, specially treated in heliotrope oil. In an extraordinary Amber Room, caskets, boxes and chessmen, even chairs and tables, all made of amber, were displayed. Even the walls of this room were completely overlaid with honey-colored light amber panels. Peter the Great first saw these panels in the palace of Mon Bijou in Berlin when he passed through in 1717 on his way to Paris. The story is that he persuaded Frederick William of Prussia to part with them in exchange for a number of recruits, all over six feet six inches tall, for his corps of grenadiers. The panels lay unused until 1750, when Rastrelli found them. An Italian master specialist in amber work labored with Russian assistants for five years to repair them, and Rastrelli had them fitted into the Amber Room. These priceless panels were stolen by the German Army during World War II and have sadly now disappeared completely.

Rastrelli conceived a Great Hall for the palace which, because it was lighted from both sides, was more beautiful than the Galerie des Glaces at Versailles. Mirrors were very important to Russians of the 18th century, and there is a profusion of them in all the Imperial palaces. The mirror was associated with many superstitions; in Muscovite days the mirror had to be hidden in a corner, covered and gazed into only when a person was safely alone. Peter bought mirrors in great quantity, and the new freedom to gaze at oneself openly was a sign of progress and liberty.

Rastrelli's gallery was two stories high and 180 feet long. Gigantic blue-and-white tiled stoves that reached almost to the ceiling stood at either end. The spaces between the thirteen sets of double windows were completely paneled with mirrors framed with shining gilded wood frames. In these glittering mirrors, Elizabeth's last masquerades and banquets were reflected.

For the formal Dutch gardens with their fish canals and bowers and bosques, Rastrelli designed a series of charming pavilions. There was a little Hermitage painted white and green, surmounted by a golden cupola and surrounded by a canal lined with black and white marble where varieties of golden fish swam. Inside was installed a clever mechanism whereby sections of five dinner tables could be made to disappear through the floor into the kitchen so that thirty-five people could be served without any inquisitive servants. When the guests wanted to dance, the tables disappeared through the floor, sections of parquetry appeared and the banqueting hall became a ballroom. The loveliest of these many pavilions was a little hunting lodge called Mon Bijou, all sea green with white columns and decorated inside with beautiful paintings of animals. Sadly, most of these fanciful pavilions were destroyed in later years, when changing taste decreed Rastrelli's work to be out of style. The most astonishing thing was that all this enormous work of construction at Tsarskoe Selo was accomplished in little more than five years.

Rastrelli's final triumph was the great Winter Palace in St. Petersburg. Four

Winter Palaces had preceded it, starting with two simple Trezzini buildings. Rastrelli had built a third wooden palace for Anna and a fourth temporary palace for Elizabeth. In July 1754 he started work on a new permanent palace on the site of the old. Lower and even more massive than the Catherine Palace, the final Winter Palace with its long rows of enormous windows looking out over the Neva River toward the Peter and Paul Fortress has 1,050 rooms, 1,786 windows and 117 staircases. Inside for receptions and balls, Rastrelli designed gigantic halls which could accommodate thousands of people at once, with great wooden doors decorated with gold, nearly 40 feet high. The building of this palace was such a huge undertaking that it was not completed until 1817. It is Rastrelli's triumph that, massive as it is, the palace, turquoise blue with white columns and silver window frames, with its reflection shimmering in the waters of the Neva, seems almost to be floating.

Elizabeth did not live to enjoy fully these two great palaces. She died on Christmas Day in 1761. She was fifty-two, worn out and grown stout from her immoderate love for food and high living. Legend says that she left fifteen thousand dresses, many of which had never been worn.

After her death, Rastrelli fell out of favor and was quickly dismissed. But, incredibly, in little more than twenty years he had designed twelve princely and Imperial palaces and supervised the designing of their interiors. He had also designed hundreds of pavilions and smaller structures and two beautiful churches, the St. Andrew Church in Kiev and the Smolny Cathedral in Petersburg. Of his later life, few details are known. He wandered for some years in Italy and Germany; but his life was Petersburg, and there he came home to die in 1771, discarded and almost penniless.

At the beginning of the 18th century, Moscow was six hundred years old and had a population of 150,000. When Elizabeth died, Petersburg was not yet sixty years old, but it had the same population. Rastrelli had changed the severe Dutch Germanic look of the city's beginnings into something rich and full of fantasy. Between them, he and his beloved Empress had created a look, a style . . . an age.

Still faithful and loving, Razumovsky was with Elizabeth when she died. Even after death, he remained gallant to her memory. Some years later, when Catherine the Great contemplated marrying her lover, Grigory Orlov, she sent her Chancellor, Count Mikhail Vorontsov, to Razumovsky to try to obtain firm evidence that the two had really married. Cunningly, Catherine held out a golden carrot by suggesting that she would raise Razumovsky to the title of Imperial Highness and Prince Consort if he would reveal the truth and allow her to examine the documents. When this was proposed to him, Razumovsky said nothing but went over and took from a locked ebony casket a parcel of papers wrapped in pink silk. He carefully read them in silence. Then he kissed the papers, made the sign of the cross and threw them into the fire. With emotion, he turned to Vorontsov and said, "I have never been anything but the late Empress's most faithful slave. Now you can see for yourself that I have no documents of any kind."

10 · CATHERINE: "A MIND INFINITELY MORE MASCULINE"

ONE OF THE FOREIGNERS who came to St. Petersburg in the middle of the 18th century stayed on to become Empress. In 1744 just two years after her coronation, Elizabeth moved to assure the succession. Her decision to do this so early seems strange; she was still a young woman who could have expected to have children herself. Possibly it was because she had lived through the confusion of succession as a girl; perhaps she had indeed married Razumovsky and knew she would never marry another.

She chose her nephew, a lad of fifteen, Karl Peter Ulrich, Duke of Holstein, the son of her much loved older sister, Anne. It seemed a good choice. Peter was the grandson of Peter the Great and the grandnephew of Charles the XII of Sweden, old enemies and two of the most powerful monarchs of Europe. But Peter lost his mother when he was three months old, and his father at the age of eleven. All his life he had lived without love, raised by a stern father whom he hardly knew and a sadistic Prussian tutor who bullied and tormented him. He was starved for affection, introverted, nervous and painfully shy.

Peter was brought to Russia with great fanfare. Elizabeth was ready to love him. She lavished attention and affection on him with all the expansive generosity of her nature; it was no use. He hated everything Russian and openly scorned the

PETER II AND PRINCESS ELIZABETH RIDING TO HOUNDS. Valentin Serov. 1900. *Page 109*

FOUNTAIN AIGRETTE: sapphires and diamonds. MATCHING SAPPHIRE AND DIAMOND EARRINGS. RUBY AND DIAMOND EARRINGS. BOUQUET FOR CORSAGE OF DRESS: gold, enamel, yellow, rose and white diamonds. (Part of a set which included matching earrings and bandeau for the hair.) All, 1750s. *Page 118*

CATHERINE PALACE CHAPEL DOMES, detail.
VIEW OF THE FACADE OF THE CATHERINE PALACE,
Tsarskoe Selo.
Architect: Francesco Bartolomeo Rastrelli. 1752–56.
Page 124

PORTRAIT OF MLLE. E. KHRUSHCHEVA AND PRINCESS E. KHOVANSKAYA,
rehearsing for a play at Smolny. Dmitry Levitsky. 1773.   *Page 138*

SMOLNY CATHEDRAL, St. Petersburg.
Architect: Francesco Bartolomeo Rastrelli. 1748–64.   *Page 123*

THE PETER THE GREAT EQUESTRIAN STATUE
("The Bronze Horseman"). St. Petersburg.
Etienne Maurice Falconet. Erected 1782.
Page 143

THE LITTLE HERMITAGE, St. Petersburg.
Architect: Thomas de la Mothe. 1764–75.
Page 137

THE IMPERIAL CROWN. Jérémie Posier. 1762.   *Page 132*

PORTRAIT OF A PEASANT WOMAN.
Ivan Argunov. 1784. *Page 138*

CELEBRATION OF A MARRIAGE
AGREEMENT, detail.
Grigory Shibanov. 1777. *Page 138*

PORTRAIT OF CATHERINE THE GREAT WALKING IN THE PARK AT TSARSKOE SELO.
Vladimir Borovikovsky. 1794. *Page 138*

PALACE SQUARE, ALEXANDER I COLUMN, GENERAL STAFF BUILDING, St. Petersburg. Architect: General Staff Building, Carlo Rossi; Column, Auguste Montferrand. Erected 1832.   *Page 155*

TRIUMPHAL ARCH. General Staff Building from the Nevsky Prospect, St. Petersburg. Architect: Carlo Rossi. 1829.

VIEW OF THE MOIKA CANAL *Page 247*

THE ADMIRALTY, St. Petersburg.
Architect: Adrian Zakharov. 1806–23.
Page 155

ST. ISAAC'S CATHEDRAL, St. Petersburg.
Original architect: Auguste Montferrand.
Begun 1818, finished 1858. *Page 155*

SPHINX in front of the Academy of Fine Arts,
and view over the Neva River
toward St. Isaac's Cathedral.

HALL OF WAR, Pavlovsk Palace.

PAVLOVSK PALACE. Architects: Charles Cameron, Giacomo Quarenghi, Vincenzo Brenna, Andrei Voronykhin, Carlo Rossi. 1782–1825. *Page 160*

LITTLE LANTERN ROOM, Pavlovsk. Architect: Andrei Voronykhin. 1807. *Page 164*

STEEL CHESSMEN. Andryan Sukhanov. 1782. *Page 162*

MAST-TREE GROVE. Ivan Shishkin. 1898.   *Page 336*

MINA MOISEYEV. STUDY FOR PEASANT WITH A BRIDLE. Ivan Kramskoy. 1882.   *Page 332*

PEASANT DRESS, region of Novgorod. 1912. *Page 199*

CHURCH OF THE TRANSFIGURATION OF THE SAVIOR, Island of Kizhi. 1714. *Page 185*

WOODEN TOYS. Hussar and Lady. Village of Bogorodskoe, Vladimir Province; Troitse-Sergeieva Posad, Moscow. 19th century. *Page 189* WOODEN KETTLE for washing hands. Archangelsk. 19th century. *Page 188* DISTAFFS. 19th century. *Page 188* WOODEN SPOONS. Khokhloma. 20th century. *Page 190*

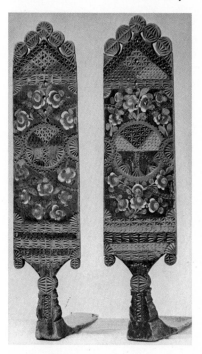

IZBA (peasant house). Fragment of a pediment. Region of Nizhny Novgorod. 1882. *Page 186*

SAMŌVAR-COCKEREL. Copper and ivory. Late 1870s.   *Page 193*

EMBROIDERY ON HAND TOWEL. Yaroslav Province. Early 19th century.   *Page 197*

ILLUSTRATION FOR FAIRY TALE: "Go I Know Not Where, Fetch I Know Not What." Ivan Bilibin.   *Page 179*

ALEXANDER PUSHKIN. Orest Kiprensky. 1827.   *Page 223*

PORTRAIT OF PRINCESS ELIZAVETA SALTYKOVA.
Karl Briullov. 1841. *Page 222*

AFTER THE REAPING, SUMMER. Alexei
Venestianov. 1830s. *Page 224*

REVIEWING OF THE GUARDS ON TSARITSYN PLAIN, ST. PETERSBURG 1831, detail. G. G. Chernetsov. *Page 235*

PORTRAIT OF COLONEL DAVYDOV. Orest Kiprensky. 1809. *Page 235*

A BALL AT PRINCESS M.F.
BARYATINSKY'S, ST. PETERSBURG.
Grigory Gagarin. 1830. *Page 233*

JORDAN STAIRCASE. Winter Palace, St. Petersburg.
Original architect: Francesco Rastrelli; Restored by
Vasily Stasov. K.A. Ukhtomsky. 1860s.   *Page 276*

HALL OF STANDARDS (LATER THE WHITE HALL) IN 1837.
Winter Palace, St. Petersburg. Adolph Ladurner.
Page 276

VIEW OF THE WINTER PALACE AT NIGHT. V. Sadovnikov. 1856. *Page 276*

VIEW OF THE NEVA AND THE FORTRESS OF SAINTS PETER AND PAUL. V. Sadovnikov. 1847.
Page 250

SLEDGING WITH THE PRISTYAZHKA (SIDE HORSE). St. Petersburg. F. de Haenen. c. 1912.
Page 261   ICE CUTTING ON THE NEVA. St. Petersburg. F. de Haenen. c. 1912.   *Page 249*
FROZEN MEAT MARKET. St. Petersburg. F. de Haenen. c. 1912.   *Page 267*

THE LAKE. RUSSIA 1899–1900. Isaak Levitan.   *Page 292*

ON A TURF BENCH. Ilya Repin. 1876.　*Page 292*

FAIR. Boris Kustodiev. 1906.　*Page 300*

FYODOR DOSTOEVSKY. Vasily Perov. 1872. *Page 319*

LEV TOLSTOY. Ivan Kramskoy. 1873. *Page 316*

MODEST MUSSORGSKY. Ilya Repin. 1881. *Page 350*

Orthodox Church. Elizabeth decided that only a good wife might save the situation. The choice finally fell on young Sophia of Anhalt-Zerbst, a second cousin of Peter's whom the young prince had met when he was eleven and she was ten. Sophia's family were well connected and, on her mother's side especially, very aristocratic, but they were one of the poorest and most obscure of the numerous German princely families. For that very reason, Sophia was uncontroversial politically and, it was reasoned, could even be sent home if things did not work out.

Sophia and her mother arrived in Russia in February 1744. Sophia was a clever fourteen-year-old girl, intelligent and anxious to please. She, too, craved affection and approval. Her mother had paid little attention to her and had shown a marked preference for her brother.

Very early in life, Sophia had determined that she had to win people by her merit. The only person to whom she had been close was her governess, Babette Cardel, the daughter of a Huguenot refugee living in Germany. Later she described Mlle. Cardel as "patient, just, cheerful and constant" and all of her life spoke of her with gratitude. Even in her old age, she still signed some of her letters to Voltaire as "Mlle. Cardel's pupil." Babette Cardel taught the young Sophia to speak French and to love French culture. Her influence had far-reaching effects in Russia.

From the very moment she arrived in Russia, Sophia shrewdly realized that to be popular she needed to show an interest in the Russian language and the Orthodox Church. Methodically, she set about learning. She worked so hard and stayed up so late over her books that sitting up in her nightgown she caught cold and developed pneumonia. Her own mother showed little interest and the doctors had almost given her up when Empress Elizabeth shooed them away and nursed her back to health herself. It made a splendid impression that the little foreign princess was so devoted to the Russian language that she had risked serious illness to master it, especially when contrasted to young Peter, who even refused to take baths because it was the custom in Russia.

After a few months of such model behavior, there was no question of sending her back. The clever girl had even managed to make a friend of her difficult fiancé. Sophia was formally betrothed in June, five months after she had arrived in Russia. Sophia was a very common name in Russia, but unfortunately, the name of Peter the Great's usurping sister, so it was decided that she be rebaptized into the Orthodox Church with the more felicitous name of Catherine.

Things might have developed differently if a catastrophe had not struck

Peter in the winter of 1745. He suddenly fell ill with smallpox. As soon as she heard the news, Elizabeth set out and drove at top speed to reach his bedside. During the whole course of his illness, she stayed with him, ignoring the risk of catching the terrible disease which might have killed her or destroyed the beauty of which she was so proud. After it was over, Peter was left disfigured, swollen, pockmarked. When Catherine saw him, she was horrified. "He had become hideous," she wrote. Peter was adolescent, already painfully self-conscious and psychologically wounded. The ravages of the disease ruined for him forever any possibility of normal human relationships. He behaved even more disagreeably and started to drink. He retreated into his past and acted more and more German. Catherine, with intelligent calculation, acted more and more Russian.

Despite everything, Elizabeth pressed on with plans for the wedding, which was set for August 21, 1745. Catherine was sixteen years old. It was to be an extremely important occasion, the first Imperial marriage ever held publicly in Russia. Elizabeth supervised all the preparations herself. She wrote to Versailles for precise information about the wedding of the Dauphin and to Dresden to ask about celebrations at the time of the marriage of the son of the King of Poland. Couriers came back with carefully detailed descriptions and sketches.

Catherine's wedding dress was magnificent—shining cloth of silver with silver embroidery all over the underskirt. ("Horribly heavy," Catherine recalled.) The dress had a tiny eighteen-inch waist, a wide skirt like those of the Infantas of Spain and a short-sleeved bodice with silver embroidery. An immense cloak of silver lace was attached to her shoulders. She was covered with jewels. After the long ceremonies and a marathon of festivities, including a procession of flag-bedecked boats on the Neva River, the young couple were escorted to their bridal chamber, all done in poppy-colored velvet with a bed embroidered with pilasters and garlands in raised silverwork. There, nothing happened. When, eight years later, Catherine gave birth to her first son, Paul, rumors insisted that the father might not be Peter at all, but a courtier named Sergei Saltykov.

Catherine had to wait eighteen years to become Empress, years she later referred to as "full of tedium and loneliness." She despised the frivolous court of Elizabeth. She did not like dancing, had no ear for poetry or music; indeed, she could not carry a tune. Later, as Empress, when she was annoyed by the noise of an orchestra between the acts of a play, she very often silenced it. Instead, she went hunting and fishing alone, or horseback riding, sometimes for hours at a time. And she read heavy books, mostly philosophy and history—Voltaire's *Histoire Universelle*, Montesquieu's *Esprit des Lois* and the *Annals* of Tacitus.

The one courtly pleasure she loved was gambling. As Grand Duchess, she lost more than half of her annual allowance at cards. As Empress, her passionate love of gambling was carried over to the intricate game of diplomacy at which she proved to be expert. The element of risk excited her and the possibility of world attention fed her vanity.

Catherine grew up in the Russian court. While she waited, she served a long apprenticeship as a courtier. She knew all the factions and grew adept at intrigue and survival. She always understood that she must seem more Russian than the Russians to be popular, so she continued to work at the Russian language, although her whole life long she never really mastered it, made mistakes in grammar and spelling and spoke with a heavy German accent. She had no real feeling for native traditions or the church. Although in her lifetime she traveled a great deal throughout Russia, she saw it through the windows of her carriages. Other than her servants, she never knew any ordinary people. The court was her life, and when she later referred to "my subjects" it was the nobility she meant. She never went against their interests.

Catherine had always been certain that she was not pretty, and this was in large measure true. She had black hair, a long face with a determined chin. Her mouth was tight-lipped and hard. She wore the eternal, inscrutable smile of the courtier. She could be charming and gay when she wished, but her clear gray penetrating eyes behind the gaiety were cold. She strove to make up for these deficiencies of nature by cultivating wit and exquisite manners and by developing her intellect and culture. She was full of passionate desires, but she also possessed the extraordinary cool self-control necessary to bring them to fruition. Power, not pleasure, intoxicated her. She had, by her own description, a mind "infinitely more masculine than feminine."

Even in her celebrated love affairs, she had a knack for making love coincide with her ambitions. During her years of waiting, as she and her husband grew ever more estranged from one another, she took two lovers. One was the charming Polish aristocrat Stanislas Poiniatowski, whom many years later she made King of Poland. After Stanislas left for Poland, Catherine took up with a dashing Guards officer named Grigory Orlov. This was very out of character since he was lowborn and appearances were always very important to her, but it turned out to be an inspired choice. Orlov was handsome and dashing, a simple man, full of physical strength and courage, who was dazzled by the rank of his new mistress. He also had four brothers, all tall and strong, fanatically devoted to each other and to their regiment.

By the time Elizabeth died, Catherine was pregnant by Orlov. She had secured her position at court and carefully built up her influence and supporters among the nobility. With the Orlovs, she had powerful partisans in the Guards. Peter had made only enemies.

Six months after Elizabeth's death, during one of the luminous White Nights of June, Catherine waited quietly at Mon Plaisir by the Gulf of Finland, while back in St. Petersburg, the Guards, led by the Orlovs, organized and executed the coup d'état that proclaimed her Empress. Ten days later, Peter died in mysterious circumstances, after a wild night of drinking with a group of men, including Grigory Orlov's brother Alexei. Catherine had finally triumphed. She was Empress at last.

All the Orlovs were suitably rewarded with estates and decorations. Grigory hoped that Catherine would marry him but she steadfastly refused, despite the fact that he was at her side for ten years and that they had three children together.

• • •

The magnificence of Catherine's coronation outdid even the most opulent of any previous tsar. With a sure instinct for showmanship, she was determined to prove without a shadow of a doubt that she was indeed a true autocrat and Imperial Empress. Her dress of golden silk had gold-embroidered double eagles scattered all over the skirt. Her coronation robes included an ermine mantle made of four thousand ermine skins.

By tradition, a new crown was made for the coronation of each tsar. The Treasury through the centuries had accumulated many dazzling examples of jewelers' art and the vast wealth of Russia. But for Catherine, a masterpiece was created. It was the work of the gifted jeweler Jérémie Posier, who had come to Petersburg from Geneva at the age of thirteen in 1728 as an apprentice to a jeweler. He spent his whole life in Russia and provided three empresses and their courts with exquisite baubles. He had great feeling for diamonds, especially, and often a resplendent brilliant was the only gem to adorn his jewelry. The crown he created for Catherine was the apotheosis of 18th-century jewelers' art. Its perfection was never surpassed, and after it no other crown was made for a coronation. It remained the symbol of Imperial Russia until the Revolution, gleaming in changeless beauty beyond the reach of time. When Catherine saw it, she was so delighted that she immediately gave Posier the rank of a brigadier general at court.

To select the gems that he needed, Posier had been given free access to the Imperial Treasury; in his memoirs he noted, "I picked out the biggest stones, diamonds as well as colored gems . . . and I thus obtained the richest object that ever existed in Europe." The crown was studded with 5,012 diamonds totaling about 3,000 carats. In two arcs 76 perfectly matched oriental pearls curved over the crown, and on the top, surmounted by a diamond cross, was an enormous spinel ruby of 415 carats bought "for a load of golden ingots" by Tsar Alexis from a Manchu Emperor in 1676. The blazing beauty and grace of the crown made it look very light, but as Posier wrote, "in spite of my greatest care to make the crown as light as possible by using strictly indispensable materials necessary to fasten the stones, it yet proved to have a weight of five pounds." To wear it for several hours during a coronation was a feat; Nicholas II complained that it gave him a headache.

To the solid gold Imperial orb, Catherine added a brilliant band of diamonds and a magnificent 47-carat sapphire. In her golden scepter she later placed the 193-carat Orlov diamond, the fourth-largest diamond in the world. The legend of this bluish-white rose cut stone says that it was the eye of an Indian idol stolen by a French soldier, which then fell into various shadowy hands until it finally landed in an Amsterdam bank. There Catherine's lover, Grigory Orlov, found it and bought it for her for 460,000 rubles. In a grand gesture, he gave it to her when she ended their ten-year liaison. Not that he went away empty-handed; she gave him a specially ordered Sèvres service worth 250,000 rubles, 150,000 rubles a year for life, and an estate and 6,000 serfs.

• • •

Catherine's style was completely different from Elizabeth's. Elizabeth ruled from the heart; Catherine, from the head. Her métier was administration, and she worked incessantly at it. In contrast to Elizabeth's disordered pleasure-loving existence, Catherine was usually in bed by eleven and rose at five in the morning, and worked ten, sometimes fifteen hours a day. She pored over state papers and wrote not only her own laws but the arguments in their favor and philosophical commentaries on them. Heavy reading, especially philosophy, remained one of her main activities.

Compulsively she had a need to be admired, to dazzle, to be loved. Her intellect was one way to capture admiration; money was another. Catherine was even more widely extravagant than Elizabeth and spent on a scale to then unknown in Russia, which is saying a great deal, since lavish spending has always been, and still is, a Russian characteristic. She spent millions, not only on building palaces and country houses, but also buying art collections, jewels and clothes for herself. She knew that money was a powerful weapon to win people; the love she felt she could not command on her own merits, she bought. She lavished estates and presents on her entourage and favorites, and once presented Orlov with a gold-embroidered coat said to be worth the extraordinary sum of one million rubles. Overflowing with wealth and trade, grain, cattle, wood, leather and furs, Russia provided her with the means.

As a ruler Catherine was always a shrewd follower of trends and people rather than an initiator. Always the opinion of people who "mattered" meant a great deal to her. Rather acidly, a contemporary wrote of her, "It was necessary to have come from some distance to please her and to have acquired a great name to be entitled to her suffrage; and particularly to obtain any recompense. Genius might be born at her feet without being noticed. . . ." Above all, what counted most was the opinion of Europe and especially France. The ideas of the French philosophers were very fashionable in the Europe of the 18th century. In Russia, already in Elizabeth's time, Voltaire's writings were very popular; three thousand copies of Voltaire's volume on philosophy were sold in St. Petersburg alone in 1756. France was far more palatable in the Russian court than Germany. Under Catherine, French became the language of the court. This perhaps was due to a tender remembrance of Mlle. Cardel, but Princess Dashkova, Catherine's close friend, offered another, more subtle explanation of this strange phenomenon. "She [Catherine] did not know either Greek or Latin and if she spoke French . . . in preference to her native German, it was only because she wished Russia to forget that she was born in Germany." Under Catherine, French language and culture became the badge of the aristocracy, which they used to give themselves a common identity and to set themselves off from all other Russians.

In a very modern manner, Catherine considered publicity an essential arm of government, and she developed a supreme talent for publicizing herself and her activities. At first she had her speeches translated into foreign languages and distributed abroad, but she shrewdly realized that she needed other voices to spread her fame. These she obtained by entering into regular correspondence with some of the greatest and most influential men of her day. She wrote hundreds of letters to Diderot, Voltaire, d'Alembert, the Prince de Ligne, Frederick the Great of Prussia and Emperor Joseph II of Austria. (At the request of Catherine, who spent years attempting to compile a Universal Dictionary of all the languages of the world, General Lafayette wrote to General Washington asking him to collect some words of the Chippewa Indians and other tribes.) Her major correspondent was a man who could be described as an 18th-century press agent, Frederick Melchior Grimm, a German who lived in Paris. Grimm published a periodical called *Literary Correspondents*. In exchange for a handsome fee, privileged and influential subscribers received his magazine. Catherine was one of his best clients and contributors. Her letters were all the more appreciated because she showered all her correspondents not only with bon mots but with more substantial tokens of her flattering admiration: expensive fur coats and rare jeweled snuffboxes. Not surprisingly, they responded enthusiastically, and a chorus of praise for "Minerva" and "Semiramis of the North" began pouring out all over Europe.

Not many of these gentlemen actually got to know their correspondent personally. Diderot did come to Russia, but the visit was less than successful; he tapped Catherine on the knee and called her "my good woman" and spoke about revolutionary ideas which she did not like a bit. When Voltaire, stung by jealousy, wanted to come too, she wrote frantically, "Tell him not to come. Cateau is best known from a distance."

• • •

All over Europe and in America as well, the 18th century offered a spectacle of extravagant splendor and sordid misery side by side. It was a time of enormous contrast between ideas of liberty and reality. In Europe, religious persecution was cruel; bloody executions were public spectacles in the squares of London and Paris. The most extraordinary wealth existed with miserable poverty. The Duke of Bedford in England kept four hundred servants at Woburn Abbey. Six sturdy men were employed only to mix and pour the King of France's cup of morning cocoa. At the great seventy-thousand-acre Middleton Plantation in South Carolina, owned by Henry Middleton, a signer of the Declaration of Independence, hundreds of slaves worked for ten years to plant alleys of thousands of camellias. Enlightened English parliamentarians turned their heads as England briskly plied the slave trade. The idea of slavery and bondage, even among intelligent and enlightened men, existed as a right and even a natural state of affairs. Even by Thomas Jefferson this right was never seriously questioned. In the 18th century, Russia, too, lived with this paradox. The system of serfdom, first begun in the 17th century in an effort to keep peasants from wandering off the land, gradually developed into a gigantic system of bondage. The serf, in principle, was not a slave. His landlord did not own him personally, only the land he worked on. By the second half of the 18th century, this distinction had been blurred.

In Catherine's time, Russian noblemen kept armies of servants. The very rich had a staff of from 300 to 800 people; 100 to 150 was considered extremely moderate. Noblemen spent a great deal of time on their estates, which, widely separated by huge distances, were like little cities in the provinces. The rich nobleman kept his own serf tailors, shoemakers, saddlers, carpenters, grooms, stableboys, dairymaids, and apothecaries, not to speak of his dishwashers, laundresses, footmen, butlers, carvers, coffee servers and valets. It was considered quite normal, in addition to all these, to have entire musical companies, actors and actresses, poets, architects and painters.

When noblemen moved from one estate to another or from town to country, they took their private theaters and orchestras with them. Twenty large carriages of entertainers accompanied one nobleman when he stopped for the night. To the already lavish standards of traditional Russian hospitality was added the desire among the nobility to keep up with the extravagances of Catherine herself.

At the beginning of her reign, Catherine talked and wrote a great deal about "liberty" and inflamed the aristocracy with ideas of freedom. In the last years of the 18th century, just as they were in Europe, voices in Russia were being raised against bondage. Some enlightened nobles had begun freeing their serfs.

But Catherine refused to hear such opinions. As she became older she became more and more conservative. She called Washington "a rebel," imposed censorship on Voltaire's writings and, to the point of ridiculousness, even on some of the laws she had written herself.

• • •

More than Catherine ever liked to admit, the artistic achievements of her reign were based on foundations laid in Elizabeth's time. It was Peter's wife, the unassuming Catherine I, who had raised Peter's school of drawing into a department of art in 1727. It was Count Ivan Shuvalov, Elizabeth's favorite in the last years of her reign, who was responsible for founding Russia's first Academy of Art.

Count Shuvalov was a brilliant and cultivated man who traveled extensively in Europe, spoke several languages and corresponded with Voltaire and the French *philosophes*. He and his friend, the scholar Lomonosov, had founded Moscow University in 1755. A few years before Elizabeth's death, Shuvalov wrote a persuasive memorandum to the Senate proposing that a permanent Academy of Art be founded and be given a building of its own. On one of his trips abroad, he had commissioned sketches in Paris; he summoned the French architect Jean Baptiste de la Mothe to St. Petersburg to teach. De la Mothe, working with the Russian architect Kokorinov, designed a graceful building which was finished in 1759.

This new academy made a great impression on Catherine, and she quickly commissioned de la Mothe to build the first Hermitage, next to the Winter Palace. Catherine wanted a sort of European town house, a private and more intimate residence to which she could retreat from the huge Winter Palace and where she could house her growing personal art collection and library. At the same time, she dismissed Shuvalov as head of the Academy of Art, elevated it to official status, and named her own man, Count Betsky, as director. Count Betsky was much more a disciplinarian and less imaginative than Shuvalov. In its earliest days, the aim of the Academy had been to create artists; under Catherine, its purpose began to change in the direction of developing an official art form rather than fostering individuality. The regulations were copied from Europe, but unlike France, painting, sculpture and the minor arts were all housed under one roof.

From the time of its founding by Shuvalov, the best students were sent abroad in groups of twelve, at the expense of the crown, to spend two to four years studying at the Academy in France and in the ateliers of Paris, Italy and Germany. The great sculptor Fedot Shubin, the son of a White Sea fisherman, entered the Academy in 1761, a year before Elizabeth's death. He studied under Nicholas François Gillet, director of the school of sculpture, and won one of the scholarships to Paris where he studied for six years. When he came back, Shubin did a series of superb portrait busts of the great men of Catherine's time. His work was so graceful and truthful that it still represents the best of Russian sculpture.

Because of their background of icon painting, Russian painters, beginning with Peter's "fledglings," were drawn from the first to the human personality. In their portraits, they tried to show not only the physical likenesses but the souls of their subjects, without glossing over any of their less attractive characteristics. The result was that the portraits of 18th-century Russia are much more informal and warmer than those of their European contemporaries. There is something relaxed, almost cozy, about them. The greatest portraitists of Catherine's time were both from the Ukraine, Dmitry Levitsky and Vladimir Borovikovsky. Boro-

137

vikovsky was by profession a soldier of Cossack origin, who came from a family of icon painters. His famous portrait of an elderly Catherine walking her dog in the park of Tsarskoe Selo is so unusually informal, so unaffected a portrait of a sovereign, that it greatly influenced later portraits of royalty.

Dmitry Levitsky, who has been called "the Russian Gainsborough," is considered the greatest portraitist of the time. Levitsky was the son of a priest who worked in the engraving office of the famous Monastery of the Caves in Kiev. Very much as Van Dyck did in England, Levitsky created an image of the Russian aristocracy for posterity, painting many of the great figures of his day.

In 1764, inspired by Fénelon's *Education of Women*, Catherine decided to found a school for girls. She established this school at the Smolny Convent, where there was already a school for orphans founded by Elizabeth. In the beginning at Smolny, five hundred girls were enrolled, half from noble parents and the other half from lesser families. Emphasis was placed on the study of languages, but the girls were also taught sciences, a daring departure that placed Smolny far ahead of other schools for girls in Europe. Between 1773 and 1776 Catherine commissioned Levitsky to paint her favorite pupils, and he executed seven tender and charming portraits of these young ladies in the bloom of adolescence. Among these is the portrait of Princess Khovanskaya and Mlle. Khrushcheva acting out their roles in a play before the Empress. Levitsky captured perfectly their shyness and delight. His success with these portraits prompted Catherine to commission a series of full-length portraits of herself, but she never sat for him, so they are, for the artist, uncharacteristically stiff. Levitsky surrounded her with Imperial symbols and covered her stoutness with flowing Roman-style robes.

The first two painters of Russian peasants also appeared in Catherine's time, Ivan Argunov and Mikhail Shibanov. Both were serfs. Argunov profited from the artistic interests of the powerful Sheremetev family, which provided him with his training. His 1784 painting of a rich peasant girl is the first portrait of a peasant done by an artist fully trained in the Western style. Shibanov, a serf of Prince Potemkin, created the first purely Russian painting of manners. Reminiscent of the French painter Greuze, Shibanov created scenes that gave glimpses of peasant life, such as his *Betrothal*, painted in 1777, which shows a peasant wedding.

In general, Catherine valued art not so much for its sensual beauty as for its intellectual content and the prestige that it conferred. So, rather than actively encouraging native painters, Catherine collected foreign masterpieces. She bought entire collections for herself—fifteen Van Dycks from Sir Robert Walpole's collection in Houghton Hall in Norfolk, and works by Raphael, Rembrandt and Rubens. Whole boatloads of paintings being unloaded on the dock near the Winter Palace were a regular sight. In time, her priceless personal art collection included four thousand masterpieces. It is this collection that forms the nucleus of the superb art collection that can be seen today in the Hermitage Museum.

• • •

Not everybody agreed with Catherine's sweeping imitation of French ways and her dismissal of the traditional values and morality of old Russia.

Among the nobility, one of those who criticized her was a princess, Catherine Vorontsova-Dashkova, who had been one of her closest friends in the early days when Catherine was a Grand Duchess. Princess Vorontsova was from the highest nobility; her godparents had been Empress Elizabeth and the luckless Peter III. She had been given a superb education; she studied mathematics at the University of Moscow, read widely in foreign literature and spoke several languages. When they met, she was fifteen and Catherine was sixteen; Vorontsova became Catherine's closest friend and confidante. She enthusiastically championed Catherine's cause among the nobility and helped to bring her to the throne. Princess Vorontsova married Prince Mikhail Dashkov, an officer in the Imperial Guards who died six years later while on active service. Dashkova never married again. She opposed Catherine's liaison with Grigory Orlov and twitted her in verse for her yes-men, her imitative foreign ways and the loose morality of her court. Her Imperial Majesty was not amused, and so for fifteen years Dashkova was banished from the court. During that time she lived on her estates or traveled widely in Europe.

Dashkova was a striking example of the independence possible for Russian noblewomen at the time. They had come a long way from the isolation of the *terem*. In Russia, as distinguished from other European countries of the period, women had civil equality. They had a legal right to keep their own fortunes and lands. A husband could languish in prison for debt, yet his wife was not legally responsible for paying his debts. Women of substance could therefore exercise a considerable degree of independence in managing their lives. Dashkova was a brilliant woman who corresponded with the *philosophes* and made friends with many notable personages in Europe, personalities as different as Frederick the Great of Prussia and the famous English actor David Garrick in London. In the years that she was away from St. Petersburg, she traveled all over the Continent, visiting the major European courts and meeting with the greatest men of the day, including, of course, those idols of 18th-century intellectuals, Diderot and Voltaire. Her son was educated at Westminster in England and at the University of Edinburgh, where Dashkova visited him and conversed with Adam Smith and the Scottish historian William Robertson. These eminent gentlemen were much impressed with her intellect and erudition.

In Russia, the powerful Prince Potemkin admired her greatly and the two corresponded regularly. In 1783, perhaps influenced by him, Catherine called Dashkova back to court and named her head of the Academy of Sciences, a post which she occupied with great distinction for fourteen years, the only woman in Europe to occupy such an exalted intellectual position.

Dashkova was extraordinarily energetic and farseeing in her post as director and did a great deal to encourage native scholarship. At a time when French was being encouraged as the language of the court, she founded a Russian Academy whose main goal was the perfection of the Russian language, and she became its first president. Under the auspices of the Academy, she organized public summer lectures open to all, which were a great popular success. She managed to raise professors' salaries and to double the number of scholarships for talented students of all classes, including peasants, whose education was completely taken over by the crown. Persistently, she raised large funds for the support of the Academy and the School for Foundlings.

She was anxious that Russians should have the benefit of reading the best of foreign books, so she established a department of translation, under whose auspices a series of translations from classical languages was published, thus establishing a tradition of Russian excellence in foreign translation that has been preserved until our day. Under her direction, the first Russian dictionary was compiled; she herself collected the abstract words. She directed that a collection of Russian theatrical works be printed and began a magazine, *Lovers of the Russian Word,* in which the leading literary lights, including the poet Gavrila Derzhavin, were published. Sixteen issues were published in one year. For the first time the Academy began regularly to publish scientific treatises in journal form. Yet somehow, with all this, she still found time to write poems and plays of her own.

On one of her many trips abroad, Dashkova visited Ireland, a country she loved, and toward the end of her life she invited a young Irish girl, Martha Wilmot, to visit her. Martha lived with the princess for several years and became almost a daughter. It was she who finally persuaded the Princess to write the fascinating memoirs that Martha's sister, Catherine, managed to bring out of Russia. The Irish sisters left an entertaining account of their picturesque life in Russia, full of lively descriptions of the notable people of the day, as well as a vivid portrait of Dashkova herself.

. . .

"You should know our mania for building is stronger than ever. . . . The mania for building is a diabolical thing, it consumes money and the more one builds, the more one wants to build; it is a disease like drunkenness. . . ." Thus Catherine wrote to Grimm in August 1779.

With her cool, rational personality and her love for methodical order, Catherine hated the atmosphere of whipped cream and gilt and the bright, vibrant colors of Elizabeth's day. Peter and Elizabeth both loved to live publicly and the buildings they ordered reflected their gregarious love of people. Catherine was very different. She had developed very early a public and a private face, and she liked to separate very distinctly her public and private existences.

As soon as she became Empress, everything Elizabethan swiftly fell out of style. Catherine had no deep love or feeling for native forms of art and architecture. She did not like Moscow and she complained of the hostile atmosphere she found there, saying she felt herself surrounded by people "whose attachment appears doubtful." She had the marvelous decaying wooden palace at Kolomenskoe torn down, although she did order a model built which still can be seen today. Annenhof, a wooden palace built in the Kremlin for Empress Anna by Rastrelli and said to be the most beautiful wooden palace in the world, was also torn down. Catherine even entertained the astonishing idea of enclosing the Kremlin with a gigantic palace surrounded with classical columns, which would have meant tearing down a great part of the Kremlin walls. She spent thousands of rubles on plans for this project, which was about to be executed when, blessedly, she lost interest. She closed down monasteries, all symbols of old Muscovy, on a grand scale. In some monasteries she had pseudoclassical bell towers installed which were strangely out of place in their surroundings. At the beautiful Catherine Palace at Tsarskoe Selo, the gilded decorations had weathered badly. Catherine had the surfaces stripped and covered in duller paint, which ruined the esthetic effect. Some of the contractors offered her nearly half a million silver rubles to be permitted to collect the fragments of gold which were left. The

Empress haughtily refused, saying, "I am not in the habit of selling my old clothes."

What was to replace Elizabethan–Rastrelli exuberance was a sober and grand neoclassical style that perfectly accorded with Catherine's interest in government and philosophy. Henceforth public buildings were to present imposing facades which fit her Imperial conceptions of her reign. Not only did this neoclassicism conform to her personal taste, but, as always, she was ever mindful of fashions in Europe, and in the middle of the 18th century antiquity was in vogue. For the first time Russians were completely involved in the intellectual trends of Europe. Russians, not only aristocrats, but artists and architects as well, were traveling all over the Continent, seeing other countries and absorbing the remarkably homogeneous ideas of the period. Antiquity was so popular in the 18th century that the same style of architecture became the symbol of aristocratic romanticism in England, democratic republicanism in the United States and authoritarian autocracy in Russia. Once again, Russians absorbed foreign ideas and then went on to construct something very much their own. What make the Russian classical style different from that of any other similar classical style in Europe are its immense size, the greater boldness in use of materials and a more theatrical, dramatic approach.

Under Catherine, St. Petersburg was transformed into a stately granite capital. At the beginning of her reign, Catherine used as architects an Italian, Rinaldi; a Frenchman, de la Mothe; and Bazhenov, a minor clerk's son from Yaroslavl who had studied in Moscow and in St. Petersburg with Rastrelli. (It was to Bazhenov that she entrusted her plan to enclose the wooden churches and buildings of the Kremlin.) Thomas de Thonon, a Frenchman who arrived from Nancy in 1790, planned the whole end of Vasielevsky Island as a monumental setting for civic and commercial ceremonies. He designed the Exchange, using as his inspiration Greek temples to Poseidon, and he also constructed granite quays, ramps and two large rostral columns crowned with lighthouses with huge seated figures of marine divinities at their feet.

Yury Velten was a Russian-born architect whose father had come from Danzig to be Peter's master cook. Velten had studied abroad and was an excellent engineer. It was he who faced the Neva quays with Finnish granite. These severe and beautiful embankments, with steps at regular intervals which go down to the river, stretch for more than twenty-four miles. They gave to St. Petersburg an elegant, grand, and unified look. Velten also designed the granite and ironwork gates and fences of the Summer Garden. These beautiful grilles were the first in a series of traceries in iron which are one of the city's distinctive charms.

In 1767, perhaps inspired by Diderot, who was an enthusiastic admirer of his work, Catherine summoned the French sculptor Etienne Falconet to Petersburg and set him to work on a heroic equestrian statue of Peter the Great. The base of this statue is a huge block of granite hewn from a cliff twelve miles from the city. Peter was supposed to have climbed this cliff, which was 21 feet high and 40 feet long. The cliff had been split by lightning, and inside the cleft birch trees grew and the whole cliff was covered with moss.

Four hundred men worked for nearly two years, from December 1768 to October 1770, to move the huge block of granite. It was somehow put on a platform made of several layers of huge logs which was laboriously rolled on copper balls on a road that had been specially constructed up to the sea. Blacksmiths continually worked on this platform to repair the copper balls, which had to be replaced as the juggernaut advanced. Hundreds of men turned windlasses in unison to the sound of drummers who stood on the stone and signaled each turn with a ruffle of drumbeats. Stonecutters chipped away as the platform moved. At the seashore, it was floated down to St. Petersburg on an enormous specially constructed barge 180 feet long and 66 feet wide and was finally deposited on the bank of the Neva. Even after the great stone had been reduced to half its original size, it weighed 1,600 tons. Excitement about this great rock, which was nicknamed "the rolling mountain," was so high that small fragments of it were used for making earrings; Catherine had a pair made for herself and sent a pair to the wife of King George III of England.

Falconet took eleven years to complete his statue; it was finally cast in 1782. To get the proper pose for horse and rider, he watched Guardsmen exercising and doing maneuvers. His pupil, Marthe Callot, did the magnificent head of Peter, copying masks made in his life and at his death. The statue was placed on the great stone in Senate Square overlooking the Neva River. Peter's arm is imperiously flung out toward the West. Under the hooves of his rearing horse lies a crushed and writhing snake. This, one of the world's great sculptures, became a symbol of St. Petersburg. Just so there would be no mistaking in what company she placed herself, Catherine had the words "To Peter I from Catherine II" engraved on the great granite base, in Latin on one side and in Russian on the other.

Throughout her life, Catherine's building mania continued unabated. During the second half of her reign, Catherine brought the Italian architect Quarenghi, one of the great architects of his time, to Petersburg. Among many other works, she commissioned him to design a palace for her grandson, Alexander I, at Tsarskoe Selo.

Starov, a priest's son educated in Moscow, Petersburg and then abroad, redid the Alexander Nevsky Cathedral and designed the Tauride Palace for Potemkin. This palace was considered one of the most beautiful in Europe, and Starov's designs had enormous effect on Russians. Because of him, Russians came to love columns as much as they had once loved the dome, and for forty years after Starov noble country houses, whether of wood or stuccoed masonry, were designed with columns.

Every summer Catherine went to Tsarskoe Selo, arriving in April or May. Even on vacation she worked hard, rising early and dealing with a mass of state papers. But after her work, she took walks in a plain dress, exercising her dogs and mingling with her subjects in the great park that was open to the public. She did not like the ornate Rastrelli palace with its sweeping line of public rooms and its formal gardens. With her customary energy, she set about to design an atmosphere more pleasing to her tastes. First she decided to change all the Dutch and French formal gardens. She wrote to Voltaire, "Now I love to distraction gardens in the English style, the curving lines, the gentle slopes, the ponds, like lakes, archipelagos on dry land, and I hold in contempt straight lines and twin alleys. I hate fountains that torture water and force it into a course contrary to its nature, statues are consigned to galleries, halls, etc. In a word, anglomania rules my plantomania." In fact, she had never seen an English garden, only sketches and engravings. But with an Imperial edict, all the formal gardens were to be obliterated. First she ordered the gardeners to leave the trees unclipped and then she advertised in England for an English landscape gardener. A certain John Busch got the job because he spoke German.

To design her personal living quarters, she chose a Scotsman, Charles Cameron. A book he had written on the baths of the Romans had reached Catherine and it so pleased her that, without further ado, in 1772 she summoned Cameron to Russia. Cameron, a man little known in his own land even today, became famous in Russia. Very little is known about his background. Catherine wrote of him, "Scottish by nationality, Jacobite by persuasion, great designer trained in the antique manner." Cameron arrived, moved into the English gardener's cottage and subsequently married the gardener's daughter. He spent thirty years in Russia without ever bothering to learn the language but quickly adapted himself to Russian taste and standards.

First Catherine set him to work designing a Chinese village of nineteen houses set among pagoda-shaped fir trees in the palace park. Then, apparently satisfied, she asked him to redesign the Imperial apartments in the Catherine Palace and to design a series of private apartments for herself.

Nothing could be more different from Elizabeth's warmth and exuberance than Catherine's miniature rooms decorated in milky white glass and submarine colors. Away went the clear bright hues, the bright blues, the gilt. They were replaced by muted tones—bronze for gold, lavender for blue, olive and dove gray. Only the inlaid doors and the warm woods of the floors still echoed the warmth of the Russian nature. Her little boudoir, called the "Snuff Box," was like the inside of a jewel case, elegant but brittle. Dominated by Catherine's wide couch, built into the width of the room, the walls were paneled with white glass, the doors framed in columns of blue glass. The Empress's bedroom was lilac, with slender molded glass columns in deeper violet and small bases and capitals of bronze. The ceilings were glass, decorated with sphinxes and bronze eagles. Rock crystal lamps illuminated the room and the marble mantle was decorated in white amethyst and gold, studded with Wedgwood medallions.

Onto an unfinished portion of the palace, Cameron attached the Agate Pavilion, a series of six rooms including reception rooms, a library, and a covered gallery. For the Pavilion, Cameron used the wealth of Russian semiprecious stones—lapis lazuli, alabaster, agate cunningly pieced together with malachite; in the Jasper Room, the walls are solid jasper interspersed with red agate. He ordered red, black, gray, green and white marble from Karelia, Finland, and Siberia. From the Urals came agate and porphyry. Only in Russia could Cameron have been so lavishly generous with these vastly expensive poetic materials. To help him, Cameron brought from Scotland stonemasons and bricklayers: 60 or 70 of them, along with their families, 140 people in all. An Imperial decree regulated their hours of work. Some stayed till the end of the contract; others settled down in Russia for life.

In the Agate Pavilion are marble fireplaces and huge chandeliers shaped like women. All the furniture is in Pompeian style—very imposing but hard and formal. Underneath the Pavilion, Cameron designed elaborate baths based on Roman models of Titus and Diocletian. A frigidarium with a swimming pool led into comfortable rooms with divans, an open fire and a warm bath. One of the baths was white marble, copied from a Roman model, with a stone canopy supported by four columns and taps made of gilded bronze.

To the Pavilion, Cameron added a covered gallery where the busts of thirty of Catherine's favorite philosophers were placed. There she liked to stroll on rainy days or take her meals in summer, surrounded by their stony glances. Among them, between Cicero and Demosthenes, stood an unusual choice, Charles James Fox. Catherine explained that the great English statesman and orator was accorded this singular honor because by his eloquence he had prevented England from going to war with Russia. "I have no other way of expressing my gratitude"; besides, she added, "Pitt will be jealous." But at the time of the French Revolution, in a rage Catherine threw both Fox and her former idol Voltaire onto the rubbish heap because their views differed from hers.

The gallery doors led out onto an impressive, sweeping staircase divided into two branches, and when Catherine grew older and could no longer climb so many stairs, Cameron designed for her a *pente douce*, a gentle, inclined ramp leading down into the garden. Catherine was delighted by Cameron's work and his designs which were, in her words, distinguished by their "strength and elegance." For her, he was the perfect architect and she paid him the unusual compliment of naming the Philosophers Gallery after him.

Catherine's title of "Great" is due mainly to her conquests. With a certain hypocrisy, she wrote, "Peace is essential to this vast empire," but she made war. She gained immense territories. One-fourth of the area of Europe was added to Russia—Poland, the Crimea and large parts of Turkey. The army and navy were doubled. Obviously, she did not accomplish all this alone.

Catherine had a great talent for surrounding herself with clever and gifted men. Among these great statesmen and soldiers, who came to be called the "Catherinian Eagles," were some of the greatest military men that Russia has ever known, Field Marshals Suvorov and Rumyantsev and the young General Kutuzov. But the most remarkable was the fiery Grigory Potemkin. For seventeen years he ruled with her. He was her lover, her closest adviser, her foreign minister, her commander in chief and probably her husband. He supported her throne, executed her vast projects, founded cities and conquered a kingdom. Theirs was an extraordinary physical and intellectual communion. Catherine ruled Russia, but Potemkin ruled Catherine. Much of her greatness is due to this mighty Russian colossus. He leaps out of the pages of history, forceful, masculine, contradictory.

Grigory Potemkin was a brilliant if erratic young man, the son of a colonel from Smolensk. He studied at the University of Moscow and received a prize for being the best student, only to be expelled a short time later because he did not attend to his studies. He went off and joined the Horse Guards in St. Petersburg. He was a recklessly bold soldier, who all his life was interested in theology. From bouts of high living, he would abruptly retire to a monastery and several times almost became a monk. Even when he was the most powerful man in Russia, he would interrupt important political discussions to receive a priest and continue a theological discussion.

Catherine first saw him when he was twenty-three, a sergeant in the Guards, who boldly rode up and handed her a sword knot at the time of her coup. He was tall, with flashing dark eyes, wide cheekbones, a sensuous mouth and a dark complexion; "a veritable Alcibiades," she called him.

After she became Empress, the Orlovs introduced him into her little gatherings of friends. Potemkin had quite a reputation as a mimic; Catherine asked him to do one of his famous impersonations. He proceeded to do a devastating imitation of her thick German accent. The company gasped. Catherine laughed. She never forgot him after that. He admired her openly and boldly. He wrote verses to her; it was the only poetry she ever really liked. Naturally the Orlov brothers soon began to look askance at all these attentions, and the story goes that one night they all fell on Potemkin and gave him a good beating to teach him a lesson and that as a result he lost one eye. From then on, Potemkin was known as "Cyclops." He disappeared for a time, but he was firmly fixed in Catherine's memory, and after she broke with Grigory Orlov she called Potemkin back to court.

She found him a brilliant conversationalist, a shrewd adviser with a "wonderful head." He had a phenomenal memory and knew Greek, Latin, French and German. Full of ardor, his moods would swing from boundless enthusiasm to total despair. Fascinated, Catherine wrote, "He is the greatest, the most bizarre, and most entertaining of eccentrics." In 1774, when she was forty-four and he was thirty-four, she took him as her lover. The same year, the French Ambassador confidentially reported to his government that Catherine and Potemkin had stolen away to a church in St. Petersburg and married.

For the first time in her life, Catherine was totally, madly in love. She wrote him every day, sometimes many times a day, even when they were only 20 yards apart. She wrote hundreds of letters and notes, full of the most extravagant endearments: my peacock, my Cossack, my golden pheasant, lion of the jungle, dearest, darling . . . and even "my husband." They pored over state papers and documents together, they took baths together, she sent her Russian letters to him so that he could correct her spelling and grammar. No matter how he treated her —and they were always having violent scenes—even when he would envelop himself with gloom, with him she was always submissive and tender.

After two years, their passionate sexual relationship cooled. He was a man incapable of faithfulness and perhaps he grew tired of her. But to the surprise of everyone, far from losing influence, he remained her closest friend and adviser. He chose all her subsequent lovers with the exception of the last. There were fifteen in all, all young, all handsome, all like lapdogs. All were subordinate to him. Potemkin remained the real master of Russia. He continued to live in the Winter Palace, which he used as his headquarters, until he moved into the Hermitage. Catherine gave him the Anichkov Palace and he also had his rooms in other Imperial palaces at Tsarskoe Selo, Peterhof and Moscow. In 1787 Catherine presented him with the magnificent Tauride Palace, one of the wonders of Europe, which she had ordered built for him. Her letters never changed. They simply adjusted their love. She continued to cover him with honors, estates, decorations. After his conquest of the Crimea, she named him Prince of Tauris and conferred on him the title of Serene Highness, "Serenissimus."

It is easy to understand her fascination with this wayward genius. "Bold mind, bold spirit, bold heart," she called him. It has been said that power and poetry are the two things that most fascinate women. Potemkin had them both on a Russian scale, still quite astonishing to peoples of more moderate passions. He was mighty in his desires and poetic in his execution of them, a creature of extraordinary contrast, like the land itself. He was an immensely wealthy man who owned estates worth nine million rubles and 35,000 serfs, and yet he was always in debt. He was capable of enormous concentrated effort when it was required, and yet could be totally indolent. He would work furiously to accomplish a goal, only to be bored and melancholy when he had attained it. He could be at once both coarse and refined. He would often receive visitors in his bathrobe, naked underneath, hair disheveled. If he was chilly, he would simply throw a fur coat over his shoulders. Then, a few hours later, he would appear, elegantly turned out, having bathed in his bathtub of solid silver and smelling of French cologne and covered with diamonds. A contemporary wrote of him, "When he was absent, he alone was the subject of conversation; when present, he engaged every eye."

At his lavish receptions, sterlet soup was served in great silver tubs; yet he loved simple Russian *kvas* and cabbage soup and in a very Russian manner could, whenever the occasion demanded it, get along with almost nothing. One English visitor told of traveling with Potemkin in his carriage on a trip to the south. Wryly, the Englishman said that while Potemkin's followers were dining sumptuously, Potemkin himself munched on a raw carrot or a turnip and expected his guest to do the same.

In the field, he slept on the ground, but his military headquarters were like those of an oriental potentate. At his underground headquarters in Ochakov in the south, a narrow dark passageway led down to a massive door. When the door was pushed aside, his visitors, amazed, beheld an enormous marble hall with gilt decorations and huge mirrors on white walls. The mirrors were arranged so that the room doubled in size wherever one looked. Rows of pillars of lapis lazuli and other precious stones supported the ceiling. Heavy curtains between the pillars separated the reception rooms from the others. Enormous chandeliers hung from the ceiling and candles cast a warm light on long, luxuriously set banquet tables. Rows of lackeys in powdered wigs and gold brocaded coats stood at attention, ready to execute the slightest wish. In the Crimea, silken tents were pitched and oriental rugs spread on the ground. In his own private court, he was surrounded by many exotic Orientals and even a French poet.

All his life, Potemkin adored women and they simply raved about him, which is understandable. He was a master of the lavish, romantic gesture. He thought nothing of dispatching a courier hundreds of miles to fetch a melon from Astrakhan or a bouquet of flowers to please one of his mistresses. Entertaining as Governor General of the Crimea, he passed around crystal cups full of diamonds after dinner and bade each lady to choose one for herself. A lady ruined her dancing slipper; on the spot Potemkin dispatched an officer to fetch her a new pair in Paris. From his carefully tended hothouses, every New Year's he presented Catherine with a bowlful of fresh cherries, which she loved.

His generosity was legendary; in the Russian manner he liked to anticipate requests and crown desires before they were expressed. He spent fortunes on presents; people besieged him for favors. The streets in front of the Tauride Palace were lined with carriages; the courtyards were full of ordinary people. When one of his school friends, rather a snob, suggested to him that in his exalted position there was no need for him to receive common people, Potemkin gave orders that this man, and this man alone, should no longer be admitted to his presence.

Unlike Catherine, Potemkin loved music and poetry. He was a great patron of the arts and organized famous musical programs. He kept a two-hundred-man orchestra at his camp and tried very hard to have Mozart come to Russia, but Mozart died too early. He himself composed poetry, ballets and a Te Deum with a salvo of a hundred guns to be rendered on an organ. Catherine put all her court entertainments in his hands; their fame spread throughout Europe. Whenever any important foreign visitor came to Russia whom she particularly wanted to impress, Potemkin planned every detail of the welcome.

In 1787, Potemkin organized for Catherine and a group of distinguished and titled visitors from Europe a lavish trip down to the Crimea and the new harbor of Sevastopol, which he had built. As they floated down the Dnieper River on eighty Roman galleys painted red and gold, each with its own orchestra, the guests passed new towns, some already constructed and others only planned. For the latter, Potemkin ordered that painted facades be erected and peasants transported from miles away to give the appearance of real towns. The term "Potemkin villages" has passed into the language as a synonym for hoax, although this is not wholly accurate.

In April 1791 he gave a reception in honor of Catherine that eclipsed anything ever seen in Russia before. Three thousand guests were invited to the Tauride Palace. Potemkin received Catherine in a handsome red silk tailcoat with a collar of precious black embroidery. The coat had solid gold buttons, each decorated with a diamond. There were so many jewels on his hat that he could not wear it; the hat was carried on a pillow behind him. There were in various rooms orchestras, Greek choirs, poets reciting, a French comedy and a ballet composed by Potemkin himself. The house was lit with 140,000 lanterns and 20,000 candles; the wax alone cost 70,000 rubles.

A few months after this extravaganza he left to return to the army in the south. There, he suffered a recurrence of the malaria that he had caught some years earlier in the Crimea. Nevertheless, he continued to push himself on. One day he abruptly demanded pen and paper, locked himself away and composed ten religious songs, pouring his heart out to God. He grew steadily worse and finally decided to return to one of his estates where the climate would be better for his health. On the way, he suddenly ordered his carriage to be stopped. "Take me out of the carriage," he said, "and put me down. I want to die in the field." There, in Moldavia, lying on a blanket by the side of the road, he died. Everyone searched for a gold coin to shut his one eye, but there was none, and a Cossack offered a copper five-kopeck piece.

When Catherine heard the news, she fainted three times and was thought to be dying; she was bled several times. She wrote to Grimm, "A terrible blow struck me yesterday . . . toward six o'clock a courier brought me the very sad news that my pupil, my friend, my almost idol, Prince Potemkin died after a month's illness." She ordered the court into mourning. She was inconsolable and cried hopelessly, "Whom can I turn to now?" For many weeks, her secretary entered in her diary, "Tears and despair," or simply, "Tears."

She lived on for five years after him. Death came to her unglamorously. In November 1796 at age sixty-seven she fainted on her way to the toilet and fell into a coma. She never regained consciousness; three days later she died, uttering a terrible scream.

Despite her little army of paid lovers, Catherine never did find the love she so desperately wanted. Her beloved Potemkin was unfaithful; her son and heir, Paul, hated her. Her oldest son by Orlov had fallen into a life of dissipation and been banished to Estonia. Intellectually she left the Russian aristocracy stimulated but not satisfied, and because of her extravagances she had enserfed millions of previously free Russian people. The last years of her reign were a bleak period for Russian culture. Her magnificence was like her boudoir—brittle, elegant, but cold.

Her story has a macabre epilogue. Peter III had not yet been crowned when he died and so had not been accorded burial in the chapel of the Peter and Paul Fortress. Paul had his father exhumed in the Nevsky Monastery. He placed a crown on his coffin and had Catherine and Peter buried side by side. With an added vindictive twist, Paul ordered Alexei Orlov, the man who had killed Peter, to lead the funeral procession holding the crown on a golden cloth.

Most ironically, the society that Catherine had encouraged to worship French culture and language was only fourteen years later to be invaded by a Frenchman and called on to rediscover its Russian qualities of endurance and faith.

11. THE YEARS OF WAR AND PEACE

Paul detested his mother. As a young man he had wanted to learn and be active in government. He was interested in sciences and had sentiments of order and justice. A student of everything from astronomy to contemporary authors, he had taken the trouble to annotate the one hundred great books of his day. He spoke perfect French with an unusual sense of nuance and style. But all these gifts withered away from want of being cultivated. Catherine ignored and humiliated him all his life.

At nineteen, the Empress married him off to a German Princess, Wilhelmina of Hesse-Darmstadt. Wilhelmina was a self-centered, frivolous lady, but Paul was madly in love with her, and when she died three years later giving birth to a stillborn child, he was overcome by despair. In short order, Catherine found him another German wife, Dorothea of Württemburg, who was rebaptized Maria Feodorovna. This Princess was cultivated and kind, a lovely, tall blonde with a rosy complexion. Amazingly, she also loved the difficult Paul and through everything remained completely loyal to him. Together they had nine children; two of their sons—the first, Alexander, and the third, Nicholas—became tsars.

Almost as soon as they were born, Paul and Maria's two eldest sons were simply appropriated by the Empress while the young parents were sent off on a lengthy grand tour of Europe, traveling "incognito" as the "Count and Countess of the North." In May 1782 Paul and Maria visited Paris. Although the savagery of the French Revolution was only a few years away, they were received with wild rejoicing by the population and entertained with a staggering round of parties, fetes and fireworks. They visited the factories at Sèvres and Gobelins and became friendly with Louis XVI and Marie Antoinette, with whom, after their return to Russia, they continued to correspond.

But when they returned it was frustratingly the same; Catherine refused to involve or consult Paul, her heir, in state affairs. She set him up in a little separate court at Gatchina, twenty-nine miles away from St. Petersburg. She, who was so profligate with money, was stingy with her son. While her favorites, younger than he, were covered in luxury at court, Paul lived retired and insignificant, a figure of pity and ridicule. All that was left to him was his mania for military dress and exercise.

At Gatchina everything revolved around his military companies. Paul's soldiers were dressed in early-18th-century uniforms with powdered wigs and tricorns. Paul supervised their endless drilling, tapping on the ground with his special cane that had a watch embedded in its head. Just before she died, Catherine decided that he should not rule at all and she began the process of rearranging the succession. When a special messenger arrived at Gatchina in 1796, Paul was sure that he was indeed disinherited and exclaimed to his wife, "We are lost!" But he was wrong. The messenger came announcing Catherine's second and fatal stroke. After forty-two years of waiting, Paul was Emperor.

The revenge of the thwarted son was swift; on the day of his coronation he changed the law of succession. From henceforth only males could rule Russia. He dismissed Catherine's architects, banished her friends and closed off contacts to the West. He so hated Potemkin that he turned the beautiful Tauride Palace into a stable and garrison for the Horse Guards. The mausoleum that Catherine had built for Potemkin in the Crimea was destroyed and Potemkin's body was exposed to the birds.

Paul was a bizarre and eccentric ruler, alternately a reformer and tyrant. His passion for Prussian drilling continued. He prided himself on being able to withstand subzero temperatures without an overcoat and made his aged generals do the same. He demanded that people once again prostrate themselves before him—the old Muscovite practice that Peter hated and had abolished. Now, even richly dressed ladies had to sink down in a low curtsy into the mud of the streets as the Emperor passed. Paul tore down Elizabeth's beautiful wooden Summer Palace built by Rastrelli in the Summer Garden where he had been born. In its place, at the end of the Summer Garden he had the gloomy fortresslike Mikhailovsky Palace erected, and surrounded it with a moat and five drawbridges. There Paul was haunted by nightmares and thought he saw ghosts in the halls. Suspicious, he saw enemies everywhere and he was not far wrong. Paul was so widely detested that, in the fourth year of his reign, on March 10, 1801, a group of drunken officers entered his rooms and demanded that he abdicate. What followed is still debated, but the end is not; the Emperor died in his nightshirt.

His oldest son, Alexander, while not directly involved in the plot, nevertheless suggested the best night for the action. He had been told when it would take place but he had extracted a promise that his father would not be killed. After the coup, when the officers found him, he was sobbing in the arms of his wife. Roughly he was told, "That's enough. Come now. Reign."

Great hopes centered on Alexander, for he had been reared by Catherine to be the ideal ruler. She called him simply "Monsieur Alexandre" and had carefully supervised his education along the philosophical lines that she favored. He was not to be smothered in furs like a Russian child but to sleep like a modern Spartan in fresh air on a simple cot with light covers, a habit he kept up his whole life. He was to be put near guns to make him brave, but unfortunately the noise only deafened him in one ear. His education was to be brilliant; the best teachers were to be found for him. Catherine wanted d'Alembert, the encyclopedist, but since this turned out to be impossible, she named a Swiss scholar, Frédéric César de la Harpe, a liberal who sympathized with the ideals of the French Revolution.

De la Harpe had enormous influence over his pupil and Alexander was a gifted student. However, as in so many things, Catherine's aspirations stopped short of final results. She interrupted Alexander's education at sixteen to marry him off to a German princess and he was left with many vague liberal ideals but no practical experience. His sense of justice had been stirred, but he was never required to follow his ideas through to their logical conclusions; he had never been given any examinations or homework.

Still, when Alexander became Tsar, he seemed the golden prince of everyone's dreams. He was tall, blond, majestic, with a classic forehead, a straight nose and intense bright blue eyes which gave him a look of amiable serenity. He could charm anyone when he wished to, and the French said he was a master of the "smile of the eyes." At first he surrounded himself with a group of liberal young men. He abolished censorship and permitted those landowners who wished to do so to free their serfs. Schools and universities sprang up; books were published

154

in great quantity. He set the historian Nikolai Karamzin to writing a comprehensive history of Russia and corresponded with Thomas Jefferson about the constitutional structure of the United States. In a simple uniform without decorations, he rode through the streets of the city alone. When he first appeared in Moscow, crowds emotionally kissed his boots, his clothes, his horse. The people idolized him and called him "the Blessed."

Alexander was determined to make St. Petersburg the grandest and most elegant capital of Europe. Like Catherine, he employed numbers of architects and commissioned many new buildings. He created a Committee of Construction to supervise private as well as public construction and he himself decided the size of buildings, not only in St. Petersburg, but all over Russia. Foreign and Russian architects, able to work with no thought of cost, created a new and monumental classical style. Only in Russia and in the United States in the 1820's and 1830's was this neoclassical style used for so many public buildings.

In 1806 the Russian architect Adrian Zakharov, who had studied in Paris and Italy, rebuilt Peter's Admiralty. In his design for this enormous building, Zakharov fused medieval, baroque and classical elements into an original Russian style. Built of brick and plaster, painted a golden yellow and white with a tall golden spire that could be seen from all over the city, Zakharov's Admiralty became one of the most distinctive landmarks of St. Petersburg.

Carlo Rossi, born in St. Petersburg, the illegitimate son of an Italian ballerina, became Alexander's favorite architect. Rossi went to Rome rather than Greece for the inspiration for his designs. His elegant neoclassical buildings, most often in yellow and white and adorned with starkly elegant heroic statues in black, were the final triumphs of Petersburg classicism. From Rossi, the Tsar commissioned some of the most famous buildings of the city. Rossi designed the Senate and Synod buildings and completed the design of the huge Winter Palace Square by building an enormous semicircular General Staff building. Embracing two sides of the vast square, with two triumphal arches ornamented with trophies and figures of warriors, this building with its sweeping unadorned facade complemented the fanciful baroque design of Rastrelli's Winter Palace directly opposite. Rossi also designed the Alexandrinsky Theater and the noble unadorned street known as Theater Street which it dominates. In the later 19th century, one side of the street housed the famed Imperial Ballet School. To this day, the building remains the official ballet school.

In 1817 Alexander decided to replace the existing St. Isaac's Cathedral with a new and monumental cathedral. A little known French draftsman, Auguste de Montferrand, who had worked on the Church of La Madelaine in Paris before enlisting in the Imperial Guard, submitted an album of sketches and surprisingly the committee decided to award the commission to him.

The dome of this colossal structure is higher than that of St. Paul's Cathedral in London, 87 feet in diameter, supported by twenty-four huge columns encased in granite; the lantern on top of the dome is 40 feet high. The work on this cathedral, begun in 1818, was not finally completed until forty years later in 1858 in the reign of Alexander's grandson, Alexander II. The interior is a symphony of gold, marble, lapis lazuli, malachite and porphyry. Walls and vaults were decorated with paintings and mosaics executed by several of the leading artists of the day.

Montferrand also later designed the largest monolith column in the world, which was erected in the Palace Square to commemorate the Russian victory over Napoleon. The transportation and placement in the square of this granite monolith, 98½ feet high and 13 feet in diameter, is considered one of the engineering feats of the century.

In the first quarter of the 19th century, sixty bridges spanned the canals, many of them of beautiful design. Built in 1825, the Lion Bridge, with lions seated on massive pedestals that acted as corners for iron abutments securing suspension cables, was one of six such suspension bridges over the Gribeyedov Canal, the first of their type in Europe.

Alexander's reign marked the end of the great building phase of St. Petersburg which had continued unceasingly for more than a century since Peter.

• • •

Alexander, despite his early good intentions and considerable talents, turned out to be a contradictory and puzzling man with strangely ambivalent attitudes toward his responsibilities. From his mother Alexander had inherited his blond good looks, from his grandmother the art of dissembling and hypocrisy. Chateaubriand called him "crafty as a Greek"; others called him "Talma of the North" and "The Sphinx."

In the course of his twenty-five-year reign (1800–1825), he veered unevenly between liberalism and despotism. He was pursued by guilt over the death of his father and by a mysterious religious mysticism that grew stronger as he grew older. Alexander loved Russia, but he did not really feel comfortable with Russians; they seemed to him lazy, hard to understand and unruly. He felt more at ease with Germans and the neat, obedient and sentimental German personality. Personally, he lived a life of compulsive cleanliness and order. Extremely vain, his uniforms were immaculately tailored, his whiskers always perfectly curled. He was a clean-desk man, who demanded that papers submitted to him always be of uniform size. The furniture always had to be lined up as precisely as a military formation. Like his father he doted on military reviews and parades.

In diplomacy and his dealings with other nations, Alexander was often enigmatic. In his relations with the new ruler of France, Napoleon, he behaved in a complicated and crafty manner. Russia and France fought in Austria and Prussia; then in a surprising about-face, Alexander allied himself with Napoleon at Tilsit. Napoleon even proposed that he marry Alexander's fifteen-year-old sister and was ready to abandon Josephine to do it. But in the end, relations between the two rulers were abruptly severed and in June 1812 Napoleon invaded Russia with his Grand Army of 600,000 men. Arrogant and sure of victory, Napoleon confidently drove for Moscow.

The Russian people's fierce defense of their land against Napoleon is one of the most magnificent examples of national courage in history. Contemporary Europeans were completely astonished. Used to the old Western stereotype of a Russia full of downtrodden peasants oppressed by an indolent aristocracy, they were surprised instead by a nation united in feeling in which both lord and peasant fought fiercely side by side with inspiring unity of purpose and patriotism. Brigadier General Robert Thomas Coxe, an Englishman on a diplomatic mission in Russia during the war, wrote in astonishment: "No person had previously to this war a just knowledge of the power and resources of the Russian Empire. . . . The reinforcement and provisioning of the assembling army was one of the most extraordinary efforts of national zeal ever made. No Russian who possessed any article which could be rendered serviceable to the state withheld it; horses, arms, equipment, provisions, and in brief, everything that can be imagined, was poured into the camp. . . . Militia performed the most remarkable marches, even for Russians, to reach headquarters. . . . Old and young, over and under regulated ages, flocked to the standards and would not be refused service. Fathers of families, many seventy years of age and upwards, placed themselves in the ranks, and encountered every fatigue as well as peril with all the ardor of youth."

Peasants poured in from as far away as Siberia to offer to fight. Nobles spontaneously donated enormous sums for the war, equipping whole regiments at their personal expense and contributing 200 million rubles to the state, more than half of the annual budget. Peasants burned their own fields and crops to deny them to the enemy.

Led by their crafty commander in chief, the one-eyed General Kutuzov, who was known as "the Fox of the North," the Russians retreated, burning as they went. Kutuzov stood against the French at Borodino, only sixty miles from Moscow, but then after appalling losses he retreated once again. Within a week, the French occupied Moscow. A day later, the city was burning.

Coxe reported: "This morning I waited with Count Rostopshchin, the Governor of Moscow, to see him fire his palace and all surrounding premises. It was a magnificent act, executed with feeling, dignity, and philosophy. The motive was pure patriotism. . . . We rounded the burning city, whose flames fired the whole sky. . . . All the houses of the nobility, all the warehouses of the merchants, all the shops, were fired and notwithstanding every effort of the enemy, the conflagration raged and rendered Moscow one flaming pile; so that as the enemy stated themselves, they occupied only a site where the city stood and their embarrassment was increased by the erroneous calculation that their needs would be supplied by the resources of Moscow. . . ."

The city was totally destroyed, said Karamzin, the historian. "Nothing was left of Moscow save the remembrance of the city and the deep resolution to avenge its fate." Napoleon watched the conflagration from the top of the Ivan Bell Tower in the Kremlin and later wrote that "such terrible tactics have no precedent in the history of civilization. . . . To burn one's own cities. . . . A demon inspires these people! What savage determination! What a people! What a people!"

Cut off from their supplies, finding nothing but scorched earth, the French began to retreat. Napoleon had callously quartered a cavalry regiment and its horses in the revered Uspensky Cathedral. From that cathedral alone, the French took away five tons of silver and five hundred pounds of gold. As they fled, winter came. Miserable, dying by the thousands in the frost and blinding snow, the Grand Army struggled back. They were harassed by peasants whose vengeful cries echoed in the forests and who attacked with pikes as terrible as any bayonets. The Cossacks rode down upon them and recovered most of the booty taken from the cathedral. (Later the Cossack leaders presented the nation with a massive silver chandelier with forty-six arms and weighing nine hundred pounds, which was hung in the cupola of the cathedral.) A Russian account says that 36,000

French dead were found in the Berezina River alone. In all, 125,000 men perished in battle; 132,000 succumbed to fatigue, hunger and cold; 193,000 were captured. Only 40,000 men returned alive from what was one of the greatest military catastrophes in history.

It was after this great victory of 1812 that the strange mysticism of Alexander began to grow stronger. As he explained to a Lutheran bishop, "The burning of Moscow brought light to my soul and judgment of God on the icy fields filled my heart with warmth and faith which I had not felt until then. I owe my redemption to God's redemption of Europe from destruction." As Alexander traveled into Europe behind the advancing Russian Army, he seemed to be on a religious pilgrimage. He read the Bible every day and stopped off to see the Moravians in Livonia and Saxony. He made a special trip to London alone to see the Quakers and invited a group of them to come to St. Petersburg.

The Russian Army arrived as triumphant liberators in Paris. On March 31, 1814, to the wild cheering of crowds, Alexander rode a white horse down the Champs Élysées, followed by his Cossacks and officers in white uniforms with flowing capes.

An Easter liturgy for the Russian Army was held on the Place de la Concorde on the exact spot where Louis XVI had been beheaded. Cossacks were stationed in Montmartre, and it is still said in France that the word *bistro* comes from the word *bystro* (pronounced bystr*a* in Russian), which means "quickly."

In Paris, Russian officers developed a passion for politics and constitutions. They were encouraged to fraternize with French Masons; they talked of the rights of man, of liberty, equality, fraternity.

In 1815 Alexander fell under the influence of a celebrated European mystic, Baroness Krudener. On her advice, he conceived the Holy Alliance to subordinate policies of major European powers to the principles of eternal Christianity. The signing of this alliance brought the crowned heads of Europe to watch as 107,000 Russian and French troops paraded at Chalons.

When he returned to Russia in 1816, Alexander grew increasingly restless. He traveled incessantly, making fourteen trips around Russia and four trips abroad in nine years. More and more, his responsibilities seemed to frighten him. He talked about abdication and grew ever more conservative. Finally, in 1825 he and his wife traveled to the Black Sea. At the small town of Taganrog on the Sea of Azov, after a mysterious solitary visit to a monastery, Alexander developed a fever and there on December 1 he died. Even in death, he remains a riddle. To this day there is a legend that Alexander did not die, but instead only pretended his death, actually going to Siberia where he died many years later as a holy man. It is one of the intriguing mysteries of Russian history to which there has never been a resolution.

· · ·

Not far from Tsarskoe Selo, 17 miles from St. Petersburg, is a palace, Pavlovsk, which reflects all the beauty of this great period of war and peace, this time of great victories for Russia, when Russians were hailed as champions of liberty and their influence was at its zenith in Europe.

The palace is set in a vast park of more than fifteen hundred acres, full of silvery birches and huge dark firs. Rolling meadows are dotted with wild flowers. Secret pools and lakes, disposed serenely throughout the park, reflect the passing clouds. It is most beautiful in the fall when the yellow birch leaves and dark green of the firs show off the yellow and white colonnaded palace and its graceful neoclassical temples and pavilions to their greatest advantage.

For forty-three years, from 1782 to 1825, all the last great architects of St. Petersburg had a hand in the design of the palace, its gardens and its brilliant interiors. Although the palace underwent several changes and was badly damaged by fire in 1803, this progression of architects, beginning with Cameron and followed by Quarenghi, Brenna, Gonzago, Voronykhin and Rossi, managed to create an extraordinarily unified and harmonious whole. Its style gracefully encompasses the delicacy of the late 18th century and the full flowering of the elegant neoclassicism of the early 19th century, summing up all the ideas of Russian decoration and the beauty of a great epoch.

A delighted Catherine at the birth of her first grandson, Alexander, gave the estate to her son, Paul, and his eighteen-year-old wife, Maria Feodorovna. There they built two rustic chalets called Paullust and Marienthal. A few years later, in 1782, Catherine directed her favorite architect, Charles Cameron, to build a palace and design its interiors. The palace bears the stamp of his genius; it was he who designed the central block and the wing galleries of the first story, which was built between 1782 and 1786. Cameron, with his taste for antiquity, ordered statues from Italy and furniture in Paris. From the great French master Henri Jacob and his son, he commissioned sixteen sets of furniture, more than two hundred pieces in all. These were executed from detailed instructions and designs sent from Russia, and planned specifically for the rooms and spaces the furniture was to occupy, for instance, sofas to fit into semicircular recesses. One of the reasons that interiors of Russian palaces are so harmonious comes from this custom of having furniture designed specifically for them by great architects.

As the work progressed, Maria Feodorovna took an interest in every detail. She herself turned ivory and worked with amber, and she had very definite ideas of her own about the designing of the interiors. She and Cameron fought; she did not agree with what she thought were some of his old-fashioned ideas, so he was eventually dismissed and others set to work, carrying out Cameron's general ideas and designs and adding many of their own. Since Paul preferred Gatchina, in the end it was Maria Feodorovna who over the years took the greatest interest in the continuing work at Pavlovsk. After Paul's death, she preferred to live there, and it remained her palace, the work and artistic interest of her life, completed only three years before her death.

The palace became a treasure house of the artistic talents of Russian craftsmen. Russian carpenters excelled at making beds, chairs, cupboards and cabinets. Architects added to these designs their own lavish decorative ideas of gilding and inlay, ormolu, marble and semiprecious stones.

Using the extraordinary skill of Russian workmen in wood, magnificent inlaid floors were designed using a whole palette of rare woods—amaranth, sandalwood, mahogany and palmetto. For each room there was a different design and pattern. Crystals were cut at Peterhof, and the St. Petersburg chandelier makers provided special designs, all forms and shapes, lanterns and bowls. There are chandeliers with stems of transparent ruby and blue glass whose frames seem to melt away among the rainbow prisms of almond-shaped crystals. There are others made of ormolu glass and silver, with crystal lilies of the valley and green enamel leaves.

For Pavlovsk were purchased several examples of the rare steel furniture made by the Tula armorers whose metalworking skills in the 18th century and throughout the 19th century were renowned throughout Europe. The Tula masters had been famous long before the formation of the earliest Russian factories. Tula, some 120 miles south of Moscow, with its fortress kremlin, was a keystone of the defensive borders of old Muscovy, and the smiths lived in a special suburb. From the 16th century the smiths of Tula were famous for their fine arms, and in the 18th century they began making richly decorated hunting weapons, which Catherine frequently gave to distinguished foreigners as presents.

The Tula workers had developed unique skills. By heating metal in a spe-

161

cial furnace, they achieved shades of burnishing from dark green to lilac to pale blue and pink. Blue was particularly effective in combination with light tones of unworked steel and they added decorative details with gilt and bronze to achieve delicate effects of color.

In the late 18th and 19th centuries these skilled metalworkers made all manner of delicate luxury objects and even furniture. The finest samovars were made in Tula. Dresses were decorated with beads and spangles of shining steel. Faceted steel jewelry splendidly imitated the sparkling of precious stones, executed in a variety of shapes, spherical and oblong, and in different sizes, some as minute as beads and used as fringe. The surface of the objects was polished until it was smooth and shining as a mirror. So renowned was the skill of the Tula workers that they figure in a famous story written by Nikolai Leskov in 1881. To prove their metalworking superiority, the English sent a steel flea to Russia. A left-handed Tula worker surpassed them; he was able to put horseshoes on the flea.

One of the masterpieces of the Tula metalworkers was an extraordinary chess set of forty-four pieces made in 1782. The king and queen are made to look like towers, with cupolas and spires. Rich ornamentation of black cut-steel heads are used against white. The burnished black pieces are decorated with gilt leaves, flowers and palmettes. The knights are bluish-black, with gold manes and fish tails, set with rose cut-steel heads; the manes and tails of the white knights are polished silver.

At Tsarskoe Selo once a year in May was held a famous fair at which the Tula masters exhibited their work. From the Tula craftsmen who made it, Catherine bought for Maria Feodorovna and Pavlovsk at the 1787 fair a rare dressing table and toilet set in steel, gilded bronze with silver encrustation. To Pavlovsk came the priceless sixty-four piece jeweled blue-and-gold Sèvres toilet set given to Maria Feodorovna by Marie Antoinette during Paul and Maria's triumphant visit to Paris in 1782. It can be seen in the Pavlovsk Palace today, the initials of Marie Antoinette still on it.

Maria Feodorovna's favorite architect and designer was Andrei Voronykhin, one of the most interesting talents of St. Petersburg of his time. Voronykhin had been born a serf of Count Stroganov, and early in life had shown such outstanding artistic talent that Stroganov sent him to Moscow to study painting. Although he continued to paint throughout his life, architecture interested him most, so he enrolled at the St. Petersburg Academy. After his studies, Voronykhin went on an extensive trip to Europe with Count Stroganov's son. He spent several years in Paris studying with the best craftsmen of the day and was in France at the time of the French Revolution. He went to Rome to study classical architecture. After six years, he returned to St. Petersburg. Emperor Paul had decided to commission the building of a new cathedral to house the miraculous icon of Kazan, one of the most sacred icons of Russia, which had been brought to St. Petersburg from Moscow in 1710, and the Tsar wanted the cathedral to be an all-Russian creation.

Andrei Voronykhin won the competition, and went on to design the huge Cathedral of Kazan which, with its many columns, has echoes of St. Peter's in Rome. General Kutuzov, the hero of the war of 1812, was buried in this cathedral. There also were placed the 103 banners, flags and eagles captured from Napoleon, which gave a very martial air to the church. In 1801, the year of Paul's death, Maria Feodorovna asked Voronykhin to come to work at Pavlovsk, and his work so pleased her that she appointed him architect to her court. In 1803 Pavlovsk caught fire and its interiors were largely destroyed. Voronykhin set about the work of restoration almost the next day, working from Cameron's original sketches and using surviving fragments of the original decor, available drawings and even the advice of people who knew how the apartments had looked. But he added a great deal of his own, using his own ideas of antiquity. He used Roman and Egyptian motifs which were much in vogue, reflecting the lively interest of Russians in Napoleon's Egyptian campaign. This fascination with the antique appeared in fashion too. Crinolines and wigs disappeared, to be replaced with slender loose dresses with soft folds, hair in smooth knots crowned by Grecian diadems.

Maria Feodorovna asked Voronykhin to design not only the furniture but also chandeliers and decorative objects which were to be executed in the workshops of St. Petersburg. He worked out new lighting arrangements modeled on Roman lamps with long chains of bronze. In the Grecian Hall, lamps were of white marble with chased ormolu; for the Empress's boudoir, he designed lamps of translucent green crystal and bronze. New crystal chandeliers were made to his designs. He used the wealth of the vast mineral deposits in the Urals and designed a whole series of decorative vases in green and red jasper, rhodonite, agate and dark-brown porphyry, which were executed by the master stoneworkers of the Urals.

In the great library, he adjusted the walls to better accommodate the magnificent set of crimson "Don Quixote" tapestries given to Emperor Paul by Louis XVI and brought to Pavlovsk from the Mikhailovsky Palace after Paul's death. A delightful touch were the chairs he designed, whose backs were ornamented with little cornucopias to hold tiny bouquets of fresh flowers.

The Little Lantern Room, part of the private apartments of Maria Feodorovna, is one of the gems of early-19th-century decoration. For it, Voronykhin designed bow windows which look out onto a secret garden full of pansies and white roses. Maria Feodorovna loved flowers; in the park was a Rose Pavilion in which two thousand varieties of roses were grown. And, reminiscent of Marie Antoinette, a little wooden dairy was tucked away in the forest. For the Little Lantern to bring nature and flowers indoors and to create the feeling of airiness and unity with nature which the Russians love so much, Voronykhin designed metal plant stands whose uncluttered classical lines look very clean and modern. The furniture is black and gold; the rugs are scattered with flowers, and the bookcases are white. There is, in this room, a remarkable sense of intimacy, a mood of comfort, serenity and privacy. Voronykhin had devoted fifteen years to his work at Pavlovsk when he died prematurely in 1814.

Nothing illustrates better than the rooms at Pavlovsk the radiance of the Russian interior. Russians were able to create a sort of sumptuous coziness which made even the most formal apartments seem warm and livable. The architect who put the finishing touches on Pavlovsk was Carlo Rossi, Alexander's favorite architect who had done so much work in Petersburg. In his own classical style Rossi put his hand to decorating some rooms. He preferred native woods, Russian and Karelian birch, poplar and walnut, and he, too, had all the furniture for his rooms designed to his specifications. To achieve a wider color range, he used a variety of stained woods and gilding. In the Lavender Drawing Room are tall doors of warm Karelian birch, and the colors characteristic of the day—violet and lilac, draperies of golden-yellow silk with lilac edging and white silk trimmed with yellow. In this room, Maria Feodorovna received visitors at her desk in front of a window solidly banked with flowers. Always loyal to her husband, she had a casket on her table in which she had placed the bloodstained nightshirt that her husband was wearing when he died. When her son Alexander came to call, she always received him first in this room, keeping the casket between them as a silent reproach.

The palace became a kind of Parnassus, a gathering place for the noted men of the day. To Pavlovsk came generals and statesmen, writers and musicians. Both intimate receptions and great evenings were held there; music filled the halls.

Pavlovsk can still be seen today in all its beauty. For a remarkable part of the story of the palace has taken place in our day. The palace was largely destroyed during the Second World War. Its ceilings were caved in, the walls blackened rubble, its rooms exposed to the weather. Under the direction of Anatoly Mikhailovich Kuchumov, a dedicated man who was its curator for thirty-five years, the palace, like a phoenix, has arisen once again from the ashes of war. It has been perfectly restored by an army of Russian craftsmen retrained in the skills of the 18th and 19th centuries. Silks were rewoven and curtains hung according to the sketches of Maria Feodorovna herself. Inlaid floors that had been destroyed by the fire of 1803 that even Voronykhin had never attempted to restore were restored to perfection in 1967.

Scattered through the palace is a rare collection of clocks which were much prized at the time. At the striking of the hours, through the halls sounds a symphony of tinkling silver bells and chimes playing old melodies, gavottes and waltzes—the last graceful echo of a great past.

•　•　•

Pavlovsk and Alexander's reign saw the final great flowering of the aristocratic arts which, beginning in Peter's time, had dominated the intellectual and artistic life of the land. In the 18th century the aristocracy had replaced the church as the principal patron and inspiration of the arts. In architecture and the decorative objects made for their courts, rulers and nobility had taken Western forms and in a very Russian way tried to outdo them in splendor. In much they had succeeded, leaving buildings and works of art whose awesome opulence and beauty still amaze.

The great war against Napoleon had made Russian aristocrats deeply conscious of Western political ideas. Fighting side by side with simple Russians, they had become conscious of the rights of all people. Officers and aristocrats, exposed to new ideas of liberty, came back from their pursuit of Napoleon determined to take the lead in making their country worthy of the high calling they had won by their victory. When Alexander died in 1825, a group of aristocratic officers took advantage of the temporary confusion between Constantine, the older of his two younger brothers, and Nicholas, as to who was to become Tsar. With sweeping idealism the officers determined to bring to an immediate and swift fruition the liberal Western political aspirations that had been awakened in them by Catherine and Alexander. On December 14, 1825, they led an uprising in which they demanded many political reforms, including a constitution. For the

Decembrists, as they called themselves, the United States was the model; one actually proposed that Russia should be divided into thirteen colonies. But Alexander's stern and inflexible younger brother Nicholas, on becoming Tsar, crushed this rebellion utterly, and among the aristocracy it was never revived.

The Decembrist rebellion marked not only the end of aristocratic domination over the political ideas of the nation but also of Western ideas over the culture. During the rest of the century, with increasing force, Russia was to reassert its own personality.

Ironically, the period that was to see native talent become world famous was presided over by the descendants of the unhappy Paul, who were all far more German than Russian. Paul was, in fact, the last Tsar who was Russian at all. His mother was German, his father still a question. If it was Saltykov, he was Russian; if it was Peter III, then he was half German on his father's side as well. Paul married a German princess, and all the later Romanov tsars, with the exception of Alexander III, who married a Danish lady, married German princesses. The last French Ambassador to St. Petersburg, Maurice Paleologue, carefully calculated that Nicholas II was only ½₅₆ Russian. All these tsars were law-abiding, correct, conservative; and although intensely patriotic, nevertheless more Teutonic than Russian in their love of military precision and order. During the 19th century, the English, too, were ruled by Germanic kings not dissimilar in temperament and personality, but a Parliament stood between them and the people, and their solid personalities brought stability and continuity to the nation.

It is a paradox that Russia is a country which seems to inspire in rulers and would-be conquerors alike a desire to order it. But Russians hate conformity and resist it. Sooner or later, all attempts at imposed order are doomed to failure; what the Russians cannot at first resist, they eventually swallow up. "Patience and time" was General Kutuzov's motto. The Mongols learned this, and so did the last Romanovs.

Trying to establish order over an epoch that saw the expression of the greatest diversity of ideas and opinions seen before or since in Russia, the last tsars of Russia veered between patterns of the old and the new. In a very Germanic way, too often they clung inflexibly to what they saw as their God-given duty to preserve an outmoded pattern of absolute autocracy bequeathed to them by Muscovy.

Alexander II, the enlightened son of the "Iron Tsar," Nicholas I, liberated the serfs in 1861, two years before Lincoln freed the slaves, but, tragically, he was assassinated before he could complete all the reforms he planned. His son, Alexander III, an intensely patriotic Russophile, reacted by veering once again to the right. His son, Nicholas II, a gentle but limited man burdened by personal tragedy and the impossible demands of the absolute autocracy born in the days of the Mongols, was overwhelmed.

It is perhaps Russia's greatest tragedy and glory that she has more talent for art than for politics. If the Russians only imperfectly assimilated the political forms of the West, they absorbed the cultural forms brilliantly. Once again, as she had done with Byzantium, Russia took the seed, this time given her from Western Europe, and nourished it in her own way to bring forth something entirely new and distinctly Russian which, in many cases, surpassed the original. And she accomplished this with astonishing speed.

What was to be the extraordinary Russian 19th century began with the spectacle of Tsar Paul tapping out his drills in powdered wig and Prussian uniform. In the West, the Russians were regarded condescendingly as barbarians who, no matter how richly, were still imitating a foreign culture. Less than a hundred years later, fusing the forms she had borrowed from the West with her own rich native culture, Russia was leading the world in music, ballet and literature. After Alexander, the arts ceased forever to be influenced from above. In the 19th century emperors and aristocrats faded into the background, to make way for a new aristocracy of talent which sprang up from the Russian land.

12. THE OLD AND TRUE WAYS

The past is not a bad witness.

Russian proverb

THE SPLENDOR of the tsar's palaces and the magnificence of the churches all declared the might of the Russian land. Yet extraordinary as they were, they were not the nation's finest treasure. More precious than jewels and gold, the real wealth of Russia lay in its imaginative people and their rich peasant culture which lay disdained for more than a hundred years.

Peter the Great with his titanic energy had wrenched his country away from the old patterns of Muscovy and tried to unite Russia irrevocably with the West. He and his successors were able to impose their will on the nobility, but the emperors did not succeed in changing the ways of the people. They, in their patient way, quietly kept their own counsel and resisted. During the 18th century the arts of the people were separate from those of the court. The two cultures ran along side by side, one imported and the other native, barely touching. Art in the service of the nobility developed along Western lines, but in the country native traditions remained unchanged. In the 19th century, this ancient cultural legacy, which stretched back to the days of Kiev and even beyond to the earliest days of the Slavs, took on a new importance. Gradually at first, and then with ever-increasing strength, it began to reassert itself.

168

Far away from the distant capital and the perfumed drawing rooms where the ideas of Western philosophers were feverishly discussed, isolated in the immense fields and forests of Russia, people clung tenaciously to their old ways. They kept their simplicity of manners, their frank hospitality and compassionate charity. They continued to follow their church in their own way. They repeated their old tales, cherished their songs and round dances and a thousand superstitions about house and forest goblins. They carefully preserved ancient folk patterns, which they embroidered in linen and carved into wooden gables.

Every province and even districts within the provinces kept their individual styles of clothes for both daily life and holidays. The gentry and townsfolk might dress in Western style, but not the peasants. They took a long view. Let polite society ape foreign ways; they were sure they were right. The land was theirs, no matter who the landlord might be; the old ways, the true ways, no matter how some foolish people might try to copy the customs of other lands. Such airs they slyly ridiculed in their wood toys and popular prints; "the Devil," went one old proverb, "is always dressed in the latest fashion." And in the end they prevailed. It was this rich folk culture, rediscovered in the course of the 19th century by the great artists of Russia, that came to first inspire them and then astonish the world with its color and vitality.

If, by the beginning of the century, people of elegant society in Russia had come to regard all that was native to their culture as unworthy and plebian, they were only reflecting the overwhelming Western view of their country. Understanding nothing of Russian traditions, it was a European stereotype to refer to the Russians as "barbarians," connoting at the same time something both glamorous and backward. Imbued with this *idée fixe*, many Westerners came to Russia and, like the Marquis de Custine, saw nothing there but the reflection of their own opinions.

But there were other more discerning foreigners who perceived the special qualities of the Russian people. The sensitive Madame de Staël, who passed through Russia in 1812, contradicted the prevailing opinion of her time when she wrote: "I saw nothing barbarous about these people. On the contrary their forms have something elegant and gentle which one does not find anywhere else. . . ." She spoke of the courtesy of the Russian people, their love of song, their courage and endurance: "The character of this people is that they fear neither fatigue nor physical suffering; there is both patience and activity in this nation, gaiety and melancholy. One sees the most striking contrasts united in them and this presages

169

great things, for ordinarily it is only superior beings who possess opposing qualities; masses are, for the most part, gray."

Observant foreigners remarked that appearances were more deceiving in Russia than anywhere else; a useful thing to remember even today. The shaggy sheepskin coat, long hair, loud voice and bushy beard of the Russian *muzhik* gave him a rough appearance which often shocked the casual observer. Despite Peter, the Russian continued to regard his beard as a treasure. Said the proverbs: "A beard is a mark of honor, even a cat has whiskers" and "No matter how fine the mustaches, you'll never cut a beard out of them." The dignified faces to be found among the peasants and Russian tradesmen in markets were striking. One visitor wrote, "When you observe old men with lofty brow, flowing beard and soft mild eye carrying beef and chickens, one would pay a wager that they were all philosophers."

Those who took the trouble to look beyond the rough surface and speak to the Russian in his native language invariably found that the most striking thing about the simple Russian was his mildness and good nature.* Peasants addressed everybody as Brother and Sister, and older people and superiors as Mother and Father. The Tsar himself was known as Father, or simply as Alexander, son of Nicholas. Of every name the Russians immediately made an affectionate diminutive; Ivan became Vanya; Maria, Masha. Diminutives (Vanyushka, Mashenka) were even made of diminutives.

Johann Georg Kohl, a German who lived in Russia for six years and spoke Russian fluently, wrote this about the simple Russian in 1842: "Address a few kind words to him and you will discover a good nature and friendly disposition. 'Good day, Father,' he will say. 'Thank God, I am well.' At the same time, the whole face relaxes into a smile, hat and gloves are taken off, bow after bow is made, your hand is grasped with as much politeness as unaffected cordiality. A few words often suffice to draw from him long stories and anecdotes. The mild, gentle hospitable spirit of the nation can be seen when two peasants meet with each other, who make more ceremony than gentlemen with us. The lowliest Russian day laborer salutes his poorest cousin with the same politeness, takes off

---

* It is striking to note the great difference in the accounts of travelers who knew the Russian language and those who did not. This knowledge seems to have made such a marked difference in their perception of the country that, in some cases, it makes one wonder if the travelers were visiting the same country.

170

his hat three times to him, shakes him by the hand, calls him brother, father, grandfather, and bowing repeatedly, inquires with the greatest interest how he does and wishes him the grace of God, the blessing of Heaven and the protection of all the saints as he would do to a person of first distinction."

When questioned, a peasant was never at a loss for words. His answers, according to Kohl, were "always apt and sometimes full of sarcastic wit," revealing a sharp sense of humor and great independence of spirit. Russians salted their conversation with the pithy proverbs of their folk wisdom. They were patient: "What is well done is slowly done." They were skeptical: "The truth has seven sides"; "The stranger's soul is murky"; "To know a man, you have to eat sixteen puds* of salt with him." Their sense of humor was sly and earthy: "A pretty girl is not afraid when men see her in the bath, but an ugly girl is frightened to death," and often touched with irony: "Fear life, not death"; "We don't live uphill, but downhill." They were extraordinarily adaptable, able to put their hands to anything, and they were shrewd: "If you don't oil the wheels, you won't get there"; "From honest toil, you don't build mansions."

The Russian peasant was also cunning, an expert at agilely circumventing authority when he did not wish to bend to it. The Russian Aesop, Ivan Krylov, tells a tale of a peasant evading the laws of religion, which carefully specified that "Ye shall not eat on fast days any kind of flesh, nor shall ye boil eggs in water upon your hearths and eat such eggs." A peasant who had no intention of depriving himself of eggs on a fast day drove a nail into the wall and hung an egg from it by a wire. He then placed his lamp under the egg and cooked it. Caught in the act by a priest, he explained slyly that he thought that in this way he was not breaking the commandment. "Why the Devil must have taught you that!" exclaimed the priest peevishly. "Ah, yes, Father, forgive me, I will confess; it is true, the Devil did teach me." At this point the Devil, who had been sitting unobserved on the stove chuckling at the sight of the suspended egg, cried out, "No, indeed, it is not true. I have not taught him, for upon my word, this is the first time I ever saw the trick!"

The contrasts in the Russian character astonished and often perplexed foreigners. Certain Russian habits were downright startling; the custom of the public baths, for instance, a tradition for centuries, astonished Europeans, who had far less exacting standards of cleanliness. Anthony Jenkinson, the Tudor merchant

* A pud = 36.11 pounds.

171

captain of the 16th century, described these baths with the sort of round-eyed wonder that was a typical foreign reaction even in much later times: "They use bathstoves twice or thrice weekly. All the winter time and almost the whole summer, they heat their stoves that so warm the house that a stranger shall first hardly like it. You shall see them sometimes (to season their bodies) come out of their bathhouses all of a froth and fuming . . . and presently to leap into the river stark naked or to pour cold water all over their bodies and that in the coldest of winter time."

The impression that foreigners sometimes had that Russians were dirty was mainly due to the ever present and often richly pungent sheepskin coat. In town and country all went to the baths, some every day and all at least once a week. The wealthier of them scented the steam with herbs. Russians simply could not understand how Europeans could do without such baths. In old Muscovy, ministers often met in the baths to discuss matters of state. When Versailles was built of rock and stone, it had no conveniences, let alone baths. Yet at the very same time, Tsar Alexis had constructed at Kolomenskoe baths not only for members of his family but three for the servants. Every village had a wooden bathhouse very much like the Finnish sauna, usually built near a stream or river.

The Russian writer Melnikov-Pechersky described the bathhouse of a rich peasant of the Volga in the 19th century. "The bathhouse, similar to the bathhouses of other peasants, stood on the bank of the river Shishenka, most importantly for reasons of safety from the danger of fire, and for another reason: in summer, after getting steamed in the bathhouse, one could at once dip oneself into the cool water of the river. After taking a hot steam bath, a Russian peasant loves to roll about in the snow if it is winter, or to bathe in icy water if it is summer. The bathhouse was high, full of light, roomy—even from the outside it did not differ from that of a nobleman. Inside, everything was tidy and well cleaned. Linden tree shelves, benches and even the floors would be scrubbed with a spokeshave several times a year. The windows in the bathhouse were large, glassed and there was a clean dressing room especially attached to it."

Once inside, Russians would steam themselves to full exhaustion, beating themselves with birch-twig brooms and then emerge rosy and naked to plunge headfirst into the icy waters of the river. The Russian writer Alexander Kuprin described the experience: "The first sensation was that of burning, a stopping of perspiration, a kind of instantaneous terror, an arresting of the heart. But soon the body would get used to the cold and when the bathers ran back to the bathhouse, they would be seized by a feeling of inexpressible lightness, as if every muscle and every pore were permeated with a blissful joy, sweet and yet energizing."

In 1805 an Englishman wrote incredulously, "Russians have a cure for every disease, two glasses of brandy, a scourging and soaping in the vapor baths and a roll in the Neva or the snow."

The exuberant intemperance of the Russians in both eating and drinking was even more shocking to some foreign observers. Said the proverb, "A feast is only happy when everyone is drunk." But, writes Kohl, while drinking made the Germans coarse and boisterous, the English brutal and beastly and the Spaniards gloomy and revengeful, it made Russians cheerful and humorous. "At the first stage they begin to chat and tell stories, they sing and fall into each other's arms, hugging, kissing nearly stifling one another. By and by even enemies become reconciled and mutually embrace; former animosities are forgiven. All strangers of whatever class or age are then cordially saluted, kissed and cuddled. . . ." The Russian, says he, did not fight when drunk, but often threw or broke things, chairs, tables, windows. "The more he drinks, the brighter seems the world and at last his jubilation subsides into a continuous song; and extended on his sledge, talking with himself . . . he arrives fast asleep at his farm whither his sober and intelligent horse has found his way without a conductor." When Kohl asked a peasant about this propensity to drinking, the Russian answered with equanimity, "God has made Russians so, what to do? Who can alter them?"

In any case, it was all part of being human. Warmly brought up as children, the Russians were never tortured with the puritanical idea of unredeemable guilt. Their church taught them that any sin, as long as it was sincerely repented, could be forgiven. It was the great strength of the Russian that through all misfortunes and adversity he kept with him this enduring sense of rightness and security. "A scolding," said he, calmly, "does not show on the collar" and "One opinion does not make a proverb." Direct and unsentimental, he had a great tolerance for human failing and weakness: "Don't rejoice in the misfortune of another; yours is there in your vegetable patch."

As he lived close to nature, the Russian was unaffected and near to both the crudities and pleasures of life, and therefore was above all a realist. "If you make yourself a canal," says the proverb, "someone will pour water through you."

The life of simple Russian people was measured in the slow rhythms of nature and regulated by the church. Both taught them patience. "The Devil's work is quick," said they. "It is bright and flashing. God works slowly; look at nature." Faith in God was so characteristic that the word for peasant in Russian, *Krestyanin*, is simply "a Christian." After visiting Russia in 1867, the Canon of St. Paul's Cathedral in London wrote, "The sense of God's presence, of the supernatural, seems to me to penetrate Russian life more completely than that of any other of the Western nations."

The Orthodox Church taught that "God is always among us," so as a reminder, icons were hung not only in the "beautiful corner" of every *izba*, but on wells and near springs in honor of Saint Evprakhia of Good Friday; in stables, in shops and restaurants and offices; even in railway stations.

In old Russia, almost one-third of the year was consumed by Holy Days in church, and until the Revolution, Orthodox fast days outnumbered all other days of the year. There were two fast days (Wednesday and Friday) every week, the St. Peter's Fast of five weeks that ended on July 13, the two-week Fast of the Assumption in August, the Christmas Fast of six weeks before Christmas, and the Great Fast of seven weeks before Easter. These frequent fasts were kept not only by the peasants but by all classes of the population. In villages at Christmas, Epiphany and Easter, a priest visited every house and held a short service.

Next to his skin, a Russian wore a cross which he received when he was baptized and never took off for the rest of his life. His Name Day or Angel's Day was the festival of his own personal saint. People sent greetings to all their friends and relations on their Saint's Day rather than on their birthday. Peasants regulated their whole lives according to church festivals and the Calendar of Saints, which once and for all established the times for doing certain things. Cattle were turned out on April 17 because it was St. Stephen's Day, and the priest blessed them and sprinkled them with holy water. Peasants plowed on St. George's Day. Apples, whether ripe or not, were gathered on Transfiguration Day in August because the peasants believed that apples eaten earlier would be like poison; after that, even if green, they would not be harmful.

In fact, wrote Kohl, "Nothing distinguishes the Russian of the lower class more than his trust in God. 'God be with thee,' 'God grant,' are expressions that meet the ear at every step . . . the common Russian may be said to live and move in God." In the bustling Hay Market of St. Petersburg, Kohl went from peasant dealer to dealer asking, "How is business?" The answers were: "Glory be to God, well." "Glory be to God, tolerably." "Glory be to God, I am satisfied." And when one man responded, "Glory be to God, awfully bad," Kohl asked him how he could say this. The man answered peaceably, "I praise him when I am unlucky as well as when I am prosperous." The Russians, continued Kohl, could be called the "Mohammedans of Christianity" because of the phrases "I can't tell, God knows" and "if it pleases God" that prefaced and ended their sentences.

This calm acceptance of fate and the sympathy for human suffering are perhaps the greatest strength of the Russian people and the most basic expression of Russian Christianity.

There is a slightly patronizing French expression, *l'âme slave* (the Slavic soul), which is usually followed by the codicil, "they love to suffer." This is incorrect. Russians do not "love" to suffer, but through their history they have often had to suffer and to endure. Their experience has bred in them a serene knowledge that there is a limit to what human beings can understand or change, and an acceptance of everything that life has to offer of both joy and tragedy. This fatalistic view is perhaps best summed up in those two quintessential and comforting Russian expressions which can be at the same time both merry and sad: *Vsyo proidyot*—"Everything will pass" and *Nichevo*—"Never mind."

In the early years of the 20th century, Maurice Baring, an English writer who spent many years traveling in Russia, wrote this about the simple Russian people: "The Russian soul is filled with a human Christian charity which is warmer in kind and intenser in degree and expressed with a greater simplicity and sincerity than I have met with in any other people anywhere else; and it is this quality being behind everything else which gives charm to Russian life, poignancy to its music, sincerity and simplicity to its religion, manner, intercourse, music, singing, verse, art and acting—in a word, to its art, its life and its faith. . . . What I admire in the Russian people is nothing barbaric, picturesque or exotic, but something eternal, universal and great—namely, their love of man and their faith in God."

Yet the deep faith in God which so much characterized the Russian people did not prevent them from surrounding themselves with a world of poetic superstitions reaching back into their pre-Christian past and founded in the nature of which they felt themselves so much a part. Peasants clung stubbornly to these ancient Slavic beliefs and sometimes even assimilated them into their religion.

These superstitions, which permeated their lives, seemed eminently sensible to them, helping to decipher a whole mysterious world of omens and signs which the church could not entirely explain.

175

The old Slavonic gods were the Wind, the Sun, the Frost, and above all, the warm fertile Earth Mother, who taught her children kindness and mercy. Peasants believed in a whole universe of sprites and spirits, like the *rusalki*, the dangerous and wanton female water spirits whose pleasure it was to lure young men and either tickle them to death or to drown them. Ancestors were revered and remembered and were thought to inhabit birch trees. In old Russia, ten days a year were designated by the church as Parents' Saturdays. Even today, perhaps in atavistic memory, Russians like to visit graveyards, where they feel comfortable and calm. They still plant birch trees by the graves of their dead.

The chief of the ancestors was the patron of the house, the house spirit or *domovoy*. Every peasant house had its own house spirit who was thought of as an old dwarf living under the threshold or in the stove of the horse stall. Statues of him dating from as early as the 12th century have been found. The *domovoy*, according to belief, disliked being seen and punished people for both curiosity and neglect. He had to be fed and treated with respect. At carnival time, pancakes were put on the windowsill for him. When a family moved, it took some of the ashes from the stove along, so as to be sure to bring the *domovoy* to the new abode. An English lady writing in the 1850's commented, "Peasants have the greatest faith in ghost stories, sorcery and the evil eye, and the tricks of a mischievous kind of Puck called the Domovoy or House Spirit, who is a very useful being in a household. If the horses become thin, it is not because the groom sells the hay and the corn, if the wine diminish or the sugar vanish, it is the neer-do-well Domovoy. If the tray of china falls down and the best set is destroyed, of course it is *his doing*, in fact there is scarcely a wicked act *he does not do*."

So important and all-pervasive were these folk beliefs that in 1845 the St. Petersburg Academy of Sciences carefully compiled a comprehensive encyclopedia of folk customs in two thick volumes entitled *Beliefs, Habits, Superstitions, Songs, Riddles and Games of the Russian People*. Every day of the year had its special duties and properties and many were marked with ceremonies. Peasants even had their own names for the months. September was called "Women's Summer." On September 1 old mattresses were burned and new ones bought to placate evil spirits. On that day children took showers through sieves to prevent illness. The date also marked the time of an old and charming rural custom, begun in the time of Yaroslav the Wise of Kiev in the 12th century. When a boy reached the age of seven, either on the first of September or on his Name Day three locks of his hair were cut and put in an amulet that he wore to the end of his days. He was taken to the courtyard where his father had a horse prepared before which his mother had laid a carpet. His godmother and godfather also were present. Both godfather and father bowed to the boy, and the father then ceremoniously seated his little son on the saddle. The godfather took the bridle and, while the father steadied his son, together they led him around the courtyard to the threshold of the house. There gifts were exchanged; normally the godfather presented the horse. A cake was crumbled over the boy's head as a sign of good luck for the future.

October and November were aptly named "Leaf Fall" and along with January and February were the months of marriages. The people also read the stars in their own way. Venus, it was said, "tells a person what to do and helps a person to see the truth." "Do not travel against the star on the first, eleventh or twenty-seventh of October." "Do not go to the baths on the third, thirteenth or twenty-third. It will bring disorder to the house." "If a maiden sees Venus on her right, her fortune will come true." If she saw the Milky Way, it predicted another year of maidenhood.

If wolves were seen about the village on October 30, it meant that cattle would die or famine or war. Witches, it was believed, flew south on January 18. Ancient belief dictated that fences should be built only then, for the picturesque reason that on that night, as they flew toward Bald Mountain, the witches caroused and got drunk and so did not pay attention.

"The thistle," says the encyclopedia of folk customs, "is full of properties. It cures diseases and the aching heart of love, sends away demons and preserves cattle. Everyone loves and keeps the thistle; everyone believes in it, most especially the thistle of Kiev which has especially miraculous and mysterious properties. Boil and wax the thistle and wear it on a trip." And so day after day, it continued, this wealth of beliefs, traditions and customs.

Not only among the peasants, but among better educated classes, superstitions abounded. An Englishwoman in the late 19th century, wrote that "in very few houses were thirteen allowed at table; they even call a servant to dine so there may be fourteen. It is unlucky to hand the salt unless both parties smile at the same time. There were lucky and unlucky days. Anything begun on Saturday will cause misfortune. No Russian would think of commencing a journey on Monday. There is the greatest faith in love philters and charms, talismans and crosses."

One of the most ancient symbols of the Slavs, reaching back into antiquity and persisting to our own day, is the bear. Venerable and mighty, the bear in ancient days was a totem representing the greatest of the Slavic pagan gods,

Perun. When Christianity came to Russia in 988, the pagan high priests were banished and their idols destroyed, but the bear symbol remained. The ribald *skomorokhi*, the jesters and buffoons of old Russia, continued to lead bears about, and sometimes bears and goats. On the arms of Lord Novgorod the Great there was a bear. In the frescoes of Yaroslav's Hagia Sophia Cathedral in Kiev is a scene of two men fighting, one wearing the mask of a bear. Even on icons the bear managed to sneak in. In the 15th century, Saint Sergius, patron saint of Moscow, is shown with a bear, presumably tamed, near him. In medieval days there were bear fights on the ice of the Moscow river. A man wrestled a bear with his bare hands and if he won he was decorated with favors from the tsar. At carnivals and festivals there were numerous mock bear fights between men dressed in bear suits, and at New Year's men similarly costumed frolicked in the streets.

Trained bears and bear handling, first mentioned in Western accounts by Olearius in the 17th century, were still being reported in the pages of St. Petersburg newspapers in the 19th century. Bears were trained to dance, to put on makeup like young women, to carry buckets of water over their shoulders. In the middle of the 19th century, they played out all sorts of satirical scenes of everyday life and spoofed pompous civil servants. Despite the fact that the clergy constantly opposed the bear cult, leading bears and bear handling for money were prohibited only late in the 19th century. Even as recently as twenty or thirty years ago, bear handlers were still seen in the streets of Leningrad. Today, Filatov's motorcycling bears in the Moscow circus carry on this tradition, although they no longer satirize the contemporary police and members of the government as they used to under the tsars.

Among the people a whole vocabulary of superstitions revolved around the bear. It was believed that on December 12, the bear, while hibernating in his lair, turned over on his other flank. After that, so the folk saying goes, "Winter wears a bear's coat," that is, the weather turns colder. On the sea, if the name of the bear is pronounced, tempest will come. To frighten away evil spirits and make the ground and cattle fertile, a bear should be led around the house and courtyard. A bear crossing the road means good luck. To cure a man of fever, turn him face down and let a bear step over him, being sure that the bear's paw touches him. So that the cattle be peaceful and the mischievous *domovoy* not bother them, hang a bear's head in the stable. To smoke out evil spirits, burn bear's fur. Hunters believed that the Great Bear constellation helped them to find their quarry because bears lay under the protection of these stars which made them hibernate because bears were thieves. Hunters should go into the forest only when the constellation shines brightly, for when it is visible the bears become peaceful and do not attack humans. And there are many more such beliefs. Resistant to all change, the bear, symbol of the most ancient Slavic god, has endured and remains the symbol of Russia itself.

Nothing gives a better idea of the wealth of fantasy and imagination that filled the life of the Russian people than fairy tales. No other country has such a storehouse of folk and fairy tales which are so round and fat and full of life. Unlike German fairy tales, there is no fear of fatal destruction. Instead, stories of the survival of the weakest, they are full of charm and earthy humor. In these Russian tales are stressed the values of the humble over the rich and powerful, the strength of the true and clean heart, a closeness and respect for nature; fish and wolves are talked to as brothers; characters are full of fantasy. There is Baba Yaga, the wicked witch who flies through the air in a mortar, rowing with a pestle, and who lives in a house built on rooster's feet that can run after its victims. And there is Kaschei the Immortal, an evil sorcerer who keeps the secret of his power, a needle, inside an egg. There is the fisherman and his greedy wife who bursts from asking for too much, and the Snow Maiden, born from the snow, who melts in the spring sun; Grandfather Frost, whose breath brings icicles and whose hair is the blizzard.

Ivan Durachok, the simpleton, appears over and over, always asleep on the stove but always much smarter than anyone gives him credit for. Equally universal is the good Ivan Tsarevich, the purest and usually the youngest of the tsar's three sons, who is so courteous and true to his word that, in one tale, he accepts a frog as a wife. In one of the many tales of the Firebird, Ivan is so faithful to his mission of guarding his father's orchards that he manages to pull a feather from the tail of the Firebird and uses it to overcome the evil Kaschei and gain his heart's desire.

Told over and over again by nurses and grandmothers from time immemorial, these beloved tales of the people were the inexhaustible well of imagination from which Russian artists in the 19th and early 20th centuries were to draw their inspiration. The colorful themes, the rhythms and sounds of these tales found their way into the poems of Pushkin, the stories of Gogol and the work of scores of other Russian writers.

Full of wisdom and melodious poetic repetition, these tales of the people with their soothing and mesmerizing phrases, "morning is wiser than evening," "love is a golden vessel, it bends but never breaks," are almost like music. And this is no mere coincidence, for at the very heart of Russian folklore was the song.

The Russians are a profoundly musical people who from their earliest days have marked the whole course of their lives and history by singing. In these songs, language and rhythm, word and melody are closely interwoven; says the Russian proverb, "Not a word can be omitted from a song." The people had their heroes' songs, their rounds and dance songs, their carols at Christmas and fortune-telling songs at Epiphany, their harvest songs and soldiers' tales, their laments and love songs. They recorded everything—work and play, joy and sorrow —in song.

The beauty of these songs and the vitality of the folk dances of Russia were still unknown to all but a few Westerners in the early 19th century, but the music of the great Russian composers was to grow from these roots. Glinka, Mussorgsky, Rimsky-Korsakov, Tchaikovsky and Stravinsky all found in the folk lore and songs of the people the themes and sounds that haunt their music. The colorful folk dances of the Russian people eventually found their way to the ballet and the Ballets Russes of Diaghilev where they electrified Europe and found a popularity undimmed to our own day.

One is struck in reading travelers' accounts down through the centuries by their descriptions of the universal love of music which existed in old Russia. Unanimously visitors commented not only on how much, but how well the Russians sang. The country, it seems, was full of music. Russians sang to their horses, while rowing boats, while selling their wares in the street, while working in the fields or simply when they were standing about. Said John Carr, "Where a German smokes for comfort, a Russian sings."

William Coxe, the traveling tutor of an English nobleman's son, in the late 18th century wrote: "In our route through Russia, I was surprised at the propensity of the natives to singing. Even the peasants who acted in the capacity of coachmen and postillions were no sooner mounted than they began to warble an air, and continued it, without the least intermission, for several hours. But what still more astonished me was that they performed occasionally in parts; I frequently observed them engaged in a kind of musical dialogue, making reciprocal questions and responses, as if chanting their ordinary conversation. The postillions sing from the beginning to the end of a stage; the soldiers sing during their march; the countrymen sing amongst the most laborious occupations; public houses re-echo with their carols and in a still evening I have frequently heard the air vibrate with the notes of surrounding villages."

In the mid-19th century, a traveler described the boatmen she saw on the river in far northern Russia: "The boatmen are fine-looking men, of the real and pure Russian race . . . their gaily colored shirts show off to much advantage their sturdy forms, their manly beards and light flaxen hair. They were singing a monotonous and yet pleasing air as they walked to and fro the whole length of their bark, propelling it with their long poles through the shallow part of the river."

In central Russia, "Nearly every house in the village has a bench in front of it, where in the evening, we frequently saw groups of peasants sitting to have a chat or to sing the national airs of which they are very fond, along with the lilting accordion and balalaika." In the mid-19th century, Baron Augustus von Haxthausen, a German, in his voluminous three-volume account of his travels in Russia, wrote: "The lightness and physical grace of the Great Russian peasant make him delight in dancing. When women dance by themselves, or with men, their movements are slow and serious, but the men, dancing on their own, especially the Cossacks, give themselves up to the dance with a passion, a vivacity of gesture and mimicry which are very characteristic. The men's voices, when they sing, are of a range, timbre and sweetness truly remarkable. Whatever the volume, it is never harsh."

Nowhere could one see how integral music and song were to every ceremony better than at a wedding, which was a joyous festival for the whole village. Weddings, usually arranged by venerable old-lady marriage brokers called *svakhi*, proceeded according to time-honored custom.

The evening before the wedding the young man was conducted to the baths and then spent the evening with his friends, while the bride by tradition sat weeping in a corner of her *izba*, surrounded by maidens who sang sad songs —she who was free was now to become a slave. On the day of the wedding, the bridegroom arrived in a troika or a carriage gaily decorated with ribbons and bells and red handkerchiefs. He knocked at the door and gave to the father of the bride a few symbolic kopecks. While everyone celebrated and feasted, the promised couple sat quietly side by side in a corner, not even speaking to each other. In a moving ceremony, parents and children, cousins, young and old of both families filed before them and each in turn blessed the young couple who bowed low before them. Each person then received an icon and some black bread sprinkled with salt. Then it was off to church for a long ceremony. Crowns held over the bride's and groom's heads during the entire service symbolized their new roles as king and queen of a new line and served also as a reminder of the suffering of Christ.

Afterward there was feasting and dancing and singing for the whole village. By tradition at all Russian wedding feasts the guests gaily cry, *"Gorko! Gorko!"* meaning *"Bitter!"* and at each cry the newlyweds must kiss to sweeten the meal.

An English lady visiting in the north of Russia in the 1850's was invited to the wedding of the daughter of the headman, or *starosta,* of a remote village on the Dvina River. She writes, "We had no sooner landed on the bank of the river when the Starosta came out to welcome us and conduct us to his house. A great number of people were assembled in front of it; they all seemed very merry and were gaily dressed in their best attire; we passed through the crowd and followed our host who ushered us with many profound bows into the best apartment, where we found a numerous company already arrived. There were at least thirty women seated in straight rows around the room; most of them had their arms crossed and remained almost motionless. Their gaily colored silks and showy headdresses had a very striking effect. The bride herself, a pretty-looking girl of about seventeen, was seated at the upper end of the room with the bridegroom at her right hand. A table covered with a white cloth and tastefully arranged, ornamented with festoons of artificial flowers and bows of pink ribbon, was before them, on which was placed the wedding cake made of flour and honey, with almonds on top; several dishes of sweetmeats, preserves and dried fruits were arranged around it. It was, as I was told, the etiquette for the bride not even to speak to the bridegroom; but we went up to her and offered our congratulations, which they both acknowledged by a graceful inclination. The Starosta ordered chairs to be placed just opposite the table . . . so we had a good opportunity of examining and admiring the bride's dress. It was composed of a coiffure nearly a foot high; it was of gold, enriched with pearls and fastened on by a knot of gold tissue behind, which was edged with lace; her ears were decorated with handsome rings, and round her neck were innumerable rows of pearls. Her jacket was of gold cloth, with a border of pearl embroidery, the sleeves of cambric, short and very full, tied up with a blue ribbon and finished by a lace trimming. This is the national costume, but it varies in different provinces and is not equally rich. But then the Starosta was well-to-do; he was not only head man of the village but he had shops of his own in Moscow and St. Petersburg. I noticed that the bride's fingers were loaded with rings . . . indeed she seemed to have on all the finery the whole family could muster. As for the bridegroom, he was a good-looking young man of twenty-two or so, very respectably dressed in a long blue coat called a caftan, closely buttoned up to the throat. We were presented with tea, coffee, wine, bonbons, cakes, fruit, etc. . . . The spoons I remarked were of Tula work, and had the appearance of being gold but were in reality of silver gilt, with arabesque flowers all over them, which they say are done with some kind of acid: I believe the secret is not known out of Russia.

"All of the women assembled were of the upper class of petty shop keepers and farmers, and they were dressed in the same costume as the bride. During the whole time we were in the room, their amusement consisted in singing, one after the other, in a low kind of chant, songs improvised in honor of the occasion. One song praised the bridegroom and his possessions: 'He had plenty of cows, pigs and horses and could take his wife to church in a droshky!' After we had remained a reasonable time with the young couple, we went outside to see the guests assembled in front of the house; there we found several women dancing . . . they moved forwards and then backwards in pairs to a singsong kind of air. . . . On the opposite side of the yard the men were having a ball among themselves; we laughed heartily at a comic pas de deux by a couple of young men who capered about in a very diverting style. Another peasant danced a solo and after the dancing, the men sang some national airs; each took the hand or leaned on the shoulder of his neighbor, 'in order to unite the tones,' as they said. . . . We took our leave of the Starosta and his family but were not allowed to depart until we had drunk to their health in champagne . . . a wine which the Russians give upon all extraordinary occasions.

"As we were stepping into the boat, the peasants gave us a parting cheer, and far away, when the village was quite lost to view in the distance, we heard their wild voices still singing in chorus their beautiful national airs in honor of the young Russian bride."

13. THE TREASURE HOUSE

THE SAME EXUBERANCE and vitality that characterized the songs, the dances and the tales of the Russian people were also everywhere evident in their folk arts. The variety, the beauty and extraordinary craftsmanship of this folk art belie the popular myth of the Russian peasant as a gloomy, downtrodden creature and reveal instead a rich life of the soul and a jubilant attitude toward life.

Borrowing themes and decorative motifs from nature and their beloved folk tales and beliefs, village craftsmen all over the land lavished decorative care on even the humblest objects, surrounding themselves in their everyday life with articles that were overflowing with color, humor and imagination. Not only did every cottage have its tracery of ornament, but every sleigh and the wheels of every cart were covered with decoration and gaily painted; bowls, spoons, salt-cellars, candleholders, craftsmen's tools and the distaffs of women all were elaborately painted and carved. Taking the simple materials given to them by nature —wood, flax, clay, straw and bone—craftsmen often produced work of such beauty that it is impossible to call it "folk" art. Rather it is art, pure and simple. It was this proud tradition of fine individual craftsmanship on every level of Russian life which made possible the intricate workmanship with richer materials in the palaces of their tsars.

Above all, Russia was a land of great carpenters with a genius for wood.

Throughout history, the limitless forests of Russia provided wood in vast quantities. Everywhere in every epoch, wood was cheap and smaller pieces were often to be had for nothing.

In old Russia, whole villas, palaces and spectacular churches were entirely constructed of wood. Count Sheremetev in the early 18th century built an astonishing wooden villa at Ostankino outside Moscow, using all serf architects, artists, carvers and cabinetmakers. The entire construction was of wood—oak, linden, birch, and nut. Columns were carved from whole tree trunks and plastered to look like marble. Carved gilded work framed windows, doorways and entrances; vast carved panels were inset into the walls. Magnificent parquet floors of many varieties of wood were laid. Chandeliers, huge vases, sphinxes, all were made of wood and coated with gold and bronze. The scrollwork on the furniture, frames and candelabra—intricately carved flower garlands, roses, cornflowers, daisies and ears of grain, figures of people, snakes, lions and mountain sheep— all were carved of wood.

The wooden churches of Russia, which preserved their ancient shapes and forms dating from the earliest Christian days, were particularly beautiful. With their tent roofs and octagonal shapes, these poetic churches echoed the forms of the flowers and trees that surrounded them. Sadly, these architectural masterpieces of earlier days have suffered terribly through the centuries because of fire and war. Before the Revolution, many still existed, but today most have disappeared and none dates earlier than the 18th century.

A triumph of wood architecture and the skill of Russian carpenters which has survived, however, is the Church of the Transfiguration, one of two churches which stand on the small island of Kizhi, one of the 1,625 islands in Lake Onega. The church was completed in 1714, according to legend, to celebrate Peter's victory at Poltava. Some stories even say that Peter himself designed it on one of his trips to the north; other versions attribute it to a peasant named Nestor who threw his axe in the lake after it was finished so that the axe would never be used for a lesser purpose. Whoever designed it, it is a miracle. Pyramid-shaped, it stands 120 feet high and has twenty-two cupolas. It was built without a blueprint or surveying instruments, simply, as the Russians say, "by the eye." Not a single nail or metal part was used. Carpenters, experts at joinery, fastened the parts together by notching them at the ends and the corners. The only tool used for the basic structure was an axe; chisels and drills were used only for decorative details. Inside the church, the iconostasis and the candelabra are all carved of wood, delicate as lace, and gilded. From across the lake, the church rises unreal, alone in the snow like a fantastic fir tree in a poet's dream.

Russians were so extraordinarily skilled with the short axe that even well into the 19th century it was often the only tool they used. Lev Tolstoy observed that some of the carpenters he saw were so adept that they could even carve a spoon with an axe. Baron Haxthausen in describing the Russian carpenter wrote: "He knows no other tools than the axe and the chisel. With them he travels over the whole Empire, finding work everywhere. If you look at the delicate carvings that adorn the peasant's cottage, it seems impossible that they have been made with such heavy and inadequate tools. In the north, where wood is superabundant, the peasant who needs a plank cuts down a tree and molds the wood with his axe to the desired thickness."

Russian villages generally were composed of a long line of wooden houses on each side of a road lined with birch trees. The shape of the simple wooden house, or *izba,* remained through the centuries much as the English mariner, Richard Chancellor, described it in the 16th century: "The common houses of the country are everywhere built of beames of Fir tree, the lower beames do so receive the round hollowness of the uppermost, that by the means of the building thereupon they resist and expell all winds that blow, and where the timber is joined together, there they stop the chinks with moss. The forme and fashion of their houses in all places is foure square, with straight and narrow windows, whereby with a transparent casement made or covered with skin like parchment, they receive the light."

Overflowing imagination was lavished on their decoration. Every peasant cottage had its delicate tracery of ornament—wooden embroidery, lace, crosses and fleurons all executed from the inspiration of axe or saw. Ancient traditions of building and carving were carefully kept and passed down from generation to generation. Many of the decorations echo the designs first made for the Volga river boats. Some idea of the picturesque look of these now vanished boats comes from an English lady traveling in Russia in the 1850's: "Native barks glided calmly past us, strange-looking things, gaudily painted red, black and yellow designs on rough wood; some were in the form of a serpent, others in that of a fish, a griffin, or some other fabulous creature and decorated with streamers of scarlet, all fluttering in the slight breeze that swept down the stream. The heavy one-masted vessels reminded me of Saxon boats some thousand years ago."

Russians used these same patterns of flowers, fruit, animals, birds and trees to decorate their houses. The image of the lion was among the most ancient, handed down by folk carvers from unknown antecedents. The lion appeared on 12th-century copper buckles from Novgorod, on cathedrals in the 15th century, and on 18th- and 19th-century peasant cottages. The figure of the siren, or mermaid woman, appeared very often, for ancient Slavs believed her to be the protectoress of meadows, plowlands and hearths. Horses' heads were said to ward off trouble and possibly came from the pagan Slavic God of the Sun, whose flaming chariot was drawn by three fiery steeds.

Whimsical carved wooden starling and other birdhouses stood outside *izba*s with curiously carved weather vanes on their roofs. Houses and their decorations were brightly painted with diamonds and squares in blue, red and green. On a carved board over balcony windows, bright-green lions might lie against a turquoise background. The inside of the eaves was boarded and painted with large red and blue flowers and bunches of grapes; shutters with thin black branches, dark-red berries, roses and flowers. In the north, the aspen shingles of houses acquired a silvery hue and a silken sheen. Nestled among the white birches, their painted fronts and gables stood brightly contrasted against the snow. Inside the *izba*s were painted wooden cupboards, tables and benches with intricately carved boards along the edges.

The wooden houses of rich peasants could be very large and elaborate. Melnikov-Pechersky described the house of a rich peasant of the Volga: "Chupurin's house, big and recently built, stood in a small village. The house was built for two households, with a summer attic under the roofs and four wings attached to the house. The house had a brick foundation, folding windows were painted white with clean glass, and each window was draped with calico curtains decorated with red cotton fringe. The front of the house was painted ochre . . . and the roof was red. The edge of the roof and the space above the windows were decorated by fancy-cut woodwork. The gates, too, were decorated in the same fashion and to make them look yet more beautiful, a carved wooden ship was mounted on top of them."

The Russians raised whole towns and even cities of wood; carpenters spoke of "cutting" rather than "building" a town. For foreigners, the sight of these wooden cities with their bright colors and carvings was one of the most striking sights of old Russia. Even as late as 1898, a house completely constructed of wood and completely furnished without any metal at all was shown in Paris at an International Exhibition.

The Russians used wood not only to construct their houses but to fashion every kind of object used in their daily lives. Like the houses, all these articles were brightly painted, covered with flowers, trees, animals and lively scenes from folklore and life.

Spinning was such an integral part of the life of the country that the custom was to make the wooden distaffs that women used as beautiful in shape and decoration as possible. These carefully crafted distaffs were often a mark of love —a father's gift to his daughter, a young man's to his fiancée. Many bore touching inscriptions: "Thee I love, to thee I give, with love from my heart to thee for all time." Or "Spin, preserve the distaff and pray God for thy father." They were kept in families as heirlooms and handed down for generations from mother to daughter. Intricately carved distaffs were also made to order and to sell at fairs and on the banks of the rivers along the busy trade routes. Techniques of carving and decoration were closely linked with local tastes and tradition. The distaffs of Kostroma and Yaroslavl were carved with a pierced tracery of wood. In other regions, distaffs were covered with designs of bright colors, with red often predominating.

Every household had a number of elaborately decorated and carved molds or stamps to make gingerbread. These molds were a precious part of each family's possessions; from the 16th century on, the custom of making gingerbread cakes, or *pryaniki,* assumed proportions unknown in any other country. From the tiniest village to the Imperial court, no celebration was complete without *pryaniki.* Family and friends gathered at individual feasts especially to eat gingerbread or make presents of it. Children were given small cakes in the shape of animals, and maidens received cakes inscribed "I love you" or "In testimony of love." Magnificently decorated cakes were made for weddings, births and even for funerals.

Gingerbreads "of honor" were sometimes more than a yard wide and weighed as much as 150 pounds. They were offered as a welcome, a gift by workmen to their patrons, by the young to the old as a sign of respect. On the birth of Peter the Great, more than 120 huge gingerbreads of various designs were presented to his father, among them one bearing the arms of Moscow and two others each weighing 100 pounds with enormous double-headed eagles, another in the form of a badge weighing 125 pounds, and others in the shape of a duck, a parrot and a dove, as well as great decorative gingerbreads representing the Kremlin with its turrets, surrounded by horses and soldiers.

Children everywhere in the land played with a whole variety of clever and whimsical wooden toys, a craft at which the Russians excelled. Carved wooden toys first received mention in 1636, when a whimsical toy cart with wooden horses was ordered from the Troitsky Monastery for the royal children. In 1721 Catherine, the wife of Peter the Great, acquired from the monastery a whole set of wooden toys including "three cows, two roosters, a deer, two rams, two pairs of swans, one duck and three ducklings and a town with soldiers." Russians were remarkably versatile and imaginative at turning out little toys from chips of wood, and because children got tired of playing with static toys, craftsmen devised animated ones—pecking roosters, woodpeckers, coachmen with carriages and sleighs pulled by trotting horses, and bears that danced, sawed wood, or carried buckets. In the 19th century, wooden toys satirized the vagaries of the rich with a great deal of humor. Toys poked fun at snobbish Hussars and feather-brained gentlewomen aping the styles of the West.

A wonderful example of the close connection between folk belief and daily life and the most internationally famous Russian wooden toy is the *Matryoshka*, the doll that contains inside herself a whole nest of other dolls, one inside the other. No one knows the exact origin of this characteristic doll, whose name comes from the diminutive of the woman's name Matryona, but there are many legends. One of them is that she springs from a very ancient goddess named Jumala of an ancient country in the Ural foothills. Russian chronicles speak of a goddess of the Ugrians that was made of pure gold, which the Vikings tried unsuccessfully to find. Baron Heberstein, in 1549, told that he had heard that she was a statue with a hollow interior containing three figures, one inside the other, and that she stood in an ancient sacred forest where no one was allowed to behold her. Every Ugrian who passed by left hanging on a tree an offering of value, which was mysteriously collected. When enough gold was collected, it was melted and a new shell was fashioned for the goddess. The English Ambassador, Giles Fletcher, in 1584 sent an expedition to the Urals to search for this mysterious and legendary golden goddess, but he, too, failed to find her. Various searches continued until 1917, and even as late as 1967 an old hunter living in the town of Tyumen said that she had been taken away and hidden so that her treasures might never be found.

The first *Matryoshka* doll contained first a girl in *sarafan* and kerchief, then a boy, another girl, and finally a baby in swaddling clothes. Over the years, these dolls expanded to include a series of boyars, which included the boyar, his boyarina wearing a pearl *kokoshnik*, a clerk, a falconer, a warrior. There were also nests of fairy-tale characters. An eight-piece doll showing Kutuzov and Napoleon with members of their staffs appeared in 1912 to commemorate the centenary of the famous war, and in 1913 the grand champion was a nest of forty-eight dolls made for a toy fair in St. Petersburg.

Through the centuries in town and country Russians ate their kasha with wooden spoons and from wooden bowls, drank their *kvas* from wooden dipper-shaped *kovshi,* and passed around the round wooden *bratina* cup at weddings and festivals. For all of these the festive color red was the favorite for decoration. On drinking vessels, horses' heads often were carved on the handle for good luck. It was said in Russia that "flowers are the artist's teacher," and in their designs craftsmen took note of every twig and blossom. In the north, objects were decorated with splendid floral decorations or birds and berries, painted against a blue, black or gold background. Whole villages became famous for making one sort of object, which they could work on during the long months of winter and sell to supplement their incomes.

From the 15th century, Volga woodsmen were especially famous for their fine wooden articles. The treasurer of the Troitsky Monastery outside Moscow reported in 1642 that the villagers had made and sold 9,750 drinking cups and 17,000 wooden spoons painted in cinnabar and red. From as early as the 16th century, the towns of Khokhloma and Semyonov in the south near Nizhny Novgorod were famous for their wooden spoons and bowls. These villagers developed a technique of making wood look like gold by bathing it in linseed oil and rubbing it with powdered tin. The distinctive rich black, red and gold woodenware of Khokhloma with its rich floral patterns painted on with fine brushes was sold every year at the Makariev Fair, until 1817 the grandest fair on the Volga.

In 1797 the mayor of the town of Semyonov reported that the city population carried on no farming at all and that in one year they had produced and sold 500,000 bowls, 300,000 platters, 100,000 cups and 800,000 wooden spoons. In the 1880's a craze for everything in the Russian style infected the bourgeoisie, and beds, chairs and tables were created in what came to be known as "the cockerel style."

The Russians, in fact, put every kind of wood, not only fir, but oak, nut, linden and birch, to their uses, from the grandest to the simplest. In the tsar's palaces as many as twenty kinds of wood were sometimes used to make splendid floor designs as rich-looking as oriental rugs.

They put the beloved birch tree which graced their fields and forests to an enormous variety of uses. An old folk maxim went "The birch tree can do four things: give life, muffle groans, cure the sick and keep the body clean." Birch splinters were used to light the fires in the *izba*, birch grease was used for cart axles, birch jars were made for medicines, and a switch made of birch twigs was used in the bath. The sledge of the peasant was made of birch. Wrote one traveler, "It is admirable, as light and regular in composition as the sledge of a person of distinction. The form is elegant, and being composed of birch wood, extremely light and manageable." Magnificent furniture was made of the warm, toast-colored Karelian birch; one region of Russia was famous for its beautiful boxes of burled birch. Birch buds were infused in vodka to give it a faint amber color and a delicious aroma. Peasants used birch bark for their sturdy sandals, or *lapti*, and for buckets so tightly and expertly woven that not a drop of water escaped. They made gaily painted birch-bark berry and bread baskets. In Novgorod in the 11th and 12th centuries, long before the use of wallpaper was introduced to Europe by the Moors in the 17th century, gaily painted birch bark was used to cover walls.

Russian craftsmen raised birch-bark work to a high level of art. In the village of Kurova Navalok in Vologda, a territory that in bygone days had been ruled by Lord Novgorod the Great, the villagers specialized in transforming birch bark into objects that seemed made of lace. In May and June they scoured the forest to find twenty-year-old birch trees, from which they stripped the upper layer of swollen bark. Carvers cut a rectangular piece out of the bark and, using a cobbler's awl, impressed on it a pattern of interweaving flowers and branches. Then, using a very sharp knife, they sliced away all the superfluous material. The lacelike stuff was glued onto previously prepared boxes or caskets, trays, cigarette boxes and tea boxes to make objects so lovely and delicate that they look as if they had come from a distant fairyland of snow. Such glove boxes were especially in demand in Europe in the 19th century, and in 1900, at the Paris World's Fair, a Russian peasant craftsman, Ivan Veprev, won a gold medal for the birch-bark objects he exhibited there.

The popular penny prints or broadsides called *lubki* were first made by using wood blocks. Mostly made around Moscow and sold all over the land on streets and at fairs from the beginning of the 16th century, the first *lubki*, which were religious in character, appeared at the time of Ivan the Terrible and were sold in great quantities outside the Spassky Gate of the Kremlin. All classes of the Russian population, including the tsar, quickly grew to love them. It is recorded that in 1635 Tsar Michael Romanov bought a whole series of these lively prints for his seven-year-old son, Tsarevich Alexis.

Bright and cheerful, the drawing of the prints was simple and straightforward; perspective and scale were usually absent. They were colored by hand, usually by women, in three or four bright colors, generally red, purple, yellow and green. Merry and full of fun, very often irreverent, *lubki* covered a wide variety of subject matter and often commented sharply on the issues of the day. Biblical pictures hung in wine shops and taverns; there were also almanacs and calendars of nine sheets showing the signs of the zodiac and the ornate ceiling of Tsar Alexis' palace at Kolomenskoe. In Peter's time *lubki* poked fun at his Westernization by showing bemused men unceremoniously getting their beards chopped off or Peter as the Anti-Christ with Satan's face. The most famous *lubok* of Peter's time, printed after his death, was called "How the Mice Buried the Cat." It ran through six reprints in one century.

Lubki were widely used as advertisements and to commemorate newsworthy events such as the first Persian elephant seen in Moscow, the big news of a huge whale caught in the White Sea in 1760 or the startling appearance of a meteor in 1769. All through the 18th and 19th centuries folk tales were favorite subjects and popular folk characters pursued a long series of varied adventures. In the 18th century in the provinces, *lubki*, were often used to instruct the children. One of the greatest favorites, "The Seven Deadly Sins," which was first printed in the 16th century, was still being hawked in the 19th. The strolling *lubki* peddler, holding at shoulder level his pictures of red and green devils, wandered through the markets and streets gaily crying, "Who wants 'The Seven Deadly Sins'? 'The Fallen Adam'? 'Life After Death in Paradise'?"

In the early-20th-century marketplaces, favorite motifs were still being sold and avant-garde artists turned to the simplicity and the technique of the ancient *lubki* as inspiration for their own drawings and hand-printed books. It was not until the Revolution that these jolly popular prints which had been loved by the Russian people for two and a half centuries disappeared forever.

Second only to their skill in using wood was the Russian excellence in metalworking of many kinds. In the 11th and 12th centuries only Byzantium was more famous than Russia for its fine silver filagree work. The skilled goldsmiths of the 13th and 14th centuries made *nimbi,* or crownlike settings, for icons of finely worked cloisonné gold. In the 16th and 17th centuries the city of Chernigov became famous for its exceptional niello work, a special Byzantine technique of engraving on metal which only the Russians preserved. Gold or silver was engraved and the hollows filled with a mixture of copper, silver and sulphur. The object was then heated, and the melting powder filled the hollows. Once cold, the work was polished and the design appeared on its surface in either a light color or a dark velvet black. Niello work was used to decorate all kinds of objects—spoons, forks, cups and tea-glass holders.

As always, the Russians connected their art to life, embellishing all metal objects, however utilitarian, with imaginative shape or rich decoration. In the 18th and 19th centuries several towns were known for their blue and black lacquered metal trays, painted with exuberant explosions of flowers—roses, dahlias, peonies and tulips.

The samovar, a metal urn in which water is kept boiling for tea, came to Russia from Persia and the Middle East in the 18th century. Charcoal or wood is burned in a vertical pipe through the center of the samovar, at the top of which is a holder for a small teapot in which strong concentrated tea essence is brewed. In Old Russia, tea drinking was a cherished ritual, a way of life. The friendly steaming samovar was everywhere, in homes and restaurants, on trains and street corners. Typically, as with everything else, the Russians immediately turned the samovar from a strictly utilitarian object into a handsome object of art surpassing its Eastern models.

In the famous metalworking center of Tula, samovar production began in 1820. First dozens and then hundreds of factories vied with one another for technical and artistic mastery. So famous did the samovars of Tula become that the Russian folk saying that parallels the English "coals to Newcastle" goes "You don't take a samovar to Tula." At the end of the 19th century, there were forty samovar factories in Tula, producing approximately 630,000 samovars; one of the most famous factories, the Batashev, alone produced 110,000 samovars annually.

The proportions, ornaments and structural details of Russian samovars were varied and imaginative. They were made in all shapes and sizes—round and squat, tall and imposing. Some of them were huge: two or three feet high and one foot in diameter. There were traveling samovars shaped like cubes, octagonal samovars whose curved legs were removable and fitted with special sockets. Some made in the north were like traveling kitchens and had three compartments for preparing three different dishes at the same time. Some made of bronze or silver were elaborately decorated and very beautiful.

Another fine showcase for Russian metalworking skill were the bells whose sound filled the land. From the 10th century on, Russians marked their days by the various pealing of bells. There was a whole language of bells; they sounded

193

alarms and warned travelers during snowstorms; they told of disasters, funerals, holidays and festivals. By the 16th century bells were considered sacred instruments of worship. Bells were cast in copper, bronze and silver in many sizes, with an innumerable variety of timbre and power of sound. Complicated tonal effects were created by these many choirs of bells. Every church and monastery had its tower where bells, hung in number and size proportioned to the wealth of the community, guided the life of the parish. By the particular tolling of larger bells and the clang when all were struck together, the worshiper knew to what service he was being called and when it would begin. (The largest bell in Rostov could be heard twenty miles away.) Over the dark forests, across the plains and still lakes and winding rivers of the land the bells sent their harmonious peals. The peasant crossed himself as he listened and believed that the saints were near.

Bells were not rung by swinging them from the top as in Western countries. Instead, the tongue was manually swung against the side, and the large bells required the united efforts of several men. One traveler says that "on a feast morning in Moscow, we saw in a low, open church tower, a man ringing half a dozen bells at once by ropes in his hands and attached to his arms."

In the Tower of Ivan the Great, 320 feet high and whose golden dome could be seen all over Moscow, story after story was filled with bells, the largest weighing 64 tons, the smallest of silver, sweet and musical. The people regarded the Tower of Ivan with reverential awe, and at important festivals, when its huge bell boomed like an artillery discharge from the Kremlin, they listened to it as if it were the voice of God.

So important were bells that the tsars sometimes got angry with them. There is a story that once a bell frightened Ivan the Terrible's horse and he ordered the bell punished by having its ears chopped off. Because one bell had been used in a mutiny against Catherine II in 1771, she ordered its clapper removed so that it stood silent for thirty years.

Anna Ivanovna in 1734 ordered the huge Tsar Bell, the largest bell in the world, to be cast. The work was completed a year later, in 1735, but in 1737, before it could be hung, a fire broke out in the structure around the Tsar Bell, and when water was poured on the huge bell, it broke. A chip weighing 11½ tons fell out of it. The Tsar Bell is 26 feet tall, has a circumference of 66 feet and weighs 200 tons. It lay in the ground where it had fallen for a century before the French architect Montferrand, who designed St. Isaac's Cathedral in St. Petersburg, succeeded in raising it in 1836 and placing it where it now stands in the Kremlin. Forty men can stand in it and sometimes services were held inside it.

Both bells and cannons were often made by the same masters and like all other objects were elaborately decorated. Some bells bore floral designs along their shoulders and lips. Cannons in the 16th and 17th centuries were decorated with lions, elks, griffins and birds, and with Biblical motifs. Cannons in the Kremlin were decorated with side grips shaped like dolphins and given names—Eagle, Unicorn—and decorated accordingly. The Tsar Cannon, the largest cannon in the world and which can be seen in the Kremlin today, was cast by Andrei Chokov in 1586. Like the Tsar Bell that never rang, the Tsar Cannon has never been fired.

There was, in fact, scarcely any craft which the Russians did not use to express their love of decoration and joy of life. Whole towns were famous for their porcelains and cheerful ceramics. Russians painted and decorated the tiles that covered the large stoves they used for heating and also placed these bright tiles as decorative motifs on the roofs and walls of churches, where they gleamed in the sun in all the colors of the rainbow. In 1656, the 60-foot roof of the New Jerusalem Temple of Moscow was entirely lined with tiles. Arches and portals were faced with large tiles composing a vast design of yellow flowers and herbs in flower bowls against a blue background. Windows were framed with wide strips of tiles with the tiled head of a lion above them. For the first time in Russia, the iconostasis was made not of wood but of panels of tiles, each about 24 feet high and 12 feet wide, of yellow, green, white and rusty tiles with raised designs. A tiled head of an angel topped each panel and tiled cherubs adorned each row of icons on the tiers.

The same love and sensitivity for color were abundantly evident in the fine enamel work for which the Russian masters were renowned since the days of Kiev. In the late 19th century, when there was a great revival of Slavic arts, several masters took inspiration from these designs of the past and, incorporating the spirit of Art Nouveau, created a whole variety of beautiful objects—tea services and tea-glass holders, bowls and spoons whose colors have the vivacity of gems. Transparent enamel, *plique à jour*, a Russian skill which has been lost since the Revolution, was used for the edges of bowls and the bottoms of tea-glass holders which glow like stained-glass windows when they are held against the light.

Using the semiprecious stones abundantly available from the Urals and sold everywhere at fairs and in the merchants' arcades in Moscow—rich green malachite, blue lapis, jasper in rich dark reds and greens, agate and porphyry—the Russians fashioned all manner of beautiful objects from tabletops to inkwells, using the stones in intricate designs.

From the East the Russians took the technique of lacquerwork and raised it to a level rivaled only by the Chinese. In fact, ninety panels that decorated Peter's Chinese Room at the little palace of Mon Plaisir and were long thought to be Chinese work because of their great delicacy were found after the Second World War to be Russian, painted on wood, using the same techniques as for icons.

In the 19th century the lacquered snuffboxes made in the Lukutin workshops of Fedoskino outside Moscow were very much in vogue not only in Russia but in Europe. In 1821, 48,000 such snuffboxes were made by the Lukutine craftsmen. Formed of glued paper which was coated with glue and chalk, then varnished, boiled in flaxseed oil and oven-dried, and then polished, ground and varnished again, this lacquerwork was both sturdy and water-resistant. Plates, caskets, cigarette boxes, pencil holders and boxes for needles were made in this manner. Some pieces were inlaid with mother-of-pearl; others were painted to look like tortoiseshell, birch or mahogany and embellished with strips of silver and gold. Many were meticulously painted with miniatures of high quality—reproductions of paintings, landscapes and scenes of everyday peasant life, which provided much information about the customs and life of the people.

Perhaps the most distinctive Russian craft was the bonework which was valued in the West as much as the precious gems and rainbow silks of the Orient. As early as the 12th century a Byzantine author composed odes to the carved bone of the Slavs, which was known in Europe as "Russian ivory." The distant northern villages that lay beyond impenetrable forests and swamps were spared the Mongol invasions. There the people kept their freedom and preserved the old artistic customs of the Slavs. The inhabitants of the town of Kholomogory near Archangel on the White Sea, close to the spot where Chancellor first landed, made finely crafted hunting knives, caskets and fancifully decorated combs out of walrus tusks. In the 17th century Tsar Alexis brought some of these master carvers to the Kremlin's Armory Palace, the center of decorative and applied art, and there they worked with deer horn and the bones of various wild animals. So much was this bonework considered a purely Russian art that the Tsar often presented bonework gifts to important ambassadors for their rulers. These craftsmen of Alexis' time created a "Moscow style" that echoed the richness of the richly decorated clothing of the time. Their openwork was as fine as lace and they sometimes inlaid their objects with mother-of-pearl and tortoiseshell.

Bonework reached its high point in the 18th century. Caskets, snuffboxes, vases and tankards were made of carved bone. Peter the Great became a skilled bone carver, and often carved in bone while discussing matters of state. Whenever he went to Archangel, he stopped to see the craftsmen of Kholomogory. Mikhail Lomonosov, the great Russian scholar and scientist of Elizabeth's time, was taught his first letters by a bone carver. Lomonosov's brother was a celebrated carver who founded a professional school for the training of carvers and taught Fedot Shubin the elements of his craft. Shubin went on to become the most famous sculptor of Catherine's time and carved in bone a portrait of Lomonosov. In this heyday of the art, magnificent chests, mirror frames and toilet chests were made of white and tinted bone with traceries of flowers and delicate carvings of animals.

In Siberia were other centers of bone carving. Prehistoric mammoth tusks, which were a wonderful material for carving, were found all over Siberia and offered in great quantities at the crowded fairs of the city of Tobolsk. The tribes of Siberia carved miniatures of animals and, before hunting trips, would utter incantations to them. The Siberian craftsmen of Tobolsk won a gold medal at the Paris World's Fair of 1900 for their work.

The fertile land that provided the limitless forests for carpenters also provided its children with rich fields of grain, flax and cotton. Peasant girls learned to spin early in childhood, and the soft linen of Russia was once among the finest in the world. Poetically, in Vologda, the village ancients believed that flax represented sunbeams and that its flowers were blue because they had swallowed the sky.

From the time of Kiev, Russians were known for their beautiful fabrics. Even in those ancient days, Russian linen was exported to Asia and the markets of India. The extraordinarily beautiful weaving and embroidery of cotton, linen and, in the late 18th century, silk, were among the glories of the nation. All over Europe, Russian women were famous for their skill at embroidery. Peasant women, gentlewomen, nuns in convents, all worked miracles with stitch and thread. For the church they embroidered with gold and silver thread, pearls and precious gems, magnificent vestments, delicate veils as fine as cobwebs to cover revered icons, and winding cloths which were used to symbolize the body of Christ. In every household was a whole variety of embroidered tablecloths and sheets, pillowcases and towels. In the countryside in the winter the friends of a young girl would gather to help her embroider her trousseau. Traditionally, she herself embroidered the handkerchiefs for the bridegroom, his best man and all his male relatives to use on her wedding day. The handkerchief called the *chirinka*, made for her wedding and elaborately embroidered, sometimes with pearls, was an indispensable article for Russian women, for it was the custom to hold it in the hands when going to church, during all visits and ceremonies.

In the *izba*, special cloths were used to decorate the house on holidays and to cover the icons in the "beautiful corner." Embroidered towels were hung on crosses and in the trees near wells and springs to honor particular saints. Special covers were woven and embroidered cloths worked for the ceremonial bread and salt which was presented to all newlyweds, and also to important visitors as a sign of welcome.

Every region had its own special variations and styles of embroidery; distances were so great and communication so difficult that many villages lived in isolation and preserved their own special traditions in ornaments and stitches unchanged for hundreds of years. Red was used everywhere, but otherwise it was easy to tell a region by its own cheerful and distinctive composition of colors.

Like the motifs carved in wood, every design had a symbolic meaning and designs were handed down for generations. What the men carved, the women embroidered with wool and silk threads of many colors. The oldest motifs were those handed down from ancient Slavic cultures—the lozenge meaning a new house, the sun, the sign of the Earth Mother worked in red and black. Multi-figured compositions full of a wealth of fantasy sprang from folklore and nature. Birds and lions, flowers, horses and fantastic trees, all the magical symbols of fertility and nature were a kind of incantation in thread against evil spirits. In the 18th and 19th centuries to these old motifs were added merry and joyful scenes of everyday life.

There was also a tremendous variety of lace making; Russian gold and silver lace became so famous in Europe that in the late 19th century it was known and sold in Paris simply as *guipure russe*. Fine shawls were woven of light wool, covered with explosions of flowers in brilliant colors. Some rare and valuable shawls which took many years to weave were so finely done that the design is identical on both sides. Silk shawls were covered with fine embroidery of gold and silver threads. Cloth prints were saturated with decoration; peasants used colorful homespun carpets on the floor.

At the end of the 19th century, clothes became even more colorful when inexpensive machine-made printed calicos and cottons came widely into use, and colorful national costumes continued well into the 20th century. In 1913 at the Russian National Handicrafts Exhibition the abundance of fabrics and weaving was astonishing. For this exhibition every area of the Russian Empire, not only Great Russia, but the Ukraine, Lithuania, Poland and the Grand Duchy of Finland, produced and exhibited fabrics reflecting its own character, local conditions and supplies, from simple peasant broadcloth to wool and linen. In November 1914 *The National Geographic* devoted an entire issue to Russia. A picture of a peasant woman walking home from the fields carried the following caption: "In Russia one may see in the harvest fields women wearing needlework on their dresses that many an American society woman might envy."

Traditional dress was very graceful and elegant, full of rich color and decoration. An English lady traveling in the Russian countryside in the 1850's wrote: "There is something quite classic in Russian dress and we frequently stood to admire the people at their employment. The straight, half-moon shaped head dress of the girl's is almost a copy of that on Diana's brow; the narrow band confining the hair of the men could find its counterpart on many antique heads; the closely setting folds of the women's sarafans are very like those in Greek paintings and on Etruscan vases; the loose shorts tied round the waist worn by men, their mustached and bearded faces, looked very like the friezes of the Athenian temples. . . . Let the visitor see these people not wrapped up in their sheepskin coats but in their summer attire. . . . Let him witness a 'chariot race' between two peasants standing upright in their small country carts and driving at the top of their horses' speed, holding the reins with outstretched arms, their heads uncovered, their fine figures clothed in red or white shirt fluttering in the wind, and their faces if not classically handsome, not devoid of manly beauty, say then whether it does not recall to his mind the Greek chariot races, when Greece was Greece."

Women wore the *ponyova,* one of the most ancient costumes of the Eastern Slavs. It was a sort of skirt made of three lengthwise strips of homespun. The *ponyova* was worn with an embroidered shirt and attached about the waist with a braided cord. The apron over the *ponyova* was very important and lavishly decorated; sometimes it was completely covered with rows of rich embroidery. Everyday *ponyovy* were decorated with calico, and, for holidays, with embroidery and spangles. Women also wore the *sarafan,* a long, flowing, pyramid-shaped jumper with or without buttons in the front, with a billowy sleeved blouse of muslin or batiste beautifully embroidered or of hand-printed linen. Most common in the north was a white linen shirt embroidered in red and a *sarafan* of indigo blue and red. In Tambov, costumes were embroidered in gold, black and silver; in Tula, in white, red and blue; in Kaluga, in red and green; in Smolensk, bright orange, red and gold with touches of blue and black. *Sarafans* were sometimes belted in gold lace, decorated with gold galloons and trimmed at the bottom with silk and wide bands of ribbons.

Rich peasant women wore superb festival *sarafans* of Russian woven silks and brocades of silver and gold and many colored threads. The *sarafan* might be of cream satin brocade with rose, blue and green floral embroidery and gold lace galloons and buttons. With this went an overblouse of white satin in a floral pattern and embroidered brocade lined with russet silk. Little overjackets were heavily embroidered, often with gold, and trimmed with sable or fox. With this costume were worn fine, high-heeled leather boots with tooled designs.

The men wore overcoats lined with fur or sheepskin; rich peasants often chose beaver or fox. Kaftans were sewn with copper or silver buttons, and sometimes embroidered in silver with a belt of damask. Richer peasants wore soft leather boots, sometimes banded in silver and decorated with many colored leathers. Lesser peasants wore birch-bark or bast sandals and, in the winter, felt boots, often embroidered. Men's belted shirts, in linen or silk, were bright-colored and in some regions embroidered.

Some of the festival clothes for church holidays, weddings, funerals and big occasions such as the beginning of the harvest or the first driving of the cattle in the fields were so rich and magnificent in decoration that they were passed down from mother to daughter or father to son. The richness and decoration of the material often characterized the whole family. Since these holiday clothes were often passed down, size or length of sleeve mattered little.

But it was on the headdress—the *kokoshniki*, the *kikas, povoyniki*, the crowns and the diadems—that the most thought was bestowed. The headdress was of greatest importance because by tradition a married woman had to hide her hair from strangers' eyes. The long plaits of a Russian woman were her pride; the greatest treasure of a Russian maiden was a single, long plait intertwined with ribbons down her back. So important was the Russian plait that it figures over and over again in song and tale; an old wedding song begins "The young man with the black curls sits at the table and asks, 'Fair Russian plait, it is true that you are really mine at last?'" Married women wore a closed cap and maidens a flowered scarf kerchief or a hoop or diadem leaving the top of her head open. The change of hairdo and headdress at a Russian wedding was accompanied by special ritual and lamentations. The single plait was carefully rebraided by the bride's female relatives and close friends into two braids.

Kokoshniki varied from region to region in a whole variety of picturesque and poetic shapes. They were peaked like diadems or round and high like crowns; sometimes they were crescent-shaped. Each town had its own style and by her *kokoshnik* one could tell exactly where a maiden came from. The *kokoshniki* of the north were heavily embroidered with gold and silver threads and river pearls, with a mother-of-pearl network which fell low over the brow. In the central regions, the *kokoshniki* were high; in Nizhny Novgorod, round, in the form of a crescent. Sometimes long veils of muslin or gauze were attached to them. The headdresses were made of silk in bright colors, in red and raspberry-colored velvet, in cloth of gold that was ornamented with pearls, decorative glass, mirrors and foil. In the south, they were peaked with a pearl net descending over the forehead. In Ryazan and Tambov strange-looking *kokoshniki* with little horns were called "magpies" and had long tails of goose down or many colored feathers. In the Ukraine, maidens wore crowns of flowers with bright, flowing ribbons. Beautiful and rich, gracefully framing the face and emphasizing soft eyes, these headdresses were in a very real way the crowning glory of Russian women.

Everything was there in this treasure house of Russian folk culture: color, music, imagination, fantasy—life. But as in the fairy tales, it was invisible to those who could not see its beauty. Someone had to discover it and understand its importance and richness. Someone had to fuse the two elements that had separated Russian culture and find a way to combine Western form and Russian content. Someone had to fashion for Russia a new image of itself. Such a genius, a poet, appeared in the early 19th century. Delving into the Russian land for his inspiration, he led the way. And after him nothing was the same again. Russia had found her new voice which was to grow ever stronger until it was heard all over the world.

14 · ALEXANDER PUSHKIN

Pushkin is our all.

Apollon Grigoriev

Opon Tsar Alexander's victorious return to Russia in July 1814 his mother, the Dowager Empress Maria Feodorovna, gave a splendid reception at Pavlovsk. The most famous generals and statesmen attended. As a high honor the Dowager Empress had invited the boys of a special lycée, newly created in the wing of the Catherine Palace in neighboring Tsarskoe Selo by Alexander for the sons of the best families.

Dressed in their special uniforms—blue serge jackets piped in red with high red collars and gilt buttons, white piqué vests and rakishly plumed three-cornered hats—the boys watched from a box hung with rose garlands an elaborate ballet which was staged in the outdoor theater. The court overflowed with admiration and praise for the Emperor, one courtier extolling, "Our Agamemnon, pacifier of Europe, Conqueror of Napoleon shone with all the majesty that can be attained by a mortal."

A triumphal arch had been erected on the way from the palace to the pavilion and was inscribed grandiloquently:

O you who return from war,
This arch is too small for you . . .

202

One of the boys from the school, instead of being awed by the Tsar's magnificence, was immediately inspired to spoof Alexander with a drawing. With an irreverence for authority that was to characterize him all his life, the young man, whose name was Alexander Pushkin, showed a corpulent Tsar, stuffed with too many state dinners, bearing down on the Triumphal Arch whose gate was too narrow to receive him while his panic-stricken generals rushed ahead to try to avoid disaster by enlarging the arch with their swords. Pushkin's friends were delighted with his wicked wit.

Only a few days earlier, this mischievous fourteen-year-old had burst into print with a poem published in a St. Petersburg newspaper and so had gained a certain fame at school. Although no one could guess it then, this boy, whom his friends characterized as "half monkey, half tiger," was destined to bring to Russia greater glory than the Tsar who had defeated Napoleon.

For the Russians, Pushkin became, and remains even today, their single most beloved writer and the quintessential romantic figure of his country. Swashbuckling and overflowing with life, he always retained the free spirit that moved him to spoof a tsar, continuing to believe that, above all, individual freedom must be preserved if life is to have dignity. Pushkin was at once merry, skeptical, enthusiastic and sad. Because he savored life so much, he lived hard and died young, leaving a legend and a poetry that continue to inspire a unique enchantment in the hearts of his countrymen.

Alexander Sergeievich Pushkin was born in Moscow on May 28, 1799, into an old boyar family of distinguished ancestry and strained means. Among his forebears was án exotic, romantic figure of whom he was very proud. On his mother's side, his great-grandfather was an Abyssinian prince named Ibrahim Hannibal, whom he later immortalized in an unfinished novel, *The Negro of Peter the Great*. Ibrahim, the story goes, had been taken in battle by the Turks and brought to Constantinople as a hostage. At the age of eight he was taken from the Seraglio and brought to the great Tsar Peter as a present. Peter grew to love the boy so much that he adopted him, sent him to study abroad and made him his comrade in arms. It was from his ancestor Hannibal that Pushkin claimed his fiery looks and dusky complexion.

The Pushkin household was disorganized and badly managed; the horses were thin, and often for receptions the servants had to borrow dishes from neighbors. Pushkin's father was irresponsible and his mother an authoritarian and selfish person who was often cruel to her little son. But luckily, from the time of his birth, Alexander was brought up by a serf woman who had refused her freedom when it was offered and elected to remain with his grandmother. Arina Rodionovna was forty-five years old when she became Pushkin's *nyanya*, or nurse. She was a warm, mild-tempered woman of the country who was steeped in all the old proverbs, lore and tales, and she had a tremendous impact on Alexander's sensitive imagination.

Like everyone else of their society, Pushkin's family had wholeheartedly adopted the French language and culture. Young Alexander was taught by tutors to read and write in French, but from his beloved nurse and other servants in the household he also grew up surrounded with Russian fairy tales and folklore. During his long stays at his family's modest estate in the country, he gained a profound love and knowledge of Russian life and customs. Later, in his poetry and stories, he could describe brilliantly the dizzying whirl of society in Moscow and St. Petersburg, and yet also evoke just as vividly the smell and feel of the country, the long line of the Russian horizon, the fresh air, the bracing gallop over the wide fields which ends by stamping the feet free of snow on the threshold of a welcoming house, and the cozy bubbling samovar by a crackling fire.

At twelve Pushkin was sent to Tsarskoe Selo to the new and prestigious establishment that had been created by the Tsar "for the training of young men destined for high office in the state." The Emperor was so anxious that this school provide the finest education possible that he lent his own library and hired the best teachers available. (Curiously, one was the brother of the notorious French revolutionary Marat.)

Pushkin's teachers were not overly impressed with him. True, they agreed, young Pushkin did have a phenomenal memory, but one wrote that he was "frivolous, hypersensitive, talkative, superficial, hot-tempered"; in philosophy "he understands quickly, grasps subtleties but is incapable of applying himself and makes absolutely no progress." "A useless scamp, nothing more," concluded another. Among his classmates he was famous for his epigrams and sly wit.

The boys were rarely allowed to leave the school, but somehow, whenever they were, the sensual Pushkin fell in love with every lady, young or old, he managed to encounter. He romanced them, wrote verses to them, sighed over them. He began to write poems, first in French and then in Russian, for the school newspapers.

Although the poem which had been published in the newspaper before the

Tsar's reception had gained him a reputation at school, a far more important event occurred a year later on the occasion of a qualifying examination for admission to the upper school. Pushkin, then fifteen, read his poem *Recollections of Tsarskoe Selo* before a large audience that included the Minister of the Interior and the famous old poet of Catherine's time Gavrila Derzhavin. Derzhavin was elderly and hard of hearing, but when Pushkin began reciting, the distinguished old poet suddenly sat up and cupped his hand to his ear. By the time Pushkin had finished, Derzhavin was so moved that his wig had slipped and tears streamed down his wrinkled face. The "useless scamp" had scored a resounding success. Later the same evening Derzhavin singled him out and proclaimed that Pushkin would be his successor and the new hope of Russian poetry.

By the time Pushkin was sixteen, the Minister of Education had commissioned the young student to write poems; one he composed for the wedding of the Grand Duchess Anna Pavlovna, sister of the Tsar, to Prince William of Orange. The Dowager Empress Maria Feodorovna was so pleased she gave him a gold watch. In his last year at school, when the boys were allowed a bit more freedom, Pushkin naturally went a step further. He would sneak out and spend whole nights carousing with a group of Hussars who were garrisoned at Tsarskoe Selo after the war, drinking champagne and soaking up their heady conversations of liberty and love.

By the time he graduated at eighteen in 1817 he was already famous. Small and lithe, he was brimming with vitality. He swam well, was a redoubtable swordsman and an accomplished rider. He was given a minor state appointment —tenth undersecretary in the Foreign Office—and immediately began a rollicking life in St. Petersburg. He wanted to see everything, know everybody. Pushkin loved women and, although he was not handsome, such was the force of his expressive eyes and the charm of his conversation that in his company a woman felt herself totally captivating; there were few who could resist him. He dressed eccentrically and sparkled in drawing rooms. He spent evenings at the ballet and romanced the ballerinas. As his conquests multiplied, he began keeping "Don Juan" lists, dividing his conquests neatly into "Platonic" and "Sexual."

It was not only the fashionable world that he frequented. Pushkin also had a thirst for gambling that lasted all his life. He drank and embroiled himself in fistfights in dives. He knew the city prostitutes and was on friendly terms with tavern owners. By the time he was twenty-one a friend had written, "Pushkin fights duels every day; thank heavens they are not fatal and the adversaries come back unscathed." He was, in fact, very like the fashionable young man about town whom he later described in *Eugene Onegin:*

His hair cut in the latest mode;
He dined, he danced, he fenced, he rode.
In French he could converse politely,
As well as write; and how he bowed!
In the mazurka, 'twas allowed
No partner ever was so sprightly.
What more is asked? The world is warm
In praise of so much wit and charm.

Those early decades of the 19th century in which Pushkin grew up were a heady time. Alexander I had inflamed intellectual society with ideas and hopes of liberty. Masonry was the fashion; secret societies sprang up on every side. In these societies, Russians found some of the intensity of feeling and commitment that they were seeking so avidly. There were great dreams and talk of constitutions. Revolutionary ideas were in the air—only old bores praised the government. Young Pushkin, barely twenty-one, was the literary idol of the city. His poems on liberty circulated everywhere; his saucy epigrams twitting the church and the Tsar were quoted with delight in smart drawing rooms. But his provocative writings, coupled with his notorious reputation as town madcap, were too much for the authorities, and they decided to cool him off by sending him on assignments far away in the south, to serve under the administrator of the colonies of New Russia in Bessarabia.

In Kishinev, far from quieting down, Pushkin continued his daredevil ways, playing cards, romancing ladies and fighting duels. For a duel with an officer he had accused of cheating at cards, he arrived nonchalantly eating a bag of cherries and continued spitting the stones in the direction of his opponent, who fired and missed. Pushkin did not even bother to shoot back. He unconcernedly strolled away, still eating his cherries. Legend says that he joined a band of gypsies and wandered around the steppes of Bessarabia with them. With comrades he traveled about the Crimea and the Caucasus, and in 1822 he was sent to Odessa to join the staff of the Governor General of the Crimean Region, Count Vorontsov.

In Odessa, he went to the Italian opera and became a passionate fan of Rossini's music. He ate oysters at Caesar Otton's noted French restaurant and, being Pushkin, also entangled himself in several romances. Somehow he managed to conduct two love affairs simultaneously; one of these ladies became the subject of some of his greatest love lyrics, and the other was Count Vorontsov's wife. For the Count and the authorities in Saint Petersburg this was the last straw. Obviously exile to the provinces had not had the proper sobering effect. Pushkin was dismissed from government service in disgrace and banished to his family estate of Mikhailovskoe in the countryside near Pskov, with only a handful of local gentry and his old nurse, Arina Rodionovna, for company.

In the ramshackle old wooden house of his grandfather's time, Pushkin set himself up in a rough and carpetless room overlooking the courtyard and began to write. His four years in the south had greatly enriched him as a writer. Now bored and restless in the undisturbed quiet of Mikhailovskoe, forcibly removed from the distractions he loved, Pushkin set himself to reading Russian history and working. His old nurse entertained him through the long wintry nights by telling him fairy tales. In November 1824 he wrote to his brother, "Do you know how I spend my time? Before lunch, I write. I eat late. Afterward, I ride. In the evening I listen to my nanny's tales and fill the gaps in my wretched education! What wonders they are, her old tales! Every one is a poem. . . ." He often read his work to her, and she sometimes made suggestions. Wrote Pushkin, "Sometimes she is cleverer than I am, because her impressions are more direct and she is closer to the truth."

At Mikhailovskoe he was enormously productive. He wrote many lyric poems, and finished *The Gypsies,* a long poetic tale based on his experiences in Bessarabia. When he was only twenty, Pushkin had written *Ruslan and Ludmilla,* a charming and imaginative long poem which for the first time used native Russian tales and folklore for its inspiration. But now, as he began what was to be one of his greatest works, *Eugene Onegin,* he introduced visual images of his own age. Inspired by his reading of Shakespeare, he wrote a play, *Boris Godunov,* for which he innovatively went to Russian history for his theme. With these works he began a body of literature that was to be called by his countrymen "an encyclopedia of Russian life." His wit and his peculiarly Russian realism—a realism that is poetic without idealizing or surrendering reality—led the way to future achievements in Russian literature and influenced a host of later writers, most notably Ivan Turgenev. The heroine, Tatyana, that Pushkin created for *Onegin* became the prototype for the ideal Russian women of Tolstoy and Dostoevsky.

In 1812 Madame de Staël had made a prophetic observation. Although she could not speak Russian, she wrote, "the sweetness and brilliance of the sounds of their language is noticeable even to those who do not understand it. . . ." The Russians, she believed, were making a mistake to try to imitate French culture. "Their writers should mine poetry from everything most intimate which they have in their souls. Genius will come to them in the arts and especially in literature, when they have found the way to bring their own nature into the language as they show it in their actions." It was Pushkin's genius that he found that way. In his work he developed not only a new content but new literary style, modernizing the Russian language and bringing it to a perfection that has never been matched. Retaining all the grace of the classical poetical form of the 18th century which the Russians had absorbed from the French, Pushkin removed the rhetoric and brought his literary language closer to ordinary speech without ever sacrificing its harmony. Although he lived in isolation in Mikhailovskoe, back in St. Petersburg where his works were published and enthusiastically read he was hailed as "the Byron of Russia" and the greatest poet of the land.

In 1826, after the death of Alexander I and the crushing of the Decembrist Revolt by his brother, the new Tsar Nicholas I, Pushkin was recalled to Moscow where Nicholas made him a startling suggestion. Since Pushkin was the finest poet in Russia, henceforth the Tsar, and only he, would be responsible for looking over his verses. It was a compliment in a way, an imperious recognition of Pushkin's unique stature and popularity. From that moment, all Pushkin's work passed under the stern eye of the Emperor, who annotated and edited it personally. Pushkin was put in the uncomfortably ambiguous position of being both the protégé-pet and the captive of Nicholas I.

From the beginning it was an impossible relationship. There was no way in which two men so different could understand each other. Nicholas was a starched, pedantically official man. The Marquis de Custine wrote of him: "The Emperor of Russia is a military chief, for whom every day is a battle." Indeed, Nicholas believed in military discipline in all things and would have been happy if every man in the land had been a soldier. In the army, said he, "there is order and no impertinent claims to know all the answers. No one commands before he himself has learned to obey." In character and even appearance, Nicholas was totally Germanic. Queen Victoria, herself a German princess, wrote of him: "He is stern and severe, with fixed principles of duty which *nothing* on earth will make him change." (More tartly, she added, "very *clever* I do not think him.")

During his thirty-year reign, he was known as the "Iron Tsar." He moved the political clock backward, introducing tight censorship and sternly trying to impose an inflexible Teutonic order on the land. Nicholas was tall and imperious. He always wore a uniform and as a result his movements were stiff and strained. He always spoke of "we military men" and "we engineers," and most of all loved dress parades and mathematics. Happily he designed uniforms for everyone from generals to schoolchildren. His personal habits were spartan; he slept in an austere bedroom with carpetless floors and a few gravures of Sevastopol on the walls. There, he stretched out on an iron camp bed, wrapped in his army cloak; under the bed was a pair of slippers which he wore for years and which were often mended. Although he was considered extremely handsome and somewhat of a flirt, Nicholas was a strict moralist, deeply attached to wife and family, a man who favored constitutional walks and conventional propriety.

No two men could have been more at odds in temperament and personality than this rigid conservative monarch and the sensual, free-spirited poet, champion of love and personal freedom. In Nicholas' eyes Pushkin was a threat to order, not to the order of the state but to the proper established order of society in general. He gave him court appointments, but he also kept him under close surveillance.

Naturally, after his return Pushkin resumed his giddy life. He gambled excessively and, no matter how successful his writings, most of what he earned was lost at cards. In a melancholy pattern that poisoned his life, he was constantly in debt. The passion for cards in those days and the sums spent for gambling were phenomenal. People devoted whole weeks to gambling. A French count exclaimed, "What gold! What bank notes! People staked all they possessed!" Pushkin described this gambling fever in the terse opening lines of his classic tale of the gambler's passion, *The Queen of Spades:* "One day they played cards at the rooms of Narumov of the Horse Guards. The long winter night passed away unnoticed, and it was after four in the morning when the company sat down to supper. Those who had won ate with good appetites; the others sat staring absently at their empty plates." During one of those long nights of cards, he chalked the epigraph for *The Queen of Spades* on his sleeve. It began:

In days of bad weather
They gathered together
Often.
And staked, God forgive them,
Fifty or a hundred
Cash.

As the stakes doubled
The cunning, unruffled, were gay.

Pushkin was so well known in the shadowy gambling world that in the Moscow police register he was listed simply as "No. 36, Pushkin, well-known gambler."

But in the salons of the new intellectuals, where people were reading Schiller, Goethe, Byron—and Pushkin, it was different. There he was received as a hero. Paradoxically, despite the stern and inflexible Nicholas, it was a time of enormous diversity of ideas and achievements in the arts. All those connected with art, which was considered a divine mystery, had enormous prestige. The poet, especially, was considered a sublime being, an instrument of God, privy to mysteries denied to ordinary mortals. This was a very Russian idea, for Russians love song, poetry and poets with a passion shared only by the Irish. Poets are quoted, loved and revered as national treasures even today. The 1820's and 1830's were a golden age of poetry in Russia, a time when it not only established itself as the equal of, but in many cases surpassed any poetry in Europe. Pushkin was not only the greatest of this generation of gifted poets but he also came wreathed in the additional romantic charm of his notorious exploits.

When he was nearly thirty, in the winter of 1828–29, Pushkin fell in love again, by his own accounting for the 113th time. But this time it was different. He was determined to marry. When Pushkin first saw Natalya Goncharova in Moscow, she was sixteen years old and a poet's delight. Dressed in an airy white gown, a simple circlet of gold in her dark hair, she was pure, distant—and as it turned out—empty. Alas, this seems to have escaped Pushkin's loving eye. He had fallen under the spell of his own imagination, and

He loved as in our age
People already do no longer; as only
The wild soul of a poet
Is still condemned to love.

Natalya, beyond the fact that she could dance, embroider and speak some French, had little education. Her family was living on the remains of a fortune made by an ancestor who manufactured textiles and had been raised to the gentry. Natalya's mother was absolutely determined to marry her most beautiful daughter to the best financial advantage. Like any romantic teen-aged girl, Natalya was flattered by a famous poet's attentions, but her mother was quite opposed. Pushkin was rejected.

Madly in love, he tried to forget. He went off to the Caucasus where his brother was serving in the army. There, in his own words, "half soldier-half tourist," he joined a campaign against the Turks and was seen galloping in pursuit of the enemy, waving a saber. To his intense disappointment, the Turks retreated across the border before he could engage in battle. He stayed for several months in the Caucasus, collecting the colorful folklore and legends of the Caucasian people.

Finally, Natalya's mother relented and agreed to the match he longed for. But, returning to Moscow with his desires crowned, Pushkin inexplicably fell into a depression. Forty-eight hours before his wedding, haunted by mysterious premonitions, he went to hear the gypsies and wept.

Natalya and her poet were married in Moscow on February 18, 1831. Natalya was eighteen, Pushkin almost thirty-two. During the ceremony, there were disturbing omens—his crucifix fell to the ground and his candle went out. Yet despite all this, it seemed a perfect match; the greatest poet had married a great romantic beauty of the city.

For a short time things went well. The famous young couple went back to St. Petersburg. The Tsar gave Pushkin an appointment in the Foreign Office and a salary of five thousand rubles. During his honeymoon, Pushkin wrote *Tsar Saltan,* one of his loveliest poetic tales.

Shortly after his return to Petersburg, at a reception given for him and his new bride, the poet was introduced to a nervous twenty-two-year-old man who hero-worshiped him. With his straight blond hair, intense piercing eyes and aquiline nose, he looked like a strange species of bird. He was from the Ukraine, the son of a modest Cossack landowner in the province of Poltava in the south. His name was Nikolai Gogol. He aspired to be a writer but was not having a great deal of luck. In school he had been told that he had no talent for prose and should confine himself to poetry, but his first published poem had been so massacred by the critics that, stung by shame and humiliation, he had scoured the Petersburg bookshops for every copy and burned them all. Discouraged in his literary efforts, Gogol, a talented mimic, had applied for a job as an actor in the Imperial Theater and had been rejected. He managed for a while to hold a position as a minor clerk in the Ministry of Public Works. Gogol was fiercely ambitious and anxious to be accepted by society. At the time he met Pushkin he was trying the career of teacher and private tutor.

The career of tutor was considered a potentially rewarding position, one that could prove a stepping-stone to more important things. Every spring, crowds of private tutors recruited in Europe—in Germany, Switzerland, France and England—debarked along the quays of St. Petersburg as soon as the ice broke. But even these were not enough, for such was the passion for education that native Russians were also being trained as tutors in the schools of the city. Private education could be a lucrative profession; salaries were high, three to four thousand rubles a year in the cities and much more, up to seven thousand and ten thousand rubles a year, to entice someone to the provinces or faraway Siberia. The tutor occupied an important position in the family—especially among the provincial gentry where every tutor was a prophet and each governess an oracle. It was a kind of lottery, a road that could lead to nothing but boredom or, on the other hand, prove a convenient way to all classes of honorable posts, including future ease and independence. If the governess was pretty and amiable, she might capture the heart of some young aide-de-camp or even a colonel and thus become Mrs. Colonel. If the tutor was personable, his connection in a high family might lead to a government post. Tutors were so numerous that they were a special class in themselves. In St. Petersburg alone, there were more than six thousand tutors and by an 1834 law they were given special privileges by the state, including the right to wear the "little uniform" of public instruction and the right to an automatic ranking in the state after a specified number of years of service, as well as pensions.

Many visiting foreigners noted in astonishment this "frenzy for education." One of these was Johann Kohl, who had studied law at Heidelberg and Munich and served for six years as a tutor in the home of a Baltic baron. After his service, Kohl traveled all over the country and left several valuable volumes of specific and detailed information on the life of the time. He wrote, "Ever since Peter the Great, Russia has been seized by such a prodigious enthusiasm for education as no nation in the world had ever exhibited. Academies, universities, gymnasiums and popular schools sprang up all over the country as if by magic, and still continue to spread with astonishing rapidity over the whole surface of the gigantic Empire. The successors of Peter have made schooling an important affair of state."

Great numbers of scholars at colleges and other establishments were maintained at the expense of the crown. In St. Petersburg, for boys there were innumerable establishments for the education of officers, starting with the prestigious *Corps des Pages* for sons of the nobility, continuing through gymnasiums and fifty other schools. There were commercial schools for the bourgeoisie and priouts for poorer children, shopkeepers and domestic servants. Educated Russians spoke several languages as a matter of course. Many ordinary Russians spoke several European languages as a normal part of their lives; merchants and shopkeepers found it essential, and even coachmen tried their luck in broken Italian and German. In the passports of servants, along with their height and other physical characteristics, was also in many instances listed that "he speaks languages," after which were listed, "Russian, French, German, English, and Turkish."

Kohl commented on the new Pedagogical Institute established in 1832 for the training of teachers. Boys entered at twelve and were taught five languages at the same time. He heard boys translating "very readily" from Greek into German and Latin into French, German and Russian. Each class was taught in a different language and the children answered the questions in the language in which the class was held.

Although wealthy families still preferred private education for their daughters, all the Russian empresses since Catherine had particularly concerned themselves with the formal education of girls and had established many schools. The principal colleges or institutes for young ladies in St. Petersburg in the 1830's and 1840's were the Catherine, to which none but aristocratic girls were admitted; the Smolny, which was divided into two parts, one for children of the nobility and the other for the bourgeoisie; the Patriotic, for daughters of officers; and the Elizabeth, for daughters of merchants and employees. There was also the Marie, where girls of humbler origins were educated and then at age eighteen provided with respectable situations or married with small dowries; the Foundling, for orphans and others; and various priouts similar to those for the education of boys.

The young ladies entered for six years and lived almost as if they were in a convent. Every summer there was a long recess, but otherwise, during the entire time at school, girls were not allowed to be absent on any pretext whatsoever. They never went for a walk on the city streets, and only twice a year for a drive. One of their rare public appearances was at carnival time, driving in a long line of modest carriages. The schools were entirely self-contained establishments. The Catherine Institute had a church, hospital and splendid ballroom. Attached to the Institute were a priest, comptroller, architects, a carpenter, a band of musicians and an immense number of servants all educated for the purpose. Kohl wrote, "Everything is found for the use of the pupils by the crown, their dresses, linen shoes and even their pocket handkerchiefs."

The excellent education provided in these schools played an important role in forming the reading public for the work of the new Russian writers. In all these schools the program was the same—modern languages (French, English and German) followed by geography, religion, ancient and modern history. Madame de Staël wrote that at Smolny in 1810 the girls sang psalms in harmony before they sat down to dinner, executed Russian dances with great grace and recited the most eloquent passages of her father's work in perfect French, which brought tears to her eyes. Most startling for foreigners, including John Quincy Adams, then the American Ambassador, their program also included physics and mathematics. During designated weeks the girls were instructed in singing, dancing, embroidery and cooking. Their only unoccupied time was one hour after dinner, which they spent walking up and down the immense corridors of their schools.

Every effort was made to find the finest professors for these schools, and Gogol had managed to secure an appointment at the Patriotic Institute. There, for four years (1831–35), he taught history to young ladies of the junior classes, sitting in neat rows before him and demurely attired in their brown dresses and white aprons. To supplement his income, in the summer of 1831 just after he had met Pushkin, he tutored the children of several great families in their country houses at Pavlovsk. His pupils remembered him as a curious, thin little man whose face twitched nervously, who dressed conspicuously and wore high cravats up under his chin. Pushkin and his wife had taken a house at Tsarskoe Selo, not far away. Longing to consolidate his new acquaintance, Gogol took to walking regularly in the lovely Imperial parks of Pavlovsk and Tsarskoe Selo, hoping to run into Pushkin, which he sometimes did. Racking his brains to find some way of having closer and more regular contact with him, Gogol hit on an ingenious solution. Telling Pushkin that he had no fixed address in St. Petersburg, he asked if he might have his mail sent in care of Pushkin. The poet was a little startled, but he agreed, and Gogol's aim was achieved.

From his early childhood, Gogol's vivid imagination conjured up strange fantasies all around him. Gogol's mother was an extremely religious woman, and when he was a boy she filled him with descriptions of the torments of hell; perhaps as a result, he was pursued by nightmares. Even in broad daylight he sometimes thought he heard voices of departed spirits calling him. He had been brought up in the rich and fertile countryside of the Ukraine, surrounded by peasants and their colorful legends and folk tales. When he arrived in St. Petersburg, he found that the reading public of the capital quickly bought up these stories. Always seeking ways to increase his earnings, Gogol had published a few short stories based on Ukrainian folk tales in magazines, disguising his identity under a series of inventive pseudonyms to protect what he saw as his professional dignity.

In the winter of 1831 a collection of these stories under yet another assumed name was published as *Evening on a Farm in Dikanka,* by Rudy Panko, Beekeeper. When he went to collect his book at the printers, he found all the typesetters laughing as they read it, and he rushed the proofs over to Pushkin, who devoured the whole book at one sitting and bubbled with enthusiasm. Pushkin wrote to the editor in chief of the Literary Supplement of the *Russian Veteran* to recommend the book, saying it was "entrancing . . . sincere and spontaneous" and, he added, "for heaven's sakes defend him if the journalists, as is their usual practice, criticize the impropriety of the expressions, his want of taste, etc. It is high time the *precieuses ridicules* of our Russian literature got their comeuppance." The book was a huge success and Gogol followed it with a second volume in 1832. But Gogol dreamed of writing something more solid and of making for himself an established position in the world. He decided to write a serious history of the Ukrainians and, despite his meager academic background, to apply for a chair of history at the University of Kiev. He was bitterly disappointed when he was not accepted. But in 1834, thanks to the help of friends, including Pushkin, he secured an appointment as assistant professor of medieval history at the University of St. Petersburg.

His first lecture was a great success, but afterward things went speedily downhill. Gogol could not seem to find much to say and came to his lectures ill prepared. One of the students who attended his lectures was the future novelist Ivan Turgenev, who wrote later that Gogol missed two out of three classes, spoke indistinctly and seemed "dreadfully confused." He soon lost his job. Between his courses at the Patriotic Institute and the University, Gogol kept writing. His *Arabesques* and *Mirgorod*, which included "Taras Bulba," were published without much critical success. Pushkin defended him and introduced him to the readers of his new literary magazine, *The Contemporary*, with a warm review of his works.

It is interesting to note that in addition to all the literary achievements, the decades in which Pushkin lived were also important as a period which began the uninterrupted growth of Russian journalism. Despite the pressure of Nicholas' censorship, several journalists made strong stands for independence, especially in literary matters. Many new magazines sprang up in Moscow and St. Petersburg, and dedicated journalists did much to spread the new literature and form public opinion. Pushkin, among all his other gifts, was a first-class critic, and his beautifully written critiques and reviews were distinguished by their sound judgment and lucidity. His neat and precisely aimed irony could sting his enemies unforgettably. He was also an innovative editor, quick to recognize new talent. In the pages of his magazine he introduced the work of many new writers; it was he who first published the verses of Turgenev. When Gogol's short story "Nose" was rejected by the editors of the *Muscovite Observer* as "trivial," Pushkin published it in his magazine with these graceful words: "N. V. Gogol withheld the publication of this sketch for a long time, but we found it so out of the ordinary, fantastical, droll and original that we have persuaded him to allow us to share with the public the pleasure it has given us."

Pushkin respected Gogol's talent and always helped him when he could, yet they could never be really close friends. The two men were completely different in personality and spirit. Pushkin was open, all grace, warmth and generosity of spirit. Gogol was devious and often lied. He was a hypochondriac, a tight person who, people said, "never unbuttoned himself" nor gave very much to others. Indeed, with his dark and secretive disposition, he made people nervous. Self-conscious, yet consumed with unbridled ambition, he was always on guard, silently following people with his sharp glance, mentally recording conversations and reactions. Pushkin loved women; Gogol was afraid of them and never married. In Pushkin's artistic world there were measure and harmony; in Gogol's everything was distorted and fantastic. Gogol longed to describe beauty in life and virtue in mankind; he tried, but to his despair, never succeeded. What he saw in humanity was the grotesque and the surreal. He had the eye of the caricaturist for the telling detail that revealed character. Like Dickens, he could brilliantly hold up to the light the foibles of man and society. Pushkin recognized this gift.

For a time, Gogol had a small apartment on Little Morskaya Street which he had decorated himself, down to painting the walls and sewing the curtains. There he entertained his friends, and sometimes Pushkin came too. The one hearty side to Gogol's character was his love of good food; his descriptions of great meals in many of his stories are mouth-watering. He gave little dinners for which all who came shared the cost. Wearing an apron around his waist, Gogol would do the cooking, preparing tasty Ukrainian specialties of *varenniki* (dumplings) and *vatrushki* (pastries), which he loved.

One night, during a four-hour discussion in Gogol's apartment, Pushkin urged him to attempt something bigger and more important than short stories. In his notebooks, Pushkin had recorded a strange event which had taken place somewhere near his estate at Mikhailovskoe and which he intended to use himself one day for a verse comedy. A clever swindler had hit upon the ingenious and dastardly scheme of buying up dead serfs cheaply and mortgaging them to the State Bank at the going rate for live serfs. Pushkin gave the idea to Gogol and suggested that he write a novel like *Don Quixote* which would be divided into cantos and in which the hero would travel all over the provinces. Gogol seized the idea and started working on it immediately, calling the book *Dead Souls*. But he found that writing a novel was a much longer and harder job than he had expected, and after finishing three chapters he wrote to Pushkin that he was longing to write a play, which he could finish quickly and perhaps earn some money. "Do me a favor of giving me a subject and I shall instantly write a five-act comedy which I promise you will be diabolically droll. In the name of heaven. My mind and stomach are both famished. *Arabesques* and *Mirgorod* are not selling at all. The devil knows what that means. Booksellers are such foul creatures that they should be hanged without remorse from the nearest tree."

Again Pushkin consulted his notebooks and found a small entry based on another real event—a man is mistaken for an inspector general on a tour of duty. Gogol excitedly begged him to let him have the idea. Pushkin agreed, but later said good-humoredly, "You must be on guard with that Ukrainian, he skins me so adroitly that I never even have time to scream!" Gogol wrote *The Inspector General* in less than two months and on January 18, 1836, he read his play to a group of friends including Pushkin. Gogol's gift for mimicry was so great that all were convulsed with laughter and one person wrote, "I am not sure the play will not lose something in performance, for few actors will be able to play it as he read it!"

Gogol coached the actors himself, and the play had its premiere on April 19, 1836, in the beautiful yellow and white Alexandrinsky Theater which had been recently completed by Rossi. The actors were a little uncertain how to play it, and the *beau monde* how to take it. People craned their necks to glance surreptitiously at the Imperial Box to see the reaction of the Tsar. The imperious Nicholas seemed to be enjoying himself hugely, chuckling and vigorously clapping. Afterward the Tsar exclaimed, "Now, there's a play! Everyone has taken a drubbing, and myself worse than anyone else!" The play excited a tremendous controversy. People rushed to buy seats and there was a flourishing black market in tickets. Critics sprang to their pens. Many of the upper crust did not have the sense of humor of the Tsar and they huffed furiously. "Intolerable insult to the nobility, the civil service, the merchants! Doesn't show a single decent man!"

One month after its opening in Petersburg, *The Inspector General* was given in Moscow. The role of the mayor was played by one of the most famous actors in Russia, a Ukrainian named Mikhail Shchepkin, who also directed the production. Shchepkin had once been a household serf, but his master had given him permission to study and then act in plays in Kursk and Poltava. After performances, he would rush home, don his livery and serve his master his dinner. At the age of thirty, thanks to a subscription raised by the Governor General of the province, he bought his freedom and went on to triumph in every theater in Russia. Shchepkin begged Gogol to come to Moscow to read for the actors and see the performance, but Gogol refused. He was hurt and stung by all the publicity and furor generated by his play. He, who so much wanted to be accepted as a solid member of society, was now simply a subject of scandal. "My play repels me!" he cried. He decided to run away from it all, to Italy and to Europe. Shortly before he left, Pushkin came to see him and asked him to read him the beginning of *Dead Souls*. Gogol read almost through the night. It was the last time they saw each other.

15 · "SOUL-INSPIRED FLIGHT": THE ARTS IN PUSHKIN'S TIME

Pushkin's epoch was a rich and vital period in Russian artistic history, one which witnessed great achievements not only in literature but in all the arts. It was a time which saw the beginning of a Russian school of painting and music, a time when the Russian ballet rose to preeminence. Pushkin was the universal artist of his era who epitomized in his work the finest artistic ideas of a dynamically creative epoch. The generosity of spirit that prompted him to act as a literary godfather to Gogol was typical of his character. With his curiosity and intelligence, Pushkin interested himself in all the arts of his day, and, as the first poet of the land, exerted an enormous influence over them all. He loved music and was an excellent dancer. He sketched, and left many witty and sensitive drawings of himself and his contemporaries; he was painted by many of the leading artists of his day.

During Pushkin's lifetime, painters left off being apprentices and began to assume an independent course. Extraordinarily swiftly the Russians had mastered the techniques of Western painting which for them was less than a century old. The Academy of Fine Arts in St. Petersburg, although rigidly formal and classical in its structure and approach, had with great success taught Russian artists strict principles of draftsmanship, design and composition, which they had now fully absorbed.

The Russian *pensionnaire* system of sending the most gifted art students abroad, begun under Peter the Great, was continued as an organized program under the succeeding tsars. Paintings were exhibited every year at the Academy and the students who won top prizes were sent, at the expense of the crown, to study in various countries of Europe for a period of two to four years, so that they "might have the possibility of seeing the work of men of genius and profiting by them." In addition, in St. Petersburg in the early years of the 19th century, three wealthy patrons founded a Society for the Encouragement of Artists, whose goal was to help young painters with awards and purchases and to provide funds to send them abroad.

Traveling abroad was such a characteristic of old Russia that a foreign stay was considered the obligatory crowning of any proper education. Russian scholars and artists sometimes lived in European capitals for many years; Turgenev spent much of his life in France. Russian aristocrats visited the literary shrines of Europe, the homes of Goethe and Schiller and, because of the enormous interest in Shakespeare, the pond where Ophelia was supposed to have drowned and the castle of Elsinore that loomed on the coast of Denmark.

In Pushkin's time Italy, especially Rome, replaced Paris as the mecca for Russian writers and artists to such a degree that an important and lively émigré colony flourished in the northern part of Rome, not far from the Piazza del Popolo. Russian artists carried on their conversations at their favorite Caffe Greco and met in the salons of wealthy patrons. Gogol spent twelve years abroad living mostly in Italy. Many painters, including Karl Briullov, Alexander Ivanov and Orest Kiprensky, made long stays in Italy.

Russian artists and intellectuals were so completely in touch with all the intellectual currents of Europe that they now were growing ever more skeptical of a purely imitative approach and were exploring new ways of their own. In the same way that Pushkin succeeded so brilliantly in poetry, painters were trying to fuse the classical forms which they had learned from Europe with a new Russian content. There was a growing pride and interest in the special spiritual and cultural qualities of the Russian people, an increasing feeling that, as the painter Ivanov expressed it, "to be Russian is happiness."

In St. Petersburg several weekly salons were frequented by Russian and

Western painters, writers and esthetes of the time. They met to recite poetry, to sketch and to discuss the many diverse ideas which now gripped them. It was the beginning of those discussions between the "Slavophiles" and the "Westernizers" which were to continue throughout the 19th century and into our own, between those who felt that the way for Russia was a closer linking to Europe and those who felt that Russia because of her own characteristics and history was called on to play a special and redemptive role for Christianity. There were heated all-night discussions on the existence of God. There was a tremendous swing away from the rationalism and skepticism of the 18th century, which were alien to the Russian personality, toward greater mysticism and spiritualism. People interested themselves in the occult. The role of that very Russian figure, the *starets,* or holy man, whom Dostoevsky was only a few years later to immortalize in literature, once again became important.

Perhaps because the Russians were so keenly sensing this duality, the most popular literary character through the early decades of the 19th century was Hamlet. Russians felt a strong kinship to the brooding prince and Shakespeare's play became so popular that simplified versions were given all over the country.

Russian society divided itself into many factions and new artistic principles emerged. There was great questioning of the validity of purely classical forms in art, a searching for new codes and a more individualistic, mystical world view. Painters had to do more than simply "copy" nature. Feeling and imagination now had to play dominant roles; the artist had the right to express his own subjective response. There was great interest in self-portraiture and in the psychological portrait, a form at which Russian painters excelled.

Some of the new artists recorded the glamorous life of the capital and the sensitive and searching faces of their patrons and friends, while others began to paint people at their daily work in the cities and in the fields. Although many of these portraits exhibit the romanticism of the time, there was already emerging in portraiture and landscape something which gave an indication of the future direction of Russian art. As in Pushkin's poetry, in these paintings, many of which glow with the rich colors the Russians loved, there is an uncompromising psychological realism which is essentially Russian, rendered in a superbly executed classical form.

Because of these two strong trends in the first half of the 19th century—one cosmopolitan and the other an embryonic interest in Russian themes—those Russian painters who traveled in the West, exhibited in the salons of Europe and competed for the same prizes as their European colleagues gained great fame in the West. Others, who chose to stay in Russia, were unknown in Europe and in great measure still remain so today.

The first Russian painter to enjoy an international reputation was Karl Briullov, the son of a Huguenot artist in ornamental woodcarving who had emigrated to Russia and Russified his name. Briullov, who was an exact contemporary of Pushkin, entered the Academy of Art in St. Petersburg when he was ten years old and in 1822, at the age of twenty-three, received a fellowship to study in Italy from the Society for the Encouragement of Artists. He lived in Rome and Naples and from 1830 through 1833 painted a huge canvas, *The Last Days of Pompeii*, which received worldwide acclaim. This painting, inspired by the enormous interest in the excavation of Pompeii, was hailed as a masterpiece in Italy and Briullov became instantly famous. He was made a member of the Academies of Bologna, Milan, Parma and Florence, and received an Imperial Medal from Nicholas I and the Grand Prix at the Paris Salon in 1834. The most celebrated artists and foreign visitors flocked to his studio in Rome, including that hero of the romantics, Sir Walter Scott, who, Briullov wrote home with joy, sat in front of his painting for an entire morning and pronounced it an epic.

When Briullov returned to St. Petersburg, where he lived from 1836 to 1849, he was received as the darling of society and he became a professor at the Academy, where he had a great influence on the following generation of painters. He was enormously productive. As friend and portraitist of literary and artistic celebrities, Briullov painted Gogol, Lermontov and Glinka, as well as many of the notable aristocrats of the day, among them Princess Saltykova, the daughter of the president of the Academy. This portrait, which ranks among his finest works, perfectly captures the atmosphere of the time. The gleaming silk and delicate lace of the Princess' dress are splendidly rendered. The portrait is romantic in its touches of exoticism—the soft leopard skin rug at her feet, her peacock feather fan and the profusion of tropical plants—but also exhibits a very Pushkinesque realism in the direct gaze of the subject who looks out at the world with a thoughtful and searching expression.

The two other most famous portraitists of Pushkin's day also exhibited in their lives and their work the emerging trends of the time. One, Orest Kiprensky, traveled extensively in Europe; the other, Vasily Tropinin, never left Russia. Both were sons of serfs. Tropinin was sent to St. Petersburg by his master to learn pastry making. Secretly, he attended the free drawing classes at the Academy as an auditor. In 1823 he was given his freedom and went on to make his artistic career, eventually becoming an Academician in Moscow.

The handsome Kiprensky was the son of a serf and the master of the estate. His genius was recognized when he was still a child and he was sent to the Academy in Petersburg where, in 1805, he won the Gold Medal and a traveling scholarship. He spent much time in Italy, where he met the great French painter Ingres, and his work was so respected that he was the first Russian artist commissioned to do his self-portrait by the Uffizi Gallery in Florence. In 1830, Kiprensky was named a professor at the St. Petersburg Academy. He became the portraitist of the aristocracy and painted many of the great men of his time.

In his work Kiprensky caught the romantic yearning for exploits which marked his epoch. There is profound integrity and feeling in his works, which are marked by the artist's sensitive understanding of the individuality of his subjects. Tropinin, although he also painted portraits of the great figures of his day, innovatively began to paint portraits of simpler people—a peasant boy, a washerwoman, a lace maker.

Pushkin was painted by both Tropinin and Kiprensky; he died on the day before he was to sit for Briullov. In Kiprensky's painting, done in 1827, when Pushkin was twenty-eight years old, the painter caught all of the warmth and impetuous charm of the poet: his head is slightly turned, there is fire in his eye, a plaid scarf is casually draped, in the romantic manner, over his shoulder.

What is most striking about this art of the first half of the 19th century is the diversity of ideas and styles. Russian painters were already beginning to think of their new art as a strong weapon in the struggle for social reform that was starting to grip society. In this artistic idea, which had nothing to do with Europe, the Russians drew directly from their own spiritual experience and their ancient ideal that the purpose of art was to serve God and uplift humanity.

Alexander Ivanov, a close friend of Gogol, although he lived in Italy most of his life, was a passionate believer in this very Russian conception of art. Excited by Briullov's *Pompeii*, Ivanov spent twenty-five years of his life working on an immense canvas, *The Appearance of the Messiah*, for which he made three hundred magnificent sketches. He was totally consumed by this painting, which he believed could bring the message of the Gospels directly to the people and regenerate mankind by the power of art. A fanatical believer in Russia, in 1847 he wrote a credo which concluded that the Slavic people would bring about a Golden Age when mankind would live in perfect peace, wars would cease, and eternal peace would be established.

Alexei Venetsianov, who spent most of his life away from St. Petersburg, set himself to record systematically for the first time the quiet and unchanging life of the peasants on the large country estates in central Russia. Venetsianov, the son of a merchant of modest means, studied painting on his own. In 1802 he went into government service as a draftsman and surveyor and also began to paint. He placed an advertisement in a newspaper offering his services and took private lessons from Vladimir Borovikovsky, who had painted Catherine in her old age. From him, Venetsianov learned the very Russian traits of simplicity and directness.

Although Venetsianov had not graduated from the Academy, he was nevertheless accorded the title of Academician for portrait painting. In 1815 he bought a small country estate in Tver province east of Moscow and retired there to devote himself to painting. He encouraged young peasants and local people to paint and founded a school that flourished during Pushkin's time in the 1820's and 1830's. In his school, which enrolled seventy students, seven of them serfs, he encouraged greater freedom of expression in painting. His aim, he explained to his students, was "to depict nothing in any way different from how it appears in nature, and to obey it alone."

Venetsianov painted the peasants with simplicity and tenderness, paralleling Pushkin's lyric evocation of the countryside. Like Chardin and Le Nain, he captured the dignity of peasant life and the individuality of his subjects. His most talented pupil, Grigory Soroka, was a serf, the son of a gardener, in whose paintings one can breathe the fresh air and the peace of the spacious countryside.

In their dedicated searching for new paths, all the artists of Pushkin's remarkable decades led Russian art in new directions and left behind them a rich pictorial legacy of a great moment in their country's artistic history.

• • •

Because of the grace of his expression, which combines passionate feeling with exquisite form, Pushkin has very often been compared to Mozart. His verses are so full of music and movement that from the beginning of his career they inspired musicians and choreographers; by the time he was twenty-one, his poem *Ruslan and Ludmilla* had already been made into a ballet in Moscow.

Indeed, it is hard to imagine Russian music and ballet without Pushkin.

He left such a rich legacy of poetic material—*Eugene Onegin, The Golden Cockerel, Tsar Saltan, Boris Godunov, The Queen of Spades, The Fountains of Bakhchisarai,* to name only a few—that throughout the 19th century Russian composers including Glinka, Mussorgsky, Tchaikovsky, Rimsky-Korsakov and Rachmaninov continually drew on his plots for librettos for ballets, music and opera. Pushkin not only witnessed the beginning of a national style of music with the work of his friend Mikhail Glinka, but also lived during a time when the Russian ballet drew ahead of any in Europe to become the finest in the world.

By Pushkin's day, ballet, generously supported by the tsars, had reached a position of great artistic importance. In 1766, Catherine the Great had consolidated the new interest in the performing arts which had blossomed under Elizabeth by creating an Imperial System of Theaters. She placed under a committee and a director the responsibility for all opera, drama, ballet and theater, as well as their schools. At first the system was designed primarily to assure a high level of performances for the court, but even in Catherine's original decree Russian actors and dancers were also expected to "give public performances for money in city theaters."

This Imperial theatrical system was augmented by a uniquely Russian phenomenon, the private serf theater, which reached its height during Catherine's time in the last quarter of the 18th century. In those days, extremely wealthy noblemen often kept their own acting troupes, orchestras and ballet companies. These troupes sometimes reached a high degree of professionalism and put on elaborate productions. Serf performers were often highly trained; taking classes each day under the direction of foreign music teachers and dancing masters who were brought to Russia for the purpose, they were also sometimes sent to Moscow and St. Petersburg for further training.

The most famous and accomplished of these serf theater companies was that of Count Nikolai Sheremetev, who in 1789, at his wooden palace at Ostankino outside Moscow, kept a theater staffed by 166 serfs, 26 of whom were dancers. All his actors bore the names of precious stones, such as "The Ruby" or "The Emerald." Sheremetev, a learned man who had studied at Leyden, read Voltaire, and possessed the finest collection of art books in Russia, fell in love and married one of his talented serf actresses, Praskovya Kovalyova, who was known as "Zhemchuzhina," or "The Pearl."

By the first years of the 19th century, bankrupt landowners could no longer afford such luxury, and the serf theaters were gradually disbanded. In 1806 the management of the Imperial Theaters in Moscow acquired the last large group of serf dancers and musicians, and before the end of the first quarter of the 19th century, the private serf ballet was no more. Ballet and opera became available to anyone who could afford a ticket. Prices were cheap and there was always a "paradise" where people of the humblest means could sit on wooden benches and see good theater.

By the late 1820's, in Pushkin's day, an enthusiastic public was flocking to performances. The best singers and dancers of Europe came to the well-appointed St. Petersburg theaters to perform with Russian companies. The largest of these theaters, the Bolshoi Kamenny Theater* (The Great Stone Theater), built in 1783 for opera and ballet, seated two thousand. (Its illumination being provided by candles, this theater burned several times. It was often rebuilt and finally replaced entirely.) There were also two other theaters where ballet was performed—the Maly (Small) Theater, like the Kamenny, open to the public, and the Hermitage Theater, exclusively for members of the court.

Count Sheremetev was instrumental in bringing to Russia Charles Didelot, a French dancer and ballet master who had worked in Paris, Bordeaux and London and at the Swedish court. Didelot had contracted to dance as well as to be ballet master of the theater. His arrival proved to be a decisive factor in the course of Russian ballet. When he first came to St. Petersburg in 1801, he found a company of 114 dancers with its own repertory, a school, and a flourishing ballet culture. The three well-equipped theaters, all subsidized by the state, had workshops capable of producing wardrobes and scenic decorations far superior to those in England and France. Didelot immediately set to work molding the company according to his ideas of excellence.

In 1809 Alexander I ordered a reorganization of the ballet school. Pupils were to be systematically taught academic subjects as well as music and the theatrical arts. There were to be regular examinations of the pupils by doctors and every six months a performance attended by other artists, teachers, students and parents. Emphasis was to be placed on developing native talent.

During his first years in Russia, Didelot was forced to share the limelight with a Russian ballet master, Valberkh, and although Didelot was an inventive and gifted choreographer and created many ballets for the court and the theater,

* Not to be confused with the Bolshoi Theater in Moscow, which was rebuilt in its present form in 1856 by the grandfather of the painter Alexander Benois, Alberto Cavos.

he was also proud and choleric and made enemies as well as admirers. In 1811 a dispute arose over the renewal of his contract. In a temper Didelot left Russia and was only persuaded to return in 1816. This time he was given a position of undisputed authority and remained in Russia until his death in 1837.

It had always been Didelot's aim to create a troupe that could rival Paris, where he felt he had never been properly appreciated. In the twenty-eight years that he was director of the ballet in Russia, he more than achieved his goal, molding the school and company into the best in Europe. Under him, ballet took a prominent place in Russian art which it never lost.

Didelot imposed an iron discipline on his dancers. A perfectionist, short-tempered and despotic, he would sometimes in his anger pull the ears or hair of his dancers if he was displeased with a performance. He habitually carried a stick or riding crop to class, which he applied liberally. This stern regimen developed outstanding dancers. Didelot doubled the size of the corps and by 1828 had a troupe of 186 dancers. He was among the first to introduce dancing on point.

Living in an era of great poets, it was perhaps natural that Didelot insisted that dancing should be "poetry in action," that not only systematic training but dramatic spirit was essential. The Russians began to put great emphasis on character and emotion in their dancing. What Pushkin called "the Russian Terpsichore's soul-inspired flight" became the ideal of the Russian ballet, one which still remains today.

From the beginning Didelot was warmly accepted as one of their own by all the writers and artists of St. Petersburg. He was the first to begin staging ballets with dramatic content, and to find subjects he read history. Being an excellent artist, he also made beautiful drawings of his ideas. It was suggested to him that he borrow poetical subjects for ballets from Pushkin's poetry. In 1824, when Pushkin had been dispatched to Kishinev, Didelot used Pushkin's poem *The Prisoner of the Caucasus* as a theme for a ballet only four and a half months after the poem was published. The same year he did a new staging of *Ruslan and Ludmilla* for the St. Petersburg Bolshoi Theater Ballet. Didelot's greatest years coincided with Pushkin's own lifetime, and Pushkin, who had for a short time studied classical technique with one of Didelot's dancers, was a great admirer of his work, writing that he found Didelot's ballets "full of lively imagination and extraordinary charm."

Didelot was a master of special effects and the stage of the Bolshoi Theater in St. Petersburg was so well equipped that he could realize the most amazing

227

technical feats, especially aerial flights at which he was a wizard. (Under Didelot, the "flight" of which Pushkin spoke was interpreted both literally and figuratively; ballerinas actually flew about the stage on wires.) There was no machinery which the theater could not supply. Mountains fell, ships sank and cupids flew. In one glorious scene the chariot of Venus was propelled into the air by fifty live doves attached to specially constructed little harnesses. His ballets were full of exotics caliphs, feudal lords, nymphs and gods; his productions sometimes so moving that spectators would burst into tears. So enchanting were Didelot's ballets that Pushkin found no way to better describe the epitome of Onegin's world-weariness than by saying that "even Didelot" could no longer amuse him.

Ballet was so popular that full-length performances were given several times a week. Adding to the marvelous spectacles on stage were the colorful and elegant characteristics of theater-going in St. Petersburg, which Pushkin described with his customary grace and wit.

In the square before the theater, in six large specially constructed stone pavilions, bonfires burned continually to warm the crowd of waiting coachmen. In the lobby, dignified bearded retired military men in uniform took coats and furs. The theater was all crimson velvet and gold, with a profusion of rococo ornamentation, garlands and curlicues. On the huge curtain were scenes of Peterhof, with its green painted roofs, its fountains, arcades and statues. Boxes were lined with crimson velvet and decorated with white medallions framed in gold on a rose background. Dominating everything, facing the stage, two stories high, was the immense Imperial Box framed by heavy velvet and gold-fringed curtains and surmounted by an enormous gilded double eagle. The first row of boxes around the Imperial loge bore the name of "beautiful floor" and, although there was no formal arrangement, these boxes were by custom reserved for the highest aristocrats and dignitaries of the court.

As a mark of respect for the performers, by custom everyone always dressed for the theater, adding great brilliance to the scene—men in white gloves, dinner clothes and glittering uniforms; women beautifully coiffed and jeweled. Dandies wandered up and down the aisles carefully scrutinizing the *beau monde*, making sure they were seen. Pushkin often joined the groups of young officers and state servants who were a permanent fixture at the ballet, always seating themselves in the first rows of the left side of the theater. Styling themselves "the left flank," these young men passionately applauded their favorite ballerinas, covered them with flowers and clamored for curtain calls. In *Eugene Onegin*, Pushkin immortalized these scenes and the dancing of one of the greatest ballerinas of the day, Avdotia Istomina, who made her debut in 1816 and still is considered one of the finest ballerinas Russia ever produced:

The house is packed out; scintillating
the boxes; boiling pit and stalls.
The gallery claps—it's bored with waiting—
and up the rustling curtain crawls.
Then with half-ethereal splendor,
bound where magic bow will send her,
Istomina, thronged all around
by Naids, one foot on the ground,
twirls the other slowly as she pleases,
then suddenly she's off and there
she's up and flying through the air
like fluff before Aeolian breezes;
she'll spin this way and that, and beat
against each other swift, small feet.

Istomina, a dazzling, dark-eyed creature whose "pure Russian beauty" set many hearts aflame (including Pushkin's, who pursued her briefly), provoked the greatest theatrical scandal of the time when two successive duels, one fatal, were fought over her.

During his long career in Russia, Didelot invited many foreign ballerinas to dance with his company. From these foreign dancers, whom the Russians carefully studied, they absorbed the best of European virtuoso techniques, which they incorporated into their own style. In 1837 the supreme Italian ballerina Maria Taglioni made a triumphal debut in Petersburg, dancing *La Sylphide*. She was idolized by the press and the public. There were Taglioni caramels and cakes, coiffures à la Taglioni. Nicholas I was a great ballet enthusiast, often visiting backstage and on several occasions providing extra funds for productions when they were needed. In 1836 the Tsar even set himself to choreographing the military drills for the harem girls for a ballet based on Titus' *Uprising in the Seraglio*. Nicholas was so enchanted with Taglioni that he left his accustomed seat to sit in the first rows of the theater so he could see her better. He had a statue of her placed in the Imperial Box and showered her with gifts, including an ermine cape. Gogol extolled her as "the symbol, the synonym of air!" and she returned to Russia every year for five seasons, dancing over two hundred performances.

The first Russian performance of *Giselle* was in 1842 and its author, the

French poet Théophile Gautier, visiting St. Petersburg in 1858, wrote that such was the enthusiasm for dance that ballet subscriptions were cheaper than opera, the ballets four or five acts long and the public so discriminating that "the fire of their lorgnettes is redoubtable."

• • •

One of Didelot's innovations was to use Russian folk dancing and exotic local color in his ballets, and for this there had to be new music. One of Didelot's and Pushkin's admirers was a young musician named Mikhail Glinka, who shared the new interest in Russian themes. Glinka, who was five years younger than Pushkin, was the son of a wealthy landowner of Novospasskoe in Smolensk province. As a child he had developed a passionate love for music, learning piano from his governess and violin from a member of his uncle's serf orchestra. At school in Petersburg, Glinka continued his musical studies and was such a gifted linguist that he mastered Latin, English, French and German and later both Italian and Spanish. Glinka's father had secured him a position in the Ministry of Communications and, from 1824 to 1828, much as Pushkin had done, he lived the rollicking life of an elegant young man about town and developed his good tenor voice with an Italian singing master. Like Pushkin, Glinka was an ardent lover of the ballet and he studied dance for two years, becoming so proficient that he was able to perform entrechats and other difficult steps. He also shared his friend Pushkin's love for Rossini's operas—and for women. Glinka was such a charmer that all of his life, not only when he was young, but even at forty-five, the youngest and most beautiful girls would surrender themselves happily to him. (Perhaps part of his secret is revealed in his memoirs, where Glinka writes that he was "very romantic" and loved to "weep tears of sweet emotion.")

In 1830 Glinka went off to Europe to study music and stayed away for four years. He spent three years in Italy where he met Donizetti and Bellini and watched them conduct their operas. He came to the conclusion that beautiful as it was, their music was better suited to sunny climes because "we who live in northern countries feel differently; impressions either leave us cold or penetrate to the depths of our soul. With us, it is always a matter of great joy or bitter sorrow." He continued on to Berlin, where he studied counterpoint, fugue and harmony with the finest German teacher of the day. But, he wrote, as he composed, "homesickness gradually led me to write in Russian."

Very much in the spirit of his times, Glinka, like the Russian painters whom he knew in Italy, felt that imitation of Europe was not enough. He began

230

to dream of creating a national work in a Russian spirit, writing to a friend in St. Petersburg, "I want my countrymen to feel the spirit of their homeland." When he came home, Pushkin's close friend, the poet Vasily Zhukovsky, suggested to him that he write an opera based on the Russian story of Ivan Susanin and the first Romanov tsar, Michael. It was the first opera with a purely Russian national theme and contained suites of lively Polish and Russian dances. Nicholas I attended many of the rehearsals, and Glinka dedicated his opera to the Emperor, who gave it its name. *A Life for the Tsar* had its gala premiere at the Bolshoi Theater in St. Petersburg on December 9, 1836. Glinka was called to the Imperial Box, and a few days later in appreciation for his work the Emperor sent him a ring worth four thousand rubles.

After this success Glinka was named director of the Court Chapel with a handsome salary and was hailed as the first composer of the land. In a fervor of romantic passion, in 1835, like Pushkin he made the mistake of marrying a beautiful, foolish seventeen-year-old girl who knew nothing about music; after four years of turbulent married life, they separated. Glinka retreated to the country where he finished his second opera, *Ruslan and Ludmilla*, based on Pushkin's early narrative poem. Although it was a finer work than his first, full of melodic, romantic Russian sound, its reception was cool and the opera was only fully appreciated after Glinka's death. In 1845 Glinka resigned his commission in the chapel and once again began traveling all over Europe studying and writing music.

At the age of forty-one, he went to Spain and was so enchanted by the country that he took an apartment in Madrid and spent much of his time writing down melodies sung and played to him by singers and guitarists. A muleteer gave him many of the airs he later used in his *Night in Madrid*. He spent three months in Granada, listening to the gypsies, and even tried to learn Spanish dances himself but found the castanets too difficult. Typically he fell in love with a fiery gypsy girl named Dolores, whom he spirited away to live with him for a time in Madrid.

For several years Glinka traveled between Russia and Europe. He lived in Paris and Berlin, sojourned in Warsaw, returning finally to Petersburg in 1854, leaving a string of broken hearts behind him in several countries. In 1855 Glinka composed a "Festival Polonaise" for the coronation ball of Alexander II, and in 1857, on yet another trip to Berlin, he died suddenly after a chill and was brought home to be buried in Petersburg.

Glinka would no doubt have written more music had he led a slightly more disciplined life, but as it was, he left behind two operas, five orchestral works, chorales, chamber and piano music and many songs. His contribution was vital to the later development of Russian music, for after him Russian dancing and the strains of national melodies became a beloved part of both the opera and ballet. Because Glinka was the first to seek inspiration for his work in the national heritage, he is still revered as the father of Russian music, and his work was much admired and studied by all the later Russian composers of the 19th century.

16 · DEATH OF THE POET

THE RUSSIAN LOVE for dance and music, which brought so many to the ballet, was echoed in society. In Pushkin's day, the connection between "ballet" and "ball" was more than a similarity of words. Members of the upper classes were all carefully instructed in complicated dance steps. As a boy at the *lycée*, Pushkin was taught the gavotte, the minuet and other stately dances, for dance was one of the social skills that was needed to climb the rungs of the Imperial bureaucracy. In his poetry, Pushkin speaks of dance with an almost professional knowledge: *Eugene Onegin* is full of flashing feet and thundering heels. Spectators of Pushkin's era came to the ballet with a serious appreciation of the demands of technique, for the social dancing of the day required the knowledge of *battements*, five positions and graceful arm movements. All through the 19th century, people in Moscow and St. Petersburg danced—not only the lovely, elegant mazurka, but the polonaise, the quadrille, the waltz, the English waltz and the galop. Ladies, who in transit from their homes were enveloped in fur, danced through the northern night in light gossamer dresses under pale lamps that glimmered like moonshine. In Pushkin's day they wore soft little beribboned and flat-heeled slippers, dresses with billowing sleeves, and their hair piled up and held tightly in back, cascading with curls. Couples dipped and swayed under the flickering lights of a multitude of candles, among orange trees and flowers. Under whirling skirts, white silk stockings and lace petticoats occasionally flashed excitingly.

Spurs jangled musically and diamond epaulettes and stars were as plentiful as mushrooms after a rain.

Pushkin's young wife Natalya adored all these balls. Pushkin, wanting to make her happy, escorted his dazzling wife to one after another. He, who had once loved nothing more than dancing, and had written that he "worshipped balls," now stood on the sidelines, bored and preoccupied. Natalya, it seemed, was interested in her husband's fame only to the extent that it made possible her social success. It was said of her that she had "a soul made of lace" and one of Pushkin's friends wrote that she "preferred the glitter of the ballroom to all the poetry in the world."

And there was no lack of handsome partners, for even in peacetime in the early and mid-19th century, St. Petersburg was filled with officers and soldiers. Some 60,000 men were garrisoned in the city, including among them nine elite infantry guards regiments and seven crack cavalry regiments. One out of every ten inhabitants was a soldier; whole blocks of the city were apportioned off as their headquarters and named after their regiments. There were 100,000 more men than women in St. Petersburg; ladies of quality never set foot out of doors unaccompanied. It was said that no other city in Europe had so many handsome men as St. Petersburg. This was due partly to the skill of the tailors, who by artful stuffing contrived to make something elegant out of any man, but also it was due to the effect of so many uniforms. If one in addition counted those who wore civil and private uniforms, the police and the cadets, half of the city went about be-starred and belaced. No city, not even London, had tailors so expert at making uniforms and liveries.

Hulans, Cuirassiers, Chevaliers Gardes, Hussars and Cossacks strode or rode the streets in full regalia, for it was prohibited for any soldier, private or officer, to go out without epaulettes and arms, and so they appeared, perfectly turned out, buttoned and plumed in their gleaming equipments.

Infantry officers wore green, with high stiff feathers in their caps. Their shiny mustaches, pinched and blackened and contrasting sharply with their beards, which were whitened, gave them a fierce appearance. The fiery Cherkes horsemen, looking like the Saracens of old with their closely fitting burnished helmets, their silver cuirasses and shirts of linked mail, rode with their sharp daggers ready and firearms loaded. Cossacks galloped through the streets with their 8-foot-long lances, pistols and sabers. There were the "blue" Cossacks, who wore a dark-blue tunic, large full trousers with a bright-red stripe down the sides,

boots, capes and high sheepskin hats from which hung a small red bag ornamented with a chain of white worsted lace and tassels; and "red" Cossacks,
clothed all in red with even higher caps made of red velvet. The Garde à Cheval
and the Chevaliers Gardes were in white, with red capes and sleeves, high stiff
jackboots and silver helmets surmounted with a shining double eagle. Their
uniforms gave them such a thin wasp-waisted look that one feared they might
fall over. The Hulans wore blue with red returns and gold, and the Hussars
draped their jackets embroidered in gold and trimmed with fur jauntily over one
shoulder.

Both Alexander I and Nicholas I loved nothing more than reviewing their
troops. On the Field of Mars or in the Admiralty Place in front of the Winter
Palace, there were constant reviews and parades, great spectacles for the whole
city, which came in crowds to watch. Accompanied by martial music and the
stirring ruffles of drums and trumpets, thousands of men were lined up in immaculate rows, pennants fluttering and lances shining in the sun. Every day, even
in winter, the Emperor personally reviewed his troops in front of the palace, some
thousand men and a number of generals and senior officers. Nicholas I, tall and
of impressive bearing, considered one of the handsomest and most martial monarchs of Europe, would ride by with his son and officers. The soldiers crisply
presented arms and the spectators uncovered their heads. "Good day, my lads!"
cried the Emperor. "We thank Your Majesty" was the simultaneous response
which burst like thunder from a thousand throats.

In those times, among those legions of military men, lived famous soldier-poets
and poet-soldiers, renowned for their daring feats in battle and their equally
prodigious capacity for carousing. One such soldier, the prototype of the dashing
liberty-loving officers of Alexander's time, was Denis Davydov, the scion of a
noble military family from Moscow whom Tolstoy later used as his model for
Vaska Denisov in *War and Peace*. Orest Kiprensky painted Davydov in 1809 in a
nonchalant pose, the very picture of the chivalrous Hussar officer in his red jacket
and skin-tight white elkskin pants. As a young colonel, Davydov was a hero of
the war of 1812, commanding a band of 130 Hussars and Cossacks who operated
behind the French lines so effectively and fiercely that Napoleon twice asked
General Kutuzov to call them off.

Davydov, who was one of the most famous and popular soldiers of his day,
was also a talented writer. He wrote a lyric journal of military life in war and

peace, about those brave swordsmen of romantic aspirations and high ideals who hated moralizing and hypocrisy. His memoirs of General Suvorov and other military leaders and his *Journal of the Partisans* earned him the reputation of being one of the great prose writers of his day. The foremost critic of the time, Belinsky, described him as "a pure Russian soul, broad, mighty, bold and gay." Davydov was also a poet, the bard of the soldier's life, singing the joys of wine and battle. His patriotic verses and poems to love and the merrymaking Hussar life circulated briskly from hand to hand. Pushkin greatly admired the soldier, eighteen years older than he, and called him "Father, commander, bard and hero!" Davydov's originality and his direct, down-to-earth style of writing impressed and influenced Pushkin greatly.

Another Hussar officer was Mikhail Lermontov, who, after Pushkin, is Russia's most beloved and quoted poet. Fifteen years younger than Pushkin, Lermontov also had a romantic ancestry. He was descended from a Scottish mercenary in the Polish service who had been taken prisoner by the Russians in 1613. This Scottish forebear traced his ancestry to one Learmont who fought with Malcolm against Macbeth and, even further, to a 13th-century Scottish bard who, legend said, had received his gift of poetry from the Fairy Queen herself. Lermontov was a spoiled, precocious boy, raised by a rich grandmother. Although he was not handsome, he had a talent for breaking hearts and first fell in love at eleven. Between the ages of fourteen and seventeen, he wrote three hundred lyrics, fifteen long narrative poems, three dramas, and one prose tale.

Having graduated from military school, Lermontov plunged headlong into the giddy existence of the Hussar, an existence he once described as "poetry drowned in champagne." Hot-tempered, hiding a sensitive soul behind a facade of arrogance and cynicism, he was periodically banished from the capital for fighting duels, although Nicholas I, with whom he often had stormy relations, nevertheless once said of him "his verses are wonderful and truthful. Because of them you can forgive all his madness." He fought in the Crimea and the Caucasus, winning many citations for bravery and daring.

Lermontov loved the wild scenery of the Caucasus, which he described in his poetry with great lyric power. He was also a talented artist who made many sensitive drawings and watercolors.

In his lyrical verses, many of which were later set to music by his contemporary Glinka and many other later Russian composers including Rimsky-Korsakov, Mussorgsky and Tchaikovsky, he wrote of the futility of human sufferings and the aimlessness of life. His most famous work and only novel, *A Hero of Our Times,* is a chronicle of the life of a Byronesque and worldly-wise officer serving in the Caucasus, whose devastated heart is as cold as an extinct volcano. Although it is short, in this ironic, tragic and visionary novel Lermontov raised Russian prose to such a refined level that many Russian critics consider it the greatest novel ever written in Russian, greater even than *War and Peace,* and continue to assign to it the highest importance.

These dashing soldiers, described so often in Russian literature as ready to duel at any pretext, or to fight battles for days, could, with hardly a pause to change, be ready to dance away the nights. And how they danced! Skill in dancing was obligatory for all gentlemen and officers. Tolstoy in *War and Peace* wrote a vivid description of their prowess. Natasha Rostova has decided to ask the famous Hussar Vaska Denisov, "celebrated even in Poland for his masterful dancing of the mazurka," to dance with her. At first he demurs, saying that he is getting old, but then abruptly changes his mind:

"The little enchantress can do what she likes with me!" said Denisov, and he unhooked his saber. He came out from behind the chairs, clasped his partner's hand firmly, threw back his head and put one foot forward, waiting for the beat. . . . At the right beat of the music, he glanced sideways with a triumphant and amused air at his partner, suddenly stomped with one foot, bounded from the floor like a ball and spun round the room, whirling his partner with him. Noiselessly he flew half across the floor on one foot, and apparently not seeing the chairs in front of him, was dashing straight at them when suddenly, clinking his spurs and spreading his legs, he stopped short on his heels, stood so for a second, with a clanking of spurs stamped both feet, twisted rapidly round and striking his left heel against his right flew round in a circle again. . . . First he spun her around, holding her now with his right hand, now with his left, then falling on one knee, he twirled her round him, and again, jumping up, dashed so impetuously forward, that it seemed as if he intended to race through the whole suite of rooms without drawing breath. Then he stopped suddenly again and executed some new and unexpected steps. When, at last, after dextrously spinning his partner round in front of her chair, he drew up with a click of his spurs and bowed to her.

To the endless stream of balls, wrote Pushkin:

. . . hussars on leave
Hurry to appear, to thunder,
To flash, to captivate, and flee.

Cascading compliments and promises of love, they were ready to commit any foolishness—up to and including death—for the favor of a lady.

All winter long with never a pause the balls continued, and yet, wrote a visiting Irish lady, "all so lively you dance until you drop." In the Moscow season of 1805, another visiting foreigner wrote, "There is one ball after another and I can't understand how it is that they do not all drop from exhaustion. If this madness goes on all winter, every single one of them will expire and the next season will have to open with a mass funeral for all the dancers." In the Petersburg season of 1834, a gentleman wrote, "What a carnival as Lent drew near . . . a veritable frenzy with balls, masquerades and suppers. Sometimes there are two balls a day. . . ." And in April 1834 Pushkin himself wrote, "Tomorrow is another ball. . . . It has thrown everyone into a turmoil and made conversation all over the town. There are to be 1,800 guests, and on the basis of one carriage per minute, the arrival of the guests is calculated to last ten hours; as the carriages are going to come up by threes, which will require only one third as long."

Pushkin's wife loved to be the center of attention. Natalya was the reigning beauty of society, and the Tsar himself, though a devoted family man, was not impervious to her charms. On occasion Nicholas even took to parading under her window on horseback and making his horse rear. So that the couple could more easily be included in court functions, he gave Pushkin a court appointment. Pushkin wore a court uniform, stood on the sidelines and fumed, while the imperious gaze of the martial Tsar turned benign, as he decorously flirted and danced with Natalya.

Although Pushkin had made many men jealous because of his charming way with women, he was now enraged by the attentions paid to his wife. As he did not suffer fools gladly and had a sharp and stinging wit, he made many enemies in high places. His work suffered. The social whirl left him no peace or leisure. In 1833 he was able to get a four-month leave of absence from the ministry and he withdrew to Boldino, a small estate of his near Nizhny Novgorod. In the space of a few months, working furiously, he wrote *The Bronze Horseman, The Queen of Spades* and *The Pugachev Rebellion* as well as two folk tales.

He was constantly worried about money. His gambling debts were always pressing. Natalya's mindless frivolity, her constant need for dresses and feathers also sorely strained his resources. He had long ago mortgaged his small estates and, other than his small court salary, he had no income but from his writing. Pushkin invented the profession of literature in Russia. Not only was he the first to defend his rights as a writer, but the first to pretend to live by his pen. He worried when his books did not sell well. He pawned his valuables; he owed money everywhere, even to his own valet. He tried to resign from his court appointment and begged the Tsar to release him so that he could go off and concentrate only on his writing. The Tsar refused, wanting to keep him and the lovely Natalya under his eye. Pushkin began a magazine in 1835, *The Contemporary*, modeled after English literary journals, which he desperately hoped would save his precarious financial situation. In 1836, after the birth of his fourth child, he wrote, "Money, Money, I need it so desperately, I would go on screaming for it with a knife at my throat." Despite all this pressure, in 1836, the year that was to be his last, isolated and proud, Pushkin wrote these ringing lines that asserted the independence of spirit he never lost:

To be dependent on a monarch or a multitude
To me, one is not better than the other. I want to live
My way, serve no one but myself and please no other,
Not bend my mind, my honor, or my knee
To any power or livery. I want to go
Here and there, wherever my fancy leads,
To admire the divine beauty of this world,
Tremble with ecstasy, happiness and love
For the creations of art, for genius . . .

That same year he also finished his magnificent prose tale *The Captain's Daughter*, which Tolstoy considered his masterpiece and about which Gogol wrote, "In comparison with *The Captain's Daughter*, all our short stories and novels are like watered porridge."

All her husband's problems did not seem to touch Natalya, and although in five years she had four children, nothing, not even pregnancy and motherhood, interrupted her social whirl for long. Soon she would again be coming home at four or five in the morning, lunching at eight in the evening, hurriedly dressing to rush off, with Pushkin in tow, to yet another festivity. And so it went, month after month.

It was in 1835 at one of those countless balls that Natalya first had met Baron Georges-Charles D'Anthès, a glamorous French émigré from Alsace. D'Anthès had come to Russia seeking adventure, secured an appointment in the

Horse Guards and was a protégé of the Dutch Ambassador. In his red and white uniform, he cut a dazzling figure in the salons. At twenty-four he was tall, blond, with an elegant mustache. Women buzzed around him. Superficial, insolently charming and a wonderful dancer, he was considered one of the most fashionable men in society and one of the handsomest men in the Guards.

As the year passed, the beautiful Natalya and the seductive D'Anthès found more and more occasions to meet. At one ball after another, they flirted and danced while Pushkin, wrote one of his friends, aflame with jealousy, "fixed wild animal eyes on them."

One morning Pushkin received an anonymous letter mocking him as a cuckold. Infuriated, on November 5, 1836, he challenged his rival to a duel. He was persuaded to withdraw his challenge only after D'Anthès surprisingly announced that he intended to marry Natalya's sister. The marriage took place on January 10, 1837, and yet only a few days later D'Anthès continued his pursuit of Natalya so warmly and openly that the whole town gossiped. Pushkin received another anonymous letter telling him that D'Anthès and Natalya had met alone. Enraged, he repeated his challenge, and this time would not be dissuaded.

They met on the dueling ground in the late afternoon of January 27, 1837, a bitterly cold, snowy day. D'Anthès fired first, shattering Pushkin's thigh near the pelvis. Pushkin managed to fire, but only slightly wounded his adversary. Mortally wounded, bleeding profusely, Pushkin was rushed home in a sleigh. When his wife saw him mounting the stairs, bloodstained and supported by his valet who had tears in his eyes, she screamed and fainted. As it was late and difficult to find his own doctors, he was treated first by the only one available, an obstetrician. When the Pushkin family physician, Dr. Spassky, finally arrived, Pushkin asked that a priest, the first one that could be found on the streets, be summoned. He confessed and took Communion. Spassky found his pulse weak. Pushkin said wearily, "Death is coming," and then added, "I am waiting for word from the Tsar to die in peace." Around midnight, when the surgeon, Dr. Arendt, came to examine him, Pushkin repeated these same words. After his examination, Dr. Arendt hastened to the palace and, finding that Tsar Nicholas was at the theater, left a message with his valet. The poet Vasily Zhukovsky, Pushkin's close friend, was also at the bedside and upon hearing his words also went himself to try to find the Emperor.

Hardly had Arendt returned when a messenger arrived from the Tsar, urgently asking that the doctor provide him with all details at once, and adding,

"I shall not sleep. I shall be waiting to hear from you." There was also a personal note written in pencil by the Tsar which he asked to be delivered immediately to Pushkin and then returned. The letter said, "If we are not destined to see each other again, here is my forgiveness and my last advice to you: die like a Christian. Do not worry about your wife and children. I shall care for them." Pushkin, according to his close friend Prince Vyazemsky, who was at the scene, "was extremely moved by these words."

Meanwhile, Zhukovsky had gone to the Winter Palace and found the Tsar waiting for news. He told Nicholas that Pushkin had taken Communion and that, as dueling was both against the law and considered a sin by the church, he was concerned about the fate of his second, Danzas. The Tsar, according to Zhukovsky, said, "I cannot change legal procedure, but I will do everything I can." He then congratulated Pushkin on his compliance with his Christian duty and repeated his promise to care for his wife and children. Wrote Zhukovsky, "I returned to Pushkin with His Majesty's answer. Having raised his hands heavenward impulsively, he said, 'How I am consoled! Tell His Majesty that I wish him a long reign, that I wish him luck with his son, that I wish him happiness with his Russia.' He said these words weakly, with difficulty, but distinctly."

Pushkin lingered for two days, suffering horribly. In moments of calm, he called his wife and comforted her. "Do not worry—you are innocent of my death. It has nothing to do with you." He sent word to D'Anthès that he pardoned him. D'Anthès, who was barely wounded, only laughed lightly and said, "Well, tell him that I forgive him, too."

To the grief-stricken friends who had kept constant vigil by his bedside, he said, "Farewell. Be happy." During the last hours before his death, he asked that Natalya spoon blackberries and syrup into his mouth, a last warm memory of the generous Russian countryside. A short time later, he sighed, "Life is over." At thirty-seven, he was dead. Collapsed over his body, Natalya screamed hysterically over and over, "Forgive me! Forgive me!"

When the news of his death was known in the city, a spontaneous phenomenon, which startled all the authorities, occurred. In the streets an unexpected movement began and grew. A contemporary wrote, "All Petersburg was astir. There was an extraordinary commotion. At the Singer's Bridge on the Moika near his home, no one could walk or ride. Crowds and carriages besieged the house from morn until dusk. Cabdrivers all over the city were told simply, To 'Pushkin,' and that was enough. It seemed that everyone, including those who could not read or write, considered it their duty to pay their last respects to the body of the poet." For three days, while the body remained in the house, a multitude of people—32,000 in a single day—filed in a continuous line around the casket; a wall of Pushkin's house had to be torn down to accommodate them. They were from all walks of life—students, soldiers, children, common people in sheepskin coats, coachmen, merchants. Two thousand copies of *Eugene Onegin* were bought up in three days and the bookseller Smirdin sold forty thousand rubles' worth of Pushkin's works in a week. Pushkin's death was a national calamity; even peasants spoke about it on the street. One old man stood quietly sobbing by his coffin. He was asked by Prince Vyazemsky, "You knew Pushkin personally, no doubt?" The old man, tears streaming down his face, answered simply, "No, but I am a Russian."

The Literary Supplement of the *Russian Invalid* printed a notice bordered in black which read: "The sun of our poetry has set. . . . Every Russian heart knows the meaning of this irremediable loss, every Russian heart is rent by it. . . . Our poet, our joy, the glory of our people!" "Russia without Pushkin," wrote Gogol, "how strange. . . . My life, my highest pleasure died with him. . . . Everything that is good in me, I owe to him." The direct, brave Davydov, now a general, grief-stricken and bewildered, wrote, "Is it possible that a French fop has killed our greatest poet?"

Lermontov reacted to Pushkin's death with all the fiery indignation of his passionate nature. He sprang to his pen and in the space of a single day wrote an emotional and angry elegy, "The Poet's Death." In it he attacked the Tsar and the *beau monde* for having caused Pushkin's death and called for revenge against the foreigner who had killed him. This poem instantly made his fame and brought down the wrath of Nicholas I, who had Lermontov placed under house arrest and then dispatched to a dragoon regiment in the Caucasus.

So heated were feelings that the government feared demonstrations. People wanted to kill D'Anthès. There were murmurs against "foreigners," even the foreign doctors who had attended Pushkin. D'Anthès was stripped of his rank and commissions and immediately deported from Russia.

Pushkin's body was sent by special convoy, galloping through the night, to Mikhailovskoe. Police were posted at every station and stood guard over the coffin while fresh horses were harnessed. And there, in the peace of Mikhailovskoe, where he had listened with such pleasure to the stories of his old nurse, and written so much that was incomparably beautiful, the turbulent, vibrant Pushkin was finally laid to rest, his ringing silvery laugh to be heard no more.

• • •

The "Iron Tsar" kept his final promise to Pushkin. In his own hand he decreed that the following measures be taken for Pushkin's family:

1. Pay all Pushkin's debts (these amounted to more than 120,000 rubles).
2. Clear the debt on his father's mortgaged estate.
3. A pension awarded to the widow and a pension to the daughters up to their marriage.
4. The sons to be made pages and 1,500 rubles upon completing their education.
5. A complete set of Pushkin's works to be published at the government's expense; profits to the widow and children.
6. An immediate grant of 10,000 rubles.

He further ordered that any works prejudicial to Pushkin's memory be destroyed, that letters to him from other persons be returned to their authors, and that Pushkin's own writings, together with those submitted to him for publication in *The Contemporary*, and similar papers be preserved after cataloging, and documents from the state archives returned to their rightful places.

Lermontov followed Pushkin to his death in 1841. At the age of twenty-seven in the wild Caucasus mountains he loved so much, he was killed in a duel with a fellow officer whom he had mercilessly gibed over a woman they were both courting. Eerily, in one of his most famous poems, "The Dream," written in 1839, he had foreseen his own death, writing:

By hot noon in a vale of Daghestan
Lifeless, a bullet in my breast, I lay;
Smoke rose from a deep wound, and my blood ran
Out of me, drop by drop, and ebbed away.

As for Gogol, after he left Russia in 1836, only a year before Pushkin's death, for twelve years he traveled restlessly all over Europe, returning only irregularly to Russia. *Dead Souls* was intended to be a trilogy, with a Hell, Purgatory and Paradise. Gogol continued writing in Vevey, Geneva, Paris and Rome the first part which he had read to Pushkin. In 1839 he came back to St. Petersburg and lived for a time in the Winter Palace in the apartments of his and Pushkin's friend, the poet Vasily Zhukovsky, who was the tutor of the heir to the throne. Despite his success, Gogol was always in debt and continually lived off his friends. This time the warmhearted Zhukovsky persuaded his pupil, the future Alexander II, to lend Gogol four thousand rubles from his personal allowance so that he could return to Italy. In 1842 the first part of *Dead Souls* was finally published with a cover designed by Gogol himself, but Gogol left Moscow before the reviews, to resume his travels in Europe. More and more he plunged into a strange and personal mysticism that led him to make a pilgrimage to Jerusalem. He struggled to write the second part of *Dead Souls*, trying unsuccessfully to introduce "positive types," and twice destroyed versions he had begun. He never saw himself as a social critic and could not fathom why people could not understand this. Gogol was not interested in abstract debates on social ideals and watched with amazement and dread the impression produced by his work which was so unlike his own conception. In his *Selected Passages from My Correspondence with Friends*, published in 1847, he defended the Tsar and serfdom and enraged the liberals who had idolized his satires. He spent his last years living in Odessa and Moscow. Fallen under the influence of a fanatical priest who convinced him that writing—and even his friend Pushkin—was an instrument of the devil, one night in February 1852 he burned the completed second part of *Dead Souls*. Afterward, consumed with his own strong religious fantasies, he refused to eat, took to bed and ten days later died at the age of forty-two.

Gogol lived his life in darkness. He remains one of the most merciless and devastating dissectors of the foibles of humanity. But Pushkin far surpassed him and indeed everyone else, because despite his painful knowledge of sorrow and the ignominy of man, he was always able to see light and to celebrate life in all its magnificence. Years before, in one of his poems, Pushkin had prophetically written:

As long as there is one poet here
My name will ring through Russia . . .
. . . For having taught my lyre to sing
Of noble hearts and freedom in a cruel age.

Pushkin gave the Russians their Russianness, fashioning for them eternally an image of themselves that embodied their deepest and most precious feelings. They responded to his gift by according him an adulation that no other country has ever lavished on a literary figure. Even today, their love of Pushkin survives intact, and there is almost no Russian who cannot recite some of his lines. These lilting lines have the effervescent beauty of the ballet which he loved. They are as shimmering as a butterfly's wings, graceful as a hand kiss. Pushkin brought the Russian language to such pure elegance and unaffected precision that it has proved impossible to transfer successfully the magic of his spare, evocative lines to any other tongue. It is not too much to say that it is worth learning Russian if only to read him, for there has yet to be published a complete edition of his works in English.

Thus, for foreigners, Pushkin has never represented his country the way that Dostoevsky, Tolstoy and Gogol do. Sad for the world. For, as Henri Troyat wrote in his biography of Pushkin, "To his compatriots, regardless of time, changing fashions and passing regimes, Pushkin's work remains the most masterful evocation of their cherished memories. In it they find the eternal image of their land, the simple line of the horizon, the long roads leading to the end of the earth, the flight of sleighs over moon-soaked snow, the trembling of the leaves through the lindens in provincial parks, the scent of tea and lilacs and the laughter of girls. In him, they find the authentic spirit of their nation, which is not disenchanted and morbid, as too many foreigners tend to believe after reading the great novelists, but prodigiously gay, naive, and healthy. . . . His love of life awakens a desire to live."

It was Pushkin, after all, who wrote:

Live radiant day! Perish darkness and night!

17 · THE BABYLON OF THE SNOWS

The Neva is clad in granite,
Bridges hang poised over her waters,
Her islands are covered with dark green gardens
And before the younger capital ancient Moscow
Has paled like a purple clad widow
Before a new Empress. . . .

I love you city of Peter's creation, I love your
Stern harmonious aspect. . . .

. . . the transparent twilights and moonless gleam
Of your pensive nights. . . .
Alexander Pushkin, The Bronze Horseman

My God, what a clatter, what a din, what lights! Four story facades rose up on both sides; clogs clumped and wheels creaked so noisily that their sound became a thunder reverberating off the walls; the houses grew larger and seemed to spring out of the ground at every step; bridges shook; carriages flew; cab drivers and postillions shouted; the snow squeaked under thousands of sledge runners gliding in every direction; pedestrians crowded and jostled each other at the foot of houses hung with lanterns, and their enormous magnified shadows danced along the walls and crept upward until their heads reached roofs and chimneys.
Nikolai Gogol, Christmas Eve

P

USHKIN AND GOGOL were the first to immortalize St. Petersburg in literature, the beginning of a long line of artists who were inspired and even obsessed by the spirit of the capital that Peter the Great had created in the northern marshes.

The young city of St. Petersburg—younger than New York, the contemporary of New Orleans—was a magical city that inspired myths, dreams and art as few other cities in the world. In the 19th century, when it was one of the most cosmopolitan and glamorous capitals of Europe, it was called the "Babylon of the Snows," the "Venice of the North," the "Northern Palmyra." When, from the decks of an approaching steamer, the French poet Théophile Gautier first viewed the long horizon of the city broken by its golden spires and towers, he was moved to write, "Nothing is more beautiful than this city of gold, on a horizon of silver, where the sky retains the paleness of dawn."

The grandiose buildings of the city which surprised the eye with their colors of yellow, turquoise, green, orange and red; the wide avenues and squares which seemed made for parades and reviews; the swift-flowing river, the misty canals, the rippling green islands and parks; all gave to the city a unique mystery and charm. But like every great city, St. Petersburg was far more than a collection of buildings; it was also a state of mind. Its way of life, which poetically adapted the tastes of both East and West to the northern latitudes, evoked for Europeans a special romance. The city was born from the collision of two cultures, and the tension arising from this collision became the persistent theme of a remarkable succession of artists. In this city, suspended between water and sky, illuminated by iridescent white nights in the summer and sunk in gloomy darkness in the winter, human relationships attained a strange intensity. It was a city of power, of fortune seekers, of officials, of the court. It was also a city of dreamers, of poets and artists.

Pushkin, Gogol, Dostoevsky and Tolstoy all assumed that their readers knew the vibrant, bustling life of St. Petersburg. Their characters played out their lives in its streets, markets and parks, their dreams of the heart at its balls and in its salons, their tragedies of the soul in its courtyards and streets. Dostoevsky called it "the most abstract and intentional city on earth"; the poet Blok, "a point of departure into infinity."

Like Venice, St. Petersburg is a water city, and its life was intimately bound up with the river. Peter had wanted to build the city on the Petrovsky Island, where the Peter and Paul Fortress now stands, but because of frequent floods it was decided to build the main part of the city on the mainland. During the 18th and 19th centuries St. Petersburg grew rapidly and spread over the many islands of the delta, and each of the islands had its own characteristics and life.*

The Great Neva, three-quarters of a mile wide and nearly three miles long, flows through the city and separates the mainland from the two largest islands, the Vasilievsky and the Petrovsky. Its branches wind among the numerous other islands of the delta; the river has six mouths to the sea. Like the Nile, the Neva provided everything for its inhabitants. All the water for the city came from the river; there was no other clear source in the marshy land. In the mid-19th century, the water of the Neva was one of the most pure and unmixed of river waters, as clear at its mouth as it was at its source. People returning there from a journey were always happy to have it once again to drink; Emperor Alexander I had bottles of Neva water sent after him when he traveled. It was wonderful for brewing tea and coffee, and beer brewed with Neva water was sent all over the Empire.† Horses and carts with their huge water casks were a daily sight, and in the winter special holes were cut in the ice for drawing the precious clear water. Winter and summer, women washed their clothes in the river and the canals, and special rafts were built for this purpose.

From mid-November, for six months the vital artery was frozen, and then it became a shining road. The best paths across the ice were marked by a little line of fir trees. Wooden ramps decorated with columns and balustrades hewn of ice were built down to the river so that sleighs could more easily cross it. There was a great ice industry on the Neva. Russians used a prodigious quantity of ice

---

* In 1842 the population was 500,000; in 1914 over 2 million.

† Alas, such was the pollution from the rapid growth of population and industry that before the end of the century the water was undrinkable and there were outbreaks of cholera in the city. In 1914, Baedeker advised tourists to drink only bottled or boiled water.

for domestic purposes. They loved to cool their beverages with ice, to drink frozen juices which were sold all summer long in the streets of every town. They drank iced water, iced wine, iced beer and even, to the astonishment of foreigners, iced tea. Because of the short hot summers, everyone, even the peasants, had ice cellars, and Russians could not conceive how a household could operate without one. There were thousands of such ice cellars in St. Petersburg, and every winter the Neva provided 500,000 sledgeloads of ice. Long sledges laden with ice were seen coming from the Neva and there were numberless ice quarries in all arms of the river where thousands of men were engaged in this ice production. They cut and heaved large blocks which were used to line cellars with walls of perpetual ice that did not melt even in summer.

Usually not before April and only very rarely at the end of March were the waters warm enough to break up the ice. This was an event eagerly looked forward to by the entire population. Odds were carefully calculated and large sums were bet on the exact day, usually between April 6 and 14, when the ice would break, and it was the cause of rejoicing all over the city. As soon as the ice broke, the cannons of Peter and Paul Fortress were fired to announce the happy event. The commander of the fortress, wearing the insignia of his rank and accompanied by his officers, would board a splendidly decorated barge and cross over to the Winter Palace directly opposite to carry to the Emperor some of the clear Neva water in a handsome crystal goblet. He would present it to the Emperor in the name of spring, informing him that the power of winter was broken and the river once more free. The Emperor drank the water to the health of his capital and returned the goblet, filled with gold pieces, to the commander. Attracted by the guns, the population would flock to the banks of the river to watch the commander in his gilded barge make the crossing, and as soon as it was safely accomplished, the river was once more covered with oars.

Although there were sixty bridges over the canals, it was difficult in the mid-19th century to build permanent bridges over the Neva because of the ice. Over the river there were only nine wooden pontoon bridges built in sections so that they could be speedily taken down and rebuilt in a few hours. In the summer these bridges remained lying at anchor and moored to poles. When the Neva froze, they were taken apart and replaced on the ice. When the guns fired, they were once again removed and for a short time the only communication between the islands was by boats or by men daring enough to leap from one ice block to another. As soon as the waters were clear, the bridges on pontoons reappeared with magical swiftness. Sometimes, while the ice was still flowing out to sea, the bridges had to be put up and taken down many times a day.*

Ships of all nations waited outside for the moment they could enter after the breaking of the ice. Then, the Americans, the Swedes, the Dutch, the English and all the other nationalities of Europe sailed triumphantly from seaward in their tall-masted ships and steamers, while Russians and tribes from the interior came in on rafts and barges. Forests of masts once again appeared along the quays, which swarmed with skippers and sailors from every land. Ships every hour brought something new and wonderful—parrots, macaws, oranges, oysters and articles of fashion.

In the spring and summer, the canals and all arms of the river were full of boats, large and small, sailing and rowing. In 1842 over a thousand boats were owned by tradesmen for delivering their goods. The gilded pleasure boats of the rich were lined with velvet and covered with silk canopies. The boatmen wore livery; the wealthy Prince Yusupov's family boatmen wore cherry-colored uniforms with richly embroidered jackets and feathered hats. All the ministries, the Admiralty, the Office of Public Instruction, had their own special boats and boatmen's uniforms. For the ordinary public there were boat landings all over the city; in the late 19th century it cost four kopecks to cross the Neva and one kopeck to cross the canals. Kohl wrote, "Most of these boats are uncovered and rowed by two men, but there are some which are covered and very large, with six, ten or twelve rowers who are skillful hands at their profession and usually entertain their passengers with singing and music into the bargain."

Winter and summer, the Neva provided fish in great abundance. To help nature, the river was also stocked with fish from other regions, including sturgeon imported from the Volga. The Russians were famous for their skill in the management of everything connected with the catching, curing and selling of fish. Along the canals of St. Petersburg, especially the Moika, small handsomely painted houses stood on rafts anchored near the shore, with bridges leading up to them. These were fish rafts, called *sadki*. On two sides of the house there were rooms, one for the crew and another for the customers who came to sit at tables and eat caviar. The main room in the middle was full of smoked and salted fish, hung,

---

* Today there are 480 bridges over canals and rivers. The bridges are opened every night from 2:30 A.M. to 4:30 A.M. to allow the passage of ships. During that time the islands are cut off from each other.

writes Kohl, "like hams and sausages of Westphalia." In the corner were large images of saints with burning lamps underneath, "as if," wrote Kohl, "it were the temple of a river goddess and the fish were suspended as offerings to her." Besides smoking and salting, the Russians had another method of preserving fish which was completely unknown in Europe—freezing. Large chests, like flour bins, were full of frozen fish—halibuts, herrings from Archangel and Lake Ladoga. Behind the house, stored under the water in huge barrels, were reservoirs of live fish, for the Russians were such epicures with regard to fish that they liked to put their fish live into the pot, and one could buy a whole live sturgeon from the Volga.

The city gave the impression of overwhelming space and size. It was airy, light and new. The streets were wide, the public places regular, the courtyards spacious and the houses roomy. Kohl wrote, "In London and Paris and likewise in some of the German cities, there are quarters which seem to be the real residences of hunger and misery . . . where the houses present the same squalid, wretched appearance as their inmates. This is not the case in Petersburg. The notions current among us, that in Russian cities magnificent palaces and wretched huts are huddled together, are founded on falsehood or misconception. In no Russian town whatever are there such glaring contrasts between indigence and luxury as in almost every city of Western Europe."

Even in the mid-19th century, many Russians, including the wealthy, still clung to their wooden houses. Otherwise the Russians used brick and plaster; marble and granite only when they were forced to, for moisture would seep into granite blocks and in the extreme cold they would freeze and burst.

Because of the shortness of the season and the impatience of the Russians, buildings were constructed with astonishing speed, almost as quickly as theatrical decorations. Russians loved redecorating and thought nothing of removing doors and windows, even knocking out walls, for a party. Despite the cold climate, windows were large; Russians were fond of using immense panes of glass which gave their houses, says Kohl, the "look of crystal palaces."

Some of the buildings of St. Petersburg were immense and housed several thousand inmates—the Winter Palace, six thousand; the Military Hospital, four thousand; the Corps of Cadets quarters, several thousands. Very early, the people of St. Petersburg preferred roomy apartments to houses. Even in the early 19th century these large apartments incorporated many modern ideas—an open plan, central heating, smokeless fires, a combination sitting room–bedroom, hanging plants and a separate entrance hall. Rents included water, light in the hall and on the streets, and the fuel for heating and cooking. Water was brought in great vats and there were always wooden steam baths in the courtyards; to wallow in one's own dirty bath water, as Europeans did, seemed unspeakably unclean to Russians.

These long, low buildings, some of which stretched for several blocks, often had several wings unseen from the street. These were connected by the famous Petersburg inner courtyards (some large enough for a cavalry regiment to exercise in), which figure often in Dostoevsky's novels. In these huge apartment complexes lived whole varied communities. Kohl speaks of one of these buildings: "On one side of the street floor it contained a bazaar, and on the other, a row of German, French and English shopkeepers. On the second floor resided two senators, and the families of several wealthy private individuals. On the third, there was a school with academicians and professors, and in the rear, besides many nameless and obscure people, several majors and colonels, some retired generals, an Armenian priest, and a German minister."

Every one of these houses had a guardian angel, watchdog and keeper called a *dvornik*, often a retired soldier. He attended to the state of the courtyards, saw the roof was free from snow, brought water from the river and was at everyone's call night and day. The other characteristic figure of the streets was the *budoshnik*, or ordinary policeman, who sat in a little hut on each street corner, so as to be always available.

Because of all the wooden buildings, fire was a danger in every Russian city. Gauthier complained bitterly that because smoking was prohibited on the streets of Petersburg he could not smoke his favorite cigar; once he tried to hide a lighted cigar under his sleeve, only to have it freeze. Old watchmen continually walked around special watchtowers erected all over the city, ready to place red flags for peril from water and black leather or sackcloth for fire in the daytime, and at night, shining red lamps.

St. Petersburg was a bustling international city. The streets buzzed with the sound of many languages. Along the wide prospects walked people from all nations of Europe and most of those of Asia; black, white, yellow faces; all races in as many different costumes as populations. There were British and American sea captains, blond Norwegians, Bokharians and Persians wrapped in silks, Indians, Chinese with their long black pigtails, white-toothed Arabs and sturdy Germans.

Foreigners were welcome in St. Petersburg, and during the 19th century they flocked there to try their luck, make their fortunes or just to visit. People came from all walks of life—soldiers and ambassadors, tutors and governesses, writers and artists, tradesmen and craftsmen. Many of them left full and lively accounts of their experiences, commenting on everything, recording the most minute details of everyday life.

Those foreigners who wished to settle and work were given many privileges. There were large colonies of English, French, Swedes and Germans who were everything from ministers of government to bakers. In the city these foreigners established their own theaters, their own clubs, their own newspapers. In the free and easy Russian society, far less class-conscious than France or England, no stigma was attached to being a tradesman, and many an elegant tailor or shopkeeper mingled freely at balls with his customers from the cream of Russian society. Many of these foreign tradesmen made fortunes and married their daughters to aristocrats.

A great proportion of the population was transient, for Russians, too, from every part of the Empire streamed freely into the city. The varied uniforms of Cossack and Grenadier, Cuirassier and Hulan mingled with the red and blue *sarafans* and flowered scarves of peasant girls and the blue kaftans of coachmen and merchants. Wet nurses wore a special and colorful costume that endured until the Revolution: a bright blue *sarafan* if they were nursing a boy, bright pink for a girl. Their dresses were embroidered in gold and on their heads they wore a diadem-shaped *kokoshnik* of rosy or blue velvet. They braided their hair in two long pigtails down their backs, and around their necks often wore a large necklace of amber beads because Russians believed that amber warded off illness.

The Nevsky Prospect was the bustling center of city life. A wide street that stretched nearly three miles from the yellow and white Admiralty with its golden spire to the blue and white Alexander Nevsky Monastery, it intersected the city from the quarters of the poor to the abodes of the wealthy. A walk along the Nevsky was almost the first thing that any foreigner did when he arrived in Petersburg. At the lower end, around the monastery, there was a village atmosphere of wooden houses painted red and yellow in the old Russian style, as well as warehouses and ironworks, and the Winter Market, where sleds and carriages for peasants were sold. From the Anichkov Bridge to the Admiralty was the most stylish and fashionable side for strolling, as it was the northern or "sunny" side; because of this the shopkeepers on the "sunny" side paid higher rents.

Visitors always exclaimed over the profusion and originality of the shop signs, a very special form of popular art. Signs were carved in decorative gilded Cyrillic letters on azure-blue or black backgrounds with, alongside, a handy translation in French or German. Just in case one did not understand any of these three languages, the contents of shops were pictured on signs intricately carved or colorfully painted: boxes of caviar, glacé hams, sausages and beef tongues for the charcutiers; the lamp maker's sign showed all his lamps. Every barber had the same picture: a lady leans back fainting in a chair; before her is a surgeon bleeding her white arm, and a boy stands ready with a basin while a man sitting nearby is getting shaved—the whole picture encircled by tooth-drilling instruments and cupping glasses. Coffeehouses showed a whole company sipping coffee and smoking cigars; goldsmiths, a whole row of ministers whose breasts and fingers were alight with diamonds, gold crosses and pearls. The butcher had pictures of oxen, cows and sheep; the baker, all his variety of breads; the lacemaker, her caps and finery. Russians were very proud of these signs and the streets were made very entertaining by these whimsical and imaginative advertisements.

Signs decorated with giant purple and white grapes announced the 250 wine cellars along the Nevsky and elsewhere in the city, where French, English, Dutch and Rhenish wines were sold. Fine wine was so popular that until the Revolution half of the wine production of France was sold to Russians. In a practice and arrangement of wine cellars which prevailed throughout Russia, bottles were carefully wrapped in fine paper and provided with several labels showing the name, birthplace of the wine and the name of the firm as well as the address of the dealer from whom the bottles came. Many wine cellars added a drinking room to their establishments. Some were elegant places where people could sip champagne, while others for the ordinary public served beer, vodka and wine. The walls of these were covered with popular woodcut *lubki* in bright colors, showing God, heaven, hell and the creation of the world, presumably to serve as uplifting reminders.

Beneath the signs, the windows of the shops were beautifully arranged for a showy display of commodities from dried fruit to mushrooms to gold and silver was a very Russian trait. It was the custom for apothecaries to place in their windows large globular bottles filled with bright blue, red or yellow liquid. When light was placed behind them they produced the effect of Chinese lanterns and could be seen for long distances at night. Grocery shops imaginatively disposed crystal vases full of coffee beans and bell glasses covering sugar loaves in the mahogany cases that lined their walls.

Along the Nevsky Prospect were churches of every denomination. Peter the Great had first given land for this purpose, and along the Prospect in 1858 Théophile Gautier noted Dutch, Lutheran, Catholic, Armenian and Finnish denominations as well as Orthodox churches for both Old Believers and new. He wrote, "There is no religion, no church that is not represented on this wide street and all practice their religion in total freedom." The religious tolerance of all Russians and the charity in religious belief prevalent in all ranks of society was noted with surprise in the accounts of many foreigners in the mid-19th century. Kohl wrote, "The capital of Russia displays temples of all other professions of faith which worship God free and unmolested after the manner of their forefathers and feel themselves under no such restraint as in modern Rome or in German Vienna; nay under less than any other capital Catholic, Lutheran, Christian or Mohammedan." The differences of religion, he said, changed the aspect of the public even more than the vagaries of the changeable climate. On Friday, the Sabbath of the Mohammedans, appeared the turbans and black beards of the Persians and the shorn heads of the Tatars; on Saturday, the black silk kaftans of the Jews. On Sunday the streets were thronged with Christians of diverse sects (he noted with special approval the German families strolling by with hymnbooks under their arms). On Catholic festival days out came the Poles, the Lithuanians, the French and the Austrians. On other days, the thousand bells of the Orthodox churches would peal and then the streets would buzz with the swarms of bright red, green, yellow, violet and blue-clad wives and daughters of Russian tradesmen. On Imperial Days or state festivals, wrote Kohl, "all the costumes, all colors, all fashions current between Peking and Paris made their appearance." It was, he says, as if Noah's ark had been stranded in the Neva and discharged its freight.

The most fashionable foreign stores were on the upper Nevsky. The English Magazine, in the liveliest and wealthiest part of the city, not far from the Winter Palace, was founded by an Englishman at the end of the 18th century but by the mid-19th century it was owned by Russians. In this vast estabishment, one of the grandest in Europe, everything was sold. There was one room for jewelry; one for Harris tweeds, English soap, gloves and hose from London; another for toilet articles from Paris and Vienna. There were articles in bronze and silver, silk cloths and umbrellas, ink and sealing wax and even stove blacking, all in elegantly labeled bottles. Beyond was Cabussué's, which specialized in French gloves, ties and handkerchiefs. Almost across the street was Brocard's, which, every time its door was opened, poured out fragrance from its splendid assortment of French perfumes and soaps.

Not far away was the Dutch Magazine, Au Petit Bazaar, and the famous Gamb's furniture store, all on the "sunny" side. Gamb's made all manner of fine furniture; the carving, a supreme Russian talent, was magnificent. The store employed fifty or sixty skilled cabinetmakers as well as sculptors, painters and carvers who worked exclusively for them. Several rooms were filled with one of Gamb's specialties—articles for travelers (a "thing of no little importance in Russia," according to Kohl). There one could find beds which with bedsteads and pillows could be packed into a case 40 inches long, 6 inches wide and 4 inches high, as well as the equipage of a nomadic tent complete with chairs, tables and other conveniences compressed in a single chest. Near Gamb's was Aux Gourmets, the foremost French confectioner, and just below the Imperial Library the famous Filippov's Bakery with its fifty kinds of bread and twenty varieties of *pirozhki*.

The seeds that Peter had sown had borne fruit. The Gobelins workers he had summoned from France were long dead, but the Russians had developed a thriving domestic tapestry industry. Elizabeth's porcelain factory was known all over Europe. Enormous mirrors of superior quality and huge panes of glass were manufactured in Petersburg. Some branches of transplanted industry were carried to a higher perfection here than they were in Europe. The best sealing wax in Europe, except for England, was made in Petersburg. In 1814 Alexander I had invited English papermakers to come to Russia. They built a factory and brought machinery and within twenty years the Russians were making a specialty of fine papers in great quantities, including delicate tinted notepapers for *billet doux* and a vast variety of other fine writing papers of all kinds. These papers were sold in England and even in America. "It is a singular fact," wrote Kohl, "that nowhere are more elegant letters now written than in Russia. The post paper is of the best quality, calligraphy most carefully studied and the envelope always accurate and handsome. Hence, in the meanest Russian stationer's shop, you find what you might hunt for in vain even in German capitals, envelopes of the finest and coarsest paper constantly for sale."

Kohl, an indefatigable visitor of factories, which were hospitably thrown open to foreigners, went to visit the paper factory and found eight hundred workmen all from the Foundling Hospital of St. Petersburg. Their clothing was white as snow, like that of cooks, and all of them were wearing imaginative paper caps of their own design.

Along the Nevsky and other fashionable parts of the city as well as in Moscow were distinctive special tea shops. Gold letters inscribed on the window announced "Here is sold all sorts of Chinese tea." Ever since Tsar Alexis had brought tea to Russia from China in the 17th century, the Russians were passionate drinkers of tea. "No sooner has the traveler crossed the frontiers of Russia than he smells the excellent tea with which he is everywhere served," wrote Kohl. "*Chai* is one of the mighty idols of Russia . . . the morning and evening beverage as the *Gospody Pomiluy* (God have mercy) of their morning and evening prayers." Whoever has once tasted the genuine China caravan tea as it was drunk in Russia, he continued, would never forget it; "the mess we call tea would be thought scarcely drinkable by the Russians."

Stepping into one of these tea shops was like stepping into China. As tea was so vital to the Russians, people of quality usually made their purchases in person, so everything in the shops was arranged as elegantly as a drawing room. The furniture and everything else were of Chinese workmanship: the floor was covered with Chinese carpets, the walls tapestried with embroideries. Over everything, Chinese lanterns cast an artificial moonlight. A haunting, delicious fragrance filled the air. The varieties of tea sorted and named amounted to several hundreds, and the price kits sent to customers looked like botany lists. The tea was packed in a great variety of cases in rows like books in a library. In the little chests which the Chinese called *lansin*, the precious tea was wrapped in soft paper and encased in lead so that none of its precious fragrance could escape. The *lansin* were encased in painted and lacquered boxes, the most expensive teas decorated with bas-reliefs of Chinese duels and Mongol battles.

Although tea was the main commodity, other things were also sold in these charming shops—paintings, pipes and tea services, mosaics and wood carvings, Chinese papers smooth as velvet, gold and embroidered silks as fine as spiders' webs. There were automatic dolls and playthings of exquisite workmanship. Shopkeepers allowed customers to wind them up—a toy gentleman would ride an elephant, another would fly across the table on a dragon. Russians adored these intricate Chinese toys.

In addition to these special tea shops, all over the city and all across Russia there were *chainayas*, or teahouses for ordinary folk. They announced themselves with a colorful sign, a samovar surrounded by white teacups on a blue ground. In the *chainaya*s, *drozhki* drivers, peasants and tradesmen, all in chatting groups, sat at small tables placed down a line in a room, drinking tea from glasses and holding, in the style of the Russian common man, a sugar lump in their teeth.

The best foreign bookstores, which offered to the public the latest as well as the classical fruits of their own national literature, were also located mainly on the Nevsky. The old firm of Bireff and Garde had German and French books. At Wolff's it was possible to buy books, magazines and newspapers in seven languages. Pluchard's was the best French bookseller. Smirdin, the most prestigious Russian bookshop and printer, was noted for its rich assortment of Russian literature and the elegance of the books it published. Smirdin printed Pushkin and Gogol as well as many other writers and in the bookshop noted writers and poets would often meet for literary lunches.

The reading public was so enthusiastic that, Kohl wrote in 1842, "If anything in Petersburg excites the astonishment of foreigners, it is the extraordinary fondness for reading now observable among Russian servants. Most of the antechambers of Petersburg grandees where part of the servants are constantly assembled, look like reading rooms, all of them being engaged with some book or other. It is no uncommon thing to find six or eight of them in different corners of the room, absorbed in their books; and if this sign astonishes the foreigner who expected to find here nothing but barbarism, sloth and ignorance, he will be still more astonished if he takes the trouble to inquire the subjects of the works they are reading. A translation of Bourrien's *Memoirs*, Karamsin's *History of Russia*, Polewoy's *Sketch of Universal History*, Krillov's *Fables*, a translation of the *Aeneid*, such are the titles which present themselves to the inquirer. Enough is now written in Russia to make the diligent reader acquainted with everything new that is worth knowing, and the book market and circulating libraries in Petersburg distribute it promptly among the people."

The stock of many booksellers in Moscow and St. Petersburg was often well over 100,000 volumes. Very high prices were paid for favorite authors. Some Russian authors acquired by their pens estates of several square miles. Persons of importance were paid from five thousand to seven thousand rubles for lending their names to favorite journals and periodicals, which had upward of twenty thousand subscribers.

The fashionable hours for promenading along the famous Prospect were after breakfast between noon and 2 P.M., when the ladies drove to the shops. Gentlemen came to meet them and pay their compliments. Then, between 2:00

and 3:00, after the daily military parade, when the Exchange was closed and commercial business was over, fashionable people strolled by the river on the English Quay in front of the Admiralty.

A number of original characters made it their business to be seen every day on the quay—a baron so fat it was said he had not seen his toes in thirty years, a fellow who made it a point always to go without a hat and another who, in the mid-19th century, still dressed in the style of Emperor Paul with a flowing wig and a silver-headed walking stick. Alexander I preferred the Palace Quay in front of the Winter Palace; on his daily strolls he sometimes ran into John Quincy Adams, the American Ambassador, and courteously inquired how he was faring in St. Petersburg. Nicholas I preferred the English Quay, and there he and his family daily strolled among their subjects, followed by two gigantic lackeys dressed in purple coats who accompanied the Empress wherever she went to carry her packages and to open doors.

• • •

To convey all the busy crowds that filled the Nevsky to their many errands and destinations were throngs of coachmen and cabdrivers. These coachmen were, in fact, such a distinctive and picturesque part of the life of old Russia that they figure prominently in the songs and tales of the nation and remain a cherished part of every traveler's memories. Wrote Pushkin:

Our dapper coachmen are astounding,
Our troikas tireless, forward bounding . . .

Whether galloping their horses across the wide expanses of land from one city to another or simply conveying a passenger briskly from one end of a long street to another, the coachmen were a breed apart. The profession was often passed on from father to son. All coachmen, whether rich or poor, in service or in business for themselves, dressed the same. In rich families where the servants wore livery, the coachman still dressed in his own national way, although his hat might be of red velvet and his kaftan of fine cloth. Not until the 1920's did they give up the characteristic garb which Théophile Gautier described in 1858:

"His low hat with its rounded crown is tight around his head with brim turned up like wings in front and back. Dressed in a long blue or green kaftan fastened under the arm with five silver buttons, pleated over his hips and cinched with a Circassian belt ornamented with gold; his small high collar encircled with a cravat, spreading his full beard over his chest, his arms outstretched straight in front of him with a rein in each hand he has a triumphant and superb air. . . . The fatter he is, the more he is paid; if he enters service thin, he demands a raise if he gains weight. As he drives with both hands, the use of the whip is unknown. The horses are led by the voice alone. A Russian coachman addresses compliments or invectives to his beasts; sometimes diminutives of an adorable tenderness, and other times insults so horribly picturesque that contemporary modesty does not permit us to translate them. . . ." (It was a question of personal pride, however, for a coachman of a respectable house never to raise his voice.)

And there was plenty of use for coachmen, for Russians never liked to walk, even for half a block. "A Russian without a carriage," wrote Gautier, "is like an Arab without a horse." With streets snowy in winter and muddy in spring, a carriage was not a luxury but a necessity. In every city all over the land there were numbers of these *izvozchiki*, or taxi drivers. In the mid-19th century there were some eight thousand in St. Petersburg alone, one traveler calculated, twenty-five to each three-quarters of a mile.

Although foreigners came to swell their ranks, most of the *izvozchiki* were Russian. They came into the cities from all over the countryside and apprenticed themselves to another coachman until they earned enough money to buy their own horse and sledge or carriage. Their profession was free; if they did not like one city or found fodder too expensive, they could leave to go to another town and try their luck anew. In provincial towns where fodder was cheap, they usually had two horses, in Petersburg only one.

To accommodate them, disposed conveniently on the streets of St. Petersburg and Moscow were little wooden troughs where coachmen could come to get fodder, for they always carried about with them a nose bag, which they fastened onto their horse's head in quiet moments. Hay was sold in portions suitable for one or two horses in a great number of booths, and water was always available from the canals.

The streets of Petersburg were filled with all sorts of carriages, pulled by all kinds of horses, from the ordinary sturdy Russian horse, patient and enduring, to the magnificent high-spirited gray Orlovs. Russians admired flowing manes and tails, so much so, that when nature failed to provide them they often added false ones. (One traveler estimated that in Petersburg 20 to 30 percent of the long manes and tails of the horses were false.)

Gautier marveled that the bustle in the streets was greater than in Paris itself. Carriages ranged from the rough vehicles of the peasants to the sleek, elegant equipages of the rich. The most common was the very distinctive *drozhki*, a little open vehicle like a phaeton, designed for what the Russians loved—speed rather than comfort.

The harness of the *drozhki* was so light that it seemed to be mere ribbons of leather; a wooden arch, the *duga*, extended from one shaft to the other, making the head of the horse appear as if set in a picture frame. *Drozhki* were usually black, with blue or apple-green decorations, seats of leather, an oriental rug on the floor and a fur blanket to wrap the passenger. There were *drozhki* called "selfish," for only one person, and others for two, but so snug that one had to put one's arm around one's partner in order to fit. "Nothing is more lovely and fragile than this little carriage which seems to have come from the coachmaker of Queen Mab," exclaimed Gautier. The Tsar himself, wrapped in his regimental cloak, drove about the city on his many errands in an open *drozhki* or a small sleigh drawn by a single horse.

Since all coachmen dressed the same, a little worldly deception was very possible. Those on their way up in the world, who wished it to be thought that they owned their own carriages, could hire special *izvozchiki* called "blue tickets." These, the limousines of the day, were elegant equipages—black horses with coats shining like satin and harnesses adorned with precious metals, with smartly dressed drivers who provided bearskins to wrap around their customers.

Izvozchiki were so numerous that a pedestrian had but to look around and ten appeared immediately, said Kohl, and "If you seemed not disposed to accept their services, they would eloquently descant on the inconveniences of walking, they would tell you the heat of the day was enough to make you faint, and that you had better get into their clean *drozhki* rather than wade through the mud."

In a city where buildings might take up several blocks, and it might take half an hour to go on foot from one end to the other, the most determined pedestrian usually soon gave up and called *"Davai!"* Nose bags would be off in a minute and bargaining would begin. There were no fixed rates; on holidays the *izvozchiki* might not come down a penny, but on ordinary days they were so courteous and good-natured that out of civility they might carry a pedestrian across a muddy street from one pavement to another for nothing.

Even if one spoke no Russian at all, said Kohl, "he will understand you. He knows how to behave fitly, courteously to each class, from beggars to Emperors and understands all languages." If his passenger happened to be Italian, the *izvozchiki*, to be polite, would scold and abuse his horse in a broken patois of Italo-Russian (*"Ecco Signore, kakoy canaille!"*). He would thank a German in his own tongue and when a Mohammedan chanced to be with him he would doff his hat and say, "May Allah grant you prosperity!" The English the *izvozchiki* called *"Eissaiki"* because of their habit of repeating "I say."

In St. Petersburg it was said that the German driver was the most intelligent, the Finn the poorest and quietest, the Pole most restless and the Russian, who never used a whip, and carried on a running conversation with his horse, the most eloquent. *"Davai,"* he would say, "what is the matter now? Art thou blind then? Brisk, brisk, mind, there's a stone. Dost thou see it? That's right. Well done. Hopp! hopp! Keep to the right. What dost thou look for? Straight forward Hussa! Juch!"

Always in high spirits, their horses always ready for a new ride, the drivers were disposed to singing, fun and gossip. They called to each other when passing on the streets. They lounged by their carriages while waiting and sang some song from their native village. Glinka mentions in his memoirs a song of a Luga driver which stuck so firmly in his mind that he used it for some of the phrases of his main hero in *A Life for the Tsar*. When they met comrades on the corners of almost every street, they threw snowballs, wrestled, cracked jokes until a pedestrian called and then they were off again.

In the winter, *drozhki* and carriages were instantly transformed into a varied caravan of sleighs. During six months of the year nature furnished a road of snow and ice better than any pavement and on which sleighs glided as agreeably and noiselessly as gondolas in Venice. The Russian sledge, a traveler wrote, "surpasses in lightness, elegance and adaption to its purpose the same kind of vehicle in all other countries. It is the result of the experience of centuries and a creation of Russian national ingenuity which passes half its existence on the ice roads of winter." There was as great a variety of sleighs in winter as carriages in summer, sleighs gaily decorated with red, gold and silver, with strange carved work and whirligigs of iron, with silver and brass bells and jingles. Members of the court were identified by their scarlet sleighs with wolfskin furs. One nobleman of the mid-19th century was famous for his sleigh banded in silver and pulled by reindeer. Harnesses were studded with polished brass or silver embossed with silver, and scarlet cloth and hundreds of colorful tassels.

Of all of them, what Gautier called "the most sublime of the species" was the romantic troika. The troika was a large sleigh, gaily painted and gilded, like the chariot of Neptune, made for four people plus the coachman. It could go at great speed and demanded enormous skill from the driver, for it was drawn by three horses but only the middle one had a yoke and a harness. The other two on each side were held by only a single rein. The three horses pulled separately, in fan shape; one outside horse was called "the flirt" and the other "the furious," and the coachman had only four reins to drive all three horses.

Russians loved speed; it was the mark of the importance of a passenger. In *Dead Souls*, Gogol wrote, "What Russian does not like to drive fast? Which of us does not at times yearn to give his horses their heads and let them go crying, 'To Devil with the world!'?" Every foreign traveler commented incredulously on the swiftness and skill of Russian coachmen. With their arms straight out before them, they would start off at a gallop and, despite the fact that there were stiff penalties if one so much as touched a pedestrian, they flew through the streets crying briskly, "*Beregis! Beregis!* [Take care!] *Padi! Padi!* [Make way!]"

• • •

Along with the coachmen, it was the swirling native marketplaces, lively and full of color, which most captivated the attention of foreign travelers. Many devoted whole chapters to their description.

Russians had the custom of exhibiting all sorts of native goods in one building, much like the bazaars of Constantinople. Every town and city had its own Gostinny Dvor (Merchant's Inn), usually located in the center of the community. In addition, there were many kinds of special markets for provisions, eggs, fowl, meat and vegetables. Western European merchants and shopkeepers were entirely excluded from these completely Russian bazaars. Russian merchants, their wives and families formed a special group, and until the Revolution, they continued to dress as they had for centuries in their own native style and kept their conservative customs intact.

St. Petersburg's Gostinny Dvor had been built for its purpose in the late 18th century under Catherine the Great. A gigantic yellow building several blocks long, with white colonnades, it enclosed a number of large courtyards. Facing the Nevsky Prospect on one side and on the other Sadovaya Street, it had several wings and appendages. All the streets around it were lined with shops, so that the quarter all year long looked like a continual fair. It was the universal Russian custom to group all those who sold the same goods together in lines or rows, called *ryady*. There was a line of wool drapers nearly a mile long, a long line of stationers and a colonnade of dealers in toys, in confections, in bells and jingles. Every commodity in fact had its long line of shops. Said Kohl, "Long is the dimension for everything Russian. Their streets of houses are long, the files of soldiers are long, the regiments of verst poles which they set up on their interminable roads are long, all their buildings are drawn out to great length; their ranges of shops are long, and their trains of carriages and caravans are long." People would simply ask, "Where is the Fur Row?" "The Petticoat Row?" "The Cap Row?"

In the Petersburg Gostinny Dvor and its appendages were ten thousand merchants says Kohl, "all extremely sharp fellows with flaxen or light brown hair and beards," dressed in the blue kaftan and blue cloth cap worn by shopkeepers all over Russia. In the winter, as no fires were allowed, to keep warm merchants wrapped themselves in their characteristic wolfskin cloaks. From their little shops they would entice passersby with the most extravagant recommendations of their goods. "Clothes, the very best!" "Kazan boots, first rate!" "Have I nothing that suits you? A bearskin? A wolfskin? Just step in!" In the corners of their shops an icon light was always burning, and they loved to surround themselves with cages of nightingales and other songbirds. When a purchase was made, they calculated the accounts with lightning speed on the abacus, the national method of calculation. On their wooden tables stood a steaming samovar which provided them all day with piping-hot cups of tea. When not busily engaged in chanting invitations or bargaining with customers, they passed the time playing backgammon on wooden tables and benches in front of their little shops or sometimes played ball in the long corridors, adroitly kicking the ball to each other over the heads of the passing customers.

The Gostinny Dvor contained all the better kinds of Russian goods and imitations of foreign goods, but only a little farther down Sadovaya Street were two enormous markets, the Apraxin Rynok and the Shchukin Dvor, which were frequented by peasants and the common people of the city. Together these two markets encompassed the huge area of 2 million square feet, almost entirely filled with shops, booths and tents—some five thousand of them—so closely packed that the little buildings nearly touched at top and only narrow alleys were left between them. Icons were suspended over the narrow wooden gates leading into the market. Wooden bridges and arches were thrown across the streets from roof to roof, and these too were festooned with icons and their little burning lamps.

Inside the market it was dark, smelling pungently of sauerkraut and leather. Wood-carvers sat at their wheels and sang songs of their own composition as they worked, organ-grinders played, and throngs of bearded Russians in their sheepskin coats crowded the narrow passageways. Interspersed among the booths, often side by side with common taverns, or *kabak*s, which sold vodka and wine, were many small chapels papered with icons in front of which the peasants knelt or piously crossed themselves.

Secondhand goods of every kind were sold in a huge Flea Market. The transient Petersburg population was constantly ebbing and flowing. People came and left, seized by what Kohl called "the nomadic vertigo of the Russian population. . . . Thousands of persons enter the gates of the city daily, not knowing whether on the morrow they are to be cooks or carpenters, bricklayers or painters." The markets were so well provided that "were the Samoyeds of Siberia and hordes of Huron or Chippewas naked as they grew up in their native forest to enter the gates all at once, they might sally forth again in a few moments equipped as civilized people."

In one corner of the market were all the dealers in icons, which were piled in heaps like gingerbread and sold by the dozens. Brass crosses and amulets hung outside the shops and the walls were completely covered with glittering icons in false gold and silver in all forms and dimensions. Gautier was impressed by the sight of the bearded men who sold them, observing that with their gentle faces they could have posed for the images of Christ they were selling. Some of the icons were newly painted by the pupils of the St. Petersburg Academy; but many were old, and the smokier and darker they were, the more they were valued by the peasants who would ask if they had been in churches.

As there were over fifty weddings a day in the city, there were rows of shops which sold nothing but bridal ornaments at very reasonable prices—metal crowns and artificial wreaths of roses entwined with silver wire for a few kopecks. By custom, the pitch and chalk shops were decorated all around with rows of hanging balalaikas. Groups of shops sold nothing but incense, others the white butter of Odessa. Some sold nothing but honey from Kazan and Tula and neighboring provinces, in every hue from white to black, all in vessels of linden wood. A whole quarter was occupied by fruit shops which sold prodigious quantities of dried fruit. These shops were fantastically decorated with pedestals on which were arranged bottles and boxes of Kiev preserves and confections. All around the walls were little chests full of raisins, currants, almonds and figs. In the corners stood large bags full of plums, nuts and juniper berries. At the door were hogs-heads of cranberries, which Russians loved. In winter, the cranberries, frozen like little red pebbles, were measured out with large wooden scoops. All these shops were festooned inside and out with long strings of dried mushrooms, a beloved article of food for all classes. Tables of money changers stood at the corners of the streets, piled with all kinds of money, and yet, even when these were in charge of a twelve-year-old boy, stealing was practically unknown. When a table was some-times overturned by the passing hurrying crowd, people scurried about to find the coins and return them all.

In the Shchukin Dvor was the poultry market which announced itself by the quacking of ducks and cooing of pigeons. Two long lines of shops, built of wood and open to the street so that one could see inside, were stocked entirely with birds, large and small, alive and dead—chickens, geese, ducks, swans, larks, bullfinches, linnets and nightingales. Above them on wooden bridges strung across the narrow street, pigeons peacefully roosted, curiously enough often side by side with cats, which were kept to keep down the mouse population and which, for some reason, coexisted peacefully with the birds. Russians refused to eat pigeons, believing them to be representatives of the Holy Ghost. They bought them only to feed and play with and to watch them fly. The shopkeepers got them down from their perch simply with a stick to which were fastened bits of rags and which they waved about in different ways to tell the birds whether they were to fly higher or come down, which amazingly they did obediently. Nightingales, larks and bullfinches were sold to merchants who loved to hang their cages about their shops and coffeehouses. The best fowl came from Moscow, the best pigeons from Novgorod. Finland provided the most singing birds; even China sent geese, which made a five-thousand-mile journey to arrive at the Shchukin Dvor. Squir-rels, hedgehogs and rabbits ran about their cages. In the back of every shop were icons, with burning lamps, surrounded by cages of larks.

Frozen birds in great quantity were sold for the table: Saratov partridges, swans from Finland, grouse from Estonia and bustards from the steppe, all packed frozen in large chests and distributed not only to the capital but all over Russia, for there were similar market customs everywhere—whether it was Tobolsk, Odessa or Archangel.

The immense Hay Market, immortalized by Dostoevsky in *Crime and Pun-ishment,* took up an entire square at the end of Sadovaya Street. The streets leading to it were lined completely with secondhand bookshops which sold every kind of

Russian and foreign book. Wax chandlers sold candles of all shapes and sizes, candles embellished by gilding, or garnished with glistening pieces of metal and red and blue glass, candles as thick as a man and tall as a pillar or spun out to the fineness of yarn. The Hay Market was so thronged with people every morning of the week that the police had difficulty keeping a clear passage for carriages in the middle. One whole side of the square was devoted to the dealers in hay and wood, trees and plants. Hay was an enormous business; in the mid-19th century there were over sixty thousand horses in Petersburg. The peasants spread hay all over the ground and divided it into small parcels so that the *izvozchiki* could conveniently buy.

On the other side of the square, peasants sold meat and fish, butter and vegetables, which they brought to the city in caravans. Piles of eggs and mountains of butter were piled up on sledges, which also served as shops and counters. Geese were cut up in many pieces; one could buy necks and feet separately in dozens and half dozens. Russians loved suckling pig, and whole sledgeloads arrived with them strung in a line like so many thrushes. As in all Russian towns there was a huge frozen meat market; foreigners found it startling to see sledges of standing oxen and calves frozen stiff arriving at market, where they were cut up with axe and saw, chips flying. One did not ask for a steak or a chop, but for a slice or a block. Large sledges brought in frozen hare as well as elk, reindeer and bear. Tiny, almost transparent little fish called *snitki* were brought in large sacks and put on the scales with shovels. Pike, salmon and sturgeon were covered with snow and lumps of ice to keep them frozen. Live cattle, horses, peasant carriages and sledges were sold at yet another enormous market near the Alexander Nevsky Monastery.

All over Russia, numbers of itinerant peddlers roamed as they pleased from town to town disposing of their goods. Of all the characteristics of the Russian personality, perhaps the one most often mentioned by foreigners was this love of restlessly moving from place to place. "The serf has more freedom of movement than the German peasant," commented Kohl in 1842 with some astonishment. At any time in St. Petersburg, as in every Russian city, there were always thousands of wandering pilgrims and itinerant vendors swarming in the alleys, the bazaars and the markets.

Tea sellers set up their tables at all the street corners. In the middle of a large table, surrounded by teakettles of all shapes and sizes, glasses large and small, and slices of cake and lemons, a copper samovar sat boiling all day. Tea sellers either sat at their tables or wandered around the streets. Round their waists they fastened like a belt a leather case that held cup and glasses, and slung over their shoulders a bag full of cakes and lemons. Carrying their samovar wrapped in thick cloths, they cried as they wandered through the streets, "It boils! It boils! Will nobody drink?" In the summer, these sellers of tea and *sbiten* (a kind of eggnog) were metamorphosed into sellers of *kvas*, a mild rye beer of which there were as many varieties as the juice of the fruit mixed with it. Russians loved their *kvas* and pitied other nations when told that *kvas* was not available there. "Honey *kvas*! Raspberry *kvas*!" called the vendors, plainly showing the glass pitchers in which *kvas* was always sold, so that buyers could better judge the contents.

Vendors sold *ovsyany kisel*, soft oatmeal pastes which they would slice off and spread with oil. They pushed carts and sledges full of gingerbread and *pryaniki*, little cakes flavored with mint, honey or spices. Some sold oranges, apples and watermelons. Still others carried about plates and forks and sold entire breakfasts of caviar, sausages and boiled eggs, for Russians loved to eat outdoors and in many towns and public places were tables where people could sit and banquet in the open air.

Sometimes, not content with talking, the vendors sang in praise of their goods. Kohl chuckled to hear one old bearded fellow in Kharkov incongruously singing in the streets, "I am a young sausage-maker and a handsome fellow, too. All the lasses are peeping after me, whom God made, and all the lads are after my sausages that a German made!"

The milk women in Petersburg, often Finnish, with their long braid fastened with a bright-yellow ribbon, their bright handkerchief and long earrings, and dressed in scarlet *sarafan* and short jacket lined with rabbit fur and with bright-green shoes with red binding, went from house to house calling, "Milk! Fresh milk!"

In Russia it was the men, not the women, who carried things about on their heads—pyramids of oranges, whole shelves of eggs and even troughs of water full of live fish—without spilling anything. Along the canals and along the streets they wandered—boot sellers; sellers of *lubki* from Moscow; Tatars selling bright silken robes; perambulating mechanics; sellers of cabbage and parsley, beef and chickens; sellers of toys and busts of Greek philosophers; even sellers of singing birds, with cages hung all about them from head to foot. The cries of "Rolls! Rolls! Whole wheat and crusty!" "Cultivated, stewed, fat plums!" "Beautiful violets, carnations, geraniums!" "*Pirogi, pirogi* with carp! With peas! With mushrooms!'' ''Lollipops!'' ''If there is something, we will sell it! Who will buy it? We will sell it!'' were part of the music of the streets.

For more than six months, the city lay frozen under ice and snow with only a few hours of sunlight. St. Petersburg lies on the same parallel of latitude as southern Greenland, the northern part of Labrador and Hudson Bay, a parallel which favors only the growth of birch trees, wild berries and thornbushes. During these long dark days, man had to learn to cheat nature by growing everything in hothouses, and in St. Petersburg all manner of fruits and vegetables were grown in huge temples of shining glass. In 1842 Kohl wrote, ''In the art of forcing fruit and vegetables, Russian gardeners excel those of every other nation. Russians are the best cultivators of vegetables throughout the Baltic provinces. No sooner is there a new town added to the Empire when a party of bearded gardeners settle in its suburbs and its walls are speedily surrounded by extensive kitchen gardens; first cabbages, then onions, cucumbers, gourds, pumpkins, and finally peas and beans. A party of gardeners unites together and farms a piece of land a half a square mile.'' For cucumbers and beans, Russian gardeners prepared little hotbeds and by using a few old windows ingeniously constructed miniature greenhouses in which the tender shoots were protected by special mats of plaited straw that were sold in the plant markets of the city. In this artful way gardeners managed to use every ray of the January and February sun and to counteract the frost. They were so watchful of their plants that on spring nights, when the weather was warmer but frost still a danger, Russian gardeners would lie wrapped in their sheepskins next to their green charges, keeping one bare foot exposed. If frost came during the night, the foot would wake them better than any thermometer. The result of all this careful attention was that Russians always brought the first asparagus and beans to market, to the extreme annoyance of competing German gardeners.

In December, the month of darkness, no amount of art would help, but as soon as the first rays of sun appeared in January and February, so would fresh spinach, asparagus and lettuce appear from the hothouses. Kohl reported that toward the middle of March red strawberries and cherries appeared in the windows of the best fruit shops of the Nevsky Prospect, as expensive as so many pearls at that early date. They were followed by beans and apricots in late March, and after the ice broke, ships brought figs and oranges. To his surprise, southern fruit was for some reason obtained earlier and cheaper in St. Petersburg than in Germany.

Kohl visited the Imperial hothouses and orangeries of the former Potemkin Tauride Palace on February 28 and found thirty rooms of various dimensions filled with flowers, vegetables and fruit trees. Vines were planted in low rows and the vineyards were partly in bloom; grapes were expected to be ripe at the beginning of June, "fifty hundred weight" of them. In other alleys, rows of apricots and peach trees were ranged in full bloom. All the plants were fostered with extraordinary care and perfect order: 20,000 apricots would be ready for harvesting at the end of May, 15,000 pots of strawberries, 6,000 pots of beans, and 11,000 pots of stocks and flowers.

Special cherry tree houses, like the orange and lemon houses of Florence, were exposed to the air only in the summer months. Some wealthy Russians had their own cherry houses with glazed roofs and wooden walls sealed with pitch in the gardens of their summer houses.

Gautier remarked that, unlike France, there seemed to be no special season for vegetables in St. Petersburg or Moscow, since peas and beans appeared on tables even in the middle of winter, and that the love of fruit was as widespread as the taste for chocolate in Germany. On his walks along the Nevsky Prospect in 1858, he passed fruit shops full of pineapples and watermelons. Apples were sold on the street corners and oranges by passing vendors. From foreign countries, vast amounts of fruit were brought—grapes from Astrakhan and Málaga, large cargoes of apples from Stettin in Germany. Quantities of apples came, too, from the Crimea, where Tatars grew them in their extensive orchards and conveyed them to all parts of Russia by great fruit caravans. Both in Moscow and St. Petersburg a favorite fruit was the "glass-apple," a species peculiar to Russia; perfectly round in form, its skin, transparent and green as glass, showed the flesh through it. "It is delicious," wrote Kohl, "to eat these ripe glass-apples in the magical twilight of a Russian summer night."

In summer, fragrant strawberries were brought in vast quantities from Finland and Estonia. Wild blackberries, cranberries, bilberries grew plentifully in Russia as well as gooseberries and raspberries, which grew to enormous size and perfection. Various species of berries eaten were unknown to Western Europeans, including the delicate golden cloudberry, which grew among the mosses of northern Finland and was sent to Petersburg preserved in sugar.

Fruit shops were scattered throughout the city, the most elegant forming a low and colorful row from Number One to Number Ten on Nevsky Prospect. Not only fresh but preserved fruits were sold, for Russians used their native berries to make many varieties of jams and preserves. Kohl found that "a St. Petersburg shop in which berry jam is sold contains as many different articles in vats and galley-pots as an apothecary's." It was the custom, especially among merchant families, to hand round on a salver after dinner a variety of preserved fruit, which the visitor spooned along with his tea. Displayed in great abundance in the fruit shops were "preserved pears and confections from Kiev, Nieschin jam, Moscow preserves and berries, American sweetmeats, Tartar alwahs, Russian pastelas made of berries, raisins, almonds and figs from Smryna, Crimean nuts and Sicilian oranges . . . all Russia is inundated with dried apricots and peaches from the Caucasus and Persia."

As all other shops in Russia, the fruit shops, too, loved to display their fruit, jam glasses and confections boxes in ingenious ways. They were arranged to represent buildings or monuments. Tempting pyramids of fruit were built up in front of the door or arranged in figures on shelves. Among the fruits and preserves were placed bright glasses filled with sparkling candy and sugar water. Each of the long pillarlike glasses rested on a confection base which served as a pedestal and the whole was surmounted by a pineapple or a melon. Every opening was filled with a nosegay, a small strawberry plant or a tiny cherry tree bearing fruit.

The demand for plants and seeds was very high. In St. Petersburg, large markets, like the flower markets of Paris, were devoted exclusively to the sale of young plants and trees; stock, roses, orange trees and magnolias could be purchased or hired for the evening for decorating a table or a ballroom. One-half of Russia was supplied with foreign plants and new species from Petersburg. So successful, in fact, were the Petersburg gardeners in their constant combat with nature that Kohl writes that if they did not come off with laurels for trophies, "then at least with cherries, strawberries and roses."

This thriving commerce in plants was very necessary as Russians, especially in winter, loved to fill their houses and apartments with a profusion of greenery and bloom, a custom which surprised and delighted visiting foreigners. Victor Tissot, a French journalist traveling in Russia in 1893, remarked that "even in the poorest taverns of the countryside, one finds flowers. Very often the room of a traveler is papered with ivy growing in pots." In St. Petersburg, apartments overflowed with blooms. An English lady writes, "In every sitting room, there are plants: heliotrope, jasmine, roses and hanging plants." Gautier exclaims, "Flowers! There is really a Russian luxury! The houses are stuffed with them!

Flowers receive you at the door and climb up the stairs with you; Irish ivy festoons the bannisters, jardinieres are on the landings, magnolias, camellia bushes are in the cornices, orchids like butterflies, around the lamps. Crystal vases on the table are full of exotic flowers. They live as if in a hothouse, which is what a Russian apartment is. Outside you are at the Pole, indoors, you would think it was the tropics.''

These flower-filled apartments were rambling, with vast rooms. Gautier, in 1858, remarked that ''our Paris architects who like to design beehives could put a whole apartment and maybe two floors in one Petersburg salon.'' The vestibule was most important, for all the heavy outdoor clothes, furs, caps, galoshes and fur-lined boots, were stored there. Rooms were kept very hot, heated by huge stoves fed with birch logs. Double windows needed no shutters, but were covered by heavy curtains. The furniture, wrote Gautier, was larger than in France, with enormous leather divans, poufs and bearskin rugs, and sometimes little stuffed black bears were used as footstools. There was always a special corner, sometimes set off by a screen, where the hostess received her guests. Rooms communicated with each other, often with sliding doors. The bedroom was not as important to Russians as Europeans. Wrote Gautier, ''Russians, even in elevated classes, are still nomadic and not especially attached to bedrooms. They sleep wherever they find themselves, sometimes in their capes on those large green leather sofas which one meets in every room.''

All this space was needed, for Russian households were sprawling and much more informal than those of Europe. A usual household would include many relatives—maiden aunts, cousins and adopted children—besides an educational staff of German, French and Russian masters and tutors and serving folk.

Russian hospitality was unbounded and legendary. In the summer months some generous nobles with estates on the islands of Petersburg threw open their grounds to the public and provided refreshments, bands, dancing, sailing, fishing, swinging, and bowling, and ended with fireworks. A friendly invitation in four languages inscribed over the entrance of the gates authorized everyone of ''decent appearance and behavior to amuse himself there.''

Madame de Staël tells of a dinner with an eminent merchant in Petersburg, who, when he was dining at home, simply ran up a flag on the roof which served as sufficient invitation to all his friends. The house of Count Orlov, she wrote, was open every day during his lifetime. ''Everyone, once presented there, could return. He never invited anyone for dinner on any special day. It was simply agreed that once admitted, one would always be well received, and often he hardly knew half the people who ate in his home." Every household had an open house at least once a week, which was called the *jour fixe*, during which friends and acquaintances were received.

Foreigners were received with great amiability, and when they were present, the conversation usually took place in French. According to Madame de Staël, "Their flexibility makes imitation easy for them; they are English, French, German in their manners according to the circumstances, but they never cease being Russian." Gautier noted that the educated spoke French easily, idiomatically, as if "they had learned it on the Boulevard des Italiens." Their manners were "polite, caressing and of a perfect urbanity." They were aware of the most minute details of French literature. "They read a great deal; such and such an author, little known in France, is more read in Petersburg." They knew all the gossip of Paris and "we learned there many piquant details about Paris that we had ignored."

Meals were lengthy and abundant. It was, and still is, a Russian custom to serve *zakuski*, little snacks of salted and pickled fish, meats and various cold salads before the main meal. These were usually taken standing up, from a special table, or sometimes even in a separate room. With the *zakuski* were served various flavored vodkas. One Russian lady writing in the 1920's remembered that her grandfather had a little revolving table on which he kept forty flavors of vodka (lemon, caraway, birch buds, buffalo grass, pepper, cranberry, etc., etc.). These *zakuski* were on occasion so elaborate that unsuspecting foreigners sometimes thought they were the whole meal, and to their sorrow were then confronted by the groaning board which Russians favored.

An English lady, visiting in 1853 in the household of a relatively modest family where the host had the rank of colonel, reported on a midday meal for twenty people: "There was *zakuski* of sardines, radishes, caviar, bread and butter washed down with vodka. Then borsch and sour cream and meat pies, blini, little pancakes spread with butter and caviar. There were native fish in white sauce with truffles and capers, followed by boiled fowls in white sauce, preserved peas and French beans, tongues cut in slices and sautéed potatoes, grouse roasted in sour cream with cranberry sauce and salted cucumbers and finally, iced pudding. The wines were French, Rhenish, also sherry and port. Each dish was served separately, in the Russian style." In Russian ice cellars food was kept fresh, even in summer, and there was plentiful use of sour cream and yoghurt. An interesting culinary note is that sugar extracted from beet root and melons was the only kind used, since Tsar Nicholas I did not allow slave-grown sugar, a direct result of Quaker influence on his older brother, Alexander I.

Like a true son of France, Gautier devoted pages to his meals in Russia. In houses that were well-to-do but not extravagantly wealthy, black bread was always served along with white, the Russian *kvas* and Grand Crus from Bordeaux appeared, along with a curiosity, "a delicious champagne which one finds only in Russia"—Champagne de la Veuve Cliquot, a wine developed in France for Russian taste and which Gautier first sipped there. (One of the delights of Russia, Gautier found, was that one could chill a bottle of champagne in a few minutes simply by placing it between the double windows, which he regularly did in his hotel room.) On different occasions, he was served bear hams and reindeer steaks as well as the magnificent sterlet of the Volga, huge asparagus native to Russia—"tender, white and no green at all," and marvelous melons from the south. He commented on the delicious *shchi*, or cabbage soup, which appeared ubiquitously in homes of rich and poor, the pullet with juniper berries and the cutlets Pozharsky, which the Emperor himself had discovered in a provincial country inn near Torzhok. For dessert there was always fruit in great profusion—oranges, pineapples, grapes, pears and apples piled in elegant pyramids. One evening, Gautier recalled, nestled among the nougats and petits fours were little bouquets of violets which, after dinner, the hostess graciously distributed to her guests.

In the capital, throughout the 19th century right up to 1914, the St. Petersburg "season" officially began on New Year's Day with a reception given by the tsar for the diplomatic corps at the Winter Palace. This reception was held in the vast white St. George Hall, 154 feet long and 65 feet wide, with its marble Corinthian columns and six immense chandeliers. There, the Emperor, seated on a large red velvet and gold throne with a huge Imperial coat of arms embroidered in gold on velvet behind him, received the good wishes of the assembled diplomats. Thereafter, until the beginning of Lent, through the wintry weeks when the capital was wrapped in ice, elegant society moved through a staggering round of concerts, banquets, balls, operas, private parties and midnight suppers.

In the winter a fashionable lady rose late and did not appear in her salon until two or three in the afternoon. Then, perhaps, there was time for a promenade in a sleigh before receiving her guests for tea. Supper was early, about six, and then it was off to the ballet or the opera. She returned in time to rest for a ball which began at midnight and from which she did not return until three or four in the morning. Suppers which continued until five or six in the morning were very much the fashion.

There was a "Bal Blanc" at which unmarried girls in virginal white danced quadrilles with young officers, carefully watched by vigilant chaperones, and a "Bal Rose" for young married couples where the swirl of waltzes, gypsy music, flashing uniforms and jewels made a person feel, said the English Ambassador's daughter in 1912, "that one had wings on the feet and one's head in the stars."

The most coveted of all the invitations in St. Petersburg was to one of the festivities at the Winter Palace. At the Palace, the setting of the most splendid court in Europe, Their Majesties held balls and receptions for 2,000, 5,000 and on occasion 10,000 people, and a summons to one of these evenings was equivalent to an invitation to fairyland.

The court was a world unto itself, governed by intricate protocol and custom developed since the days of Elizabeth and Catherine. The grandiose Winter Palace was inhabited by 6,000 people. Its 1,100 rooms, illuminated by 2,000 windows, were filled with art treasures, mirrors, chandeliers, paintings, rich Persian rugs, mahogany and rosewood furniture upholstered in fine silks and satins. The Golden Salon was filled with mosaics in the Byzantine style, and the Malachite Room, a salon which seemed like the Royal Chamber of Neptune, was all white and gold with columns, tables and huge urns of solid, rich green malachite.

Through these silken rooms and polished halls, up and down the 117 staircases of the Palace, silently moved an army of servants and retainers, all in gorgeous livery. Equerries in capes bordered with Imperial Eagles and hats with long waving red, yellow and black ostrich plumes stepped noiselessly on the soft soles of their patent-leather slippers. Footmen resplendent in snow-white gaiters ran before visitors on the carpeted staircases. At every door lackeys stood, as if carved of stone, in varied costumes according to the room to which they were attached. Some wore the traditional black frock coat, others the Polish surcoat with red shoes and white stockings. At one door stood two handsome lackeys with crimson scarves on their heads caught with tinsel clasps. There were tall Negroes in turbans and pantaloons whose only function was to silently announce the arrival of Their Majesties by opening the doors before them.

Balls were held in the immense Nicholas Hall, 200 feet long and 61 feet wide, with its great doors, made of mahogany ornamented with gold. For a hundred years the ceremonial for these vast assemblies did not change. Descriptions of balls held in the time of Nicholas I are almost identical to those of the reign of Nicholas II, more than fifty years later, the only difference being the exchange of electricity for candlelight.

Théophile Gautier assisted at one of these wintry revels in 1858. That night all was silent and frosted with snow, and "the moon, rising pure and clear shed its ghostly light on this nocturnal whiteness, turning the shadows blue and giving a fantastic appearance to the immovable silhouettes of the equipages. . . . The Winter Palace flamed in all its windows like a mountain pierced with holes and lit by an internal fire."

Along the Grand Staircase of the Jordan Entrance with its enormous columns and steps of Carrara marble, stood troopers of the Chevaliers Gardes with gleaming silver breastplates and helmets surmounted with double eagles, along with Cossack Life Guards in scarlet tunics. The halls were lined with lackeys in Imperial livery all standing immobile and silent. Wrote Gautier, "The gallery stretched long and deep with its polished columns and gleaming floors in which were reflected the gold, the candles, and the paintings. . . . It was like a furnace of light and heat, so bright that it seemed a conflagration. . . . Cordons of fire ran along the cornices, torchères with a thousand arms were like burning bushes and hundreds of chandeliers descended from the ceiling like flaming constellations. . . ."

There was the smell of fragrant wood burning in the huge porcelain stoves and of the incense which lackeys swung in silver censers to perfume the rooms. Vases of scented flowers in porcelain and silver basins, baskets of orchids and plants filled the rooms. For these great evenings, the Nicholas Hall was transformed into a Winter Garden with long *allées* of laurels and rhododendrons.

The uniforms of the men were encrusted with gold embroidery; their chests were ablaze with broad ribbons, diamond orders and medals. Young Hussar officers in scarlet and blue tunics and gleaming boots wore elkskin britches so tight that it took two soldiers to put them on.* Bringing with them a breath of

---

* How this feat was accomplished is explained by A. A. Mossolov in his book *At the Court of the Last Tsar.* "It was essential that the breeches should not have the slightest crease. To attain this result, they were damped, smeared with soap and put on. The operation called for the services of a couple of vigorous soldiers. I hope my readers will pardon me for descending to a slightly vulgar detail. There is no other way of giving an exact idea of the function performed by the two soldiers. Have you ever watched a miller trying to get the flour into an insufficiently filled sack? He punches the sack. That is just what the two soldiers had to do. 'They punched the elkskin breeches,' and in due course the officers settled down into them."

distant parts of the Empire were the elegant Circassian and Mongol officers in their exotic oriental uniforms. The night that Théophile Gautier attended, Tsar Alexander II was dressed in narrow blue trousers and a white knee-length tunic bordered at the hem and sleeves with blue fox. His collar and chest were ablaze with decorations.

For all official court ceremonies and many of the balls, all the ladies of the court wore the beautiful and elegant court dress. Worn over a white silk or satin underskirt with gold braid or embroidery around the hem and down the front, the body and train of this dress were of crimson, green or blue velvet embroidered in gold, with velvet sleeves reaching almost to the ground. The ladies' hair was coiffed low and caught in a net of gold. Over it they wore a diadem or *kokoshnik* of velvet matching their dress, heavily embroidered with gold and jewels, and attached to the diadem a veil of tulle or lace falling to their shoulders. The Empress and the Grand Duchess wore the same dress, only more profusely embroidered, with a longer train sewn with diamonds. The net in which they caught their hair was sprinkled with diamonds.

A court ball began at 9:00 P.M., when the Grand Master of Ceremonies appeared and tapped loudly three times with his cane embossed with a golden Double Eagle. The sound brought an immediate hush. The Grand Master of Ceremonies called out, "Their Imperial Majesties," and hundreds of dresses rustled into a deep curtsy as the huge doors opened and an imposing procession began. First came the Master and Mistress of the Emperor's and Empress's household, followed by the Emperor and the Empress, great officials of their household and pages, then the Tsarevich, Grand Dukes and Duchesses. The solemn and moving national anthem was played. The effect produced by this entrance of the Tsar was so awesome that Mrs. Lothrup, the wife of the American Minister in 1895, marveled, "I have come to the conclusion that Their Majesties are to people here what the sun is to our world. . . . I do not expect you to understand it—it must be seen and felt."

Court balls always opened with a polonaise; "not a dance," wrote Gautier, "but a parade, a procession that has much character." All the guests formed themselves into two lines, leaving an aisle down the middle of the ballroom. When everyone had taken his place, the orchestra played a majestic melody. (Mrs. Lothrup recalled that the orchestra played the polonaise from Glinka's *A Life for the Tsar*.) Then the promenade began, led by the Emperor, who gave his hand to a princess or to a lady he wished to honor. As the cortege proceeded, officers and gentlemen one by one detached themselves from the company to offer their hand to a lady and thus couple after couple joined the dance as the music quickened. They made a tour of the hall, and returning, formed again. "The ladies pass lightly," wrote Gautier, "under their plumes, their diamonds and flowers, lowering their eyes modestly or letting them float innocently about the room, maneuvering with an inflection of the body, or a little movement of the heel, their clouds of silk and lace, occasionally refreshing themselves with a rapid fluttering of their fans."

Following the polonaise, just as in Vienna or Paris, it was waltzes, quadrilles and cotillions, except for the mazurka, which was danced in St. Petersburg with an elegance and perfection unknown anywhere else.

The passion of Russian women for jewels was displayed on every head, neck, ear, wrist, finger and waist. Dresses of tarlatan, taffeta and tulle had ribbons of diamonds catching the ruffles of their skirts; velvet ribbons clasped with pearls and ropes of fine oriental pearls were entwined in the hair and cascaded onto white bosoms.

Watching the scene from a balcony, Gautier wrote that he was reminded of a brilliant kaleidoscope, changing and rearranging its colors constantly, "the whirlwind of the waltz billowed the dresses like those of whirling dervishes and in the speed of evolution, the knots of diamonds and the strands of gold elongated themselves in serpentine flashes like lightning and little gloved hands placed delicately on the epaulettes of waltzers looked like white camellias in vases of solid gold."

About 11:00, he continues, Emperor Alexander II led the way into another gallery where tables were set for supper. As he stepped over the threshold of the hall, the five thousand candles of the room simultaneously burst into flame, brilliantly illuminating the room. This miracle was achieved by linking fine threads of cotton soaked with an inflammable liquid from one candle to another. Lit in six or seven places, the fire spread itself almost instantly. The same method was used to light the thousands of candles in the Cathedral of St. Isaac's.

At supper the Empress seated herself at a large horseshoe table on a dais. Behind her gilded armchair against the marble wall was an enormous spray of camellias and pink roses, blooming, in Gautier's words, "like a gigantic vegetal fireworks." Twelve black men, wearing twisted white turbans, green jackets with gold corners, wide red pantaloons sashed with a belt of cashmere, the entire outfit braided and embroidered on every seam, walked up and down the dais steps, giving or taking dishes from the lackeys. Others also remember these gala suppers: an English Ambassador in the time of Alexander III speaks of the beautiful "Bal des Palmiers," where supper was served in an immense salon transformed into a Winter Garden. Tables were laid around the base of palm trees brought from the conservatories of Tsarskoe Selo and embedded in parterres of flowers, giving the hall the effect of a tropical grove.

Mrs. Lothrup wrote, "In the hall where supper was served, a balcony ran all around, and at each end were projecting balconies where two orchestras played alternately. Two thousand people were seated at supper and served at the same time with no confusion. On the tables which were six feet wide were arranged great pieces of silver in a design of horses and knights perhaps three feet long, then a silver vase with palms and flowers, then another design, then a silver candelabrum holding fifteen candles and another fine piece, all of pure silver. For every two people, there was a salt cellar of silver in different shapes; mine was a bear. Forks, knives and spoons were all very handsome, many of silver gilt. In one fine room was an immense round table and a buffet all around it for cakes, tea, etc. Another buffet in a corridor must have been 150 to 200 feet long. At all there were champagne, tea, lemonade, cakes—all very handsome. During the evening, ices in the shape and color of fruits were handed around."

Mrs. Lothrup remembered that Alexander III was dressed in dark trousers and the scarlet tunic of the Chevaliers Gardes and carried a brass helmet with an eagle on top, and that his small and vivacious wife, Empress Maria Feodorovna, was in white gauze striped with silver, with strings of diamonds about her neck, great diamonds in her ears and a tiara of "superb diamonds." After supper the waltzes continued until one-thirty. At the departure of Their Majesties, the company immediately dispersed in a flurry of furs and cloaks into the frosty air and the glittering scene disappeared almost as if a magic wand had been passed over the company.

• • •

The dark days of winter lasted so long in the northern capital that the coming of spring and the few sunny days of the year were greeted as a miracle. For a short time of intense beauty, the Neva sparkled bright blue, the days lengthened into the opalescent midsummer white nights, and St. Petersburg blossomed in green.

During their reigns both Alexander I and Nicholas I had sponsored the creation of public parks and gardens in every city. Nowhere were these green parks more beautiful, or more of a triumph of man over nature, than in Petersburg, where trees and flowers were lovingly made to grow in a climate and ground as dreary as the moss plains of Siberia.

The Summer Garden, on which Peter the Great had lavished so much attention, was the most famous and beloved of the people of the city and the inspiration of its poets. Centrally located in the mainland part of the city, it was bordered on one side by the Neva and on the other sides by canals. Long, tree-lined *allées* with graceful white sculptures were interspersed with parterres of flowers. In winter, the flower beds were packed with straw and mats and the statues covered with little wooden huts. In April, when people took off their furs, the trees and statues took off their winter coverings. In spring and summer the gardens were perfectly kept; the grass was continually watered and the paths swept. The tall railings and the large iron gates of the Summer Garden with their iron wreaths, arabesques and bars had been made by the renowned metalworkers of Tula. They were so famous for their beauty of design and composition that in the mid-19th century one Englishman traveled from London especially to see them and, after making sketches of them, returned home contented.

Pushkin loved the Summer Garden and, as he lived not far away, on early summer mornings when the garden was quiet and deserted he would often go there. In 1834 he wrote to his wife, "The Summer Garden is my backyard. I wake up and go there in my robe and slippers. After dinner I sleep there, read and write. It is my home."

The Summer Garden was the promenade and recreation field for the youth of St. Petersburg. Young ladies came with their governesses, teachers with pupils, nurses with infants. There one could happily observe little children at play. All through the 19th century, it was the custom of all classes to dress their little boys until they were seven or eight in Russian peasant fashion—hair cropped close all around, neat kaftans with smart little belts after the fashion of the merchants of Gostinny Dvor, and high Tatar caps like the sledge drivers', or those of the Cherkes, with fur borders. Not until nine or ten were well-to-do boys dressed in the European fashion; even the little Grand Dukes in the palace dressed in this same way. With their nurses from all over Europe, the children learned all languages at once. The foreign nurses took up the rich words of endearment of the Russian language, which is full of affectionate and tender diminutives: *lyubezny* (my dear), *milenki* (my little darling), *golubchik* (my dove), and *dushenka* (my little soul). Tchaikovsky opened his opera *The Queen of Spades* with a charming scene set in the Summer Garden: nurses are watching their charges and the children break into a merry chorus.

Throughout the month of May, especially on Sundays, the Summer Garden was the scene of outdoor *fêtes*. A military band would play and ladies in their finery would stroll on the arms of officers in their resplendent uniforms. On Whitsunday, the second Sunday in May, Russian merchants gathered there for a special ceremony which endured until 1917. All their marriageable sons and daughters would meet there on that day, the sons to gaze, the daughters to be gazed at, all in a row along the flowery parterres, with their mothers stationed behind them. The young men in their best kaftans and furred hats, their beards finely curled, would walk with their fathers along the blushing row of silent damsels. The girls wore their best holiday dresses and were covered with as much gold and as many jewels as they and their mothers could rummage from their own or their grandmothers' wardrobes. This was called the "Showing of the Brides." If a choice were made, eight days later there would be a second meeting of all the principals which took place in private. Similar Bride Shows for merchant families took place in every provincial town on the eve of great religious processions.

Some parks in the city were favored by special groups; the German artisans especially loved one public garden where they gave concerts, balls and illuminations. On the various islands were many parks; in Petrovsky Park in the late 19th and early 20th centuries historic naval battles were re-enacted on the lake for the public, using period uniforms and real ammunition, followed by great fireworks displays. At Ekaterinhof, there was a traditional May Day promenade of carriages at which the Emperor always appeared. Outside Petersburg, in the Imperial parks, there were many special summertime events: at Peterhof in July, *fêtes* were held to which the entire population of the city was invited.

In 1837, the first railroad was constructed between St. Petersburg and Pavlovsk and Tsarskoe Selo. The shopkeepers and tradesmen especially loved to go to Pavlovsk for their Sunday outings. At the train station on the edge of the lovely park was a well-known restaurant, the Vauxhall, and close by it a concert hall where free concerts were given every weekend. The waltz king, Johann Strauss, came from Vienna to conduct these concerts every summer from 1865 to 1872.

The vast Imperial parks and gardens at Tsarskoe Selo were always open to the public, with the exception of a small garden around the Alexander Palace where the Imperial family could stroll in private if they wished. These gardens, wrote an American traveler in 1909, "are one of the most beautifully kept enclosures in the world. On account of the severity of the climate, its trees and flowers have to be watched and cultivated with the utmost tenderness. An invalid soldier commands an army of 500 gardeners. After each falling leaf, a veteran runs and every spear of grass is carefully drawn from lake and river . . . the result is a park that is kept in the order of a ballroom." Baedeker in his voluminous, meticulous guide to Russia in 1914 noted for the traveler that there were popular concerts with good bands every Sunday in the summer in the parks of Pavlovsk and Oranienbaum; that in Peterhof a military band played in the park daily and the Imperial Court Orchestra gave free concerts every Tuesday, Thursday and Friday nights.

Petersburgers loved boating in the summer when the glistening river encompassed the finest parts of the city in a frame of silver. There were forty islands in the archipelago of the Neva delta, and in the summer there was a general exodus of the population to the islands. On many, like Kamenny Island, there were dachas and summer houses.* On some there were famous night spots—in Alexander II's time on Apothecary's Island, the famous Samarkand and Ingels restaurants, where gypsies sang until dawn. A popular excursion was to the point of Elagin Island where a military band gave concerts while all gazed out over the sparkling water. Many islands had swings, parks and amusements. On one of these, the Krestovsky, in the mid-19th century, countless wild paths still crisscrossed each other and opened onto pleasing views of the Gulf of Finland. To this island, the favorite place for the ordinary people of Petersburg, the peasants and merchants rowed over in their painted boats. Numerous sliding hills and swings were erected there, and the beloved samovar could be seen steaming on the grass beneath every group of pine trees, with a noisy party singing and talking around it.

About sunset, Kohl suggested, the traveler should "hire a boat with a half-dozen stout active boatmen and having rowed through the branches of the Neva, enter the Gulf of Finland. There, stop for a while to gaze at the broad disc of the summer sun descending into the horizon . . . then your boatmen, singing, drinking all the time, will briskly skim over the surface of the water, rowing

---

* Even in the mid-19th century, nature was so close to the city that a lady sitting in her garden in the environs of Petersburg was startled by the appearance of a bear whom she frightened away by throwing a volume of George Sand at his head.

completely around some of the islands. You will see the glimmering night lights of the fishing villages, a blaze of light from the brilliantly illuminated dachas and the midnight movement and bustle on the islands which are no less active during these nights than in the daytime."

All during the midsummer nights of the end of June and early July, the six mouths of the river were dotted with boats. Boatmen in rich and fantastic colors played reed pipes, tambourines and horn music. Many pleasure boats were full of musicians, and sometimes parties of friends would hire a boat and all perform on various instruments. The rowers of pleasure boats were often chosen for their fine voices, and sometimes, having rowed against the stream, groups of boats would then drift on the current and the rowers gather in a circle to sing together. They made such exquisite harmony that people came out on their balconies or to the river's edge to listen to the music, and when the concert was ended, the impromptu audience would go their ways, repeating the songs and echoing them in every part of the city.

These northern nights of perpetual light—the "White Nights"—are of magical beauty. "Imagine an atmosphere enchantingly clear and bright," wrote Kohl; "the source of light not visible over the horizon; a night in which nothing secretes itself, neither twittering birds nor wakeful man, nor plants and flowers, whose colors are distinguishable; in short, a night possessing all the charms of night together with all the convenience of day." Imagine, he continued, "all this animated with thousands of boats. Englishmen of nautical experience, proud of their superiority to all others in the management of their elegant little barks; German citizens indulging at night with their families in forgetfulness of the cares of the day; Russians pouring forth over the waters the harmonious airs of their national songs. . . . Step into one of these boats. All the magic scenes of Venice and the canals of gondolas are insignificant in comparison with the picturesque life of the summer north. In vain would you seek a city on the face of the globe which can afford anything to be compared with the charms of these summer nights' excursions in Petersburg."

18. THE EXPANSIVE COUNTRYSIDE

The notion that the Russian common man is a creature apart by himself, oppressed and without influence, and that the higher and more civilized classes of the country float above him like oil over water is entirely false. On the contrary, all within the bounds of the empire are intimately connected, perhaps more intimately than anywhere else, and less divided into distinct and permanently separated classes and castes than we in our Western European aristocratic states. One and the same spirit pervades all, and the same peculiarities which we discover in the bearded muzhik appear, though it is true, under different forms and masks in the topmost pinnacles of the Babel Tower of Russian society. . . .

These bearded fellows are the same people that we meet, groomed and polished in the drawing rooms; they are the caterpillars and the nymphs which have been transformed into those butterflies whose gorgeous colors and whose skill in diplomatic transactions amaze us. They constitute the roots and the trunk whose sap is transmitted to all the leaves of the wide spreading tree . . . and from which its good as well as bad fruit has proceeded.

J. G. Kohl
Russia and the Russians in 1842

IF St. Petersburg was the window through which all Western ideas entered Russia, it was also the focus of the cultural debates which dominated the second half of the 19th century. The 1860's and 1870's ushered in an era of unparalleled searching and examination, when the whole of Russian society was scrutinized. An enormous variety of opinions and ideas existed. Controversy is life blood to a Russian, and never did it flourish as during the fifty-seven years before the Revolution. Writers were contemplating the national character, painters went back to the land, musicians found the sounds of a new music in folk songs. Such was the quality of the cultural renaissance that in many fields Russia drew ahead of the West.

Within two decades, many of the most famous works of Russian literature were created, novels full of startling encounters and relentless discussion about life, death, religion and destiny, works so gigantic and powerful that they are still a standard against which the novel is measured. They brought to the world a rich emotional life, different from anywhere else, characters so alive and scenes so vivid that they now seem part of our lives.

This time of torrential creativity began in the reign of Alexander II, who took the throne in 1855, succeeding his stern father, Nicholas I, who had dominated Pushkin's time. Although Alexander had been raised as a conservative by his father whom he admired, his reign was one of innovation. Thanks to Nicholas, who had the foresight to bring his son into the Councils of State, Alexander came to the throne more fully trained with practical administrative experience than any previous tsar. He was blessed with an excellent memory and spoke five languages fluently. His mother saw to it that from the age of nine the tutor appointed for him was a cultured and kindly man, Vasily Zhukovsky, one of the best poets and finest translators of Russia and a close friend of Pushkin and Gogol. This patient and idealistic tutor, the illegitimate son of a Russian nobleman and a Turkish captive, had an enormous influence on Alexander and is credited with giving the Tsarevich a "predilection for good." Zhukovsky set Alexander an excellent example. When Alexander had done his lessons well, money was given to him to be placed in a box for charity. Zhukovsky taught his pupil history and accompanied Alexander on a trip through Russia and Siberia, pointing out what he thought was significant along the way. Long before Alexander came to the throne, Zhukovsky freed his serfs and, out of his own savings, bought serfs from other masters and then gave them their liberty.

At the time of his wedding in 1841, Alexander asked his father to grant a general amnesty for all prisoners. Nicholas refused to go this far, but all imprisoned debtors were released from jail and told that the Tsar had paid their debts. Many prisoners and exiles were set free. In 1847 Alexander asked to be appointed to a commission inquiring into the abuses by serf owners and afterward begged his father to liberate the serfs. At his coronation in 1856, Alexander ordered a general amnesty, pardoned the Decembrists and ordered cancellation of tax arrears for the poor. In 1857, on his birthday, he expressed his desire to release more prisoners, but it was found that there were no prisoners still confined in the fortress of Peter and Paul.

As soon as he came to the throne, Alexander addressed himself to the most burning question in Russia, the problem of serfdom. Even before he was crowned, in the spring of 1856 he spoke before an assembly of the Moscow nobility and counseled, "Better to abolish serfdom from above, than wait until it abolishes itself from below." He engaged a committee to thresh out the problem and urged it to action with these words: "I wish and demand of our committee general conclusions how to approach this business, not making all sorts of excuses to postpone a plan of legislation until the Day of Judgment. . . . I hope that after all the palaver you are actually going to make a move to do something." But the committee dragged its heels, despite the fact that the Tsar's brother Constantine, an ardent reformer, also kept urging it on. At the same time, Alexander's aunt, the Grand Duchess Helen, a woman active in both social and cultural affairs, drew up a plan for the emancipation of the serfs on her estates and submitted it to the Emperor.

Serfdom was an extremely thorny problem, one which called into question the entire structure of Russian agriculture. Serfdom had come gradually to Russia. Before the 17th century, it was unknown.* As an institution it paralleled almost

---

* Serfdom in some form existed in almost every nation and did not finally end until the 19th century. In Western Europe, the French Revolution of 1789 brought it to an end in France. Between 1807 and 1816, similar reforms were enacted in Spain, southern Italy and most of Germany. In the remainder of Germany and the Hapsburg dominions, serfdom was abolished by the Revolution of 1848. Remnants of serfdom were not abolished in the United States until 1833, when the patroon system in New York State finally ended. As for slavery, the British Empire abolished it in 1833, the French colonies in 1848, the Dutch East Indies between 1859 and 1869. It continued in Argentina until 1853, Venezuela until 1854, Peru, 1856, the United States until 1863 and in Brazil until 1881.

exactly the span of slavery in the United States. Wanting to prevent the constant wandering of peasants and the stealing of labor from one landlord by another, successive tsars enacted laws which circumscribed the right of free movement. In 1649, thirty years after the first slaves were brought to Virginia, Tsar Alexis issued a decree that definitely bound a large portion of peasant families to hereditary labor on their landlords' estates. No serf could marry without his landlord's permission. He could be taken off the land and made into a domestic or house serf.

The fine distinction between Russian serf and American slave was that every serf family, other than house serfs, owned a piece of land where they could labor when the lord's needs had been satisfied, and from which they could sell the surplus for their own profit. In principle the serf was tied to the land, not the master, but in the 18th century Peter the Great established a tax on all the male population which the landlords, not the peasants, were responsible for paying. Thereafter, the tendency was overwhelming to regard the serf as the landlord's property, to be bought and sold without the land, although later this was strictly against the law.

Even when serfdom was most pervasive, not all peasants were enserfed; there were always free peasants, and serfdom did not exist everywhere in Russia. In Great Russia around Moscow, serfdom under individual proprietors was the rule. But in many regions of the north, the south and Siberia, serfdom was unknown. And it was never segregation; lords and serfs worshiped side by side in the same churches. Serfdom was an estate, not a class, and within the estate were many variations. When Alexander II came to the throne, 37.7 percent of Russians were classified as serfs, according to the census of 1858. Of these, half were state peasants, whose only obligation was to pay a tax to the state and who could, with authorization from their community, leave to seek work freely in the cities or anywhere else. For the others, tied to individual landlords, obligations varied widely; for some it was a sum of money, for others it was labor. Increasingly, in the 19th century, serfs availed themselves of a system called *obrok*, which meant that they paid a tax to their landlords and worked elsewhere at a variety of occupations. In 1858, just before emancipation, 67.7 percent of all serfs were on *obrok*.

Some serfs living on rich lands became rich themselves. Peasants were shrewd and capable traders and in the 19th century they controlled much of the trade of the nation. Peasant entrepreneurs sometimes remained serfs even after they had amassed fortunes; paradoxically, some even had serfs of their own. Abuses of the system were sometimes horrible; there were monsters and misers, but there were also warm and responsible relationships between landlords and serfs. The worst evil of the system was that serfs, like slaves, had no civil rights and were without redress, totally subject to the arbitrary will of their owners.

From the end of the 18th century onward, many enlightened Russians had been agitating for the freeing of the serfs. Some noblemen unilaterally freed the serfs of their estates. In the 19th century there was an ever mounting concern over the issue and the majority of Russian opinion was in favor of correcting this injustice. But there were people, much like the plantation owners of the American South, who firmly believed that it was natural for some individuals to be born free and others in slavery, that God had not desired equality in nature and that it was wrong for the Christian to rebel against inequality in society.

The tenacious myth that old Russia was inhabited exclusively by fabulously wealthy nobles and miserably poor peasants has little basis in fact. The entire question of emancipation was further complicated by the fact that, like the peasants, the "nobility" was not a well-defined class but an estate which contained many different classes. There were rich noblemen—according to the census of 1858, 1,400 of them in a land of 60 million. But a wide abyss yawned between such families as the Vorontsovs, the Sheremetevs and the Yusupovs and the rest of the gentry estate.

In an effort to create a meritocracy which would reward ability, Peter the Great had established a system of ranking for every one of his subjects. Peasants were tied to the land, merchants and traders to trading, and the nobles and gentry had the obligation to enter state service, either military or civil. Everyone was recognized as belonging to one of these estates. Any educated person could apply to enter state service, regardless of background, entering at rank fourteen and aspiring to rank one. As soon as a person reached the eighth rank, which corresponded to a colonel in the army or a captain in the navy, he automatically became a "noble." (Pushkin entered service at the tenth rank, Gogol as a fledgling professor at the fourteenth rank.) Titles in themselves were unimportant, and pedigree counted for little if it was not linked to a suitable state ranking. There was a high degree of social mobility; one could move from one estate to the other, sometimes with alarming speed. Nobles in Peter's time, if they did not educate themselves or if they concealed serfs, were automatically thrown out of rank and sent to the army as common soldiers to start climbing the ladder all over again.

Serfs in the army could rise in two generations to noblemen. Dostoevsky, whose father was a modest doctor, was classified as a noble. Lenin's grandfather was a serf, but Lenin was born a nobleman because his father had achieved the civil service ranking of hereditary major general. So much more important was rank than pedigree that there was a popular saying in Russia that *"Chin, chai and shchi* [rank, tea and cabbage soup] are our gods."

In this matter, Russia was completely different from Western Europe and England, where title and lineage counted for everything. In Europe, titles were held only by the eldest sons, and fortunes tended to accumulate and grow in the hands of a few noble families, encouraging a snobbishness and exclusiveness of class which even today are difficult to bridge. Both because of the ranking system and the informality of the Russian character, there never was a perfumed, haughty aristocracy, except for a small circle around the court. To a Russian, the profound respect shown by the English working class for a "gentleman" was incomprehensible. Even in 1790, Alexander Radishchev, a liberal writer of Catherine's time, wrote proudly that "boasting about one's ancient lineage was an evil eradicated from Russia." Early in the 20th century, the English writer Maurice Baring wrote that he could find no feeling of aristocratic class consciousness among the Russian nobility as compared to the landed families of Britain.

In Russia, once daughters were provided for, lands and fortunes were equally divided among all the sons. Each son had a right to bear the family title and to pass it on to his sons in turn. Under this system, family lands tended to disappear in three or four generations. In the 19th century the majority of the gentry in Russia were living modestly. Penniless princes proliferated; there were wandering peddlers who could legitimately be called prince. Tolstoy's family butler was a prince, while Tolstoy, a count, considered himself "upper middle class." According to the 1858 census, only 18,500 nobles could live independently on their estates; in the province of Ryazan, 1,700 lived as one family with their peasants, plowing the fields and sharing the same kinds of houses.

At the time of emancipation, one-third of the landowners had fewer than ten serfs apiece. Consequently, the reapportionment of land and equitable repayment were an enormously complicated business. Emancipation without reimbursement meant ruin for the landlord; emancipation without land, ruin for the peasant. Nevertheless, when, after four years, Alexander saw that little headway was being made, in 1860 he liberated all the crown serfs. Then, overriding all objections, he spoke as an autocrat: "This I desire, I demand, I command," and set a deadline for the rest of the nation. On March 3, 1861, he signed the emancipation decree into law, two days before Lincoln's first inauguration, and two years before the United States freed the slaves.

In the United States, the nation was so bitterly divided over the question of slavery that the landlords of the South went to war to preserve their way of life. In Russia, although there was grumbling, the landlords accepted the Tsar's will peacefully. But perhaps even more than for America, emancipation was an enormous and shaking change for Russia. Five times as many people were involved. After emancipation, many landlords simply did not know how to operate independently and promptly went bankrupt. Many peasants, forced to buy their own tools and deprived of the use of common lands, lived worse than before. They began leaving the land in droves to seek work in the cities. In the United States it required a century for the nation to adjust to the social changes brought about by emancipation—and the process still remains unfinished. Russia still was attempting to solve the myriad problems brought by emancipation when the Revolution came.

. . .

In the years immediately following the emancipation, everyone was talking about the land and "the people." Russians by nature love the country. Lyric descriptions of a visit to a commodious and placid country house fill the pages of their literature. Even those members of the gentry who were forced by their work to live in cities would pass long visits at the family country house, however modest. Merchants and professional men bought country houses, called *dachas*, as soon as they could afford them, and there they hurried whenever their work permitted. But now the whole life of the countryside took on a new importance. Great attention was paid to the masterpieces of folk art. Intellectuals idealized peasant life. Beginning in the 1860's, there was a back-to-nature movement among university students, who affected long hair and beards and disheveled peasant blouses. Singing folk songs and mouthing socialist slogans they had learned at school, they flocked idealistically to the countryside to immerse themselves in peasant life. The peasants looked at these newcomers with some astonishment, sometimes turning them over to the local authorities.

Russian artists turned to the simple peasant and set themselves to depicting his life with realistic accuracy. In the second half of the 19th century, it was from the provinces that many of the foremost artists of the land appeared. The provincial landed gentry contributed more perhaps to Russian culture than any other group. Pushkin, Gogol, Turgenev, Tolstoy, Glinka, Tchaikovsky, Rimsky-Korsakov, Mussorgsky and Diaghilev, as well as a host of other painters and poets, all sprang from the countryside. Even Dostoevsky, generally thought of as a man of the city, remembered with joy the summers he spent as a boy in a little country house that his father had bought in the countryside outside Moscow. Chekhov was a grocer's son, from the small provincial town of Taganrog.

Yet, ironically, just as artists were turning their closest attention to the life of the country, it was beginning to change, and they had little idea that they were recording a way of life that was already disappearing.

Life in the provincial countryside was placid. Gogol pictured it this way in "The Fair at Sorochintsy":

Not a sound in the fields. Everything is as though dead. High in the heavenly gulf a single lark flutters, his silvery song climbing down the stairways of the air towards the enamored earth. . . . A myriad of insects, like emeralds, topazes, rubies, rain down upon the many hued vegetable patches shaded by giant sunflowers. Great streaked haystacks and sheaves of golden wheat stand ranged as in an encampment covering the endless plain. The boughs of cherry trees, plum and apple and pear sag with the burden of their fruit. . . . What a delight, what easy leisure lies in those summers of Little Russia!

When Pushkin described a country family in *Eugene Onegin*, he wrote:

You have a Russian family setting
With tea and jam and endless tattle
About the weather, flax and cattle.

The country house, half hidden by trees, was a warm and familiar feature of the landscape of old Russia. These houses, the majority of them wooden, were comfortable and cozy rather than luxurious. There were no châteaux in Russia—in the European sense—no walls, no moats, no manicured parks or formal flowery parterres. Just before the First World War an English visitor wrote this description of a typical country house: "The house stands preferably on a river bank, or on a hillside. It is half-hidden amidst a grove of trees. Frequently, it has a veranda and a balcony supported by massive white columns. Near the house there is almost sure to be a linden tree avenue leading to an orchard of apple, pear and cherry trees. . . . Indoors, a wide entrance hall, a big dining room, a drawing room, a kitchen full of busy chattering life, stairs leading to all sorts of quaint nooks and corners, well-stocked storerooms, libraries, often containing old and valuable books, old-fashioned mahogany furniture, family portraits on the walls and generally a snug and soothing sense of leisure, security and remoteness from the bustle of the world. Such is the home of the average landowner or country squire."

In 1873 an English lady visiting central Russia wrote of the calm and beautiful countryside surrounding such a country home, "There were plains, extending far and wide unenclosed by hedges, bright green fields of flax and waving corn in the midst of forests of sombre pine; the numerous eagles careening aloft in the clear blue sky; the peasants in their gaily colored costumes merrily singing their native airs while at their work, or sitting down under the shade of the birch trees taking their repast, whilst in the background the white house of the proprietor is half-buried among the trees and close by the white church with its blue dome bespangled with gold stars, its tapering gilt spire and numerous glittering crosses all rendered doubly brilliant by the rays of an unclouded sun. There, both lord and peasant offer up their prayers every Sunday and Saint's holiday. When the peasants have finished their repast they devoutly turn towards the church and make the sign of the cross as they bow down in the shade to take their midday nap for two hours during the excessive heat.

"During the summer the inhabitants of a Russian country house live almost entirely out of doors; they pass their time in sitting under the trees, reading or smoking (for many of the ladies smoke), embroidering and chatting, or they stroll into the woods in parties to look for mushrooms which form a favorite dish at their tables. Nothing indeed can be more pleasant than the life in a country house; everything is easy and without restraint. There is not that splendor and opulence we see in England, on the contrary, the rooms are but scantily furnished—only what is necessary for use is kept there."

No people understand the extremes of both pleasure and peace better than the Russians, and many painters captured in their canvases the enveloping serenity of their national landscape. Isaak Levitan caught the broad still expanses of lake and meadow; Boris Kustodiev, in his painting of his wife and baby at their country house, the warmth of wood and freshness of lilacs. In one of his finest canvases, Ilya Repin, himself the son of a peasant from the Ukraine, painted several generations of a Russian family all sitting peacefully reading while a luminous sunlight streams through the trees.

Enormous distances and bad roads separated people in the provinces, and because of this, hospitality was open and generous. An old Slavic proverb goes,

"A guest is always welcome." Victor Tissot, traveling in the isolated Russian countryside in 1893, commented, "Never is the unexpected arrival of a visitor or a stranger a surprise, and it was always a pleasure. Family life is ample and free. You are received if anyone at all has sent you, or even simply by presenting yourself. Guests are welcome to stay as long as they please, one night or six, or several weeks." Rather than allow their guests to return home at night, every apartment in the house was turned into a sleeping room. Beds were made up on sofas and chairs, accommodation found for a dozen acquaintances with as little care about the trouble as if "it were merely a shakedown of straw in the stable."

The relaxed informality of life in such houses often confused Europeans who sometimes found the easy manner between servants and masters embarrassing. In 1805 Martha Wilmot commented, "'Tis by no means uncommon to see masters and servants mingle in the same dance, and in visiting a strange house I have more than once been puzzled to find out which was the mistress and which the *femme de chambre*."

Amusements in the country were simple. People played *gorodki*, a kind of quoits, rocked on swings and seesaws, and went swimming in streams and ponds. Stanislavsky wrote of water festivals at his family's country house near Moscow at the end of the 19th century. A tremendous rowboat carrying a brass band would precede a procession of gaudily painted boats, and the day would be given over to rowing contests and swimming for prizes. On St. John's Night in the summer, "young and old would take part in making an enchanted forest. Costumed in sheets or masked for the purpose, some of us would go into the trees and wait for the coming of the fern seekers on whom we would mercilessly descend from our hiding places. If we hid in the bushes, we would rush out, and if in the grass we would crawl out. . . . Often on summer nights, all the neighbors would come together for the purpose of spending the whole night outside and meeting the dawn." Name Days and holidays were great events, such evenings as Pushkin described in *Eugene Onegin*, when after the evening's dancing and cards, a place was found for every guest on tile stoves, divans, couches; some even curling up in cozy eiderdowns on the stairs.

Lev Tolstoy's youngest daughter, Alexandra, tells of life at Yasnaya Polyana where at Christmas everyone put on fancy dress and told fortunes at New Year's:

All the household servants, thirty in all, dressed themselves in their best and came into the house where they joined in all sorts of games and danced to the fiddling of old Grigori.

It was very jolly, there were mummers, always a bear with its master, a goat, peasants and women dressed up as Turks.

Sometimes gypsies would come and interrupt their eternal wandering to sing and dance. She writes:

The gypsies used to gather at the home of some person living in the outskirts of Tula. The members of the chorus took up their places: the women—in their bright-colored dresses, vivid kerchiefs, with gay shawls draped over one shoulder—in a semicircle in front. Behind them were ranged the slim, swarthy men with their guitars, in silk shirts of various colors and velvet sleeveless coats. The leader stood facing them. He would run his fingers over the strings of his guitar and faintly, barely audibly, in harmonious unison, the song began; louder and louder, faster, more piercing rang out the rich powerful chords of the guitarists. The tempo increased, the guests stamped the rhythm; now the guitarists were striking the strings full with their whole fists. Suddenly in floated the gypsy women dancers, serenely, one after another. In they came stretching their arms out as if to someone, first throwing themselves forward, then withdrawing, their heads proudly tossed back, and all the while tapping the rapid rhythm with their feet. Their teeth flashed, the golden coins on chains around their necks jingled. The men of the chorus yelled and whooped, the women dancers urged themselves on with guttural, staccato exclamations, the guests shouted. . . . Suddenly from the back row bounced a male dancer. He slapped his knees, the floor and like some demon whirled around two of the women, flitting in and out at a frantic rhythm. The tempo went still faster, the whooping grew louder, the guests yelled, the excitement reached a peak. . . . The music stopped, the dance was over.

Horses played an important part in country life. Russians loved fine horses and were such excellent horsemen that for three years in succession they captured the prestigious King Edward Cup in England for dressage and jumping. In 1914 Russia had more horses than any other country in the world—35 million as compared to its nearest rival, the United States, with 24 million. Many fine breeds were raised in Russia; the dapple-gray, chestnut and black Orlov, developed in the 18th century, was among the finest carriage horses in the world. The government put such importance on horse breeding that it sponsored breeding farms to keep lines pure and even had a special Ministry of the Horse. Tolstoy loved horses so much that with his earnings from *War and Peace* he bought a large estate of ten miles square in Samara, and there established a stud farm where at one time he kept four hundred English Thoroughbreds, Rostopshchins, and Kabardian Trotters; at this estate he often organized lively horse races with the local Kirghiz tribesmen.

Russians considered fox hunting much too formal and hunted instead for wolf, bear and elk. The swift Russian borzoi was trained for wolf hunting. Hunters set off on horseback accompanied by a group of these fleet, elegant dogs. Two borzois would set out in pursuit of a wolf across the broad fields, and, coming in one on each side, would bite the wolf behind the ears and bring him down. Stanislavsky wrote, "With the beginning of the hunting season and until the coming of the frosts, the kennels came to life. With dawn there would come the sound of the hunting horn, pedestrians and mounted kennel men surrounded by full packs of dogs would rush hither and thither and the hunters would arrive in their equipages, singing and followed by a wagon with provisions for the breakfasts in the forests. On their return they would show the animals they had killed, usually hares and wolves . . . at night there would be music, dances, games."

Tissot tells of staying in a country house in the Ukraine. His room had floors of polished oak, wolfskin rugs on the floor and bright blue and red curtains on the windows which looked out onto a little wooden balcony. "The nights of the steppe were brilliant. They have a reflection of gold and blue. It seems as if the sky is illuminated with a thousand tiny flames that sparkle like diamonds. . . . After the hunt coming back at night by the light of torches and the sound of hunting horns, pistol shots and the hurrahs of the hunters and beaters, all would dance all night."

The Russian countryside was rich. There were wild game and birds in forest and field, fish rippling in ponds, streams and rivers. An English traveler to the steppe in the time of Peter the Great marveled at the luxuriant growth of wild flowers and herbs which "spring up like a garden as soon as the snows are departed. Asparagus, the best I ever ate, grows so thick you may in some places mow it down." In 1792, William Coxe, in his *Travels*, wrote, "Mushrooms are so plentiful as to form an essential part of the peasantry's provisions. I have seldom entered a cottage without seeing an abundance of them, and in passing through markets, I was often astonished at the prodigious quantity for sale; their variety was no less remarkable than their numbers; they were of many colors, amongst which I particularly noticed white, black, yellow, green and pink. Russian peasants are skilled at recognizing them and hand down their lore from peasant to child. Many mushrooms never ventured on in this country are in daily use by all classes in Russia." Thousands of basketfuls, thousands of wagonloads, he says, were brought from the country to Moscow. Peasant women and children carrying painted birch-bark baskets gathered mushrooms in great quantities and sold them in the towns. Peasants used mushrooms to make preserves and pickles, which they substituted for fresh vegetables during the long winter.

Another Englishman, traveling in the countryside in 1873, wrote, "Immense quantities of strawberries and raspberries grow wild in Russia, also red and black currants. . . . In the northern provinces there is a kind of yellow fruit in the shape of a mulberry, called *maroshka*, which makes an excellent preserve, and also is used medicinally as a remedy for dropsy. Various wild berries, such as cranberries, bilberries, etc., abound in the forest."

Russians loved rich and lengthy meals and nowhere more so than in the country. The pages of Gogol and Chekhov contain many descriptions of succulent country meals; Tolstoy wrote lovingly of *pirozhki* that melt in the mouth. The rich peasants of the Volga made it a practice to "set up tables" at least twice a year, to which they would invite 100 to 150 less prosperous peasants for huge feasts. They hoped that their generosity would be appreciated and that the peasants would make themselves available for help when they were needed. Pavel Melnikov-Pechersky, describing the high tea of a rich peasant in the late 19th century, spoke of the samovar, polished until it "gleamed like fire," placed on a table surrounded by "all kinds of sweetmeats, candies, pastila, cakes, honey cakes, treacle cakes, walnuts, American nuts, almonds, pistachios, raisins, dried apricots, figs, dates, Kiev glazed fruits, fresh apples and apples stewed with cranberries. There was also fresh caviar, *balyk* [cured fillet of sturgeon], ham and pickled mushrooms . . . carafes of colored vodkas and a bottle of Madeira."

A great deal of effort went into the preparation of various specialties, starting with the cabbage soup that was the staple of every peasant meal. Country houses had large storerooms and were completely self-sufficient, ready to survive the long isolated months of winter. A Russian lady writing in the early 20th century described the storerooms in the province where she lived as "large bright rooms with large windows and the walls entirely lined with shelves. On one side of the walls from ceiling to floor were set poles upon which hung smoked hams, smoked tongues, whole sides of bacon, homemade sausages, homemade cheese. Under the shelves stood buckets with butter, sacks with buckwheat and cereals for kashas, small barrels with salted apples, pears and mushrooms. Casks with salt and flour, dried beans, mushrooms, soup greens, peas, sacks of dried apples and other dried fruits and cones of sugar. On higher shelves were large jars full of all sorts of pickles, mushrooms of several varieties, beets, carrots, turnips, tomatoes, cauliflower, onions, cucumber, string beans, red and white cabbage, leeks, melon, watermelon, cherries, crabapple, pears, and gooseberries. On other shelves were all the jams, all sorts of berries and fruits in immense jars, and then johns and demijohns of syrups used in winter for ice creams, creams and jellies, and homemade fruit candies and dried fruits. Plus a large cellar packed with ice.

"Sauerkraut was put away in great quantities. At harvest time a cart load of cabbage was bought for a middle-sized family; more if the family was larger. At the end of August most yards looked alike—the cabbage was dumped in one corner of the yard while in the middle some half dozen women armed with chopping knives were busily occupied with chopping cabbage in two or three troughs set on tables. Then, cucumbers were salted. Carrots, turnips, beets were placed in large boxes with their roots buried in sand, eggs kept in ashes or oats or dipped in lime water or in olive oil. Cauliflowers were hung along the walls or from the ceiling of the cellar itself.

All liquors, brandies and sparkling drinks were prepared and put away for the winter, as well as vinegar and mustard, vegetable oil and yeast and various meats and fishes. . . ."

The single volume that gives the most accurate idea of the bountiful hospitality considered normal in a Russian household is the famous cookbook of Elena Nikolaievna Molokhovets. Elena Molokhovets was a housewife from a military family. An excellent cook, she was forever collecting and jotting down recipes. In 1861, when she was thirty, as a surprise present for her Name Day, her husband had her recipes printed and the book quickly took wing, becoming the staple culinary guide of Russia until the Revolution. Called *A Gift to Young Housewives; or How to Diminish Household Expenses,* this remarkable cookbook ran through twenty-eight editions from 1861 to 1914, selling more than 600,000 copies. Russians still gleefully quote passages from her now legendary pages: "If twenty-six people arrive unexpectedly for dinner, do not worry. Go to the cellar and take down one or two hams hanging there. Take one pound of butter and two dozen eggs. . . ." In her enormous cookbook, a thousand pages long, there are more than four thousand recipes, among them recipes for the preparation of a dozen kinds of game birds and more than twenty varied pâtés. The extraordinary diversity of her book is quite startling. In her section on babas, she includes fifty-two different recipes, the first being the well-known "baba au rhum" and the last being a "snow baba" that uses 24 egg whites. In her four egg yolk varieties, she includes "lacy baba," a "baba for friends" which uses 36 egg yolks and six whole eggs. There are also listed a "coffee baba hastily made," chocolate, almond and poppy seed babas and a remarkable creation called the "capricious baba" followed by her sobering comment, "delicious when successful, which rarely happens."

There are also sections on how to make jam, wine and liquor (including thirty-two flavored vodkas), sausages and pickles. In her first edition, in 1861, she included a section on how to thaw and use frozen meat, much used in Russia but unthought of in the West. Along with her pages of recipes for every conceivable meat, fowl, vegetable and sweet, she offered ideas for meals both modest and fancy, feast and fast for every day of the year, as well as menus for children's lunches, servants' meals, balls and dances, and all the major holidays—more than eight hundred menus in all.

She fills her book with practical ideas, suggesting, for example, that with the vegetable peelings from the kitchen one can thriftily feed two little pigs. (As many people even in Moscow kept cows and other domestic animals in their courtyards until late in the 19th century, this was useful advice even for city dwellers.) She also suggests that water in which rice had been boiled is efficient as a hand softener; that calves' stomachs washed and dried can be used to keep cheese fresh and that the blood of slaughtered animals be poured under the fruit trees in the orchard as plant food. She explains how to dye eggs for Easter (wrap around the eggs pieces of silk or cotton or put onion skins in the water for yellow and then boil) and tells how much special Easter egg dyes cost (gold and silver: two kopecks). She also explains how to set tables for every occasion and includes careful drawings of all necessary culinary utensils, even plans for apartments and houses. Counsels Elena Nikolaievna, "There should always be a room for prayer" and "privacy for each member of the family is important."

In 1911, when Elena Nikolaievna was eighty, a Golden Jubilee edition of her cookbook was printed. All the major Russian newspapers ran editorials of praise. A lengthy preface to this edition included congratulations which poured in from all over the nation. The preface states, "Very few books in the language have been printed in as many copies. There is not a single corner of Russia where this book cannot be found and hardly a single family who does not have its own book." The continuing popularity of Elena Molokhovets' culinary advice is evident in the fact that its last edition, in 1914, was 280,000 copies.

. . .

Even at the end of the 19th century, Russia was still a rural land of villages and small towns. In 1897 there were only eighteen towns with a population of 100,000 or more, and most of these were near the frontiers and the trade routes. Moscow was the only large city in the interior of the country; otherwise there were five hundred villages and small towns ranging in size from 1,000 to 10,000.

In the streets of these small towns walked all the characters whom Gogol and Turgenev described so graphically—the civil servants in their uncomfortable high collars and green hats, the magistrates, a few gilded youths awkwardly aping Western manners, peasant women with bright flowered scarves on their heads and *muzhiks* in bast shoes. When the priest passed in the street, most people bowed; the merchants in the Gostinny Dvor who spent their time playing cards and telling stories would doff their caps. Not far away, in the rundown manor house sat the impoverished nobleman, fatalistically awaiting better times. These types were so well known to readers that when Nicholas I on a tour of the provinces was asked if he wished to inspect the local provincial offices, he is supposed to have answered, "No, it is not necessary. I have read Gogol."

Americans can recognize a little of the rough-and-ready spirit of the Old West in these small, rural, isolated towns. Victor Tissot, traveling through Russia in 1893, noted down the rules posted in a newly formed social club in the provincial town of Chernigov which included the following admonitions:

1. It is prohibited to enter the club in tarred boots. In case of bad weather, when the streets are muddy all members of the club are required to wear galoshes so as not to dirty the floors.
4. The dancing of the cancan during the quadrilles is prohibited and in general all kinds of conduct beyond the limits of propriety.
6. It is strictly prohibited to get drunk beyond the boundaries of decency as is usually practiced at present; if this happens, the buffet manager of the club who has served the drinks shall be punished by a fine of three rubles a person and the sum of these fines shall go toward the building of a library.
10. It is prohibited to fight while playing cards. In case of billiards, it is prohibited to strike one's partner with a billiard cue. A fine of 40 kopecks will go toward paying the club secretary's wages.

The first of Russia's painters to address himself to life in the provinces was Pavel Fedotov (1815–53), one of the painters of Pushkin's remarkable decades. Fedotov was born on the outskirts of Moscow and grew up in a small provincial town. An army officer, Fedotov did not begin to paint until the age of thirty, and although he studied briefly at the St. Petersburg Academy, he was more influenced by the paintings of the Dutch masters in the Hermitage, which he studied carefully. Fedotov was fascinated by anecdote, costume and detail. His paintings, sly satires on the emergence and manners of a newly rising middle class in the provinces, have the sharp bite of Gogol. In his *Major's Courtship*, he shows the excitement of a rich provincial merchant family when a middle-aged impecunious nobleman comes to call. There is an overdressed mother, bubbling with excitement, urging her daughter to be charming, and a father, still wearing a traditional kaftan, standing by, obviously bewildered. Fedotov's paintings were the first to reflect a new critical attitude toward Russian life, an attitude that was to grow much stronger in the 1860's, and his work greatly influenced the realistic painters of the last quarter of the century who were to call themselves "The Wanderers."

The centers of life in all provincial towns were the open markets, full of goods which peasants brought from the countryside, and the colorful fairs and bazaars held regularly throughout the countryside with their accompaniment of gypsies, wandering players and dancing bears.

In Europe, such fairs disappeared during the Middle Ages, but in Russia they remained widespread until the Revolution. They were held in many cities; some specialized in products of a particular region; in all, several thousand fairs of medium and small size were scattered through Russia. Only in the late 19th century, with the coming of the railroads, did their importance gradually begin to wane.

The greatest fair of all, the largest in Europe and, indeed, the world, was the huge fair at Nizhny Novgorod, which took place from July 15 to September 10 every year. The city of Nizhny Novgorod* is located southeast of Moscow in what was one of the richest agricultural districts of Russia. Situated at the junction of two great rivers, where the Oka meets the Volga, goods could be transported there easily by water, and from the middle of the 14th century onward a fair had been held in the neighborhood. In the 19th century, goods were brought there

* Today, the city is called Gorky.

300

from Europe and western Russia by railroad, and from the East by the old trade routes of sledge, barge and caravan.

The Nizhny fair was one of the spectacular sights of old Russia, a swirling kaleidoscope of sights, sounds and varied humanity, which Mussorgsky set to music in his "Fair at Nizhny." Millions of peasants and merchants from Europe and Asia thronged to this immense fair; some Asiatic travelers spent the entire year traveling there and back. During the two months of the fair, the population of the city swelled from 40,000 to 200,000—the daily count of additional visitors was calculated from the amount of bread sold. The equivalent of 200 million dollars' worth of goods was sold or exchanged in six weeks, and the fair established the prices of goods all over the Empire. Even as late as 1914, during those two months of summer, the Nizhny fair attracted more than 400,000 visitors.

In 1872 one of the visitors was an enterprising American, Edna Dean Proctor, who wrote a detailed and vivid account of her visit to the fabled fair. "From the station, we drove at once to the Hotel Russia. . . . The first floor opened to the street, where a throng of vehicles of all sorts was constantly arriving and departing. The next floor was given up to dining rooms in which you might see all the costumes and hear all the languages of Europe. . . . Tanks of running water bordered by growing ferns and flowers were filled with the famous sterlet of the Volga, swimming at ease and ready to be served up at any moment to the epicurean guest. . . .

"At the door of the hotel we took droshkies for the Fair was a mile away. The street was filled with people on foot, and with carriages and drays and carts of every description going back and forth; and as we whirled down the steep slope that leads to the bridge over the Oka, the crowd was so great that it was with difficulty that we could make our way. Cossacks, as mounted police, with flashing eyes and fiery horses which they sat like centaurs, were riding up and down; and what with the strange costumes and languages, the blinding dust which the rising wind swept through the air, and the hum from the boats on the river, we began to understand what is meant by the Fair at Nizhny."

The wharves along the banks of the Oka, which stretched for miles, were piled high with iron, cotton bales and tea, and so crowded with craft that they seemed an extension of the town. As far as the eye could see, the river was alive with steamboats, barges with roofs, tugboats and rowboats; a floating bridge of boats, a half mile long and as wide as an avenue in New York, led to the main fairgrounds. The confusion and animation of this bridge were like nothing else in

Russia. *Drozhki* drivers careened at top speed over this floating road, which was thronged with peasants and pilgrims; Persians and Armenians in long black and blue robes girdled by brilliant sashes and wearing huge turbans, conical fezzes, or high Astrakhan hats; Tatar workmen in rust-colored work jackets; Chinese; Greeks in red tarbooshes; dark-eyed Georgians and Turks in baggy pants.

The bazaar and its suburbs were a separate stone city, specially built for the purpose after a fire in 1824, on a low marshy point of land. It was surrounded on three sides by canals and on the fourth by an open square on which were the residences of the governor and other officials. Twelve long avenues crisscrossed with streets divided the central bazaar area which comprised five hundred or six hundred shops. Along either side, the crowds strolled, watching jugglers or listening to bands of music, while vendors of sweet drinks, sherbets and small wares wandered in the crowd hawking their goods. Around this central area, stretching out in every direction were thousands of buildings made of brick, wood and even yellow, green and red mats, some six thousand shops in all.

Like a human beehive, the bazaar buzzed with life. Along the streets the long lines of restaurants and inexpensive lodgings were crowded with people. Men, women and children gathered about tubs of pickles, or sat on benches munching on sunflower seeds, fruits and nuts, eating cakes and dried fish washed down by *kvas*. Watermelons were sold everywhere. They lay in heaps on the wharves and on wagons, and every man, woman and child both in town and at the fair seemed to be gorging themselves on the luscious red fruit. Steam from the samovars of the tea vendors curled in the air, barbers shaved heads under the open sky, and flocks of pigeons, which no one was allowed to kill, fluttered and cooed on the rooftops and in the trees.

The bazaar overflowed with colorful goods and people. There were piece goods from England and France, perfume from Constantinople. Mrs. Proctor wrote: "Beneath the Governor's house we entered the bazaars, the first devoted mainly to articles of dress and personal adornment. First were Russians from beyond the Urals, with various stones cut at their works at Ekaterinburg, or by artisans at their homes with a foot lathe in the evenings or on holidays; brooches and buttons and seals of perfect malachite; that vivid green overspread with mysterious figures which made it the favorite amulet of antiquity; crystals of amethyst, violet enough to be still a charm against wine; of aquamarine with a clear sea tint in shade or sun; and of topaz from the pale yellow to the orange brown—and rose and pure white crystals cut into globes for necklaces or wrought into twelve-sided seals engraved with the signs of the zodiac—and rarest of all, paper weights where, upon a base of jasper, were grouped the semi precious stones of Siberia fashioned into fruit and leaves.

"Nearby were men of Khorassan and Bokhara with ornaments and slender bars of lapis lazuli and turquoise, and Prussians from the Baltic with amber for the Chinese to burn as fragrant incense before their gods. Then came the Persians from the south shore of the Caspian displaying carpets and shawls and cashmeres —handsome, dark-bearded men in kaftans of their own silk trimmed in gilt bands and speaking French with ease to foreigners. Beyond were men of every race between Nizhny and the Atlantic with the varied fabrics and small wares of their respective countries.

"Russian manufactures were in the ascendent," said Mrs. Proctor. Abundantly displayed were "piles of silks and satins and tissues of Moscow, some of them woven with gold and silver threads to suit the markets of the East and heaps of printed cloths, gay colored for the same buyers; elegant articles of silver and leather, cutlery from Tula and stores of samovars." Peasants, she said, might rather go without shoes than without a samovar and none were so poor to be without one; more than 72,000 samovars were sold at Nizhny every year. In the line of trunk shops were piles of wooden trunks strapped in brass or iron, painted scarlet, green and blue, ornamented with fruits and flowers and strange figures in Persian and Arabic patterns. There were stores full of pictures and portraits of the tsar, stacks of boxes filled with beet root sugar from central Russia and long lines of kegs of caviar from the sturgeon fisheries of the Volga, Kama and the Ural. Most attractive were the vast stores of furs, from wolfskins which one could buy for a few kopecks, bear and tiger skins "elegantly prepared and so cheap!" to the fine glossy sable. Near to these were felts, both fine and coarse for hats and blankets, and winter boots and rugs of Siberian wool for carpets and sledge covers.

Many of the merchants were former serfs who, wrote Mrs. Proctor, although in the past had been allowed by law a credit of only five rubles, had such reputations for honesty that on the security of their word alone they had annually been entrusted with large sums. Now, said Mrs. Proctor, "they trade in their own right and pay tribute to no master. Some were men of noble mien and rare business ability, able to hold high place in any commercial center in the world."

The most important article of merchandise at Nizhny was tea. Of the 15 million pounds of fine quality tea brought to Russia from China through Kiakhta, some went directly to Moscow, but the larger part found its way to the fair, where it was distributed throughout the Empire.

In the Chinese quarter of the bazaar, in houses covered with yellow paint and Chinese characters, with projecting roofs hung with bells at the corners, were the offices of the great tea merchants. There, rare teas wrapped in paper and packed in cases of lead protected by a wooden chest and finally packed in cowhide were tasted. Using a long steel auger with an oblong groove and sharp point the merchants bored into the case and brought out an auger full of tea, which the prospective buyer rolled in his fingers and smelled or chewed. Piled in the tea warehouses on the quays were thousands of such leather-covered packages, each about two feet square. Their precious contents had taken eighteen months to come from Kiakhta four thousand miles away. Securely fastened on boats, camels and sledges, they came first to Perm, and from there down the Kama River and up the Volga to Nizhny. In these warehouses were all sorts of special teas for Mohammedans, for the Kirghiz and Kalmuck tribesmen, as well as the great bulk of teas for Russia proper. "Pure black teas raised in northern China and brought fresh and unimpaired to the market; almost colorless when drawn but possessing an exquisite flavor and bouquet and stirring the blood like wine," according to Mrs. Proctor. "Here too was rhubarb, of which China sends annually through Kiakhta some half million pounds, and silk in curious bales and robes embroidered in brilliant hues."

Under a mile-long gallery by the river and even piled up on the sand banks was the iron of Siberia, the second most important article of traffic at the fair. It was heaped up in every form, from solid bars and sheets and rails to cauldrons for wandering tribes and small household utensils for the cabins of peasants. Skirting the river were warehouses full of cotton, rags for papermakers and hides from the steppe and grain from the productive fields of the south. A little distance away, a broad space was covered with timber which had been floated to Nizhny in rafts and barges; and close to the water, lying in piles on the ground or waiting to be removed from boats, were tons of dried fish from the Caspian and lower Volga, "the principal food of the poorer classes during church fasts which occupy one-third of the year."

To come to Nizhny from the distant oases of the Tatar desert, every spring caravans of five or six thousand camels left for distant points on the Russian frontier. Peter the Great had first seen the importance of these oases and had opened roads from the lower Volga to the Oxus which were still in use in the late

19th century. In two months the camel caravans arrived in Orenburg, eleven hundred miles away, and from there their goods were transported to the Volga to reach Nizhny. The Moslems of Bokhara and its sister states brought wheat and barley from their irrigated fields, cotton in bales and the jet-black curly lambskins of Karakul. The handsomest skins went to Teheran and Constantinople while the less valuable black, white and gray skins made the hats of ordinary Persians and Tatars, and those, which under the name of Astrakhan, went to Europe and America. There were the striped and embroidered *khalat*s of Khiva, garments cut like dressing gowns and highly prized by the Tatars of Russia; gay silken shawls and handkerchiefs of the soft, loosely woven fabrics of Bokhara. The caravans also brought the unrivaled dried fruits of the region—peaches, grapes, apricots and the delicious green and yellow melons of the Oxus.

Mrs. Proctor noted, "Part of this Asiatic merchandise is exchanged for money but most is exchanged for manufactured articles at great profit to the Russians; for iron kettles, cutlery, large copper samovars, jewelry, coral beads, leather, broadcloth, white muslin, chintzes, velvet, gold thread for embroidery, bright-colored shawls and ribbons and sugar—but neither guns nor ammunition, for Russia will not furnish these to her turbulent neighbors.

"Along the wharves were many Tatars carrying merchandise to and fro. Some were clad in kaftans of blue cotton, some in coats of sheepskin with turbans on their heads, or caps with a rim of fur. The most devout among them said their prayers daily in the mosque which rises beside the Armenian chapel and the handsome Russian church beyond the bazaars . . ."

Near the mosque, announcing themselves with flags and streamers and the booming of drums and brass bands, were outdoor circuses, ballets and dramas. Along the river stretched rows of bathhouses built of logs and planks, painted in all the colors of the rainbow and frequented by both men and women. Beyond the bazaar were restaurants, concert and dancing halls, meeting rooms for merchants and a multitude of small inns and teahouses. To the fair crowded theatrical companies, bands of Tyrolese and Hungarian musicians, French concert hall girls, fortune-tellers, showmen of every kind. In the cafés and gardens, gypsies sang and danced. In some *traktir*s choruses of peasant lads in belted red blouses sang and danced wild Russian dances accompanied by tambourines and accordions while the patrons gulped beer and vodka and munched on their *zakuski* of caviar and cucumbers. The Germania Hotel presented choruses of twenty or thirty singing girls; Russians, Germans, Hungarians and Poles.

"At evening," continued Mrs. Proctor, "the city was given up to diversion. Myriad lights gleamed through the streets and along the Oka whose placid waters reflected distinctly every object on shore. Colored lanterns lent their glow to the grounds; music and hum of voices filled the air . . . and in momentary lulls, the peeping of frogs was heard, showing that civilization has not yet wholly reclaimed the ancient marsh."*

* After her visit to Nizhny, Mrs. Proctor continued on to Saratov, where she noted for sale in the stores of the shop windows little busts of Abraham Lincoln, "his grave, kindly face having the same charm on the Volga" as it did at home.

19. HEROES AND ANTI-HEROES

It is difficult for us to carry ourselves back to the days of the early nineteenth century to picture the life of the Russian landowning nobility that produced Pushkin, Lermontov, Gogol, Turgenev and Tolstoy. There can be no doubt that the life of men of that class disposed them to creativeness. They spent unhurried days, traveled by carriage, had time to think, to read; they produced children and trained them in accepted traditions of chivalry, courage, love of their country; they studied languages, believed in the stability of the state, in their own incontrovertible right of dominion over the peasants; they observed holidays, attended church services; when they were ill they rarely had doctors to attend them, they died quietly, resigned to God's will.

They had everything for their needs on their estates. There were cows, sheep, hogs, chickens, turkeys, ducks, heavy sweet cream, fresh butter, rich breads—a full measure of good things. Dogs and horses played a large part in the lives of these landed proprietors. They took pride in their high-spirited mounts and hounds, made a show of smart turnouts and expert coachmen. No one fussed because of the slowness of getting about, because of snowdrifts, blizzards, lack of bathrooms, remoteness from civilization. They knew no other life.

Alexandra Tolstoy
A Life of My Father

307

OF ALL THE COUNTRY HOUSES of Russia, the most famous was Yasnaya Polyana, or Clear Glade, the home of Russia's most renowned country gentleman, Count Lev Tolstoy. Through his books and stories, Tolstoy impressed the life of the Russian countryside indelibly on the consciousness of the world and, over the years, his beloved Yasnaya Polyana became the symbol of its enduring values and spirit.

Lost in the countryside 130 miles south of Moscow, Yasnaya Polyana was an estate of some four thousand acres, which had been owned by Tolstoy's aristocratic grandfather, Prince Volkonsky, and left to Tolstoy. All his life Tolstoy drew strength from this peaceful place which he called his "inaccessible literary stronghold." The grounds were filled with venerable linden trees, birches, firs, elms, elders and huge bushes of lilacs. There were four ponds, a deep stream and four little hamlets of humble *izbas* inhabited by 350 peasant families. The white wooden manor house, embellished by a peristyle of columns and a neoclassical pediment flanked by two pavilions, looked out on this calm rolling landscape.

It was in this house, in 1828, that Lev Tolstoy was born, on a wide leather couch which throughout his life he kept in his study. On this same couch, all his thirteen children were also born. It was at Yasnaya Polyana that Tolstoy wrote two of the world's greatest novels, *War and Peace* and *Anna Karenina*. There he began his teaching experiments with peasants; there he developed the religious philosophy that dominated his later years. It was from Yasnaya Polyana that he fled as an old man of eighty-two, determined to finish his days in religious contemplation. It is at Yasnaya Polyana that he lies buried, in a wooded glade where as children he and his brother had searched for a magic green branch on which they believed was written the secret of happiness for all men.

Tolstoy identified deeply with the Russian peasant; in his mature years he wore a peasant blouse and plowed his own fields. Yet he always remained very much the master of the estate and proud of his aristocratic forebears. Peter the Great had given the title of Count to a Tolstoy ancestor who had been his ambassador and adviser. Tolstoy's mother, Princess Volkonskaya, was the only daughter of a descendant of the original founders of Russia.

Tolstoy's mother died when he was eighteen months and his father when Lev was eight years old. Young Lev was raised at Yasnaya Polyana by a cousin and a Russian nurse to whom he was devoted. Later he was sent to live with various aunts. Even as a child, he had a passionate temperament and could easily burst into tears, either of affection or rage. As a man, his angers could be fearful, although afterward he would always repent bitterly. Always he was split between the two poles of his character, seesawing between his passionate nature and the desire, which he felt even early in life, to find religious and philosophical truth.

At sixteen, Tolstoy was sent to the provincial University of Kazan where he studied Arabic and Turkish. Not succeeding very well, he switched to law, did even more miserably, and after two years was expelled from the university. He went back to Yasnaya Polyana where he embarked on an ambitious program of self-education, voraciously reading the classics, the Bible and Jean-Jacques Rousseau. He spent some time in St. Petersburg, living a disorderly life. He drank, had a passion for gypsy music and singers and, although he always felt himself to be ugly and awkward, loved many women. He gambled so constantly that in 1850, when he was twenty-two, his losses forced him to sell the main part of the house at Yasnaya Polyana, which was dismantled, board by board, and sent to another estate. As his favorite brother, Nikolai, was fighting in the Caucasus, Lev volunteered and there fell in love with a Cossack girl whom he later made into the heroine of his novel *The Cossacks*. He did so well as a volunteer soldier that he was admitted to the regular army as a gunner and took part in the fierce defense of the city of Sevastopol. It was during those turbulent years that Tolstoy wrote his *Childhood, Boyhood, Youth* and his stories of Sevastopol, sending *Childhood* to a distinguished literary magazine in St. Petersburg signed only with the initials "L.N.T."

These first works were hailed; his stories of Sevastopol so moved the Empress that she wept. Alexander II upon reading them was so impressed by the young writer's talent that he ordered him transferred to a less dangerous position. When Tolstoy returned to St. Petersburg after seven years in the south, he was welcomed as a triumphant hero by the writers of the capital. But Tolstoy had begun a school for peasants at Yasnaya Polyana and was deeply absorbed in educational ideas and theories. To study the teaching methods of other lands, he made two extensive trips abroad in 1857 and 1860, visiting France, Germany, Switzerland, Belgium and England. In London, during his second trip, he met his literary idol, Charles Dickens, whose works he always kept by his bedside. He went to visit his brother, Nikolai, who suffered from tuberculosis and was living in the south of France. There, during his visit, Nikolai died in Tolstoy's arms.

Tolstoy later wrote that the death of his beloved brother was "the most powerful impression of my life."

All during his turbulent and often lonely youth, Tolstoy dreamed of a pure and great love. At thirty-four he married a girl of eighteen, Sofia Behrs. Sofia was one of the three daughters of a lady three years older than Tolstoy, whom he had once loved and who had married a Moscow doctor. After their marriage, Sofia devoted herself to Tolstoy and bore him thirteen children, five of whom died. Their forty-eight years of married life were often stormy. Living with a genius was not easy. Sofia did not share her husband's overwhelming love for the peasants and life in the country, and in later years she watched with growing consternation as the writer became increasingly a religious ascetic.

It was in their first bloom of married life at Yasnaya Polyana that Tolstoy began the book that was to become the single most famous Russian novel, *War and Peace*, the immense saga of two families during the years of the Napoleonic war. At first, Tolstoy had thought of writing a novel based on the Decembrists, as he himself identified with the hopes of these idealistic and liberal aristocratic officers of Pushkin's time. Gradually, realizing that these men had formed their ideas during the years of the Napoleonic war, he changed his focus; to understand them, he felt, one had to understand their roots. He began by immersing himself in the atmosphere of the period, doing meticulous research, reading newspaper accounts of the time, ordering stacks of books which were sent from Moscow. Later he was to write, "Whenever, in my novel, historical personages speak and act, I have not invented anything. I used materials of which I have a whole library full."

During the seven years it took Tolstoy to write this colossal novel, which finally ended with the publication in December of 1869 of the sixth and final volume, his young bride, who was only twenty when he began, shielded him from everything. She took over the household accounts and the management of the estate. She cared for a large household, gave birth to four children and still found time to painstakingly recopy his pages in her beautiful curling script. Tolstoy covered his pages with a tight, microscopic, almost illegible handwriting, scribbling innumerable corrections, crossing out sections, adding thoughts between the lines, in the margins and on the backs of pages. As he wrote, he often added trial adjectives in the margins, bits and fragments of ideas from which he then constructed a scene. After the babies slept and the servants had retired, Sofia would begin her work by flickering candlelight. Skillfully, often working far into the night, Sofia deciphered amputated words and half-finished sentences. When she was finished, she would return the neatly copied pages to his night table where he would find them in the morning, only to have to face them again, entirely covered with corrections the next evening. Tolstoy made many drafts of each chapter, usually five or six, and was always unhappy when he had to give up a manuscript and could make no more changes. Patiently, Sofia recopied them all. Before he finished, she had recopied most of *War and Peace* seven times.*

Tolstoy's first drafts were hesitant, even amatuerish, but the more he worked, pouring all of his vitality and energy into his pages, the more he gained power. His characters were both real and imaginary. He drew some of them from people he knew or had known, sometimes hardly bothering to change their names. He would model one character on his grandfather and another on his mother whom he had never known but always idealized, then he would mix them and infuse them with what he called "the juice of fiction." Constantly plotting and replotting events, he would lay out games of solitaire in the evenings, forecasting aloud, "If this game comes out, I'll have to change the beginning" or "If this game comes out, I'll title it . . ." only to fall silent.

By the time he had finished his first chapters he was so consumed with his story that even a fall from a horse which dislocated his right shoulder did not stop him. During the weeks he was forced to spend in Moscow for treatment, he continued to dictate feverishly to his sister-in-law, Tanya Behrs, with his arm in a sling. He would go on for days on end, not noticing her exhaustion, occasionally stopping abruptly in mid-flow to exclaim, "No! That's no good. . . . It won't do! Scrap all that." In the evening, to assembled friends and family in a drawing room lit only with a few candles, he would sometimes read chapters of his book, taking on all different voices of his characters.

In February 1865 the first part of the book, Chapters I through XXVIII, was published under its original title, *The Year 1805,* in *The Russian Herald.* (It was only later that Tolstoy renamed it *War and Peace.*) Shortly before, he had written to a friend, "In a few days there will appear to you the first part of a novel laid in

---

* Sofia carefully saved the rough drafts of Tolstoy's writings and never threw away a scrap of paper on which he had written. The manuscripts for *War and Peace* were laid aside untouched for many years in an unused room. Eventually Sofia had twelve wooden cases made, put all the manuscripts in them, and sent them for safekeeping to the Rumyantsev Museum in Moscow where they remain today.

1805. Give me your unvarnished opinion of it. I would wish that you would take some of these children of mine to your heart; there are some fine people among them, and I love them very much." But the first reactions to his work were disappointing. Critics found this first portion long and slow moving. One whose opinion Tolstoy anxiously awaited was that of his fellow writer Ivan Turgenev. Turgenev, who was ten years older than Tolstoy, had been one of those in the St. Petersburg literary world who had first acclaimed Tolstoy's stories of Sevastopol and his *Childhood, Boyhood, Youth.*

The two writers had been friends, but as the years went by, as they warily circled each other's work, their exchanges had grown increasingly acid. In 1862, when Tolstoy was thirty-three, their differences exploded. Tolstoy suggested that perhaps the real reason for their quarrel occurred when one evening he stopped at Turgenev's estate at Spasskoe. After the kind of lengthy and copious dinner which Turgenev enjoyed, at which wine flowed freely, Turgenev settled Tolstoy in a comfortable armchair in his parlor and gave him his new book, *Fathers and Sons,* to read. Tolstoy fell asleep over the pages and to his embarrassment awoke to see the proud Turgenev's back retreating through the door. Turgenev said nothing about the incident, and the next day the two went to visit the poet Afanasy Fet. Over dinner, Turgenev and Tolstoy quarreled so bitterly over a triviality that Turgenev's horses were summoned and he summarily left. Tolstoy, in a cold rage, sat down and wrote him a letter challenging him to a duel and dispatched a man for weapons and ammunition. Meanwhile, Turgenev wrote a letter of apology and did not receive Tolstoy's challenge until he was already in Paris. The duel between two of Russia's greatest writers did not take place, but Tolstoy and Turgenev did not communicate again for seventeen years.

Nevertheless, when the first chapters of *War and Peace* were published, Tolstoy was anxious for Turgenev's opinion, writing that "he is a person I love less and less as I grow up and yet whose opinion I cherish. He will understand." Turgenev's judgment was harsh: "The thing is positively bad, boring and a failure . . . it is bad because the author has not studied anything, knows nothing and under the names of Kutuzov and Bagration puts forward some slavishly copied portraits of contemporary generals. . . . And who are these young ladies? Some kind of affected Cinderellas?" (Turgenev revised his opinion later, writing to a friend in 1868, "I have just finished the fourth volume of *War and Peace.* There are some intolerable things in it and some which are admirable. The admirable ones, which on the whole predominate, are so magnificently good that nothing better has been written by anyone in Russian and probably nothing so good has ever been written. . . .")

But Tolstoy was too deeply immersed in his creation to be destroyed by these first negative reactions. Although sometimes he was discouraged—reading over the clean pages which Sofia returned to him and saying, "It seems pretty foul to me"—he continued to grasp at every shred of information about the period, even advertising in the newspaper for a complete set of the *Moscow Journal* of the time. He immersed himself in the lives of Napoleon and Alexander I.

The longer he worked, the closer he came to his characters and their lives, absorbing them in some mysterious way from the people close to him. Sofia's vivacious sister Tanya always came to visit at Yasnaya Polyana in the summer. Unlike her sister, Tanya shared Tolstoy's passion for hunting and riding. Together they would set off for long rides and woodchuck hunts. While they rested under the trees, they had long conversations and Tolstoy questioned the pretty and lively Tanya about her flirtations and romances (one of her unhappy passions he transformed into the unscrupulous and seductive Anatoly Kuragin). Later Tolstoy wrote, "I took Tanya, did her over in combination with Sonya [his wife] and came out with Natasha."

He poured much of himself into his heroes—his dreams and aspirations of charity into the idealistic Pierre, his strong love of life and pragmatism into the proud Prince Andrei, his passion for nature and experience of soldiering into Nikolai Rostov. He went to see all the places where the events he wrote about took place. He sketched out the positions of the troops at Borodino in his manuscript and went with his brother-in-law to visit the battlefield. Happily, he wrote to his wife, "I have just come back from Borodino. I am pleased with the trip, very. If only God will give me good health and tranquility, I'll write the best Battle of Borodino yet!"

Nevertheless, when the entire book was published in December 1869 there were many critical reviews. Tolstoy had written his book during the time of the great reforms of Alexander II when serfdom had just been abolished. The popular press, the theater and fiction were filled with lurid denunciations of serf flogging and corrupt nobles of the past. One of Tolstoy's deep desires in the creation of his novel was to show that his serf-owning grandparents, parents and, indeed, even himself were not the inhuman monsters of the popular imagination, but decent men and women who lived the best they could with an unjust institution which they had not created. But it seemed that no one was pleased. The conservatives said that he had belittled great Russian commanders; the liberals fussed because their circle was not represented at all; the radicals reacted shrilly, screaming about "infamous products of an age of serfdom" and "an apologia for gluttonous aristocrats, sanctimony, hypocrisy and vice." Tolstoy was accused of historical inaccuracies and of using too much French. For a while he simply stopped reading all the criticism. While the critics fulminated, the public flocked to buy the book, recognizing it immediately for what it was—an extraordinary literary achievement. *War and Peace* gained a popularity that it has never lost. Without leaving Yasnaya Polyana, Tolstoy had conquered Russia.

• • •

After the titanic creative effort of *War and Peace*, Tolstoy was exhausted. In February 1870 at Yasnaya Polyana he wrote, "All this winter I have done nothing but sleep, play bezique, ski, skate and run, but mostly lie in bed." Drawing strength from nature, he took long walks among the firs and white birches. All his life Tolstoy loved sports and playing games with children. During those winter months he taught his children to ice skate, skimming over the ice doing figure eights and threes with his beard streaming in the wind. He taught the children to ride early, holding them on the horse at first, then letting them go alone as soon as they could manage. He had a passion for hunting. One day while out riding with his sister-in-law Tanya, her saddle slipped. Hanging head downward, she screamed, "Lyovochka, I am falling!" Tolstoy, in mad pursuit of a hare, only called out over his shoulder, "Wait a minute, dear," as he galloped past.

Nevertheless, for Tolstoy "inactivity" was relative. During the three years that followed *War and Peace*, he threw himself back into his theories of teaching. He and all his family joined to instruct thirty-five peasant boys in a school held in a wing of the house. Tolstoy himself wrote a primer and four readers and was terribly disappointed when the first edition did not do well. At the end of his primer, he had appended some general remarks for teachers which included the following precepts: A student can only study well when he studies gladly. The material used for teaching must always be interesting. A child should never be embarrassed in front of teachers or comrades. A child should never fear punishment because of failure to understand, because, said Tolstoy, "The mind of man can only operate when it is not oppressed by external influences."

His family was growing so quickly that an addition had to be constructed onto the house. There, secluded from the bustling life of the household, Tolstoy worked in his little study, which was divided in the middle by bookshelves. In it were his writing table and the leather-covered couch on which he was born. In a little niche stood a bust of his favorite brother, Nikolai. On the walls were portraits of Dickens, Schopenhauer, Fet in his youth, and a group of writers from the circle of *The Contemporary* magazine in 1856, which included Turgenev, the playwright Ostrovsky and a young Tolstoy in his officer's uniform; on the wall there was also a stuffed deer's head and some antlers brought by Tolstoy from the Caucasus on which he hung his towel and his hat. From his windows he could see the lawn which sloped down to the ponds and, far off across the fields, the trains on the newly built railroad flashing by.

He threw himself into reading the classics, Molière, Goethe and Shakespeare. He began a novel about Peter the Great, then abandoned it. He decided to learn Greek and threw himself so intensely into his study that within three months he was reading Herodotus. He dreamed of writing a pure and severe work in the style of the ancient Greeks and wrote to his friend the poet Fet, "Now I firmly believe that I shall write no more gossipy twaddle of the *War and Peace* type."

And yet, through all of this activity, a new idea was germinating. As early as 1870, his wife wrote in her diary, "Yesterday evening he told me that he had in mind the type of woman who is married, in high society, but who ruins herself. He said that the problem was to make this woman only pitiful, and not guilty, and as soon as he found her type, then all the other characters and male types he had thought of earlier fell into place and grouped themselves around this woman." Tolstoy made an outline of this idea, but then dropped it. However, in 1872 an event occurred in the neighborhood which made a profound impression on Tolstoy. The mistress of a neighboring landowner, jealous of the governess in the household, threw herself under a train. Tolstoy went to the railroad station where the autopsy was being performed and was deeply affected by the sight of the broken body. But it was not until a year later, in March 1873, that everything that had been working in his mind suddenly took flame. One night, Tolstoy found a volume of Pushkin's *Tales of Belkin* in the living room and began reading passages of it out loud to his wife. He was struck by the opening sentence: "The guests arrived at the country house." "That's the way for us to write," he exclaimed. "Anyone else would start by describing the guests, the rooms, but he jumps straight into the action." Later that same evening, he went into his study and began writing *Anna Karenina*, whose original first sentence (which eventually began the sixth chapter) was "After the opera, the guests gathered at the home of young Princess Vrasskaya."

For the next two months he wrote furiously. The coming of spring to Yasnaya Polyana always filled him with renewed life and power. He planted trees, sowed seeds and worked with the peasants. In his notebook, he wrote this lyric description of a May night at Yasnaya Polyana: "The leaf on the birch is full grown, like a tender little kerchief. There are mounds of pale blue forget-me-nots, yellow fields of wild garlic. . . . A gray black bee hums, weaves its way and feasts. Burdocks, nettles, the pipestems of rye push upward hour by hour. Yellow primroses. The dew is iridescent on the sharp-pointed tips of grass. They are plowing for buckwheat. . . . The peasant women are pounding the hemp and spreading their gray sacking on the grass. The songs of nightingales, cuckoo birds and peasant women in the evening. . . ." By May 16 he had finished a rough draft of his novel. But then he put it aside, as he did many times during the four years that it took him to complete *Anna*.

Nothing demonstrates better how a character can come to life and overpower its author than the transformation of Anna during those years. Tolstoy's first description of her was "she is unattractive, with a low, narrow forehead, short turned-up nose, rather large. . . ." In the earliest of his five drafts, she was called Tatyana Stavrovich, and she was loud-voiced, domineering and selfish. The men in the life of this unpleasant creature were noble and dignified. But as the drafts progressed, Tolstoy fell in love with his heroine. The horrid Tatyana was gradually transformed into the lovable and irresistible Anna, while the men in her life gradually became more and more reprehensible.

Once again, Tolstoy found his characters in the world around him. He listened to details of the society scandals of Moscow and St. Petersburg. Anna was modeled on two different ladies; her appearance on Pushkin's granddaughter, a beautiful lady with, said Tolstoy, "lively Arabian ringlets and a smooth gait," and her character on a noblewoman famous for her learning and intelligence. He put himself into the novel as Levin, and traits of his wife in both Kitty and Dolly.

While Tolstoy was writing *Anna*, the painter Ivan Kramskoy came to Yasnaya Polyana to do his portrait. Although Tolstoy strenuously resisted the project, Sofia finally persuaded him and the painter caught the writer in his full powers of creativity. Strong and massive, dressed in his gray peasant blouse belted with leather, Tolstoy's intense eyes under their bushy brows seem to pierce the canvas.

Kramskoy later found that those keen eyes had been observing him as well, for he later discovered himself in *Anna Karenina* as the painter, Mikhailov.

Many things interrupted the writing of *Anna*. In 1873–74 there was a failure of crops in Samara where Tolstoy had bought a large estate. He interrupted his work to organize relief, writing so eloquent an appeal to the *Moscow News* that help flowed in from all over Russia to the amount of 1,887,000 rubles and 756,000 pounds of grain. There were family sorrows. The years of *War and Peace* had seen the birth of four children. While writing *Anna*, three were born and died—their youngest, Peter, at eighteen months; another little boy, Nikolai, who lived ten months; and a little girl who lived only long enough to be baptized. Sofia, although deeply affected by these deaths, nevertheless continued as usual to carefully recopy all her husband's drafts.

The first fourteen chapters of *Anna* were published in January 1875 in *The Russian Herald*. The reviews acclaimed the book as brilliant. But Tolstoy had trouble continuing and it was only a year later, in 1876, that he delivered additional chapters of *Anna*. While he was in Moscow he called several times on Tchaikovsky. Meeting the writer whom he idolized as a demigod made Tchaikovsky very nervous. "It seemed to me," he wrote, "that this great searcher of hearts could see right through me and discover my innermost secrets." Tolstoy loved music, and to please him, Tchaikovsky asked Nikolai Rubenstein, director of the conservatory, to arrange a special musical evening. Tolstoy was deeply moved and Tchaikovsky wrote in his diary, "It may be that never in my life have I as a composer been as flattered and touched as I was when Lev Tolstoy, sitting beside me and listening to the andante of my quartet, burst into a flood of tears." When he was back at Yasnaya Polyana, Tolstoy in gratitude sent Tchaikovsky a collection of folk songs which he suggested that he use in his compositions.

Anna Karenina was finally published in its entirety in 1878 when Tolstoy was fifty. Many acclaimed it; a friend wrote Tolstoy that Dostoevsky was running about St. Petersburg "waving his hands and calling Tolstoy the god of art." But others were less kind. Turgenev crackled, "He has gone off the track. The whole thing is sour; it smells of Moscow and old maids." Others called it "a vulgar love affair, permeated with the idyllic aroma of diapers." Tolstoy had lost interest and could hardly bring himself to read the reviews, good or bad. Two years later, he wrote to an admirer, "Concerning *Anna Karenina*, I assure you this that abomination no longer exists for me, and I am only vexed because there are people for whom this sort of thing is necessary."

His books had made him the most famous author in Russia. His royalties from *War and Peace* and *Anna Karenina* amounted to more than twenty thousand rubles a year. At Yasnaya Polyana there were footmen in red waistcoats and white gloves, governesses and tutors. But these trappings of wealth and fame only made Tolstoy more and more uncomfortable. He had always sensed the great power of faith of the Russian peasant and admired his endurance and calm acceptance of all that life could bring of suffering and sorrow. Often, he went out on the Moscow–Kiev road near his estate and encountered groups of wandering pilgrims with eyes full of faith, whom the peasants called "God's People." Tolstoy always took them in for the night and fed them. After *Anna*, he went to church more often and visited a monastery with a friend. He began to put literature aside and intensify the search for religious truth which was to consume him for the last thirty years of his life.

It was in his mood of religious penitence and brotherhood that in 1878 Tolstoy wrote a letter to Turgenev and asked him to forget their past differences. Turgenev greeted the letter happily and came to call on the Tolstoy family at Yasnaya Polyana. All spent a gay evening of witty talk and jokes. But the reconciliation was never deep, and the two were never really friends again. Turgenev was an admirer of Western ideas, a man who had studied in Berlin and who spent most of his life living in Paris as an intimate of Flaubert, Daudet, de Maupassant and the French literary world. He had little sympathy for Tolstoy's deep interest in the Russian peasant and even less for his religious questing, which Turgenev found ridiculous and a useless waste of Tolstoy's talent. In 1880 Turgenev came to ask Tolstoy to participate in ceremonies connected with the unveiling of a monument to Pushkin in Moscow, and found him translating the Gospels into Russian. Tolstoy, deeply immersed in his study, refused to come. Turgenev, a fervent admirer of Pushkin, could not understand this and left offended. Upon his return to Moscow Turgenev ran into Dostoevsky. Although Dostoevsky admitted often being envious of Tolstoy's position and fame, in his column, "Diary of a Writer," he had praised *Anna Karenina* as "a perfect work of art . . . unlike anything published in Europe. . . . There is something in this novel of our 'new word' . . . something that has not yet been heard in Europe although the peoples of Europe have great need of it, however proud they may be." Dostoevsky was then planning to go to Yasnaya Polyana to see Tolstoy, whom he had never met. But Turgenev discouraged him, telling him that Tolstoy was so absorbed in his religious theories that "he could not talk of anything else." Accordingly, Dostoevsky gave up his plan and wrote to his wife that people were saying that Tolstoy was "half mad."

It is interesting to speculate what a meeting between these two giants of Russian 19th-century literature, so different in their backgrounds and their writing, might have produced. Fyodor Dostoevsky was seven years older than Tolstoy, the son of a merchant's daughter and a staff doctor in a Moscow hospital for the poor. Shy and nervous as a youth, Dostoevsky keenly felt his lack of breeding and culture and bitterly resented those of his contemporaries who were richer, better-looking and more elegantly dressed than he. He spent three unhappy years at a School of Military Engineers in St. Petersburg, at night plunging himself into a program of self-education. He devoured books—Schiller, Balzac, Dickens and Hoffmann, melodramas and books on crime. Boldly, Dostoevsky decided to resign from the school and devote himself to literature. In 1846, with the publication of *Poor Folk,* he enjoyed a brief limelight, being praised by the foremost critic of the city, Belinsky, as a rare new talent. But he was teased and made fun of by the city's literary lions, including Turgenev, which deeply offended him.

Idealistically, Dostoevsky embroiled himself in a young socialist group and in 1849, at the age of twenty-six, he was accused of conspiracy against Nicholas I's government and sentenced to death. He had been taken out to face the firing squad when, at the last minute, he was informed that he had been reprieved and sentenced to four years in a penal settlement in Siberia.

It was while he was in prison that Dostoevsky became a believer in the Christian doctrine of salvation through suffering. He believed this so fervently that later, when a friend remarked that his punishment had been unjust, Dostoevsky heatedly replied, "No! Just! The people would also have condemned me had they had to judge my crime. And you know, perhaps the Almighty had to send me to Siberia . . . to teach me something." After his sentence he was drafted into the army and sent to a remote city where he married a local widow, unhappily as it turned out. He rose to officer's rank but then had to resign because of recurrent attacks of epilepsy. In 1859 he was fully pardoned by Alexander II and eventually returned to St. Petersburg. His powerful *House of the Dead,* about his prison experiences, was published in 1864, just as Tolstoy was beginning his work on *War and Peace.*

But while Tolstoy lived secure from financial worry, as a respected figure in the country, Dostoevsky was forced to eke out a living from his earnings as a writer and editor. An inveterate gambler, always in debt, suffering from epilepsy,

Dostoevsky lived a life as turbulent and tragic as any of his heroes and heroines. While still married, he fell madly in love with a tempestuous young woman who became the prototype of all his independent, proud heroines. He traveled with her to Europe, only to have her leave him for a Spaniard in Paris, while he returned to his dying wife. After her death, the magazine he had started failed. *Crime and Punishment,* his first novel on the theme of redemption through suffering, began its serialization in 1866 at the same time that *War and Peace* was appearing in the pages of *The Russian Herald.* As he was working on the last part of *Crime and Punishment,* Dostoevsky suddenly realized that within three months he owed another novel to an unscrupulous publisher from whom he had accepted an advance. Failure to fulfill this agreement meant that the publisher had the right to print everything that Dostoevsky might produce for the next nine years without paying him. With the help of a nineteen-year-old stenographer, Anna Snitkina, he worked feverishly and, drawing on his own experiences, produced *The Gambler* in one month. Then he married the young stenographer and fled to Europe to avoid his creditors.

For four years he and his new wife lived in Germany, Italy and Switzerland; *The Idiot* was written almost entirely while Dostoevsky was abroad. His devoted wife provided him with great emotional support and during their fourteen years of marriage he produced several great novels, culminating with *The Brothers Karamazov.* With his wife's help, Dostoevsky was finally able to reorganize his finances and even to acquire a house in the Russian countryside.

Dostoevsky was a deeply religious man and politically a strong conservative Slavophile. For a short time, he became editor of the archconservative magazine *The Citizen* and later a regular contributor. He waged war against the liberals and the revolutionaries, who repaid him by calling his work "corruption" and "lunacy." For Dostoevsky, Western society was too materialistic and commercial; instead he felt the values of the simple Russian people—meekness, compassion and acceptance of the will of God—were what society should emulate.

During their parallel careers, as Tolstoy was writing about the world of the country gentry, a class and a way of life which were gradually disappearing, Dostoevsky was creating the anti-heroes who haunted the dark streets of misty St. Petersburg. Yet, although they were very different—Tolstoy the champion of nature and man, the brilliant recorder of reality in its most precise detail, and Dostoevsky the relentless explorer of the dark recesses of men's souls—they were joined in their belief that in the Russian people lay the virtues that could illuminate the world.

At the unveiling of the Pushkin monument in 1880 Dostoevsky delivered an impassioned speech in which he proclaimed Russia's mission of regenerating the world through the universal service of its people and the brotherly love of the Orthodox faith. So moving was his speech that flowers were showered onto the platform. Some in the crowd cried, "Prophet," "Saint," and a student fainted from emotion. Tolstoy later regretted not going to meet Dostoevsky then, and shortly after wrote to a friend that he had just reread *House of the Dead*, saying, "I do not know of a better book in all modern literature . . . including Pushkin. If you should see Dostoevsky, tell him that I love him." This letter gave Dostoevsky great pleasure. But then suddenly, on January 28, 1881, Dostoevsky died, and the two great writers never met. Although at various times of their lives both wrote critical remarks of each other's work, Tolstoy was deeply saddened by Dostoevsky's death. To a friend he wrote, "How I wish I could say all I feel about Dostoevsky. . . . I never saw the man and never had any immediate relations with him; and suddenly when he died, I realized that he was someone very close, dear and necessary to me. I felt him to be my friend, and never dreamed but that we should meet, just that this had not yet happened, but was in store for me. And suddenly . . . I read, he is dead? It was as though one of my supporting pillars had buckled. I had a moment of panic . . . and then I realized how precious he was to me and I wept, and am still weeping."

In the 1880's and 1890's such was Tolstoy's fame, not only in Russia but throughout the world, that he became almost an oracle, and Yasnaya Polyana a place of pilgrimage. The house swarmed with visitors—friends and admirers both famous and humble, religious teachers and philosophers, followers of Tolstoy's religious precepts of nonresistance who called themselves "Tolstoyans." As the nearest railroad station was three miles away and there were no hotels, Sofia, in the open and generous way of the Russian countryside, offered hospitality to everyone. The house was full of people who came to stay, sometimes for a week or even a month.

Turgenev, on his rare visits, was always gay and full of stories from Paris; during one lively evening of games, despite Tolstoy's lofty disapproval, he merrily danced the cancan. To the end of his days Turgenev continued to be profoundly distressed at Tolstoy's preoccupation with religion. Only a month before his death in 1883 he wrote Tolstoy a touching letter saying, "My friend, return to your literary activity . . . you, great poet of the Russian land." But although in his last thirty years Tolstoy wrote two plays and three novels—*The Kreutzer Sonata, The Devils* and *Resurrection*—he devoted himself to his religious preoccupation, writing countless articles on religious matters. In his later years when he was asked which of his works he considered best, he answered the two popular tales "What Men Live By" and "Where God Is, Love Is."

Beginning in 1891, he devoted two years to helping in the relief of severe famines which struck Russia after an especially dry summer. The entire Tolstoy family assisted in the effort, working in devastated regions and organizing worldwide appeals for famine relief. As the children grew up and went to the university, Sofia insisted that they buy a house in Moscow. Tolstoy finally agreed but bought a house as much like a country home as possible, set behind huge walls in a large park. He hated the city, finding in it nothing but "stench, stone, opulence, poverty, debauchery." While his wife attended balls and social gatherings, which she enjoyed, Tolstoy would often slip through the gates of his house disguised as a worker to join the men working on the river and help them to saw and chop wood. He asked to participate in the census taking so that he could study for himself the conditions of the poor of the city.

At every chance, he fled back to Yasnaya Polyana. He became a vegetarian and scorned material comforts. Visitors would arrive to find him working in the fields or cobbling his own boots. Numerous artists came to sculpt and paint him. The painter Nikolai Ge became such a close friend of the family that the children called him "grandpapa" and Tolstoy encouraged him to paint religious subjects. Ilya Repin, whose work Tolstoy greatly admired, came often. As Tolstoy hated to pose, considering it a waste of time, Repin, unruffled, would quietly sketch him at work in his study, and when Tolstoy plowed the fields Repin would run around from one end of the field to the other, trying to capture him on paper. Once, Repin even tried to plow himself, but the horse would not obey him.

At Yasnaya Polyana, Tolstoy received all the leading magazines and newspapers, foreign as well as Russian, and kept up with most of the significant books published abroad. His desk was piled with letters from all over the world; his correspondents over the years ranged from Thomas Edison to Gandhi. In 1895, when his *The Power of Darkness* was staged at the Imperial Theaters of both Moscow and St. Petersburg, Yasnaya Polyana was overrun with production, set and costume designers, who came to make sketches of peasant cottages, buy up peasant women's costumes, take photographs and learn the correct pronunciation for various folk expressions.

Himself the last survivor of the race of great writers of the 1860's, Tolstoy in his old age interested himself in the work of a new generation. He loved

Chekhov's short stories so much that he often read them aloud, saying, "Chekhov is Pushkin in prose." Chekhov came to visit him in 1895 and the two men became close friends. But although he loved Chekhov's stories, Tolstoy thought his plays were terrible, "worse than Shakespeare's." At the Moscow Art Theater, Tolstoy was bewildered by *The Sea Gull* and hated *Uncle Vanya*, writing that "there is no real action, movement, toward which the endless conversations of the neurasthenic intellectuals tend. It is incomprehensible what Chekhov wants to say anyhow." One day Tolstoy put a paternal arm around Chekhov and said, "Listen, my friend, do me a favor. Don't write any more plays." Such was the warmth of their friendship that Chekhov did not take offense.

In 1900 Maxim Gorky came to visit. Gorky, dressed in his customary black Russian blouse, trousers stuffed into his boots, with his long chestnut hair forever getting into his eyes so that he constantly had to throw it back, and Tolstoy, with his flowing beard and rough peasant clothes, made an unlikely pair. And yet, surprisingly, the revolutionary firebrand and the old aristocratic writer got on very well. Tolstoy told Gorky, "You are a true peasant. You will find it hard going among the writers but don't be afraid. Always say what you feel; it may be coarse in expression, but never mind!" After their first meeting, Gorky wrote to thank Tolstoy: "I confess, I never expected that you would treat one so well." To which Tolstoy cheerfully replied, "Some people are better than their books and some are worse. . . . I liked your writing, yet I found you better than your writing."

On subsequent visits, the two took long walks together, Gorky writing, "he strides along the paths with the quick step of a connoisseur of the earth; not one pebble, not one pansy escapes his penetrating eyes that look everywhere, measure, weigh." Gorky could not persuade Tolstoy about Marxism, which Tolstoy hated, nor could Tolstoy convert Gorky to Christianity. Yet such was the imposing presence of the great man that Gorky wrote, awestruck, "I do not believe in God, but I looked at him, I don't know why, with a great deal of circumspection and a little fear, too. I looked at him and thought, 'This man is like God.' "

In his diary Tolstoy noted, "Gorky has something to say, he exaggerates untruthfully, but he loves, and we recognize our brothers where we have not seen them before." However, Tolstoy was very disappointed by *The Lower Depths*, finding in the play a lack of sincerity. Tersely, he wrote in his diary, "Gorky is a false impression."

Over the years the stream of visitors to Yasnaya Polyana never stopped.

From the United States came George Kennan, who was studying the penal system in Siberia, William Jennings Bryan and Jane Addams. In 1908 Thomas Edison sent Tolstoy a Dictaphone; but Tolstoy was so excited when he tried to speak into it that he stuttered and forgot what he wanted to say. "Stop the machine," he cried, "it's dreadfully exciting." Then he added with a sigh, "Probably such a machine is good for well-balanced Americans, but it is not for us Russians." Fyodor Chaliapin came to sing for Tolstoy. Although Chaliapin, like Gorky, was of very humble birth, there was nothing bitter or gloomy about him, instead he was buoyant and joyous. As he sang, Tolstoy kept murmuring, "Marvelous, wonderful." When Tolstoy was eighty, at Christmastime Wanda Landowska came to Yasnaya Polyana to play Mozart and Haydn.

In his later years, because of his total involvement with his religious theories, Tolstoy's relations with his wife became increasingly acrimonious. One night, telling only his daughter where he was going and leaving a note for Sofia saying that his departure was definite, he fled the house dressed as a pilgrim, determined to join his followers in the Caucasus. When she found the letter, Sofia tried to drown herself in a pond and was rescued by her daughter. On the way to his destination, Tolstoy caught pneumonia and died in a small railroad station on November 7, 1910, while the world looked breathlessly on and newsreel cameramen waited. His last words were "The truth . . . I love man . . . How are they . . ."

Tolstoy had lived under four tsars and his life spanned the greatest creative century Russia had ever known. Where everything had begun, everything ended. Lev Tolstoy was brought to his final rest in the earth of Yasnaya Polyana in the peaceful glade shaded by the ancient trees he had loved.

20 · THE WANDERERS AND THE MIGHTY HANDFUL

IN TOLSTOY'S LONG LIFETIME he had been a witness not only to great changes in the life of the peaceful countryside that he so much revered but in all of Russian society. In addition to the sweeping transformation of life brought about by the emancipation of the serfs, Alexander II had also instituted many other important reforms. The legal system was overhauled and trial by jury introduced. Local self-government for rural districts and large towns was instituted, with elective assemblies possessing restricted right of taxation.

Alexander's reforms concerning education and the press had especially far-reaching effects. Already in the time of Nicholas I, Russia had seen the rise of a new group that came to be called the "intelligentsia." This term referred to a layer of educated, socially concerned people, who were not necessarily of the gentry; people such as priests' sons, middle-class professional people and peasants with higher school training. Even under the stern Nicholas, the university population had increased, and despite censorship, in the years from 1845 to 1848, 2 million copies of foreign publications were imported into Russia. In 1857, shortly after coming to the throne, Alexander II threw open the universities to

325

everyone. Thousands quickly grasped this opportunity and the universities over-flowed. Fees were nominal and richer students often organized committees of assistance to help needier students. Higher education became a national hobby. In the democratic and critical atmosphere of Russia's new universities, ideals of all kinds, including the most avant-garde socialist and radical ideas then popular in Europe, were hotly discussed. Lecture halls were crowded, with students wedged in to the doors. For the youth of the day the most popular entertainment was a four-hour evening lecture followed by two hours of intensive debate.

Russian students traveled abroad, studying in universities in Bonn, Jena, Berlin, Paris, Zurich and London. Foreign professors, many of them German, came to Russia. In women's education, Russians were ahead of Europe. Girls were admitted to the universities; women of thirty-five came to study for careers. As early as 1868 two pioneering girls went to study medicine in Zurich; by 1873 seventy-seven were granted medical degrees there. In 1868 a girl who wanted to be a midwife was admitted to the University of St. Petersburg Medical School, and four years later five hundred women applied. By 1913 women held many important positions, including professorships in men's colleges. Russia was the first country to establish a technical school for women, and the first woman civil engineer was a Russian.

In Alexander's time this rapidly burgeoning student population became an important political and cultural force, and the "intelligentsia" gained an influential public voice. Alexander had lifted the restrictions on the press that had existed during his father's time, and during his reign, a whole group of radical writers and philosophers began to express their ideas vociferously. The most famous of these was Alexander Herzen, whose lifetime spanned the reigns of Nicholas I and Alexander II. Herzen, the illegitimate son of a wealthy nobleman, inherited a large fortune and lived mostly in Europe. After being expelled from France for openly supporting their Revolution of 1848, he spent his time in Rome, England and Switzerland. Herzen was a man passionately devoted to individual liberty who dedicated his life to rebellion against every form of oppression, social and political, public and private. He was a gifted writer and his essays and autobiography are ranked as masterpieces of Russian prose. He was also a journalist of genius, and in London in 1857 he founded a weekly newspaper, *The Bell* (*Kolokol*). In articles written with brilliance, gaiety and passion, he dealt with any subject that seemed to be of topical interest, deriding, exposing and denouncing abuses and misgovernment in Russia. Although *The Bell* was officially prohibited, innumerable copies poured into Russia. In fact, during the years 1857 to 1861, Herzen's newspaper was the principal political force in Russia and its articles often led to immediate action. The newspaper was found on the desks of ministers and even of Alexander II, who read it regularly and carefully and tried as he could to correct the abuses it cited.

In Alexander's time, newspapers and magazines began to proliferate, a process which continued unabated until the Revolution. Alexander's reign saw the first appearance of weekly and bimonthly journals of literary comment and criticism, of specialized journals for doctors, engineers and lawyers. There were fashion magazines and magazines for children.

This new press of Alexander's time often was highly critical of the government. To be official became a reproach. Opinions varied widely; there were extreme conservatives who thought everything should go backward, extreme radicals who wanted to sweep everything away, and liberals who grumbled but were not sure what to do. In the 1860's among young Russian intellectuals there was an overwhelming conviction that science was the answer to all the world's problems. Life was to be based on scientific reality and "common sense," which meant dispensing with old-fashioned beliefs such as marriage, laws and God. Sons were arguing with fathers that the values of their civilization were outworn and should be thrown out the window.

From the mid-19th century into the beginning of the 20th century the great desire of the majority of students and intellectuals was for representative government. The novelist Ivan Turgenev became the spokesman for this progressive and reforming enthusiasm that had taken hold of Russian society. But in the new, open atmosphere there were also spawned extreme radical groups, small in number but totally dedicated, and in their psychology and tactics precursors of the terrorist movements of our own day.

The best summation of the mood of the radical students of the epoch was Turgenev's novel *Fathers and Sons,* published in 1862. In it he brilliantly dissected the characteristics of these rationalist students through the person of his hero, Bazarov. Turgenev coined a word for them, "Nihilist," because they accepted no traditions or authorities and wished only to destroy. With the blithe insouciance of the theorist, the leading Nihilist critic, Dmitry Pisarev, urged, "Destroy to the right and the left! No harm can come of this."

In the late 1860's and early 1870's, one such small group, calling themselves the "People's Will," determined according to their principles to sow chaos in society by committing acts of terrorism. They attacked municipal officers and provincial governors and threatened to burn down the wooden city of Kostroma. As they feared that Alexander's reforms might render their extreme revolutionary ideas useless, the Emperor was their worst enemy. Determined to kill him, they put out a "warrant" for his arrest; the first attempt was deliberately set for the first anniversary of Lincoln's assassination. After several bungled attempts, which included blowing up a train and killing many innocent people, and setting off a bomb under the dining room in the Winter Palace, killing fifty-seven Finnish guards and servants, they finally succeeded. On March 14, 1881, they assassinated Alexander with a bomb. Fatefully, in his pocket on the day he was killed was a draft of a constitution which was to be published in the newspapers on the following day.

During those decades of increasing political controversy which culminated in the tragic assassination of Alexander, in literature, music and art, the philosophical and cultural controversy between the Slavophiles and the Westernizers sharpened. Did Russia because of her unique history and character have a special destiny, or did the answer to her problems lie in closer connection and assimilation with the West? Was Russia to evolve toward constitutional government or dramatically sweep everything away for some new and all-inclusive idea? Was the goal of art to preach or to exist only for itself? All the artists of the second half of the 19th century were in some way caught up in this discussion; all made statements of their views in their work.

It was during this turbulent and searching time that a new movement in art began. Realistic in style and social in intent, for thirty years it reflected all the trends and discussions of the changing society.

The second half of the 19th century in Russia was above all a time of commitment. To their discussions of both life and art the Russians brought an extremely moral attitude. Idealistically, they wanted to put their new ideas into action immediately, to sweep away the false for a better and purer world. Art, they felt, could help accomplish this lofty goal. It could transform, inflame, regenerate man. Although these ideas seemed new, they were not really so new at all, but only a transmutation of the most profoundly Russian convictions about art which had been held since their early Christian days. The ideals of integrity and total commitment of the artist and the moral function of art lay at the very heart of the national esthetic. Although these ideas now came clothed in the new social concerns of the late 19th century, as fervently as they had in the days of the devoutly dedicated icon painters, the Russians continued to believe that the artist was a special transmitter of truth, with a responsibility to uplift humanity and lead man toward his higher spiritual nature and destiny.

The writers of the day were examining their society under a magnifying glass. It was natural that this ferment of ideas about the destiny of Russia, and the spirit of reform and social commitment, would spill over to the painters. More and more they began to rebel against the constricting formality of the Academy of Art, which in the mid-19th century dominated their lives and careers.

• • •

When Catherine the Great established the Academy of Fine Arts as an institution, her aim had been to enrich the cultural life of the nation, to make of art an honored and legally protected profession. Her statutes specified that graduates of the Academy were to work as independent artists, free of military service. She attached a boarding school to the Academy which gave its students, rich or poor, a fine education and sent them off prepared to take their places among the cultural elite of the nation. Paul and Alexander I interfered little in the Academy's affairs, but when the imperious Nicholas I, with his passion for military precision, came to the throne, it was a different story.

Nicholas did make a great contribution to art in Russia when in 1839 he ordered the construction of the New Hermitage to house the rich Imperial art collections. Completed in 1852, this was the first building to be constructed specifically as a museum and Nicholas opened it to the public, admission free. The vast collections included rare artifacts, Roman and Greek sculptures and more than two thousand canvases gathered by Catherine and her successors. The new museum was immediately ranked as one of the finest in Europe because it included so many works of the best periods of Raphael, da Vinci, Titian, Giorgione, Velásquez, Van Dyke, Rembrandt and the Dutch masters, and it provided a great impetus for artistic study in Russia.

But under Nicholas, life at the Academy began to change. The Tsar had been trained as an engineer and was an accomplished draftsman. For this rather tenuous reason he considered himself a great connoisseur of art. He quickly began to bureaucratize the Academy along his favored military lines, making it conform to his own close and narrow conceptions. Art was to conform to his own taste and that of his court. Neoclassicism, which he favored, was the official doctrine; artists were to be transformed into obedient servants of the state. The Tsar popped in to visit classrooms and studios, peering over the shoulders of young artists, exhorting them to do better and work harder.

Previously there had been a simple, flexible grading system; now a strict grading system governed everything. Students who finished the curriculum received the title Class Artist 1st Class; various complicated ranks delineated Academicians. For the annual competitions for scholarships abroad, a subject was assigned. Artists had no choice in the matter and even had to follow their originally approved sketches without changing a line. As the official Academy gradually came to dominate the fine arts, the few private art schools began to fade away. Artists, who in the 18th century and early 19th century had been honored members of society, were now lowered to the rank of petty government employees.

When Alexander II came to the throne he appointed a more liberal director to the Academy and changes were made. In 1860 Vasily Perov won the Gold Medal and a three-year traveling scholarship abroad by painting a subject of his own choosing called *A Village Sermon*, a sharp, satirical scene of a village church where the sermon is being preached to a peacefully snoring landowner, his flirtatious wife and a crowd of ragged peasants.

But in the pages of the magazines and newspapers which were springing up like mushrooms, writers and critics were noisily propounding their new ideas. "Art," wrote the fiery radical critic Pisarev, "consists in preaching morality to the people." Paintings, said he, should evoke "energetic protest and dissatisfaction." Artists were urged to come out of their musty halls, take their proper place in the great reforming of society and contribute their solutions to the moral and social problems of their day.

These new ideas were in the air when in 1863 the Academy announced that the subject of the annual competition would be "Odin's Entrance into Valhalla." Outraged at being assigned a subject so far removed from reality, a group of thirteen graduating students led by Ivan Kramskoy, the son of a lowly copy clerk from a provincial town in southern Russia, refused to compete at all and resigned from the Academy in protest, thus giving up all their chances for civil rank and government commissions.*

There was also a rather more human side to their crusade. All but one of the original group of protesting art students, and the vast majority of other paint-

---

* At the same time in France, the French Academy had grown so pompous and formal with its insistence on subjects from antiquity that they refused to permit the paintings of the Impressionists to be shown in their annual Salon. The Impressionists formed their own exhibition in 1862 and called it the "Salon des Refusés."

ers who came to be associated with them later, sprang from the humbler ranks of society. Perov was the illegitimate son of an impoverished baron; Repin and Maksimov, the sons of state peasants. Among the new intelligentsia of the 1860's, education and the intellectual prestige that accompanied it were all important, and the Academy was not considered by them the equivalent to the university education which qualified a person as an "intelligent." (The artists felt their lack of polish very keenly. Ilya Repin, one of the most gifted artists of his day, once bemoaned the fact that he knew so little about the ways of the fashionable world that when a gentleman patron of his gave him a stipend to attend the Academy and extended his hand, his first reaction was to kiss it.)

These young artists were anxious to be accepted as full-fledged members of the new cultural elite. They wanted to be taken seriously, to paint real subjects from real life which would parallel the literature of exposé which was then so much in fashion, to have their paintings considered as important to the national culture as the written word. Therefore, they enthusiastically and idealistically adopted the idea of service to society that was the *idée fixe* of the new intellectuals whom they so much admired. They decided to form an Artel, or cooperative, which would incorporate ideas of a new and unselfish life, far from bureaucratic control; to dedicate themselves idealistically to painting pictures that would raise the consciousness of their society. In doing this, they considered themselves liberals, not revolutionaries. They had no desire to sweep away institutions, but merely to make people think. Repin later wrote, "The pictures of those days made the viewer blush, shiver and look carefully into himself . . . they upset the public and directed it on the path of humaneness." Kramskoy, in his very Russian way, saw the mission of art as close to that of religion. "Art should uplift," said he, "fill man with power to rise, strengthen his spiritual makeup."

During the day, the members of the little Artel worked at various jobs, painting icons, retouching photographs, doing illustrations, accepting any work that was offered to them and sharing the profits. Full of youthful zeal, in the evenings they conducted self-education programs led by Kramskoy at which they discussed contemporary history, literature and philosophy, and once a week invited their friends and supporters to join their discussions. To popularize their paintings and their ideas they held private shows in their apartments and organized a group exhibit in 1865, which they took to the great fair at Nizhny Novgorod to try to sell to the large gathering of merchants.

Although they continued to go to Europe to study as artists from the Academy had always done, Perov in 1863 asked to come home early from his traveling scholarship because he said he found no inspiration in France. When the most socially conscious of them all, Kramskoy, went off to France and Germany in 1869, he wrote some enthusiastic letters home, but made the charge, familiar to us today, that Western artists were motivated by sensation and publicity. The new artists preferred to examine the Russian rather than a foreign atmosphere; the process which had begun in Pushkin's time was now complete. They began to make regular study excursions into the countryside to study and sketch people as they really were. Maksimov, the son of peasants, resigned from the Academy in 1866 to live and paint among the people of his native village. Perhaps because many of the artists were from humble origins themselves, they rejected what they considered the false tears and sentimentality with which drawing-room intellectuals regarded the life of the peasant. As a result, in their best paintings they showed the peasants not in a moralistic way but as individuals with qualities and characteristics that were their own and merited respect. One of Kramskoy's finest portraits, *Mina Moiseyev*, shows an old peasant not as a miserable creature but as a wise and experienced old fellow with silver beard, friendly wrinkles and twinkling eyes. Repin postponed taking his European scholarship and spent the whole summer of 1870 sketching and living with the boat haulers of the Volga to prepare for his painting *The Boat Haulers*, perhaps the single most famous painting of the time. Although it was later hailed as a kind of political icon by the radicals, Repin himself, whose portraits were always robust and unpitying, did not view his subjects as symbols of human misery but as individuals. He later wrote about each man, vividly describing his specific memorable qualities.

In 1870, finding that communal living posed problems, the original Artel broke up because of "dissension and arguments," but by then they had another idea. Four of the original group along with eleven other artists from Moscow, all friends from their school days, decided to form a new organization called "The Association of Traveling Exhibits," or, as they came to be known, "The Wanderers." The founding group included, besides Kramskoy, Nikolai Ge, Konstantin Makovsky, Grigory Myasoedov and Ivan Shishkin. Later, many other artists grouped themselves around The Wanderers, among them Repin, Arkhip Kuindzhi, Vasily Surikov, Viktor Vasnetsov and Vasily Maksimov; in all, over the years they numbered 109 active members and 440 participating artists. In their original proposition to other artists, the founding group wrote: "All of us have agreed on a single idea . . . concerning the usefulness of an exhibition managed by the artists themselves. We think there is a possibility to free art from bureaucratic control and to widen the circle of those interested in art and subsequently to widen the circle of buyers."

Calling themselves "The Wanderers," their imaginative idea was to bring their new art to the people directly, by means of regular art exhibits which would open in Petersburg and Moscow and then go on to provincial towns both to provide a higher artistic level for the provinces and serve as a pictorial commentary on the problems facing Russia.

They placed an advertisement in the newspapers and held their first exhibition on November 28, 1871, in the imposing halls of the very Academy they had rejected. In this original exhibit were forty-six canvases, among them the famous Ge painting, *Peter the Great and His Son Alexis.* The exhibition was praised by the press and warmly received by a receptive public. Then they began a series of traveling exhibitions. How popular the traveling art shows became is vividly demonstrated by the fact that in the years that followed there were forty-eight such exhibits; they were not finally discontinued until 1923.

From their beginning, The Wanderers were financially supported and greatly helped by a shy and retiring man, Pavel Tretyakov, whose father had been a petty merchant of no education who operated a small retail store in the Moscow arcades. Their father had provided a good education for his two sons, Pavel and Sergei, who went on to increase the family fortunes by re-equipping their textile mills in Kostroma with modern Western machinery and expanding the firm's marketing facilities in Moscow.

Pavel Tretyakov was from a class disdainfully looked down on by the aristocracy as well as the liberal and radical intelligentsia. Writers of the day, including the most popular playwright, Alexander Ostrovsky, made scathing fun of this merchant class whom they portrayed as being uncouth, money-grabbing boors. This was very far from reality, for although this new merchant class did not usually attend university, they were provided with excellent tutors who gave them an excellent education.

Tretyakov's family was rich but not hugely wealthy, and yet Pavel Tretyakov altruistically decided to devote a large sum of his money to promoting Russian art. From the time he was a young man, it was his goal to bring together a representative collection of all Russian painters, a collection which would serve as an inspiration for the current generation of artists and for future generations. The magnificent collections of the Hermitage Museum in St. Petersburg were mostly Old Masters. Tretyakov dreamed of a museum devoted to Russian art, something which did not then exist. In 1857, when he was only twenty-five, Tretyakov began collecting. At twenty-eight, he made out a will which gave 150,000 rubles, almost half the capital he had at the time, to set up a museum of Russian art. Furthermore, the will carefully specified that the gallery not be run by bureaucrats and that its governing board be composed of persons selected for their knowledge of art and not their birth or social position. Patiently, step by step, he collected Russian art of all periods—icons, 18th-century portraits by Levitsky, early-19th-century portraits by Kiprensky. In 1869 he commissioned from The Wanderers group a series of paintings of national celebrities, among them Tolstoy, Dostoevsky and the scientist Mendeleev. In 1871 it was he who bought most of the paintings of the first Wanderers' exhibition. His support of the group was massive; between the years 1870 and 1897 he spent the huge sum of 893,000 rubles on purchases. He invited many of the Wanderer artists to spend summers on his estate. His commitment and dedication to his ideal were so strong that on many occasions painters would sell him works for less, sometimes even donating paintings outright because they were going to hang in a "national" gallery.

By 1872 his collection had grown to 1,567 items and his house was overflowing, so Tretyakov began construction of a gallery in the Muscovite-Slavic style. In 1874 he began transporting paintings and personally supervised the placing of each painting according to chronological order, and opened the collection to the public. Through the years, as he continued collecting, Tretyakov simply kept adding more rooms to his gallery. Many artists had rooms devoted entirely to their works; when in 1880 he bought seventy-eight sketches by Vershchagin, he was obliged to add six more rooms.

Tretyakov was a quiet man, with thin, finely chiseled features and long sensitive fingers, a man of old-fashioned religion, strongly conservative Slavophile views and regular habits. Throughout his life, every day he worked from nine to twelve and again from two to six, sitting on a high stool before his desk, surrounded by nine clerks. Each day he visited his Moscow store to supervise and give instructions. Whenever he could get away from his business, he loved to travel and he made many trips abroad, visiting Switzerland, Belgium, Austria, Hungary and the Scandinavian countries, traveling long distances on foot. Everywhere he went, he visited art museums, exhibitions and artists' studios, tirelessly recording everything that interested him in his meticulously kept travel diaries.

334

He had excellent taste and refused to be drawn into using art for the political purposes of any faction. To the annoyance of the "cause" people, he coolly chose what was best artistically. Scenes, he said, should be painted with a feeling for "truth and poetry . . . poetry should be everywhere."

In this view Tretyakov was strongly supported by the two greatest writers of his time who also did not believe that "art should serve the people and preach." Tolstoy wrote vigorously, "The goal of the artist lies not in solving a question in an indisputable manner, but in making people love life, in its infinite, eternally inexhaustible manifestations." Dostoevsky was against artistic creations with "preconceived tendencies." When he went to the exhibit in 1873 at which Repin's *Boat Haulers* was first hung, he went expecting to see a moralistic picture that attacked the upper classes, something of which he did not approve. Ironically, this picture, considered by the radicals as a call to revolution, did not strike Dostoevsky in that way. He wrote a criticism for the conservative weekly *The Citizen*, saying that happily it was not one of those pictures which screamed at people, "Look how unfortunate I am!"

About his own talents Tretyakov was always modest. Even when visitors to his gallery numbered more than fifty thousand a year, he wrote to Tolstoy in 1890, "And now, let me say a few words on the subject of my collection of Russian painting. So often and already long ago, I have asked myself: Is what I am doing worthwhile? . . . and I continue to complete my collection without being sure of its usefulness."

Retiring by nature, he did not like publicity, but his efforts were enthusiastically endorsed by other industrialists who followed his example and founded galleries of Russian art in Kiev and other provincial cities. It was largely due to his influence and others like him that Alexander III founded the Russian Art Museum in St. Petersburg. In 1892 Tretyakov gave his enormous gallery to the city of Moscow "to contribute to the establishment of useful institutions in his beloved town and further the development of art in Russia." He died in 1898, having devoted forty years of his life to his art collection. The Tretyakov Gallery remains today as a rich legacy of his foresight and generosity.

By the late 1870's the thrust of The Wanderers had changed. No longer merely a spur to social change, they had become something else, a national school. The most influential critic of the day, Vladimir Stasov, strongly supported this idea, writing, "The Association had taught artists to generously and seriously understand the land, love the Russian people, the Russian nature, the Russian way of life and Russian society with its worries and adversities." Kramskoy and a few others continued to flail away at the overriding importance of social consciousness in art, but unsuccessfully. When Repin took his delayed three-year scholarship in Paris and was happily painting French cocottes and learning from the Impressionists, Kramskoy wrote him a frantic letter calling him to task and exhorting him not to forget Russia's problems. Unruffled, Repin stoutly defended his right to paint whatever struck him. One of his loveliest paintings was done soon after his return from Paris in 1876. Called *On a Turf Bench*, it shows a serene Russian family setting full of softness and Impressionist light.

Landscapes became a favorite theme of The Wanderers. The poignant beauty of the Russian land had been celebrated in poetry and literature but not in art, and the Wanderer paintings of snow scenes, wild spaces and dark forests stirred the public tremendously. Ivan Shishkin painted forests in botanical detail, carefully recording the individuality of each tree. Naturally, the "cause" people did not like him at all. They considered landscape useless except for background, but Shishkin captured and still holds a popularity with ordinary Russians which has lasted to this day.

During the 1880's many of The Wanderers turned to painting historical subjects, choosing themes from old sagas, medieval Muscovite days and the Russian past. These paintings were scrupulously exact as to historical detail. In 1885 Repin finished his famous *Ivan the Terrible at the Death of His Son*. In 1887 Vasily Surikov completed his massive canvas, *The Boyarina Morosova*, heroine of the Old Believers of the 17th century. Vasnetsov did many scenes of medieval Moscow. For his colorful paintings Andrei Ryabushkin, a late and transitional Wanderer, traveled all through Russia studying old cities, icons, precious objects and handicrafts. So carefully researched are his paintings that he was often consulted about the details of life in earlier centuries. Ryabushkin loved to show his work to peasants to get their reactions; he would do them over if they did not understand. He designed sets for the operas *Boris Godunov* and *Khovanshchina* and did mosaics in churches. His influence was enormous on the later avant-garde painters, especially Boris Kustodiev and Natalya Goncharova.

Tsar Alexander III, who came to the throne in 1881, was a passionate Russophile, so much so that he changed the uniforms of the army from their Western look to the familiar baggy trousers, boots and fur caps we know today. He was vitally interested in promoting the study and preservation of the national heritage. From the time of its founding in 1866 when he was still Tsarevich, he headed the Russian Historical Society. He was a committed patron of the arts, generously supporting the restoration of Russian antiquities, notably in Kiev. He opened the Russian Historical Museum in Petersburg and sponsored a network of provincial art museums and schools. During his reign, appropriations for the Academy were greatly increased, as were the state funds for commissions and constructions.

Alexander III warmly embraced The Wanderers as the national school and extended his Imperial patronage to them. He was so enthusiastic that he became Tretyakov's strongest competitor; at The Wanderers' exhibition of 1888 Tretyakov bought ten canvases and Alexander five. In 1889 Tretyakov bought two and the Imperial family twenty-seven. The Tsar took down all the Western paintings in his palace at Tsarskoe Selo and replaced them with Russian art.

As they prospered, not only were The Wanderers accepted into polite society, they bought and renovated estates from the impoverished nobility in the years after emancipation when these were easily available. They lived in elegantly furnished apartments and worked in well-appointed studios. In 1889 Alexander invited the Association to help in the reorganization of the very Academy from which they had resigned in disgust thirty years before. Five Wanderers, including Repin, Kuindzhi and Myasoedov, sat on the government commission that drafted the new statutes approved in 1893. Repin, Shishkin and Kuindzhi became professors and twelve others joined the governing assembly. The Academy was completely reorganized; artists were allowed to freely select their subjects; they were to have independent studio training and no more civil service ranking. The circle was complete; what had started as a breaking of tradition had become the tradition. By 1905 the rebels had become the Establishment.

Now that they were in authority it was their turn to come under attack by the new generations of artists who resented the dominance of realist painting over national art. Doboujinsky and Benois of the new "World of Art" movement as well as the more avant-garde advocates of neo-primitivism and Cubo-Futurism all demanded more recognition by the Academy and derided The Wanderers as far behind the times.

Once again the battles heated and the discussions continued until April 18, 1918, when after 174 years the St. Petersburg Academy of Fine Arts in which Elizabeth and Catherine had placed such hopes was extinguished as a useless institution, and the imposing doors with the motto "For the Free Arts" chiseled over the entrance were then closed.*

---

* In 1934 the Academy was reopened under the new name of Repin Institute and exists today as an official organ of the Ministry of the Arts of the U.S.S.R.

Through the thirty years of their existence, The Wanderers had faithfully recorded the vast changes that Russian society was experiencing. They had painted the impoverished gentry, the rising merchant class, the conflicts between fathers and sons, the migration of the peasants, the workers in the factories and the coming of the railroads.

Although The Wanderers have since been severely criticized for their overtly realistic and moralistic approach to art, what the Russian public loved and still loves is the element of storytelling in their works. In the 1880's the painter Mikhail Nesterov, who was not in The Wanderers group, wrote, "The public went with pleasure and readily to their beloved *Peredvizhniki*, the same way it loved reading favorite authors." This, of course, was a great compliment to those artists who had wanted their work to be considered as important as the written word.

•　•　•

During the same years that painters broke away from the formality of the Academy and went to seek their inspiration in the land, a similar movement was happening in music.

Today, the strains of Russian music are so familiar and beloved a part of the world's musical heritage that it is hard for us to imagine a time without their sound. Yet during the century and a half of Westernization—from the end of the 17th century to the middle of the 19th—Russia's national music had almost disappeared from view.

The Russians are a profoundly musical people. Their magnificent liturgical music has completely different roots from that of the West. Like the icon, its form first came to them from Byzantium and Greece, but once on Russian soil it was quickly nourished and changed by the folk melodies that filled the life of the people. From the 11th century to the 13th century, in the days of Kiev, church songbooks were carefully compiled. In the 16th century, a golden age of music in Russia, hundreds and perhaps thousands of these songbooks were carefully copied and kept, written in strange *neume* notations which date back to early Christian days. Sadly, much of the heritage of past masters is still obscured because of this complicated and still largely undecipherable musical alphabet. Western musical notation was introduced to Russia in the late 17th century, and with it Russian music became strongly influenced by musical ideas brought in by Poles and Ukrainians and later by the many Italian singers who came to sing at the court.

But the Russian earth was fertile, and the Russian musical heritage remained alive, flowing like a spring of clear water under the earth. From the
beginning of the 19th century there was a widespread cult of music and musical
pastimes, especially singing. Music was present everywhere: in the *izbas* of the
peasants, the mansions of landowners, the roadside inns; in villages, towns and
cities. In the smartest restaurants there were orchestras of stringed instruments;
in simpler *traktirs*, or taverns, barrel organs or bands and later Gramophones.
Military bands played in the parks. There were the wandering gypsies, which all
Russians loved. Church choirs were highly valued; even private institutions such
as banks had choirs trained to sing in church, and the competition between them
was lively. Certain churches became famous for the fine bass voices of their
deacons. Some talented deacons were given a complete musical education and
invited to sing both secular and ecclesiastical music in private homes.

Beginning in the early decades of the 19th century, there was an increasing
interest in collecting folk songs. Expeditions were made to the countryside to
collect and set down native songs on the spot. One of those most passionately
interested in this rich national musical tradition was Mili Balakirev. Balakirev, the
son of a humble public official in Nizhny Novgorod, was befriended by a rich
neighboring landowner, an enlightened dilettante and author of the first Russian
biography of Mozart.

Balakirev's benefactor took him to St. Petersburg to widen his musical
knowledge and introduced him to the famous composer of Pushkin's day, Mikhail
Glinka. Balakirev became a fervent admirer of Glinka, and after the composer's
death dedicated himself to perpetuating Glinka's dream of a national music that
would draw its inspiration from folk songs and themes of Russian folklore. Balakirev was strongly supported in his ideas by Vladimir Stasov, archivist of the St.
Petersburg library and an influential critic who was also the staunch supporter of
the nationalist Wanderer painters. Beginning in 1856 Balakirev, a man of very
definite opinions who was happy only when he could direct or instruct, gathered
about him a group of friends and musicians who met regularly for musical evenings. None of this little circle had any formal musical training. They were drawn
together by their mutual interest in exploring the possibilities of a "new" music,
which would be different from the Western tradition. In 1858, Balakirev himself
made an expedition to the countryside to collect folk songs. He took a boat down
the Volga to Nizhny Novgorod, stopping at various places to write down the
songs of the bargemen and haulers. One of these, which he orchestrated, became
famous the world over as "The Song of the Volga Boatmen."

Balakirev's strongest supporter and collaborator was Caesar Cui, a military engineer from Lithuania, a professor of fortifications who was also very knowledgeable about opera. Although Cui, except for a few songs, never became a very successful composer, he assumed the role of critic for those more talented in their little circle. In 1857, at one of their weekly musical soirees, a foppish seventeen-year-old officer, newly graduated into the Preobrazhensky Guards, introduced himself to Cui. His name was Modest Mussorgsky and he was, as it turned out, a talented amateur pianist. Balakirev was happy to discover someone who could join him in playing the classic and romantic composers in four-hand arrangements. Mussorgsky had had no systematic musical training and he persuaded Balakirev to give him lessons in musical form. Together they played through all Beethoven's symphonies in piano arrangements and analyzed their form. Thanks to these sessions, the young man began to try his hand at composing.

In 1861 a young naval cadet, Nikolai Rimsky-Korsakov, who had composed a few short piano pieces, came to Balakirev for advice. To Rimsky's delight, he was invited to join the group's discussions on instrumentation and part writing and, rather amazingly, Balakirev encouraged the completely untrained young man to begin a symphony. Rimsky began enthusiastically, only to have to leave for his obligatory three-year graduation cruise with the Imperial Navy. Shortly afterward, in 1862, Mussorgsky introduced another fledgling composer into the circle, a doctor-chemist, Alexander Borodin.

For several years the little group of friends met regularly to play, listen to and criticize each other's works. Balakirev was despotic, determined to impose his own ideas and quick to anger when his suggestions were not accepted. Increasingly, as his talented pupils began to mature and develop ideas of their own, they resented his dominating personality and ruthless criticism. Eventually they broke away from his influence and went their own ways.

But despite their differences, the little group (Balakirev, Cui, Rimsky-Korsakov, Borodin and Mussorgsky), which came to be called the "Mighty Handful,"* remained united in their desire to get away from imitation of the West and to look to Russian roots for inspiration.

In their basic idea of forming a Russian school of composers, Balakirev and

---

* Stasov coined the name. In May 1867, after a Pan-Slavic concert in St. Petersburg conducted by Balakirev, Stasov spoke of the new composers as "a small but mighty handful." Some unfriendly critics later used the term to mock them.

his little circle were swimming strongly against the current of fashion. Their principal opponent was Anton Rubenstein, a great pianist and champion of the Western school of musical thinking. Anton and his brother Nikolai were piano prodigies from southwestern Russia whose ambitious mother had carefully nurtured their careers. She took them to Europe, where they performed with great success and also acquired a strong German musical training. Periodically Anton would return from his prolonged stays abroad, trailing clouds of European glory. His prestige was enormous. He had a generous Imperial patroness, Grand Duchess Helen, sister of Nicholas I. It was Rubenstein who in 1862 was asked to expand the courses of the Imperial Music Society into a full-fledged conservatory, of which he became the first director. Among the first pupils of the newly formed Conservatory was young Peter Tchaikovsky, who had recently left his post as a clerk in the Ministry of Justice to devote himself to music.

Tchaikovsky idolized Rubenstein, who was his teacher, but Anton failed to see any great talent in his moody and introspective pupil. In 1866 Anton's brother Nikolai went on to found a similar conservatory in Moscow. Short of funds and searching for professors, he asked the young senior student Tchaikovsky to be his first Professor of Harmony.

At the time, Anton Rubenstein could not imagine how anyone could be interested in Russian music. In the 1850's and 1860's, a solid German musical education counted for everything. Europe was dominated by Mendelssohn, by the operas of Verdi and the mighty personality of Richard Wagner. Critics hailed composers of the Western school. Verdi himself came to St. Petersburg in 1862 to conduct the premiere of his opera *La Forza del Destino*, which had been commissioned in Russia at a cost of 22,000 rubles, and was greeted with the applause of the *beau monde* and of Emperor Alexander II; Wagner made a visit in 1863. Critics hailed composers of the Western school. St. Petersburg was already full of German musicians from the large colonies of Germans in the city. Now, the new Conservatory attracted many more—German theoreticians and teachers who had no idea of the Russian musical past and were often totally ignorant of the language as well. These German professors were not only to train professional musicians but to educate composers.

It was in reaction to the powerful forces of Rubenstein that in 1867 Balakirev formed the Free Music Society to play the music of the "free" Russian musicians and became its first conductor.

•   •   •

The three most famous members of the Mighty Handful, Borodin, Mussorgsky and Rimsky-Korsakov, were very different in personality and their approach to work, yet they remained close friends; their lives and often even their compositions closely intertwined. What is remarkable and, despite all explanations, mysterious, is the fact that although none of them had the usual grounding of classical harmony, counterpoint, fugue and orchestration, they all composed music of the highest order. They arrived as a fresh breeze to the Teutonically-dominated European musical world, bringing with them the sounds of a new national music.

Although he was their contemporary, Tchaikovsky was not one of their group. As the first important graduate of the St. Petersburg Conservatory, he took what he needed from his German masters, and then went off on his own stormy personal path, combining European methods with his love for Russian melody. Although Tchaikovsky lived most of his life in Moscow and also spent long periods traveling abroad, during his lifetime he made frequent visits to St. Petersburg and often consulted with Balakirev, who in 1869 suggested to him his "Romeo and Juliet" overture. Tchaikovsky loved to sit up until three o'clock in the morning with Rimsky-Korsakov and Glazunov in their favorite restaurant talking about music; Rimsky noting in passing that Tchaikovsky could drink a tremendous lot of wine without losing command of his faculties—"very few of us could keep up with him in this respect." A moody, melancholy man who all his life loved Mozart, spoke French and German fluently and diligently studied English because he loved to read Dickens, Tchaikovsky was nevertheless very close to his compatriots in his deep love for his native land. He once wrote, "I passionately love Russia, the Russian language, the Russian way of thinking, the Russian facial beauty, Russian customs. . . ." His music was of such force that it made itself felt in every phase of Russian music for the remainder of the century and beyond.

In the Balakirev circle, Alexander Borodin was a composer whose work was always refined and scholarly, but nevertheless reflected in a highly original manner the spirit of Russian music. Music historians agree that if Borodin had been able to devote more time to composing, he would have played an even greater part in the evolution of music. But the musician was also a dedicated doctor and scientist, who spent his life balancing his two careers.

Borodin was the issue of a romantic liaison between a twenty-four-year-old daughter of a soldier and a royal Georgian prince who fell madly in love with her when he was sixty. When he was born in 1833 in St. Petersburg, Borodin was registered as the son of one of his father's serfs, Porphyry Borodin, but the spirit of his true father remained in the strains of the Caucasus which later haunted his music. Despite the fact that she never acknowledged him officially, and always insisted that he call her "Auntie," he was cared for tenderly by his mother. As a child, he loved the military band concerts that were given in the parks of the capital and one bandsman taught him to play the flute. By the time young Alexander was twelve, he was an avid concertgoer. He taught himself to play the violin and, although he knew nothing of counterpoint, at thirteen he wrote a concerto for piano as well as a trio for two violins and a cello. Borodin also loved science and, as his mother thought music an undignified calling, he was enrolled at the St. Petersburg Academy of Medicine in 1852, the same year that Tchaikovsky, the son of an Inspector of Mines from the province of Votinsk, enrolled at the School of Jurisprudence.

As a medical student, Borodin formed a string quartet and would often walk several miles with his cello under his arm to meet his friends and play all night. In 1856, when he was twenty-three and working as a house physician in a military hospital, he met a young lieutenant, Modest Mussorgsky, who was assigned to the hospital as an orderly. The two spent many hours discussing their mutual interest in music. Borodin graduated in 1858 as a Doctor of Medicine, having done his thesis on acids. The next four years he spent in Europe, sent by the Imperial government with a group of students and the great Russian chemist Mendeleev to study the latest scientific developments.

In Heidelberg, Borodin fell in love with a charming Russian girl named Catherine Protopova, an accomplished pianist who was studying there. The two went to concerts, where she introduced him to the music of Schumann and Chopin. Besides their shared interest in music, Catherine so keenly interested him in women's rights that, a few years later, after he married her, Borodin began a campaign to permit higher education for women which eventually resulted in the establishment of a women's medical school.

After Borodin's return to St. Petersburg in 1862, Mussorgsky took him to meet Balakirev, who, in his usual forceful way, encouraged Borodin to begin work on his First Symphony. The work went slowly. Borodin was then a young instructor at the Academy of Medicine and devoted to his students. Cultured and witty, he loved teaching, and his students loved him. The atmosphere in his laboratory was cheerful. Borodin often hummed a tune as he conducted his experiments and was always ready to talk about music with anybody who seemed interested. At night, the sound of his piano floated through the halls from his apartment in the Academy. After Rimsky-Korsakov's return from the sea, the two became great friends. Rimsky often came to spend the night so that they could play each other's works on the piano, the cello and the flute. Rimsky remembers that Borodin was always so delighted to talk music that he would sometimes leave an experiment bubbling to play fragments of compositions, only to leap up suddenly in the middle of a discussion and rush back to his laboratory to find something about to explode.

It was no wonder that, with all his activities, five years went by before Borodin finally finished his First Symphony in 1867. He conducted it himself in 1869, at one of the Free Music Society concerts. The public was warm but the critics, who favored the Rubenstein circle, were chilly. One wrote cuttingly of "a symphony by somebody of the name of Borodin that pleased only the friends of the composer, who applauded so persistently that he was obliged to appear on the platform and take a bow." They sneered at Balakirev's circle as "that little coterie of soldiers, sailors and chemists."

In 1869 Stasov suggested to Borodin that he write an opera based on the 12th-century epic poem *The Lay of Igor*. Borodin immediately set to work, only to have to set his opera aside for his medical work or other musical compositions, including his Second Symphony. As a full professor at the Academy, he had a busy teaching schedule and many duties. He was known for his compassion and was constantly being asked to help the needy and to assist numerous charities. In addition, his wife loved cats and their house was full of them, according to Rimsky, "chiefly strays." When Borodin came home from his laboratories at night, he would find students waiting for help with their work.

Rimsky wrote in his memoirs that "their apartment was often used as a shelter or a night's lodging by various poor (or 'visiting') relations, who picked that place to fall ill or even lose their minds. Borodin had his hands full of them, doctored them, took them to hospitals. . . . In the four rooms of his apartment there often slept several strange persons of this sort—sofas and floors were turned into beds. . . . At dinner and tea too, great disorder prevailed. Several tomcats that found a home in Borodin's apartment paraded across the dinner table sticking their noses into plates, unceremoniously leaping onto the diners' backs. . . ."

When his apartment was full, Borodin would amiably give up his plans for composing, afraid that the sound of his piano might waken his guests. His wife developed asthma, decided that she could not live in the damp climate of St. Petersburg and went to live in Moscow. Borodin spent more time traveling back and forth and writing voluminous letters. With all this to distract him, Borodin worked at his music when he could, often sitting at the piano in an overcoat because the stoves in his apartment were constantly broken. He once ruefully wrote to a friend that it was almost impossible for him to find time for composing except on his rare holidays or when he was sick.

When, in 1875, *Prince Igor* was still not finished, Rimsky tried to spur Borodin on by arranging for him to play some pieces of his composition at a concert. But, when the moment approached and Borodin was not ready, Rimsky, in desperation, offered to help him with the scoring of the Polovetsian dances and the final chorus. Unruffled, Borodin brought over his unfinished scores, and he, Rimsky and another composer, Liadov, worked together far into the night. "To save time," wrote Rimsky, "we wrote in pencil." Borodin then daubed the sheets with a special liquid gelatin of his own invention so that the pencil would not rub off. Then, continued Rimsky, "we hung them on lines to dry like so much washing."

But *Prince Igor* was still unfinished at the time of Borodin's sudden death in 1887. At fifty-four he collapsed of a heart attack while dancing dressed in Russian costume at a carnival ball given by the professors at the Academy. His friend Rimsky-Korsakov, along with Alexander Glazunov, completed and orchestrated the score after his death.

Borodin was the first of the "Five" to win international acclaim when his first two symphonies were played in Europe in 1880. Liszt, whom Borodin had met in 1877 on one of his trips abroad to visit laboratories, wrote to him that "the greatest connoisseurs as well as the general public applauded you heartily." In 1885 when Borodin visited Belgium for an International Exhibition, his music received enormous acclaim. On several occasions he was asked to conduct his music himself, but he always modestly refused, thinking himself not sufficiently experienced.

It was a loss for music that this kindly, talented man was able to devote so little time to it in his life, but the handful of works he left behind are of such brilliance that they set a course both in his own country and in the West, affecting European composers from Liszt to Ravel. And, obviously, Borodin did not regret anything, for he wrote to a friend, "Music, for my friends, is the principal occupation of their life, the end for which they live. For me, it is a relaxation, a pastime that distracts me from the absorbing duties that tie me to a professional chair. . . . I love my profession and my science. I love the Academy of Medicine and my pupils. . . . I have to keep constantly in touch with both the men and women students because young people's work requires close supervision. If, on the one hand, I want to finish a composition, I am, on the other hand, afraid to devote too much attention to it lest it should react unfavorably upon my scientific studies."

The strange and wayward genius in the midst of the Mighty Handful was Modest Mussorgsky. His music penetrated deep into the soul of the Russian people, and in a short and turbulent lifetime he poured forth a series of brilliant and innovative ideas. Baffling, contradictory and self-destructive, he was never understood even by his closest friends, and ended his life in alcoholic ruin.

Mussorgsky was a man of the country, born in 1839 in Karevo in the district of Pskov, on his father's estate of sweeping meadows and vast forests. Before he had a single lesson, he began to improvise on the piano. At nine he played a concerto for family guests. At thirteen he was enrolled, as his grandfather had been, in the cadet school for the elite Preobrazhensky Guards. In his childhood, the greatest influence on Mussorgsky, as on Pushkin, was his nurse, whose fairy tales he loved and from whom he learned to understand the spirit of the Russian people. "Modest," wrote his brother, "was always uncommonly partial to everything connected with the people and the peasantry." But when he graduated into the Guards at seventeen, no one could have imagined this partiality from his appearance. He was a conceited, dandyish dilettante with a taste for expensive champagne. Borodin described him in those days: "He was a smallish, elegant little officer like a lieutenant in a picture book; brand-new, close-fitting uniform, shapely feet turned neatly outward, hair scented and curled with utmost care, aristocratic and exquisitely manicured hands. His manners were elegant and stylish . . . his conversation very affected and liberally interspersed with French phrases. All the ladies smiled upon him . . . he sat at the piano and played very pleasantly some pieces from *Traviata* and *Trovatore* with coquettish movements of the hands."

Yet only one year after he met Balakirev and persuaded him to give him lessons in musical form, much to the surprise of the little circle, who considered him rather a joke, Mussorgsky resigned his commission to devote himself to music. He studied Mozart's *Requiem*, the operas of Gluck, Beethoven's "Moonlight Sonata," and earnestly tried to compose music himself. During that year of turbulent searching, he fell ill with a strange nervous disorder that continued to afflict him periodically the rest of his life, driving him to depression and drink.

That year, 1859, he made a trip to Moscow and visited St. Basil's Cathedral, the Kremlin, the Spassky Gate and the Bell Tower of Ivan the Great. These sights of the holy city of Moscow made a lasting impression on Mussorgsky. Thereafter, he revered Moscow as the true repository of Russian tradition and he devoted the last thirteen years of his life to two majestic operas celebrating its history.

From the beginning, Mussorgsky had an idea that music should reproduce the accents of human speech and follow its natural flow. "Nothing that is natural," he wrote, "can be wrong or inartistic." This realistic counterfocus to melody in his music baffled and annoyed his professor, Balakirev, who found him finally "unteachable." It also confused his friend Rimsky-Korsakov, a melodist who drew his music directly from folk songs. It was this confusion that later caused Rimsky to try to make corrections in Mussorgsky's music to render it smoother and more understandable. Mussorgsky totally rejected sentimentality, melodrama and classical art forms. He looked for his sounds in the poetic repetitions of Russian fairy tales, in liturgical chants, the bustle of the marketplace at Nizhny Novgorod, the sounds of nature and the world around him. From the window of his brother's house, he once heard the voice of the village idiot proclaiming his burning passion to the belle of the neighborhood, and from this wrote a strikingly realistic song.

Mussorgsky's friends joked about his ambition to become a composer. They found his piano playing quite brilliant, but they underrated his musical intelligence. Stasov wrote that "he seems like a perfect idiot." Balakirev acidly agreed: "Mussorgsky is practically an idiot."

Only the kindly Borodin, to whom he played one of his compositions, "Scherzo in B Flat," in 1860 did not agree. Borodin wrote, "I was quite astonished . . . it did not please me at first, though I was greatly impressed by the novelty of it. . . . I had not taken seriously Mussorgsky's assurance that he meant to devote himself to music. . . . I had regarded it as an arrogance, but after hearing the Scherzo, I hesitated."

After the emancipation of the serfs Mussorgsky's family fortunes, like those of so many landowners, declined dramatically. To keep afloat, he accepted a minor government appointment in the Ministry of Communication and, some years later, a clerkship in the Forestry Department. He plunged ahead with his composition and started planning an opera, but in 1865 his mother died, and once again he lapsed into depression and started drinking so heavily that he fell seriously ill.

It was in 1867, a year after Tolstoy had begun serializing *War and Peace* and Dostoevsky had published *Crime and Punishment*, that Mussorgsky suddenly burst out with his astonishing "Night on Bald Mountain," a piece describing the evil ceremonies and revels of the witches' sabbath on a mountain near Kiev. Saying that "it was boiling" within him, he wrote it in only eleven days one summer when he had to spend some time looking after affairs at a small estate in the countryside. It is a work which seems to explode out of the Russian people; there is nothing comparable to its startling sounds.

Hopefully, he dedicated it to his teacher, Balakirev, who rejected it coldly. But this piece marked an important change in Mussorgsky's creative self-confidence. Exultantly he wrote to a friend, "It is not a conglomeration of Teutonic profundity, but produced from native fields and nourished with Russian bread." To Balakirev he answered stoutly, "I consider it is a good work and shall continue to do so. I may have produced trifling efforts in the past, but this is the first significant thing I have written and whether you like my witches or not, I refuse to alter the general plan of my work or my development of it."

Mussorgsky loved Gogol, whom he felt to be closer to peasant culture than any other writer. He set to work on an opera based on Gogol's story "Marriage," writing the first act in twenty-seven days, working alone in a peasant hut and surviving chiefly on milk. Borodin rather liked it; the others were once again horrified at his daring harmonies. It was the preparation for his masterpiece. That year, 1868, an eminent professor and authority on Pushkin suggested to him that an opera libretto be taken from Pushkin's great tragedy, *Boris Godunov*. Mussorgsky seized the idea and set to work. He wrote his opera in little more than a year, in the time he had free from his work as a ministry clerk. Parts of the Pushkin drama he used verbatim; others he changed according to his own inspiration. As a cadet at school, Mussorgsky had been introduced to church music by a priest at the Court Chapel, and it had made a lasting impression on him. In *Boris* he used the form and sound of this mighty Russian church music. He played parts of his opera to the little circle for approval and criticism, and in 1870 submitted it to the director of the Imperial Theaters. In *Boris*, Mussorgsky concentrated the beauty and vigor of Russian folk art. His work was so radically different from the melodic Verdi operas with their lilting tenor and soprano arias that it shocked the committee because of its "extraordinary modernism." They objected to the fact that, contrary to accepted convention, there was no leading female character, and rejected the opera by six to one.

Mussorgsky immediately began a second version. He and Rimsky were then sharing an apartment where they had only one table and a single piano. In the morning Mussorgsky used the piano while Rimsky did his copying and orchestration at the table. In the afternoon while Mussorgsky was at work at the ministry Rimsky used the piano. Stasov often came to wake them and over their simple breakfast of bread and cheese they told him about their work of the preceding days. As work progressed, Mussorgsky sent humorously worded invitations to his friends to come and listen to parts of his opera. ("Come . . . we will pull Boris by the hair.").

In 1872 he submitted his revised second version of *Boris* to which he had added the Polish noblewoman Marina as a leading female role as well as the revolution scene in the forest, which Pushkin had not written. Once again, the selection committee rejected it, but by then the opera had won many admirers. Three scenes were successfully performed at the Maryinsky Theater in 1873. During the years that passed between the first and second versions, Mussorgsky had also begun work, along with many other compositions, on his second opera based on 17th-century Muscovite history, *Khovanshchina*.

At thirty-three Mussorgsky's contradictory personality alternately delighted and repelled people. Rimsky's wife wrote of him that "his face was not very expressive but suggested a mystery concealed in it. . . ." His manners could be elegant and his singing delightful; he was a brilliant pianist. He could act the part of Ivan the Terrible or Boris with deep dramatic feeling. He hated the routine and commonplace in every branch of life. Strangely, for someone who loved peasant life, he "hated ordinary simple words." He often twisted people's names. His letters were witty, and often humorous, but sometimes there was a certain affectation in his brilliance. His work was constantly interrupted by attacks of bleak depression and bouts of heavy drinking.

In those times his friends could not restrain him. One of these friends, the painter Ilya Repin, wrote sadly, "It seemed unbelievable that a well-bred officer of the Guards, with beautiful manners, a witty conversationalist with the ladies, an inexhaustible punster . . . could have sunk so low." Many times Stasov went to retrieve him in cellars where Mussorgsky had passed the night carousing with rough companions and found him shabbily dressed and bloated with drink. Unsuccessfully Stasov tried to persuade him to come to Germany to meet Liszt, but Mussorgsky refused to leave St. Petersburg.

Finally forced, it was said, by a leading singer who had been given the right to demand a new opera and threatened to resign unless she got her way, a full production of *Boris Godunov* was performed on February 8, 1874, with the costumes and sets of the original Pushkin play. Mussorgsky directed some of the rehearsals personally. Despite the sniping of the academicians and critics who could never forgive Mussorgsky his lack of musical education, it was an outstanding success. But the opera was so strange and new that a sad progression of events followed. First cuts, then longer and longer intervals between performances and then, after only twenty performances, his opera disappeared from the repertoire entirely. Its first success had made Mussorgsky arrogant and overambitious, and when it did not go on, he was devastated.

The downfall of *Boris* was followed by the total decay of Mussorgsky. His all-night bouts of drinking increased. Stasov wrote, "Mussorgsky is changed completely . . . his face is swollen and dark in color, his eyes are dull and he spends days on end in a Petersburg restaurant with a cursed bunch of drunkards." During these last sad years, he traveled about with a well-known contralto and her accompanist and tried with difficulty to continue work on *Khovanshchina*. In 1880 he began to have convulsions. His friends took him to the Nikolaievsky Military Hospital, where after a few weeks of care he seemed to revive a bit. His friends tried to comfort him; they brought him his favorite books and papers and Cui lent him his favorite dressing gown. When Ilya Repin came to visit, the painter did a sad portrait that uncompromisingly recorded Mussorgsky's decline; he is wild-eyed, with scraggly hair and unkempt beard, his face bloated by drink. In his last weeks sometimes he talked coherently, at other times he raved. One day he called out twice and collapsed. He died on March 16, 1881, the morning of his forty-second birthday. His last words were: "Everything is finished, ah! How miserable I am!"

Mussorgsky was one of the great songwriters of the 19th century. In his lifetime he wrote sixty-five songs, many to his own words, which evoke scenes of Russian life with sensitivity and insight. In these songs, melodies conform realistically to the natural inflections of the voice and language. During his last year, in a sudden burst of creativity, Mussorgsky composed a last, great cycle, "The Songs and Dances of Death." These final songs, along with the piano cycle "Pictures at an Exhibition" and parts of an opera based on Gogol's "Fair at Sorochintsy" were found in a heap of paper scraps when he was taken to the hospital.

Only a few weeks after Dostoevsky, Mussorgsky was buried in the Alexander Nevsky Monastery, in the same month Alexander II was blown to pieces. Four years later his friends erected a memorial to him. Yet it was not until our own century that the genius of this strange and tortured man was fully appreciated. Because his work was so boldly innovative, many have tried over the years to put it into a more comprehensible frame. *Khovanshchina* was completed and orchestrated by Rimsky-Korsakov, who worked from an arrangement for piano and voices. He changed it so much while scoring it that many of its original characteristics were completely obliterated. "Pictures at an Exhibition" was orchestrated in its present form by Ravel many years later.

As for the mighty *Boris Godunov,* no other opera has had such a strange lifetime, nor been subjected to so many changes and versions. Mussorgsky's friend, Rimsky, saddened at the opera's disappearance from the repertoire of the Imperial Theater twice, in 1896 and again in 1906, made various changes in order to try to make the opera less rugged and more acceptable. Several additional modifications were made for Diaghilev's 1908 production in Paris, in which Chaliapin sang the leading role. *Boris* was not performed in America until 1914, at the Metropolitan Opera, with Chaliapin singing and Toscanini conducting.

It is these Rimsky-revised versions of *Boris* which are the most often performed on the world's stages. Not until 1928 was there a revival of Mussorgsky's original score in Russia, and later, in 1935, in Europe, but only in French, English and German translations. Not until 1975 was the full Mussorgsky score published and made widely available in the West. Today, almost every opera house has its own version of this compelling work, which is now considered to be not only the finest Russian opera ever written, but one of the greatest of all the world's operas.

The youngest of the Mighty Handful, and the one who, unlike his unhappy friend Mussorgsky, enjoyed enormous recognition in his own lifetime, was Nikolai Rimsky-Korsakov. Rimsky taught, composed and conducted with equal ease and self-confidence, enjoying great success in all three fields. As a composer he was astonishingly prolific. He wrote fifteen operas, all but one on themes suggested by Russian folklore, three symphonies, numerous symphonic suites and poems, chorales, piano and chamber music. As a loyal friend, he also stepped in to finish some of the work of Borodin and Mussorgsky.

Rimsky was the "colorist" who went straight to the folk song for inspiration, drawing his themes and rich melodies directly from them; those he remembered and those he heard around him. (He wrote that he once spent a long time trying to catch a tricky rhythm from the singing of Borodin's maid, a native of one of the Volga provinces.) He saw individual characteristics in various keys. For him, A major was the key of "youth and brilliance"; D flat he associated with love and warmth, D major with light and brilliance and A minor "with the glow of the sunset over a snow-covered winter landscape."

Rimsky-Korsakov became a master of orchestration, yet he never heard an orchestra in his childhood. He was born in the north in 1844, in the small town of Tikhvin in the region of Novgorod where his father was a civil governor. Although his family was of respected gentry, he was always especially proud of his two humble grandmothers. He liked to say that from one, a priest's daughter who had five illegitimate sons, he had inherited a love for religious ceremonies, and from the other, a serf, his love for folk songs. As a child, he spent many hours listening to the choir of the monastery which was not far from his house. He learned to play the piano and, at eleven, tried to compose an overture for piano in six movements. But his admired older brother was a naval lieutenant who later rose to admiral, and young Nikolai avidly read his brother's letters from far-off places, constructed model ships and dreamed of the sea. The only musicians in his little town were a bumbling violinist and a house decorator who played the tambourine. Not until Nikolai was fifteen, and a cadet at Naval School in St. Petersburg, did he first hear two of Beethoven's symphonies and Glinka's operas, and he quickly grew to love these operas so much that he spent hours making musical arrangements of them for piano. He took piano and cello lessons, and one of his teachers introduced him to Balakirev. To his delight, he was included in "really serious discussions of orchestrations, part writing," among "real, talented musicians."

During his Christmas holidays in 1862, when he was only eighteen, he finished the first movement of the symphony that Balakirev had encouraged him to write. By April he was off on his graduation cruise around the world on the cruiser *Almaz*. When his ship was forced to spend four months at Gravesend for repairs, Rimsky and his shipmates happily explored London and went to Covent Garden to hear the Royal Italian Opera. Balakirev wrote to urge him to continue working on his symphony. Since there was no piano on board, Rimsky was forced to go to the local pubs in Gravesend to try out his second movement on their pianos. In 1863, Alexander II dispatched a Russian fleet to the United States to demonstrate Russia's support for Lincoln and the Union during the Civil War. Tall-masted ships, the *Almaz* among them, flying the red, white and blue Imperial flag, dropped anchor in New York Harbor. Rimsky stayed in the United States

MASLENITSA. Boris Kustodiev.   *Page 366*

ICE SLIDE. St. Petersburg. F. de Haenen. c. 1912. *Page 363*

SPRING FLOWERS EGG. House of Fabergé.
1890.   *Page 375*

STRAWBERRIES. House of Fabergé.
Page 374

EASTER VIGIL. Boris Kustodiev. *Page 379*

EASTER GREETING. Boris Kustodiev.
Page 380

BELL RINGERS. F. de Haenen. c. 1912.
Page 194

MOSCOW TAVERN. Boris Kustodiev. 1916.   *Page 388*

PORTRAIT OF F. CHALIAPIN AS BORIS GODUNOV IN OPERA OF M. MUSSORGSKY.
Alexander Golovin. 1912. *Page 394*

IVAN MOROZOV. Valentin Serov. 1912.   *Page 405*

SWAN PRINCESS. Mikhail Vrubel. 1900. *Page 395*

ANNA PAVLOVA (original poster for the *Ballets Russes*).
Valentin Serov. 1909.   *Page 432*

SERGEI DIAGHILEV AND HIS NURSE.
Lev Bakst. 1905.   *Page 425*

SET FOR THE BALLET <u>PETRUSHKA</u>. Alexander Benois. 1911.   *Page 441*

SET FOR THE BALLET <u>SCHÉHÉREZADE</u>. Lev Bakst. 1910. *Page 437*

COSTUME DESIGN FOR TAMARA KARSAVINA IN THE
BALLET <u>FIREBIRD</u>. Lev Bakst. 1910.   *Page 436*

PORTRAIT OF NIJINSKY AS THE FAUN
from *L'Après-midi d'un Faune*. Lev Bakst. 1912.
Page 447

THE WEDDING. Marc Chagall. 1910.   *Page 451*

DANCING PEASANTS.
Natalia Goncharova. 1911.
Page 451

ROOSTER: RAYONIST STUDY.
Mikhail Larionov. 1912.   *Page 451*

SUPREMATIST COLORS. Kasimir Malevich.
c. 1915.   *Page 454*

NICHOLAS II. Valentin Serov. 1900. *Page 425*

from October 1863 until April 1864. He visited Annapolis and Baltimore and went up the Hudson to Albany and then Niagara Falls, where he says he was "shown to rooms in a magnificent hotel." In New York, he says, "we visited restaurants and lounged about eating and occasionally drinking" and also "heard a poor performance of Gounod's *Faust*." On his ship, accompanied on the violin by the American pilot, Mr. Thompson, Rimsky played American songs and anthems. There was a grand ball at the Academy of Music, where hoop-skirted ladies were whirled about by Russian and Union officers. Later Rimsky sailed to Brazil, and it was almost three years before he finally returned from the sea to his beloved group of musicians.

In 1865 his First Symphony was ready and was performed at a Free Music Society concert. The audience was enthusiastic, and quite astonished when the composer, who came out to acknowledge their cheers, turned out to be a twenty-three-year-old naval officer in a stiff uniform with gold buttons. As he matured, Rimsky found Balakirev's dominating personality more and more confining, and he began to strike out on his own, composing an opera and working on the orchestration of the works of his friends. In 1871, because of his growing reputation as a young "modern" composer, the director of the St. Petersburg Conservatory, that bastion of the opposition, quite unexpectedly asked him to become Professor of Practical Composition and Orchestration.

At first he hesitated, recalling in his memoirs, "If I had made a study of music and possessed even a fraction more knowledge than I actually did, it would have been obvious to me that to accept the appointment would be foolish and dishonest. . . . At the time I could not properly harmonize a chorale, had never attempted a contrapuntal exercise and knew little about the structure of a fugue. . . . In my compositions, I had aimed at correctness in part writing . . . and had attained it instinctively. . . . As for the art of conducting, I had no conception of it whatever, never having directed an orchestra or rehearsed a single choral work. . . ."

But his friends urged him to accept anyway and "I was young and self-confident." Thus, at twenty-seven, Rimsky became a professor of music while still retaining his commission in the navy. He stayed up all night studying, struggling to keep ahead of his students. "I had to pretend I knew everything and understood their problems, and at the same time glean information from my pupils without letting them know. . . . By the time they had learned sufficient to see through me, I had also learned something! . . . having undeservedly accepted a professorship at the conservatory, I soon became one of its best—perhaps its best—pupil!" In time, Rimsky became one of Russia's finest music teachers. His students loved him. He was simple and unprofessorial in manner, went about in worn clothes and old boots and always exhibited delight over a good piece of work by one of his students.

In 1872, with Mussorgsky as best man, Rimsky married Nadezhda Purgold, a pianist, who became the mother of their seven children. As he was still a naval officer, in 1873 a special post was created for him—Inspector of Naval Bands, the first of many official positions he was to hold. He traveled back and forth to the Black Sea and typically, to better supervise his bands, he quickly learned to play simple tunes on the flute, the clarinet and the trombone. In 1874 Rimsky was asked to conduct a benefit concert for the famine victims in Samarkand at the Club of Nobility, and with his characteristic confidence, accepted, despite the fact that he had never conducted anything more than the orchestral class at the conservatory. To make up for his deficiency he once again stayed up all night, scrutinizing the score and, alone in his study, practicing the motions of conducting. At rehearsals he managed to control his extreme nervousness and, he wrote, "appeared to perform like an old hand." The same year he took over the directorship of the Free Music Society when Balakirev gave it up; he immediately organized a grand concert in the City Hall.

Along with all these activities, which also included the assembling of a collection of a hundred Russian folk songs, he was busy composing. The same year that Tchaikovsky composed *Eugene Onegin*, Rimsky was at work on his lovely opera *May Night*, which had its premiere at the Maryinsky in 1880 with the father of Igor Stravinsky as a member of the chorus.

In the summer of 1880, while living in a summer house in Luga in the heart of the Russian countryside, Rimsky wrote his opera *The Snow Maiden*, considered by many to be his masterpiece. It is a fairy tale of pagan Russia, whose characters shade from human to half-human to personifications of nature. While he was writing this opera, he was completely immersed in the Russian atmosphere and delighted with everything around him—"the remote villages with their ancient Russian names . . . the beautiful garden with its cherry and apple trees, currant bushes, strawberries, gooseberries, its flowering lilacs . . . the triple echo from our balcony seemed like the voices of wood sprites . . . the vast forest, the fields of rye, wheat, oats, millet, flax . . . the little stream where we bathed." Perhaps because of the profound joy he felt, for *The Snow Maiden* he created orchestral scenes of dazzling beauty. In this opera, perhaps his finest work, it is impossible to tell precisely what he took from the folk melodies of the people and what came from his own soul.

On the accession of Alexander III in 1883, Balakirev was appointed Intendant of the Imperial Chapel and Rimsky became his assistant. Together, they worked on the music for the coronation, for which Tchaikovsky also composed a march. When Mussorgsky died in 1881, Rimsky immediately dropped his own work to take over the preparation of his friend's work for publication, and when Borodin died, in 1887, Rimsky once again laid aside his own work to finish *Prince Igor.* He and the young composer Alexander Glazunov spent the summer in a little village working on *Igor* together and while there Rimsky, with his usual overflowing energy, also composed "Capriccio Espagnole," which became one of his most popular pieces. (The first time it was performed, the orchestra burst into applause, and so Rimsky dedicated it to them.)

As his fame continued to grow, Rimsky often traveled abroad. In 1889 he and Glazunov along with other Russian artists went to Paris where Rimsky conducted two concerts of music at the Palais du Trocadero. He was so highly regarded by the French that, in 1900, he was elected as the one corresponding foreign member of the French Academy, replacing the Norwegian composer Grieg. In the years between 1889 and 1906 the prolific Rimsky composed seven operas, the most famous of which were *The Tsar's Bride, Tsar Saltan* and *The Golden Cockerel,* the last two based on Pushkin's narrative poems, as well as *Schéhérazade,* an orchestral fairy tale that remains one of his most popular compositions, and a piano concerto. In 1902 he became the director of the Imperial Russian Symphony concerts and in 1907 conducted his music in Paris at a series of concerts organized by Sergei Diaghilev. Although in his last years Rimsky suffered from angina pectoris, he always refused to follow his doctor's orders for long, and in 1910, after a period of furious composing activity which included finishing the proofs of *The Golden Cockerel,* he died suddenly at the age of sixty-six.

Of all the arts, music is perhaps the most mysterious. Even with all the explanations, there is still something baffling about how these composers of the Mighty Handful managed to write great music without the usual classical musical education. Yet, in the end, perhaps it was an advantage, for they were not weighed down by tradition and convention and were able, each in his own way, to strike out in new paths.

The end of the 19th century and the beginning of the 20th saw yet another great flowering of music in Russia—Sergei Rachmaninov and Alexander Scriabin in Moscow, Sergei Prokofiev in St. Petersburg. Musical prodigies sprang up in great number: the pianist Vladimir Horowitz in Kiev; the violinist Jascha Heifetz, who came from Vilnius to St. Petersburg to study with Leopold Auer; and in Odessa, which had a rich musical culture, the violinists Nathan Milstein , Mischa Elman, Toscha Seidel and Joseph Roisman, all of them trained by the two remarkable teachers, Max and Alexander Fiedelmann.

At the end of his life, Rimsky-Korsakov became the first music professor of a young law student, Igor Stravinsky. To this young man, his most extraordinarily talented pupil, Rimsky imparted his secrets of orchestral wizardry. Stravinsky went on to become the greatest and most influential composer of the 20th century—the culmination and the crowning of the powerfully independent anti-conservatory tradition begun by the Mighty Handful.

21 · ICE SLIDES AND EASTER EGGS: RUSSIA CELEBRATES

The glories of these frosty days
Like secret promenades in sleighs . . .

Alexander Pushkin
Eugene Onegin

On the frozen snow, see how sleighs glide light and silent! In a night sparkling with stars, gallop in a troika across the vague and frozen spaces where there are no roads, no bridges, no villages, and you will feel that delicious sensation of the infinite and the unknown, so well described as the "vertigo of the north." When a sleigh is thus taken in a rapid whirlwind you are no longer on earth, you are in space, in the clouds, in the moon! Going up in a balloon which is taking off and in its flight dissolving the silver layer of the clouds!

Victor Tissot
La Russie et Les Russes

ALTHOUGH RUSSIAN LIFE was changing rapidly in the second half of the 19th century, some things did not change. Among the glories of old Russia were the beloved popular festivals and church celebrations that punctuated the year

357

like exclamations of pleasure, gay holidays when the whole populace, rich and poor, joined together to celebrate with exuberance and joy.

The coming of winter ushered in the year's celebrations. For the West, it is the rigors of the Russian winter that are legendary. In tones of awe, stories are told of how the snow begins in October and lasts until April, how the houses are sometimes buried up to their roofs and the winter nights last twenty hours. So intense is the cold that houses crack; travelers sometimes arrived in town frozen stiff and dead in the sleighs. Considering all this, one would suppose that Russians would dread the coming of the frost. Yet to the astonishment of Westerners, Russians also found great magic and delight in winter. They greeted the first snow with joy and excitement. Robert Ker Porter, an English artist who lived and traveled extensively in Russia, wrote in 1813, "They sing, they wrestle, rumbling about like great bears among the furrows of the surrounding snow." It was a custom to make a wish as the first soft snowflakes began to cover the ground. The sensual Pushkin wrote:

. . . how healing
Is winter with its frosts and sleigh-rides o'er the snow
Your love beside you close, her trembling fingers stealing
Beneath the silken furs to curl around your own
Their hot, their burning touch designed for you alone!

And in another verse, he joyfully exclaimed, "How hotly kisses flame under the snow!"

Théophile Gautier wrote lyrically of his first winter in Russia. In the extreme cold "winter takes on character and poetry. It becomes as rich in effects as the most splendid summer. The snow sparkles like diamonds and is redoubled in whiteness from the frost which hardens it. Trees crystallized with frost look like great ramifications of beaten silver, the metallic flowering of a fairy garden." The Folk Encyclopedia of 1845 begins its sections on winter with these sentences: "Snow is an important matter to the Russian land. The respect that people accord to snow in the villages sometimes takes on very unusual proportions; around snow there are many myths, legends and customs."

In the deep forests the immense firs covered with snow stood like sentinels of an enchanted silence. The branches of the birch trees, bare of leaves but flowering with frost, had the fineness and elegance of ostrich plumes. On sunny days, the glittering land stretched to infinity, evoking that sense of unlimited space which in Russian is lovingly called *prostor*. For travelers, it was like being on the sea, the endless expanse broken only rarely when suddenly, from behind a forest, would emerge immense caravans of sleighs, 100 to 150 together, one driver for each seven horses, laden with wares they were carrying to every part of Russia. Ker Porter wrote, "In the morning, as they advance toward you, the scene is as beautiful as it is striking. The sun, then rising, throws its rays across the snow, transforming it into a surface of diamonds. From the cold of the night, every man and horse is encrusted with these frosty particles. The manes of the horses and the long beards of the men have a particularly glittering effect."

In the villages winter was the time for carving and embroidery. Girls and women gathered together around the great stove. These gatherings had a name, *posedelki*. The girls embroidered and sang; the young men came to laugh, joke and flirt a little; old *babushka*s told stories.

In village and city, houses were heated with great stoves in which birch wood, long-burning and smelling of fresh bread, crackled. The tall stove occupied a central part of all modest houses. In the *izba*s of the peasants, the stove served for cooking and heating, baking and sleeping. Benches ran all around it, and there were hollows and cornices for drying wet socks and clothes. On the platform of the stove, people slept. Russian stoves were the most efficient of their kind ever invented. Made of earthenware, they warmed slowly and heated all day. In the city, for six months a year houses were warmed from top to bottom by these great stoves. Sometimes there was one in each room; sometimes they were in the basement of houses which were centrally heated. It required great skill to set such stoves, and the Great Russians, especially the Muscovites, had attained a complete mastery of this business.

In the cities there was a whole winter way of life. Sledges glided along the frozen streets; people were wrapped in furs of every variety—the humble in sheepskin and wolf coats, the rich in fox and sable. In buildings, public rooms for the poor were constantly heated; bonfires were kept in the streets for drivers and pedestrians. When the thermometer fell lower than twenty-three or twenty-four degrees below zero, the police went around day and night to keep the sentries and *budoshniki* awake and to watch for drunks who, if they once went to sleep in the snow, simply froze. People on the streets watched each other for telltale signs of frostbite. Without ceremony they would say, "Thy nose, daddy," and proceed to rub with snow a nose white as chalk. Despite the cold, the parades in front of the palace took place every day. The officers wore no cloaks; neither did the Emperor, who exposed himself to wind, snow and hail.

In Petersburg, wrote Kohl, "From all the houses, and likewise from the churches, which are heated too, whirl thick columns of vapor, which appear as dense as if there were a steam engine in every house, and reflect all sorts of colors. The snow and ice in the streets and on the Neva are pure and white as though all were baked of sugar. . . . The snow as you tread on it crackles and howls with the strangest melodies; all other sounds assume unusual tones in this frigid atmosphere; while a slight rustling or buzzing is continually heard in the air, arising probably from the collision of all the particles of snow and ice that are floating there."

The windows of shops and restaurants blossomed with tracings of frost that looked like mysterious jungles of icy palms and fronds. In apartments and houses, people enclosed themselves behind double, triple and even quadruple doors. Double windows were put in in October, and not until May were they removed and windows opened once again to the air. Salt or sand was put between the windows and heaped up in fanciful forms or planted with artificial flowers, each household arranging its windows differently, so that it was entertaining to make a tour on a bright winter's day to observe the fanciful ways in which these double windows were decorated.

All in all, "Winter in Russia," wrote the visiting French journalist Victor Tissot, "is not that grumpy and rheumatic old man who visits us and comes crying in our gutters and coughing in our chimneys. Winter in Russia is an invigorating shock. Winter here is a young man, full of verve and enthusiasm to whom festivals are owed." Summer was short and a time for work; winter was the time for holidays, and January and February the months of love and marriage. Many of the major church holidays took place in winter.

At Christmas, there was caroling in the streets of towns and villages. Through the streets, boys carried a brightly painted star with a candle before it, turning it as they went and stopping in front of churches and houses to sing. Everybody participated in this caroling, not only the peasants. In the 17th century the tsar himself in a sleigh, followed by his boyars and courtiers and led by two drummers, would go from house to house in Moscow and sing for the owners, who were expected to give gifts and treats. Peter the Great went thus to congratulate his friends, but in his own forceful style he kept a list of carolers and those who did not go were punished.

Christmas Eve was the last day of the six-week Christmas fast, and for all the devout, ancient custom dictated that no one eat until the first star glimmered in the sky. The traditional dish was *kutya*, boiled wheat sweetened with honey and sprinkled with poppy seeds, or boiled rice with raisins and nuts. In some of the villages of southern Russia a custom prevailed which lasted well into our own century. Into the *izba*s was brought a mixed sheaf of barley, wheat and buckwheat tied together with a handful of hay. The sheaf was placed in the corner under the icons and beside it a pot of *kutya* with a candle stuck in the middle. Hay was spread on the table and covered with a white cloth in memory of the manger. Dinner began with a prayer for the New Year, and finished with *kutya*. The head of the household first threw a spoonful outside for Grandfather Frost, saying, "Here is a spoonful for thee; please do not touch our crops." A spoonful was thrown up on the ceiling; the grains that stuck prophesied the number of bees there would be in summer. Finally, upon rising from the table, everyone left some *kutya* in their bowls for their departed relatives. On Christmas Day, it was the custom for everyone in town and village to go visiting in their finest clothes. According to the Folk Encyclopedia of 1845, tables were always spread in a special manner, traditionally with at least five varieties of nuts, from Greece, the Volga and Siberia, as well as many kinds of pickled mushrooms, several sorts of special gingerbread cookies made from recipes of the various towns of Russia. "Apples, fresh and of all kinds, were spread on the table; some sweet as pears, others scrunchy as winter, those that were yellow and red together, apples preserved in sugar and dried, Ukrainian apples and apples stewed in *kvas*. Along with them, many dried fruits, large and small raisins, currants, cherries and two kinds of prunes, stewed and dried pears and dates."

The period between Christmas and New Year's had, in old Russia, a special joy and a special name, *Svyatki*. It was one of the gayest and happiest times of the year, "a time," says the Folk Encyclopedia, "when could be seen the boundless revelry which stirs Russian hearts and represents their true expansiveness. It was a time of closeness, which brought all those who were separated by generations together . . . for it was a time for love, dedicated to those who are fated for each other. In the villages the young could hold hands freely, and because old people remembered the joys of the past they too grew younger. Old ladies reminisced tearfully of the days when they were maidens, they told stories and gave advice." During the week of *Svyatki*, and most especially on New Year's Eve, it was the tradition to tell fortunes every day in a whole variety of ways. Several mirrors were placed to reflect one into another, and a candle was placed before them; one's fate might appear in the mirror. A shadow of a burning paper would be thrown on the wall or a large candle melted into a bowl of water, and the figure made gave a clue as to who would be the future beloved. In the villages, maidens and boys would make a circle, and in front of each maiden a little pile of grain was placed. A hungry rooster would be brought in and the one whose grain he pecked first would be married within the year. Girls went out into the courtyard or street and asked the first passerby his name; that was a clue to the name of the beloved. All this was immortalized by Pushkin in *Eugene Onegin*. Of his heroine, Tatyana, who kept the old customs of the country and who was hoping that Onegin might love her, he wrote with gentle humor:

Tatyana in the court appears,
And, careless of the cold, is training
A mirror on the moon, now waning;
The image trembling in the glass
Is but the wistful moon's, alas . . .
The crunch of snow . . . a step approaches;
Straight to the stranger Tatyana speeds,
Her voice as tender as a reed's,
And rash the question that she broaches:
"Your name is—what?" He passes on,
But first he answers: "Agafon."

Only during *Svyatki*, says the Folk Encyclopedia, was "Ancient Russia resurrected . . . customs passed down from times immemorial, no one knew from where, unwritten, unexplained, passed on from the people of bygone years."

The snow of the night before Epiphany, January 5, was considered the most precious. In the villages old women collected it from the top of the haystacks, believing that it could whiten linen as not even the sun. Villagers believed that the snow collected on Epiphany Eve would keep well water fresh and preserve a spring even if there was not a drop of rain in summer. It could cure poor circulation, dizziness and cramps in the joints; placed on the hearth, it could protect the household from the fiery snakes which flew through the air waiting only to fly down the chimney and transform themselves into a handsome young man so charming that a maiden could not resist his wiles. "Bright stars bring white lambs" went the old proverb; the colder it was on Epiphany, the better would be the harvest.

In both Moscow and St. Petersburg, on the day of Epiphany, January 6, one of the most brilliant of religious ceremonies, the Blessing of the Waters, took place. This ceremony, a sanctification based on the immersion of Jesus in the Jordan, was a rite dating far back into antiquity, one which foreign visitors found both moving and mysterious.

In St. Petersburg on the ice of the Neva an open temple, painted and gilded, supported by pillars, surmounted by a golden cross and embellished with icons of John the Baptist, was erected. Inside, the temple was decorated with crosses and holy books and in the middle of the sacred enclosure a hole was cut in the ice and called the Jordan. An enclosure of fir boughs twisted together was placed at a distance from the temple and carpeted with scarlet cloth as was the temple and the platform for the procession.

After a liturgy held in the Court Chapel, the bishops and archimandrites issued from the Winter Palace in their richest habits, sewn with pearls and glistening with gold, and with lighted tapers proceeded to the Jordan singing anthems. In splendid attire, the Imperial family and the court followed, and while the service was being performed, all the troops in the city were drawn up in an enormous ring on the ice of the Neva, with their standards waving and artillery planted ready to fire. After many prayers, the priest blessed the water with his uplifted hands three times and consecrated it by immersing a holy cross in the water three times, while cannons reverberated in solemn cadence. After the ceremony, mothers hastened to dip their children in the opening in the ice to bless them, and people flocked to draw water, for it was believed that the water so consecrated remained for years as fresh as when drawn from the river and had the power to cure the sick of their diseases.

In winter horses were raced on the frozen rivers. The Samoyed tribes sometimes came down from the north to St. Petersburg and gave reindeer sleigh rides on the Neva. In the villages there were snow forts and games. But of all the winter amusements, the most beloved and typically Russian were the ice slides or ice mountains which were erected in all villages and towns. Ice hills and the carnival towns which grew up about them on holidays were a very old and popular amusement, known since the 15th and 16th centuries. In a flat country such as Russia, hills are a sensation; Russians of all ages loved whizzing down these artificial ice mountains, a sport at which, having practiced from childhood, they were very proficient.

As soon as winter came, in squares and public places all over the land, ice hills were erected, usually near a river. They were constructed of wood—a narrow long-legged temporary stage that rose to a height of 30 or 40 feet and sometimes even higher. The platform, to which one ascended by wooden stairs, was supported by tree trunks and wooden pillars. Two such platforms were constructed to face each other and were set parallel so that the force of sledding down one would carry a rider all the way down to the steps of the other. He would then climb up and start back the opposite way. Like the side of an abrupt cliff, the slope was at first very steep. It then flattened out at the bottom, with sand at the very end of the course to slow down the flying sleds. The whole surface of the course was covered with large blocks of ice, frozen shining and smooth in a few seconds from torrents of water thrown over them. In the villages, on simple ice hills, boys and girls went down swift as arrows, and kept the slope in good condition by bringing snow and pouring water on it. They carved small sleds of ice cakes or blocks, placing straw in the hollows and boring a hole at one end for a rope. In cities, in the large courtyards of houses, ice hills were erected for children.

Kohl wrote that one day, walking early through the streets of St. Petersburg, he saw a snow hill constructed up to a roof from which children and servants, looking as if they had just gotten out of bed, were happily sliding down on mattresses. The fun-loving Empress Elizabeth had a glorious ice hill at Tsarskoe Selo designed by Rastrelli. It had a 150-foot course and a central building topped by a golden cupola 80 feet high. From it extended slides and switchbacks to the length of 900 feet. An apparatus driven by donkeys brought sleds up to the top of the hill.

The huge ice hills of Moscow and St. Petersburg erected at Christmas and festival times, at the expense of the municipality, were extremely elaborate and an amusement for the entire population. The platforms were gaily decorated with open pavilions, often in a Chinese pagoda style, complete with bright fluttering flags. The sides of the course were ornamented with little fir trees. The slide was wide enough to accommodate as many as thirty sleds at a time and stretched the length of several city blocks. Workmen were engaged to smooth it until it was mirrorlike. Special sledmen wearing heavy stiff leather gloves stood at the bottom of the platforms with sleds, ready for a few kopecks to guide one expertly down.

Two and sometimes three people flew down on a sled. Ker Porter described the ride this way: "A sort of sledge, without projections of any kind, but in shape and flatness like a butcher's tray most fantastically ornamented with carving and colors is placed on the summit of the hill. The native sits himself upon it, very far back, legs extending in front perfectly straight. The person to be conveyed places himself in front in similar attitude, and both remaining steady, pass down the frozen torrent. The native guides with his hands, and so cleverly that they steer around groups of upset persons. Many go down alone, and others on skates, who fly forward in a perfectly upright position. . . . The sensation excited in the person who descends in the sledge is at first extremely painful, but after a few times, passing through the cutting air, it is exquisitely pleasurable. This seems strange, but it is so; as you shoot along a sort of ethereal intoxication takes hold of the senses which is absolutely delightful!"

In principle, tricks were prohibited on these slides, but sometimes daredevil boys would go down lying flat on their backs on their sleds, arms crossed over their chests, or on their stomachs, head first, going so fast that the police could not catch them. People lined the course to watch, and although sometimes people tumbled all over each other at the end of the ride, surprisingly there were very few accidents. Decorous visiting English ladies seem to have worried most about the shocking immodesty of having their petticoats flying over their heads.

Gautier wrote with obvious delight that in St. Petersburg, "Often, after the theater or an evening with friends . . . when the snow sparkles like pulverized marble, the moon shines clear and glacial and the stars scintillate with the vivacity which frost can produce . . . a group of young men and girls wrapped warmly in their furs, make up a party to go sup on the islands; they climb in a troika and the rapid team, with its three horses spread fan-shaped, starts up with a tingling of bells, stirring up a silver dust. . . . A sleepy tavern is roused . . . the samovar heats, champagne is cooled, plates of caviar, ham, herring . . . and little cakes are arranged on the table. They chat, laugh and joke and then for dessert climb up one of the ice hills lit by torches and slide down; then it is back to the city around two or three in the morning, savoring in the midst of the whirlwind of speed in the lively, raw and healthy air of the night, the voluptuousness of the cold."

The Russians loved sliding so much that even in apartments there were slides made of polished wood. The last Tsarevich, Alexis, and his sisters had such a slide of gleaming mahogany in the ballroom of the Alexander Palace and delighted in sliding down on pillows and whirling long distances on gleaming waxed floors. In the summer, the outdoor hills were sometimes converted to polished wood and people slid down on scraps of carpet, large pieces of smooth tree bark or little carts with wheels. In the late 19th century these carts were mechanized and these mechanized carts and hills in parks came to be known, quite inexplicably, as "American Hills," while everywhere else they were called, as in France, "Russian Mountains" or, as in America, the roller coaster—a Russian gift to the world.

Just as winter began to seem unbearably long, preparations for Easter began. In old Russia, the coming of Easter was a yearly drama, with a beginning, a middle and an end, and even a curious epilogue. Two months of every year were spent preparing for and celebrating the Resurrection and the coming of spring. The celebration began in the snow, with a pagan and earthy carnival celebrating life, and was followed by a long fast; it culminated in the beginning of spring and the new explosion of re-creation and happiness which are at the core of the Christian belief.

First there were the eight days of stuffing, feasting and carnival called *Maslenitsa*, or "Butter Week." During every day of *Maslenitsa*, before the long weeks of Lent when all butter was prohibited, Russians consumed huge quantities of blini, little pancakes smothered in butter, at every meal. All restaurants and taverns served blini, always cooked a few at a time and brought piping hot to the table.

Depending on the date when Easter fell, shortly before *Maslenitsa*, as a harbinger of the sky and warmth and the jollity to come, little cakes in the shape of larks, with wings, thin legs and eyes made of currants, were sold. Russian writers have left many glowing descriptions of the joys of *Maslenitsa*. Alexander Kuprin wrote:

Only yesterday, Moscow was still eating "larks." And today, the real Tsar, knight and hero of Moscow is the thousand-year-old blini. . . . The blini, rosy and hot, as hot and warming as the sun, blini smothered with butter, a memory of the sacrifices brought to the mighty stone idols of yore. Blini: a symbol of the sun, of beautiful days of good harvest, happy marriages and healthy children.

O pagan, independent principality of Moscow! She eats blini hot as fire, eats them with meat with sour cream, with fresh caviar and pressed, with red caviar, herring, with *kilki*, sprats, sardines, with salmon and sterlet sturgeon, with the famous smelts of the White Sea.

366

To ease the way, with each blini, pour a little of the varied vodkas—forty different kinds, forty different infusions. First the classic, then with black currant but smelling of the garden, and caraway and anise and German Kummel . . . absinth and buffalo grass and infused with birch buds and poplar and lemon and pepper . . . and . . . impossible to count them all!

And how many blini are eaten in Moscow during the Butter Week, no one can count for the figure would be astronomical. The count would start in puds, go on to berkovs* and then to tons and then to whole freight loads.

They are eaten in glory, paganly, admitting no refusal. The old men say with disdain, "Eh, people aren't what they used to be. Frail they have become. No capacity at all. Judge for yourself. Petroseev, a merchant of Oganchikov, made a bet with Tryasilov as to who could eat the most blini. And what do you think? On the thirty-fourth blini, not budging from his place, he gave up his soul to God. Yes-s-s, people have changed. When I was young, a long time ago, the merchant Korovin easily consumed fifty blini at one sitting and washed them down with lemon and Riga balsam vodka."

Maslenitsa began on the Sunday eight weeks before Easter, usually in February, and rose to a pitch of merrymaking which ended abruptly eight days later on the evening of the Sunday following. In Moscow, in St. Petersburg, in provincial towns and tiny villages, there were carnivals and celebrations—figures in masks raced through the streets, traveling troupes of actors entertained the peasants, bear trainers came with their dancing bears. Ice slides and swings were erected.

In Moscow on the Novinsky Boulevard and in Petersburg on the Admiralty Place, the preparations began several days before *Maslenitsa*. Long trains of sledges laden with planks and lumber came into the city, and on the Admiralty Place, smack in the middle of the court, the Senate and the Synod, enormous ice slides were erected which stretched from the Winter Palace several blocks down to the Senate Square, where Peter's famous stone statue stood. Around the slides a whole town of booths, theaters and restaurants was erected at the expense of the city, with everything neat and all in a row, gaily decorated. These carnival towns for *Maslenitsa* and other popular festivals during the year were specially designed and architected by a man employed by the city solely for this function. The most famous of such designers of popular festivals at the turn of the century was Alexei Alekseev-Yakovlev, who made elaborate mock-ups for each of these St. Petersburg carnival towns. Some of the theaters held as many as five thousand

* The pud = 36.11 pounds; the berkov = 10 puds, or 361.12 pounds.

people. Booths and theaters were adorned with wooden columns and balconies, wooden urns and other architectural decorations. There were the puppet theaters for the Petrushka characters, known and loved since the 16th century. There were merry-go-rounds with flags. Jugglers, buffoons and mimes, ventriloquists, bear handlers, and Neapolitan and German comics who delighted the crowds with their funny Russian accents performed day and night.

This gay scene was transformed into art in 1911 in that most Russian of ballets, *Petrushka*, with music by Igor Stravinsky and the colorful sets of Alexander Benois, who as a child had loved the carnival towns.

Along with the ice slides, up went all the varieties of swings, or *kacheli*. Swinging was so popular that as soon as families went to the country for the summer, the repairing of swings and the building of new ones was the first order of business. In the spring, the peasants went to the woods and cut young, supple birch branches and twisted them into swings. Every town had a public park, or if not a park, a field, which had swings. There were swings with sails like windmills, easily set in motion by a simple piece of machinery or, even more simply in the villages, by many hands. The appearance of the first swings at *Maslenitsa* brought enormous merriment to everyone. From the lowest peasant to the highest members of the court, everybody went swinging. Peter the Great loved to swing and at carnival time would come along with his officers to whirl merrily on the *kacheli*. During *Maslenitsa*, according to Kohl, "The swings never stood still. Numerous as they are, they keep turning all day like the windmill giants of Don Quixote. They put young and old who fill the hanging seats in the best humor and the place incessantly resounds with the choruses of the lasses and the music of the lads who take up a flute, a clarinet or a balalaika along with them."

In front of the theaters and booths, tea vendors set up their tables lined with whole rows of teapots of different sizes, and the large samovars boiled away, the steam playing about their chimneys like flags. During *Maslenitsa* there were even more nut vendors than tea vendors, for this, too, was a tradition of carnival. The nut vendors set up large tables in a long row covered with tents. The surface of their tables was like a large writing desk with compartments filled with hazelnuts, Welsh and Greek nuts, Ukrainian nuts and a type of huge hazelnut called *funduki*, large as a pigeon's egg, which they shoveled with their bright brass hand shovels. In two or three days, says Kohl, "the snow looked as if an army of squirrels had encamped there." There were also gingerbread vendors and bonbon vendors—but no wine shops, for they were not allowed in the carnival town.

As there was usually still snow, it was a time of sleigh riding in gaily beribboned sleighs with bells jingling on horses' necks and harnesses. Thousands of Finns from nearby villages would swamp the city with their brightly painted and carved sleighs which looked like boats and that children loved. At *Maslenitsa* and Easter, there was always a *gulyanie*, or procession of sleighs or carriages. *Drozhki* drove down to the carnival town and proceeded slowly along the barrier separating them from the booths. In provincial cities, the display was even grander because no ordinance specified the number of horses, and people could drive as many as they pleased. Everybody had a right to join in, and humble vehicles took their places in line with fashionable ones. In Moscow, Ker Porter wrote with amazement, "Their favorite amusement is what is called 'the promenade.' It consists of all the carriages of the city, perhaps to the number of seven thousand trailing after each other in regal procession filled with all the beauty and splendor of Moscow; in my life I never beheld so many lovely women at one time." In St. Petersburg the promenade included twenty carriages, each drawn by six horses, full of the modest young ladies from Smolny, the only time in the year they were allowed out in public, while in others rode English merchants, German artists, Swedish scholars, ladies wrapped in sables, governesses with their children, merchants with their wives in high *kokoshniki* and holiday dress.

All the theaters in the city performed every day, twice a day, in French, in German, in Russian and Italian. There were special mime and festival performances in the theaters of the carnival city. A special listing of the carnival events was published each day in a little flyer called simply *Blin*.

By tradition at the end of the week in Petersburg, there was a great public masquerade in the Bolshoi Theater, which was specially adapted for the purpose by the building of a platform floor over the seats so as to turn it into a huge hall. Every decently dressed person of whatever rank in society was welcome. The theater was full of strange masks and people dressed as frogs and birds. Servants and peasants loved masking and were better at devising ingenious costumes than genteel society. By tradition, the Emperor always made an appearance at this masquerade, and masked young ladies could approach him, so it happened sometimes that he would promenade about the hall with a shop girl or a milliner on his arm. Kohl once overheard a conversation between Nicholas I and a masked milliner who exclaimed, "Oh, but how handsome you are!" to which the Emperor replied, "Ah, but if you could have seen me as I once was!"

During the last three or four days of carnival, business came to a standstill.

All serious affairs were stopped. School was suspended, public offices closed. Wearing their finest jewels, the wealthy ran to dancing lunches and then to yet other balls in the evening. The theaters performed morning and evening, the *bajazzos* and buffoons every five minutes. Ordinary people began drinking in the morning and were so full of high spirits that they applauded everything. Finally, the Emperor and the court and all high officials joined the promenade in their carriages.

In the villages a straw Prince Carnival was seated before a bountiful table on a sled and drawn through the streets. "Stay, stay!" cried the crowds. "Stay with us forever!" But, at the end of his ride, he was enthroned on a bonfire and ceremoniously burned. In the cities, the sleds on the ice hills dashed faster and faster, the swings whirled and the buffoons began to look at their watches and announced to people from hour to hour how much longer the carnival would last and then . . . the church bells tolled at six, and everything, like Cinderella's ball, stopped dead. Everyone went home to prepare for the Great Fast.

After the carnival, whole squares looked like ballrooms after the ball, littered with nuts and orange peels. The swings were taken down, the ice hills broken up with crowbars. Everybody was dejected and listless. The seven-week Great Fast preceding Easter was the most important fast of the year and observed by everyone. No meat of any kind, either animal or fowl, was permitted; no milk, eggs or butter, or sugar. Instead, it was mushrooms, cabbage, oil, fish and potatoes, coffee with milk of almonds. In the 18th century the sale of caviar during the Great Fast surged because the Muscovites used caviar instead of butter for all their sauces. The first, fourth and seventh weeks of Lent were the strictest. The most devout excluded even fish in the first and last weeks and ate nothing at all on Wednesday and Friday of those weeks. Society fasted the first and last weeks and Wednesday and Friday of all the others.

As the Great Fast began, some people purchased birds and then set them free as a sign of hope that God would liberate them from their sins. For seven weeks public amusement, dancing and theatrical performances were forbidden, or took on a different and more circumspect character. Operas became concerts, plays public declamations and *tableaux vivants*. Wealthy ladies put away their brilliant jewels and wore only simple pearls and corals or a few modest turquoises scattered like forget-me-nots through their hair. Singing and conversation replaced dancing; it was the golden time for musicians and singers who came from

Paris and Vienna. Those whose Name Day fell during Lent were fortunate, for everyone came to visit and bring presents to relieve the monotony.

The one happy interruption to the Great Fast was Palm Sunday, which the Russians call *Verbnoe Voskresene*, or Branch Sunday. In old Russia it was a festival for children. In the villages, peasants went into the woods and cut great quantities of pussy willows which they brought in bundles to the cities. There were very large branches as big as young trees and extremely small ones, a hundred of which went to a bundle. The rigidly Orthodox father would buy a whole tree, which he would have blessed in church and then plant behind the image of his saint.

On the Thursday before Palm Sunday, in the cities, a special market or Fast Fair took place, a cheerful and animated exhibition of toys and flowers. The Palm Market in St. Petersburg was full of every variety of branches, which were bought for children who carried them about the streets. Not satisfied with nature alone, to the bare branches Russians added paper leaves, large and small, and gaily colored paper flowers. One branch would become the stem of a lily, another a gigantic bunch of tulips or a prodigious hyacinth. On some boughs were hung all sorts of fruit embossed on wax, birds and a little wax angel tied on with a blue ribbon. In the Palm Market many booths were devoted exclusively to these wax angels, in whose attitudes and occupations there was a great deal of imagination; some reposed on waxen clouds, others chattered beneath green wax bushes. Orientals and Greeks sold Eastern sherbets and confections from Constantinople; there were sellers of icons and crosses—even crosses made of gingerbread.

For Palm Sunday servants made toys to give to the children in their houses and the cooks made confections of sugar. Wealthy uncles and godfathers frequently sent richly decorated palm branches to their nieces and godchildren. For such branches the angel was of gold, the leaves of silver and the fruits, usually hollow, filled with costly presents. Along with the sale of branches there were huge markets of real flowers from the rich greenhouses of St. Petersburg, booths full of moss roses, violets, hyacinths, orange and lemon trees, and nosegays of bright flowers. Among the flower sellers were the toy dealers who offered miniature houses, palaces and furniture, and miniature churches with cupolas, turrets and crosses; coach sellers who sold all the Russian coaches reproduced in miniature down to the nails, wood and tin; glass workers who offered miniature dishes of all kinds. Writes Kohl, "Out of the most paltry materials in the world, chips of wood, ice and dough the Russian contrives to make something or other. Thus in

371

the Palm Market, you see old soldiers going about with all sorts of little machines, mull and clapper works when the wheels are put in motion. An old discharged marine carried a complete frigate about on his head, all her sails were spread and she was so large that she looked as if she were sailing away with him fastened to the rope. Another invalided soldier had reproduced a Russian peasant's courtyard with all its appurtenances in wood and straw."

All classes of society participated in this joyous Palm Market, and, like any one of his subjects, the Emperor always appeared with his family and conducted his sons and daughters through himself.

On the eve of Palm Sunday, in commemoration of Christ's entry into Jerusalem, a great procession was held in all cities and towns in which the whole population joined. Singing hymns, people carried the branches, plain or decorated, which they had bought or cut for themselves. In church all the branches were consecrated. After the priests blessed them, then everyone—fathers, mothers and children—walked home carrying their branches. The peasants attached a special importance to Palm Sunday and regarded the blessing of the branches as a benediction pronounced on their trees.

The next morning it was the universal custom for the children to get up early and happily beat slugabeds with their branches. They were so excited at the prospect that they hardly slept all night. Stealing through the house in their nightgowns at dawn, they happily beat all those they found in bed, crying delightedly, "The rod beats, beats to tears. I beat thee not, the rod beats!"

At the Palm Market and during the days just before Easter, millions of decorated eggs were sold, for eggs played an important role in the great festival. The symbol of the egg is one of man's most ancient. The Greeks and the Romans renewed their faith in life by eating eggs; the Chinese presented red eggs at the birth of a baby. The creed of the ancients was that the egg signified life and hope, here and now, and the early Christians took it as a symbol of Resurrection and the life beyond the grave. In Russia, the custom was described as early as the 16th century by the Tudor mariner Anthony Jenkinson: "They have an order at Easter which they always observe; to dye or color red a number of eggs of which every man and woman giveth one to the priest of their parish upon Easter morning. And moreover, the common people used to carry in their hands one of these red eggs, not only upon Easter day but also three or four days after; and gentlemen and gentlewomen have their eggs gilded. They use it as they say, for a great love, and in token of the Resurrection, whereof they rejoice."

In Russia, the Easter season was a regular orgy of eggs. Not only was it customary to put an egg in the hand of every acquaintance one met, but people played games with eggs, ate them and used them in huge quantities for the traditional Easter bread and Easter dessert. Moscow was amply supplied with eggs from its environs and sent quantities to St. Petersburg before Easter. Caravan after caravan filled with eggs came into the city. Eggs were boiled hard and stained red. All the shops were filled with eggs, the demand for which Kohl says was "incredible." He says that 3 million eggs were sold in the last days of the Fast, and the total Easter consumption in St. Petersburg, for a population of approximately 500,000, was estimated in 1842 at an astounding 10 million! A lady of my acquaintance remembers that in the early years of the 20th century the annual Easter consumption of eggs in her family alone came to 100 dozen.

Before Easter, all over the city there were hundreds of special markets and stalls selling eggs, red eggs with white shadings in a hundred different patterns, many with short sentences written on them—"This present I give to him I love," "Take, eat, and think of me," "Christ is risen," and many more. From the Ukraine came the exquisitely colored and intricately decorated Ukrainian eggs called *pisanky*.

At the Imperial Glass Works, Kohl found two rooms where everyone was exclusively employed in grinding flowers and figures on colored and uncolored glass eggs. The Porcelain Factory produced a huge quantity of eggs, large and small, painted and gilded, and provided with bright ribbons so that receivers could hang them up as they pleased. The makers of wax eggs and the confectioners outdid themselves. During the whole of the Fast season, in the shops there were rows of handsome boxes containing wax and sugar eggs of all sizes, from the smallest wren's egg to the eggs of swans and ostriches. There were giant egg-shaped boxes covered with gold paper and full of chocolates to be sent to ladies; transparent eggs into which one could look and see a bouquet of flowers, little wax trees, or images of saints; still others held a cradle in which cherubs lay sleeping. The provinces sent their eggs to St. Petersburg and St. Petersburg sent back all over Russia the products of its talented artisans.

Today the most famous of all these eggs are the magnificent Imperial Easter eggs made for the last two tsars of Russia, Alexander III and Nicholas II, under the supervision of the master jeweler of the day, Peter Carl Fabergé.

• • •

Russians have always had the sense to invite and accept direction, as well as the ability to absorb quickly and then to carry the idea still further. This has been as true of the architecture and icons they borrowed from Byzantium as it has been of the ballet. Russia managed to transform everything it touched, to infuse art and stamp it with its own genius. Nothing illustrates this better than the art of Fabergé, which was the product of centuries of European craftsmanship infused with the Russian spirit.

Peter Carl Fabergé was a third-generation Russian of distant Huguenot ancestry. In 1685 the Fabergé family fled the bloody religious persecutions of the Protestants in France. Hiding, changing their name, they wandered all over Europe for 150 years. Finally, in 1835 Fabergé's grandfather settled in Estonia and became a Russian. Only then did the family feel safe enough to resume the family name. Peter Carl's father came to St. Petersburg and apprenticed himself to a Russian jeweler and in 1842, only five years after Pushkin's death, established his own little goldsmith's shop. Young Peter Carl was sent to Europe to study for a few years and when he returned was apprenticed as a goldsmith in the family business. In 1870, when he was twenty-four, he took over the management of the firm in which his two brothers and later his four sons all worked.

The height of Fabergé's art was from 1881 to 1917, the period of the last two tsars. In its heyday, seven hundred craftsmen of extraordinary skill worked in independent workshops of the House of Fabergé. There were Fabergé establishments in Moscow and Odessa, branches in London and Paris. In St. Petersburg, the House of Fabergé was at 24 Morskaya Street. There, Fabergé both lived and worked, with almost all the workshops gathered under one roof.

Peter Carl Fabergé was a quiet, reserved man with a ready and dry sense of humor. His English colleague and biographer, Henry Charles Bainbridge, writes that he favored well-cut tweeds which gave him the look "of an immaculate gameskeeper with large pockets." An intense person who did not waste actions, gestures or speech, Fabergé was acutely sensitive to details of life around him, as if, said Bainbridge, he had always "a magnifying glass to the eyes and an amplifier to the ear." He was tolerant of people, but a perfectionist at work. He did not, of course, personally design every one of the thousands of objects that bore his name, but it is said that he personally inspected all the sketches and every piece of finished work. One story has it that if a piece did not measure up to his exacting standards, he smashed it with a little hammer he carried about for that purpose.

The Fabergé craftsmen made hundreds of "objects of fantasy"—cigarette boxes and umbrella handles, picture frames, exquisite miniatures and jeweled flowers, a whole menagerie of little animals, and figures of Russian peasants, gypsies and Cossack horsemen in nephrite, crystal, lapis lazuli, obsidian, jasper and agate. In their Moscow shop, the silversmiths of Fabergé made rich tea sets and beautiful enameled objects in the Slavic style. Some of these articles were not particularly expensive, costing only a few dollars. In everything, it was the crafts-manship that was exquisite; the objects felt good, the hinges were perfect. Fa-bergé objects grew so famous that kings and queens of Europe, the mandarins of China and the maharajahs of India, not to speak of the thousands of ordinary people, all patronized him. The King of Siam, Chulalongkorn, whose son had been sent to study at the Corps des Pages and spoke Russian fluently, summoned Fabergé to Siam, and the House of Fabergé made hundreds of objects and com-memorative medals for the Siamese court.

Bainbridge says that the tradition of the Imperial Easter eggs began because of the assassination of Alexander II. Empress Marie, the wife of Alexander III, had been so shaken by the sight of the bleeding and shattered body of her father-in-law that she had difficulty in recovering. Her husband was looking for something that might raise her spirits and delight her at Easter. In 1883 Fabergé proposed to the Emperor a surprise egg. He produced one which looked like a simple hen's egg, made of gold, enameled with opaque white, which, when opened, revealed a yolk, also of gold. The yolk opened, and inside was a chicken made of gold of different shades, with a model of the Imperial crown and inside it a tiny ruby egg. The Emperor was delighted and, beginning in 1884 or 1886—the exact date is not known—he ordered an egg every Easter for the Empress. The agreement was that Fabergé would have an absolutely free hand in the creation and the Emperor would never know beforehand what it would be. Fabergé always kept his design a careful secret. When once, bursting with curiosity and unable to keep his promise, Alexander asked what the egg would be that year, Fabergé serenely answered only, "Your Majesty will be content." Eleven Easter eggs were created for Alexander and after his death his son, Nicholas II, continued the tradition, increasing the order to two every year—one for his mother and one for his wife, Alexandra. Probably fifty-five eggs were made, of which forty-three are known to exist. The Provisional Government did not allow Fabergé to deliver the last two, made in 1917, and they have disappeared.

Fabergé made most of the deliveries personally each year, ceremonially bringing the egg encased in a specially made velvet box. When in later years there were two, he sometimes sent his son or chief assistant. In 1912 his son Eugene traveled the whole of Russia to go to Livadia to deliver the egg to Nicholas, and

Fabergé went personally to the Dowager Empress. Fabergé never forgot that the egg was always a symbol of life, joy and hope. However magnificent they were, the surprises inside were always earthy and lively. The 1906 egg of mauve enamel, Alexandra's favorite color, and latticed with diamond ribbons opened to reveal a swan four inches high. The swan rested on a large aquamarine that served as a lake and was surrounded with tiny gold water lilies. Lifted from the aquamarine lake and set in motion by means of a tiny device under one wing, gold webbed feet guided the tiny swan. Its head and neck raised and lowered, the wings spread to disclose each feather separately.

Another, of transparent rock crystal, made for Empress Marie in 1908, has inside a tree of gold with flowers of enamel and tiny precious stones. On the tree sits a peacock of gold, richly enameled. When wound up, the peacock struts about, spreading and closing its tail. Other eggs contained a tiny coronation coach, a basket of spring flowers, tiny miniatures of the royal family or little easels on which scenes were painted on mother-of-pearl. In the egg of 1892 was a tiny gold model, exact in every detail of guns, chains, anchor and rigging, of the battleship *Pamyat Azova* on which Nicholas as Tsarevich had made his trip around the world. In the Great Siberian Railroad Egg of 1900 was a tiny scale-model train of the newly built Trans-Siberian railroad, ⅝ inch wide and 12 inches long. A miniature locomotive with a ruby headlight pulled the train; each car was perfectly reproduced even to the church car with a Russian cross and bells on the roof.

Until his death in 1903, the Easter eggs were created by Mikhail Perkhin, an artist from Petrozavodsk, and of all Fabergé's workmasters perhaps the most remarkable. Perkhin started his life as a peasant, acquired training in goldsmiths' shops and in 1886 opened a workshop of his own. From that time on, he worked exclusively for Fabergé. His assistant and chief workman, Henrik Wigstrom, a Swedish Finn who had worked with Perkhin from the beginning, took over when he died. Often the surprises, including the marvelous miniature yacht and train which were primarily jeweler's work, were carried out in the workshop of August Holstrom, another Swedish Finn from Helsinki, who had received his training in St. Petersburg and who was considered the finest jeweler in Europe. The rich enamels that glow like jewels were the work of two remarkable Russian masters, Alexander Petrov and Vasily Boitzov, who, along with their staff, executed every enameled piece of the House of Fabergé.

The House of Fabergé made thousands of lesser eggs, from the tiny enamel eggs which brothers and fathers presented each year to their wives, mothers and daughters to hang on necklaces worn to church on Easter, to extremely elaborate large ones, but the dazzling Imperial Easter eggs were made only for the Emperor. Their cost was approximately $15,000, but today they are priceless. Exquisite works of art, they have become a symbol of their age.

In 1918 the Bolsheviks nationalized the House of Fabergé and took everything in it. Fabergé asked only for ten minutes to take his hat and left. He lived his last years in Cannes, a sad and lonely old man, repeating over and over, "This is not life." There he died in 1920 at the age of seventy-four.

When he closed the door of 24 Morskaya Street, Fabergé left behind seventy-six years of his family's work, and much more. The Fabergé workshops were the culmination of five hundred years of inherited work and experience. There were no better craftsmen at work in the applied arts than those assembled in the House of Fabergé. In their fields, they were the best craftsmen of their time, and Fabergé, the last great goldsmith in the tradition of Benvenuto Cellini.

With him the careful craftsmanship in gold and stone, and the secret of the vibrant ruby and mauve, green and blue Russian enameling, disappeared, along with the eggs, forever.

• • •

The merrymaking of *Maslenitsa* and the somber abstinence of the Great Fast were only prologue to the most profound and joyous festival of the year. For nearly one thousand years Easter has been the principal feast day of the Russian calendar. "The goodness hidden in the hearts of the holy shall be revealed in their risen bodies just as the bare trees put out their leaves in the spring" promises an old sermon.

In Russia the season of flowers and the leaves is so brief that it holds a special poignancy. The transformation from snow to flowers comes almost overnight; the ice breaks, the trees flower. Spring in Russia is a waterfall; once it begins, there is no slow growth of buds. Suddenly, everything seems to bloom at once, helped by the covering of snow—pussy willows, violets, anemones and apple blossoms, all together. There are no primroses in Russia, no daffodils, but in the deep forests bloom masses of little snowdrops, called in Russian "under the snowlings," bluebells, and fragrant lilies of the valley which peasants used to bring to the cities by armfuls, along with cowslips and sweet-smelling violets. The glorious peak of spring is the lilac, which grows in profusion everywhere; the smell of lilacs floats through streets and perfumes the clear White Nights of June. The queen of the flowering trees is the *cheryomukha,* or bird cherry, with its soft white flowers which, when they fall over the canals of St. Petersburg and blow through the streets of Moscow, are poetically called "summer snow" by the Russians.

Easter marked the start of this joyous season, the true beginning of the year, for the Orthodox Easter generally falls later than Catholic Easter, often in late April. The date depends on the Jewish calculation of Passover. According to the New Testament, Jesus made his entrance into Jerusalem at the beginning of Passover; thus the Russian Easter always falls one week after Passover.

In the life of old Russia, it was the climax of the year toward which everything flowed and from which everything flowed. Houses were scrubbed from top to bottom, furniture repaired and repainted. Elaborate preparations were made for the Easter feast and the giving of gifts. It was so important that it was called simply "The Festival."

On Good Friday, the churches were kept dark. In the tabernacle was a sarcophagus draped with a cloth embroidered with the body of the Redeemer. The doors of the churches were kept continually open and people solemnly made a tour of the churches to kiss the wounds of the Savior. Many people attended church every day during the week before Easter. Everyone fasted; the devout took no food at all on Wednesday and from Friday until Easter night. The air was tense with expectation. Everything was quiet. People were tired from fasting and standing during the lengthy church services. All day Saturday people continued to visit the churches. The priests did not appear until shortly before midnight; therefore it was the custom for one of the public to read the Gospels. A Bible stand was placed in every church for this purpose; persons of any class, as long as they could read Slavonic, could come forth with a burning candle in their hands to read from the Bible to all those willing to listen. Kohl writes of making such a tour of the churches in 1837. In one he found an old scarred soldier in his long gray coat standing at the lectern. Around him was gathered a crowd of children, all listening intently. In another an old man with long beard and feeble voice was reading the account of the sufferings of Christ, surrounded by a rapt crowd of women young and old, youths and men, all listening while people continued to go and kiss the representation of the corpse. "I could not tire of witnessing these scenes and found them in all the churches addressing themselves with equal force to the heart."

Toward midnight the churches in every city filled more and more until they overflowed. People gathered in St. Basil's in Moscow and the hundreds of churches of the city, in the huge Cathedral of St. Isaac's and the Cathedral of Kazan in St. Petersburg, in all the churches in all the cities of the provinces; in every small village people came together both inside and outside the churches and waited.

The court gathered in full dress in the Court Chapel. The governors of every province appeared in their gold embroidered uniforms in their churches. The civil officers, the curators of every university along with all the professors and the pupils of all the schools—everywhere it was the same, high and low the whole nation gathered together for the Easter vigil.

As the hour approached, the priests read a Mass slowly, sadly, while the people stood with their unlit candles. As midnight neared, gradually each person took a flame from another until all the candles were lit, the illumination general and the bright flickering flames a living symbol of the spirit. And then, at midnight, Easter burst forth in all its glory. The golden doors of the iconostasis were thrown open and the representation of the tomb and cross removed. The priests led a procession of all the people out of the church; then, joined by all those assembled outside, all went around the church three times singing, in symbolic search of the risen Christ. When they returned to the front of the church for the third time, the doors were thrown open and a priest joyously announced three times to the assembled crowd, "Khristos Voskrese!" to which came the ringing response, "Voistinu Voskrese!" All returned into the church to the magnificent singing of the choir, punctuated with the happy refrain, "Christ is risen," and its response, repeated joyfully over and over again. At the moment of the singing of Khristos Voskrese in the churches and the lighting of the thousands of tapers, the outside of the church was illuminated. After seven weeks of virtual silence, joyously the bells began to ring all over Russia, starting with the great sixty-five-ton bell in the Tower of Ivan in Moscow which was rung only three times a year, spreading to all the bells of Moscow, of Petersburg, and every town and village, until the whole land was full of the ringing of bells which continued all through the next day unabated and at intervals throughout the week.

At midnight in Petersburg and Moscow, the streets and public buildings were suddenly brightly illuminated. Above the lighted Kremlin and the Winter Palace rockets and fireworks exploded and the cannons of the Peter and Paul Fortress were fired at measured intervals. At the turn of the century an observer wrote, "The roaring of the bells overhead answered by the sixteen hundred bells from the illuminated belfries of all the churches in Moscow, the guns bellowing from the slopes of the Kremlin over the river and the processions of priests in their gorgeous cloth-of-gold vestments with crosses, icons and banners pouring forth amidst clouds of incense from all the churches of the Kremlin and slowly wending their way through the crowd, all combined to produce an effect which none who has witnessed it can ever forget."

At the end of the Easter service, which lasted more than three hours, the priests gave every member of the congregation a blessing and a kiss. When church was over, no one thought of going to bed. Everyone went out to feast. On passing through the streets at two or three in the morning, one could see through the windows all the tavern tables covered with white cloths and lighted for customers. In homes, rooms were decorated with plants and flowers. Dinner began at three or four in the morning, and often the sun shone in upon the dessert. It was the tradition that anyone who entered the house was welcome; the table was set with food at night and all through the next day.

Every household had been preparing the Easter feast and dyeing eggs for most of the week. Tables spread wide were decorated with pots of white lilacs and fragrant hyacinths. Lambs carved of butter covered with curly butter wool were set in the middle of the table along with sugar flags and crosses. There was a staggering array of cold salads, hams, veal and roasted birds. Many foods were in egg shape or served in eggs; confectioners hid their sweets in egg-shaped crusts. There were assorted cakes, babas and *mazurkis*, but on every table in town and village were placed the same two traditional Russian Easter dishes. One was the rich Easter bread, *kulich*, thick, round and cylindrical, decorated with frosting and the letters XB signifying "Christ is risen," and always accompanying it, the thick sweet creamy white *paskha* made in a special triangular mold that also bore the symbolic letters. Bakers added all sorts of whimsical touches to their *kulichi*; little *kulichi* adhered to the large ones like oysters, plums were put in the plaited dough decorating the top, or sprigs of the branches of Palm Sunday. Each family had its own cherished recipes which were passed from one generation to another. (Elena Molokhovets lists seventeen recipes for *paskha*.) All over Russia, high and low enjoyed the identical Easter breakfast: they spread *paskha* on their *kulich* and ate it with a hard-boiled egg dipped in salt and washed down with a tumbler of icy vodka.

Most people—certainly all the peasants—had their Easter breakfast first blessed by the priests. Toward the end of the Easter service, they carried in their *paskha* and *kulich* on plates wrapped in brightly embroidered cloths. They set them down in the middle of the church and the priests passed between a double row of plates the whole length of the church blessing each. There were often so many that the tasty line continued outside the church and even around the building. It was a curious and beautiful sight—the tall loaves, large and small, surrounded with flowers, the triangular towers of *paskha* decorated with leaves and red eggs, and even sometimes pots of preserves or honey.

Beginning on Easter night and continuing throughout the next day, everyone visited everyone else. Gentlemen made it a point to call on all the lonely old ladies. The curator of a university was visited by all his professors, the Chief Justice by all his judges, the governor by all his colleagues, court and civilians of the town in which he lived. Everyone greeted everyone else with the same traditional greeting, "Christ is risen!" "Indeed He is risen!" and they kissed three times. This visiting and kissing went on all week. First all members of a family without exception kissed each other. Coachmen, footmen and servants made the tour of the household on Easter Sunday, kissing all the children and giving them eggs. In the army, the general of a corps (eighty thousand men) kissed all his officers; the commander of a regiment, all the officers of all the regiments and a select number of privates. A captain kissed individually every soldier in his company. And it was the same in all the civil departments. The head kissed all his underlings, who hastened to visit on Easter Sunday in their state uniforms. And what amazed Kohl was that these kisses were not polite little kisses, but "downright hearty smacks."

The Emperor was the busiest of all. Not only did he kiss his own huge household, plus all the hundreds of visitors he received on Sunday morning, but the meanest sentry he passed on Easter was greeted with an Imperial kiss and a *Khristos Voskrese*. At the parade on Easter Sunday he kissed a whole assembled corps of officers and a large number of privates. (In 1904 Nicholas II recorded in his diary that he had exchanged Easter greetings with 280 people following midnight Mass and later on Easter morning with 730 of his soldiers.) All over the streets *muzhiki* met and kissed, the next phrase usually being, "Let's go, Brother, and have something to drink," and off they would go to the nearest tavern. In a provincial town, Kohl saw a watchman kiss every pretty girl whose basket or cart he examined.

Everyone drank joyously; whole villages were drunk at Easter, "a time," says Kohl, "when no Russian can be kept under control."

In the provinces and the cities, there was another show of carriages with all the ladies dressed in their high *kokoshniki* and bright-colored holiday dresses. The balls began anew and everybody was running to court, to visits, to the churches, to breakfasts and to the swings, for the swings were once again erected in public squares and fields, more numerous even than during carnival. "At Easter," wrote one visitor, "every swing of the *kacheli* is ringing with the singing of the lasses and balalaikas and a more confusing scene for the eyes cannot be found than some dozen of these swings in full play."

Instead of tea and nuts, the vendors immediately began selling oranges and ices. There were so many, says Kohl, that, "when you survey the heaps of oranges which are piled up at Easter in public places you would imagine that this agreeable fruit must grow in Russia on the birches and the pine trees." In preparation for Easter, the first orange ships waited for the breaking of the ice in the Baltic ports, and oranges were sent from the Baltic to as far away as Kharkov, where vendors piled them up in huge pyramids on their heads and somewhat incongruously called out, "Oranges, lemons, genuine Petersburg fruit!" Kohl continued, "It is a fact that throughout Russia, as far as the utmost limits of Siberia, all places where swings are erected at Easter are inundated with oranges and lemons."

Along with the piles of oranges, Easter day brought the first appearance of ices sold outside and they were carried about for sale in all public places. Kohl wrote, "This custom, to which we in other countries are strangers, is greatly promoted by the cheapness of ice and sweetened juices of Russia. On Easter Sunday you see all at once a great number of young fellows who like showy butterflies have burst forth from unsightly chrysalises. . . . The same lads who were only a few days before selling hot dry cakes for the Fast now appeared in thin red-flowered blouses which fell over their black velvet breeches. Like the ribbon of an order, over their shoulders, and tied over the left hip they wore a large white napkin with a long red fringe, which fluttered in the wind. In this costume they were to be seen from Easter Day in Petersburg, Moscow, Odessa and Russian cities in general. . . . They carried their ices in two tin jars standing in a wooden tub covered with ice which kept their ices frozen even in the sunshine, and enticed their customers with a stream of good cheer and jokes, 'Ice! Ice! The freshest, the coolest: chocolate, vanilla, coffee and rose ice and the best of all, flower ice! Who will taste my delicious ice? Flower blossom? Yes! Come, my pretty dear, will you have a poppy blossom ice? You will like it better than a kiss from your sweetheart.' "

All week long everybody played with eggs. Children bowled with eggs on a cloth on the floor. They had egg fights; holding eggs tight in their hands and almost covered they hit the tops to see which had the toughest shell. It was the custom to give presents. Wrote Kohl, "The confectioners' shops make an extraordinary display at this season and exhibit all sorts of devices to entice customers. You will see there every possible thing executed in sugar—numberless household utensils, whole churches, fancy tarts which look like Chinese pagodas, pictures in sugar, crucifixes in handsome boxes."

During the whole of Easter week the doors of the iconostasis in all the churches, otherwise kept shut all year except for certain moments in the service, were kept continuously open as a symbol of the welcome of heaven. The devout continued to go to church every morning before merrymaking. Finally, on the Sunday following Easter, there was a special service at which the priest distributed a ceremonial bread, baked and stained red on the outside, with gilt letters reading, *Khristos Voskrese*.

Easter had this curious epilogue. The Monday evening vespers and the Tuesday liturgy following the last Easter week service made up what was called Remembrance Day, or *Radonitsa*. Russians went to the graveyards to place food on the graves of their departed ancestors, and many had cheerful picnics there. All the food was blessed by the priests, and some people gave away all their provisions to the poor at the cemetery. With this curious and very Slavic veneration of the clan, the bright Easter season ended.

22. MERCHANT PRINCES

Moscow, those syllables can start
A tumult in the Russian heart.

Alexander Pushkin
Eugene Onegin

I'll marry him. I'll consent—only let's go to Moscow. I implore you, let's go! There's nothing better than Moscow on earth!

Anton Chekhov
The Three Sisters

IN THE LAST DECADES of the 19th century, the city of Moscow, eclipsed for so many years by the glamorous northern capital of St. Petersburg, assumed a new importance. After 1861 Russia industrialized at a rapid pace. Moscow became the center of this swiftly growing new external and internal commercial activity. It was the largest manufacturing town in Russia; within its walls and suburbs were two hundred factories for the weaving of the famous Moscow silks alone. Between 1870 and 1912 Russia, in an enormous spurt of fertility, doubled in population; a still unexplained phenomenon which put great strains on the cities. Laborers came streaming in from the countryside seeking work, and Moscow swelled from 602,000 inhabitants in 1873 to 1,617,000 in 1912.*

* Today the population of Moscow is regulated by law and special permission is required to live there.

384

This burgeoning business activity created a new class of wealthy merchants and industrialists who began to support the arts in a generous and highly creative manner. In the late 19th century, as Russian artists of all kinds became ever more interested in Russian themes, it often happened that Moscow was quicker than St. Petersburg to acclaim and recognize these new native talents; the music of Modest Mussorgsky and Peter Tchaikovsky, the singing of Fyodor Chaliapin, the painting of Mikhail Vrubel. A brisk rivalry sprang up between the two great cities, which were as different in style as they were in appearance.

In his autobiography, *My Life in Art,* Konstantin Stanislavsky wrote: "The new capital considered Moscow to be a provincial town and itself one of the cultural centers of Europe. All that was of Moscow was a failure in Petersburg and vice versa. The Muscovites lost little love on the bureaucrats of Petersburg with their formalism and cold affectedness. They lost no love on the city itself, with its fogs, its short and gloomy days, its long white summer nights. Moscow was proud of its dry frosts, of the bright glitter of white snow under the winter sun, of its hot, dry summers."

The panorama of Moscow was a striking contrast to the neoclassic granite palaces, the severe straight prospects and the misty canals of St. Petersburg. With the Moskva River winding sinuously through its heart, Moscow radiated in concentric circles from the Kremlin, its five main districts separated by walls or boulevards. Like an overgrown village, the city sprawled over seven hills for more than 27½ square miles, an area greater than any other city in Europe except London. One-tenth of the city was occupied by gardens and ponds, giving it in many places the look of the country. Wide boulevards contrasted with crooked, irregular streets and narrow alleys that zigged and zagged only to finish abruptly in dead ends. Painted wooden houses in all colors of the rainbow, from pearly violet to pale yellow, stood side by side with houses of stone and brick. Above the city rose the towers and spires of its five hundred churches and twenty-five monasteries and convents. Under the trailing light of the sun, their gilded and multicolored cupolas reached up and flowered like speckled carnations, tulips and dahlias, and their golden crosses gleamed like lines of fire against the sky. "One who has not lingered in the streets of Moscow," wrote Victor Tissot in 1893, "will never understand Russia. There, Europe comes face to face with Asia—everything is contrast."

In its 1914 edition, the famous Baedeker guide described the "extraordinarily animated traffic" in the streets. "What is known here as German (Western) dress is predominant, but side by side with it we see the bearded *muzhik* in his bast slippers, caftan and sheepskin, the Russian in his old Russian fur cap and his wife adorned with strings of genuine pearls, Circassians, Tartars and Bokhariots, all in their national dress, Greeks in red fezzes, Persians with high conical caps and other types too numerous to mention." Coachmen with their long kaftans of dark cloth and their distinctive caps rattled by at their usual breakneck speed. Gypsies in brightly colored dresses and gold chains were a common sight. Tatars, much in demand because of their sobriety and intelligence, were employed as servants and waiters and in wine establishments to roll about the huge barrels of wine. This was a far cry from the days when the Grand Duke of Muscovy went out to meet the haughty Tatar ambassadors by spreading a mat of rich sables for their feet and presenting them with a goblet of mare's milk, humbly licking the drops that fell on the manes of their horses.

All the various costumes of the Muscovites, said Baedeker, were best seen at popular festivals and in the markets: "the most interesting being the Okhotny Ryad [The Hunter's Line] market for vegetables, eggs, poultry and game near the Imperial Theatres, the Sunday Market, the most important market for flowers and fruit held near Bolotnaya, the chief Flower Market on the Tsvetnoy Boulevard, the Horse Market in Konnaya, birds and dogs in Trubnaya." For above all, the city of Moscow was a city of merchants, great and small.

In the open marketplace of the Arbat, a huge market was held daily. Sellers of hot sausages, herring, apples and lemons, socks and woolens circulated through the crowds. On their heads, boys carried wooden trays of beef and calves' feet. Throughout the city men carried buckets filled with pickles, selling them to the peasant crowd as a relish for black bread. Peasants came straight from the countryside to sell enormous bowls of fresh sour cream and baskets of wild strawberries and mushrooms in the streets of the city.

The famous merchant arcades off Red Square had been built according to the directives and personal specifications of Ivan the Terrible. In the *ryady* of fabrics, tourists found the bolts of silken cloth woven with gold and silver that were a specialty of the great Moscow textile mills. In the rows of furs, the most prized pelt was the blue fox; the finest capes made of the paws alone. In the lapidary section, rock crystals, gold chains, bracelets and earrings were piled up in wooden containers. Fine turquoises were sold by Tatars who had gone to Persia to find them. The so-called "Upper Rows," facing the Kremlin on the northeastern side of Red Square, were housed in a huge building built between

1888 and 1893. Three stories high, 275 yards long and 95 yards deep, it was intersected in each direction by three glass-covered corridors with bridges on the second and third stories. The Upper Rows contained a thousand offices and shops for both the retail and wholesale trade; an excellent restaurant was located in the basement. (This huge building still exists today and is known as G.U.M.)

Among the many sights of Moscow recommended to tourists by Baedeker were the dozens of museums, which, as in St. Petersburg, were generally admission free, and the huge Bolshoi Theater for Opera and Ballet rebuilt by Alberto Cavos in 1854. The Ionic portico of this impressive theater was surmounted by a colossal group called Phoebus in the Chariot of the Sun; its interior, decorated in white and gold with five balconies, seated four thousand. Also interesting to visit, said Baedeker, was the famous Foundling Hospital founded by Catherine II and maintained by the state, at a cost of one million rubles a year entirely obtained from a tax on the sale of playing cards. This hospital, which housed twenty-five hundred babies with thirty thousand more boarded out in neighboring villages, could be visited on Thursdays and Sundays. There, visitors were surprised by the sight of six hundred wet nurses all dressed in *kokoshniki* and bright *sarafans* standing in neat, colorful rows beside the white beds of their tiny charges.

In Moscow, the center and fortress of the Orthodox Church, colorful religious processions were seen winding through the streets almost daily. Every morning, in a carriage drawn by six horses and accompanied by priests and servants, the icon of the Miraculous Virgin of Mount Athos was toured through the streets to visit the bedsides of the sick and the dying. Everywhere, at churches and street shrines, passersby gave the sign of the cross, and some even prostrated themselves. Above the Spassky Gate to the Kremlin was the revered Icon of the Redeemer, placed there by Tsar Alexis in the 17th century, who also decreed that no man should pass through the gate without removing his hat in respect to it. Miraculous properties were attributed to this icon. According to legend, once when a band of marauding Tatars attempted to seize the Kremlin, the icon blinded them all, and in 1812, when Napoleon tried to pass through the gate with his head covered, a sudden violent wind blew off his famous tricorn hat. In 1914 the decree of Alexis was still strictly observed and a guard stood by to remind the forgetful.

Even in a city famous for its churches, one of the greatest sights in the late 19th century was the Cathedral of the Redeemer, which stood on the banks of the Moskva River within sight of the Kremlin. Begun in 1839 and financed entirely by a popular subscription of 15 million rubles (almost 8 million dollars at the time), as a thanksgiving to God for the defeat of Napoleon, this immense cathedral took forty-four years to build. The huge white cathedral, constructed in the form of a Greek cross, was 335 feet high and covered 8,020 square yards. It was surmounted by five gilded domes, the largest of which had a diameter of 100 feet. The outside walls were sheathed in marble, and broad flights of steps led to twelve fine bronze portals. The roof was bordered by a gilded balustrade and forty-eight marble reliefs. All the materials were Russian; many of Russia's finest architects, artists and artisans had worked on it.

The interior of the cathedral was a blaze of colors; murals by celebrated artists lined the walls. *The National Geographic* in November 1914 said that "the effects obtained by the blending of red, white, gray marbles with gold quite beggar description." Sixty windows elaborately decorated with gold and marble provided light; at festivals, the cathedral was lit with thirty-seven hundred candles. The music of its choirs was celebrated. Seven thousand worshipers could be accommodated at one time, and on Sundays so many men came that women often went on other days of the week. The structure was regarded by artists and architects alike as a masterpiece of cathedral construction. It was, according to the *Geographic*, "one of the memories which every visitor will always cherish." *

It was in Moscow where the ebullient "wide nature" of which the Russians were so proud could most readily be seen. The city was full of restaurants and *traktir*s which served, far more than in St. Petersburg, exclusively Russian meals and specialties in dizzying abundance. At the well-known Testov Restaurant the specialty of the house was a remarkable many-layered *kulebyaka*, each layer composed of a different filling—meat, fish, mushrooms, chicken, game. There was also the Slavyansky Bazaar, where over the *zakuski* table hung a large painting by Repin, and a diner might choose the sterlet for his supper from those swimming about in a tank, Filippov's café and the famous confectioneries of Petrovka Street.

Merchants were famous for their gargantuan appetites and lavish hospitality. They drank vodka "by the yard," lining up little glasses neatly in a row. At the turn of the century the highly respected mayor of Moscow, himself a merchant, would sometimes turn up at a restaurant with a group of his merchant friends for lunch, place his high top hat on the table and order champagne. When the hat was chock full of corks, they would get up, pay and return to their offices.

---

* In 1931 the cathedral was blown up on orders of the Communist government. Today, a public swimming pool occupies the site.

Tissot, in 1893, interrupted his visits to factories and interviews with Nihilists to describe with Gallic gusto his meal at the famous *traktir* of Lupachev, a restaurant frequented by merchants. The restaurant was decorated entirely in the old Russian style; huge copper urns stood along the walls which were decorated with carved paneling and old tapestries of golden cloth. The tables were set with 16th-century pitchers of gold and beaten silver. On the sideboards were spread a "mosaic of *zakuski*"—caviar, radishes, butter, anchovies, sausages, smoked salmon, herring, stuffed crayfish, smoked goose *en croûte,* smelts, olives stuffed and glazed, and slices of pineapple. In a hedge around the table stood vodka in various old bottles with multicolored labels—vodka of mountain ash, cassis, red currant, oak; vodka called "Passage of the Danube," "Pushkin," "Bulgaria," "Peter the Great" and "Nordenskold," this last with pieces of ice floating about in it. The restaurant then offered its guests a bewildering variety of soups, for, Tissot says, "the essence of Russian cooking is variety"—sterlet with eelpout livers ("The Russians invented it—a feast for the gods!"), also soups of stuffed cabbage and "à la Grecque," with nettles, with Warsaw croutons, of duck, of purée of ham or purée of hare, "little Russian" buckwheat consommé, potage Pozharsky, Ukrainian borsch, lazy *shchi* soup, soup with veal kidneys, mushroom bouillon, and many more. Along with these came a variety of *pirozhki*—Russian patties stuffed with Polish noodles, with blini dough, with truffles, *viziga,* carrots, sauerkraut, onions, rice and wild mushrooms, or prepared Caucasian, Livonian or Muscovite style. This was followed by yet another soup, the fish soup *ukha,* and then Tissot was served a typically Russian dish, suckling pig with kasha, followed by *kisel,* a fruit paste. The whole meal was polished off with a Russian punch for which Tissot gives the recipe: "In a silver bowl, in which one has poured two bottles of champagne, add slices of pineapple, a pound of fine sugar, and a half a glass of kirsch. Can be served cold or hot, by setting it on fire." He added that on his table he was surrounded by a forest of glasses of all shapes and sizes, all bearing mottos such as "For a robust man everything is healthy" and "Not to drink is not to live," and that the meal was, by merchant standards, "extremely modest," since merchants who came to Lupachev's to feast never ordered fewer than twelve main dishes!

In the numerous teahouses all over the city, waiters in white tunics served delicate overland tea of faint amber color and delicious aroma with a slice of lemon, to the ladies in cups and the gentlemen in glasses. To these quiet tea tables, friends came to chat and buyers and sellers to consummate their bargains, for no bargain was complete without a cup of tea to seal it.

On Sundays, which were holidays for everyone, people went off to one of the ornamental gardens of Moscow, where, according to an American traveler in 1893, they relaxed "among trim hedges, plots of bright flowers, linden, elms, and locusts, somber firs and thin birches stretching away to the horizon." There Russians, both men and women, smoked and played cards, which they loved, while the Germans drank beer, smoked their pipes and listened to the music of an orchestra, the singing of some Tyrolese or a gypsy band.

In certain parks there were the gypsy restaurants where the Russians loved to go to finish up an evening; in the Petrovsky Park was the famous Yar where Rasputin went to carouse. At the Yar the renowned gypsy singer Vera Panina performed. She became the heroine of a celebrated scandal when one night, pining with unrequited love for a member of the Imperial Guard, the passionate Vera took poison and died on the stage in front of her beloved, singing, "My Heart Is Breaking." At another restaurant, the Strelna, there was a Palm Court with a glass roof and walls, filled with palm trees and tropical plants surrounded by little artificial caves, each holding white tables at which diners sat among fountains playing into basins. At the Strelna there was also a large room with an open roaring fire where choruses of gypsies, the men dressed in white brocaded Russian blouses and the girls in bright silk dresses, sang. The Vice-Consul of England in 1912, Robert Bruce-Lockhart, was so moved by their singing that he wrote: "The gypsy music is more intoxicating, more dangerous than opium or woman or drink! . . . There is a plaintiveness in its appeal which to the Slav or Celtic races is almost irresistible. For better than the words it expresses the pent up and stifled desires of mankind. It induces a delicious melancholy which is half-lyrical, half-sensuous. Something there is in it of the boundless width of the Russian steppe. It is the uttermost antithesis of anything that is Anglo-Saxon. It breaks down all reserves of restraint. It will drive a man to moneylenders and even to crime. . . ."

By the end of the 19th century, once again, as they had in the Middle Ages, all roads led to Moscow. The city had nine railroad stations and was the hub upon which the new railroad lines from all over the Empire converged like the spokes of a wheel.

Moscow profited from the coming of the railroads which transformed Russian life as dramatically as they were doing at the same time in the United States. The St. Petersburg–Moscow line was begun in 1842 after Nicholas I ended a dispute over possible routes by taking a ruler and drawing a straight line between the two cities. The man responsible for finishing this main line and for standardizing the wide gauge, which made Russian trains ride so comfortably, was an American engineer, Major George Washington Whistler, father of the famous painter. While in Russia, Whistler also supervised the construction of a locomotive factory, designed a new roof for the city's Riding Academy, assisted in the construction of some bridges across the Neva and constructed new docks for the naval base at Kronstadt. When Whistler died in St. Petersburg in 1848, his body was carried by the Tsar's private barge to Kronstadt, where it was placed on a steamer for New York.

From 1857 on, railroads spread rapidly all over the land, assuming such an importance in the consciousness of the nation that they even entered into literature. Some of the greatest scenes of Dostoevsky's *The Idiot* take place in railroad stations. In Tolstoy's *Anna Karenina* the train looms over the story and becomes almost a character in its own right. Russian railroads were built with great thoroughness and their luxurious equipment competed with the best of European railroads; in first class there were plush red velvet seats and lace curtains. Samovars steamed at each end of each car. Station houses were handsome structures built of brick, surrounded with carefully kept grounds filled with trees and plants. Victor Tissot observed in 1893 that "the stations are clean and elegant. At each station they offer you newspapers or books and render a thousand services and seem to know the manual of courtesy. They have the best railroad buffet restaurants in the world, the most commodious railroad cars, and in each station there lies an open book where travelers may register their complaints." Conductors wore tall sheepskin hats and smart black tunics belted with a scarf. (The scarves were different for each railroad company.) Such was the pride of all officials connected with the railroads that the Director of Communications in St. Petersburg personally attended the departure of the daily mail train for Moscow and, as the train pulled out, he took off his hat and drew stiffly to attention. All lines but one, the Trans-Siberian, were built by private enterprise. Moscow had its railroad barons, a new breed of pioneering entrepreneurs who not only laid the groundwork for the industrial expansion of the last two decades of the century, but began to use their fortunes in a number of creative ways. These were men like Samuel Polyakov, the son of destitute Jewish parents, born in a small town of Mogilev province. Polyakov rose from a modest job as a post office employee where his intelligence attracted the attention of Count Ivan Tolstoy, the Minister of the Post.

Polyakov began building railroads in the south and eventually became an immensely wealthy man who gave a good part of his fortune for educational purposes. Some two to three million rubles went to provide educational facilities for the youth of remote country areas. In 1867 he founded a high school and technical school for railroad personnel, financing it by drawing twenty-seven rubles from the profits of each mile and assigning them to a school fund.

Another was the engineer Karl Von Meck, who helped to construct and later to administer the railroad line from Moscow to Tambov province. Von Meck became a millionaire, and when he died left most of his money to his widow, Nadezhda. Madame Von Meck was among the first to recognize Peter Tchaikovsky's genius, and for thirteen years she generously subsidized him. In what was surely among the most curious friendships in history, the two maintained a long and intimate correspondence but, by mutual agreement, never met. She worshiped him from afar, preferring to know him only through his music.

The most remarkable of these new railroad magnates was Savva Mamontov, a man of extraordinary breadth and imagination who divided his talents between art and business and achieved spectacular success in both. As a railroad magnate, he turned his interest to the north. From Yaroslavl, he pushed the railroad through dense forest regions to Vologda and finally in 1898 through to Archangel on the White Sea. In the arts, Mamontov and his family came to play a decisive role in the development of a new Russian art, and in the renewal of the theater and the art of theatrical decoration at which the Russians were to excel.

As a result of Westernization and the growing industrialization, native folk and decorative arts had been severely weakened and were in danger of disappearing. It was a group of Moscow businessmen who, realizing this threat to the national heritage, set about to encourage cottage industries in rural areas. Mamontov was the most important and influential of these. In 1870 he bought a summer house, Abramtsevo, in the countryside thirty-five miles from Moscow, not very far from the ancient Troitse-Sergeieva Monastery. The estate had once belonged to Sergei Aksakov, a writer and close friend of Gogol. Gogol had often visited the comfortable wooden house (where, said Aksakov, "the mushrooms come up to the door") and written part of *Dead Souls* there.

Mamontov made his new estate into the meeting place of the leading painters, sculptors and musicians of the day. Ilya Repin and his family came to live there for several summers, as did the painters Viktor Vasnetsov, Konstantin Korovin, Mikhail Nesterov and Mikhail Vrubel. The great portraitist Valentin Serov, whose luminous portraits have been compared to Renoir's, was virtually adopted by Mamontov, and lived at Abramtsevo for many years. The simple homey interior of Mamontov's house at Abramtsevo became the background for many famous Russian paintings of the day, including Repin's renowned *They Did Not Expect Him*.

The Mamontovs turned Abramtsevo into an important artistic center for the preservation and furthering of native decorative arts. They built special studios for sculptors and workshops for craftsmen skilled in the traditional arts. Many objects made in the pottery and other workshops of Abramtsevo were so distinctive, and of such artistic value, that they left a lasting mark on the decorative art of Russia.

Mamontov's energetic wife, Elizaveta, had an enormous influence on all these artistic activities. She collected all sorts of native handicrafts, embroidery and carvings, which became the nucleus of a fine museum. She was a deeply devout woman, very involved in the revival of the liturgy of the Orthodox Church. Both she and her husband were inspired by ideals of bettering the life of the people. When they first arrived at Abramtsevo they began their stay by building a hospital and then followed it with a school, the first in the region, for the neighboring peasant children. Elizaveta herself took over the teaching and organization of this school. It was her forceful personality which inspired the building of a little church on the estate, a project which was so spectacularly successful that it led to a revival of interest in Russian medieval art and architecture and had great influence on the development of modern art in Russia. The Mamontovs' circle, which included several of the most talented painters of the nation, plunged into this project enthusiastically. They searched out archeological documents and historical information. All of the friends contributed ideas and work for the decoration and building of this church. It was designed by Viktor Vasnetsov in the highest traditions of 14th-century Novgorod architecture. The wooden ornaments were painted by Repin; Vasnetsov decorated the windows and painted icons. The gifted landscape artist Polenov designed the iconostasis. Women embroidered vestments and covers to Polenov's designs. Vasnetsov executed a mosaic floor in the shape of a spreading flower, and the lovely church was constantly in use until the Revolution.

Mamontov loved music and had spent several years in Italy developing his fine baritone voice. He was also a talented playwright and a gifted stage manager. In his mansion in Moscow, Mamontov held literary and musical evenings every week. In the Russian tradition of those days, amateur productions were often staged by his family and friends. Stanislavsky, a cousin of Mamontov, described these cozy and intimate theatricals:

"Young people and children, relatives and acquaintances came from all over and assisted in the common cause. Some ground up the paints, others primed the canvas . . . still others worked on the furnishings and props. Mamontov was in charge of all these activities and at the same time wrote plays, joked with the young people, dictated business letters and telegrams connected with his complicated railway affairs. . . ."

For his productions Mamontov innovatively turned to some of the artists he knew for the scenery and costumes. Rimsky-Korsakov's operatic masterpiece, *The Snow Maiden*, was first performed in 1883 in a little theater in Mamontov's house, with sets by Vasnetsov. The costumes of the peasant chorus were borrowed from the government of Tula province and the authentic objects collected by Mamontov's wife were used as props.

In 1888 Mamontov decided to found a private opera company to acquaint the public with the music of Russian composers who had until then received only a lukewarm reception in St. Petersburg. The first company lasted two and a half seasons and gave thirty-three operas. In 1896, the year of Nicholas II's coronation, Mamontov formed a second opera company which performed until 1904. Sixty operas were staged, forty-three by Russian composers, among them *Boris Godunov*, Tchaikovsky's *The Sorcerer* and *Oprichnik*. Mussorgsky's *Khovanshchina* was first played in his theater; Rimsky-Korsakov composed *Sadko, The Tsar's Bride* and *The Golden Cockerel* especially for Mamontov. In 1896 Mamontov met and heard Fyodor Chaliapin, who was then an obscure member of the artistic staff of the Imperial Theater in St. Petersburg. He offered the singer a job in his operatic company, tripling his salary and launching his fabulous career. Three years later when Chaliapin left Mamontov's company to go back to the Imperial Theater, he went back as a star.

Mamontov was in charge of all the productions, often conducting them himself. He was, said Vasnetsov, "like an electric current igniting those around him." He was the first to realize the importance of making scenery an integral part of a play's plot, period and music, turning over the scenery and costume design to easel painters who swept away stereotyped ideas and came up with fresh new concepts. Productions began to be looked on as a whole, and a dramatic unity emerged. This was nothing less than a revolution in the art of theatrical decoration. Before, the back cloth had been a decorative background for acting; now it became an integral part of the production. Painting found a place in the theater; Konstantin Korovin, Alexander Golovin, Mikhail Vrubel and Isaak Levitan all designed sets for Mamontov's productions. Scenery and costumes with carefully conceived patches of color became living canvases. Painters took pride in finding exactly the right tones for costumes. They searched junk shops and antique dealers for old fabrics. Thanks to Mamontov, painting began to go hand in hand with music, song and dance, profoundly affecting the course of modern theatrical decoration.

Among all his contributions to art, Mamontov was the first to recognize and support the avant-garde artist Mikhail Vrubel, a precursor of Russian Cubism and Constructivism. Vrubel was an unusually versatile artist, a painter, sculptor, architect and book illustrator whose work was pointing in a new, nonrealistic direction. In 1896 Mamontov commissioned from Vrubel two large panels for the Northern Pavilion at the All-Russian Exhibition held at the Nizhny Novgorod Fair. When the panels were rejected by the committee, which refused to exhibit them, Mamontov simply financed the building of a special pavilion for Vrubel's canvases just outside the exhibition grounds. There, Vrubel's paintings became a sensation with the public and critics alike, and Vrubel a special pride of Moscow, his work profoundly influencing the later Russian avant-garde painters.

Vrubel is almost unknown in Europe, but for Russians the story of this tragic genius has the haunting glamour of Gauguin or Van Gogh. Vrubel's tormented paintings are touched with mysticism and terror. He was plagued by strange visions which finally drove him to insanity. In 1902, during an exhibition in St. Petersburg, he remained all night in the gallery with a bottle of champagne for company, painting and repainting a huge canvas called *The Demon*. The morning of the exhibition he was found incoherent and babbling, and he ended his days in an asylum.

Because he believed that "the eye of the people must be trained to see beauty everywhere—in streets and railroad stations," the imaginative Mamontov encouraged Vrubel to paint frescoes in the Metropole Hotel, commissioned Vasnetsov to paint panels for the Donets Railroad Station in the 1880's and followed this by having the Yaroslavl Station in the city decorated with murals by Korovin, who, at Mamontov's urging, made a special trip to Archangel to make his sketches. These murals were later exhibited at the Paris Universal Exhibition in 1900.

In 1899, Mamontov suffered serious business reverses. In the ensuing investigation, he was falsely accused of embezzlement of railroad funds and sent to jail to await trial. Yet even in prison he remained busy and cheerful. From his cell he wrote to his friend, the artist Polenov, "I never understood so clearly the full meaning of art until now." In the months while he awaited his trial, he wrote a script for an opera. Called *The Necklace*, it dealt with the times of the ancient Greek colonies in Italy. He also translated the libretto of *Don Giovanni* into Russian and sculpted miniature busts of his jailers. Stanislavsky writes that when he came to visit his cousin in prison, he found these little busts all cheerfully lined up like soldiers on parade. When Mamontov was tried in 1900 and found not guilty, the courtroom audience cheered. But his days as a patron of the arts were over forever, for while he sat in prison all his belongings had been sold at public auction and his railroad acquired by the government.

Mamontov spent the last eighteen years of his life operating a small pottery workshop in Moscow. But his friends did not desert him, and the little workshop very soon became a lively meeting place for the best actors, musicians, painters and sculptors of the city.

•　•　•

Many of the new generation of enlightened merchant industrialists of the late 19th century were descendants of the traditional merchant families of Moscow who had lived for centuries in the Transriver district where the *Streltsy* of Ivan the Terrible had also once been quartered. In the Transriver district, across the Moskva River from the Kremlin and not far from the Trading Rows, houses were squat and simple, surrounded with high, strong fences. Behind the fences lay carefully swept courtyards and gardens with apple trees, gooseberry and currant bushes and little flower beds of pansies and forget-me-nots. At night the gates were locked, and the houses were kept closed, the curtains drawn. Conservative old merchant families lived in retirement and isolation. They got up at dawn and retired early. They shunned public entertainment, even considering ballet an unsuitable entertainment for the ladies of the family, who were kept carefully out of sight except on festival days.

These old-style merchants, many of them stern Old Believers, had the reputation of being a hard-working, hard-driving, hard-praying lot, despotic and tyrannical in their family life, cunning and ruthless in business. They kept their beards and longish hair; they wore Old Russian dress—peaked cap, long kaftans with stand-up collar, baggy pants tucked into their boots; their wives were wrapped in stiff brocades and shawls. The intelligentsia mocked and despised them, laughed at their style of entertaining and their gigantic meals, so lavish as to be vulgar. Although among the strongest impressions of travelers to Russia in the latter part of the 19th century were the streets full of traffic and the busy activity on wharves and in railroad yards, none of this is found in Russian literature, for the great writers of the day were all hostile to the merchant class and to the idea of a materialistic society. Tolstoy was interested in the relationship of the peasant and nobleman and extolled poverty and brotherly love as an ideal. Dostoevsky, in his great novels, railed against the accumulation of wealth as a seductive temptation, a disaster for man. Gorky, who accepted considerable financial help from a wealthy merchant, condemned and ridiculed the merchant class as a group. A wide abyss yawned between the bourgeoisie and the intelligentsia.

What was being overlooked in books and plays in this period was that the traditional picture of this class was rapidly changing, that the new merchants who were emerging differed greatly from the narrow traditional merchants of older days. Industrialization accelerated at such a pace that by the end of the 19th century and the beginning of the 20th, Russia led both Europe and America in its rate of economic growth. According to Soviet sources, in the period between 1873 and 1913, pig iron production increased twelve times and coal production twenty times. Between 1885 and 1913, oil production, organized by the Nobel family that had come from Sweden and settled in St. Petersburg in 1835, increased four and a half times. (The famous Alfred Nobel, who returned to live in Sweden in the early 1860's, exploded his first mines in the Neva River, based on work he had done on nitroglycerine with his Russian professor at the University of St. Petersburg. His two brothers, Robert and Ludwig, stayed on in Russia and went on to develop the richly productive Baku oil fields.)

In late-19th-century Russia, the new merchant princes created by this industrialization came to have as important an influence on the arts and sciences of their time as the Dutch merchants of 17th-century Holland. Among the thirty clans constituting the upper ranks of the Moscow bourgeoisie of the time, some had come from trading families of small artisans and merchants who had come to Moscow in the late 18th and early 19th centuries; others were from peasant stock; and many were Old Believers. As a group they were bold, original and colorful, and they showed great independence of judgment and freedom of action in their dedication to the arts.

Clannish and family oriented, they went their own way. They did not much like Western ideas, and remained cool toward the abstract notions and speculations of Europe which so much interested the Russian nobility in the 18th century and the intelligentsia in the 19th. Instead, they clung to native Russian culture and artistic forms, respecting the traditions of long ago.

They opposed the classical style of Petersburg architecture—"a pile of stones" they called it—and instead built themselves elaborate mansions in the Muscovite neo-medieval style, as well as some imaginative examples of the art nouveau style. They mistrusted St. Petersburg as the seat of soulless bureaucracy and foreign ideas. (One of the industrialists wrote that in his family a trip to St. Petersburg was called "a trip to the Tatar Khan.")

In the late 19th century, these independent dynasties of merchants exercised great power. In their beloved Moscow, they built hospitals, clinics and schools, old people's homes and rest homes for students. They founded magazines, assembled great art collections and played a decisive role in the renaissance of a new Russian art. The Moscow Conservatory and Symphony Concerts, founded by Nikolai Rubenstein and conducted by Tchaikovsky, were entirely supported by private money. In fact, wrote Stanislavsky, "the finest institutions of Moscow in all spheres of life including art and religion were founded by private initiative."

Among the more than twenty art-collecting merchant families in Moscow were the Shchukins, who were textile industrialists. All six Shchukin brothers became collectors. The third son, Sergei, was among the very first people in the world to appreciate the work of modern French artists when the French were pronouncing them insane and worthless. In the 1890's with great independence of taste, Sergei Shchukin began collecting all that was most significant and remarkable in the art of his time. Unprepossessing in appearance, with his sharp, dark eyes under their bristling brows, seldom seeking advice, Shchukin boldly searched out the work of "rejected" artists.

He bought paintings by Monet, Degas, Renoir, Van Gogh, Rouault, Braque, Cézanne, Rousseau and Gauguin. He was the major collector of Matisse and the first to buy Picasso, eventually acquiring fifty-one Picasso paintings. On the walls of his Grand Salon hung twenty of his thirty-eight Matisses; in his dining room were more than fifteen Gauguins. By 1914 he owned 221 works, the largest collection of Impressionists in the world. Shchukin liked to hang his paintings on the wall and live with them for a while before he committed himself to buying. Sometimes he reproached himself for weeks for buying a painting he did not understand. He told Matisse that it sometimes took him a year to get used to one of his new paintings. Nevertheless, he persisted, and thanks to his extraordinary taste, the most advanced ideas and movements in art became more familiar to Moscow than to Paris itself.

Shchukin made of his collection a public gallery and received anyone who was interested in seeing it. On Sundays, acting as host and guide, he received all visitors personally. Sometimes people showed amusement and even disgust, yet so great was his confidence that taunts did not bother him in the least. And, although he stuttered, he was so eloquent that he was always able to inspire his audiences with his own enthusiasm. Many foreign travelers made the trip to Moscow especially to see his collection. Eminent representatives of great European museums came to study it. A steady stream of art critics, journalists and students from the Moscow Art Academy poured through his house; as a result, a group of students at the Art Academy organized a Cézanne fan club. His collection had enormous influence on young artists and students, widening their horizons and, in the end, sending them off on their individual and different paths. Such was the influence of his collection that a professor at the Art Academy exclaimed, "After the spicy fare they get at Shchukin's, how can we tempt them with the bland fare we can offer them here? Everybody wants to catch up with Paris, we can teach them nothing. I can't stand it! I'll resign!"

To ornament the grand staircase of his home, Shchukin commissioned two huge panels, *Dance* and *Music*, from Matisse, who came to Moscow in 1911 specifically to help place his works. It was the only time that Shchukin was known to have had serious qualms. For a short time he was nervous about all the nude figures. Among his other philanthropies, Sergei Shchukin also became the founder of the Institute of Philosophy at Moscow University. Each of his five brothers had an extensive collection of books, furniture, arts and crafts. In 1892 his brother Peter built a museum for his collection of Russian antiquities, manuscripts, documents and objects, more than 300,000 items.

The Shchukins were not alone. Another merchant, Alexei Bakhrushin, who had grown rich from his commerce in furs and leathers, collected all things that concerned the theater, and in 1894 created a Museum of the Theater and gave it to the Academy of Sciences. In 1913 the museum contained more than thirty thousand items, manuscripts of plays, sets, designs, costumes. Thanks to this remarkable collection, the history of Russian theater can be traced from its beginnings to modern days.

Stanislavsky describes a merchant named Kuzma Soldatenkov who altruistically devoted himself to the publication of books that could not hope for a large circulation, but were useful to science, social life, culture and education. Stanislavsky writes that the "two windows of his study shone after midnight where he sat planning with artists or scientists some useful but unprofitable publication." The Ryabushinsky family collected icons of the Old Believers of Novgorod and Stroganov schools, as did the merchant Kharitenko, who gave his entire collection to the church of his estate in Kharkov. Kharitenko's living rooms were furnished with Aubussons; he commissioned Vlaminck to paint the ceilings. He entertained lavishly, giving great gala evenings for which he hired Ekaterina Geltser, the reigning ballerina of the Bolshoi Theater, to dance, then followed her performance with nocturnes by Chopin played by a leading violinist, dancing and finally, at four in the morning, had his guests transported in a fleet of troikas to the Strelna to hear the gypsies. In a sharp contrast of old and new, his aged mother never went out in society and did not leave the part of the house that was hers. With her icon lamps burning in the corner, she sat wrapped in her shawl by the samovar, dipping pieces of sugar in her tea.

• • •

The Morozovs were the kings of them all. From 1812 to 1880, in three generations, they rose from serfdom to being the leading industrialists of Russia. By the end of the century, numerous members of this vigorous clan—brothers, sisters, cousins, wives—were all making important contributions to the cultural, artistic and social life of the country.

The first Savva Morozov was a serf who in his teens worked in a small silk factory on his master's estate. When he married, his young wife became famous for her skill in dyeing fabrics and for her fine sense of color. After the burning of Moscow in 1812, when no shops were left in Moscow, the enterprising Savva took the cloth and ribbons produced by his family and went about selling them from house to house. It is said that this rugged man walked the fifty miles from his native village of Zuevo to Moscow in a single day. By 1820 he had collected enough money to buy the freedom of his family; by 1837 his woolen mill consisted of eleven buildings and employed two hundred workers. In the 1850's he converted his mills to cotton, and the employees in his factory increased to one thousand. When he died at ninety, he turned over his thriving business to his five sons. The youngest, Timofei, was the true heir of the prodigious energy and business sense of his father.

Timofei reorganized the firm, spent large sums for the training of Russian engineers, establishing scholarships for graduates of the Imperial Technical College so that they could continue their education abroad, and then offered them jobs when they returned. By 1880 Timofei was the leading industrialist of Russia. He possessed immense holdings in textiles and banks. His factories covered an area of two and a half miles, employed eight thousand people and made a profit of two million rubles a year. But he was a ruthless despot who tolerated no criticism or contradiction. His employees were terrified of him. He demanded faultless production, and to achieve high quality he imposed a system of fines on his workers. In 1885 his workers revolted. They went on strike, destroyed machinery and broke windows. The first strike in Russia, it made a deep impression on the younger of Timofei's two sons, also named Savva. Savva fell in love with a beautiful village girl who had been a machine operator in the Morozov plant and married her. After his father's death, he made it his concern to improve working conditions in their factories. He built new and airy living quarters for his workers and their families and improved medical care. His enterprises prospered more than ever.

Savva was a large, awkward man who looked like a peasant. On his massive frame European clothes hung uncomfortably. His dark eyes were sharp and quick, his movements slow and deliberate. He was a man of great physical strength and unusual will power, energy and independence. The writer Maxim Gorky, whose friend and supporter Savva became, described him as "a flatiron." Savva paid the equivalent of $7,500 to bail Gorky out of jail when he had been arrested for revolutionary activities. Savva also contributed large sums to the Social Democratic Party.

Along with his interest in social causes, Morozov had a great interest in the theater. In 1898 he was approached by one of his acquaintances, Konstantin Alekseev, better known today by the stage name he adopted—Stanislavsky—for help in supporting a new theater. Stanislavsky himself was the son of a textile merchant, whose cozy family life he vividly describes in *My Life in Art*.

Stanislavsky had been interested in the stage since childhood. His parents, who loved opera, took their children to forty or fifty performances a year. He and his sisters and brothers staged marionette shows and circuses in a little theater in their home. In 1888, when he was twenty-five, with a friend, Vladimir Nemirovich-Danchenko, the director of the dramatic classes of the Moscow Philharmonic Society, he founded an acting group. They called it the Society of Art and Literature, and it quickly became one of the most popular Moscow amateur theatrical companies because of the high standard of acting and the innovations of Stanislavsky.

Stanislavsky was a cousin of Savva Mamontov, and he later said that seeing the productions at Mamontov's house in the 1880's inspired his "realistic" theater ideas. Stanislavsky began to lead the theater away from its constricted and conventionalized traditions toward a greater freedom of expression. It was his aim to see, in authentic settings, real feelings expressed in the theater, to achieve such a synthesis of themes and characters that an illusion of real life was created on the stage.

He declared war on theatrical conventions of all kinds. Actors were called on to act from the inside out, to find emotions and feelings from their own experience which would give truth to their acting. Stage decor was changed from top to bottom to give the impression of reality. He introduced ceilings in interiors and hid the floor with little bridges and staircases. To increase the illusion of reality, sometimes he even cut the stage with furniture and placed some with its back to the audience. He and his colleagues searched everywhere for authentic costumes that would lend verisimilitude to their productions.

The little company traveled to many Russian cities, achieving enormous success. Even in Petersburg, their seasons were sold out long in advance. Students, government employees and the nobility flocked to buy tickets, warming themselves at bonfires while they waited in line. In 1897 Stanislavsky and Danchenko decided to found a professional company, calling it the Moscow Art Theater.

Although Stanislavsky and his actress wife worked for nothing and the company enjoyed great public support, finances were shaky and therefore they approached Savva Morozov for support. Morozov came to the shareholders' meeting and offered to buy up all the holdings. From that moment, not only did Morozov completely finance the company and supervise all its financial affairs, but he also plunged actively into its artistic work. It was he who took over the supervision of all the lighting of stage and auditorium. As soon as his family would leave for the country, Morozov would change the parlor of his huge neo-Gothic mansion into a laboratory for scenic experiments. The bathroom was turned into an electrical workshop, where Morozov prepared lacquers in various tones and colors for painting blue electric light bulbs and glass. He would try out the new effects in his garden, dressed in working clothes and working side by side with electricians whom he amazed with his professional knowledge of electricity.

Morozov not only completely financed the building of the famous Moscow Art Theater, but also helped conceive and design it. An old building was completely renovated. Away went the accepted gilt and ornate decoration of auditorium and foyers. The theater was simple and pure as a temple: dark wood paneling, portraits of great actors and artists on the walls, wooden benches and white walls. Everything was meant to rivet the attention of the audience to the stage. Morozov spared no expense in installing comfortable dressing rooms for the actors and, in consultation with Stanislavsky, built a complex revolving stage, something which barely existed in Europe. Not only did the stage revolve, but underneath it was a complete revolving substage with a tremendous trap which could serve as a river or a mountain chasm. The lighting system was the best available, with the newest reflectors and apparatus all worked from an electrical keyboard.

Despite his vast business responsibilities, Morozov attended almost every performance. When he could not come, he kept in close touch by telephone, supervising not only the lighting but the whole complex theater mechanism. He was often seen climbing ladders to hang draperies and pictures and carrying furniture like any stagehand.

It was one of the aims of the Moscow Art Theater to promote the interests of Russian literature by producing the works of contemporary authors on stage. So the first production in the new theater was Anton Chekhov's *The Sea Gull*. At that time Anton Chekhov was known as a writer of short stories. He had started life as the son of a poor grocer in the small town of Taganrog in the south. His grandfather had been a serf who had bought his freedom. Chekhov was sent to study medicine in Moscow on a scholarship provided by the municipality of his small town. At the age of nineteen he became the sole support of his family, and to make money began to write and publish short stories in the newspapers of Moscow and St. Petersburg. By the time he was thirty-five his success was such that he had acquired by his pen an estate of three hundred acres, where he went to live with his parents and younger sister and gave free medical treatment to neighboring peasants. All his life Chekhov was proudest of his medical calling, insisting always, "My real profession is medicine, but I sometimes write in my spare time."

His first play, *The Sea Gull*, had first been played in St. Petersburg in 1896 and was booed off the stage. The first audiences did not appreciate his new dramatic methods of "indirect action," of people reacting to events that were happening offstage. They found the play monotonous and boring. Chekhov had been present at one of the performances and was in such despair at the play's failure that he spent the whole night despondently wandering the banks of the Neva River, exposing himself to freezing winds which severely worsened the tuberculosis he had had since he was a young man. As a result, his doctors sent him to live in the milder climate of the south in Yalta. It was only with the greatest difficulty that Stanislavsky and Danchenko persuaded Chekhov to allow them to perform his play again in their theater. Even Stanislavsky, who did the staging, found the play difficult to grasp at first, and said that its power came to him only slowly as he worked on it.

The historic premiere of *The Sea Gull* in the new Moscow Art Theater took place on December 17, 1898. The sets were by the painter Isaak Levitan, who perfectly captured the autumnal mood of the play; Stanislavsky himself played the role of Trigorin. This time the play was a resounding success, so much so that a sea gull remained painted on the curtain of the theater to remind audiences ever after of its triumphant premiere. The Moscow Art Theater followed *The Sea Gull* with the first productions of *Uncle Vanya* in 1899, *The Three Sisters* in 1901 and *The Cherry Orchard* in 1904, the work which immortalized the displacement of the nobility by the rising merchant class. The theater became popularly known as "the house of Chekhov." Chekhov himself often read his plays for the actors and sat in the audience watching rehearsals. But when Stanislavsky tried to consult him, he would always say, "I am a doctor, not a stage director," and run to hide in the shadows. In 1901 Chekhov married an actress from the theater. In 1904 the two went on a trip to Germany, where he died of tuberculosis at the age of forty-four.

The Moscow Art Theater staged the plays of many other contemporary authors, notably Maxim Gorky, whose *Lower Depths* was first performed there. Inspired by Mamontov's innovations, Stanislavsky, too, asked the leading painters to design sets for his productions. In 1902 he called on Alexander Benois and other painters of the new World of Art group in Petersburg. Because of the creative impetus of the Mamontov opera and the Moscow Art Theater, theatrical decor became an extremely important part of the work of Russian painters. The Moscow Art Theater gave birth to a whole new way of thinking about acting, playwriting and staging, and had a profound influence on theater in the West. Although the actors were considered among the best in the world, their stress always was on teamwork rather than stars. In his devotion to his art, Stanislavsky expected and received complete dedication from his company and demanded from his audiences a stern discipline. Once the curtain had risen in the Moscow Art Theater, no one was allowed to enter until the first act was over. Absolute silence was required, so that audiences could hear the whisper of the wind, the clopping of horses' hooves and even the chirping of crickets. (A popular rumor had it that Stanislavsky bred crickets for this purpose on his country estate.) It was the first theater of experimentation, and it led the way for other bold experiments in the Russian theater of the early 20th century—the avant-garde theater movements of Synthesism, Rhythmic Unity, Expressionism and Futurism.

Savva Morozov came to a tragic end. In the spring of 1905 he approached his mother with a plan to introduce profit sharing among his workers, one of the first industrialists in the world to propose such an idea. His mother, the wife of the despotic Timofei and the stern matriarch of the clan, categorically refused and removed him from control of their enterprises. Savva shot himself a month later in France. Some said it was because of his mother, others because of his bitter disappointment at the direction his revolutionary friends, whom he had so strongly supported, were taking. Some even said he was murdered. He was buried in the Old Believer Cemetery in Preobrazhenskoe in what was then the outskirts of Moscow.

Many other members of the exceptional Morozov clan made great contributions to the arts. They financed magazines of philosophy and art. Varvara Morozov built up an important collection of Russian manuscripts, books and contemporary paintings. The first public library in Moscow, the Turgenev Library, was her creation. She gave lavishly to welfare organizations, old people's homes, hospitals, houses for the poor and schools throughout the country, and in the Morozov factories pioneered schools for workers' education which were copied by other industrialists. Two of her sons, Mikhail and Ivan, built up vast collections of Impressionists. Ivan Morozov's fabulous collection, which rivaled Shchukin's, numbered 100 Russian paintings and 250 French works, including 12 Gauguins, 17 magnificent Cézannes, 17 Maillol statues, and the works of all leading Impressionists as well as Matisse and Picasso. Bonnard decorated Ivan Morozov's country estate; Maurice Denis decorated Ivan's cousin Alexei's house and Vrubel did five panels on the theme of Faust for Alexei's country estate. Margarita Morozov was a fine pianist, a pupil of Scriabin. At the end of the century, she had a salon in which met the leading literary and scholarly figures of the day; among them philosophers Vladimir Solovyov and Nikolai Berdyaev and the writer Andrei Bely.

This extraordinary class of merchants hardly had time to consolidate themselves into a cohesive group, for they lasted only a generation. But, in the short time that they existed, they accomplished miracles for their country and the city they loved so much. After the Revolution, their collections were seized. Many of their magnificent Impressionist paintings can be seen today in the Hermitage in St. Petersburg and the Pushkin Museum in Moscow. Their names have been all but obliterated. No major work has yet been written on their collective contribution to the arts.

23. PETIPA AND THE IMPERIAL BALLET

AT THE END of the 19th and the beginning of the 20th century, St. Petersburg was at the peak of its cosmopolitan fame. Fast international express trains brought travelers from all over Europe (forty-six hours from Paris, twenty-eight from Berlin). Numerous steamship lines regularly served the capital. Every Friday evening a two-thousand-ton steamer left London for St. Petersburg via the Kiel Canal. Well-appointed hotels were ready to receive the weary traveler. In 1913 at the Astoria Hotel was an Anglo-Russian Bureau with a gigantic map of the London tube system and a large library of English books from Chaucer to D. H. Lawrence. As the telephone directory system in Russia was one of the most modern in Europe, it was easy to consult the St. Petersburg directory and discover the milliners, the florists and numerous specialty shops of the city, or study the floor plans of all the Imperial Theaters, which were also included. Guards regiments, doctors, lawyers of the city were all listed under their own special headings. In *All Petersburg*, the directory of 1914, in the special section "Artists," one could find Bakst, Lev, at Nadezhdinskaya 52, or Repin, I1, who also listed the address and phone of his famous Finnish villa, *Penati*. In the alphabetical listing of all the residents of the city, one could quickly look up the poets Blok, Alex, Offitserskaya 57; Kuzmin, Mikh (with the notation "man of letters"), at Moika 91; and Gumiliev, Nik, at Tsarskoe Selo, Malaya 63.

Among the excellent restaurants of the capital, the most famous were Donon's (French cuisine), Privato (Italian), the Bear and Cubat's. The draught beer at Dominique's was highly recommended, and Palkin's was known for its splendid organ music. At Leiner's, a cozy delicatessen with sawdust on the floor, Diaghilev, Benois and Stravinsky argued and planned while, wrote Stravinsky, "eating caviar, Black Sea oysters, and the most delicious pickled mushrooms in the world."

In addition, St. Petersburg had many clubs, some renowned for their excellent meals. Unlike England these clubs were not the exclusive refuge of men, but also welcomed families and guests. Among them were the New English Club for Americans and English, the Commercial Club for merchants, the Literary and Artistic Society, the Imperial Yacht Club and Imperial Automobile Club.

Baedeker advised tourists that the interiors of the Imperial palaces could be visited by depositing one's passport at the entrance and suggested watching the changing of the guard at midday. Each of the regiments of the household cavalry had mounts of one color (Horse Guards, black; Gatchina Hussars, dapple-gray; Chevaliers Gardes, chestnut). He also mentioned "horse races in spring and summer," "public entertainment and music of military bands every Sunday and holidays in all the parks." Helpfully, he informed the tourist that "news vendors are on every street corner," and foreign newspapers at Wolff's and Violet's.

The city was a mecca for the art lover. Imperial museums were free, and many private collections were also open to visitors. The traveler could view the vast collection of the Yusupovs in their palace on the Moika Canal, the Stroganov palace collection, the Semyonov collection with its five hundred Dutch and Flemish paintings. The public library opened its enormous collection of books and manuscripts to any interested foreign visitor. One could hear and see the best performers and works that Russia and Europe could provide. At the Maryinsky Theater the new operas of Tchaikovsky, Borodin and Rimsky-Korsakov were produced impeccably, as well as the operas of Wagner, with the finest German singers of the day. There were also the French and the Italian Opera which brought their world-famous stars. Rimsky-Korsakov was the regular conductor of the symphony concerts of the Imperial Music Society which invited as guests the greatest conductors and virtuosos of Europe. Sarah Bernhardt and Bartel were regular visiting members of the permanent French dramatic company of the Mikhailovsky Theater.

St. Petersburg had four opera houses. Moscow, Tiflis, Odessa and Kiev also each had an opera house with permanent companies which gave performances through eight- and nine-month seasons. In 1901 Nicholas II built the

Narodny Dom, or People's Palace, in St. Petersburg, and a number of similar institutions quickly sprang up all over Russia. Financed by municipal funds or by private individuals, the most important feature of these People's Palaces was a concert and opera theater with extremely low-priced seats as well as a nonpaying choir school, a free library and lecture halls. There were two such People's Palaces in St. Petersburg; Nicholas II's Narodny Dom contained an opera and concert hall which accommodated three thousand. Standing room cost a penny, the equivalent of five American cents. The best Russian and foreign companies performed in these People's Palaces, and they were enormously popular. A visiting correspondent of *The Times* of London wrote that they were filled with "crowds of working people, artisans and soldiers who are given the opportunity of becoming acquainted with a great variety of standard operas both Russian and foreign."

In *My Life in Art*, Stanislavsky wrote that the reason the ground was so fertile for his Moscow Art Theater was because, from the time of Alexis, the tsars had provided imperially supported schools and theaters that gathered the best artists and pupils and brought the best European artists to help in their development. No other nation supported its theaters in so lavish a manner or attracted so many distinguished visitors. At the end of the 19th century Nicholas II subsidized five theaters from his Privy Purse, as well as the Imperial Ballet, the ballet school and the Academy of Fine Arts.

One of the brightest jewels in this tiara of artistic establishments was the St. Petersburg Imperial Ballet School. The school was—and remains today—on Theater Street, housed among the noble complex of buildings designed by Carlo Rossi in the imposing neoclassical style of Alexander I. Dominated at one end by the yellow and white Alexandrinsky Theater, with its sweeping columns and black statues, the street is one of the most beautiful in the world, grand and yet with something of the austere atmosphere of a cloister.

Acceptance to the school was so difficult that only six to ten of every hundred applicants were taken. The children were subjected to a rigorous medical examination; a doctor examined their spines, their hearts, their hearing. They were asked to sing a scale and to read music. If they passed these tests, for two years they remained on probation, continuing to live at home but otherwise supplied with everything by the school. After two years, if they qualified, they entered a world apart, as strictly secluded and regulated as a monastery or a convent. A doorman in Imperial livery stood in the lobby. Portraits of the Emperor, celebrated teachers and ballerinas of old lined the walls. The school had its own yellow and white pillared chapel with its own large choir, and its own theater, where the annual examination took place, and which they shared with the pupils of the drama school. It had its own infirmary, with doctors and nurses constantly in attendance. The boys had three uniforms—black for everyday, dark blue for holidays and gray linen for summer, with a high velvet collar on which a silver lyre, encircled with palms and surmounted with the Imperial crown, was embroidered. They had two overcoats, one for winter with heavy Astrakhan collar, patent-leather boots and pumps and six changes of underwear. The girls wore serge dresses with tight bodices and a white fichu of lawn, black alpaca aprons for everyday and white tucked aprons for Sundays, white stockings and black pumps. Juniors wore brown; pink was given as a mark of distinction, and a white dress was the highest mark of all. When the girls went out for their daily walks, they wore black pelisses lined with red fox gathered in folds under a round fur collar, black silk bonnets and high boots with velveteen tops.

The students slept in spacious dormitories, twenty-five to forty in rooms large enough for fifty. Each pupil had his own private cubicle with his own icon hung above his bed. Boys and girls were strictly separated. Even when they met for ballroom dancing lessons and rehearsals, they were forbidden to talk to each other and kept their eyes lowered.

Each morning when they arose at seven-thirty, the children exchanged their handkerchiefs for clean ones. On Fridays they were taken to the baths, where maids in white linen shifts in dressing rooms full of steam scrubbed them on wooden benches. All girls up to the age of fifteen had their hair brushed by a maid. A chiropodist attended to their feet, which were tended with religious care. Every Saturday during their years at school the children underwent a medical examination.

Prayers were sung after meals; during Lent the students fasted. The senior girls, helped by the juniors, embroidered a pall or carpet for the church, while one read aloud the lives of saints and martyrs. These children, vowed to Terpsichore, were virtually adopted by the tsar and considered part of the Imperial household. The Imperial family often sent delicacies to their tables. The pupils were kept from the world as from contamination, their growth concentrated on a single purpose. In this school were formed the finest dancers in the world.

For eight years, in this cloistered and protected atmosphere, the art of dancing was taught to them by the best masters. More than any other of the performing arts, ballet depends on a laying on of hands from master to pupil; their teachers traced back in unbroken succession to the greatest masters of the art. In addition the children were schooled in mathematics, history, languages and music, ballroom dancing and manners. As seniors they were taken to the theater and given lessons in elocution, acting and singing. They were taught makeup in rooms outfitted with mirrors and lights like theatrical dressing rooms, and practiced in a rehearsal room with the floor raked as it was on the stage. For several hours every day, while their dancing masters played the violin, they went through their exercises, the boys in black trousers and white blouses, the girls provided with heavy tasseled shawls to keep them warm between breaks. As a high honor, the pupils who excelled were asked to water the floor. (This settled the dust and kept the floor from being too slippery.)

From their first year on, pupils at the school were used in productions at the Maryinsky Theater of Opera and Ballet, one of the loveliest and most welcoming theaters in the world. Designed in 1860 by Alberto Cavos, the theater with its blue hangings adorning the boxes, its stalls and barriers painted in gilt with white background, its sparkling crystal chandeliers, and chairs upholstered in blue velvet, had an atmosphere of great gaiety and yet of coziness. The vast, airy auditorium was so skillfully constructed that the stage was clearly visible from every seat.

At the theater the children were provided with their own special dressing rooms. They were taken to the Maryinsky in special carriages which accommodated six, accompanied by their governesses, a maid and a beadle in livery. Long vehicles which held fifteen were used for great occasions. Special carriages also went to fetch artists and took them home after each performance; every ballerina was given a carriage to herself.

After graduation, from the secluded atmosphere of the school the young dancers passed into this glittering world. Like the other Imperial Theaters in St. Petersburg and Moscow, the Maryinsky was supported by the tsar with an annual subsidy of 2 million gold rubles. Thanks to this steady and generous patronage, and the protected artistic atmosphere at the school, Russian ballet at the end of the century had no rival. Ballet had developed elsewhere in Europe—Paris, London, Vienna, Milan and Copenhagen—from 1800 to 1845, but by the end of the century it was in sad decline. Impresarios pitted virtuoso ballerinas against each other and male dancers were relegated to carrying them about. At the end of the 19th century in Paris, male dancers had almost disappeared, their roles given to women. In the West, with the exception of Denmark, ballet was regarded as an entertainment, hardly an art form at all.

But in Russia, ballet held a position of great artistic importance. Unlike

Paris or London, in Russia ballet was not considered just a *divertissement* to be tossed into an opera or a theatrical performance to enliven the production. Ballet performances were independent, had complicated libretti of several acts, and lasted many hours. Wednesday and Saturday were ballet nights. The competition for seats was extraordinary. Boxes were sold out for the entire season, taken by private families, clubs and regiments. Seats in such coveted boxes were passed down from father to son. Among these exalted boxholders were groups of dogmatic and very conservative balletomanes who never missed a performance. Whenever their favorite St. Petersburg ballerinas would dance in Moscow, trainloads of devotees would follow. They waited for their favorite steps and considered an occasional modification of a step a shocking irreverence. And there were also the balletomanes of pit and gallery—students, schoolboys, people of modest means who waited in line for hours for tickets—who cheered, covered their favorites with flowers and crowded around the stage door. In their enthusiasm, students sometimes threw down their coats in front of the carriages of their favorite ballerinas. A wealthy Russian once strewed a snowy street of St. Petersburg with violets, so that his favorite visiting Italian ballerina would feel more at home. Dancers performed at court and then sat down to supper with the Imperial family. Tamara Karsavina recalled that she received a cipher of the Empress in rubies and diamonds from the hands of the Empress herself. The great Kschessinska, a favorite of the Grand Dukes, danced her roles wearing large diamonds and emeralds.

At the end of the century, there were 180 dancers in the Maryinsky Theater, all strictly graded in rank, through which they progressed from cadets to captains. First came the *corps de ballet*, then *coryphée, sujet, prima ballerina* and *prima ballerina assoluta* or, for a man, *soloist to the Tsar*. Salaries corresponded to rank, proceeding through the grading system with parts given according to ability. The term of service was twenty years, after which the dancers received a pension for life. Their dancing shoes were made in Paris, and they, too, were distributed according to rank; the *corps de ballet* was entitled to one pair for every four performances, *coryphée* for every three, solo dancers for two, first dancers every night and ballerinas each act.

For forty-one years, from 1862 until his retirement in 1903 when he was over eighty, the undisputed master of this kingdom, part fairyland, part cloister, was Marius Petipa. Petipa was a Frenchman born in Marseilles, the fourth generation of a family of dancers and actors. After an apprenticeship as a dancer and ballet master in Paris and several tours, including one to America in 1839, Petipa arrived in St. Petersburg in 1857 under contract to dance. While never a great classical dancer, he was handsome, a partner of great steadiness and strength and an extraordinarily talented mime. He was also full of choreographic ideas and gradually began to create ballets. His first important creation for the Maryinsky was *The Pharaoh's Daughter*, in 1862, a massive ballet which lasted five hours and included a dance for the *corps de ballet* in which eighteen pairs of dancers carried on their heads baskets of flowers which concealed thirty-six children who popped out on the last beat.

After this triumph, Petipa was named ballet master of the theater. In the fifty-six years that he devoted to the Russian stage, he brought choreography to an apex of achievement. His dancers appeared in operas, ballets and dramatic performances. Amazingly, although he lived in Russia for sixty-three years and married two Russian dancers, he never quite mastered the language and throughout his life continued to address his dancers in a mixture of broken Russian and French, with sometimes delightfully humorous results. But they always understood him, for so deeply attached was he to his adopted country that a contemporary wrote, "A Frenchman by birth, Petipa was Russian from head to foot." His four daughters became dancers in the Russian ballet, and three of his sons were actors on the Russian stage.

In those golden years of the Imperial Ballet, Petipa ruled with firm leadership and clear direction, always exhibiting craftsmanship, wit and grace. He created forty-six original ballets, most of them of several acts, revived seventeen other ballets, created whole new scenes for *Giselle* and *Le Corsaire*, thirty-five dances for operas and five ballet divertissements, earning for himself the title of Master of the Russian Ballet.

Only one other choreographer has been so prolific and has so far advanced the art of ballet—George Balanchine of the New York City Ballet, himself a graduate of the Imperial Ballet School.

Not all of Petipa's works were brilliant, but among them are several full-length masterpieces done in collaboration with great Russian composers which were more than enough to assure his immortality: *Don Quixote* (1869, revised in 1871), *La Bayadère* (1877), *Sleeping Beauty* (1890), *Raymonda* (1898) and, with the Russian choreographer Lev Ivanov, *The Nutcracker* (1892) and *Swan Lake* (1895). The legacy of these great ballets and the standards of perfection they established still are treasured throughout the world.

Petipa was a handsome, urbane man with expressive eyes and elegantly trimmed mustache and beard. Such was the respect he commanded that, when he entered the rehearsal hall, all the dancers, including the greatest ballerinas, immediately stood up. He demanded total discipline, and that his dancers grasp everything quickly. He spoke little, amiably addressed all the girls as "ma belle" and always waited for complete silence to fall over the company before he began his rehearsals. An accomplished mime, he showed dancers their roles so well and so captivatingly that they strained, hardly breathing, to catch his smallest gesture. During every performance, he always sat watching in the wings.

He had great command of masses, using groups of dancers in intricate but always pleasing patterns of opposition and contrast. His dances for the *corps de ballet*, which was justly famous for its accuracy and discipline, were beautifully staged, providing interweaving, symmetrical groups, meticulously planned by the choreographer, who covered notebooks with complicated sketches. Often he would work out these patterns at home, using small figures like chessmen to represent the men and women dancers he was moving about. One of his greatest achievements in symphonic group movement was the "Shades" second act of *La Bayadère*. Down a ramp which stretched off into the wings, as if they appeared from nowhere, the *corps de ballet* in white tutus with gauzy white scarves attached to their wrists stepped, one by one. Like a musical scale they performed precisely the same movement, one after another, and as one complete line descended, another followed and another, until the stage was filled with ethereal white figures moving in identical harmony to the same melody. Over the years, this masterpiece of classical dance served many Russian ballerinas, and in 1903 was the ballet that brought Anna Pavlova to fame.

Petipa had great feeling for the particular style of an epoch, often doing prolonged research in the library. Solos, *pas de deux* and variations he created live at rehearsals, for he had a great feeling for the individuality of a given dancer. Unerringly he sensed which roles were right for a particular performer, and used his or her individual gifts to advantage, often creating roles especially for them. He loved to watch at the school the classes of the great Swedish teacher, Christian Johansson, sometimes taking ideas from his complicated combinations which, it was said, the master never repeated twice. Petipa interpreted them with impeccable taste, rarely giving combinations which would only show off virtuoso technique, but instead concentrating on grace of line and pose. His whole system, wrote the dancer Nikolai Legat, who knew him well, could be best summed up in these words: "Strive for beauty, grace and simplicity, and consider no other laws."

Petipa was always searching to fuse the emotional content of dance and music, and in his collaborations with Tchaikovsky, he brilliantly achieved this. Petipa gave Tchaikovsky a detailed program for writing the music, indicating the nature and duration of every dance. Together they created ballet symphonies with four parts, in which the choreography followed the music, becoming more and more complicated. From this inspired partnership, a new form of Russian music was born.

Their first joint ballet, commissioned by the Imperial Theater, was *Sleeping Beauty*, which had its premiere in 1890. Petipa created the role of Princess Aurora for Carlotta Brianza, a twenty-three-year-old visiting Italian ballerina, and designed a whole palette of roles for his other fine dancers; Enrico Cechetti was the first Bluebird and the great Pavel Gerdt the first Prince Desiré. Tchaikovsky himself played the music at some of the rehearsals. It is difficult to believe today that this ballet, now one of the best loved in the world, was coldly received at its dress rehearsal. The spectators declared that it "lacked melody," was too complicated and "undanceable." Rumors flew that the dancers found the music so incomprehensible that they refused to dance to it, and Tsar Alexander III, who was sitting in the front row, left immediately after the rehearsal without saying a word. The ubiquitous and powerful critic Stasov sneered, "French operetta" and "porcelain dolls"; still others thought it "much too serious." Tchaikovsky was berated by fellow composers for lowering himself so much as to compose ballet. But despite the carping, the dancers soon grew to love *Sleeping Beauty*, and the public made it a triumphant success.

In 1891 Tchaikovsky left for another of his extended tours abroad, this time to the United States, where he conducted concerts of his music to a tremendously enthusiastic public in New York, Baltimore and Philadelphia. He was present at the opening of the new Metropolitan Opera House, and was the guest of honor at a gala reception given at the Russian Embassy in Washington. When he returned, he and Petipa began to work on *Nutcracker*, with Petipa once again sending detailed instructions to the composer. Tchaikovsky wrote the music in two weeks, but it did not please him. In one of his moods of bleak depression, Tchaikovsky wrote to a friend that "the old man is breaking up . . . not only does his hair drop out and turn as white as snow . . . he loses bit by bit the capacity to do anything at all." And, "the ballet is infinitely worse than 'Sleeping Beauty,' so much is certain." Nevertheless, on March 19, 1892, Tchaikovsky conducted his new *Nutcracker* orchestral suite at a concert of the Russian Music Society in St. Petersburg and reported that it was "a clear success," although the composer continued to polish various sections. As the ballet production was being mounted, Petipa fell ill and, although he continued to supervise the production, the talented choreographer Lev Ivanov was called in to produce his own choreography to Petipa's specifications.

For his *Nutcracker*, Tchaikovsky ordered a new instrument, the celeste, from its Parisian inventor and wrote anxiously to a friend, "I don't want you to show it to anybody for I am afraid that Rimsky-Korsakov or Glazunov will smell it out and take advantage of its unusual effects before me." Tchaikovsky used this new instrument, which was then unknown in Russia, to produce the charming effects of tinkling bells in the dance of the Sugar Plum Fairy.

The new ballet had its premiere along with a forgettable opera, *Iolantha*, at the Maryinsky on December 6, 1892, St. Nicholas Day, the Name Day of the Tsarevich Nicholas. Afterward, in a masterpiece of understatement, the burly Tsar Alexander III is supposed to have said only, "Very nice, Tchaikovsky." Some time later Tchaikovsky wrote to a friend, "The opera was very well liked, the ballet not. Truth to tell, it was a little boring, despite the magnificence of the settings. The papers, as always, reviled me cruelly."

The idea for *Swan Lake* had grown in Tchaikovsky's mind for many years. He had started writing the music in 1875, and perhaps even earlier composed a children's ballet on the theme for his nieces and nephews. The ballet had its premiere in Moscow in 1877 with poor choreography by the ballet master of the Bolshoi and it was not a success. There are indications that before his death Tchaikovsky had begun plans with Petipa and Ivanov for a new production at the Maryinsky, but sadly Tchaikovsky did not live to see *Swan Lake*, considered the masterpiece of the Russian school. The great composer died of cholera in St. Petersburg on November 6, 1893. His death came only nine days after he had conducted at the Russian Musical Society the premiere of his Sixth Symphony, the "Pathétique," which, to his bitter disappointment, had been tepidly received by the public and judged inferior to his other works by critics.

Ivanov composed the famous second act of *Swan Lake* for a gala evening in memory of the composer in 1894. The full production with choreography by Petipa and Ivanov had its premiere on January 15, 1895, five years to the day after the premiere of *Sleeping Beauty*.

PETIPA AND THE IMPERIAL BALLET

Although the three Tchaikovsky ballets were based on French and German fairy tales, their heroes and heroines are profoundly Russian—in *Swan Lake* most of all. The swan is a very old symbol in Russian folklore, signifying faithfulness in love; the image of white swans shedding their wings at night to become maidens recurs in many tales. Ivanov used patterns of the ancient Russian *khorovod,* or round dance, in his brilliant choreography for the second act. The themes of these ballets are those which were central to Tchaikovsky's creation—the yearning for true happiness and love, the belief that love is stronger than death and that good vanquishes evil. It is because these eternal spiritual themes have been brought to life in music and movement of the highest art that, although these ballets appear to be dressed as fairy tales, they touch us so deeply still.

When the vigorous Petipa finally retired in 1903, at the age of eighty-five, the St. Petersburg company was strong and beautifully trained. The accuracy and discipline of its *corps de ballet* were renowned. It had a repertoire of over fifty ballets, including such gems of the classical ballet as *Corsaire, La Fille Mal Gardée,* and *Giselle,* all of which, but for the Russians, would have been lost forever, for *Giselle* had not been performed in Paris since 1868. Two elaborate new ballets were lavishly produced every year. The costumes were made of the best heavy silk and finest velvet, decorated with hand embroidery. Dancers wore stiff corsets, boned bodices and clouds of tulle which fell to below their knees.

At the beginning of the century, the school possessed a collection of great dancing masters: Christian Johansson, the famed Swedish teacher who was nearly ninety; the Italian Enrico Cechetti; the Russians Pavel Gerdt and the brothers Sergei and Nikolai Legat. During the second half of the 19th century the best European virtuosos had been invited to dance in Petersburg. The Russians had studied them carefully, taking from the Italians strength, from the French grace, and infusing it all with the unique Russian spirit and interest in characterization. The ballet had reached an apotheosis with a generation of extraordinary dancers, many of whom went on to become immortals of the dance. Matilda Kschessinska, who had been the mistress of Nicholas II before his marriage, was the reigning ballerina.

In 1891 Anna Pavlova, the illegitimate daughter of a poor laundress, who had studied in a school for peasant children, entered the school. Pavlova was so gifted that she never was in the *corps de ballet,* but in 1899 went straight into solo roles. Ethereal and lyric, she revived memories of the grace and lightness of the great Italian ballerina Taglioni, whom the Russians had so idolized. At the school in 1900 were Tamara Karsavina and an extraordinary young man, Vaslav Nijinsky. Nijinsky was the son of a family of talented itinerant Polish dancers. As a child he traveled with his family all over Russia, seldom staying in one place longer than a month, sleeping with peasants in places where there were no inns. His gifted father, a great classical dancer, gave him lessons and he appeared on the stage for the first time at the age of three. Even while he was at school, his leaps were astounding. Karsavina remembered that one day by chance she saw the boys finishing their classes when one boy not only rose higher than any other, but seemed to stay suspended for a moment in the air. When she asked who he was, his master chuckled and said, "It is Nijinsky. The little devil never comes down with the music."

But the ballet as an institution had become conventionalized. The sets, although opulent, were often heavy and pompous, and the music sometimes unimaginative. It was time for a change, and Mikhail Fokine, a young dancer who taught at the school and later became the ballet master of the theater, accomplished it. Fokine, who was from a merchant family, was half Russian and half German. He made his stage debut in 1898 at the Maryinsky. Not only was he a talented dancer, but proficient on several musical instruments. In his teaching and later in his choreography, Fokine stressed the role and importance of music in ballet, insisting that the dancers, including the *corps*, have an understanding of the music to which they danced. "Music," he said, "is not the mere accompaniment of a rhythmic step, but an organic part of the dance. The quality of choreographic inspiration is determined by the music."

Fokine was an irritable man with a fierce temper. His dancers had to put up with vehement harangues. Often he abruptly left the rehearsal hall and sometimes even threw chairs, but he gave the dancers new freedom in their art. He democratized the *corps*, de-emphasized Italian acrobatics and stressed strong male dancing. Gradually, he liberated the girls from their stiff costumes, which, crested and padded, were almost as rigid as uniforms. For his choreography, he read books on art and archeology, and, as he was a talented painter, he often sketched his suggestions for dancers. He drew plans on the floor, made graphs of movement and composed dances on the stage to music. In a single decade, he revitalized the dance. Two visitors to St. Petersburg deeply influenced his choreographic ideas. The Crown Prince of Siam was studying at the Corps des Pages, and in 1900 a troupe of Siamese court dancers came to the city to perform. In 1907 Isadora Duncan, the American girl from San Francisco, arrived. With her flowing garments and barefoot dancing to "important music," she stunned the Russians and especially impressed Fokine.

For ten years, Fokine was the partner of Pavlova, and for her he created *Les Sylphides, Le Pavillon d'Armide,* and the famous dance monologue, *The Dying Swan,* for a charity performance on December 2, 1907. All these works bore the imprint of his new ideas.

Fokine dreamed not only of liberating ballet from its formality but of an alliance of all the arts, music, dance decor, in ballet productions. His ideas naturally made him gravitate to the group in St. Petersburg who called themselves "The World of Art," who thought in the same way, and who were championing the ideal of the unity of all the arts.

24·THE WORLD OF ART

He painted no pictures, created no productions, ballets or operas; he hardly ever appeared as a critic on questions of art . . . but the inspiration and fire which we professional artists expressed in our work was displayed by Diaghilev in the organizing of everything in which we were associated. He published books, edited the magazine and later directed the difficult and often depressing work of theatrical enterprise. . . . The sphere of advertising and publicity was alien to us, whereas Diaghilev was marvelous at it—he was a born master of the art.

Alexander Benois
Memoirs

What did he want? Three definite things: to reveal Russia to Russia, to reveal Russia to the world, to reveal the world—new—to itself.

Robert Brussel

THE WORLD OF ART group had grown from a circle of school friends who had started meeting together in the 1890's, joined by a mutual interest in the arts and in their opposition to what they saw as the stale, overrealistic tendencies of The

Wanderers. A young man named Alexander Benois, who came from a distinguished family of Venetian and French artists who had emigrated to Russia in the early 19th century, was the heart of the original group. Benois's father was architect of the Imperial court; his uncle, Alberto Cavos, had designed two opera houses in St. Petersburg, as well as the Bolshoi Theater in Moscow. The Benois household was always full of painters, sculptors and architects. Alexander Benois, himself an artist, was a storehouse of knowledge of art history and was especially interested in the art of the theater.

His close friend and a charter member of the group was Lev Bakst, then still known as Rosenberg, a prim, redheaded fellow, the son of a respected Jewish merchant family, who was then a student at the Academy of Fine Arts. There were also Walter Nouvel, who was interested in music, and Dmitry Filosofov, a student of philosophy, who in 1890 introduced into the group his eighteen-year-old cousin, newly arrived in town and enrolled in the School of Jurisprudence. His name was Sergei Diaghilev.

Diaghilev came from an old family of country gentry; his father had been an officer in the Chevaliers Gardes. When his wife died giving birth to Sergei, his father had remarried and the family went to live in Sergei's grandfather's house in Perm. Diaghilev's stepmother was a remarkable woman who had the greatest influence on his life, and he loved her deeply. She gave him her own love for music, and strengthened his independence and determination by telling him, "Never say cannot. It is a word you must forget. For when one wants to, one always can."

Diaghilev's family represented one of the finest sides of the spacious society of those days, the all-pervasive interest in the arts among gentry and professional people. These were people who gave their leisure time, and often whatever fortunes they had, to the pursuit of artistic ideals.

Thanks to his talented stepmother, the Diaghilev house in Perm became a center for culture in the provincial town. A music group was formed and a teacher in a Classical High School who was also a talented pianist gave concerts. At large family gatherings, piano, violin and chamber music were played, and impromptu performances held of operas of which everybody knew the scores by heart. In his grandfather's library was a large collection of illustrated books of the great museums of the world. The whole atmosphere of Diaghilev's childhood was permeated with a love for art and he went on to devote his life to the discovery of talent and the creation of art. His life in the country also gave him a deep love of all things Russian, which never left him.

Diaghilev's aunt who lived in St. Petersburg was a fine singer who had on occasion used Mussorgsky as an accompanist. In the manner of those days, she was an outspoken lady, deeply interested in politics and women's rights. Her husband held an important position in the Ministry of Justice. But, although he was well connected, at first the sophisticated little group of friends found Diaghilev somewhat arrogant, the country cousin putting on airs. His appearance was unusual. He had a large head that seemed too large even for his massive body, dark expressive eyes, a small, neat mustache and a streak of white through his dark hair which earned him the name "Chinchilla." He carried himself with an air of superiority, wore a monocle and dressed elegantly with fancy waistcoats and a top hat. The group found his eager way of seeking out the "right" people and dropping his card around town annoying and pretentious. They thought him intellectually inferior; he did not show the proper respect for their god, Wagner, nor did he know any Italian melodies. Instead, he knew Glinka's operas by heart and loved Borodin, Mussorgsky and, especially, Tchaikovsky to such an extent that the group made fun of him.

The friends held weekly artistic discussions at the Benois house, with each member giving a paper or lecturing on some subject of interest, and Benois explaining the principles of art with charm and intelligence. Diaghilev attended the discussions; he sometimes yawned, but he soaked up everything. In those early days the friends could not imagine that behind the appearance of a dandyish dilettante were concealed a stubborn will and a perseverance that could overcome all obstacles, that they had met the perfect collaborator, the man who would bring all their ideas to life.

Music was Diaghilev's greatest interest then. He dreamed of becoming a composer. He had a strong baritone voice and when he met with his friends they sang entire operas through. He composed a duo for soprano and baritone to the words of Pushkin's *Boris Godunov* but, to his intense disappointment, his work made not the slightest impression on the group of friends. When he took it to Rimsky-Korsakov, under whom he was studying musical theory, the composer was so discouraging that Diaghilev never composed anything again. Instead he turned to art, with Benois as his mentor.

When, at twenty-one, Diaghilev inherited a modest fortune, he began to buy paintings and made trips abroad in 1893 and 1895. Benois provided him with introductions to artists of the Munich group. He went to Berlin and bought paintings by Lenbach and had long discussions in the studios of German artists. He went to Italy, bought antiques in Florence and fell in love with Venice. In 1895 in Dieppe, he met the painters Jacques Blanche and Aubrey Beardsley. Wrote Benois, "He stayed at the best hotels, rode about town in a closed carriage, dressed elegantly, wore an eyeglass (although he did not need one), was never separated from a very tall top hat. On his visiting cards he appeared as Serge de Diaghilev." He bought pictures and gave wonderful dinners in restaurants; for foreigners, said Benois, Diaghilev was the very picture of the "real Russian boyar." (His inheritance lasted him about three years.) Diaghilev was a great charmer. Indeed, writes Benois, "If he wanted something . . . it was almost impossible to resist the pressure he exerted, often very endearingly. . . ." He had such a passion for celebrities that he would simply present himself at their doors and, thanks to his charm, always came away with a signed photograph. Thus on his travels he met Zola, Gounod and Verdi, whose photographs, along with many others, he carefully arranged on tables in his St. Petersburg apartment. He also absorbed all that he could in Russia. He went to Yasnaya Polyana to meet Tolstoy. He traveled to Moscow where he became a close friend of Mamontov, the railroad baron, and met all of the group of artists around him. Mamontov made a strong impression on him, deeply influencing Diaghilev.

By the time he returned to St. Petersburg, his taste was honed. He had won himself a place as a full-fledged member of the group, which now had some new additions—Benois's nephew, the painter Eugene Lanceray; the painter Konstantin Somov; the French cultural attaché Charles Birlé, who worshiped Gauguin, Seurat and Van Gogh; and Alfred Nourok, who had a keen interest in the work of Beardsley. The group had also taken on a name; it now officially called itself "The World of Art." Their slogan was "art, pure and unfettered," a rebellion against the prevailing standards of both the Academy and the all-powerful realistic Wanderers. Their ideal was the solidarity and unity of all the arts; their aim to create work that was national but parallel with Western European thought, something which Peter the Great would have heartily approved. For them, individuality above all was vital.

Increasingly, the strong-willed Diaghilev became their leader. In 1897, when he was twenty-five, he organized his first art exhibition, showing the works of English and German watercolorists, and wrote a challenging article in the newspaper *Novosti*. "It is time," said he that "we stopped admiring these inartistic canvases with policemen, rural guards, students in red shirts and young women with cropped hair."

423

In those days Russian artists traveled frequently, freely and widely. In 1897 Kandinsky left his law practice in Moscow to devote himself to art, and went to join a group of Russians who had formed an art colony in Munich. Many of The World of Art painters turned toward Paris. Benois divided his time between Paris, Lugano and St. Petersburg. He lived for two years in Versailles and studied Delacroix, Daumier and Degas. Bakst resigned from the Academy because his professors had reprimanded him for his bold and unorthodox use of color and tried to turn him to sculpture. With Konstantin Somov, he left for a stay in Paris. Lanceray also came to Paris and studied with Whistler; Bakst and Benois also frequented Whistler's studio. In Europe the friends continued their discussions and made study trips all over France, Germany and Italy. Upon his return to Petersburg, Bakst became the drawing master of the family of Grand Duke Vladimir, Nicholas II's uncle, married a daughter of Tretyakov and painted society beauties. He was well on the way to becoming an official artist when luckily Benois returned, and convinced him that his talents demanded more of him.

In 1898 Diaghilev mounted another exhibition, this time of Finnish and Russian painters. Later that year, when the group decided to found an art journal, it was the energetic Diaghilev who raised the money from two patrons—his friend Savva Mamontov and Princess Tenisheva, a wealthy woman who surrounded herself with artists, commissioned many works of art, and founded extensive studios for the development of native peasant crafts on her estate at Talashkino. Diaghilev became the editor of the new magazine, Bakst its designer, and Benois the literary editor. Valentin Serov, one of Russia's finest painters, also joined them. Diaghilev greatly respected and admired Serov, who was seven years older than he, and it was Serov who became the final arbiter of disputes on the magazine board.

Diaghilev had found his vocation. Without being proficient in any of the arts, he had a creative appreciation for all of them. His organizing ability was extraordinary. He had a genius for discerning talent and he could fire anyone, even the most indifferent, with his own infectious enthusiasm.

It was the idea of the new journal, *The World of Art*, to put forward new Russian artists, to widen the artistic interests of the public and to provide them with the latest information on the art of all countries. Diaghilev designed the cover of the magazine, decided its size and its challenging tone. *The World of Art* pioneered the art journal of quality in Russia. It was lavishly printed on beautiful paper, with excellent reproductions. Diaghilev and Filosofov dug out of the Academy of Art old type characters dating from the time of Empress Elizabeth. Bakst worked all night with the printers, setting type and working on layouts.

In a pattern that became his style, the meetings of the editorial board took place in Diaghilev's apartment, around his large dining-room table. First there was good food and wine and then ideas flowed. Always in attendance was Diaghilev's old nurse, a wizened old peasant woman of indeterminate age who had been present at his birth. Although she had lived through the emancipation and been freed by it, she heartily disapproved of the reform and was constantly grumbling about "newfangled nonsense." Totally devoted to Diaghilev's family, she guarded their privileges ferociously. Diaghilev worried, shocked and teased her, then he would kiss her—she worshipped him. Her entire work consisted of preparing and pouring afternoon and evening tea. Through all their editorial meetings, she sat by the samovar and looked after the tea and jam. She was such an essential part of the room and the life of the group that in 1905, when Bakst painted Diaghilev's portrait, he painted the old nurse sitting stolidly behind him.

The World of Art had been in existence barely two years when Mamontov suffered business reverses, and Tenisheva, alarmed at the notoriety of the group, withdrew her support. At the time, Serov was doing a portrait of Nicholas II. This painting, one of the most revealing portraits of royalty ever painted, became one of his finest works. Typically, boldly, Diaghilev asked Serov to approach the Emperor and ask him to subsidize their magazine. Nicholas II agreed, and provided ten thousand rubles a year until the Russo-Japanese war in 1904. Then, because of its lavish format, the magazine could no longer support itself, and it ceased publication.

In the six years of its existence, *The World of Art* discussed in its pages all that was best in art, both past and contemporary. In his leading editorials, Diaghilev set the tone: "One of the greatest merits of our times is to recognize individuality under every guise and at every epoch. The creator must love only beauty. It is blasphemous to force ideas. . . ." Because of the group's ideal of the unity of all the arts and their belief that one art flowed into another, they devoted many pages to the decorative arts, outstanding Russian craftsmen and ancient Russian art. It was an idea of the time, championed at Abramtsevo and Talashkino, to bring the esthetic of art into the design of furniture, interior decoration and the adornment of simple objects. The talented Vrubel designed balalaikas, clay stoves, and murals for hotels. In 1900, *The World of Art* published an article on the artist-jeweler Fabergé's Easter eggs. It published articles by Maeterlinck,

Grieg ("Mozart and Ourselves"), Nietzsche ("Wagner in Bayreuth") and Ruskin. Kandinsky contributed articles from Munich and Grabar wrote an article on Picasso and Matisse, sending reproductions from Paris. *The World of Art* published the works of the poets Balmont, Briusov and Blok; it even published an essay praising American millionaires for their collections of art. In almost every issue, Benois wrote on art with a skill that won him the reputation of being one of the foremost art historians of Russia. The magazine promoted interest in the preservation of the monuments and architecture of Petersburg. Mamontov's opera company, with its exciting set designs by leading painters, had come to Petersburg in 1898, and in the pages of *The World of Art* the editors urged the idea of artists doing stage designs and discussed theater productions. *The World of Art* inaugurated and championed a school of book illustration which was second only to their innovations in theatrical decoration. Bilibin, Lanceray and Doboujinsky, one of whose pupils was a young man named Marc Chagall, all did illustrations for the magazine. In the last year of the magazine, Diaghilev approached Chekhov to ask him to become co-editor.

Every year *The World of Art* held art exhibitions which included the best of the art of the period. In the first exhibition the painters Bakst, Benois, Golovin, Vrubel, Levitan, Nesterov and Repin were exhibited side by side with Degas, Puvis de Chavannes, Whistler and many other Europeans, reflecting the artistic ideas of the world. There was a decorative arts section with embroideries and pottery from Abramtsevo in Russia, Lalique from France and Tiffany from America.

The greatest of all these exhibitions was the historic exhibit of Russian portraits from 1705 to 1905, which Diaghilev personally organized with the style and flair that was his trademark. He had written a brilliant monograph on the 18th-century painter Levitsky, and had become very interested in portrait painters. For this historic exhibition, Diaghilev traveled tirelessly all over the country, talking to governors of provinces, visiting estates, persuading owners to let him rummage into their attics and cellars, collecting and finding portraits. With patience, energy and dedication, he pursued people for loans of furniture and objects. To evoke the great days of the past, he chose a dramatic site for the exhibition: the beautiful Tauride Palace that Catherine II had built for Potemkin and which was empty and unused. Three thousand paintings, sculptures and objects were each given harmonious settings to reflect the period and styles of two hundred years of Russian glory. Bakst designed a sculptured court with green trellises in the French style, to form a magnificent Winter Garden. Benois and

Diaghilev hung the paintings. Nicholas II was the patron, the Imperial family came for the opening and a banquet was given in Diaghilev's honor. At that dinner he gave a speech in which he uttered these strangely prophetic words: "We are the witness of the greatest moment of summing up in history, in the name of a new and unknown culture, which will be created by us, and which also will sweep us away."

The years from Nicholas II's coronation in 1896 through 1918 were a period of such glittering accomplishment in the arts and sciences that the period is known as the "Silver Age" or the "Russian Renaissance." The ferment of activity included politics, philosophy, science, and unparalleled creativity in every branch of the arts. The activities of *The World of Art* inspired a whole range of new artistic endeavor in those creative years of the early 20th century. A whole group of new art journals was formed—*The Scales, The Treasures of Art, The Golden Fleece* and *Apollon,* a journal which included the work of all the leading poets and writers of the new Symbolist and Acmeist movements, as well as presenting articles and commentaries on all the leading painters. The bookstores were overflowing and the book-buying public so enthusiastic that well-known authors like Chekhov earned enough from their writings to buy estates; the poet Alexander Blok was paid five gold rubles a line. Such was the Russian love for poetry that well-known poets were mobbed by enthusiastic audiences. People, not only in Moscow and St. Petersburg but all over the provinces, knew the works of Blok and many other poets by heart.

Violent literary debates took place in the pages of the journals *Grif* and *Scorpion.* Inspired by the activities of *The World of Art,* Walter Nouvel and his friends formed a society which presented evenings of contemporary music and introduced St. Petersburg to the new music of Debussy, Franck, Ravel, Schoenberg and Prokofiev. Filosofov started a magazine called *The New Path,* which explored the religious and mystical trends of the new philosophers Solovyov and Berdyaev.

Art exhibitions proliferated. The Moscow artists formed a group called "The 36." Mikhail Larionov and Natalya Goncharova, neo-primitives who looked to peasant art and crafts with their vivid colors and animal forms for their inspiration, held the "Blue Rose" exhibition in 1907, and in 1909 their exhibition included the work of the young Marc Chagall. At the "Golden Fleece" exhibition in 1908 and 1909 the works of avant-garde Russian artists and French Impressionists hung side by side.

There was a prevailing atmosphere of culture. Businessmen and professional people were amateur musicians, poets and writers, and they provided a great public for the career artists. Inspired and influenced by Mamontov and the activities of *The World of Art,* the Imperial Theaters began to invite painters to design their productions. First, it was Korovin and Golovin at the Maryinsky Theater. Bakst was invited to design the sets for *Oedipus Rex* at the Alexandrinsky Theater in 1904, and in 1907 Benois designed the sets and costumes for *Le Pavillon d'Armide,* one of his most successful productions. On stage there was a synthesis of all the arts—music, dancing, painting. By 1904, Russian set designers were the finest in the world. Painters of every style and school found expression in the theater; they designed for puppet theaters, cabarets and even the circus.

In 1899–1900 Diaghilev was asked to edit the annual Imperial Theaters Yearbook, a job which he did brilliantly, his work accurately reflecting the fine state of the Russian theater at the time. He was asked to supervise the production of a ballet, *Sylvia,* at the Maryinsky, but his autocratic personality annoyed many of the conservative members of the theater committee, who considered that he was undermining the traditions of the theater and, after a dispute that had a great deal to do with pride, he resigned.

It was at that time that Diaghilev, finding himself blocked in his plans to reorganize the Imperial Theater, turned his prodigious energy toward Europe. He had always been different from others of his group in his passionate determination to show Europe what Russia could do. Even at the time of his first art exhibition in 1897 he had said, "I want to nurse Russian painting, cleanse it, and bring it to the notice of the West, make it big and known."

In 1900 Diaghilev had gone to Paris for the Universal Exhibition. There Russia had scored artistic triumphs: Serov won a gold Medal of Honor, Korovin and Malyutin gold medals for painting, Golovin and Vrubel honors for applied arts. Seeing this success, Diaghilev boldly decided that the time was right for mounting a large exhibition of Russian painting, much of which was totally unknown in Europe at that time, and he decided to make himself the unofficial ambassador of Russian art. Before he had a cent, in 1906, he leased space at the Grand Palais in Paris for a large exhibition of Russian art. The exhibition was to be, in Diaghilev's words, "a glimpse of our art as perceived by the modern eye." Grand Duke Vladimir, uncle of the Tsar and a great admirer of Diaghilev, agreed to be the honorary chairman. The exhibit occupied twelve rooms; there were 750 items, many lent to Diaghilev by the Imperial palaces, museums and collections. As Diaghilev always put the greatest importance on setting, Bakst once again arranged his trelliswork Winter Garden. To set off the exhibit of old icons, a special room was hung with the rare old golden brocades of which priests' robes were made. Musicians and singers performed, and such was the impact and success of the exhibition that the French offered Diaghilev the Legion of Honor. He suggested that it should be given instead to Benois and Bakst.

The following year Diaghilev organized a series of concerts of the music of Russian composers, including Glinka, Mussorgsky and Borodin. (To his intense disappointment, French musicians rejected his beloved Tchaikovsky, considering him "vulgar.") It was Diaghilev's idea that the composers should perform their own compositions, so at these historic concerts, Rimsky-Korsakov conducted, Scriabin played his compositions and Rachmaninov performed his piano concerto. Many compositions now world famous were first heard at these Paris Opera concerts.

The fame of Mussorgsky in the West dates from that time, for it was his music that made the greatest impression. The singing of Chaliapin created such a sensation that Diaghilev immediately decided to present, in 1908, the entire *Boris Godunov,* of which only fragments had been played. The painters Golovin, Yuon, Lanceray, Bilibin and Benois all worked on the decor for this production. The scenery was painted on the stage of Catherine the Great's Hermitage Theater. Ivan Bilibin, a painter and illustrator, expert on the history and costumes of old Russia, was called in to help design the costumes. The floor, the beds and the tables of Diaghilev's rooms were piled with bright-colored silks. He and Benois spent hours combing the flea markets of St. Petersburg and Moscow, buying from Tatar and Jewish dealers all the gold embroidered 18th-century neckcloths they could find—more than a hundred of them, which they unhesitatingly cut up to make the collars of the boyars' costumes. For the first time, the West saw the extraordinary standards of Russian theatrical productions, and the public was dazzled. Chaliapin instantly became the most famous basso in the world.

All things had come together. Russian musicians, painters, actors were all thinking the same way. The time was right for Diaghilev's greatest and boldest venture. For the spring of 1909, he decided to arrange another season of opera. He did not originally plan to include ballets, in which he was not particularly interested. But Benois, a great balletomane, persuaded him that the theater, and most especially the ballet, was the best way in which they could realize all their artistic aims. Ballet, argued Benois, was an interesting art form which by some miracle had survived in Russia when it had withered everywhere else; in the

Maryinsky was a group of superior dancers who had just come of age, and there was a new era of choreography with Fokine. Diaghilev hesitated, but finally agreed that they would present alternate evenings of opera and ballet. Fokine was invited to be ballet master.

The artistic committee was convened for a special meeting in Diaghilev's dining room to discuss the idea. Pencils and papers were placed in front of every member. On a small table stood the samovar, biscuits, jam and several plates of Russian sweets. Vasily, Diaghilev's faithful manservant, and his old nurse once again poured tea, while the group threw out their ideas. Around the table were Benois, sitting intently with his pince-nez perched on his nose; Bakst, with his curly red hair, fastidiously dressed and smelling of scent; General Bezobrasov, a great ballet connoisseur; Walter Nouvel, authority on music and now an official of the court; Valentin Serov; Dr. Botkin, the Tsar's physician; Tcherepnin, the composer; and many others of the elite of St. Petersburg artistic worlds. They decided to include in their program *Le Pavillon d'Armide*, the recent production of the Maryinsky designed by Benois; *Les Sylphides*, newly choreographed by Fokine; and a production of the Maryinsky *Egyptian Nights*, renamed *Cleopatra*, for which Diaghilev proposed alterations to the music. Suddenly excited by the idea, Bakst enthusiastically exclaimed, "There will be huge temples on the banks of the Nile. Columns. Sultry day, and a great many lovely women with beautiful bodies."

At first, all went swimmingly. Grand Duke Vladimir agreed to be the patron of the venture. Diaghilev was to receive a large subsidy from the Imperial Treasury, as well as the loan of scenery and costumes from the Maryinsky for some of the operas and ballets. But, in the winter of 1909, Grand Duke Vladimir died. Opposition to Diaghilev's project arose among the conservative members of the theater, who thought that he should take Petipa's ballets and who found the collaborators "too modern" and "decadent." Suddenly, no money was available from the Imperial Treasury. Luckily Diaghilev loved combat. Undaunted, he rushed off to Paris, and with his charm and connections managed to raise money from friends there. Despite every last-minute obstacle, the season that was to make artistic history went forward.

The Russians had taken the seed of Western art. They had absorbed and nourished it in their own particular way. They were now about to return it to the West as something astonishingly new.

25 · DIAGHILEV AND THE BALLETS RUSSES

On May 1, as soon as the Maryinsky season was over, Diaghilev's Grand Embassy left in waves for Paris. Borrowed from the Imperial Theaters were forty-two dancers from St. Petersburg and thirteen from Moscow; Diaghilev had over-ridden the objections of his artistic committee and insisted on having the best from both theaters. Bakst, Benois, Fokine and other members of the artistic committee, the great basso Fyodor Chaliapin and his Chinese manservant who accompanied him wherever he went, the composer Tcherepnin who was to conduct the large orchestra, choirs of singers and numerous groups of walk-ons, plus crates of scenery and costumes, all converged on Paris.

Nijinsky's mother and sister arrived to see him perform and along with them arrived large numbers of friends and relatives of other performers, who came just for the experience. Paris overflowed with Russians staying in little hotels all over the city.

At the last minute, the French, upon learning that there was to be *ballet* as well as opera, huffily declared that they could not permit their august Opéra to be used for mere dancing performances.*

---

* To show the low regard in which ballet was held in the West as late as 1910, the *Encyclopaedia Britannica* wrote of it, "a spectacle the chief interest of which is quite independent of

431

Undeterred, the indomitable Diaghilev arranged to rent the Théâtre du Châtelet, a dilapidated building used for melodramas. As he always put the greatest importance on the proper setting for his productions, with a burst of energy, in the short two weeks before opening night, he set about to remodel the theater. Several rows of stalls were ripped out to make way for the large orchestra; the walls were covered with red cloth, carpets laid, flowers and plants set all about the entrance. The stage was overhauled and the lighting improved. Dancers rehearsed for long hours either in the rooms under the roof ("an atmosphere to breed salamanders in," wrote the ballerina Karsavina), or on the stage among the carpenters as they banged away and moved scenery. There was so much noise, the dancers could hardly hear the piano. Fokine shouted himself hoarse, tore his hair and every day grew thinner. Bakst imperturbably knelt on the stage throwing paint on the scenery. There was no time for class; dancers did their warming-up exercises holding onto the scenery or a chair. There was no time for meals, so Diaghilev grandly sent out to the neighboring restaurant, Larue's, whose owner had once been chef to the tsar, for caviar and blini, roasts, pâtés and salads, which were set up in their silver service on packing crates, while behind the back cloth strayed a flock of sheep needed for the ballet *Le Pavillon d'Armide*.

The program was designed by Paris' *enfant terrible*, the poet and artist Jean Cocteau. Valentin Serov had done the poster—a charcoal and white drawing on blue-gray paper of Anna Pavlova in the long romantic tutu designed by Benois for *Les Sylphides*. On kiosks and walls, it blossomed all over the city, becoming the emblem of Les Ballets Russes.

Diaghilev and his Parisian manager, Gabriel Astruc, had carefully composed the audience for the gala opening night to include a glittering mixture of the most august names of the aristocracy and the government of France as well as a host of famous artists and writers: the sculptor Rodin; the musicians Saint-Säens, Ravel and Lalo; Paquin and Caron of the *haute couture*; the great actress of the Comédie Française, Cécile Sorel, and the chanteuse Yvette Guilbert; dancers from the Opéra, and the American dancing sensation Isadora Duncan. Astruc had hit on the ingenious idea of sending fifty-two invitations to the loveliest young actresses and dancers of Paris and seating them all together in the front row of the balcony, carefully alternating blondes and brunettes—a bevy of beauty that

---

dancing. . . . Thousands of pounds are spent on dressing a small army of women who do little but march about the stage." Russia was not even mentioned, although at that time Pavlova, Nijinsky, Kschessinska were dancing on the stage of the Maryinsky.

caused such a stir that a newspaper devoted a front-page article to the phenomenon, calling it Astruc's *corbeille* (basket) of flowers. From then on, Parisian theaters renamed the first row of the balcony *la corbeille*.

May 19, 1909, was a great date in the history of ballet and of Russian art, a night when Russia dramatically introduced new concepts of beauty to the West. The curtain rose on *Le Pavillon d'Armide*, a production of the Maryinsky Theater designed by Benois as a glorification of the French 18th century. Benois, who had lived in Versailles for two years, took great pride in showing the *style noble* even better than the French could do. For the Paris production, he had designed entirely new costumes. Onto a delicate scene of pink, green and blue stepped Nijinsky in the courtly male dancing attire of the 18th century—a white, yellow and silver costume trimmed with silk festoons, lace ruffles and ermine tails; a silk turban on his head and a jeweled collar high on his neck. At the end of a spectacular *pas de trois*, Nijinsky executed a series of airy leaps and, spurred by the applause of the audience, unexpectedly decided to leap off the stage. Almost as if he were taking flight, he soared into the wings; no one saw him land. Paris had never seen such a leap, and it produced the effect of an electric shock. The astonished audience erupted with applause.

After the exquisitely mounted spectacle in the colors of Sèvres porcelain, the audience was suddenly transported into another and unknown world—the desolate steppe of the days of Kiev for scenes from Borodin's *Prince Igor*. To give the illusion of unlimited space, the artist, Nikolai Roerich, had abolished the wings and painted his scene on a curved canvas. The set was all mottled gold sky stretching toward an unlimited horizon, with the brick red and gray rounded tents of the Polovtsy nomads in the foreground. To the music of Borodin's powerful, melodic score, slave girls undulated and sang. Then, a crowd of barbaric warriors, their faces smeared with soot, their coats green and mottled red and ocher, erupted onto the stage. Frenziedly they danced the wild Polovetsian dances, which were to be considered among Fokine's greatest creations. The whole whirling scene ended with the leader of the Khan's warriors, played by the dynamic character dancer from Moscow, Adolph Bolm, charging at the audience, spinning in the air and landing on one knee and fiercely aiming his bow at the public. Ballet in Paris conspicuously lacked male dancers; the virility of the male dancing in the Polovetsian dances was a revelation and the audience went wild.*

* The virile erotic overtones of the ballet proved so shocking in London that when it was performed there in 1911, a hundred bejeweled dowagers rose as a group and imperiously streamed out of the theater, exclaiming, "It isn't dancing—it's just savage prancing about!"

The excitement was so great that at the intermission the audience simply invaded the stage. Karsavina and Nijinsky, trying to warm up for their lifts and turns for the next ballet, had to dodge through the surging mass to the cries of "He is a prodigy!" and "It is she!" When order was finally restored, the company continued with *Festin,* a divertissement of character and national dances which took place in a medieval Russian banqueting hall. It was a rich potpourri of pieces and music from several Russian composers, including Tchaikovsky, Glinka and Glazunov, with gorgeous costumes by Bilibin, Korovin and Bakst. Karsavina and Nijinsky danced a *pas de deux* with Nijinsky as a turbaned prince wearing a mustard, lime green and golden tunic sewn with pearls and topazes. When they came on, the courier of the company, who was standing in the wings, exclaimed, "Good Lord! I have never seen such a public. You would have thought their seats were on fire!"

The next day the newspapers erupted with praise. One Paris newspaper printed Nijinsky's picture over a full page. He was hailed as "the angel, the genius, the dancer divine!" Of Karsavina they wrote, "Everything in her is poetry." One critic, in a phrase which must have specially pleased *The World of Art,* exulted, "Like a gust of fresh wind . . . dance has come back to us from the North. The Russian ballets are a triumph of unity!"

On succeeding evenings of that first historic season, ballet played on alternate nights with opera. Karsavina wrote, "Something akin to a miracle happened every night . . . the stage and the audience trembled in a unison of emotion." Chaliapin sang the role of Ivan the Terrible in Rimsky-Korsakov's opera, wearing sumptuous costumes by Golovin and Bilibin which were accurate in every historic detail. The next evening the curtain rose on *Les Sylphides,* choreographed by Fokine to the music of Chopin, danced by Anna Pavlova, Nijinsky and Karsavina. When the curtain went up on this performance the audience gasped; a critic wrote that "the dancers were like blue pearls." Of Pavlova they said, "She is to dance what Racine is to poetry, Poussin to painting, Gluck to music."

Also on the program was the ballet adapted from the Maryinsky production of *Nuits d'Egypte,* renamed *Cleopatra,* with music by six Russian composers and an exotic Bakst setting with huge columns and pink gods framing a glimpse of the Nile. The sinuous Ida Rubenstein, a private pupil of Fokine's, played the Queen of the Nile. In an entrance of stunning theater, she was brought onto the stage in a sarcophagus, wrapped like a mummy in twelve veils of different colors which were ceremoniously unwound, one by one, with the queen imperiously throwing off the last one, revealing herself to Paris. (Bubbled a critic, "She is too beautiful, like a strong essence of perfume.")

The Ballets Russes was the rage of Paris. The dancers were feted; a reception was given for them at the Quai d'Orsay where they performed Russian dances. Cartier copied the jeweled choker that Nijinsky had worn in *Le Pavillon d'Armide* and, the entire winter, elegant ladies wore imitations in jet, diamonds and pearls. The society of Paris vied with each other to entertain them. At one memorable party, the dancers performed in a garden among clumps of softly lit trees. Tamara Karsavina had her dressing room filled with white roses by admirers each day. The foremost critic of Paris fell in love with her and, piling his car full of pillows, would drive her about; after one dinner, Marcel Proust insisted on escorting her home.

Diaghilev had triumphed. He had proved that the art form conceived in Russia by Bakst, Benois and Fokine was a wonder of the world. In their first season, they had conquered Paris, with its sophisticated and discerning public. Benois, looking back on those first evenings, wrote with pride, "Every participant in the Russian season . . . felt that he was bringing to the entire world all that is Russian, all that comprises his greatest pride; Russian spiritual culture, Russian art. . . . Not Borodin, not Rimsky-Korsakov, not Chaliapin or Golovin or Diaghilev triumphed in Paris, but all Russian culture . . . the inimitable features of Russian art, its great sense of conviction, its freshness and spontaneity, its wild force and at the same time, its extraordinary refinement."

. . .

After their triumph, the "committee" happily dispersed on trips all over Europe; Diaghilev, Nijinsky and Bakst went off for a holiday in Venice. When they once again reassembled about the large table in Diaghilev's St. Petersburg dining room in the winter of 1909–10, Diaghilev announced that after such a success, it was now no longer enough simply to borrow productions from the Maryinsky. For their second season they had to create entirely new ballets.

Before each member was the usual large pad of paper and a pencil. Diaghilev sat at the head of the table with his large black exercise book, making entries. Once again the collaborators began to throw out ideas, their meetings marked by the intense creativity that distinguished all of Diaghilev's enterprises. Karsavina, who was present at some of these sessions, wrote: "Unrepeatable those days . . . unimaginable the boyish exuberance of those pioneers of Russian art." There was

Bakst, "full of exotic . . . fantastic ideas"; Benois, "inspiration coupled with clear thought"; Roerich, "all mystery"; and Doboujinsky, "a great romantic, shy, naive and simple."

After much discussion they decided to mount *Schéhérazade* to the music of Rimsky-Korsakov and to present *Giselle,* which had not been seen in Paris since 1868, with Pavlova and Nijinsky. Then Diaghilev made a surprise announcement. He had for some time wanted to mount a new ballet based on the Russian legend of the Firebird. Since the first composer he had approached could not complete the score, he had commissioned the ballet from an unknown twenty-six-year-old composer named Igor Stravinsky. He had heard Stravinsky's short symphonic poem "Fireworks" at a concert some months before and it had so delighted him that he had immediately approached the young composer with his proposition. (Glazunov had huffed on hearing it, "no talent . . . only dissonances." Happily, Diaghilev heard differently.)

Fokine read through several collections of folk tales, but the group finally decided that no single story was entirely adequate and they evolved the scenario by piecing together parts of several versions, taking ideas from various people as the story developed, even from the writer Remisov, who sometimes dropped in and bewildered the friends with his strange tales. "There are Bellyboshkies," he said one day, "evil sort of creatures, some with tails and some without." The word sounded so picturesque that the Dance of the Bellyboshkies in the train of the wicked sorcerer Kaschei grew out of it. Fokine worked as closely with Stravinsky as Petipa had with Tchaikovsky in the development of the music, going over it section by section as it was being written, the two appealing to Diaghilev wherever they disagreed over tempi.

Stravinsky was present at rehearsals, playing passages over and over so forcefully that he almost demolished the piano. Upon first hearing the new music of *The Firebird,* the dancers were dismayed; to them, it hardly sounded like music at all. Stravinsky hammered out rhythms, hummed loudly, not worrying if he hit wrong notes. Serenely confident, Diaghilev, who prided himself on seeing genius where others saw eccentricity, turned to Karsavina and said, "Mark him well, he is a man on the edge of celebrity." As he was so often, Diaghilev was right.

June 25, 1910, marked the day when Europe first heard the new sound of Stravinsky. *The Firebird* had its premiere in the august Paris Opéra itself. The music of the young composer was a revelation. Diaghilev's inspired choice of Stravinsky for *The Firebird* was the beginning of a great collaboration which was to last twenty years and give the world many masterpieces. The composer was called and recalled to the stage to acknowledge the applause of the audience. Claude Debussy came on stage to embrace him and invite him to dinner. In the evenings that followed, Stravinsky basked in his new celebrity, meeting all the *beau monde* as well as being introduced to Marcel Proust, Paul Claudel, Sarah Bernhardt and many other luminaries. Diaghilev did not see the first historic performance from his usual seat in the theater. Fokine had worried so much about the complicated lighting of the production that, to reassure him, Diaghilev was backstage working the lights personally.

If *The Firebird* was a triumph for Fokine and Stravinsky, *Schéhérazade* was the triumph of Bakst. For this ballet he designed a setting of the exotic and voluptuous Orient which became the most famous stage decor of the age, transforming fashion and decoration for the next fifteen years. Boldly, lavishly, Bakst used rich color in totally new and daring combinations. He was the first to mix blue and green on the stage; an intense jewel blue and green dominated his all-over scheme. He used no flats, but simply splashed paint on the vivid walls and ceilings of the harem. A huge looped curtain, apple green striped with sky blue, spotted with pink roses and large circular patterns in black and gold, framed the left-hand side of the stage. From it hung enormous golden lamps. In the blue background were immense doors of silver, bronze, gold and blue; on the floor coral red carpets, rose and pink rugs, piled with heaps of cushions. The Shah's divan was approached by a staircase supported by two strange carytids. What one critic called "Bakst's debauch of color" was so intoxicating, so startling and exciting that again and again, each time the ballet was performed, audiences spontaneously broke into applause when they saw the sets. Bakst's invention in the design of costumes has never been surpassed. He revealed and amplified the human body with his designs, elongating its line with feathers, highlighting movement with veils and jewels. There were blue, orange and crimson turbaned khans; scarlet eunuchs; diaphanously clad rose, pink and green odalisques and jeweled ladies of the harem; braceleted Negroes with bunched metallic lamé trousers linked to their brassieres by ropes of pearls.

For his role as the chief slave, Nijinsky painted himself a wonderful prune color with a silvery sheen that contrasted with his gold trousers. It was all unforgettable, the ballet ending with a slaughter of the wayward harem and slaves by the enraged Shah. Nijinsky, half feline, half human, leaping great distances with controlled power, inspired in the critics a whole string of animal descriptions—

"half cat, half snake," "a panther," "fiendishly agile, feminine and yet wholly terrifying," "a stallion with distended nostrils, full of energy." Renoir loved the ballet. A friend said it inspired the great artist with "wild enthusiasm." Marcel Proust said simply, "I never saw anything so beautiful."

Instantly, Bakst was established as the greatest stage designer in the world. After the first performance, not only the theater, but dressmakers, interior decorators, jewelers and all branches of decoration were affected for many years. In his ateliers the great Paris couturier Paul Poiret transformed women into svelte creatures with his harem-draped skirts and pants, and turbans with egret feathers. Until that time only flower scents had been permissible for genteel ladies; now exotic perfumes with names like "Maharajah," "Le Fruit Defendu" and "Shalimar" filled the air. Jewelers brought out ropes of pearls ending in tassels of seed pearls, gold and coral. Cartier was inspired to set emeralds and sapphires together for the first time. Rooms were paneled with exotic woods, and piled with pillows; lampshades quivered with tassels.

Before the Russian ballets, in dress and interior decoration, it was unthinkable to mix blue and green, orange and cerise. After them, suddenly vermilion, coral, the orange of zinnias and marigolds, the green of malachite, lemon, eggplant, intense turquoise and lapis lazuli juxtaposed with gold and silver bloomed everywhere. In the month preceding the first ballet season of 1909, the colors of fashion were sober and muted; myrtle green and navy blue, taupe and mauve all seen through a layer of gray chiffon. By 1911 all of this had completely changed. Colors suddenly are described as "Rose Vif," "Nuits d'Orient," "Jonquil." In 1914 the English journal *The Studio* said, "Art has danced to the strains of the Russian ballet, leaving here and there lingering notes on dress fabrics, wallpapers and cushions." Fifteen years after *Schéhérazade*, in 1925, the art historian Gabriel Moury wrote, "There is no doubt that the influence of the Russian ballet, not only on theatrical design, but on fashion, books, textile designs and indeed upon all the arts, is as strong today as it was in 1910."

The Russian love of rich colors, brought by the ballets, changed the eye and the taste of the West, and remained a permanent legacy in fashion and interior decoration affecting us even today.

• • •

Along with the vivid colors of Bakst, the choreography of Fokine and the music of Stravinsky, the Ballets Russes first displayed to the outside world the spectacular dancing of Vaslav Nijinsky. He was a dancer so extraordinary that although his career lasted only ten years—five years in Russia and five years abroad—before he went insane, it was enough to make him an immortal of the dance; perhaps the immortal.

Paris had seen beautiful and brilliant ballerinas but for more than a century no male dancer like Nijinsky. He was acclaimed as a god, the new Vestris* of the dance.

The fabled Nijinsky was small, five feet four inches tall, 130 pounds, with heavy, muscular thighs. He had a long neck and slanted eyes which gave him a strange, faunlike expression which he often accentuated on stage with makeup. Even when surrounded by people, he seemed always to be alone. He sat silently through dinner parties, smiling. When he did talk, it was shyly and softly, without looking at the person before him. He was as orderly, neat and polite as a schoolboy. He had only two suits to his name at any one time, but luxuriously wore pastel crepe de chine shirts for practice and had hundreds of pairs of dancing shoes made for him in London of special kid.

He was so unprepossessing offstage, such an ambiguous, introverted, moody and mystical person who lived so entirely within himself, that many people who had contact with him thought him a little childish and not very literate. He walked through rehearsals mechanically, and even his fellow dancers often worried that he was not really grasping a role. But once he began to get into costume for a performance, imperceptibly a gradual metamorphosis would come over his face, his body and manner, until he became the role he was playing. Once on stage, he would burst into life, bringing to each part the drama and subtlety which had in some mysterious way been developing deep in his acutely sensitive soul. Chameleonlike, he would change, enrapturing all who saw him whether he was an 18th-century court dancer, a slave in golden trousers and pearls as in *Schéhérazade*, Harlequin chasing butterflies in a candlelit garden, the phantom of a rose or a pathetic puppet thrown by his master into a black box.

His leaps were breathtaking. He seemed to hover in the air and then even more extraordinarily would come down slowly and gently as a feather. (When he was once asked if it was difficult to stay in the air, he groped for an answer and said, "No! No! Not difficult. You just have to go up and then pause a little up

* The brilliant French dancer Auguste Vestris (1760–1842), considered the greatest male dancer of his time.

there.") He was the only dancer in the world ever able to accomplish the *entrechat dix*, executing this extraordinarily difficult feat with elegance and wit. Coolly, seemingly without effort, he simply shot straight into the air. Impresarios and members of the press inspected his shoes to see if there was any rubber in them, and the stage for trapdoors and mechanical devices. The emphasis on his leaps annoyed Nijinsky, who would doggedly repeat, *"Je ne suis pas un sauteur; je suis un artiste."**

He evoked in spectators an impression of otherworldliness, as if he were poised between reality and some other existence. Paul Claudel wrote of him, "His was the victory of breath over weight, the possession of the body by the soul." Nijinsky himself seemed to experience an almost religious ecstasy when he danced. In one of the rare verbal glimpses into his spirit, he once said, "Art, love, nature are only an infinitesimal part of God's spirit. I wanted to recapture it and give it to the public so that they may know He is omnipresent. If they felt it, then I am reflecting Him."

Tragically, at the age of twenty-nine, in 1917 the divine dancer was overcome by madness. First it was paranoia; he would have men examine the stage meticulously to be sure that no one had sprinkled broken glass on it. Then one day, his memory became a blank. He lost all sense of his own identity and remained for thirty years, gentle, but lost to the world forever. Yet, like a dying star, he left behind him such a brilliant trace that the glow remains with us still.

• • •

In 1911, instead of continuing to borrow artists from the Imperial Theaters, Diaghilev decided to form his own permanent touring company. He was helped in his plan by a comic opera occurrence which some unfriendly tongues insisted he had created himself. Nijinsky decided to dance *Giselle* at the Maryinsky Theater in the short jerkin and tights that Benois had designed for him for Paris, without adding the customary more modest trunks. The briefness of his costume apparently shocked some conservative members of the audience, and in the row that followed, Nijinsky resigned from the Imperial Theater, and from 1911 on danced for Diaghilev alone.

Every year, shortly after the chestnuts bloomed in Paris, Diaghilev and his company would arrive in Paris to delight, excite and sometimes shock Parisians

---

* "I am not a jumper; I am an artist."

440

with new and wonderful ballets and operas. They brought Mussorgsky's *Khovanshchina* and *Boris Godunov*, Rimsky-Korsakov's *May Night*, and scenes from *Sadko*. Beginning in 1911, as a warm-up, they always began in Monte Carlo, following Chaliapin's regular season there. The great singer was obliged to do only a certain number of performances at the Imperial Theaters in Russia and then was free to accept any contracts he wished all over the world. He traveled everywhere, including America, and his dramatic delivery and personality became a standard which deeply affected operatic styles.

Diaghilev had resurrected ballet in the West. Because of his success, Russian dancers were in demand all over the world. By 1911 various Russian ballerinas were appearing in every one of the big music halls of London. Many formed their own companies, notably Anna Pavlova, who in 1911 began to tour with her own troupe. Although it was mounted with less taste than Diaghilev's, nevertheless she brought ballet and her unique talent to a wide public all over the world, including the United States, and did much to popularize the art among modest audiences.

In 1911 the Diaghilev Ballets conquered England when they were asked to perform at the gala in honor of King George's coronation. During that season at Covent Garden, the famous Kschessinska came to dance *Swan Lake*. In an unbelievably lavish gesture, she hired the virtuoso Russian violinist Mischa Elman, who was then playing recitals at Albert Hall, to come and play the violin solo in the second act. That same year the Diaghilev company traveled to Budapest, to Vienna and Germany, and in later years to South America and the United States.

For the Paris season of 1911, Diaghilev's Ballets Russes presented the poignant *Petrushka*, considered by many to be the company's masterpiece. The most Russian of ballets, it was the triumph of the World of Art ideal of the unity of the arts, created and developed, not only by several extraordinary talents but in several countries. Stravinsky composed the music in France and Switzerland; Benois designed and executed the sets and costumes in St. Petersburg; the ballet was finished and choreographed in Rome and perfected in Paris.

Petrushka had a curious birth: After the success of *The Firebird,* Stravinsky had decided to set to work on another ballet, one which would be based on the pagan rites of spring in Russia. Diaghilev and he had discussed the idea and Diaghilev had urged him to proceed for the following season. But suddenly, a new idea interrupted him. Stravinsky went to vacation in Vevey and Lausanne in Switzerland. Before tackling his big ballet project, he decided to write an orchestral piece for piano. Quite unexpectedly while he was composing the music, he writes, "I had in my mind the distinct picture of a puppet, suddenly endowed with life, exasperating the patience of the orchestra with diabolical cascades of arpeggi." When he had finished this "bizarre" piece, he said, he walked along Lake Geneva trying to think of a title to express in a word the character of the music and the odd puppet who had sprung into his mind. Abruptly it came to him: "Petrushka, the immortal and unhappy hero of all fairs in all countries." Diaghilev came to visit shortly after and Stravinsky played him the piano piece, which later became the second scene of the ballet. Together, Stravinsky and Diaghilev decided to do a new ballet, and they quickly settled on the scene of the action—the St. Petersburg Carnival Fair of *Maslenitsa*. Diaghilev immediately wrote to Benois and asked him to do the scenario and design the sets and costumes. Despite the fact that Diaghilev and Benois had had a serious rift, Benois, "the patriot of Petersburg," enthusiastically agreed. As a child he had loved the puppet theaters of the Butter Week Carnival, and it delighted him to bring alive his memories of St. Petersburg fairs of his childhood. As for the hero, Benois wrote, "Petrushka, the Russian Guignol, had been my friend since childhood. I immediately had the feeling that 'it was a duty I owed to an old friend' to immortalize him on the real stage." Benois conceived the character of the Blackamoor, remembering that in the Russian street performances of Petrushka there was always an intermission between the acts when two Blackamoors dressed in velvet and gold beat each other with sticks. "If Petrushka were to be taken as the personification of the suffering side of humanity . . . his lady Columbine as the incarnation of the eternal feminine, then the gorgeous Blackamoor would serve as the embodiment of everything senselessly attractive, powerfully masculine and undeservedly triumphant."

Early in the winter of 1911 Stravinsky came to St. Petersburg and played his score for Benois. Into his music he had exuberantly and imaginatively woven brightly colored threads of Russian folk songs from eleven collections, including those compiled by Rimsky-Korsakov and Tchaikovsky. Interwoven were songs sung at Eastertide and those of Midsummer's Eve, the song of singing beggars who wandered from village to village repeating over and over again that "Christ is risen," and the love song of a happy bride. The tune that accompanies the lively dance of the coachmen and grooms was a street song from Tambovsk whose words offer a lusty picture of lives made up of fish chowder, noodle soup and love. For Russians, the unexpected appearance of these familiar melodies gave the ballet special overtones of humor and warmth.

Benois designed the sets and costumes in St. Petersburg, placing the ballet in the time of Nicholas I. As it happened, the apartment he had rented was directly over the lodgings of a group of coachmen and he wrote, "unceasing revels and dancing went on there all day long to the sound of balalaikas and the laughter of gay ladies. At any other time, this would have disturbed me . . . but in the present case, the noise, the stamps and shouting only helped to inspire me—it was almost a gift of providence."

In the spring, the friends all gathered in Rome. The painter Serov came to join them and they all spent happy moments strolling through the public gardens. The pianist Scriabin was also in Rome giving avant-garde concerts and piano recitals with simultaneous projections of rays of light from an early color organ. The first rehearsal of *Petrushka* took place in smelly rehearsal rooms so stifling that the impeccable Stravinsky was forced to ask the ladies for permission to remove his coat while he played, while Benois sketched continuously, noting, "Fokine can make nothing of the rhythms. Appalling heat."

When the orchestra in Paris rehearsed the score, the musicians began laughing; Pierre Monteux, the conductor, had trouble convincing them that Stravinsky's music was not meant as a joke. (Even Fokine took a long time to appreciate it.) The scenery and costumes arrived from St. Petersburg. They were Benois's masterpiece, full of nostalgia for the great *Malenitsa* fairs. On either side of the stage were the wooden theaters with their painted signs and puppet shows, in the distance the golden spire of the Admiralty. The sails of the swings revolved and the children rode on a French carousel, an authentic one of the Napoleon III period which Diaghilev and Benois had managed to buy at a fair.* All the familiar characters of St. Petersburg came to life—the coachmen, the nursemaids in bright *sarafans* and *kokoshniki*, the organ-grinders and bear handlers.

With *Petrushka*, the "committee" had conceived a masterpiece in which many talents merged to create a perfect work of art. Nijinsky created the role of the unhappy puppet, and it became his favorite role. Miraculously he, who had glittered in gold and lamé in *Schéhérazade* and *Le Pavillon d'Armide*, turned himself into an ungainly and grotesque puppet, bringing such genius, intensity and pathos to the role that Sarah Bernhardt upon witnessing his performance exclaimed, "I am afraid, I am afraid, for I see before me the greatest actor in the world."

---

* This carousel was inadvertently dropped and lost forever in the River Platte when the ballet's scenery was unloaded in Buenos Aires.

The 1911 season saw two triumphs for the incomparable Nijinsky. Fokine choreographed for him a short ballet, *Le Spectre de la Rose,* inspired by a verse of the French poet Théophile Gautier. In this ballet Nijinsky, dressed in a costume covered with rose petals, his makeup suggesting a strange and beautiful beetle with a rose petal mouth, played the phantom of a rose which a young girl had been given at a ball. At the end of the ballet Nijinsky crossed the stage diagonally at a run and soared out of the left window in a leap so extraordinary that all those who saw it remembered it for a lifetime. He seemed to fly up and out into the night. Jean Cocteau, who was present at the first performance, described it as "a jump so poignant, so contrary to all the laws of flight and balance, following so high and curved a trajectory, that I shall never again smell a rose without this unerasable phantom appearing before me."

The effect of this leap upon spectators was mesmerizing; for the following performances people crowded the wings to watch and wait for it. Nijinsky had in fact invented a double leap by which, out of sight, he curled in the air and fell perpendicularly. His apparently effortless leap was in fact so strenuous that he was caught by four men, including his masseur, Williams, and faithful valet, Vasily, who held their hands crossed together to form a net against which he landed. As he stood there panting under the hot lights, his rose petals dark with sweat, Williams massaged his heart, Vasily applied cold towels to his nostrils, while someone else stood by with strong coffee.

Mysteriously, after a performance, his costume always seemed to disintegrate and would come up to wardrobe bereft of many of its petals. When the wardrobe mistress made a special investigation, she discovered that Vasily had been selling the rose petals as souvenirs to Nijinsky's hordes of female admirers and had built himself a house from the proceeds. Thereafter, the company dubbed it "Château Spectre de la Rose."

Dostoevsky once wrote that the specific trait of the Russian mind is its capacity for grasping the whole from its obscured and often scattered features. The indomitable Sergei Diaghilev had this trait in full measure; he could always discern the whole. It was his prodigious energy, vision and will that kept all these incandescent talents working together at a pitch of creativity which has rarely, if ever, been surpassed in history. It was his special genius to be able to bring out the best in others, and to infect them with total enthusiasm for a project. "Any work done under him acquired the charm of a fantastic adventure," wrote Alexander Benois.

A perfectionist, Diaghilev supervised every detail of his elaborate productions, capable of seeing and managing many things at once. He was everywhere. He would go into artists' studios and watch them work, supervise execution of costumes, examine scores and listen to the orchestra. Everyday he stopped in to watch the dancers practice and rehearse. Karsavina wrote with awe, "I had seen a Japanese performer once, exhibiting feats of multiple concentration. I failed to be impressed by him; I had seen Diaghilev at work." The style and elegance which were the mark of the Ballets Russes were the result of his meticulous taste and all-seeing eye, for it was he, and he alone, who made all the final decisions. The dancers said that they danced only for him and that it was his approval alone that mattered.

Diaghilev was always controversial. In Russia the establishment never understood him. In the early years of his ballets, many regarded him as a charlatan who was perverting the true meaning of art and refused to support him. But Diaghilev's iron will never admitted obstacles and for over twenty years he always managed to find funds for his enterprises. His autocratic personality, which often made him regard people as part objects and part subjects, made him enemies. Yet such were his charm and diplomacy that he always managed to get anything he really wanted. In the company there were many a tiff and row, but for the success of his enterprise he was ready to do anything, smooth any ruffled feathers, and rows usually ended up in what Karsavina called "a typical Russian way—reconciliations, tears, sobs, embraces, celebrations." He once spent five hours on the telephone convincing Fokine to return to the ballet after a rift.

Diaghilev can not be called an impresario, for he never did anything for personal gain; always it was for the love of art alone. He created works for his own satisfaction and that of his friends. In a lordly way, he presented his productions almost as if he were a host, and the performers his own. From the very beginning, all his enterprises, whether art exhibitions or ballets, were begun before he had a kopeck in the bank. Because of his mania for beauty and his luxurious tastes, he spent enormous sums on his productions. The tutus for *Les Sylphides* were thrown away after every performance; the tights for dancers were specially made in Paris; crates of shoes were ordered in Milan. His backers inevitably lost money and yet they were always satisfied and proud of their association with him. All the money he earned from one successful venture was immediately put into the next, and if a production was a failure, as they sometimes were, he was never discouraged. "The success of a production is unpredictable," he would repeat. "All I care for is its merit."

He never kept books, and although huge sums of money passed through his hands, he never diverted any of it to his own use. He paid his dancers well. Many of them ended up with comfortable sums in the bank, but Diaghilev never owned a car, and although he was always elegant in his top hat and beaver-collared coat, close observation revealed that his trousers were sometimes frayed and his boots worn. "All I gain in profit," he once said, "is my keep in the best hotels and the privilege of a seat at the Russian ballet."

From the time he formed his ballets until his death in 1929 he never had a real home, but lived in a series of hotel rooms which were always littered with half-packed trunks. Letters, programs and file boxes littered the tables; canvases and drawings were piled on chairs and against walls. He hated to get up early; so in the morning he would breakfast in bed with the shades tightly drawn against the sunlight, reading reports of his secretaries and talking on several telephones, keeping in touch not only with the innumerable business details of his productions but with his myriad social obligations which were an essential part of his everlasting search for funds.

He lunched late, in Paris often at Larue's, where he would sit with Bakst, Benois and other artist friends who changed every day. Nijinsky sat silently, listening, while Bakst sketched constantly, on menus, tabletops, napkins, scraps of paper.

Diaghilev deeply loved Russia and, despite his cosmopolitan life, remained completely Russian and true to the heroes of his youth. Shortly before his death in 1929 he still maintained, "Tchaikovsky is a genius, not fully understood in Europe." In a very Russian way, he always feared mysterious, undefinable sources which conspired against reasonable chances of success and he was highly superstitious. He would not let people throw their hats on the bed ("It means misfortune"); he was afraid of germs, and for years refused to travel by steamer because a fortune-teller told him he would die on the water.

It was a very great disappointment for Diaghilev that in the end he was never able to present his ballets in Russia. In 1912 he and his company were to perform a season at the People's Palace in St. Petersburg. The company was overjoyed. All his plans were made. He had planned to reverse the artistic process and bring to Russia a new ballet created in the West, *Le Dieu Bleu*, which he had done with French composers, the poet Jean Cocteau and Reynaldo Hahn. Then the news was brought to him that the Narodny Dom had burned to the ground. "Well," he sighed, "it seems that I was not destined to show my ballets in Russia now—which is a great pity. For I have a presentiment that after this I shall never be able to show them at all." And then he fell silent for a long time.

In 1912 Diaghilev began the first of his many collaborations with Western composers. Maurice Ravel composed *Daphnis and Chloé* and Claude Debussy *Prélude à l'Après-midi d'un Faune*. This short ballet, which marked Nijinsky's debut as a choreographer, lasted only eight minutes, but it managed to cause a scandal which rocked Paris.

Dressed in mottled tights, with a tightly curled golden wig and tiny horns, his faunlike eyes accentuated with makeup and his ears elongated and pointed with wax, Nijinsky danced with seven nymphs. At the end of the ballet, the nymphs fled, one of them dropping her veil, upon which Nijinsky fell with a convulsive erotic movement. Some in the audience hissed and booed loudly, while others shouted *"Bis!"* Diaghilev ordered the ballet repeated. The next day the newspapers of Paris exploded with shock and outrage. One critic, heading his article *"Un Faux Pas,"* huffed "decent people will never accept such animal realism." Paris divided itself into camps. The police were called in to watch a subsequent performance to determine whether or not it was obscene. The great sculptor Auguste Rodin sprang to the defense of Nijinsky in print, and then found himself the subject of attack. Tempers became so heated that Russian Ambassador Izvolsky suggested that this anti-faun scandal was a dastardly attempt to break up the Franco-Russian alliance. The reverberations even reached the United States where the *Pittsburgh Gazette* headlined the news, announcing in triumphant tones "Wicked Paris Shocked at Last!"

Yet the celebrated scandal over the Faun was only a prelude to what was the climax of the Diaghilev Ballets Russes—*The Rite of Spring*, performed on May 29, 1913, to the music of Igor Stravinsky with choreography by Nijinsky.

The ballet showed the pagan Russian rites of spring, and in the music he composed for this ballet Stravinsky overthrew the whole rhythmic system. *The Rite of Spring* appeared like a meteor for which no one was prepared. This was no spring of poets with soft clouds and daffodils but a spring exploding from the innards of the earth with primitive violence and the primordial, overwhelming urge of fertility. In the ballet's climax, a maiden frenziedly danced herself to death to renew the life of the soil. Stravinsky in his music created dramatic orchestrations in which strings and woodwinds produced new sounds in extreme registers, as well as special instrumental effects which brutally catapulted the audience into the 20th century with its pounding machines and dissonances.

For the dancers, Nijinsky created frenetic twists, jerks, asymmetrical angular movements which were closely identified with the music. In rehearsal, the dancers disliked the ballet intensely; they had to time their movements by counting bars. Diaghilev, as usual, found their disapproval a good sign. But even he was not prepared for the riot that ensued when it was first performed.

Hardly had the curtain gone up when pandemonium broke out. One of the spectators recalled, "It was like an earthquake." The audience felt personally attacked; they perceived the composition as blasphemy, an attempt to destroy music itself. People began to hoot and catcall. No one could hear the music for the noise. The lights were turned on in an effort to calm the storm, but as soon as they were lowered, the screaming and insults began again. The conductor, Pierre Monteux, threw desperate looks at Diaghilev, who motioned that the performance should continue as he shouted at the audience, "Listen first! Whistle afterward!" So heated were feelings that one elegantly dressed lady in an orchestra box stood up and slapped the hissing young man in the box next to her. Her escort stood up and exchanged cards with the offender and the two fought a duel the next day. Another man remembered that a young man stood up behind him in their box and was so intensely excited that he began to pound rhythmically on his head. What is more, wrote the man, "my emotion was so great that I did not feel the blows for some time." Ravel, red with rage, spat out crushing remarks to the demonstrators. Someone screamed, "Shut up, you bitches from the sixteenth!" The police were called between two scenes to eject demonstrators. Above the deafening noise the music was inaudible; Nijinsky stood in the wings desperately counting out the beat for the dancers, who were almost in tears.

The next day the critics called it *"Le Massacre du Printemps,"* and the dancing, "epileptic fits." The composer, they said, "had written a score for which we shall not be ready until 1940." The ballet with Nijinsky's choreography had only four performances in Paris and three in London. Several years later, when Diaghilev wanted to revive it, no one could remember the original choreography. Today, from notations of Stravinsky's original score, sketches and recollections of those who saw it, it appears that this ballet was Nijinsky's masterpiece, for which he had conceived movements far ahead of his time, shooting dancers like space travelers into the modern world.

In July 1913 Stravinsky wrote, "Nijinsky's choreography is incomparable. Everything as I had wanted it, with few exceptions," and then prophetically continued, "But we must wait a long time before the public grows accustomed to our language. Of the value of what we have accomplished, I am convinced, and this gives me strength for further work."

In one stride, *The Rite of Spring* had reached a peak of modern music which was never surpassed. Such was the scandal that it was some time before this music was heard for what it was: a titanic composition which changed everything after it.

26. THE AVANT-GARDE

During those years when Diaghilev was startling the West, in Russia artists of the avant-garde were pushing into ever more daring experimentation, striking out to the frontiers of modern art. The years from 1907 to 1917 were a period of enormous creativity and individualism not only in the arts, but also in science and philosophy. It was a time of an extraordinary diversity of ideas, ranging from the most conservative to the most revolutionary. The press, which had enjoyed an uninterrupted growth since the time of Alexander II, was never freer. By 1916 there were fourteen thousand newspapers and magazines in Russia —six thousand in Moscow and St. Petersburg alone, which reflected every shade of political, philosophical and artistic opinion. Radical and Marxist newspapers sprang up and were freely sold on the street; *Pravda* came into existence in 1912. The *tonki* (thin) and *tolsty* (thick) journals of literary comment and criticism, which had begun in Alexander's time, by 1916 numbered several thousands, appearing weekly and bimonthly. Diaghilev's *World of Art* had inspired many other similar art journals of superb printing and quality.

Russian poetry, which since 1895 had enjoyed a glorious and continual flowering, reached its maximum potential in those prewar years. The Symbolist movement, which came to Russia from Belgium and France, had produced many important poets—Valery Briusov, Konstantin Balmont, Fyodor Sologub, Zinaida Grippius, Alexander Blok, Andrei Bely and Vyacheslav Ivanov. Admirers of hierarchy and religion, the Symbolists saw the artist as a high priest, and reached

450

for another and mystical world through metaphor. For them, music was the supreme symbolistic art. The Symbolist pianist and composer Alexander Scriabin dreamed of a single harmony of music, art, light and smell. Scriabin staged exhibitions, concerts and cultural events throughout Russia and abroad, including a performance on a barge sailing down the Volga. The Symbolist poet Vyacheslav Ivanov held regular Wednesday poetic evenings in his "Tower" apartment in St. Petersburg which overlooked the gardens of the Tauride Palace. These gatherings, at which poets of different ages and reputation read their verses, were so well attended in 1907 through 1909 that Ivanov was forced to tear down the partitions between rooms to accommodate all his guests. Supper was served at 2:00 A.M. and discussions of poetry continued through the night. In the early years of the 20th century, the Symbolist movement had become the respected literary establishment; the works and artistic philosophy of Symbolist writers dominated the advanced art and literary journals of the time.

But around 1908 to 1910, in both Moscow and St. Petersburg, the supremacy of this powerful literary and artistic movement began to be challenged by a group of new young poets and artists who sought to go beyond it into other ideas and forms of art. One challenge came from a group that took the name Acmeists and included the poets Anna Akhmatova and Osip Mandelstam. These poets rejected the mystical goal of art and called for attention to the real world, to romance, warmth and concreteness.

At the same time, an even more radical group of young writers and artists who were to call themselves Futurists, excited about Cubism and Primitivism in modern painting, rebelled against everything that was connected with the old world of art. Rejecting established esthetics entirely, they boldly developed poetic styles closely patterned on developments in modern art, with its unexpected shifting of planes, its use of elementary shapes and primary colors.

In these years, such was the richness of Russian poetry that there lived and worked in the land no less than nineteen major poets, each of whom could have been counted as the central figure of a nation's poetry. Among them were giants —Blok, Biely, Mandelstam, Mayakovsky, Akhmatova, Gumilev, Esenin, Pasternak, Tsvetayeva. A hundred Russian poets made their living entirely by their published poetry, often reciting in auditoriums and theaters where they were accorded the adulation of matinee idols.

Leading the most radical wing of avant-garde was a new generation of young painters. Two of the most active were Natalya Goncharova and Mikhail

Larionov. Goncharova was born into a distinguished family of Tula—her paternal grandmother was a daughter of Pushkin and her mother was from the Belaev family, which had contributed greatly to the development of Russian music at the time of the Mighty Handful. Larionov came from a small town near the Polish border and a much humbler background; he was the son of a military doctor and the grandson of a sailor. The two met when they were both students at the Moscow School of Painting, Sculpture and Architecture and formed a lifelong association, becoming ultimately husband and wife.

Both were enormously influential in the early years of the new movements in art. Larionov was called the first Russian "Impressionist"; Goncharova created a new, neo-primitive Russian style of simple and angular silhouettes. She was strongly influenced by icons (as was Kandinsky), by the popular *lubki* prints sold in the marketplaces, by the shapes of the wooden dolls, the gingerbread molds and the folk art of the people. Her style was spontaneous; she was, said Larionov, a person who "thought with her paintbrush." In her bright and often humorous paintings she tried to evoke the ribaldry of the *skomorokhi* of Old Russia and the earthy life of Russian streets and villages. Larionov's own work included a lively series of soldiers and sailors. Although the mood of their art was different (in his early works, his more detached and restrained, and his colors muted; hers intensely emotional, glorying in color), beginning in 1906 they were joined in their determination to create a new 20th-century art stemming from Russian roots and unrelated to Europe. She foresaw a time when Russian art would play a central role in world artistic life and Europe would come to Russia for lessons. "The future is ours!" was Larionov's battle cry. "We are not a province of Paris," Goncharova insisted.

In 1909, Larionov and Goncharova launched their new Primitivism, exhibiting their work at the first of three "Golden Fleece" exhibitions sponsored by an art journal financed by the wealthy Moscow merchant Nikolai Ryabushinsky. These historical exhibitions grouped avant-garde Russian artists with the foremost artists of the French avant-garde: Maillol, Rodin, Bonnard, Rouault, Braque, Vuillard, Vallotton, Derain, Van Dongen, Picasso and Vlaminck. The new Russian Primitivism of Goncharova and Larionov had wide repercussions, not only in painting and poetry, but music as well, affecting Stravinsky and his *Rite of Spring*.

Between 1910 and 1913 there was an explosion of new ideas on art. Innumerable brochures, books, manifestos and essays flooded both Moscow and Petersburg. In addition there were countless public debates, exhibits and theatrical spectacles. Every artist proclaimed his independence. Ideas and theories proliferated with such dizzying speed that it was often difficult to classify artists into precise schools. Groups would coalesce for a time, only to break into other groupings, each going off in its own direction. Russia was not only in touch with all the latest artistic currents of Europe, she had leaped dramatically ahead. Moscow and St. Petersburg were meeting places for the most avant-garde international artistic ideas of Paris and Munich.

The new artists were influenced by the paintings of Braque, Matisse and Picasso which, thanks to the many exhibitions and the collections of Shchukin and others, they often were able to see and appreciate before Paris did. But, opposing the hegemony of the West over artistic principles, they declared that they did not have to look outside Russia for the new art, that it could be discovered in the context of their own past. For example, Goncharova insisted that Cubism was latent in Scythian art and in the wooden dolls sold at Russian fairs.

To broadcast their ideas, Goncharova and Larionov organized Russian modernist exhibitions. In 1910, at their first "Knave of Diamonds" exhibit in Moscow, they presented 250 works by thirty-eight avant-garde artists including Alexandra Exter and the Burliuk brothers, as well as several works of the Russian artists Marianna von Werefkin and Vasily Kandinsky, then living and working in Munich, and three by Kasimir Malevich. Malevich, the son of a sugar factory foreman from Kiev, arrived in Moscow in 1905 at the age of twenty-seven. One of the great innovative artists of the 20th century, he rapidly joined Larionov and Goncharova as the third leader of the avant-garde. In 1911, when Larionov developed his theory of Rayonism, which attempted to penetrate the essence of an object through rays, Malevich, along with Tatlin, launched the Russian Cubo-Futurist movement.

In 1912, uniting the two groups, Larionov and Goncharova organized an exhibition that was a bold assertion of their independence and the first conscious break of the Russian artists with Europe. This exhibit was greeted with howls of outrage by the critics. Playfully, the artists named it the "Donkey's Tail" because Repin had scornfully said that the paintings could have been done by a donkey with a paintbrush attached to its tail. To this exhibit, Goncharova, Larionov and Tatlin contributed fifty-nine works each and Malevich twenty-three. It also marked the first appearance of Marc Chagall, who sent his painting *Death*. Chagall, who was from a mystic and devout Hasidic Jewish family, had set himself to painting the life of the Jewish communities of Russia with such poetic works as *The Wedding* and *The Sabbath*.

In those same years, a succession of other art exhibits presented every new artistic current to the public. In 1911–1912 the Union of Youth, a group formed to exhibit avant-garde painters and sponsored by Levky Zheverzheyev, a wealthy merchant in St. Petersburg, introduced the work of Olga Rozanova and Pavel Filonov. Continuing to hold exhibitions twice yearly thereafter, the Union of Youth brought together the best work of all the new modernists. A striking phenomenon unique to the avant-garde movement was the great number of major women artists. Thirteen of the leading painters were women, among them: Alexandra Exter, Olga Rozanova, Sonia Delaunay, Lyubov Popova, Varvara Stepanova, Elena Guro (who was also a poet); and two of the major contemporary poets were women: Anna Akhmatova and Marina Tsvetayeva.

In both Primitivism and Cubism the Russians saw far more radical possibilities for both painting and literature. By 1910 Kandinsky had represented atomic fission in his multiple compositions. Malevich in 1913 predicted, among other things, the building of cities on earth satellites. By 1913 those two Russian pioneers of modern art had rejected representational art completely and, leading the way that European artists were to follow a few years later, moved into pure abstraction. In his Suprematist theory of art evolved around 1915, Malevich could proudly announce that through his doing "objects had disappeared like smoke."

It was also around 1910 that the daringly radical group of poets and painters who called themselves Futurists began to be active in literature. Originally brought together by the Burliuk brothers, David, Vladimir and Nikolai, the artist sons of a farming merchant who managed large estates near the Black Sea, the little group was linked by its interest in the pre-Slavic past and Russian folk and popular arts. (David Burliuk, for instance, had a large collection of the colorful signboards that decorated Russian streets.) In 1907 and 1908 they had begun to develop poetic styles which were closely linked to the developments of modern art.

The Futurists came from very diverse backgrounds. Velimir Khlebnikov, a mathematician and linguist who studied painting, was the son of a family of ornithologists from Astrakhan. Alexei Kruchenykh, the son of a peasant family near Kherson, was a high-school art teacher when he first met the Burliuks in 1907. Kruchenykh moved to Moscow to help David Burliuk organize art exhibitions and abandoned painting to become a poet and the most controversial and radical innovator of the Futurist group. There were also Elena Guro, a poet and painter from St. Petersburg, the daughter of a general and wife of the Futurist composer Mikhail Matyushin, and Benedikt Livshits, a young law student from a wealthy merchant family. The most famous of all was the handsome and flamboyant Vladimir Mayakovsky, born in Georgia, the son of a forest ranger; he had first met the Burliuks when he was studying painting in Moscow. Mayakovsky, too, abandoned painting for literature and became the foremost revolutionary poet of the land.

Because many of the Futurist poets had begun as professional artists and all of them could paint and draw, they set about to link painting and literature, trying to bring into the verbal medium what they saw in modern painting. For them, in the words of Livshits, modern painting was "not only a new vision of the world in all its sensuous magnificence and staggering variety . . ." it was also "a new philosophy of art, a heroic esthetic which shattered all established canons and opened breathtaking possibilities."

Mayakovsky set about translating poetically the Cubist and neo-primitive paintings done by his friends; Larionov and Goncharova began to illustrate poetic works.

In St. Petersburg, the ideas of these Bohemian modernists were vigorously supported by an unlikely colleague, Dr. Nikolai Kulbin, a professor at the Military Academy, physician of the General Staff, who had a civilian rank of major general. Kulbin was a fanatical sponsor of avant-garde causes, and organized art exhibitions and lectures at which the Futurists could expound their ideas. In 1910 Kulbin published a book, *The Studio of the Impressionists*, which included Khlebnikov's "Incantation by Laughter," perhaps the single most famous Futurist poem. In an effort to establish what he called *"zaum,"* or a transrational language that went beyond meaning into pure sound, Khlebnikov built his entire poem on the Russian root for the word "to laugh", adding a whole vocabulary of prefixes and suffixes.

In 1912, financed by Yury Kuzmin, a pilot, and Sergei Dolinsky, a composer, the Futurists published a manifesto, "A Slap in the Face of Public Taste," in which they rejected all previous art forms and announced, among other ringingly iconoclastic credos, that they intended to "throw Pushkin, Tolstoy, et al. overboard from the Ship of Modernity." Among the seven contributors to the "Slap" were Mayakovsky, who contributed two poems; Kandinsky, who wrote several sketches in prose; and Kruchenykh, who wrote a poem which included incorrectly stressed words and no capitals or punctuation.

In the years 1910 to 1913 Futurist poets and painters published their own books in which poetry and painting were intimately linked. These books, which are among the most striking and exciting ever published, were often hand printed and illustrated. Working together collectively, painters and poets conceived each page as a canvas visually mixing word and image. They used different type faces, printed poetry in various forms and shapes. They employed the artist's own handwriting, and inspired by the *lubki* prints, children's drawings, fairy tales and colorful signboard art, they introduced offbeat illustrations. In deliberate contrast to what they saw as excessively refined and lavish art journals, they printed one of their books on wallpaper. (Their famous "Slap" was printed on gray-brown wrapping paper with a cover of coarse sackcloth which was described by a derisive reviewer as "the color of fainted louse.") These Futurist books bore a series of outrageous titles—*Roaring Parnassus, The Mare's Milk, The Croaked Moon* (a collection of the writings of Kruchenykh, Khlebnikov and Mayakovsky). Perhaps the masterpiece of this genre was *A Game in Hell,* a burlesque and fantastic poem by Kruchenykh and Khlebnikov, the first edition of which, in 1912, was illustrated by Goncharova and the second in, 1913, by Rozanova and Malevich. In their poetry the Futurists used epithets, street language out of context, jumbled and archaic words, breaking with language until nothing was left but sound. Malevich and Goncharova designed covers that reached to the borders of abstraction.

In that dizzyingly productive time one art flowed into another. The dynamic union of painting and theater begun by Mamontov and continued by Diaghilev reached its apotheosis in 1910–11. As Diaghilev presented *The Firebird* and *Petrushka* to delighted audiences in Paris, at home in Russia a galaxy of gifted painters transposed the magnificence of their talent to the stage.

Golovin, Korovin, Doboujinsky, Roerich, Benois, Bilibin, Kustodiev, Yuon and Levitan worked on the Imperial stages and at the Moscow Art Theater, while the gifted younger generation of avant-garde painters—Larionov, Goncharova, Malevich, Tatlin, Exter and Chagall—exercised their talents in the multitude of experimental theaters that came into existence in the early years of the 20th century.

During the whole prerevolutionary period, the Russian theater was extraordinarily vital and diverse. Reacting against what they considered the excessive realism of the Moscow Art Theater, students of Stanislavsky—Meyerhold, Vakhtangov, Evreinov—broke away in their own directions. Actors would group themselves around a great innovative director, and painters would group themselves around a theater. Between 1900 and 1914, a veritable avalanche of plays was written. In that short period, 121 new plays by twenty-six playwrights were produced in Moscow and St. Petersburg, from Gorky to Chekhov to the most avant-garde Futurists.

In 1906 in St. Petersburg, Vera Komissarzhevskaya, a famous actress, began her Dramatic Theater and invited Meyerhold to be its director. In this theater on Offitserskaya Street with its curtain designed by Bakst depicting a sphinx and a Greek temple, Meyerhold staged plays by the Symbolist writers Sologub and Andreev, his most ambitious project being a series of poetic dramas by the Symbolist poet Alexander Blok, in which Meyerhold experimented with the theater as a means of conveying purified extracts of emotion. Meyerhold's startling production of *Hedda Gabler* was built around a correspondence of mood and color. As the curtain went up, the stage seemed filled with a blue-green mist. An entire wall was covered with a huge tapestry representing a silvery-gold woman with a deer. Silver lace decorated the tops of the stage and the wings. On the floor was a greenish-blue carpet and all the furniture was white. White furs were thrown over a strangely shaped sofa on which Hedda reclined, dressed in a sea-green watery-looking dress which, according to a contemporary, "shimmered and flowed at her every movement and she resembled a sea serpent with shining scales."

In 1912 a group of Moscow Art Theater actors broke away and formed an experimental theater, The Studio. Moscow also presented the witty Yiddish Theater of Mikhouels and Zipkind. In St. Petersburg, Nikolai Evreinov founded his Antique Theater to restore the methods and forms of the ancient European theater of the Middle Ages, as well as founding a small theater called the Crooked Mirror. This last, an intimate theater for social, political and literary parody and satire enjoyed an enormous success, not only in the capital but on its provincial tours. Alexander Tairov began his Kamerny Theater based on his "expressive gestures" technique of acting and opened it with a play of the Sanskrit poet Sakuntula translated by a Symbolist poet. In 1913 the works of no less than seventeen contemporary Russian playwrights were being played simultaneously in the theaters of Moscow and Petersburg.

In addition, theater was supplemented by a new phenomenon, the theater-cabaret. The first and most famous of these miniature theaters of satire was The Bat in Moscow, which, beginning in 1910, gave spectacles composed of ten or fifteen comic numbers accompanied by songs, the characters sticking their heads through sets of painted panels of wood. At The Bat whole original comic operas

457

and even ballets were staged with sets designed by Bakst and Doboujinsky. Such theater-cabarets became the favorite meeting places of writers, musicians and theatrical artists. At the end of 1911, The Wandering Dog was opened in the cellar of a large house with the walls decorated by Sergei Sudeikin. There, wrote the Futurist poet Benedikt Livshits, evenings might include anything from Kulbin's lecture "On a New World View" or Piast's "The Theater of the Word and the Theater of Movement" to purely musical evenings of avant-garde composers. At The Wandering Dog Mayakovsky recited his revolutionary poetry, and one memorable evening Karsavina danced to the music of Couperin, not on stage, but in a small space on the floor encircled by a garland of flowers.

The Futurists sponsored many evenings of public lectures and recitations which were well attended because the members of the group with their wild declamation, crazy enthusiasms and outrageous appearance were such good entertainment. Mayakovsky, Goncharova and Larionov strolled in and out of stores in outlandish clothes, brilliantly colored waistcoats, sporting radishes and spoons in their lapels, and walked about the Moscow streets with algebraic signs and flowers painted on their foreheads.

In 1914 they made a film, *Drama in Cabaret 13*, in which they parodied the excessive refinement of the Symbolists by recording their own everyday behavior. In one scene, Larionov, his eyes painted with green tears, emerged into the street carrying Goncharova in his arms, her hair flowing, a bawdy mask drawn over her face and her right breast exposed. To popularize further their ideas, in 1913–14 the Burliuks organized a Futurist tour of fifteen provincial cities which was full of their usual attention-getting antics. Vladimir Burliuk, a burly professional wrestler, carried around with him 20-pound weights while his brother had "I-Burliuk" written across his forehead. The handsome, fiery-eyed Mayakovsky dazzled and shocked audiences with his flamboyant personal declaiming style, his tremendous feeling for rhythm, his brutal but effective use of slang and dizzying stylistic originality.

The climax of these Futurist theatrical activities was in December 1913, when the Union of Youth sponsored four performances of a Futurist play and opera at Luna Park in St. Petersburg. These productions, which occurred only a few months after the riot in the Paris theater over *The Rite of Spring*, caused nearly as much of an upheaval among Russian audiences. One was a play called *Vladimir Mayakovsky: A Tragedy*, which the poet not only wrote and directed but in which he also played the leading role. As Mayakovsky wanted no professional actors, all the supporting roles were acted by amateurs, mostly university students. Filonov designed the costumes; figures of grotesque people and men without heads or ears walked about the stage. To the capacity crowds that flocked to the performance despite the exorbitant prices, Mayakovsky introduced himself from the stage as "perhaps the last poet" and promised to "reveal our new souls in words as simple as mooing."

The other work was an opera composed by the Futurist composer Matyushin and the self-styled "wildest" poet, Kruchenykh. Called *Victory Over the Sun*, the opera depicted the struggle of the future over the past, symbolized by the sun, which was eventually stabbed and captured. In a daring departure, Malevich designed the costumes and sets in a purely abstract manner; one of the back cloths was a black-and-white square on a white background. Characters such as the Fat One, whose head was two steps behind his body, the Mugger, hooded in black, and Cowards, whose faces were covered, were transformed into moving machines by cardboard and wire costumes. As for the play, casts for the opera were recruited by newspaper advertisements that discouraged professional actors. Some of the actors spoke only in vowels, others only in consonants, singers deliberately tried to sing off key. Blinding lights and ear-splitting sounds rent the theater.

Despite the fact that opening night of his play was described as a fiasco by Mayakovsky, and both the opera and the play were ridiculed by the critics, all four performances were sold out and attended by many celebrities, including the famous Symbolist poet Alexander Blok. During the performance of *Victory Over the Sun*, wild hissing and applause alternated in the audience. Some spectators became so enraged that they sprang up, shook their fists and shouted epithets; one screamed, "You're an ass yourself," and another hurled an apple.

Diaghilev, never a stranger to artistic controversy, gloried in the cultural ferment that was occurring in his native land. With his usual keen eye, it was he who had first exhibited Larionov and Goncharova at one of his *World of Art* exhibits in 1906 and invited them to accompany him to Paris at the time of the Russian art exhibition he organized. In 1913, newly returned to Paris from a visit to St. Petersburg, Diaghilev described to his dinner companions the tornado of artistic ideas that was sweeping Russia. Jokingly, but also with pride, he said, "Twenty schools sprang up in a month, Futurism, Cubism—that is ancient history, prehistory, in three days one is already a philistine. Mototism dethrones Automatism, to be superseded by Trepidationism and Vibrism, which soon goes out of existence because of the emergence of Planism, Serenism, Exacerbism, Omnipotism and Nothingism."

The creative years from 1907 to 1917 were like a magnificent burst of fireworks that illuminates a whole sky. Russian culture had ushered in the 20th century and showed every sign of continuing to dominate it. In every area of art —painting, sculpture, architecture, literature, music, theater and ballet—Russia was in the forefront, bringing to the world dramatically new concepts of beauty. The names of Russian artists were known all over the world as the symbols of everything that was daring, beautiful, and free. Among artists in Russia there was a joyous certainty that an era was coming in which the beauty of art would transform and regenerate the world.

And then came the upheaval and chaos of the great war, and in its wake tumultuous change. After 1914 Diaghilev went on to help create other innovative works, but nothing ever surpassed the genius of those first seasons when the links with Russia were closest. After 1917 he never went back. But, almost as if he had sensed the upheavals that were coming, Diaghilev had brought out much of the best of Russian art and planted it firmly in Europe. He had established ballet as a vital art form that could express a wide range of emotion and pass through all national boundaries and languages. Ballet took root in France, England and in the United States. His collaborators went on to nourish the art up to our own day; his dancers, designers and choreographers influencing every form of theatrical art. In Russia, after the Revolution, the tremendous creative surge of experimentation continued for a few short years, and then a silence fell over the land.

. . . feather after feather floated down on meadow and forest. The mischievous wind covered the feathers with grass and leaves, but nothing could rob them of their glowing rainbow colors.

Despite everything, for those who love and seek to create beauty, the glowing feathers still exist and inspire in all the extraordinary works of art created by Russians over the centuries. They glow today in the music of Stravinsky, the joyful paintings of Chagall, the inspired playing of Horowitz and Rostropovich, the incisive writing of Nabokov, the spiritual endurance of Solzhenitsyn, the brilliant choreographic genius of Balanchine. These are all part of the priceless legacy of a culture of beauty, generosity, grace and exuberance which, although it has now disappeared, continues to make the world dream.

SELECTED BIBLIOGRAPHY

GENERAL

Afanas'ev, Aleksandr, comp., *Russian Fairy Tales*. New York, Pantheon Books, 1973.

Almanakh pechati. St. Petersburg, 1909.

Anastasy (Mitropolit), *Pushkin v ego otnoshenii k religii i pravoslavnoy tserkvi*. Munich, 1947.

Andreev, I. M., *Ocherki po istorii russkoy literatury XIX veka*. Jordanville, N.Y., Holy Trinity Monastery, 1968.

Andronikov, Irakly, *Lermontov: Issledovaniya i pokhodki*. Moscow, Izdatel'stvo "Khudozhestvennaya Literatura," 1964.

Antokol'sky, P., *O Pushkine*. Moscow, Sovetsky Pisatel', 1960.

Arndt, Walter, *Pushkin Threefold*. New York, Dutton paperback, 1972.

Baring, Maurice, *The Mainsprings of Russia*. London, Thomas Nelson & Sons, 1914.

———, *An Outline of Russian Literature*. New York, 1915.

Belyaeva, L. N., comp., *Bibliografiya periodicheskikh izdaniy Rossii, 1901–1916*. Leningrad, Publichnaya Biblioteka.

Bergamini, John D., *The Tragic Dynasty*. New York, G.P. Putnam & Sons, 1969.

Berlin, Isaiah, *Russian Thinkers*. New York, The Viking Press, 1978.

Bill, Valentine T., *The Forgotten Class: The Russian Bourgeoisie from the Earliest Beginnings to 1900*. New York, Frederick A. Praeger, 1959.

Billington, James, *The Icon and the Axe*. New York, Alfred A. Knopf, 1966.

Blum, Jerome, *Lord and Peasant in Russia*. Princeton, N.J., Princeton University Press, 1961.

Bozheryanov, I. N., ed., *Nevsky Prospekt: Kul'turno-istori-chesky ocherk dvukhvekovoy zhizni S.-Peterburga*. St. Petersburg, A. Vil'borg, 1901.

Buchanan, Meriel, *The Dissolution of an Empire*. London, Murray, 1932.

Davydov, Denis, *Stikhotvoreniya i stat'i*. Moscow, Izdatel'stvo "Khudozhestvennaya Literatura," 1942.

Dement'ev, comp., *Russkaja periodicheskaya pechat' (1702–1894)*.

Diehl, Charles, *Byzantium: Greatness and Decline*. New Brunswick, N.J., Rutgers University Press, 1965.

Dobson, George, *Russia's Railway Advance into Central Asia: Notes of a Journey from Saint Petersburg to Samarkand*. London, W.H. Allen, 1890.

Entsiklopedichesky slovar', vol. 37. St. Petersburg, F.A. Brokgaus, I.A. Efron, 1908.

Fedotov, G. P., *The Russian Religious Mind*. vol. 1: *Kievan Christianity—10th to 13th Centuries*. New York, Harper & Bros., Torchbooks, 1960.

———, *The Russian Religious Mind*. vol. 2: *13th–15th Centuries*. Cambridge, Mass., Harvard University Press, 1966.

Fennell, John L. I., *Ivan the Great of Moscow*. New York, St. Martin's Press, 1962.

Fitzlyon, Kyril, and Browning, Tatiana, *Before the Revolution*. London, Allen Lane, Penguin Books, 1977.

Graham, Stephen, *Tsar of Freedom: The Life and Reign of Alexander II*. New Haven, Conn., Yale University Press, 1935.

Grekov, B., *La Culture de la Russie de Kiev*. Moscow, Ed. Langues Etrangères, 1947.

Harcave, Sidney, *Years of the Golden Cockerel: The Last Romanov Tsars, 1814–1917*. New York, Macmillan & Co., 1968.

Hingley, Ronald, *A New Life of Anton Chekhov*. New York, Alfred A. Knopf, 1976.

———, *The Russian Mind*. New York, Charles Scribner's Sons, 1977.

Horgan, Paul, *Maurice Baring Restored*. New York, Farrar, Straus & Giroux, 1970.

Karger, M., *Novgorod the Great*. Moscow, Progress Publishers, 1973.

Kelly, Laurence, *Lermontov: A Tragedy in the Caucasus*. New York, George Braziller, 1978.

Kluchevsky, V. O., *A History of Russia*. Trans. by C. J. Hogarth. 5 vols. New York, Russell & Russell, 1960.

———, *Peter the Great*. Trans. by Lillian Archbald. New York, St. Martin's Press, 1959.

Knox, Thomas W., *The Russian Empire*. New York, Harper & Bros., 1902.

Kratkaya literaturnaya entsiklopediya, vols. 1–8. Moscow, Gosudarstvennoe Nauchnoe Izdatel'stvo "Sovetskaya Entsiklopediya," 1962.

Kuprin, Aleksandr, *Yunkera*, vol. 6. Moscow, Izdatel'stvo "Khudozhestvennaya Literatura," 1958.

Kuznetsova, Evgeniya, *Russkie narodnye gulaniya*. Leningrad-Moscow, Izdatel'stvo "Iskusstvo," 1948.

Lafitte, Sophie, *Chekhov*. Trans. by Moura Boudberg. New York, Charles Scribner's Sons, 1973.

Lisovsky, N. M., comp., *Russkaya periodicheskaya pechat', 1703–1900 gg. (Bibliografiya i graficheskie tablitsy)*. Petrograd, N.M. Lisovsky, 1915.

Literaturnye pamyatnye mesta Leningrada. Leningrad, Lenizdat, 1976.

Longworth, Philip, *The Three Empresses.* New York, Holt, Rinehart & Winston, 1972.

Lossky, Nicholas, *History of Russian Philosophy.* New York, International Universities Press, 1951.

McLean, Hugh, *Nikolai Leskov: The Man and His Art.* Cambridge, Mass., Harvard University Press, 1977.

Markov, Vladimir, *Russian Futurism.* London, MacGibbon and Kee, 1968.

Mel'nikov, P. I. (Andrey Pechersky), *Sobranie sochineniy v shesti tomakh,* vol. 2. Biblioteka "Ogonyok." Moscow, Izdatel'stvo "Pravda," 1963.

Meyendorff, John, *Byzantine Theology.* New York, Fordham University Press, 1974.

———, *A Study of Gregory of Palamas.* London, Faith Press, 1964.

Meylakh, B., *Zhizn' Aleksandra Pushkina.* Leningrad, Izdatel'stvo "Khudozhestvennaya Literatura," 1974.

Miliukov, P., *Outlines of Russian Culture.* 3 vols. New York, A.S. Barnes & Co., Perpetua Ed., 1960.

Mirsky, D. S., *A History of Russian Literature.* New York, Vintage Books, 1958.

Molokhovets, E., *Podarok molodym khozyaykam ili Sredstvo k umen'sheniyu raskhodov v domashnem khozyaystve,* pts. 1, 2. St. Petersburg, 1898, 1911, 1914.

Moskva v zhizni i tvorchestve A. S. Pushkina. Moscow, Moskovsky Rabochy, 1949.

Nabokov, Vladimir, *Drugie berega.* New York, Chekhov Publishing House, 1963.

———, *Speak Memory.* New York, G.P. Putnam's Sons, 1966.

Nechaev, V. V., *Obshchy vid i vneshny rost Moskvy za XVI-XVII veka.*

Obolensky, Dmitri, ed., *The Penguin Book of Russian Verse.* London, Penguin Books, 1962.

Ocherki istorii Leningrada, vol. 1: (1703–1861). Izdatel'stvo Akademii Nauk SSSR, 1955.

Oldenbourg, Zoe, *Catherine the Great.* New York, Pantheon Books, Random House, 1965.

Oldenburg, S. S., *The Last Tsar: Nicholas II, His Reign and His Russia.* 4 vols. Hattiesburg, Miss., Academic International Press, 1975.

Palmer, Francis H. E., *Russian Life in Town and Country,* London, George Newnes, 1901.

Pares, Bernard, *A History of Russia.* New York, Alfred A. Knopf, 1960.

Payne, Robert, and Romanoff, Nikita, *Ivan the Terrible.* New York, Thomas Y. Crowell Co., 1975.

Pipes, Richard, *Russia under the Old Regime.* New York, Charles Scribner's Sons, 1974.

Platonov, Sergei F., *Ivan the Terrible.* Hattiesburg, Miss., Academic International Press, 1974.

———, *Moscow and the West.* Trans. and ed. by Joseph L. Wieczynscki. Hattiesburg, Miss., Academic International Press, 1972.

———, *La Russie Muscovite.* Paris, Histoire du Monde, 1932.

Poslovitsy, pogovorki, zagadki v rukopisnykh sbornikakh XVIII–XX vekov. Moscow-Leningrad, Izdatel'stvo Akademii Nauk SSSR, 1961.

Pushkin, Alexander, *Eugene Onegin*. Trans. by Charles Johnson. London, Scholar Press, 1977.

———, *Poems, Prose and Plays*. Selected and ed. by Avram Yarmolinsky. New York, The Modern Library, Random House, 1936.

———, *Selected Works*. Progress Russian Classic Series, Moscow, 1974.

Rambaud, Alfred, *L'histoire de la Russie depuis les origines jusqu'à nos jours*. Paris, Hachette, 1900.

Risanovsky, Nicholas V., *A History of Russia*. New York, Oxford University Press, 1963.

Sakharov, I., comp., *Skazaniya russkogo naroda*. 2 vols. St. Petersburg, 1841, 1849.

Schmemann, Alexander, *The Historical Road of Eastern Orthodoxy*. New York, Holt, Rinehart & Winston, 1963.

Selivanova, Nina Nikolaevna, *Dining and Wining in Old Russia*. New York, E.P. Dutton, 1933.

Shchegolev, P. E., *Duel' i smert' Pushkina*. Moscow-Leningrad, 1928.

Shmelev, Ivan, *Leto Gospodne*. New York, Saint Seraphim Foundation, Inc.

Shubinsky, S. N., *Istoricheskie ocherki i razskazy*. St. Petersburg, 1908.

Solov'ev, S. M., *Istoriya Rossii s drevneyshikh vremen*. Vols. 1, 2. Moscow, Izdatel'stvo sotsial'no-ekonomi-cheskoy literatury, 1959.

Soloveytchik, George, *Potemkin*. London, Thornton Butterworth Lits., 1938.

Tarsaïdze, Alexandre, *Czars and Presidents*. New York, McDowell, Oblensky, 1958.

Todd, William Mills, III, ed., *Literature and Society in Imperial Russia—1800–1914*. Stanford, Cal., Stanford University Press, 1978.

Tolf, Robert W., *The Russian Rockefellers*. Stanford, Cal., Hoover Institution Press, Stanford University, 1976.

Tolstoy, Aleksey, *Knyaz' Serebryany*. Moscow, Izdatel'stvo "Pravda," 1969.

Tolstoy, Alexandra L., *Tolstoy: A Life of My Father*. Belmont, Mass., Nordland Publishing Co., 1975.

Tolstoy, Lev, *Childhood, Boyhood, Youth*. London, Penguin Classics, 1964.

———, *War and Peace*. 2 vols. London, Penguin Classics, 1957.

Troyat, Henri, *Divided Soul: The Life of Gogol*. Garden City, N.Y., Doubleday, 1973.

———, *Pushkin*. Trans. by Nancy Amphoux. Garden City, N.Y., Doubleday, 1970.

———, *Tolstoy*. Garden City, N.Y., Doubleday, 1967.

Vengerov, S. A., ed., *Russkaya poeziya*, vol. 1, *Epokha klassitsizma*. St. Petersburg, 1897.

Vernadsky, George, *A History of Russia*. 5th rev. ed. New Haven, Conn., Yale University Press, 1961.

Vernadsky, George, and Karpovich, Michael, *A History of Russia*, 4 vols. Vol. 2, *Kievan Russia*, Vol. 3, *The Mongols*. New Haven, Yale University Press, 1943–1959.

Vickery, Walter N., *Pushkin: Death of a Poet*. Bloomington, Ind., Indiana University Press, 1968.

Volkonskaya, M. N., *Zapiski knyagini M. N. Volkonskoy*. Chitinskoe knizhnoe iz-vo, 1960.

Voyce, Arthur, *Moscow and the Roots of Russian Culture*. Norman, Okla., University of Oklahoma Press, 1964.

Waliszewski, Kasimierz, *Ivan the Terrible*. London, William Heinemann, 1904.

Ware, Timothy, *The Orthodox Church*. London, Penguin Books, 1963.

Zabelin, I. E., *Domashny byt russikh tsarits*, vols. 16, 17, *stoletiakh*. Moscow, 1869.

———, *Domashny byt russkogo naroda*, vols. 16, 17, *stoletiakh*. Moscow, 1872.

———, *Istoriya goroda Moskvy*, Moscow, 1905.

Zenkovsky, Serge, ed., *Medieval Russia's Epics, Chronicles and Tales*. New York, E.P. Dutton, 1964.

Zernov, Nicholas, *Eastern Christendom*. New York, G.P. Putnam's Sons, 1961.

———, *Russian Religious Renaissance of the 20th Century*. New York, Harper & Row, 1963.

Zhukov, V. P., ed., *Slovar' russkikh poslovits i pogovorok*. Moscow, Izdatel'stvo "Sovetskaya Entsiklopediya," 1966.

CONTEMPORARY ACCOUNTS

Adams, John Quincy, *Memoirs*, vol. 2. Ed. by C. P. Adams. 12 vols. Philadelphia, 1874–1879.

Baedeker, Karl, *Russia: A Handbook for Travellers*. Leipzig, 1914. Facsimile ed., Random House, 1971.

Bond, Edward, ed., *Russia at the Close of the 16th Century (Of the Russe Commonwealth* by Giles Fletcher and *Travels* of Sir Jerome Horsey). Haklyut Society Series, no. 20. New York, Burt Franklin, 1964.

Bruce-Lockhart, R. H., *British Agent*. New York, G.P. Putnam's Sons, 1933.

Carroll, Lewis, *The Russian Journal and Other Selections*. New York, Dover Publications, 1977.

Catherine II (Catherine the Great), *Mémoires de Catherine II*. Paris, Librairie Hachette, 1953.

———, *Memoirs of Catherine the Great*. Trans. by K. Anthony. New York and London, Alfred A. Knopf, 1927.

Chancellor, Richard, and Adams, Clement, *Chancellor's Voyage to Muscovy*. DeMoneta Russica Elzevir 1630. Edinburgh, J. McGrindle, 1886.

Collins, Samuel, *The Present State of Russia in a Letter to a Friend at London*. London, John Winter for Dorman Newman, 1671.

Coxe, Reverend William, *Travels into Poland, Russia, Sweden and Denmark*. London, 1792.

Cross, Samuel, and Sherbowitz-Wetzor, Olger, eds., *The Russian Primary Chronicle*. Laurentian Text. Cambridge, Mass., Medieval Academy of America, 1953.

Daschkoff (Princess), *Mémoires de la Princesse Daschkoff*. Edition: Pascal Pontremoli. Mercure de France, 1966.

Delmar, Morgan E., and Coote, C. H., eds., *Early Voyages and Travels to Russia and Persia* (Anthony Jenkinson and other Englishmen), vol. 2. Haklyut Society Series, no. 73. New York, Burt Franklin, 1965.

The Englishwoman in Russia: Impressions of the Country and Manners of the Russians at Home by a Lady Ten Years Resident in That Country. New York, Charles Scribner's Sons, 1855.

Fennell, J. L. I., ed. and trans., *The Correspondence Between Prince A. M. Kurbsky and Tsar Ivan IV of Russia, 1564–1579*. Cambridge University Press, 1963.

Gautier, Théophile, *Voyage en Russie*. Paris, Hachette, 1961.

Granville, A. B., M.D., *St. Petersburgh: A Journal of Travel to and from That Capital*. London, Henry Colburn, 1829.

Haxthausen, Baron Augustus von, *The Russian Empire and Its People, Institutions and Resources*. 3 vols. Hanover, 1847–1852.

Herberstein, Sigismund von, *Notes upon Russia*. (Rerum Moscovitticarum Commentarii.) Trans. and ed. by R. H. Major. Haklyut Society Series, nos. 10, 12. 2 vols. New York, Burt Franklin, 1963.

Hodgetts, E. A. Brayley, *The Court of Russia in the 19th Century*, vols. 1, 2. London, Methuen & Co., 1908.

Kohl, J. G., Esq., *Russia and the Russians in 1842*. Vol. 2: London, Henry Colburn, 1843. Vol. 1: Petersburg, 1842.

Leroy-Beaulieu, Anatole, *The Empire of the Tsars*. Trans. by Z. Ragozin. 2 vols. G.P. Putnam & Sons, 1898.

Lothrop (Mrs.), *The Court of Alexander III: Letters of Mrs. Lothrop, wife of Honorable George Van Ness Lothrop, Minister of the United States*. Ed. by William Prall. Philadelphia, John C. Winston, 1910.

Masson, Charles F. P., *Mémoires secrets sur la Russie*. 2 vols. Paris, 1800–1804.

———, *Secret Memoirs of the Court of St. Petersburg*. London, H.S. Nichols & Co., 1895.

Mossolov, A. A., *At the Court of the Last Tsar*. London, Methuen & Co., 1935.

Olearius, Adam, *Travels of Olearius in Seventeenth Century Russia*. Stanford, Cal., Stanford University Press, 1967.

Paleologue, Maurice, *An Ambassador's Memoirs*. 3 vols. Trans. by F. A. Holt. New York, Doran, 1925.

Paul of Aleppo. *The Travels of Macarius, Patriarch of Antioch*. London, 1936.

Porter, R. Ker, *Travelling Sketches in Russia and Sweden*. London, 1813.

The Principal Voyages, Traffiques and Discoveries of the English Nation, vol. 2. 12 vols.

Glasgow, Richard Haklyut, James Maclehose & Sons, 1903.

Proctor, Edna Dean, *A Russian Journey*. Boston, James R. Osgood & Co., 1873.

Putnam, Peter, ed., *Seven Britons in Imperial Russia*. Princeton, N.J., Princeton University Press, 1952.

de Staël, Anne Louise Germaine, *Dix années d'exil*. Paris, La Renaissance du Livre, 1909.

Tissot, Victor, *La Russie et les Russes*. Paris, Librairie Plon, 1893.

Vasili, Comte P., *La Sainte Russie*. Paris, Librairie de Firmin-Didot, 1890.

Wilmot, Martha and Catherine, *Russian Journals, 1803–1819*. Ed. by Marchioness of Londenberry and H. M. Hyde. London, Macmillan & Co., 1934.

Wilson, Francesca, *Muscovy: Russia Through Foreign Eyes 1553–1900*. London, George Allen & Unwin, 1970.

ART AND ARCHITECTURE

Aleksandrov, V. A., Kushner, P. I., and Rabinovich, M. Ch., eds., *Russkie: Istoriko-etno-graficheshy atlas*. Moscow, Izdatel'stvo "Nauka," 1970.

Alpatov, Mikhail V., *Andrey Rublev*. Moscow, Izdatel'stvo "Iskusstvo," 1959.

————, *Treasures of Russian Art in the 11th–16th Centuries*. Leningrad, Aurora Art Publishers, 1971.

Art Objects in Steel by Tula Craftsmen. Leningrad, Aurora Art Publishers, 1974.

Ascher, Abraham, *The Kremlin*. Wonders of Man. New York, Newsweek, 1972.

Bainbridge, Henry Charles, *Peter Carl Fabergé: Goldsmith and Jeweller to the Russian Court*. London, Spring Books, 1966.

Benois, A., *The Russian School of Painting*. New York, 1916.

Bilibin, Ivan Yakovlevich, *Stat'i: Pis'ma: Vospominaniya*. Leningrad, Izdatel'stvo "Khudozhestvo," 1970.

Boguslavskaya, I., *Russkaya Narodnaya Vyshivka*. Moscow, Izdatel'stvo "Iskusstvo," 1972.

Brion-Guerry, L., ed., *L'année 1913: Les formes esthétiques de l'oeuvre d'art à la veille de la première guerre mondiale*. 3 vols. Paris, Editions Klincksieck, 1971–1973.

Buxton, D. R., *Russian Medieval Architecture*. Cambridge, 1934.

Compton, Susan P., *The World Backwards: Russian Futurist Books, 1912–1916*. London, The British Library.

Cross, S. H., *Medieval Russian Churches*. Cambridge, Mass., 1949.

The Dormition Cathedral in the Moscow Kremlin. Moscow, Izdatel'stvo "Izobrazitel'noe Iskusstvo," 1971.

Ermitazh: Istoriya i arkhitektura zdaniy. Leningrad, Izdatel'stvo "Avrora," 1974.

Faensen, Hubert, and Ivanov, Vladimir, *Early Russian Architecture.* New York, G.P. Putnam & Sons, 1975.

Gordin, M. A., ed., *Pushkinsky Peterburg.* Leningrad, 1974.

Gosudarstvennaya Tret'yakovskaya Galereya, *Iskusstvo XVIII veka.* Moscow, Izdatel'stvo "Izobrazitel'noe Iskusstvo."

Grabar, I., ed., *Istoriya russkago iskusstva.* 6 vols. Moscow, 1909–

Gray, Camilla, *The Russian Experiment in Art, 1863–1922.* London, Thames & Hudson, 1962.

Habsburg-Lothringen, G. von, and Solodkopff, A. von, *Fabergé: Court Jeweler to the Tsars.* New York, Rizzoli, 1979.

Hamilton, George Heard, *The Art and Architecture of Russia.* The Pelican History of Art. Baltimore, Md., Penguin Books, 1954.

Holme, Charles, ed., *Peasant Art in Russia.* London, Paris, New York, The Studio, 1912.

Ilyine, M., *Les arts décoratifs populaires en Russie.* Moscow, 1959.

Ivanova, E., *Russian Applied Art.* Leningrad, 1976.

Ivanova, E. A., *Russkie samovary.* Leningrad, Khudozhnik RSFR, 1971.

Kruglova, O., *Traditional Russian Carved and Painted Woodwork.* Moscow, "Izobrazitel'noe Iskusstvo," 1974.

Kutchumov, Anatoly M., *Pavlovsk.* Leningrad, Lenizdat, 1970.

———, *Pavlovsk Palace and Park.* Leningrad, Aurora Art Publishers, 1975.

Leningrad: House of Peter I, Summer Gardens and Palace of Peter I. Leningrad, Aurora Art Publishers, 1975.

Levinson, Andre, *Bakst: The Story of an Artist's Life.* London, The Bayard Press, 1923.

Lukomski, G. K., *L'art décoratif russe.* Paris, 1928.

———, *Le Kreml de Moscou, ses cathédrales, ses trésors d'art.* 3 vols. Paris, 1928.

Marcadé, Valentine, *Le renouveau de l'art pictural russe, 1863–1914.* Editions l'Age de l'Homme. Lausanne, Metropole, 1971.

Marsden, Christopher, *Palmyra of the North.* London, Faber & Faber, 1942.

Martynova, M. V., *Dragotsenny kamen' v russkom yuvelirnom iskusstve XII–XVIII vekov.* Moscow, Izdatel'stvo "Iskusstvo," 1973.

The Neva Symphony: Leningrad in Works of Graphic Art and Painting. Leningrad, Aurora Art Publishers, 1975.

North Russian Architecture. Moscow, Progress Books, 1972.

Ouspensky, Leonid, and Lossky, Vladimir, *The Meaning of Icons.* Boston, Boston Book and Art Shop, 1969.

Ovsyannikov, Y., *Russian Folk Art and Crafts.* Moscow, Progress Books.

Pamyatniki arkhitektury Leningrada. Leningrad, Izdatel'stvo Literatury po Stroitel'stvu, 1972.

Pronin, Alexander and Barbara, *Russian Folk Arts*. Cranbury, N.J., A.S. Barnes & Co., 1975.

Pugin, V. A., *Mirovozzrenie Andreya Rubl̈eva*. Moscow, Izdatel'stvo Moskovskogo Universiteta, 1974.

Rae, Isabel, *Charles Cameron: Architect to the Court of Russia*. London, Elek Books, 1971.

Reau, L., *L'art Russe des origines à Pierre le Grand*. Paris, 1921.

Riabushkin. Leningrad, Aurora Art Publishers, 1973.

Ribakov, B. A., ed., *Cokrovisha Almaznogo Fonda USSR*. Moscow, Izdatel'stvo "Iskusstvo," 1975.

Rice, Tamara Talbot, *A Concise History of Russian Art*. New York, Frederick Praeger, 1963.

———, *Russian Art*. West Drayta, 1949.

Ross, Marvin C., *The Art of Karl Fabergé and His Contemporaries*. Norman, Okla., University of Oklahoma Press, 1965.

———, *Russian Porcelains*. Norman, Okla., University of Oklahoma Press, 1968.

Russian Folk Costume; Treasures of the Order of Lenin State History Museum.

Russia's Treasure of Diamonds and Precious Stones. Moscow, The People's Commissariat of Finances, 1925.

Snowman, Kenneth, *The Art of Karl Fabergé*. Greenwich, Conn., New York Graphic Society Library.

Taranovskaya, M. E., *Karl Rossi*. Leningrad, Lenizdat, 1978.

Taranovskaya, N. V., *Russkaya derevyannaya igrushka*. Leningrad, Khudozhnik RFSR, 1968.

Valkenier, Elizabeth, *Russian Realist Art. The State and Society: The Peredvizhniki and Their Tradition*. Ann Arbor, Mich., Ardis, 1977.

Voyce, Arthur, *Art and Architecture of Medieval Russia*. Norman, Okla., University of Oklahoma Press, 1967.

———, *The Moscow Kremlin: Its History, Architecture and Art Treasures*. Norman, Okla., University of California Press, 1954.

Waterfield, Hermione, and Forbes, Christopher, *Fabergé Imperial Eggs and Other Fantasies*. New York, Charles Scribner's Sons, 1979.

Weitzmann, Kurt, *The Icon*. New York, George Braziller, Inc., 1978.

Zabelin, I. E., ed., *Moskva v ee proshlom i nastoyashchem*, vol. 1. Moscow, Moskovskoe knigoizdatel'stvo Tovarifesta Obrazovanie.

BALLET, THEATER AND MUSIC

Abraham, Gerald, *Rimsky-Korsakov*. London, Duckworth, 1945.

Assafiev, B., *Composers of the First Half of the 19th Century*. Moscow, 1959.

Barnes, Patricia, *The Children of Theater Street*. New York, The Viking Press, 1978.

Beaumont, Cyril W., *A History of Ballet in Russia*. London, C.W. Beaumont–Wyman & Sons, 1930.

Benois, Alexandre, *Memoirs*. Trans. by Moura Budberg. 2 vols. London, Chatto & Windus, 1960–1964.

Borodin, A. P., *Pis'ma*. Ed. by S. Dianin. Moscow, Gosudarstvennoe Muzykal'noe Izdatel'stvo, 1936.

Brook, Donald, *Six Great Russian Composers*. London, Salisbury Square, 1947.

Buckle, Richard, *Nijinsky*. Harmondsworth, Middlesex, England, Penguin Books, 1975. (Hardback: Weidenfeldland, Nicholson, 1971.)

Calvocoressi, M. D., and Abraham, G., *Masters of Russian Music*. London, Duckworth, 1936.

Chaliapin, Feodor, *I, Feodor Chaliapin*. Trans. by H. M. Buck. New York, Harper & Bros., 1927.

Dandre, V., *Anna Pavlova*. Berlin, Petropolis, 1933.

Dianin, Serge, *Borodin*. Trans. by R. Lord. London, Oxford University Press, 1963.

Fokin, M., *Protiv techeniya*. Moscow–Leningrad, Izdatel'stvo "Iskusstvo," 1962.

Glinka, M., *Memoirs*. Ed. by A. N. Rimsky-Korsakov. Moscow.

Grigoriev, S. L., *The Diaghilev Ballet, 1909–1929*. Trans. by Vera Brown. London, Dance Horizons Publications, Constable & Co., 1953.

Haskell, Arnold, with Walter Nouvel, *Diaghileff: His Artistic and Private Life*. New York, Simon & Schuster, 1935. (Paperback: Da Capo Press, Inc., 1978.)

Karsavina, Tamara, *Theater Street*. London, Constable & Co., 1930, rev. 1948.

Kirstein, Lincoln, *Nijinsky Dancing*. New York, Alfred A. Knopf, 1975.

Koesler, Horst, ed., *The Concise Oxford Dictionary of Ballet*. London, Oxford University Press, 1977.

Krasovskaya, V., *Russky baletny teatr (vtoroy poloviny XIX veka)*. Leningrad, Izdatel'stvo "Iskusstvo," 1963.

———, *Russky baletny teatr (nachala XX veka)*. Leningrad, Izdatel'stvo "Iskusstvo," 1971.

Kschessinska, Mathilde, *Dancing in Petersburg*. Trans. by Arnold Haskell. Garden City, N.Y., Doubleday, 1961.

Marius Petipa: Materialy, vospominaniya, stat'i. Leningrad, Izdatel'stvo "Iskusstvo," 1971.

Montagu-Nathan, N., *History of Russian Music*. Reeves.

Nijinsky, Romola, *Nijinsky*. New York, Pocket Books, 1972.

Pleshcheeva, Aleksandra, *Nash balet (1673–1899)*. St. Petersburg, 1899.

Riesemann, Oskar von, *Moussorgsky*. New York, Alfred A. Knopf, 1929.

Rimsky-Korsakov, Nikolai A., *My Musical Life*. New York, Alfred A. Knopf, 1947.

Roslavleva, Natalia, *Era of the Russian Ballet*. London, Victor Gollancz, 1966.

Russkoe teatral'no-dekoratsionnoe iskusstvo. Moscow, Izdatel'stvo "Iskusstvo," 1970.

Seroff, Victor, *Modeste Moussorgsky*. New York, Funk & Wagnalls, 1968.

Spender, Charles, and Dyer, Philip, *The World of Serge Diaghilev*. Chicago, Henry Regnery Co., 1974.

Stanislavsky, Constantin, *My Life in Art*. New York, Theater Arts Books, 1924.

Stravinsky, Igor, *Petrushka*. Ed. by Charles Hamm. A Norton Critical Score. New York, W.W. Norton & Co., 1967.

Swan, Alfred J., *Russian Music and Its Sources in Chant and Folk Song*. New York, W.W. Norton & Co., 1973.

Swift, Mary Grace, *A Loftier Flight*. Middletown, Conn., Wesleyan University Press, 1974.

Teatr Letuchaya Mysh' N. O. Balieva, 1908–1918. Moscow, "Solntse Rossii."

ARTICLES, CATALOGUES AND MAGAZINES

The Art of Russia, 1800–1850. Minneapolis, University Gallery, University of Minnesota, 1978.

Beaumont, Cyril W., "Pushkin and His Influence on Russian Ballet," 2 pts., *Ballet*, London, Dec. 1947 & Jan. 1948.

Diaghilev and Russian Stage Designers. Washington, D.C., International Exhibitions Foundation, 1972–1974.

Diaghilev et les Ballets Russes. Bibliothèque Nationale, 1979.

"Les Futurismes," *Europe: Revue littéraire mensuelle*, Apr. 1975.

Grosvenor, Gilbert, "Young Russia: The Land of Unlimited Possibilities," *The National Geographic*, vol. 26, no. 5, Nov. 1914.

Karlinsky, Simon, "The Vanished World of Elena Molokhovetz," University Publishing, no. 8, fall 1979.

Kolb-Seletski, "Gastronomy, Gogol and His Fiction," *The Slavic Review*, 1970, vol. 29.

Nagler, Alois, "Sources of Theatrical History," *New York Theater Annual*, 1952.

Paris–Moscou, 1900–1930. Paris, Centre Beaubourg, 1979.

Russian and Soviet Painting. New York, The Metropolitan Museum of Art, 1977.

Russian Painters and the Stage: 1884–1965. Exhibition Catalogue. Lobanov-Rostovsky Collection, University of Texas, 1978–1979.

Russian Stage and Costume Designs for the Ballet, Opera and Theater. Washington, D.C., International Exhibitions Foundation, 1967–1969.

The Silver Age of Russian Art, Apollo, London, Dec. 1973. Denys Sutton, ed. 8 articles: 1. "Wanderers and Esthetes," 2. "Russian Architecture, 1880–1910," 3. John E. Bowlt, "Two Russian Maecebanes," 4. Boris Lossky, "The Popular Arts in Russia and Their Revival," 5. Eugene Klimoff, "Alexandre Benois and His Role in Russian Art," 6. Michael Ginsburg, "Art Collectors of Old Russia," 7. John E. Bowlt, "Nikolai Ryabushinsky," 8. Mary Chamot, "Russian Avant Garde Graphics."

Stage Designs and the Russian Avant-Garde, 1911–1929. Introduction and Catalogue by John Bowlt. Washington, D.C., International Exhibitions Foundation, 1976–1978.

Todd, William M., "The Russian Terpsichore's Soul-Filled Flight: Dance Themes in Eugene Onegin." Forthcoming in *Pushkin and the Dance.* New York, Dance Horizons.

Valkenier, Elizabeth Kridl, "The Peredvizhniki and the Spirit of the 1880's," *The Russian Review,* July 1975.

INDEX

473

486

(*continued from copyright page*)

Pages 239, 244. Excerpts from poetry of Alexander Pushkin from *Pushkin* by Henri Troyat, translated by Nancy Amphous. Translation copyright © 1970 by Doubleday & Company, Inc. Reprinted by permission of the publisher.

Page 243. Excerpt from "The Dream" by Mikhail Lermontov reprinted from *Lermontov: Tragedy in the Caucasus* by Laurence Kelly by permission of the publisher, George Braziller, Inc. Copyright © Laurence Kelly 1977.

Pages 206, 259, 291, 357, 362, 384. Excerpts from Alexander Pushkin's *Eugene Onegin* translated by Babette Deutsch, from *The Poems, Prose and Plays of Alexander Pushkin*, selected and edited by Avram Yarmolinsky, The Modern Library, Random House Publishers. Copyright © 1936, renewed 1964 by Random House, Inc. Reprinted by permission of the publisher.

Page 229. Excerpt from Alexander Pushkin's *Eugene Onegin* translated by Charles Johnston, Scholar Press. Copyright © 1977 by Charles Johnston. Reprinted by permission of the translator.

Page 237. Excerpt from Leo Tolstoy's *War and Peace* translated by Rosemary Edmunds, Penguin Books. Copyright © Rosemary Edmunds 1957, 1978. Reprinted by permission of Penguin Books, Limited.

Pages 294, 307. Excerpts from *A Life of My Father* by Alexandra Tolstoy, translated by Elizabeth Reynolds Hapgood, published by Nordland Publishing Company, 1975. Copyright © 1953, 1975 Alexandra L. Tolstoy. Reprinted by permission of the estate of Alexandra L. Tolstoy.

PICTURES

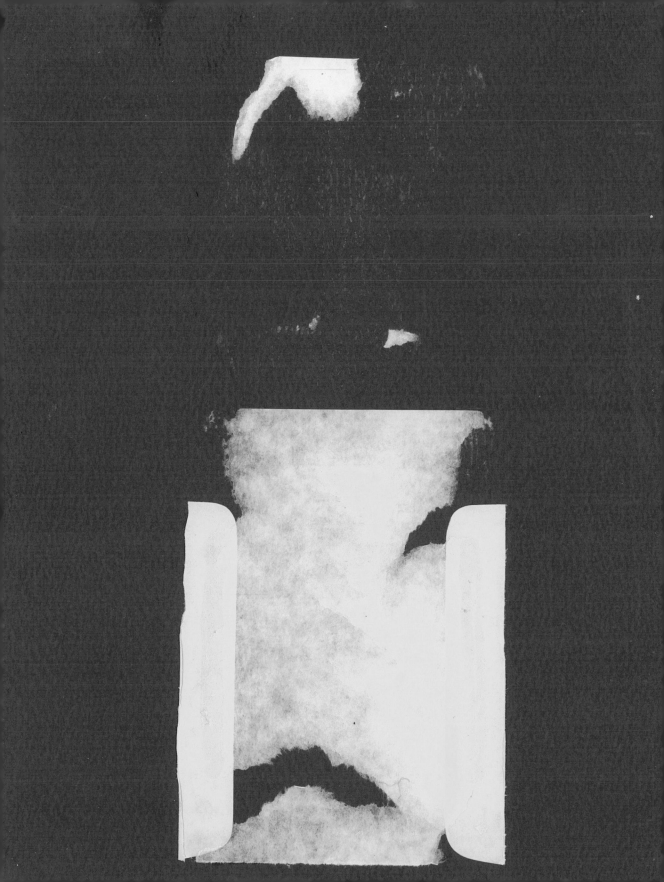